Securities Market Issues for the 21st Century

Merritt B. Fox,
Lawrence R. Glosten,
Edward F. Greene &
Menesh S. Patel, editors

April 25, 2018

Copyright © 2018 Merritt B. Fox, Lawrence R. Glosten, Edward F. Greene & Menesh S. Patel

All rights reserved

Prepared in connection with

The New Special Study

a project of

Columbia Law School & Columbia Business School's Program in the Law and Economics of Capital Markets

New Special Study Steering Committee

Reena Aggarwal
Franklin Allen
John C. Coffee Jr.
Robert W. Cook (former member)
James D. Cox
Emanuel Derman
Zohar Goshen
Joseph A. Grundfest
Maureen O'Hara
Joel Hasbrouck
Richard G. Ketchum
Donald C. Langevoort
Christine A. Parlour
Ailsa A. Röell
Hillary A. Sale
Joel Seligman
Leslie N. Silverman
Larry Sonsini
Chester S. Spatt
& *in memoriam*:
Harvey J. Goldschmid

TABLE OF CONTENTS

Acknowledgements iii

Chapter 1. Securities Market Issues for the 21st Century: An Overview 1
Merritt B. Fox, Lawrence R. Glosten, Edward F. Greene & Menesh S. Patel

Chapter 2. The Economics of Primary Markets 33
Kathleen Weiss Hanley

Chapter 3. The Regulation of Primary Markets 101
Donald C. Langevoort

Chapter 4. The Economics of Trading Markets 145
Ryan J. Davies & Erik R. Sirri

Chapter 5. The Regulation of Trading Markets 221
Paul G. Mahoney & Gabriel V. Rauterberg

Chapter 6. The Economics of Intermediaries 279
Jonathan B. Berk & Jules H. van Binsbergen

Chapter 7. The Regulation of Intermediaries 311
Allen Ferrell & John D. Morley

Chapter 8. Globalization 381
John Armour, Martin Bengtzen & Luca Enriques

ACKNOWLEDGEMENTS

This book benefited from the guidance and assistance of a number of individuals, including Reena Aggarwal, Craig Barrack, Christopher Bates, Gregg E. Berman, Tal Cohen, Andrew J. (Buddy) Donohue, Stephen Fraidin, Joseph A. Grundfest, Keith F. Higgins, Howell E. Jackson, Charles M. Jones, Richard G. Ketchum, Eric J. Pan, Joanna Perkins, Jay R. Ritter, Lanny A. Schwartz, Chester S. Spatt, and William J. Williams Jr., who each served as commentator or panelist at the Initiating Conference of the New Special Study at which the seven foundational papers in this book were presented; the various participants at the Initiating Conference; Laura L. Miller, Assistant Director of Columbia Law School and Columbia Business School's Program in the Law and Economics of Capital Markets, who provided invaluable assistance in the preparation of this book; and Riancy Z. Li, Michael F. Motala, Ingrid Y. Pan, and Corinna Su, who each provided excellent research assistance. This book also greatly benefited from the generous support of the Smith Richardson Foundation.

Chapter 1
SECURITIES MARKET ISSUES FOR THE 21ST CENTURY: AN OVERVIEW

Merritt B. Fox,[1] Lawrence R. Glosten,[2] Edward F. Greene[3] & Menesh S. Patel[4]

The 1963 publication of the Special Study of the Securities Markets marked a seminal moment in the history of U.S. securities regulation. Headed up by legendary SEC lawyer Milton Cohen, this 3000 page report evaluated every aspect of the processes by which individuals and institutions acquire direct or indirect interests in securities and by which savings are channeled through the capital markets to new real investments. The impact of this study was enormous, generating the information and ideas behind most of the important securities regulatory initiatives undertaken over the next several decades.

Fifty-five years later, however, we are in a very different world. The purpose of this book is to explore the wholly new set of securities regulation issues that we face today. As part of the first stage of a New Special Study of the Securities Markets, we asked thirteen of the world's greatest experts in securities regulation and financial economics to identify what are the most important questions going forward. They were then to assess the extent to which adequate answers to these questions can already be found by researching the existing literature, and the extent to which new thinking or empirical research is needed. The chapters that follow are the results of their efforts. They contain both important policy guides usable right now and thoughtful agendas for future research. Equally important, they testify to the need for the New Special Study

---

[1] Michael E. Patterson Professor of Law, Columbia Law School and co-Director, The Program in the Law and Economics of Capital Markets, Columbia Law School and Columbia Business School.

[2] S. Sloan Colt Professor of Banking and International Finance, Columbia Business School and co-Director, The Program in the Law and Economics of Capital Markets, Columbia Law School and Columbia Business School.

[3] Senior Counsel, Cleary Gottlieb Steen & Hamilton LLP and co-Director, The Program in the Law and Economics of Capital Markets, Columbia Law School and Columbia Business School.

[4] Post-Doctoral Research Scholar, The Program in the Law and Economics of Capital Markets, Columbia Law School and Columbia Business School.

project to move forward to completion, with a final product as comprehensive and prescient as the original 1963 study.

A better understanding of the securities markets and their regulation can generate large rewards to society. The securities markets are a central part of the U.S. financial system, serving the interests of investors, businesses, and the economy as a whole. The stock and bond markets provide investment opportunities for both households and institutions. The securities markets also act as a source of corporate financing and permit ways to hedge against the economic risks associated with the cash flows of individual firms. Further, securities markets, through competitively determined prices, provide important information about the future prospects of businesses, guiding decision-making in the real economy. In serving these various functions, securities markets are an important contributor to the efficiency of our domestic economy and its capacity to improve living standards through innovation-based growth.

This chapter presents an overview of the issues raised by the chapters that follow. It starts with a consideration of the driving themes indicating that a comprehensive study of the securities markets today is such a different exercise from that undertaken 55 years ago. It then uses these driving themes to help put in context the four main areas covered by the chapters that follow: primary markets, secondary trading markets, intermediaries and globalization.

1 Driving Themes

Any effort to understand today's securities market and its proper regulation will be a very different exercise from the original special study's effort 55 years ago. Five distinct, though interrelated, themes explain why, in terms of both changes in the phenomena under study and the power of our tools for understanding them.

1.1 Information Technology

The information technology (IT) revolution defines our age. Securities and information are inextricably intertwined and so it is hardly surprising that the IT revolution, with its extraordinary gains in fast, inexpensive communication and computational capacity, has transformed the securities markets. A security is a promise to pay dollars to its holder in the future if certain circumstances prevail. At its heart, a securities market is simply a way of helping securities buyers and sellers to find each other, i.e., persons with interests in buying such contingent future dollars (usually called "savers" or "investors") and persons with interests selling these contingent future dollars (issuers of new stock and bonds and the periodic resellers of what the issuers originally issued). Rules based information systems are how persons with buying interests and those with selling interests find each other. Moreover, investor decisions to buy or sell securities depend on information about the issuer and about what others are doing in the market.

The transformational change brought about by IT is particularly evident in the way stocks are traded in the secondary market. Traditionally, trading in the stock of each publicly traded company of any significance was largely confined to a *single* venue, either NASDAQ or the New York Stock Exchange (NYSE). At NASDAQ, a dealer was the purchaser of every share sold by a trader and the seller of every share bought by a trader. The dealer did so at quoted prices generated through the calculation and judgment of an individual human being. At the NYSE, the specialist for any given stock played a similar role but also facilitated floor trading and posted limit orders (a firm commitment, unless cancelled, to buy or sell up to a specified number of shares at a quoted price) sent to him by traders in the stock. Today, any given stock is potentially traded in each of nearly *eighty* competing venues, the majority of which are electronic limit order books, in which the quotes come entirely from traders posting limit orders that are matched by a computer with incoming marketable buy and sell orders (orders that have terms allowing them to execute at what is then the best available price in the market). A significant portion of the quotes resulting in executed trades come from high-frequency traders (HFTs). Each HFT uses high-speed communications to constantly update its information concerning transactions and quote changes occurring on every major trading venue in each stock that the HFT regularly trades. It then feeds this information into a computer that uses algorithms to change its quotes, often many times per second. Sophisticated institutional investors use similar techniques to get large purchases and sales done with the least possible market impact.

The IT revolution is having important effects in other spheres of the market as well. For example, institutional and individual investors and their advisors increasingly use computer programs as guides in their purchase and sale decisions. Also, there is considerable potential for changes in the way primary sales of securities are marketed, and in how issuers provide disclosure both at the time of an offering and to the secondary trading market thereafter, although, rightly or wrongly, current regulations hold much of this back. Also, blockchain technology could have a revolutionary effect on clearing and settlement and with it significant changes in the role of securities brokers.

Finally, the IT revolution, with our resulting extraordinarily increased capacity to collect, store and retrieve data and to make calculations based on this data, is transforming our capacity to learn what is going on in the securities markets. This makes realistic broadly effective enforcement of rules against insider trading and other undesirable trading practices, where in the past these rules were much closer to being mere aspirations of good behavior. As discussed further below, this increased capacity also makes practical empirical studies that can resolve a wide range of issues relevant for good policymaking that were previously simply the subject of contending academic theories.

1.2 Institutionalization

Relative to the time of the original special study, a much larger portion of the buying and selling of securities is handled today by institutions. Three important trends are evident. One is the enormous growth in individual investor money going into index mutual funds and exchange-traded funds (ETFs). When based on broad general market indexes, these funds allow an individual investor to enjoy at low cost the risk-reducing benefits of a much more broadly diversified stock portfolio than was practical in an earlier era when such a portfolio would need to be constructed by a large number of individual-level purchases and sales. When based on more specialized indexes, such funds provide similar cost savings for constructing individually designed portfolios that best hedge against other components of an investor's publicly traded stock portfolio that are different from what would be in a fully diversified portfolio[5] or against risks related to an investor's non-stock investments such as human capital or real estate holdings.

A second trend is the growth of investor money going into managed mutual funds and hedge funds, i.e., funds that, rather than just mimicking an index, seek to outperform the market. Use of these investment vehicles involves the delegation of the effort to find under- and over-priced securities to professional managers, an effort previously undertaken to a much greater extent by individual investors, often with the advice of their full service brokers. Associated with both the first and second trend is the huge growth in the amount of money managed by pension funds and by university and other non-profit endowments. These entities use strategies mimicking both the index funds and managed funds.

The third trend is the large expansion of private equity funds. These funds buy and sell significant stakes in non-publicly-traded stock. In doing so, they both provide firms an avenue for equity finance that does not entail the regulatory hurdles associated with a public offering, and provide the holders of already issued non-publicly-traded stock a certain degree of liquidity.

1.3 Increased Understanding of Capital Markets

In the 55 years since the last special study, financial economics has been transformed from a relative backwater, largely based on institutional description,

---

[5] These could include a share position accumulated for speculative reasons, shares with a low capital gains basis, or shares in the investor's employer.

to a major area of economics that has generated a number of Nobel prizes. In 1963, it would still be years before the term "efficient market hypothesis" would be coined, portfolio theory was in its infancy, and the inception of the game-theoretic field of micro-structure economics that studies the mechanisms by which exchange occurs would need to wait another two decades. Similarly, as already noted, the hugely increased capacity to collect, store and retrieve data and to make calculations based on these data resulting from the IT revolution, and the accompanying gains in econometric techniques have resulted in a transformative improvement in our ability to study capital markets empirically. These theoretical and empirical advances have greatly increased our storehouse of knowledge concerning the impact of a wide variety of market practices and regulations. These advances also mean that we have the capacity to answer far more of the questions that have yet to be definitively resolved empirically if we devote the needed resources to the task. This increased understanding of how markets work has also had a profound effect on the behavior of market participants themselves.

1.4 Increased Multiplicity of Markets and Market Practices

There has been a large increase in the size and sophistication of capital markets outside the United States since the original special study. There has also been within the United States the development of new types of primary and secondary securities markets for unregistered shares based on various new registration exemptions.

This increase in the multiplicity of markets and practices has important implications. First, because multiple markets give issuers and investors choices in the ways they can accomplish their securities market aims, these multiple markets compete with each other for patronage to one extent or another. This competition can push market operators and their regulators to act in ways that lead to more innovation, lower costs, and greater attention being paid to the needs of the market users, thereby leading to a "race to the top." If, however, there are significant externalities involved, this competition may result in a socially disadvantageous regulatory "race to the bottom" instead, at least absent sufficient coordination among the officials of the competing regulatory regimes. More generally, understanding the consequences of this competition for the workings of the securities markets and the process of their regulation involves some complex political economy. Competition helps shape the rules under which each market operates because it alters the views held by the various persons who have a stake in, and influence over, the content of the regulatory regime involved. For the same reasons, competition also helps shape the rules applying to the issuers whose shares trade in each market and to the rules applying to persons who trade in it and their brokers.

Second, the increase in the number of markets provides us a much wider range of experience. These markets differ from each other in terms of both their internal rules of operation and the external rules imposed upon them by their respective regulators. This wider range of experience offers opportunities to learn about the effects of different rules in terms of valued outcomes such as price accuracy and liquidity. This is especially so given the sophisticated empirical tools now available to study and compare markets.

1.5 Globalization

As recently as 25 years ago, U.S. investors held only 6% of their portfolios by value in foreign issuer stocks and investors abroad held only 3% of their portfolios by value in U.S. issuer stocks. Today, U.S. investors hold 25% of their portfolios in foreign issuer stocks, and investors abroad hold 13% of their portfolios in U.S. issuer stocks, in each case a more than four-fold increase proportionally. Each, however, still falls well short of what an ideally diversified portfolio would be for any investor whatever her nationality: approximately 40% in U.S. stocks and 60% in issuers from the rest of the world.

The erosion of home bias that has occurred in the last 25 years is explained in part by each of the four drivers discussed above. Consider first, the IT revolution. Because of it and technical change more generally, differences in the costs of timely acquisition of information from, respectively, foreign and from domestic sources have narrowed and in many case vanished. Email, transmission of documents by email attachment, the web, and links to computerized databases have essentially no cost sensitivity to distance, and international telephone calls and travel for face-to-face meetings and on-site inspections have declined greatly in cost. This reduction in the difference between acquiring information domestically and from abroad applies with respect to both information directly relevant to predicting the prospects of issuers and information about the motivations and reputation of the sources of such directly relevant information.

These same technological changes, through their effect on mass media, marketing, education, scholarly research and direct personal interaction, are working toward creating a more uniform social and economic culture among the capitalist nations of the world and toward the coalescence around English as the international language. This greater uniformity of culture and language assists the speculative investor in evaluating the information he receives from abroad and gives the passive investor more faith in how stocks of foreign issuers are priced. These same technological changes have also contributed to the development of truly transnational securities firms with the trust and control advantages of communications within a single organization.

Finally, there is a dynamic aspect to the relationship between the IT revolution and globalization. The rules by which investors and their advisers evaluate information have a "learning by doing" aspect and thus improve with experience. This means that the decline in information costs to date has likely not yet had anywhere near its full impact on reducing the impediment to global securities markets traditionally arising from the cost advantages of local information.

The increase in cross border holdings is also related to institutionalization. In part because of the division of regulatory authority along geographic lines, individual investing in stock of foreign issuers faces obstacles that domestic investing does not. One way that domestic investors can gain access to the shares of a foreign issuer is for the foreign issuer to cross list its shares on a market in the investor's home country, typically in the form of an ADR in order to make currency exchange and clearing and settlement easier. Many foreign issuers are unwilling to do this, however, because of the regulatory compliance costs, potential liability arising from cross listing, and the costs of maintaining the ADR facility. For any foreign issuer that does not cross list, the domestic investor faces the transactional complications of placing an order on a foreign exchange. This typically includes having a broker regulated by the regime of the investor's home country as well as one regulated by the regime of the country where the trade actually occurs. There are also foreign exchange and clearing and settlement complications. Because of economies of scale, these complications of transacting abroad are much less costly on a per-dollar-invested basis for an institution than for a single individual. Thus the growth of both index and managed funds has significantly facilitated the increase in cross border ownership and reduced the demand for cross listings.

Our increased understanding of capital markets has also played a significant role in the increase in cross national holdings. Although the idea that diversification had risk-reducing benefits was well understood in the academy by the time of the original 1963 study, many investors at that time did not understand these benefits or at least how significant they are. This was particularly true with respect to diversifying to include the stocks of foreign issuers. The larger principle justifying diversification in general is that a highly diversified portfolio of stocks has less risk associated with it than a single stock or small group of stocks with the same expected return. This is because the future fortunes of each firm can be affected by a wide variety of potential developments, and, to the extent the developments affecting one firm are independent of those affecting another firm, a good development for one can easily be accompanied by a bad development for another. If both stocks are in an investor's portfolio, the effects of the two developments tend to cancel each other out. Firms from different countries tend to have less in common with each other than ones from any one country. Thus, a portfolio that includes shares of issuers from multiple countries, not just ones from the investor's home country, can diversify away more risk than one confined to a single country. Today this principle is far better understood by fund managers of various types and by individual investors and their advisors.

2 Primary Markets

Chapters 2 and 3, written respectively by Katherine Hanley and Donald Langevoort, explore the economic and legal issues relating to the primary equities market. A number of interrelated issues are identified: IPO underpricing, the size of underwriter fees, the volume of IPO activity, disclosure regulation, and unregistered offerings.

2.1 IPO Underpricing

One important issue identified by both authors is the well-documented phenomenon of IPO underpricing. Many studies have shown that closing prices on the first day of trading following an IPO are on average significantly higher than initial offering prices. The gain in first day price varies by period, but in the U.S. from 2001 to 2015 the average has been almost 14%. Interestingly, the range of underpricing in recent years is not very different from that of decades earlier even though today, with institutionalization, a large portion of the offering is typically sold to institutions whereas earlier much more of the offering was placed as the result of the selling efforts of retail brokers.

At first glance at least, such underpricing would appear to be a serious issue. An initial purchaser of an offering during this period could enjoy on average a 14% gain by holding the shares she purchased just a single day. Thus, but for this underpricing, the issuer would have received 14% more in proceeds for the shares it issued, meaning that its cost of capital would have been substantially lower. This may indeed be a cause for regulatory concern, but two questions stand out. One is whether it is better to characterize this price jump as a problem of secondary market overpricing than one of IPO market underpricing? Some studies suggest that this may be the case. These studies show that returns on IPOs over multiple year periods such as five years are below market returns. Because share prices over the longer run are the better measure of firm success, these results suggest that the typical issuer received, if anything, too high a price, and that its cost of capital in the IPO was not inefficiently high.

The second question is whether the average first day price jump is simply an additional part of the cost of distribution above and beyond the underwriter commission. In other words, the price jump may be necessary compensation to initial purchasers for them to be willing to take the adverse selection risks associated with committing to the offering while they see whether there develops a liquid market for the shares at a good price. This concern suggests that a better understanding of the underpricing phenomenon is necessary for us to be able to ascertain whether or not there are regulatory changes that could enhance economic welfare.

Hanley surveys a range of potential explanations for IPO underpricing identified by researchers, each of which has at least some empirical support. Some of the explanations rely on asymmetric information problems that exist between a private company and the members of the public that it seeks to turn into a wide shareholder base. To a considerable extent, these asymmetries may be inherent in the process of going public and hence not subject to amelioration by regulation. However, existing regulation of registered offerings does alter issuer behavior in ways relevant to this problem by both restricting them from disclosing certain information and forcing them to disclose other information. It is thus important to know more about whether any of the restrictions are unnecessarily aggravating the problem as well as whether there are disclosures not currently mandated which if made would cost effectively reduce any asymmetry-based portion of the underpricing.

Other potential causes of IPO underpricing are based on principal-agent issues involving the relationships among the investment bank, the firm going public, and institutional investors. Again, some kind of collaborative effort among such players is going to be necessary for a firm to go public and any collaborative effort is likely to involve some agency costs. It is possible, however, that some kind of contractual failure is contributing to these agency costs that could be ameliorated by a regulatory change. Closely related to this problem is the possibility, discussed by Langevoort, that rents are being earned by the underwriters or the initial purchasers because of arrangements that unnecessarily restrict competition. To the extent that any regulatory change could reduce either of these problems, the resulting reduction in IPO underpricing would be welfare enhancing because these problems, to the extent they exist, raise an issuing firm's cost of capital for no good reason.

Hanley suggests that we might have a much better handle on the relative importance of these different factors if we had better data on the allocation of IPO shares by the underwriters. Currently, each underwriter's allocation data is a closely held secret for competitive and perhaps other reasons. This is an area where the New Special Study could use the help of the SEC, which could mandate its collection on a confidential basis and then either study the data itself or anonymize the data and make it available to the Study's researchers.

2.2 Underwriting Fees

Relative to other countries, the fees charged by underwriters for U.S. public offerings are extremely high, especially for initial public offerings. Much ink has already been spilled on this topic and the Justice Department closed its investigation of the banks concluding there was no evidence of price fixing. Still, it is an open question why U.S. underwriter fees are so high.

The issue closely resembles the issue of IPO underpricing in the sense that the high fees could simply reflect greater underwriter effectiveness at providing a new issuer with a liquid market, but it also could reflect some kind of contracting failure or competition constraint that could be altered by regulation. If one of the latter two possibilities plays a role, their contribution to the high fees would represent a serious, but correctable inefficiency in the economy. Accordingly, an important potential research question is to explain why U.S. underwriting fees are so high. One empirical design would take advantage of the variation in fees across countries and then look at various measures of the success of the public offering process. While the project would have to avoid complicated endogeneity and selection effect problems, it could provide important insight into the underwriting fee question. Among other questions, the analysis could focus on why book building is the predominant procedure used in the U.S. for both IPOs and seasoned offerings, when theory, and to some extent practice abroad, suggests that auctions, and for seasoned offerings, rights offerings, may be superior.

2.3 IPO Volume

Another primary market issue addressed by Hanley is the drop in IPO activity over the past two decades. Since the Internet bubble in 2000, there has been a great deal of concern among academics, practitioners, and regulators about what is a viewed as a significant decline in the number of IPOs. A more accurate description would be that we have seen a great deal of volatility in the number of IPOs both over the last century and over the period since the internet bubble, but that the volatility may be around a lower central number in the last 15 years or so. The large drop immediately after the internet bubble burst is hardly surprising, as a high level of offerings is one of the defining characteristics of a bubble and is by definition unsustainable. Still, IPO activity since then does seem to be low even relative to many non-bubble years, though it should be noted that IPO activity did pick up significantly in 2017.

If we really are witnessing a secular decline in IPO activity, this is a potential cause for concern. A share with any given expected future cash flow to its holder will be more valuable if it trades in a public market than if it does not, which, all else equal, lowers a firm's cost of capital. An IPO is a principal route for a firm to obtain public trading for its shares and hence to get this benefit. For the entrepreneur who has established a successful innovative new firm and its early investors, an IPO creates the possibility of diversifying the wealth that they have gained, and so the future availability of an IPO acts as an incentive to such entrepreneurship and investing.

Again, assuming that there has in fact been a longer term IPO decline, whether it calls for any regulatory changes depends on its causes. The overarching questions are: have the alternatives to IPOs become more attractive, or have IPOs become less attractive and in ways correctible by regulatory change? Hanley reviews a number of explanations for both the observed volatility over time and the apparent overall lower level in recent years. One explanation, which presumably does not suggest any market failure or call for a regulatory response, is that with institutionalization, the private equity market has become much more vital. Thus, some firms that in the past would have engaged in IPOs have a viable alternative that will allow the venture capitalists and other early investors to cash out, the entrepreneur to diversify her gains, and the firm to raise new capital. Also it appears more such firms are being acquired by other firms rather than going public. This might be because IPOs are less attractive, but it also might be for reasons independent of the attractiveness of IPOs.

If research were to show that there has been an increase in IPO underpricing or underwriter fees, that could help explain the IPO decline, but whether these developments would call for regulatory change goes back to the discussion above. Another explanation would be that the act of going public and the ongoing cost of being a public company have increased. One response might be to change the rules to lower such costs, an approach in fact taken with the recent reforms that allow "emerging growth companies" to disclose less. This response has some logic to it, but it is not self-evidently correct. This is because the costly regulations requiring offering and ongoing disclosure serve important economic functions including combatting adverse selection. One way to test whether the effectiveness of these functions has been diluted is to see whether emerging growth company offerings are showing signs of increased adverse selection such as greater IPO underpricing.

2.4 Mandatory Disclosure Regulation

As just suggested, understanding better the contemporary corporate disclosure environment is important, for determining whether the disclosure requirements imposed at the time of an initial offering and the continuing periodic disclosure requirements thereafter make being a public company unnecessarily costly, thereby discouraging IPOs. It is also important because of the impact of continuing periodic disclosure rules on firms that are already public and almost certainly will continue to be so. Objections to the current system range from arguments that mandatory disclosure is entirely unnecessary to the much more modest, but still potentially important complaint that the current disclosure requirements have grown by accretion without periodic review of which parts of the accumulated set of mandates have been truly shown to meaningfully inform prices.

Assessing the seriousness of these complaints, and designing remedies to any problems that are revealed, will require both further conceptual thinking and further empirical work. On the conceptual side, as Langevoort explains, one difficulty is that we lack an agreed-upon methodology for assessing the costs and benefits of disclosure, including whether the appropriate vantage should be investor protection, capital formation, or social welfare. Presumably, though, the ultimate normative standard by which the securities market regulatory regime should be judged is its contribution to social welfare, with investor protection and capital formation being instruments for reaching this end. Considered this way, we can see that a number of social goals animate discussion of securities markets and their regulation, including disclosure rules. These goals include: (i) promoting the efficient allocation of capital so it goes to the most promising new investment projects in our economy; (ii) promoting the efficient operation of the economy's existing productive capacity; (iii) promoting the efficient allocation of resources between current and future periods so as to best satisfy the needs of firms seeking funds for real investments (trading the promise of future dollars to obtain current dollars) and the needs of savers seeking to forgo current consumption in order to enjoy future consumption (trading current dollars to obtain the promise of future dollars); (iv) promoting the efficient allocation among investors of the risks associated with holding securities so that the volatility in the cash flows generated by productive enterprises is borne by risk-averse investors in a way that generates the least disutility; (v) fostering an overall sense of fairness; (vi) economizing on the real resources society devotes to the operation of the trading markets and to the enforcement and compliance costs associated with their regulation; and (vii) fostering innovation that over time can improve the capacity of the system to serve these preceding goals. The securities markets' operations impact these social goals in complex ways that result from its interacting characteristics, with the two most important characteristics being share-price accuracy and liquidity. The impact of any given practice or regulation on the goals above is most easily evaluated through a two-step process, first assessing the effect of the practice on each of these two market characteristics and then identifying the effect of the characteristic on the goals.

Empirical financial economics provides us with various measures of the informedness of share prices and liquidity. The contributions of any given disclosure rule can be assessed using these measures, examining its impact at the time it was first imposed. The best candidates for such tests are regulations that were not initially imposed on all firms at once, so that before and after comparisons are not as easily confounded by other factors changing at the same time. On the cost side, as Hanley elaborates, much could be learned from an in depth case study analysis of the compliance costs of even a small sample of issuers.

2.5 Exempted Offerings

The traditional route for a firm to raise capital through an offering that leads to liquid trading of its shares has been an IPO conducted through the disclosure oriented Securities Act registration process. Out of concern that such registered offerings are impracticably burdensome for many firms, particularly small and medium size enterprises (SMEs), Congress has reacted by creating more lightly regulated pathways for certain kinds of firms to achieve the same ends through what we might call "quasi IPOs." These pathways are the result of the interactions of a number of new statutory provisions. These provisions include the mandate that the SEC adopt the Rule 506(c) registration exemption that allows general solicitation for certain unregistered offerings, the mandate that the SEC adopt rules allowing crowdfunding, the introduction of the Regulation A+ offerings, the new §4(a)(7) exemption from Securities Act registration for secondary transactions in unregistered shares by accredited investors, and the Exchange Act §12(g) amendment that increases the number of record shareholders needed to trigger the Act's periodic disclosure requirements from 500 to 2000.

As Hanley observes, there is a need for data on results of these quasi IPOs. This data can be used to see the extent of the liquidity discount for such offerings relative to registered offerings and whether the reason for the discount is "structural" (i.e. harder for buyers and sellers to find each other easily) versus increased adverse selection due to lower disclosure. Such data might also reveal how well capital is allocated through the quasi IPO route relative to via the registered IPO/seasoned offering route by seeing how the firms making offering of each type perform over time. These studies would require gathering data, not currently available, concerning the volume, types of transactions, bid/ask spread, depth of book, quality of execution etc. on Nasdaq Private Mkt and on SharesPost, where accredited investors can trade pursuant to a 4(a)(7) exemption or Rule 144.

Langevoort in turn suggests that it would be worthwhile to examine whether there is a relationship between the returns on different Rule 506 offerings and the characteristics of the accredited investors who purchase each. The purpose would be to determine whether there are two types of offerings: one type with good returns that are purchased by sophisticated investors who truly have no need for rigors of the registration process, and another type with poor returns that are purchased by investors who meet the current standards for being accredited but who apparently are vulnerable to being the target for poor deals.

One rationale for a mandatory disclosure regime is that the disclosures involve positive externalities: the private costs to each individual firm of making the disclosures are greater than the social costs; and the private benefits to the firm are less than the social benefits. As Langevoort suggests, it is important to try to determine the extent to which the development of the new opportunities for quasi IPOs undermines the production of these externalities. The private costs of an individual issuer's disclosures include the fact that the information provided can put the issuer at a disadvantage relative to its competitors, major suppliers, and major customers, but these are not social costs because the disadvantages to the issuer are counterbalanced by the advantages confered on the other firms. On the benefit side, an issuer's disclosures can be useful to investors in analyzing other issuers, which is a social benefit, but the gain to the issuer in terms of a transparency-induced boost to share price only reflects the usefulness of the disclosure to investors in analyzing the issuer itself. Thus, each issuer has some socially optimal level of disclosure, where the marginal social cost equals the marginal social benefit. Unregulated, however, an issuer will choose the level of disclosure where the marginal private cost equals the marginal private benefit. Because the issuer's private costs of disclosure exceed the social costs and its private benefits fall short of the social benefits, the issuer's choice will be below the socially optimal level of disclosure. With a mandatory-disclosure regime that sets the required disclosure level at the higher socially optimal level, any one issuer must disclose more than is privately optimal, but this issuer will benefit from the additional disclosure of all the other issuers in the market because they are also being subject to the same mandate.

Two questions deserve an attempt at even rough empirical estimation in connection with this rationale for mandatory disclosure. First, how great is the social value of the positive externalities described above. Second, to what extent are the new quasi IPO opportunities competing with traditional IPOs and slowly eroding a system that corrects for what would otherwise be the market failure associated with these externalitites, and to what extent are new quasi IPOs simply creating liquidity for firms that otherwise would have stayed private.

3 Secondary Trading Markets

Chapters 4 and 5, written respectively by Ryan Davies and Erik Sirri and by Paul Mahoney and Gabriel Rauterberg, explore the economic and legal issues relating to the secondary trading market for equities. Both chapters address the issues raised by the transformation from the floor and dealer markets of yesterday to today's world of electronic limit order book based trading venues. This technology-driven transformation, combined with the regulatory tilt toward encouraging multiple venues competing for the trading in each stock, has given us today's super-fast multi-venue structure for trading. The issues addressed by the two chapters relate to a number of matters including (i) whether the cost of trading has declined in this new stock market and whether large institutional traders share in these reduced trading costs, (ii) HFT practices, (iii) exchange operating rules, (iv) dark pools, and (v) possible radical transformations of Reg NMS such as the elimination of Rule 611 (the order protection rule).

3.1 Cost of Trading

Davies and Sirri canvas the academic literature with regard to the question of whether, relative to the days of the NYSE specialists and NASDAQ dealers, algorithmic and high frequency trading generates benefits to the market by increasing liquidity and therefore lowering the cost of trading. They conclude that, with a few exceptions, the literature generally provides an affirmative answer to this question. The area where the most controversy remains is whether large institutional orders have shared in this lower cost of trading or whether, instead, their cost of trading has actually increased. This is a question in need of further empirical study.

It should be noted, however, that even if the trading costs for large orders is found to have increased, there would remain two issues worthy of further analysis. First, is this trading cost increase simply the product of HFTs being better than the dealers and specialists of yesterday at protecting themselves against adverse selection – i.e., better at detecting when the orders coming to them are from informed traders? Second, if so, is the cost increase for these traders on balance socially harmful or in fact socially beneficial? The possibility that it is beneficial arises because, as a general matter, the very ability of HFTs to better protect themselves against adverse selection is likely the primary cause of the decrease in the cost of trading for all other traders. Suppose, in addition, that the large orders are mostly without social benefit. This could be because, for example, they come mostly from persons who are trying to trade in the very brief time before an issuer's public announcement gets fully reflected in price or from persons trading on soon-to-be-announced inside information. And suppose that the small trades are socially beneficial. This could be because, for example, they are coming from retail level persons with no special information who are buying as a way to save and selling in order to cash in to have funds to consume. And because they are coming from persons trading on the basis of longer-term-price-accuracy-increasing fundamental value research, whose trading is not so urgent that they cannot break their orders up into less revealing small pieces and submit them over time. Empirical research, using, for example, the SEC's new consolidated audit trail data, might shed considerable light on whether this description of who uses large trades versus small trades is correct and hence on whether any increase in the cost of large trades in fact reflects something socially desirable rather than undesirable.

3.2 HFT Practices

Even if we conclude that markets work better today than yesterday overall, this does not necessarily mean that we now live in the best of all possible worlds. Among the complaints that the world could be made still better are a number of criticisms of HFTs, ones that go beyond the complaint that their role as today's market makers make large trades more expensive. Although today's HFT-dominated market appears to supply liquidity to at least most traders at lower cost than in the past, HFTs may also exploit their capacity to obtain and act on market information (information concerning newly completed trades and changes in the quotes) faster than others in ways that are perceived as unfair. These concerns are exemplified by Michael Lewis' popular book *Flash Boys* and his claim that because of such HFT practices, the U.S. equity markets are "rigged."

One such practice criticized by Lewis is what he refers to as "electronic front running." The setting for the practice begins with a trader seeking to trade a substantial number of shares of a given issuer by breaking the total up into several orders and simultaneously sending each order to a different exchange. It takes slightly different amounts of time for the different orders to reach the respective exchanges to which they are sent. An HFT then uses its speed advantages with regard to obtaining and acting on market information to detect the existence of the trader's order that is first to arrive at its destination. Based on this observation, in the brief time before the trader's other orders arrive at the respective exchanges to which they were sent, the HFT cancels its quotes on these other exchanges and submits new, changed quotes. The reason an HFT would do so is because something about the trader's trade on the first exchange makes the HFT concerned that the trader has private information. The analysis of whether it is socially desirable or undesirable that an HFT to protect itself against adverse selection in this way directly parallels the analysis above concerning whether any increase in the cost of doing large trades is undesirable. The answer to the question depends on the social value of the type of trading by the trader whose trade is being detected versus the social value of other the other types of trading less subject to electronic front running. The former is made more expensive by the practice. The latter is made less expensive because the HFTs do not need as wide a bid/ask spread to compensate themselves for the adverse selection losses associated with the former type of trading. Again, empirical research using the SEC's new consolidated audit trail data might shed considerable light on the question of the types of traders benefited and hurt by the practice.

It is worth considering as well two other HFT practices criticized by Lewis that involve an HFT's speed advantages in obtaining and acting on market information. One, that Lewis refers to as "mid-point exploitation," involves the HFT executing against a limit order priced at the midpoint between the best bid and offer (NBB and NBO) available in the market, where the determination of what is the NBB and the NBO is based on the Securities Information Processor (SIP), the public data feed. The SIP is a bit slow in reflecting changes in the actual quotes available on the various exchanges and so the NBB and NBO based on SIP do not move to reflect actual quote changes as quickly as the HFT becomes aware of them. Thus, when there is a substantial change in the actual best bid and/or offer, situations can arise where the HFT can execute against the midpoint limit order at a price based on the SIP's NBB and NBO and reverse the transaction for a profit by sending an order that will transact at the new changed actual best bid or offer. The second such criticized practice, which Lewis refers to as "slow market arbitrage," again involves exploiting the slowness of the SIP. Consider a situation where the HFT has an offer on one exchange that has been the NBO, but a new better offer arrives at another exchange. The HFT learns of the new better (i.e., lower) offer on the other exchange ahead of it being reported on the SIP. The HFT can then engage in a riskless arbitrage if, while the SIP has yet to catch up, a marketable order from some random third party arrives at the first exchange. The HFT's offer is still the NBO according to the SIP and so the third party's marketable order executes against it. Having just sold a share as a result this transaction at the old higher NBO, the HFT then profitably reverses the transaction by sending a purchase order to the exchange with the new lower offer.[6]

Unlike electronic front running, each of these other two practices is unambiguously anti-social, yielding profits to the HFT without providing any benefit to the market. Before deciding to try to stop these practices, however, it is important to establish empirically how prevalent they are. The most effective way of stopping them would likely involve some measure that would decrease or eliminate HFT market information and execution speed advantages. This would also reduce or eliminate the ability of HFTs to engage in electronic front running, which, as we have just seen, may be a socially beneficial, not harmful, practice. Thus, if these two practices are in fact not very prevalent, the cure might cause more damage than the disease.

Another criticism of HFTs is that they engage in "quote stuffing," i.e., cancelling old quotes and submitting new ones so frequently that only a small percentage of all the quotes posted are actually executed against. To the extent that this complaint is in fact distinct from complaints about electronic front running, it would appear to reflect a concern that such frequent quote changes

---

[6] Slow market arbitrage can also occur through a set of mirror transactions where the HFT has a bid that has been the NBB and it learns of a new better (i.e., higher) bid on another exchange ahead of it being reflected on the SIP.

strain the capacities of exchanges and that of the interconnections among them and with the SIP. It is unclear why the individual exchanges cannot deal with this problem by calibrating their fees and rebates to reflect the costs that such quoting behavior imposes on them. Still, as noted in the chapter on globalization discussed below, Europe, with its new MiFID II regulations, has recently imposed limits on quote cancellation, whereas the U.S. has no such limits. This situation provides an opportunity for an empirical examination of what the effects of limits are on market liquidity.

An additional factor to consider in connection with these various HFT practices is, as noted by Davies and Sirri, the concern by some market observers that HFTs are pitted against each other (and to some extent against other sophisticated traders in the market) in a competition to acquire and act on market information faster than anyone else. This arguably leads to significant social waste: the fiber optic cables, highly powerful computers and human talent required by each HFT engaging in this race are very expensive. If these resources were instead deployed elsewhere in the economy, they would permit society to enjoy greater production of other goods and services of real value.

Another concern associated with the rise of HFTs, again identified by Davies and Sirri, is that high frequency traders will trade only when it is in their economic interest to do so. When they withdraw completely, a flash crash can occur because no one in the business of providing liquidity is doing so, leaving, to be executed against, just standing limit orders well away from what had previously been the NBB and NBO. Moreover, as Davies and Sirri also report, while most existing empirical studies have found that the new, HFT-dominated stock market has led to improvements in liquidity, some have found that it has also led to greater moment-to-moment volatility, although opinion is divided on this. Concerns about flash crashes and the possible increase in moment-to-moment volatility call for both further conceptual thinking and further empirical study. On the conceptual side, we need to think more about whether the occasional, quickly self-corrected, flash crash or any possible increase in moment to-moment (or even day-to-day) fluctuations in price really matter. After all, the functions that accurate prices play in promoting efficiency in the real economy involve price levels over considerably longer periods of time. And, for individual investors buying and selling, price deviations randomly above or below some central figure are, with multiple transactions, likely to each other cancel out.

On the empirical side, at least two important questions need to be addressed. First, with regard to moment-to-moment general volatility, we need a more definitive answer as to whether the rise of HFTs have in fact led to increases. Second, even if we conclude that flash crashes are unimportant in terms of the role that accurate prices play in promoting efficiency in the real economy or the risk they impose on investors, do they have a psychological effect that reduces market confidence in ways that damage the market's functioning?

3.3 Exchange Operating Rules

To the extent that HFT practices based on the capacity to very quickly acquire and act on market information and the associated arms race are considered socially unfortunate, there are at least two ways exchanges might alter their operating rules to combat these practices. One is for an exchange to install a "speed bump," i.e., an intentional delay of traders' communication with the market center. One avenue for evaluating the effectiveness and desirability of such a speed bump is to use as a case study the speed bump implemented by the U.S. exchange IEX, which created a 350-microsecond delay by routing all external communications through a coiled fiber-optic cable. Even if an empirical study reveals that the speed bump does yield gains for IEX and those trading on IEX, two questions would still need to be given further thought. One is whether, with just IEX adopting its form of speed bump, are any gains it achieves simply the result of negative externalities imposed on the other exchanges or the persons trading on these other exchanges? The other, somewhat related question is whether there is any reason to expect if all exchanges adopted speed bumps (or speed bumps were imposed on all exchanges by regulation), would HFTs then be in the same position to take advantage of their speed as they were when there were no speed bumps, with just a pause of $1/3000^{th}$ of a second before everything begins?

A second way of solving these problems, if they are found to be real, is replacing the current structure of continuous trading on exchanges with periodic batch auctions.[7] As a theoretical matter, batch auctions can mitigate or negate the competitive advantage an HFT would obtain from a capacity to more quickly acquire and act on market information. This would diminish or eliminate both the practices based on these speed advantages and the incentive to engage in the associated arms race. However, further thought is required as to whether, for batch auctions to accomplish much, all exchanges would need to adopt them and whether the timing of the auctions on each exchange would need to be very close, perhaps impractically so, to simultaneous.

Another kind of exchange operating rule worthy of further study is the wide range of order types that exchanges allow today. Traders historically were limited to market and limit orders, with perhaps a few allowable modifiers to these such as immediate-or-cancel, all-or-none, or fill-to-kill. Today, each

---

[7] This proposal is from Eric Budish, Peter Cramton & John Shim, *The High-Frequency Trading Arms Race: Frequent Batch Auctions in a Market Design Response*, 130 Q. J. ECON. 1547 (2015).

exchange has between 25 and 50 different order types. Davies and Sirri believe that many of these order types are either rarely used or used only by highly sophisticated traders. Some commentators view the availability of these complex order types with suspicion, perhaps simply because it is HFTs that are typically the parties pushing for their adoption by the exchanges. It would be helpful to have a better understanding of these orders through empirical work that could pin down their welfare effects in terms price accuracy, liquidity and their potential for causing some kind of system collapse.

3.4 Dark Pools

Dark pools publicly report transactions in the same way as exchanges do, but differ from exchanges in that they do not publicly report the nonmarketable limit orders that are posted on them. This absence of "ex ante transparency" raises the issue of whether "price discovery" – the speed with which market prices adjust to fully reflect new information possessed by at least some traders in the market – will suffer if some portion of total trading occurs on dark pools. Davies and Sirri cite studies suggesting that this is the case, i.e., that more trading on dark pools leads to inferior price discovery.

One question that needs further thought is whether a difference in the speed of information reflection measured in seconds or even hours really matters in terms of the contribution that well-functioning markets can make to society. It is important to note that the issue of price discovery is quite distinct from the overall amount of information that is reflected in an issuer's share price. The overall amount of information has much more effect on the accuracy with which the share price predicts an issuer's future cash flows than do small differences in the speed with which any given bit of information is reflected in price. The analysis of the social significance of price discovery actually more closely resembles the analysis, addressed above, of the social importance of very short term price volatility.

On the empirical side, ceilings on the proportion of a stock's trading that can occur on dark pools have recently been imposed in Canada and, under MiFID II, in Europe. The imposition of these ceilings presents opportunities for empirical investigations of the impact of dark pools on liquidity and longer term price accuracy, as well as on price discovery and volatility.

3.5 Proposals for More Radical Reform

Both Davies and Sirri and Mahoney and Rauterberg address issues relating to NMS Rule 611, known as the "order protection rule." This rule requires that each trading venue have procedures in place that reasonably assure that if the trading venue receives an order for a given stock and the venue's best quote is less favorable than the best quote available on one or more other exchanges, the order will be sent on to one of these other exchanges. The order protection rule is perhaps the most controversial component of the SEC's whole national market system regulatory scheme and its critics maintain that it should be abandoned. These critics suggest that the rule unnecessarily complicates the system of interconnections among trading venues and claim that this complication leads to system breakdowns. They also object to the fact that the rule gets in the way of a trader that is willing to pay more than the best price if doing so will get the trade done faster.

Supporters of the rule claim that the rule guarantees small-order traders execution at the best price regardless of the diligence of their brokers, which is hard for such traders to monitor. The critics respond that monitoring brokers is not so difficult and that competitive pressures will force brokers to maintain cost-effective levels of diligence. The rule's supporters also claim that it provides a reliable incentive to reward those who submit the best quotes and gives new exchanges a better chance to penetrate the market.

In order to evaluate these competing claims, it will be necessary to examine empirically how the order protection rule has worked and its benefits and costs. The empirical analysis can rely on the fact that the rule only requires procedures that are "reasonably designed" to avoid execution at an inferior price. This "reasonably designed" standard has not been interpreted as requiring that 100% of all orders received be executed at the best quote, and in fact less than 100% are. Studying how far on average the execution prices of the orders that do slip through these procedures are from the best available quotes in the market would provide at least a sense at the outer edge of the amount of protection the rule provides, given the current level of broker diligence. A study of exchange breakdowns could examine the plausibility of the claim that complications introduced by the rule have been a significant contributing factor. Further thought also needs to be given as to whether the faster trades at inferior prices that are blocked by the Rule are really socially valuable. It is possible that they are often not, being based information of short lived value, either inside information soon to be publicly announced or information from a public announcement that has just been made and not yet fully reflected in price.

The issue of eliminating Rule 611 goes beyond how traders interact with the system as it is. It potentially goes to the system's whole structure. The NMS rules concerning automated access necessitated by Rule 611 were the death knell for the specialist system on the NYSE. As Mahoney and Rauterberg argue, elimination of Rule 611 would thus allow changes in the automated access rules. This, they suggest, would create room for a manual market to reestablish itself and with it a role for floor traders. How much this possibility strengthens the case for repealing Rule 611 comes back in part to the questions, discussed above, about whether institutional trading using large order is in fact more difficult than in the earlier era and, if it is, whether the increase in difficulty is really socially disadvantageous. Of course, even if further empirical work suggests affirmative answers to these two questions, more thinking would also be needed to determine whether it would be realistic to expect a manual market to reemerge.

Mahoney and Rauterberg go further and raise the question: why not scrap NMS entirely and encourage a different type of competition that would let each exchange set the rules with regard to the issuers listed on that exchange? An exchange's rules might well be ones that would require of all orders relating to the shares of each of its listed issuers be sent exclusively to it, but another exchange might choose rules that would allow the trading of the shares of its listed issuers on multiple exchanges. Mahoney and Rauterberg suggest that this wholesale reform could lead to one exchange doing batch auctions, another using manual trading, another maintaining an electronic limit order book, and so on. To the extent that the shareholders of different issuers would be better off trading on exchanges with different trading protocols, competitive pressures would lead different exchange operators to offer these different protocols. To the extent that certain protocols dominate certain others, competitive pressures would push out any exchanges insisting on offering the inferior protocols. For such a radical reform to even begin to be viable, however, there needs to be confidence that each issuer would in fact choose the listing exchange best for its shareholders. A sense of whether this is the case could come from a study of the factors that currently determine issuers' choices of where to list.

4 Intermediaries

Chapters 6 and 7, written respectively by Alan Ferrell and John Morley and Jonathan Berk and Jules van Binsbergen, explore the economic and legal issues relating to the intermediaries. Intermediaries include each of the different kinds of firms – broker-dealers, investment advisors, mutual funds, hedge funds, pension funds, and private equity firms – that help determine in which securities individuals and institutions acquire direct or indirect interests and in what secondary trading venue the resulting purchase and sale orders are executed. As noted earlier, one of the biggest contrasts between the time of the 1963 Special Study and today is the extent of institutionalization. While individual investors historically bought and sold stocks and bonds directly, they now predominantly do so indirectly, through mutual funds, hedge funds, ETFs, and similar vehicles. Ferrell and Morley report that about 75% of the common stock of American public companies now belongs to institutional intermediaries.

4.1 Managed Mutual Funds

As Ferrell and Morley observe, the Investment Company Act (ICA) was enacted by Congress in 1940 primarily to target closed-end mutual funds. However, in the years since 1940, the mutual fund industry has moved to being overwhelmingly dominated by open-end funds, with their assets now having more than forty times the assets of closed-end funds. Ferrell and Morley suggest that this rise of open-end funds has left significant aspects of the ICA seriously out of date, particularly its provisions requiring that open-end fund shareholders have the right to vote.

As Ferrell and Morley explain, when the ICA was enacted, shareholder voting was common in closed-end funds, but not in open-end funds. Nonetheless, the ICA imposed a system of mandatory voting in director elections and other matters for both types of funds. Ferrell and Morley argue that the shareholder voting requirements should be eliminated for open-end funds. Echoing the work of other scholars, they say that that open-end shareholders have very little incentive ever to use their right to vote if they are dissatisfied with management. This is because they have a cheaper and more effective option: redeeming their shares for their pro rata share of the net asset value of the fund's assets. In essence, this redemption right provides an especially strong form of exit. It would be helpful to test the Ferrell and Morley proposition by doing a study of the extent to which investors in open-end funds actually use their voting rights. If it turns out that the right in fact has essentially never been used in the nearly 80 year history of the ICA, the current costly process of soliciting proxies would indeed appear to be an unnecessary waste.

Without a shareholder vote, open-end fund boards of directors would presumably be simply self-perpetuating institutions. Ferrell and Morley thus go further and inquire as to whether boards of directors for mutual funds should be eliminated outright. Even if voting were eliminated, however, further thought and empirical inquiry is required before taking this further step. Maintaining the board means maintaining a group of persons who have fiduciary duties. So the key question for research is whether these fiduciary duties serve any useful purpose.

Another important issue concerning actively managed mutual funds is whether fund managers in fact have the ability to add value through buying underpriced securities and selling overpriced ones. The issue is closely tied to a second issue: whether the fees of managed funds need some kind of regulation. The two issues are closely tied because, beyond the small portion of fees related to the mechanical costs of operation that managed funds and index funds must both incur, adding value is the justification for the much larger fees being paid to the managers of actively managed funds. These two issues are in turn linked to a third issue, identified just above: whether open-end funds should be required to have directors. This is because the fund board's two primary functions are to decide whether to retain the existing fund managers and to negotiate the managers' fees.

The chapter by Berk and van Binsbergen hones in on the basic issue of whether active fund managers add value. As they explain, the consensus view is that investors are better off avoiding funds with active managers and the fees they charge; instead they should invest in low-fee passive index funds. The basis of this view is studies suggesting that when the fees for managed funds are taken into account, investors in these actively managed funds do no better than if they personally invested in stocks chosen by random selection.

Drawing on their earlier work, Berk and van Binsbergen develop in their chapter a rational expectations model of fund management that challenges this consensus view. In their model, rational investors move assets to funds having a positive net alpha and remove assets from funds having a negative net alpha. This proposition, when coupled with decreasing returns to scale to fund managers' investment opportunities, predicts that funds' net alphas will all tend to zero in equilibrium. Berk and van Binsbergen's model further predicts that in equilibrium investors are indifferent between actively managed funds and passive, i.e., index, funds. Active fund managers do add value in their view, but competition between investors causes this value to flow to the managers. Berk and van Binsbergen also conduct empirical analysis to evaluate the theoretical predictions of their model. Among other things, they find that they cannot reject the null hypothesis that the average fund net alpha is not statistically different from zero at any conventional level of significance.

There is much in this work that makes sense. Certainly it is plausible that a fund manager can generate fundamental value information, and trade accordingly with expected profits. They do so by gathering various bits of information that are publicly available or are otherwise observable features of the world and analyzing what has been gathered in a sophisticated way that enables a superior assessment of a stock's cash flows than that implied by the current market price. Microstructure economics would suggest that liquidity suppliers compensate for the profits made by such fundamental value traders simply by widening the bid ask spread that is also paid by uninformed traders and traders trading on mistaken beliefs. It is plausible as well that such fund managers could capture through their fees some portion, perhaps all, of the profits so generated.

How far should this framework be taken in terms of designing regulation? It potentially suggests that there is no need, through the maintenance of the directors requirement for open-end mutual funds or otherwise, for any legally based controls on management fees, or, as discussed below, for the regulation of the kickbacks to brokers who steer investors to these funds. More work is needed, however, before it would be appropriate to implement regulatory change based on these conclusions. First, the model is based on the assumption of rational investors adding money to positive alpha funds and subtracting it from negative alpha funds. How realistic is it to assume that ordinary investors can in fact identify which is which and act accordingly, particularly given how long it takes to separate out with any statistical confidence which funds have done well because of luck and which because of greater skill? In other words, recent historical performance is only a weak proxy for the actual abilities of fund managers. Moreover, this uncertainty concerning the alpha of different funds occurs in the context of a world where funds are heavily marketed and brokers may receive bonuses from a fund's sponsor for recommending it to the broker's clients. Investor mistakes in identifying positive and negative alpha funds would appear raise more serious questions for the conclusions of the Berk and van Binsbergen theory than investor mistakes concerning the future cash flows of an issuer raise for the conclusions of the efficient market hypothesis with regard to secondary trading markets. The price impact of mistaken traders in secondary trading markets can be arbitraged away by smart money traders with an ability to sell short but there is nothing comparable with regard to the movement of money among open-end funds. As for their empirical study, it was only unable to reject with statistical confidence the null hypothesis that the average fund net alpha is not statistically different from zero. This is not a demonstration that it in fact was approximately equal to zero. It is perfectly possible that it was not equal to zero and that the problem is that the test simply did not have the power to allow a rejection of the null hypothesis.

In this connection, Ferrell and Morley say that there is good evidence of a lot of competition in the mutual fund space, but also evidence that some funds, after fees, consistently underperform the risk-adjusted market return. They suggest that more research needs to be done as to why these corners of the market exist. This may be an area where experimental economics would be helpful because, to the extent that these corners exist, it is because of investor behavior. Once the causes are understood, it is possible that the focus should be at changing investor behavior. One possibility, they suggest, is that in place of the bland disclosure currently imposed, something akin to a cigarette pack displaying only a skull would be in order. Ferrell and Morley also point out that data suggests that almost all the class actions under ICA Section 36(b) are ones brought against big funds. This, they say, suggests that the attention of SEC enforcement officials needs to be especially focused on smaller funds, which tend to charge the higher fees.

In sum, resolving the question of how far the work of Berk and van Binsbergen can be taken in reforming the regulation of actively managed open-end mutual funds can be of great social value. It may turn out that some, or perhaps most of the current regulation may be necessary. But, to the extent that it is not, the costs of compliance with unneeded regulation represent an unfortunate extra burden on a business that generates fundamental value information. Such information improves share price accuracy in ways that are meaningful to the more efficient operation of the real economy. Unnecessary higher costs mean less of this valuable information generation will occur.

Ferrell and Morley also have things to say about closed-end mutual funds. They point to the near universal negative NAV of closed end funds. With regard at least to funds where all their investments are in liquid stocks, they ask whether this negative performance suggests that a closed-end fund is inherently such a poor way of organizing money management that it should not be allowed. Here, they suggest, empirics may be ahead of theory. Regulatory reform to discourage investment in these funds, or even their outright ban, would, at a minimum, require more thinking as to whether, and why, the open-end right of redemption is dominant in all situations as the superior form of disciplining stock fund management.

4.2 Broker-Dealers

In their chapter, Ferrell and Morley also address broker-dealers and their duties. As they explain, broker-dealers have a number of legal obligations, such as a duty of best execution and an obligation to recommend only suitable investments. However, unlike investment advisers, broker-dealers do not owe a traditional trustee-type fiduciary duty to their clients under current federal law. Part of the problem is that when a broker-dealer handles a purchase or sale order for a client through a principal transaction, i.e., by being the counterparty to the client, making a profit on the transaction would not be allowed if the broker-dealer were considered to have trustee-like fiduciary duties. Yet the broker-dealer would be providing a service to the customer just like when it instead handles such an order as a broker. This can be a problem even if the duty is watered down a notch so that the broker-dealer is allowed to make a "fair" profit on the transaction but the burden is on the broker to show that it is fair.

There is considerable policy discussion about whether broker-dealers should be subject to some sort of fiduciary duty under federal law. As Ferrell and Morley observe in their paper, that question cannot be answered in the abstract and instead requires an understanding of the specific ways in which existing broker-dealer regulation and a federal fiduciary rule would diverge as a practical matter. The relevant question is one of marginal effects – that is, whether a federal fiduciary duty on broker-dealers would impose obligations on broker-dealers beyond those they are currently subject to under prevailing broker-dealer law. As Ferrell and Morley explain, the necessary analysis requires a detailed identification of the specific ways in which the imposition of a federal fiduciary duty on broker-dealers would subject them to obligations not already mandated by existing broker-dealer regulation.

Additional empirical studies would also be helpful in determining the extent of potential benefits, if any, of imposing a federal fiduciary duty on broker-dealers. Many, but not all, states impose fiduciary duties on brokers, and those that do vary in the extent of the duty. By using cross state differences in fiduciary rules, a study could assess the effect of the imposition of federal fiduciary duties on the number of broker complaints and on the level of investment advice services provided. Information on complaints against brokers is available from FINRA.

With such a large portion of individual investor funds now going into mutual fund products rather than being used to purchase individual stocks, the broker-dealer's role in selling these products is particularly important. Consider first actively managed funds. If the rational expectations framework developed by Berk and van Binsbergen accurately describes the fund management market, the fact that a broker sends her client to a high fee fund that provides the broker a kickback may not be indicative of any breach of fiduciary duty by the broker. This is because, in equilibrium, expected investor returns net of fees will in any event equal the risk-adjusted expected market return. However, we have discussed above, there is research that would need to be done to determine the extent to which this model can reliably guide regulatory policy.

More generally, Ferrell and Morley suggest that much more work needs to be done concerning broker-dealer sales practices. Questions abound. In doing a study, what evidence should one look to, for example, to determine whether investors are being given poor investment advice that is distorted by the interests of the broker-dealer? In what ways, if any, is the nature of the competition among brokers for clients insufficient to bring fees down to competitive levels? Is the traditional transaction-based structure of fees the optimal one? With regard to this last question, Berk and van Binsbergen think that it is indeed competition that has caused the large shift over the last several decades in terms of who determines where the typical investor's money is being invested: from full service brokers, with their transaction based compensation, to fund managers, who are compensated on a funds under management basis. Presumably the key to answering the questions of both what are inherently socially defective sales practices and the effectiveness of competitive market forces in combatting them involves understanding better investor behavior and knowledge. Again, this is where experimental economics is the most likely route to finding things out, at least absent the availability of natural experiments arising from changes in law that change what a broker is and is not allowed to do in one jurisdiction relative to another.

There are potential issues as well with regard to how brokers sell passively managed mutual funds – i.e. index funds. The important question is whether currently there are a significant number of instances where a broker recommends a product with a higher fee where there is no reason to believe it will produce a different gross return, for example two index funds (a) with the same amount invested by the investor, (b) based on the same index, and (c) run in the same fashion. If the gross return is expected to be the same for each, the net return to the investor will be less with the higher fee fund. An empirical test of this question, and any regulatory remedy if the test shows there is a problem, would each share the same key challenge: how to determine that two products based on the same index are, other than their fees, essentially equivalent even though there are some variations in the way that they are run.

5 The Global Context

U.S. securities markets do not operate in an isolated state, unaffected by the laws of other countries and the actions of investors, issuers and exchanges abroad. This fact does, and should, affect U.S. regulation and is an important consideration in how all the issues discussed in Chapters 2-7 should be approached. In Chapter 8, John Armour, Martin Bengzten, and Luca Enriques address this global context.

5.1 The Increase in Global Interaction

As discussed in the first section of this chapter, relative to the time of the 1963 Special Study, today's securities markets now are much less defined by national borders. Armour et al. flesh this point out. For example, they provide World Bank data from 1970-2015 on global net inflows of portfolio equity, which provide a rough measure of the extent of globalization of the securities markets. As shown in Figure 1 in their chapter, global net inflows stayed fairly constant from 1970-1985 but ballooned in the period 1985-2015. They identify three potential sources for the increase in transnational market activity: firms raising more capital in foreign countries, investors sending more of their capital abroad, and financial institutions offering more international intermediation. In order to fully understand the implications of this changed global context for U.S. securities regulation, it will be important to identify more precisely the relative importance of these three potential channels working to globalize securities markets.

5.2 The Reach of U.S. Securities Regulation

Any given equity securities transaction has a number of dimensions: the issuer, the buyer, the seller (different from the issuer except in a primary market offering), the trading venue (or, in a primary market or a non-trading-venue secondary transaction, the place from which the solicitation of the transaction was made and the place where the solicitation was received), the intermediary involved, and the place where consideration is exchanged for the security. Unless all of these dimensions involve just one country, the transaction has some international dimension to it. This in turn can potentially give rise to claims by more than one country to regulate the behavior of some or all of the participants in the transaction. With any transaction that has at least one U.S. dimension of this sort and at least one non-U.S. dimension, the question for the United States is should it seek to so regulate.

The U.S. Supreme Court, in the *Morrison* case, used a transaction location approach to determining the reach of Section 10(b) of the 1934 Act. Some commentators and courts have extended the logic of that decision with regard to the reach of other provisions of U.S. securities laws. Whether or not the Court's opinion represented a good approach to statutory interpretation, this exclusively transaction-location approach seems simplistic policy-wise, especially across the wide range of different possible issues that our securities law touch upon. Armour et al. suggest that rather than the rigid formula in *Morrison*, the appropriate reach of U.S. securities law should depend on the specific rule at issue. For instance, the appropriate reach of private liability suits based on false or misleading issuer statements may be different than the appropriate reach of rules concerning broker-dealer behavior or insider trading. This is an important point. Drawing in the wrong place the lines of the reach of any given U.S. rule can be very disadvantageous. On the one hand, too broad a reach may unnecessarily scare away primary and secondary transactions from the United States. On the other hand, drawing it too narrowly can leave U.S. interests unprotected. Given the wide range of different U.S. securities law rules and regulations, this is an area requiring more conceptual thinking than it has been given so far.

5.3 Other Issues

Armour et al. identify a number of other research questions relating to the globalization of the securities markets. These include analysis and determination of the circumstances under which U.S. institutional investors choose to invest in foreign companies through ADRs rather than investing directly in the underlying foreign shares. They also suggest an evaluation of the welfare consequences of the observed reduction in cross-listing and further empirical research concerning the factors that determine whether foreign firms conduct IPOs or cross-list in the United States.

5.4 Learning From Others

At a number of points in this chapter, we have suggested empirical studies based on the experiences of other countries. Armour et al. suggest a number of additional such ideas. For example, European restrictions on HFT cancellation of orders, as well as their market maker obligations to post quotes, could each be good objects of empirical studies concerning their effects on the bid/ask spread, volatility, price discovery, and price informedness. The same is true of the French action against certain HFT practices of Virtu Financial. The EU "fiduciary duty" imposed on broker-dealers would make an interesting comparative study with the U.S., including how the EU duty deals with principal transactions. The performance of the AIM market in the UK could be a good source of what happens when mandatory disclosure is relaxed.

6 The Way Forward: Completing the New Special Study

There is a growing consensus that the profound changes to the securities markets highlighted in the first section of this chapter necessitate a new comprehensive evaluation of these markets. Such an effort could significantly enhance the quality of future regulatory reforms. Indeed, writing almost three decades ago, Milton Cohen, the key figure behind the 1963 Special Study, stated that while the 1963 study "still serves as an important reservoir of data and concepts, . . . much of its contents has become obsolete."[8] Since then, academics and regulators alike have echoed these concerns with increasing frequency and have repeatedly called for a new comprehensive study of the securities markets.

With the New Special Study Project, this call is finally being heeded. The Project is a multiyear effort under the auspices of Columbia Law School and Columbia Business School's Program in the Law and Economics of Capital Markets. The Project commenced in 2015 and draws on the collective insights of academics, practitioners, and regulators in order to critically and comprehensively evaluate the securities markets and the regulation of these markets. The ultimate objective of the New Special Study Project is a detailed report summarizing the project's findings and recommendations that will be directed to federal financial regulators, the U.S. Congress, interested stakeholders in the securities markets, and the general public. The final report will be built around a set of empirical and other research projects addressing the salient aspects of the securities markets and their regulation.

The seven chapters that follow are based on papers commissioned by the Project that were initially presented at the Initiating Conference of the New Special Study, held at Columbia University on March 23-24, 2017. The papers and the conference were part of Stage I of the New Special Study Project, the purpose of which has been to lay the intellectual foundations for the larger effort. The key questions for Stage I have been: what are the most important issues, for which of these issues are there already answers in the existing

---

[8] Milton H. Cohen, *A Quarter-Century of Market Developments—What Should a New "Special Study" Study?*, 45 BUS. LAWYER 3 (1989).

literature, and for which is new research required? Stage I is culminating with the publication of this book.[9]

Stage II of the Project involves the development of a definitive plan for completing the Study. This would include detailed identification and design of the necessary research studies as well a detailed outline of the final report. Stage III will be the implementation of this plan of action, leading to the completed report.

The issues discussed in this first overview chapter are but a small sample of the many timely and interesting issues developed in the seven chapters that follow. The sheer number of potential issues of inquiry identified by the authors of these papers is a reflection of the importance and necessity of a modern comprehensive analysis of the securities markets. They make fascinating reading. They contain both important policy guides usable right now and thoughtful agendas for future research for a wide community of scholars. Most importantly, they lay a firm intellectual foundation for the New Special Study Project going forward.

---

[9] The Initiating Conference also included commentators and panels commenting on each of the seven papers. In addition, the Conference included a separate panel session devoted solely to technology issues. Also as part of Stage I, on November 17, 2017, a separate conference was held at Columbia University with the presentation of papers and comments focused solely on debt markets issues relating to the New Special Study.

Chapter 2
THE ECONOMICS OF PRIMARY MARKETS

Kathleen Weiss Hanley[10]

Raising capital from the general public is a market feature of the American economic system.

Neither the securities acts, the Commission, nor the industry itself fully anticipated the problems arising from the entry of unqualified persons, the spectacular development of the over-the-counter market, the vast number of companies going public for the first time, or a variety of other striking changes.

Letter of Transmittal of the Special Study of Securities Markets (part 1) at p. iii & iv.

1 Introduction

Reading the first Report of Special Study of Securities Markets, one is struck by the similarity of the issues facing the Securities and Exchange Commission (SEC) in 1963 and today. Conflicts of interest, tensions in the appropriate level of disclosure, and the speed of issuance are all present in the Special Study. The chapter on Primary and Secondary Distributions to the Public came on the heels of a significant wave of initial public offerings (IPOs) that highlighted the potential for abuses in the market. Concerns about the amount of capital raised in unregistered or private offerings and the influence of institutional investors were central themes of the chapter. The resources available to the writers of the study were modest by today's standards. The principal

---

[10] Bolton-Parella Endowed Chair in Finance and Director of the Center for Financial Services, Lehigh University. This discussion is heavily based upon my joint work with Susan Chaplinsky, Amy Edwards, Jerry Hoberg, Charles Lee, Katie Moon, Paul Seguin, and Bill Wilhelm. Additional material is from a letter that Jay Ritter and I wrote in support of including primary market transactions in the Consolidated Audit Trail. I also would like to thank Jay Ritter for helpful comments and data as well as Matthew Gustafson, Tom Hanley, Alexander Ljungqvist, Michelle Lowry, Roni Michaely, and Stanislava Nikolova. This chapter was written with the financial support of The Program in the Law and Economics of Capital Markets, a joint program of Columbia Law School and Columbia Business School, where the author is a Program Fellow.

Figure 1: Document Size

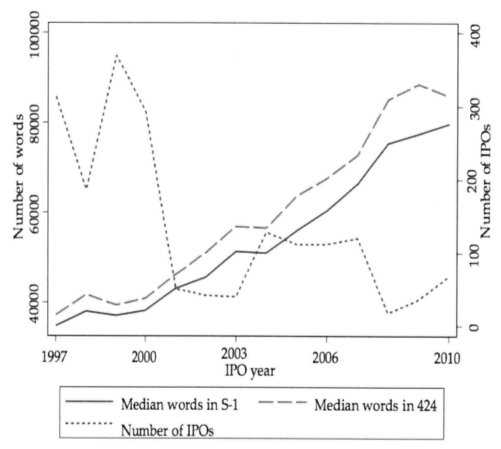

Notes: The figure is from Loughran and McDonald, *infra* note 11, and plots the median number of words contained in Form S-1 and Form 424 filings and the number of IPOs for calendar years 1997-2010. Form S-1 is the initial filing on EDGAR for registering the IPO offering with the Securities and Exchange Commission (SEC). Form 424 is the final IPO prospectus. The sample includes 1,887 U.S. IPOs during 1997 to 2010 with an offer price of at least $5.

emphasis was on only 22 new issues offered to the public between 1959 and 1961. But the conclusions of the study, despite the small sample size, are remarkably similar to those using much larger samples and more sophisticated techniques.

The similarity of issues suggests that the fundamental economic principles that guided securities offerings in the 1960s are generally still the same as those guiding securities offerings in the twenty-first century. One might argue that the solutions identified in the original study and ultimately implemented may not have been very effective in solving ongoing issues in the offering process. It is within this context that the New Special Study seeks to "enhance the quality of future regulatory reforms" through careful analysis of the current state of primary markets. Thus, the issues raised in this chapter, and those raised in the chapter on the law of these markets by Donald Langevoort, may not have easy solutions.

There are, however, notable differences in the securities markets today that necessitate revisiting the regulations put into place in the 1930s. This is most evident in the increase of available information to investors. Investors now have regular access to information on both public and private companies through media outlets, private trading markets, and the Internet. Since the Special Study in 1963, a myriad of new disclosure rules have been implemented, giving investors an unprecedented view into the workings of a public company. For example, over the past decade or so, the amount of information in IPO offering documents has ballooned. Figure 1, drawn from Loughran and McDonald, shows a steady increase in the number of words in the offering documents of an IPO.[11] For example, the 1980 prospectus of Apple Computer was 47 pages, while the 2017 IPO prospectus of Snap was 253 pages. With the rise of textual analysis, researchers and institutional investors can now process large amounts of information quickly. But it is uncertain who benefits from this increased disclosure and whether, or to what extent, it is relevant to the decision-making of less sophisticated investors.

Compared to the 1960s, there still remain definite gaps in our understanding of the securities offering process. Nowhere is this more apparent than in the economics of initial public offerings. Despite hundreds of papers that have examined the pricing of securities issued to the public for the first time, there is no clear consensus about either the equilibrium level of underpricing or the relative costs and benefits of using bookbuilding to raise capital. A number of theoretical papers have argued that discretionary allocation in bookbuilding can promote price efficiency. This discretion, however, has given rise to questionable underwriter practices and conflicts of interest that harm issuers. A question that continues to be debated is why bookbuilding remains the predominant offering mechanism when other methods that do not suffer from conflicts of interest, such as auctions, have not gained traction.[12] It is difficult, if not impossible, to

---

[11] Tim Loughran & Bill McDonald, *IPO First-Day Returns, Offer Price Revisions, Volatility, and Form S-1 Language*, 109 J. FIN. ECON. 307 (2013).

[12] Wilhelm notes that bookbuilding is simply a form of an auction whose primary benefit arises from the repeated relationships among participants. *See* William J. Wilhelm, *Bookbuilding, Auctions and the Future of the IPO Process*, 17 J. APPLIED CORP. FIN. 2 (2005). He argues that "whatever merits lie in bookbuilding probably arise from the compromise it strikes between negotiating through a

determine whether the benefits of price efficiency of bookbuilding outweigh the potential for abuse without additional information on the allocation strategy of underwriters. Yet this information, at least in the U.S., has been impossible to obtain. Thus, a central goal of the New Special Study of Securities Markets should be to persuade regulators to increase transparency in the offering process by requiring disclosure on the allocation strategy of financial intermediaries involved in securities offerings.

The prolonged decline in the number of IPOs and the rise in private market financing are both areas that also warrant additional investigation. Given the corresponding decline in public companies overall, and the consolidation of firms in many industries, it is important to isolate the economic channels that may be responsible.[13] Changes to securities regulation may not be the panacea. The preliminary evidence on the efficacy of the JOBS Act in attracting companies to the public market, for example, is mixed. While the number of companies going public shortly after the passage of the JOBS Act at first increased,[14] IPO activity has since declined despite a buoyant stock market. Furthermore, there does not appear to be a reduction in direct offering costs of going public[15] as would be expected if the Act was successful in reducing issuer's regulatory burden. Finally, the majority of the provisions of the Act increases the incentive of companies to remain private, thereby, reducing the number of IPOs.

Little is known about why firms go public and the trade-offs they make in obtaining private versus public capital. It is clear from the discussion in this chapter that a more holistic analysis of the transition from private to public markets, that incorporates both the life cycle stage of the company and its size, is needed. Papers that take firm size and life cycle stage into consideration find that both factors are important determinants of firms' choices and characteristics. For

---

reputable intermediary and generating substantial competition among a select group of potential bidders. Any such merits derive from the relationships bankers maintain with investors and issuing firms." *Id.* at 58-59.

[13] Grullon, Larkin, and Michaely argue that the decline in antitrust enforcement in recent years may be a contributing factor in the consolidation of certain industries. *See* Gustavo Grullon, Yelena Larkin & Roni Michaely, *Are U.S. Industries Becoming More Concentrated?* (working paper, 2017), https://papers.ssrn.com/sol3/Papers.cfm?abstract_id=2612047.

[14] *See* Michael Dambra, Laura Casares Field & Matthew Gustafson, *The JOBS Act and IPO Volume: Evidence that Disclosure Costs Affect the IPO Decision*, 116 J. FIN. ECON. 121 (2015).

[15] *See* Susan Chaplinsky, Kathleen Hanley & Katie Moon, *The JOBS Act and the Costs of Going Public*, 55 J. ACCT. RES. 795 (2017).

example, Lemmon, Roberts, and Zender examine the capital structure of firms by tracking their financing choices from the time before they go public and find that differences among firms pre-date the IPO.[16] Beck, Demirguc-Kunt, and Maksimovic, using firm survey responses from around the world, find that smaller firms face significantly greater obstacles to growth than larger firms and some of these obstacles are related to the country's legal system.[17] Companies do not go public in a vacuum and a more comprehensive study of how trading markets, regulation, governance, intermediaries, and the offering process are inter-related could help determine where regulatory intervention could be useful in reducing financing inefficiencies.

These inefficiencies are nowhere more apparent than in the differences in capital raising in public versus private markets. Approximately ten times more transactions occur in the private markets than in the public market.[18] Indeed, Gustafson and Iliev find that when the SEC began allowing smaller public companies to use shelf registration in 2008, these companies substituted private capital raising with public capital.[19] This transition to public capital resulted in a reduction in the offering discount (and cost of capital) of transitioning firms relative to firms that were unaffected by the regulation.

In addition, the quality or type of firm that is able to access private markets may create spillovers into the public marketplace. Bolton, Santos, and Scheinkman argue that "while retail investors may be adequately protected for the less juicy investments that are offered to them in public markets, they are being denied access to the more lucrative investment opportunities in private markets."[20] Thus, understanding the challenges firms face when deciding to enter

---

[16] See Michael Lemmon, Michael R. Roberts & Jaime F. Zender, *Back to the Beginning: Persistence and the Cross-Section of Corporate Capital Structure*, 63 J. FIN. 1575 (2008).

[17] Thorsten Beck, Asli Demirguc-Kunt & Vojislav Maksimovic, *Financial and Legal Constraints to Growth: Does Firm Size Matter?*, 60 J. FIN. 137 (2005).

[18] Scott Bauguess, Rachita Gullapalli & Vladimir Ivanov, *Capital Raising in the U.S.: An Analysis of the Market for Unregistered Securities Offerings*, 2009-2014, SEC White Paper, (2015), https://www.sec.gov/dera/staff-papers/white-papers/30oct15_white_unregistered_offering.html.

[19] Matthew Gustafson & Peter Iliev, *The Effects of Removing Barriers to Equity Issuance*, 124 J. Fin. Econ. 580 (2017).

[20] Patrick Bolton, Tano Santos & Jose A. Scheinkman, *Shadow Finance*, in RETHINKING THE FINANCIAL CRISIS 260 (Alan Blinder, Andrew Lo & Robert Solow eds., 2012).

the public market is of paramount importance to a well-functioning capital market.

This chapter loosely follows the outline of the original Special Study and is designed to provide the reader with a high level discussion of the primary themes in the initial public offering process, the issuance of follow-on offerings, and private financing. In addition, it includes a survey of the main reasons for the decline in IPOs in the past decade or so, and highlights regulatory gaps where appropriate. The primary focus of this analysis is equity offers because these securities are generally more informationally sensitive. However, the issuance of debt far exceeds that of equity and thus, an in-depth examination of debt offerings in the *New Special Study* is needed to shed light on the choices firms make when raising capital.

2 Initial Public Offerings

2.1 Offering Process in the U.S.

Although it is possible for an issuer to directly market its IPO to investors, in the U.S. almost all firms considering going public hire an underwriter to facilitate the offering. There are two primary ways in which IPOs may be underwritten. A *best efforts* offering is one in which the underwriter does not pre-commit to purchasing shares from the issuer, but instead agrees as the issuer's agent, to do its best to place the issue. If the underwriter is unsuccessful in placing the minimum number of shares offered within a specified time frame, the offering may be canceled. Best efforts offerings are generally limited to small and more speculative deals in which the underwriter may be hesitant to guarantee the purchase of unsold shares.

In a *firm commitment* offering, the underwriter guarantees to purchase the shares in the offering from the issuer, less an underwriting discount, even if the entire issue cannot be placed. Since a firm commitment underwriting exposes the investment bank to substantial risk should the offering fail, these offerings are most often conducted and priced using *bookbuilding*. This type of underwriting is the most common form of offering mechanism in the U.S. and the discussion in this chapter will focus primarily on firm commitment offerings that are marketed using bookbuilding for issues that will trade on a national securities exchange.[21]

Figure 2 describes the time line for a typical IPO.[22] The offering process begins with the selection of the underwriter that will bring the issue to market.[23]

---

[21] If the stock will not trade on a national securities exchange, the offer may be subject to individual state securities laws also known as "Blue Sky laws."

[22] This figure is only representative. Of course, the offering process may be shorter or longer than indicated here.

Figure 2: Offering Process

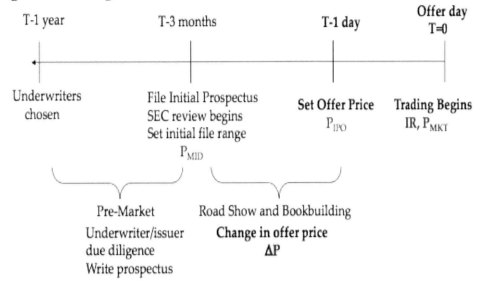

Notes: The figure presents a typical timeline for the offering process. P_{MID} is the midpoint of the offer price range in the preliminary prospectus. P_{IPO} is the offer price. ΔP is the change in the offer price from the mid-point of the offer price range. IR is the initial return measured as the percentage difference between the offer price and the pricing at the close of the first trading day, P_{MKT}.

After the issuer chooses its underwriter, it begins conducting its due diligence, which will become the basis for the disclosures in the registration (Form S-1) filed with the SEC and the prospectus distributed to potential investors. This is an important step because the issuer and its underwriter are liable under Section 11(c) of the Securities Act for any material misstatement in the offering prospectus. Therefore, adequate due diligence on the part of the underwriter can mitigate exposure to future lawsuits.[24] In addition, due diligence can aid the underwriter and issuing firm in the setting of the initial offer price range.

As noted in the next chapter by Donald Langevoort, there are a myriad of disclosure items that are required in the registration statement. Once the underwriter and the issuing firm have prepared the registration statement, it is

---

[23] Often, more than one underwriter is engaged to co-lead the offering. In addition, the lead underwriters may form a selling syndicate composed of a number of investment banks that will help place the shares.

[24] *See* Kathleen Weiss Hanley & Gerard Hoberg, *Litigation Risk, Strategic Disclosure and the Underpricing of Initial Public Offerings*, 103 J. FIN. ECON. 235 (2012).

filed with the SEC.[25] The SEC then begins its review and provides comments on the filing. Lowry, Michaely, and Volkova estimate that most firms receive between three and four comment letters, but there is considerable variation in this number.[26] After the SEC's comments have been substantially addressed and an offer price range disclosed in an amendment to the registration statement, the issuer can begin the road show and the underwriter can begin its bookbuilding.

In order to "build the book," the underwriter solicits indications of interest from institutional clients. These indications of interest are non-binding orders and can be changed or rescinded at any time until final allocations are made. Once the underwriter has finished soliciting indications of interest from its clients, it will work with the issuer to set a final offer price and the number of shares to be issued. This offer price does not need to be within the offer price range that was filed on the registration statement. However, significant changes to the offer price may necessitate amendments to the registration statement if the change in proceeds is material or exceeds thresholds set by SEC rules.[27] Once the SEC has declared the offer effective, the underwriter can begin finalizing the orders from its clients and the shares can begin trading.

Bookbuilding has two characteristics that often raise concerns. First, research has shown that the offer price does not fully incorporate supply and demand and, in some cases, even current public market information.[28] Thus, the underwriter and the issuing firm often issue shares that are "underpriced," that is, the first trading day value is significantly above the offer price. Second is that the underwriter has discretion over the allocation process. Since, on average, the

---

[25] Michelle Lowry, Roni Michaely & Ekaterina Volkova, *Information Revelation Through the Regulatory Process: Interactions Between the SEC and Companies Ahead of their IPO* (working paper, 2016), https://papers.ssrn.com/sol3/papers.cfm?abstract_id=2802599. After the passage of the JOBS Act, certain issuing firms that qualify as "emerging growth companies" can confidentially file their initial registration statement with the SEC. The issuing firm's registration statement is made public only if the firm decides to go forward with the offering.

[26] Comment letters are not released until after the offer becomes effective.

[27] Rule 430A of the Securities Act of 1933 limits the pricing flexibility to 20% of the maximum aggregate offering price set forth in the fee table. *See* Matthew J. Barcaskey, *Do SEC Regulations Constrain Offer Price Revisions of IPOs?* (working paper, 2004).

[28] *See* Tim Loughran & Jay Ritter, *Why Don't Issuers Get Upset About Leaving Money on the Table in IPOs?*, 15 REV. FIN. STUD. 413 (2002); Michelle Lowry & William Schwert, *Is the IPO Pricing Process Efficient?*, 71 J. FIN. ECON. 3 (2004).

Table 1: Average First Day Returns

Year	Number of IPOs	First Day Return
1980	71	14.3%
1981	192	5.9%
1982	77	11.0%
1983	451	9.9%
1984	172	3.6%
1985	187	6.4%
1986	393	6.1%
1987	285	5.6%
1988	102	5.7%
1989	113	8.2%
1990	110	10.8%
1991	286	11.9%
1992	412	10.3%
1993	509	12.7%
1994	403	9.8%
1995	461	21.2%
1996	677	17.2%
1997	474	14.0%
1998	281	21.9%
1999	477	71.1%
2000	381	56.3%
2001	79	14.2%
2002	66	9.1%
2003	63	11.7%
2004	173	12.3%
2005	159	10.3%
2006	157	12.1%
2007	159	14.0%
2008	21	6.4%
2009	41	9.8%
2010	91	9.4%
2011	81	13.3%
2012	93	17.9%
2013	157	21.1%
2014	207	15.5%
2015	117	18.2%
2016	73	14.9%

Notes: The table presents the number of IPOs and average first day returns from 1980 to 2016. The first day return is calculated as the equally-weighted percentage difference between the offer price and the closing price on the first day of trading. The sample includes IPOs with an offer price of at least $5.00, excluding ADRs, unit offers, closed-end funds, REITs, natural resource limited partnerships, small best efforts offers, banks and S&Ls, and stocks not listed on CRSP (CRSP includes Amex, NYSE, and some NASDAQ stocks). The data are from Jay Ritter's website (https://site.warrington.ufl.edu/ritter/ipo-data/).

shares of an IPO are underpriced, the underwriter can use IPO shares as a form of currency. This discretion has led to unethical practices, particularly during hot markets, in which investment bankers have given preferential allocation to certain investors in exchange for past or future business or other accommodations such as soft dollars. The remainder of this section will delve into these issues more deeply.

2.2 IPO Pricing

> The public eagerly sought stocks of companies in certain "glamour" industries, especially the electronics industry, in the expectation that they would quickly rise to a substantial premium–an expectation that was often fulfilled. Within a few days or even hours after the initial distribution, these so-called "hot issues" would be traded at premiums of as much as 300 percent above the original offering price.
>
> Special Study (part 1) at p. 487.

Numerous studies have documented that IPOs are, on average, underpriced on the first trading day. Underpricing (also called the "initial return") is measured as the percentage difference between the final offer price and the closing price on the first day of trading.[29] Table 1 shows the time variation in mean initial returns from 1980 to 2015.[30] During the tech IPO bubble of 1999 and 2000, average first day returns reached a high of 71.1% and 56.3%, respectively. Although first day returns are much lower after this period, the average underpricing from 2001 to 2015 is still almost 14%. Therefore, an investor who purchases shares across all IPOs can expect a positive, significantly high one day return.

This section briefly reviews the most common reasons put forth in the literature for underpricing. There have been a number of excellent review articles

---

[29] Underpricing of new issues also occurs, to some extent, in bond offerings. Cai, Helwege, and Warga document underpricing of 47 basis points for speculative-grade debt IPOs but no significant underpricing for investment grade IPOs. They conclude that the rationale for underpricing the debt of riskier firms is similar to that posited for equity IPOs. *See* Nianyun (Kelly) Cai, Jean Helwege & Arthur Warga, *Underpricing in the Corporate Bond Market*, 20 REV. FIN. STUD. 2021 (2007).

[30] Data are from Jay Ritter's website (https://site.warrington.ufl.edu/ritter/ipo-data/) unless otherwise stated.

that summarize the literature in more detail[31] and therefore, the discussion in this chapter will be limited to major themes.

2.2.1 Bookbuilding Theories

> It was not uncommon for underwriters to receive, prior to the effective date, public "indications of interest" for five times the number of shares available. Indeed, indications of interest received by the managing underwriters alone sometimes exceeded the total amount of the offering.
>
> Special Study (part 1) at p. 515.

One of the first papers to provide a theory of IPO underpricing is by Rock.[32] He models the IPO process as having two types of investors: informed and uninformed. Informed investors know the "true" value of the shares and only buy when the offer price is below that value, while uninformed investors bid in every IPO. If shares are rationed in better offerings, the uninformed face a winner's curse because they are allocated a larger proportion of offers that may be overpriced. Thus, if the participation of informed investors is necessary to place the offer, IPOs, on average, must be underpriced in order to induce uninformed investors to participate in the offering.

In Rock's model, the offering mechanism is similar to a fixed price auction where the offer price is set, investors bid on this issue, and allocation is determined by how much a bidder desires.[33] If there is oversubscription, shares are allocated on a pro rata basis. If the issuer misjudges interest in the offer, there is no ability to adjust the offer price in response.

Bookbuilding overcomes this drawback and may be one reason why this offering mechanism is the predominant method around the world.[34] Under this

---

[31] *See* Jay Ritter & Ivo Welch, A Review of IPO Activity, Pricing, and Allocations, 57 J. FIN. 1795 (2002); Alexander Ljungqvist, *IPO Underpricing, in* HANDBOOK OF CORPORATE FINANCE (B. Espen Eckbo ed., 2007); Michelle Lowry, Roni Michaely & Ekaterina Volkova, *Initial Public Offerings: A Synthesis of the Literature and Directions for Future Research*, 11 FOUNDATIONS & TRENDS IN FIN. 154 (2017).

[32] Kevin Rock, *Why New Issues are Underpriced*, 15 J. FIN. ECON. 187 (1996).

[33] There have been few auction IPOs in the U.S. (only 22 since 1999). They have been brought to market by WRHambrecht who has recently expanded into the Regulation A+ market.

[34] *See* Ravi Jagannathan, Andrei Jirnyi & Ann Guenther Sherman, *Share Auctions of Initial Public Offerings: Global Evidence*, 24 J. FIN. INTERMEDIATION 283 (2015).

offering method, the issuer and underwriter set an expected offer price range and begin the process of meeting with investors in a "roadshow." The underwriter then solicits non-binding indications of interest (quantity and/or price) and other feedback from investors, thus allowing the issuer to incorporate information generated from investors in the setting of the final offer price. It is important to note that information generated during the roadshow may be positive or negative. For example, if the demand of investors is low, the offer price will be reduced or the issue withdrawn. If demand from investors is high, the offer price may be increased.

Increasing the offer price in response to good information, however, provides a disincentive for investors to tell the truth. (There is always an incentive to truthfully reveal demand for offerings with too high an offer price.) If investors inform the underwriter that the price is too low, the underwriter will likely respond by raising the offer price. Therefore, investors prefer not to reveal good information in order to keep the offer price low. To induce investors to truthfully reveal good information, therefore, they must expect greater profits when they tell the truth than when they lie.

In bookbuilding, underwriters have discretion in the allocation of shares to investors. This means that investment banks are free to allocate as many shares to a particular investor as they wish.[35] Benveniste and Spindt, Benveniste and Wilhelm, and Spatt and Srivastava theoretically show that investors are motivated to truthfully reveal the level of demand through a pricing and allocation schedule that maximizes their total expected profit (underpricing times shares allocated).[36] If good information is revealed, underwriters can raise the offer price but allocate more shares to investors who reveal good information. If demand exceeds the available number of shares, underwriters may prefer to compensate investors for truth telling by allocating a smaller number of highly underpriced shares rather than a larger number of slightly underpriced shares.

---

[35] There may be constraints imposed by the issuer that may limit the underwriter's discretion. For example, the issuer may insist on a specific ownership structure. Brennan and Franks suggest that underpricing can be used to determine the diffusion of shareholders. *See* Michael Brennan & Julian Franks, *Underpricing, Ownership and Control in Initial Public Offerings*, 45 J. FIN. ECON. 391 (1997).

[36] Lawrence Benveniste & Paul Spindt, *How Investment Bankers Determine the Offer Price and Allocation of New Issues*, 24 J. OF FIN. ECON. 343 (1989); Lawrence Benveniste & William Wilhelm, *A Comparative Analysis of IPO Proceeds Under Alternative Regulatory Environments*, 28 J. OF FIN. ECON. 173 (1990); Chester Spatt & Sanjay Srivastava, *Preplay Communication, Participation Restrictions and Efficiency in Initial Public Offerings*, 4 REV. OF FIN. STUD. 709 (1991).

Table 2: Average First Day Returns by Revisions from the Offer Price Range

Panel A: Percentage of IPOs by Revisions from the Offer Price Range

Year	IPOs with OP<Low	IPOs Within	IPOs with OP>High
1980-1989	30%	57%	13%
1990-1998	27%	49%	24%
1999-2000	18%	38%	44%
2001-2016	36%	43%	22%
1980-2016	29%	48%	23%

Panel B: Initial Returns by Revisions from the Offer Price Range

Year	IPOs with OP<Low	IPOs Within	IPOs with OP>High
1980-1989	0%	6%	20%
1990-1998	4%	11%	31%
1999-2000	8%	26%	121%
2001-2016	3%	11%	37%
1980-2016	3%	11%	50%

Notes: The table presents the percentage of IPOs and first day returns by the revision to the offer price from the offer price range on the registration statement from 1980 to 2016. The first day return is the equally-weighted percentage difference between the offer price and the closing price on the first day of trading. OP is the offer price, Low is the lowest price in the offer price range, High is the highest price in the offer price range and Within is between the highest and lowest price in the offer price range. The sample includes IPOs with an offer price of at least $5.00, excluding ADRs, unit offers, closed-end funds, REITs, natural resource limited partnerships, small best efforts offers, banks and S&Ls, and stocks not listed on CRSP (CRSP includes Amex, NYSE, and some NASDAQ stocks). The data are from Jay Ritter's website (https://site.warrington.ufl.edu/ritter/ipo-data/).

In practice, the type of information revealed during bookbuilding and investor demand are correlated.[37] When an offering is "hot," it is not uncommon

---

[37] *See* Scott Bauguess, Jack Cooney & Kathleen Weiss Hanley, *Investor Demand in Newly Issued Securities* (working paper, 2016), https://papers.ssrn.com/sol3/papers.cfm?abstract_id=2379056.

for the IPO to be oversubscribed many times. When this occurs, the underwriter has less flexibility in the allocation of shares and therefore, must significantly underprice the issue in order to induce truth telling. Thus, when good information is revealed, offer prices only partially adjust.[38] Table 2 shows the percentage of IPOs that have final offer prices that are below, within, and above the offer price range indicated in the preliminary prospectus. As can be seen in Panel A, most issuers are priced within the offer price range. Approximately 48% of all issues from 1980 to 2016 are priced within the range, with 23% priced above and 29% priced below. While there have been fluctuations through time (notably in 1999 and 2000), the relationship remains fairly stable.

Table 2 also presents the initial return by the revisions in the offer price range. Issuers whose offer price is above the highest price in the offering price range have higher initial returns than those who priced within the offer price range. Issuers whose offer price is below the lower price in the offering price range have lower initial returns than those who priced within the range. Indeed, the percentage difference between the final offer price and the mid-point of the offer price range has strong predictive power for the magnitude of first day returns even after controlling for other characteristics of the offer and issuer known to affect underpricing. In Panel B, offers that priced above the offering price range have, on average, a 50% initial return compared to 11% for within the range and 3% below the range. Indeed, Butler, Keefe, and Kieschnick document that the offer price revision is ranked number one in predicting underpricing for those methodologies that permit such identification.[39]

More direct tests of the role of information revelation during bookbuilding use actual allocation data obtained from underwriters. Cornelli and Goldreich use allocation data for international equity issues (both IPOs and follow-ons) from a prominent European bank.[40] They find that during bookbuilding, indications of interest are solicited for approximately two weeks and result in an average of approximately 400 bids. Most of these bids are strike bids in which no offer price is indicated meaning that the bidder will take shares at any price. The authors find, however, that limit bids or bids that reveal a price, particularly those that are large and submitted by frequent bidders, are strongly

---

[38] *See* Kathleen Weiss Hanley, *The Underpricing of Initial Public Offerings and the Partial Adjustment Phenomenon*, 34 J. FIN. ECON. 231 (1993).

[39] Alexandar Butler, Michael O'Connor Keefe & Robert Kieschnick, *Robust Determinants of IPO Underpricing and Their Implications for IPO Research*, 27 J. CORP. FIN. 367 (2014).

[40] Francesca Cornelli & David Goldreich, *Bookbuilding and Strategic Allocation*, 56 J. FIN. 2337 (2001); Francesca Cornelli & David Goldreich, *Bookbuilding: How Informative is the Order Book?*, 58 J. FIN. 1415 (2003).

informative in the setting of the offer price. This finding supports the notion that information revelation through indications of interest are important in setting the offer price.

Providing additional support for the role of pricing and allocation in bookbuilding, the authors find that the underwriter allocates more shares to bidders who provide a price as part of their bid. Jenkinson and Jones, however, do not find this to be the case for the sample of issues they obtain from a different European bank.[41] In a more recent paper that uses a broader sample of underwriters that underwrote IPOs in the UK, Jenkinson, Jones, and Suntheim confirm Cornelli and Goldreich's findings on preferential allocation to investors who provide a price with their bid.[42]

Bookbuilding theories would suggest that the dominant investor in IPOs will be institutional investors who can provide information relevant to pricing. Only a few studies use U.S. data to study actual allocations. For example, Hanley and Wilhelm have data on aggregate institutional and retail allocation from one underwriter and find the favored status enjoyed by institutional investors in underpriced offerings appears to carry a quid pro quo expectation that they participate in less attractive issues as well.[43] In contrast, Aggarwal, Prabhala, and Puri, using data collected from the SEC on nine investment banks, find preferential allocation to institutional investors and argue that these investors are particularly adept at avoiding "lemons" or underperforming issues.[44]

Because of the lack of transparency in allocation data in the U.S., other studies such as Reuter, Ritter and Zhang; Chemmanur, Hu, and Huang; and Johnson and Marietta-Westberg use Form 13F data as a proxy for initial allocations.[45] But this data cannot fully capture primary market allocations for at

---

[41] Tim Jenkinson & Howard Jones, *Bids and Allocations in European IPO Bookbuilding*, 59 J. FIN. 2309 (2004).

[42] Tim Jenkinson, Howard Jones & Felix Suntheim, *Quid Pro Quo? What Factors Influence IPO Allocations to Investors?* (working paper, 2016), https://papers.ssrn.com/sol3/papers.cfm?abstract_id=2785642.

[43] Kathleen Weiss Hanley & William Wilhelm, *Evidence on the Strategic Allocation of Initial Public Offerings*, 37 J. FIN. ECON. 239 (1995).

[44] Reena Aggarwal, N. Prabhala & Manju Puri, *Institutional Allocation in Initial Public Offerings: Empirical Evidence*, 57 J. FIN. 1421 (2002). Aggarwal also uses this data to examine aftermarket trading. *See* Reena Aggarwal, *Allocation of Initial Public Offerings and Flipping Activity*, 68 J. FIN. ECON. 111 (2003).

[45] Jonathan Reuter, *Are IPO Allocations for Sale? Evidence From Mutual Funds*, 61 J. FIN. 2289 (2006); Jay Ritter & Donghang Zhang, *Affiliated Mutual Funds and the Allocation of Initial Public Offerings*, 86 J. FIN. ECON. 337 (2007); Thomas

least two reasons. First, the requirement to file Form 13F is limited to institutional investment managers with investment discretion over $100 million or more in Section 13(f) securities. Thus, smaller institutions (including some hedge funds) and retail customers are excluded. Second, institutions may engage in secondary market transactions from the time of the initial allocation to the filing of the form, obscuring allocations that occur during the filing period. Indeed, Shen finds only a 60% correlation between 13F holdings and actual allocations to affiliated mutual funds.[46] Hence, regulators and academics need access to the bidding and allocation practices of investment banks in order to understand the costs and benefits of bookbuilding as an offering mechanism.

2.2.2 Role of Disclosure

> In view of the speculative nature of many new issues, the disclosure provisions of the Securities Act assume a particular importance to the purchaser in the after-market, especially in periods of intense demand.
>
> Special Study (part 1) at p. 547.

As noted in the chapter on the law of primary markets by Donald Langevoort, numerous laws and regulations mandate specific disclosure to investors in order to aid them in their investment decisions and nowhere is this more important than when a firm issues securities. Hail and Leuz examine securities regulation in 40 countries and find that "countries with extensive securities regulation and strong enforcement mechanisms exhibit lower levels of cost of capital than countries with weak legal institutions, even after controlling for various risk and country factors."[47]

In the U.S., disclosure regulation (and its enforcement) serves as the primary mechanism to protect investors and is the main tool by which the SEC can alter the capital raising landscape. The SEC oversees the offering process through its review of registration statements. During the review process, the SEC staff provides comments to the issuer that are designed to ensure compliance

---

Chemmanur, Gang Hu & Jickun Huang, *The Role of Institutional Investors in Initial Public Offerings*, 23 REV. FIN. STUD. 4496 (2010); William Johnson & Jennifer Marietta-Westberg, *Universal Banking, Asset Management, and Stock Underwriting*, 15 EURO. FIN. MGMT. 703 (2005).

[46] Ke Shen, *Playing Favoritism? A Closer Look at IPO Allocations to Investment Bank-Affiliated Mutual Funds*, (working paper, 2016).

[47] Luzi Hail & Christian Leuz, *International Differences in the Cost of Equity Capital: Do Legal Institutions and Securities Regulation Matter?*, 44 J. OF ACCT. RES. 485 (2006).

with the Securities Act of 1933 and other disclosure rules as well as with applicable accounting standards. It is important to understand that the review process is not intended to pass judgment on the merit of the proposed offering. Investors, therefore, are tasked with reading and understanding the required disclosures in order to make an informed investment decision.

The extent to which mandatory disclosure benefits investors has been long debated. A number of studies find that there are benefits to enhanced disclosure in terms of lower costs of capital or higher equity values.[48] For example, the imposition of mandated disclosure for OTC Bulletin Board companies,[49] the effects of the 1964 Securities Act Amendments,[50] and the effects of the 2005 Securities Offering Reform on the issue costs of seasoned equity offerings,[51] generally find benefits to increased disclosure.

Not all mandated disclosure, however, may increase shareholder value. For example, studies such as Coates and Srinivasan and Leuz, which investigate whether the equity values of U.S. firms increase after the enactment of the Sarbanes-Oxley Act (SOX), characterize the evidence on this issue as mixed.[52] This characterization is largely due to the imprecise dating of the law's effectiveness, compounding financial and political events, and the lack of a control group of public firms unaffected by the law.

Proponents of increased disclosure argue that the benefits to investors

---

[48] *See* Robert E. Verrecchia, *Essays on Disclosure*, 32 J. ACCT. & ECON. 97 (2001); Ronald A. Dye, *An Evaluation of "Essays on Disclosure" and the Disclosure Literature in Accounting*, 32 J. ACCT. & ECON. 181 (2001); Paul M. Healy & Krishna G. Palepu, *Information Asymmetry, Corporate Disclosure, and the Capital Markets: A Review of the Empirical Disclosure Literature*, 31 J. ACCT. & ECON. 405 (2001).

[49] *See* Brian J. Bushee & Christian Leuz, *Economic Consequences of SEC Disclosure Regulation: Evidence from the OTC Bulletin Board*, 39 J. ACCT. & ECON. 233 (2005).

[50] *See* Michael Greenstone, Paul Oyer & Annette Vissing-Jorgensen, *Mandated Disclosure, Stock Returns, and the 1964 Securities Acts Amendments*, 121 Q. J. ECON. 399 (2006).

[51] *See* Sarah B. Clinton, Joshua T. White & Tracie Woidtke, *Differences in the Information Environment Prior to Seasoned Equity Offerings Under Relaxed Disclosure Regulation*, 58 J. OF ACCT. & ECON. 59 (2014); Nemit Shroff, Amy X. Sun, Hal D. White & Weining Zhang, *Voluntary Disclosure and Information Asymmetry: Evidence from the 2005 Securities Offering Reform*, J. ACCT. RES. 51, 1299–1345 (2013).

[52] John C. Coates & Suraj Srinivasan, *SOX After Ten Years: A Multidisciplinary Review*, 28 ACCT. HORIZONS 671 (2014); Christian Leuz, *Was the Sarbanes-Oxley Act of 2002 Really This Costly? A Discussion of Evidence From Event Returns and Going-Private Decisions*, 44 J. ACCT. & ECON. 146 (2007).

outweigh the costs to issuers because it decreases information acquisition costs that, in turn, may increase pricing accuracy.[53] Given the large amount of uncertainty surrounding the valuation of the firm at the time it goes public, disclosure may reduce information asymmetry between the issuer and the investor, thereby reducing underpricing. Theories that build upon the framework of Benveniste and Spindt,[54] such as Sherman and Titman,[55] suggest that underpricing rewards investors for acquiring information about the company, thereby increasing pricing accuracy. However, many newly public companies are in competitive, high tech industries where disclosure may reveal valuable strategic or proprietary information to rivals.[56] If this is the case, then issuers may prefer to withhold information even if the cost of capital is higher. The tradeoff in disclosure regulation is to balance the desire of issuers to protect strategic information and the need for investors to use this information to appropriately value the company.

In order for disclosure to be value-relevant to investors, it must lower the cost of acquiring information and in turn, lower the cost of capital at the time securities are issued. A number of papers have examined the effect of disclosure on underpricing in IPOs with mixed results. Leone, Rock, and Willenborg examine how specific issuers are in their disclosures about the uses of the IPO proceeds in the prospectus and find that an increase in specificity is associated with a decline in underpricing.[57] The authors suggest that specificity reduces the information asymmetry problem faced by investors. Ljungqvist and Wilhelm show that firms citing the funding of operating expenses (less specificity) as the primary use of proceeds have higher underpricing.[58] Guo, Lev, and Zhou focus

---

[53] *See* Ann Sherman & Sheridan Titman, *Building the IPO Order Book: Underpricing and Participation Limits With Costly Information*, 65 J. FIN. ECON. 3 (2002).

[54] Lawrence Benveniste & Paul Spindt, *How Investment Bankers Determine the Offer Price and Allocation of New Issues*, 24 J. FIN. ECON. 343 (1989).

[55] Sherman & Titman, *supra* note 53.

[56] Sudipto Bhattacharya & Jay Ritter, *Innovation and Communication: Signalling With Partial Disclosure*, 50 REV. ECON. STUD. 331 (1983); Masako N. Darrough & Neal M. Stoughton, *Financial Disclosure Policy in an Entry Game*, 12 J. ACCT. & ECON. 219 (1990); Sudipto Bhattacharya & Gabriella Chiesa, *Proprietary Information, Financial Intermediation, and Research Incentives*, 4 J. FIN. INTERMEDIATION 328 (1995).

[57] Andrew J. Leone, Steve Rock & Micheal Willenborg, *Disclosure of Intended Use of Proceeds and Underpricing of Initial Public Offerings*, 45 J. ACCT. RES. 111 (2007).

[58] Alexander Ljungqvist & William Wilhelm, *IPO Pricing in the Dot-com Bubble*, 58 J. FIN. 723 (2003).

on product-related disclosures in the prospectus by firms in the biotechnology industry and find a negative relation between the extent of disclosure and the bid–ask spread but do not examine if there is a link to IPO underpricing.[59]

However, a number of studies document that increased disclosure in specific parts of the prospectus actually increases, not decreases underpricing. Beatty and Ritter present evidence that more information in the Use of Proceeds section is correlated with underpricing.[60] Beatty and Welch and Arnold, Fishe, and North examine the Risk Factors section of the prospectus and find that more disclosure in this section is associated with higher initial returns.[61] The challenge in any study of disclosure is controlling for the endogeneity of the disclosure decision. In other words, it is unclear whether firms provide greater disclosure of risk factors in the prospectus because they are riskier in general, or because they are providing additional information to investors.

In order to overcome this problem, Hanley and Hoberg examine whether information in the prospectus is informative or standard by comparing an issuer's disclosure choices relative to those of other similar IPO issuers.[62] Standard disclosure is defined as information in an IPO prospectus that is already contained in both recent and past industry IPO prospectuses, while informative content is the disclosure in the prospectus not explained by these two sources. If disclosure is useful to investors, then issuers that have prospectuses with more informative content should have a lower cost of capital. Indeed, the authors find that the greater the informative content of a prospectus, the better the pricing accuracy and the lower the initial return. Content directly related to information that would be used in valuation models by investors seems to matter most.

In addition, the authors propose that information production on the value of the firm can occur either at the time of due diligence or instead, by investors during the bookbuilding process. They find that the less informative the prospectus, i.e. the less due diligence that was conducted in the pre-market,

---

[59] Re-Jin Guo, Baruch Lev & Nan Zhou, *Competitive Costs of Disclosure by Biotech IPOs*, J. ACCT. RES. 42, 319 (2004).

[60] Randolph Beatty & Jay Ritter, *Investment Banking, Reputation and the Underpricing of Initial Public Offerings*, 15 J. FIN. ECON. 213 (1986).

[61] Randolph Beatty & Ivo Welch, *Issuer Expenses and Legal Liability in Initial Public Offerings*, 39 J. LAW & ECON. 545 (1996); Tom Arnold, Raymond P.H. Fishe & David North, *The Effects of Ambiguous Information on Initial and Subsequent IPO Returns*, 39 FIN. MGMT. 1497 (2010).

[62] Kathleen Weiss Hanley & Gerard Hoberg, *The Information Content of IPO Prospectuses*, 23 REV. FIN. STUD. 2821 (2009).

the more likely that information production will occur during bookbuilding. In other words, pre-market due diligence and bookbuilding can be substitutes for each other. Thus, this trade-off suggests that underwriters make strategic decisions as to how much effort to expend in disclosing information in the prospectus and these decisions have a direct effect on the issuer's cost of capital.

2.2.3 Litigation Risk

Other papers have proposed that underpricing can be used to reduce the probability of shareholder litigation. By setting the offer price well below the expected market price, issuers and their underwriters provide a hedge against subsequent price declines that may result in shareholders claiming damages. However, there has been mixed empirical evidence in support of the relationship between initial returns and lawsuits. Drake and Vetsuypens find no relation between the incidence of a lawsuit and initial returns.[63] Lowry and Shu, on the other hand, control for endogeneity where initial returns can act as both insurance and a deterrent to litigation and find some evidence for both.[64]

Section 11 of the Securities Act allows any purchaser of securities to sue for damages if there was any material misstatement or omission in registration statement, whether or not the purchaser relied on those disclosures.[65] If underpricing is used as insurance against a future lawsuit, however, it would only be a deterrent to the original buyer of shares in the IPO. If there is underpricing, aftermarket investors buy at higher prices than IPO purchasers. The threshold for a lawsuit for aftermarket purchasers, therefore, is much lower than the threshold for IPO purchasers. Thus, underpricing cannot deter a lawsuit per se, but only deter IPO purchasers from joining the class. The benefit of underpricing is that it reduces the probability that the lawsuit will be brought under Section 11 and the likelihood that the underwriter will be named in the suit.[66]

---

[63] Philip Drake & Michael Vetsuypens, *IPO Underpricing as Insurance Against Legal Liability*, 22 FIN. MGMT. 64 (1993).

[64] Michelle Lowry & Susan Shu, *Litigation Risk and IPO Underpricing*, 65 J. FIN. ECON. 309 (2002).

[65] For a more in-depth discussion, see the chapter by Donald Langevoort.

[66] Section 11 of the Securities Act of 1933 limits damages to underwriters: "In no event shall any underwriter . . . be liable in any suit or as a consequence of suits authorized under subsection (a) of this section for damages in excess of the total price at which the securities underwritten by him and distributed to the public

Hanley and Hoberg show that if purchasing shareholders are part of the class and an underwriter is named in a Section 11 lawsuit, the underwriter loses significant market share in the year after the lawsuit occurs.[67] Thus, underwriters may have a powerful incentive to increase underpricing in order to protect their reputation. Using a nested logit model that incorporates both the probability of a lawsuit and whether IPO purchasers are in the class, they show that the higher the initial return, the lower the probability that IPO purchasers will be part of the class. Thus, the deterrent effect of initial returns is not in stopping lawsuits from occurring, generally, but in limiting the type of plaintiff that will bring the lawsuit and by extension, whether the underwriter is named in the suit.

2.2.4 Conflicts of Interest

> The pricing of new issues involves a double—and sometimes conflicting—role of the underwriter. In the words of a representative of one firm: "We wear two hats. We represent our clients and we represent these companies". . . . Several of the underwriters interviewed pointed out that the offering prices they set were often less than the maximum that might have been obtained. In part, such decisions were motivated by a sense of obligation to customers and a desire to give them a bargain.
>
> Special Study (part 1) at pp. 500-501.

Generally, issuers go public only once.[68] The issuer, therefore, likely has limited experience with how an offering is structured and how the issue may be priced, leaving them vulnerable to underwriters using underpricing for their own benefit. Investment banks may face a conflict of interest between maximizing the proceeds to the issuing firm and giving their repeat investors profits from purchasing underpriced shares in a newly public company. The combination of the issuer's unfamiliarity with the IPO process and the dual clientele of investment bankers have given rise to a number of theories to explain underpricing. It is important to note that the underwriter does not have a

---

were offered to the public." 15 U.S.C. § 77k (2017). Lawsuits may still be brought by aftermarket purchasers under Rule 10b-5.

[67] Hanley & Hoberg, *supra* note 62. There is no effect on underwriter market share if the suit is brought by aftermarket shareholders under Rule 10b-5.

[68] An exception, for example, may be reverse LBOs or spinoffs.

fiduciary duty to issuers.[69]

Because bookbuilding gives underwriters substantial latitude over allocation and pricing, there have been instances of underwriters using IPOs as a form of currency to curry favor with investors and potential customers. Allocation of IPO shares may involve quid pro quos in which preferred status in underpriced shares is granted in return for an expectation of payback. This is not a new phenomenon. The Special Study notes, "Almost without exception, participants in the offering of new issues in significant demand refused to make an allotment to any customer who had not formerly done business with them."[70] The payback may require the investor generating significant commission business either before or after the IPO.[71] Underwriters may have the expectation that investors will participate in overpriced offers in order to gain access to underpriced offers.[72] In addition, the allocation of underpriced shares can act as an inducement to get corporate executives to use the underwriting firm, also known as "spinning."[73]

In addition, underwriters may give preferential allocation to affiliated mutual funds in order to improve performance. Ritter and Zhang find some evidence that mutual funds affiliated with investment banks receive underpriced IPOs, particularly during the tech IPO bubble period.[74] More recently, Shen uses actual allocation data reported by affiliated mutual funds and confirms the

---

[69] Language in the underwriting agreement expressly discusses this tradeoff. For example, "The Company has been advised that the Representative and its affiliates are engaged in a broad range of transactions which may involve interests that differ from those of the Company and that the Representative has no obligation to disclose such interests and transactions to the Company by virtue of any fiduciary, advisory or agency relationship." *See* https://www.sec.gov/Archives/edgar/data/1719489/000119312517344053/d471396dex11.htm. *See also EBC I, Inc. v. Goldman Sachs & Co.*, 5 N.Y.3d 11 (2005).

[70] Special Study (part 1) at p. 515.

[71] *See* Jonathan Reuter, *Are IPO Allocations for Sale? Evidence From Mutual Funds*, 61 J. FIN. 2289 (2006); M. Nimalendran, Jay Ritter & Donghang Zhang, *Do Today's Trades Affect Tomorrows IPO Allocation?*, 84 J. OF FIN. ECON. 87 (2007); Michael Goldstein, Paul Irvine & Andy Puckett, *Purchasing IPOs with Commissions*, 46 J. FIN. & QUANT. ANALYSIS 1193 (2011).

[72] Hanley & Wilhelm, *supra* note 43.

[73] *See* Xiaoding Liu & Jay Ritter, *The Economic Consequences of IPO Spinning*, 23 REV. FIN. STUD. 2024 (2010).

[74] Ritter & Zhang, *supra* note 45.

findings of Ritter and Zhang that these funds are more likely to purchase "hot" IPOs.[75] However, the amount allocated to affiliated mutual funds is lower when demand is higher. Presumably, this is because investment bankers prefer to use their discretionary allocation of underpriced shares to reward a broader segment of their clientele.

Each of these types of actions creates a conflict between the underwriter and the issuing firm. In particular, the use of underpriced shares as currency by underwriters creates an incentive to recommend a lower offer price than might otherwise be obtained in order to make shares in the offering more valuable to investors who provide a benefit to the underwriting firm. The lower proceeds received by issuers increases their cost of capital when securities are sold, resulting in less investment by the firm.

Given the potential for conflicts of interest of underwriters, it is surprising that more issuers do not switch underwriters if underpricing is excessive. Krigman, Shaw, and Womack find "little evidence that firms switch [underwriters] due to dissatisfaction with underwriter performance at the time of the IPO."[76] More surprising is that they document that those issuing firms that actually do switch tend to have lower not higher underpricing at the time of the IPO. Why then don't issuers punish underwriters when there is excessive undervaluation?

Corporate executives may be willing to accept the prospect of significantly underpriced shares when they derive benefits from doing so. Insiders taking their company public may be excited about the prospect of recognition that high underpricing may bring and the ability to monetize their investment in the firm. Furthermore, insiders are often prohibited or limited by the investment bank from selling shares in the IPO. Because they do not personally participate in the IPO, they do not directly bear the cost of underpricing (other than through dilution) but may reap indirect benefits.

Loughran and Ritter use prospect theory to posit a rationale for why insiders are willing to leave money on the table.[77] Assume that good information is revealed during bookbuilding and it is clear that the offer price may be much higher than expected. Insiders may be willing to accept high underpricing (and dilution) if their wealth has increased unexpectedly. This is particularly salient if the insider does not sell in the IPO. If the aftermarket price is a reflection of the "true" value of the firm, these insiders will then transact at a higher price once they are able to trade.

---

[75] Shen, *supra* note 46.

[76] Laurie Krigman, Wayne Shaw & Kent Womack, *Why do Firms Switch Underwriters?*, 60 J. FIN. ECON. 245 (2001).

[77] Loughran & Ritter, *supra* note 28.

Ljungqvist and Wilhelm test whether prospect theory can explain the decision to switch underwriters.[78] They show, using Loughran and Ritter's behavioral proxy, that issuers are more likely to switch when they are dissatisfied. In other words, they are less likely to switch if the change in their wealth exceeds the amount of underpricing. This effect is stronger for more inexperienced CEOs. They also document that underwriters appear to extract higher fees in subsequent transactions if their IPO clients are deemed satisfied and do not switch. These findings suggest that corporate insiders may value the increase in their own wealth over and above that of maximizing the proceeds to the firm.

Other indirect benefits to the issuer may accrue primarily to the founders and managers of the firm. For example, there was a significant rise in directed share programs during the tech IPO bubble. These programs allow insiders to set aside and allocate a certain number of shares in the IPO for purchases by friends and family, thereby increasing their wealth with underpriced shares. Ljungqvist and Wilhelm document that large directed share programs appear in only 25% of IPOs in 1996 but this rises to 76% in 1999 and an astonishing 91% in 2000.[79]

The issuing firm may receive significant media attention if the IPO is expected to be popular. A number of studies document that media attention is correlated with initial returns.[80] Enhanced visibility can bring prestige and awareness of the firm and its managers to the investing public.

Loughran and Ritter suggest that issuing firms were more willing to accept high initial returns during the tech IPO bubble if it gave them access to all-star analysts.[81] Analyst coverage is a scarce and expensive resource. They note that there are typically only five Institutional Investor all-star analysts providing coverage to an industry and investment banks spent upwards of $1 billion during the tech IPO bubble on equity research. Therefore, issuers may be willing to allow underwriters to underprice an issue in order to give them access to these

---

[78] Alexander Ljungqvist & William Wilhelm, *Does Prospect Theory Explain IPO Market Behavior?*, 60 J. FIN. 1759 (2005).

[79] Ljungqvist & Wilhelm, *supra* note 58.

[80] *See* Utpal Bhattacharya, Neal Galpin, Rina Ray & Xiaoyun Yu, *The Role of the Media in the Internet IPO Bubble*, 44 J. FIN. QUANT. ANALYSIS 657 (2009); Douglas Cook, Robert Kieschnick & Robert Van Ness, *On the Marketing of IPOs*, 82 J. FIN. ECON. 35 (2006); Laura Xiaolei Liu, Ann E. Sherman & Yong Zhang, *The Long-Run Role of the Media: Evidence from Initial Public Offerings*, 60 MGMT. SCI. 1945 (2014).

[81] Tim Loughran & Jay Ritter, *Why has IPO Underpricing Changed Over Time?*, 33 FIN. MGMT. 5 (2004).

analysts.[82]

Significant enforcement and class action lawsuits resulted from these practices after the tech IPO bubble burst. On April 28, 2003, the NASD, SEC, NYSE and others announced the final terms of the Global Analyst Research Settlement against ten of the top investment banks. In addition to the conflicts noted above, underwriters were charged with submitting fraudulent research reports that increased the price of a stock. In response, the NASD and NYSE enacted rules that prohibited many of the activities that led to the Global Analyst Research Settlement.[83]

It is clear that the opaqueness in the strategies used by investment banks to allocate shares has allowed questionable underwriter practices to occur. These abuses harm the ability of firms to raise capital at fair prices and, therefore, increase the cost of capital. Underwriters have long resisted providing information about allocations and their determinants to regulators and the public. This is likely because increasing transparency on how IPOs are priced would shed light on the practice of using underpriced shares to receive indirect compensation from clients.[84] Thus, one regulatory initiative that would improve the ability of regulators and researchers to understand and monitor the practice of underwriting would be to require disclosure of bids and allocations in the primary market, at a minimum, on the Consolidated Audit Trail (CAT).[85] Doing so would improve the ability of regulators and researchers to determine whether the current mechanism of discretionary allocation employed by underwriters benefits or penalizes issuers. Such information can be used to show how strongly allocations correlate with a) buy-and-hold investing, b) soft dollars paid to underwriters, and c) other possible side payments. An additional benefit to requiring the disclosure of primary market allocations is that it may reduce behaviors that benefit underwriters at the expense of issuers.

---

[82] Liu and Ritter formalize how a desire for influential analyst coverage results in higher underpricing in equilibrium. *See* Xiaoding Liu & Jay Ritter, *Local Underwriter Oligopolies and IPO Underpricing*, 102 J. FIN. ECON. 579 (2011).

[83] *See* http://finra.complinet.com/en/display/display.html?rbid=2403&element_id=9751.

[84] The agency theory of excessive IPO underpricing does not explain why underwriters extract rents via underpricing rather than charging higher gross spreads. Loughran and Ritter suggest that the reason is twofold: the covariance of severe underpricing and good news, and the fact that opportunity costs are less salient than direct costs. *See* Loughran & Ritter, *supra* note 28.

[85] For additional information, see Kathleen Weiss Hanley & Jay Ritter, Comment Letter (July 12. 2016), https://www.sec.gov/comments/4-698/4698-1.pdf.

One mechanism that might mitigate conflicts of interest is the creation of independent IPO advisors. Jenkinson, Jones, and Suntheim document a rise in the use of independent corporate finance advisors by issuers in European IPOs over the last ten years.[86] These advisors help guide the company through the IPO process, including selecting the book-runners, setting the offer price range, and helping the underwriter in determining the allocation of shares. Because they work for the issuer, it is reasonable to expect that the advisors can monitor the underwriter's behavior and ensure that there are no quid pro quos during allocation. However, when the authors examine whether advisors mitigate conflicts of interest, they find that even when an issuer employs an advisor, underwriters are still more likely to give preferential allocation to investors based on the amount of revenues they generate for the bank. It is not clear whether advisors allow such practices because they also directly benefit from them or because an allocation strategy based on revenues is the most cost-effective method of conducting an offering. Clearly, additional research is needed to determine why this occurs.

2.3 Aftermarket Trading and Price Stabilization

> Most distributions of corporate securities are made at a fixed public offering price in markets which may be "stabilized": underwriters peg or fix the market price of a security, through bids for or purchases of that security, for the limited purpose of preventing a decline immediately prior to or during a public offering. Similar activity in the regular trading markets might be regarded as manipulative. . . . Underwriters agreed that customers who sell their allotments in the immediate after-market are to be avoided. One underwriter stated: "With respect to my personal feelings, I detest free riders."
>
> Special Study (part 1) at pp. 481-82, 523.

In addition to the pricing and allocation of securities in an IPO, underwriters also engage in creating an orderly market after trading begins. If aftermarket trading profits are related to initial returns, this may be another rationale as to why underwriters may prefer underpricing. Ellis, Michaely, and O'Hara show that the lead underwriter is always a market maker in the issuing

---

[86] Tim Jenkinson, Howard Jones & Felix Suntheim, *Quid Pro Quo? What Factors Influence IPO Allocations to Investors?*, J. FIN. (forthcoming).

firm's stock and accounts for the majority of the trading volume in the security.[87] They also document that aftermarket trading profits (either round trip trades or changes in inventory) are positively related to initial returns.

Dollar profits due to market making or trading are not the only potential source of profits to lead underwriters. During the tech IPO bubble, when underpricing of IPOs reached its peak, a number of underwriters were accused of engaging in activities that manipulated the aftermarket price of the stock through "laddering." Laddering is a quid pro quo arrangement where, in order to receive an allocation, an investor agrees to buy additional shares in the aftermarket.[88] This agreement can lead to a misperception that aftermarket demand for the stock is greater than it actually is and may artificially inflate the price, leading to higher underpricing.

Ellis, Michaely, and O'Hara also find that underwriters can accumulate substantial inventory, particularly in underpriced stocks, that may expose them to the risk of subsequent price reversals.[89] One reason why underwriters engaged in laddering practices that required investors to make aftermarket purchases may have been to alleviate net inventory.

Underwriters often overallocate shares in an IPO.[90] In other words, the number of shares sold at the offer price exceeds the available number of shares in the offering. In order to manage this overallocation, underwriters have two tools at their disposal: aftermarket purchases and the overallotment option. The overallotment option grants the underwriter the option to purchase additional shares from the issuer at the offer price, up to 15% of the offering.

If the IPO is underpriced, it is beneficial for the underwriter to exercise the overallotment option to deliver any shares that may have been sold in excess

---

[87] Katrina Ellis, Roni Michaely & Maureen O'Hara, *When the Underwriter is the Market Maker: An Examination of Trading in the IPO Aftermarket*, 55 J. FIN. 1039 (2000).

[88] *See* Grace Hao, *Laddering in Initial Public Offerings*, 85 J. FIN. ECON. 102 (2007); John M. Griffin, Jeffrey H. Harris & Selim Topalogluc, *Why are IPO Investors Net Buyers Through Lead Underwriters?*, 85 J. FIN. ECON. 518 (2007); Stephen Choi & A.C. Pritchard, *Should Issuers Be on the Hook for Laddering? An Empirical Analysis of the IPO Market Manipulation Litigation*, 73 U. CIN. L. REV. 179 (2014).

[89] Ellis, Michaely & O'Hara, *supra* note 87.

[90] *See* Kathleen Weiss Hanley, Charles Lee & Paul Seguin, *Price Stabilization in the Market for New Issues*, 34 J. FIN. ECON. 231 (1996); Reena Aggarwal, *Stabilization Activities by Underwriters After Initial Public Offerings*, 55 J. FIN. 1075 (2000).

of the number offered because the offer price is less than the market price.[91] But if the offer is overpriced, the underwriter may choose to cover its overallocation with purchases in the aftermarket and use these purchases to maintain the offer price in the secondary market.[92]

While much of the attention in both the media and the literature has been on high average initial returns, approximately 28% of IPOs issued from 2003 through the first quarter of 2015 experience zero or negative returns on the first trading day.[93] The average first day return for these IPOs is -5%, with almost one third of the offers having no difference between the offer price and the first day closing price.

The role of the underwriter in the aftermarket is particularly salient for issues that do not experience a price increase on the first trading day. Rather than allowing market forces to work, underwriters are permitted to price support an issue (at a price no higher than the offer price) under Regulation M. While the SEC envisioned that such activities be governed by a stabilizing bid that is disclosed to the market, in reality, underwriters maintain the price of the offering by purchasing shares in the aftermarket. These shares are then used to cover the short position in the number of shares allocated, a practice called "syndicate short covering."

Syndicate short covering is defined in Regulation M Rule 104 as the placing of any bid or the effecting of any purchase on behalf of the sole distributor or the underwriting syndicate or group to reduce a short position created in connection with the offering. Rule 104 has different disclosure requirements depending on whether the activity is a stabilizing bid or purchases for syndicate short covering even though each have similar economic outcomes. If a stabilizing bid is placed in the market, Regulation M requires "prior notice to the market on which such stabilizing will be effected, and shall disclose its

---

[91] Another benefit is that the underwriter earns the gross spread for shares purchased in the overallotment option but not in the aftermarket.

[92] For a model of price support in which underwriters stabilize an IPO not to reduce investor losses but to increase their own price and penalize flippers, see Raymond Fishe, *How Stock Flippers Affect IPO Pricing and Stabilization*, 37 J. FIN. & QUANT. ANALYSIS. 319 (2002). Zhang provides a theoretical model of overallocation in IPOs and concludes that overallocation can increase aftermarket demand and higher market prices. Donghang Zhang, *Why do IPO Underwriters Allocate Extra Shares When They Expect to Buy Them Back?*, 39 J. FIN. & QUANT. ANALYSIS 571 (2004).

[93] IPOs are identified from SDC and filtered as in Table 1, but includes IPOs of financial institutions. Returns are calculated using data from the Center for Research in Security Prices (CRSP).

purpose to the person with whom the bid is entered." In contrast, if stabilization is conducted using syndicate short covering, the market maker must "provide prior notice to the self-regulatory organization with direct authority over the principal market in the United States for the security for which the syndicate covering transaction is effected." Because the disclosure requirement for syndicate short covering has less transparency to the market, this practice has the potential to be misleading to investors who purchase stabilized securities in the first few days of trading.[94] Proposed amendments to Regulation M would require disclosure of syndicate covering transactions to the market and provide greater transparency to investors as to the pricing of the security.[95]

Underwriters who are engaged in stabilizing the price prefer that investors who are allocated shares do not trade or "flip" them on the first day of trading because doing so places price pressure on the price of the security. In order to discourage this practice, underwriters have threatened to withhold future allocations from customers who flip, or apply a penalty bid to syndicate members who allow flipping. A penalty bid takes back all or part of the selling commission for allocations that are flipped.[96]

Krigman, Shaw, and Womack document that flipping (defined as seller-initiated block trades of 10,000 shares or more) accounts for 45% of trading volume on the first day in cold issues but only 22% in hot issues.[97] Furthermore,

---

[94] The prospectus discloses that such activities may take place.

[95] These amendments were proposed in 2004, *see* SEC Release No. 34-50103, July 28, 2004 and 69 FR 48008, (Aug. 6, 2004), but have not been finalized due to the introduction of a controversial new rule, Rule 106, that prohibits tying arrangements whereby allocation in a "hot" offering is conditional on purchases in a "cold" offering. In traditional bookbuilding models, tying, or bundling of IPOs can be beneficial to issuers because it reduces underpricing. The opposite effect can occur if the tying arrangements are due to conflicts of interest between the issuer and underwriter. Additional economic analysis is needed to determine the cost-benefit tradeoff of allowing tying of hot and cold offers.

[96] FINRA has expressly prohibited imposing a penalty bid on only select syndicate members since 2010. Paragraph (c) of Rule 5131 prohibits any member or person associated with a member from directly or indirectly recouping, or attempting to recoup, any portion of a commission or credit paid or awarded to an associated person for selling shares of a new issue that are subsequently flipped by a customer, unless the managing underwriter has assessed a penalty bid on the entire syndicate.

[97] Laurie Krigman, Wayne Shaw & Kent Womack, *The Persistence of IPO Mispricing and the Predictive Power of Flipping*, 54 J. FIN. 1015 (1999).

flippers are able to predict poor performers subsequent to the offer. Aggarwal, using allocation data from underwriters, finds that flipping accounts for an average of 19% of trading volume overall and institutional investors flip 47% of shares with the highest initial returns but a far lower 20% of shares of IPOs with low initial returns.[98] Furthermore, she finds that penalty bids are rarely used. Chemmanur, Hu, and Huang use proprietary trading data and estimate that institutional investors sell over 70% of their allocations in the first year.[99] More importantly, they find that institutions who hold IPO allocations for a longer period, particularly those in weak IPOs, are rewarded with higher future allocations. Hanley, Lee, and Seguin, examining closed-end fund IPOs, show that the greater the selling volume after the offering, the sooner price support ends.[100] Thus, the ability of an underwriter to control the selling activity of investors in the immediate aftermarket is an important determinant of the length of price stabilization.

Miller argues that short sale constraints immediately following an IPO contribute to pricing inefficiencies in the short term.[101] The premise that short selling is difficult immediately after an IPO is based upon the perceived high cost of borrowing shares,[102] limits on underwriters lending shares during the first month of trading,[103] the lockup of insider shares which restricts supply,[104] and difficulties in locating shares prior to the closing of the offer. However, Edwards and Hanley provide evidence that refutes the notion that investors are unable to short sell securities of an IPO.[105] They document that short selling on the first

---

[98] Reena Aggarwal, *Allocation of Initial Public Offerings and Flipping Activity*, 68 J. FIN. ECON. 111 (2003).

[99] *See* Thomas Chemmanur, Gang Hu & Jickun Huang, *The Role of Institutional Investors in Initial Public Offerings*, 23 REV. FIN. STUD. 4496 (2010).

[100] *See* Kathleen Weiss Hanley, Charles Lee & Paul Seguin, *Price Stabilization in the Market for New Issues*, 34 J. FIN. ECON. 231 (1996).

[101] *See* Edward M. Miller, *Risk, Uncertainty, and Divergence of Opinion*, 32 J. FIN. 1151 (1977).

[102] *See* Alexander Ljungqvist, Vikram Nanda & Rajdeep Singh, *Hot Markets, Investor Sentiment, and IPO Pricing*, 79 J. BUS. 1667 (2006).

[103] *See* Todd Houge, Tim Loughran, Gerry Suchanek & Xuemin Yan, *Divergence of Opinion, Uncertainty, and the Quality of Initial Offerings*, 30 FIN. MGMT. 5 (2001).

[104] *See* Eli Ofek & Matthew Richardson, *Dotcom Mania: The Rise and Fall of Internet Stock Prices*, 58 J. FIN. 1113 (2003).

[105] Amy Edwards & Kathleen Weiss Hanley, *Short Selling in Initial Public Offerings*, 98 J. FIN. ECON. 21 (2010).

Figure 3: Number of IPOs and Listed Firms

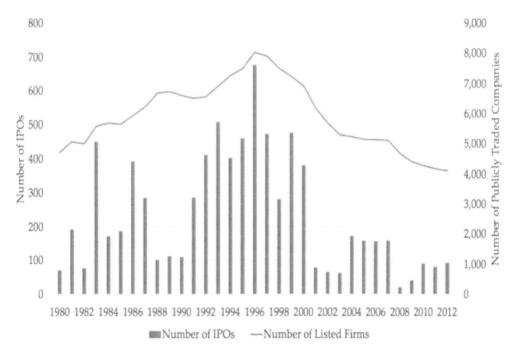

Notes: The figure presents the number of IPOs and listed firms by year from 1980 to 2012. The sample of IPOs (bar) is from Jay Ritter's website and includes issues with an offer price of at least $5.00, excluding ADRs, unit offers, closed-end funds, REITs, natural resource limited partnerships, small best efforts offers, banks and S&Ls, and stocks not listed on CRSP (CRSP includes Amex, NYSE, and some NASDAQ stocks). The number of listed firms (line) is from Doidge et al., *infra* note 108. Listed firms include domestic, publicly-listed firms in the U.S., from the WDI and WFE databases. Investment companies, closed-end funds, REITs, ETFs, and other collective investment vehicles are excluded.

trading day occurs in virtually all IPOs and the greatest amount of shorting occurs at the open.[106] Furthermore, short selling is highly correlated with under-pricing. Although short selling is highest in the first few days of trading (in excess

---

[106] Barry and Jennings document that, on average, 90% of the initial day's average return is earned on the opening trade. *See* Christopher Barry & Robert Jennings, *The Opening Price Performance of Initial Public Offerings of Common Stock*, 22 FIN. MGMT. 54 (1993).

of the typical ratio of short selling to volume documented by Diether, Lee, and Werner, it does not appear to curb observed underpricing.[107]

2.4 Decline in IPOs

It is perhaps not surprising that lack of success should be so common among new, small ventures brought to the public during a period of high market receptivity. Nevertheless the results do not suggest the adoption of a public policy of exclusion: in an economic system based on enterprise and risk-taking, neither the speculative venture nor the established one should be denied access to capital markets by the Federal Government.

Special Study (part 1) at p. 552.

Since 2000, there has been a significant decline in the number of IPOs. This decline is mirrored by the overall deterioration in the number of listed companies in the U.S.[108] and the increasing concentration of firms in many industries.[109] The drop in both the number of IPOs and listed companies can be seen in Figure 3. In 1996, the number of publicly listed companies peaked at over 8,000 and the number IPOs reached almost 700.[110] Furthermore, the average size of an IPO has increased since that time. Before 1998, most issuers raised $50 million or less in total proceeds. As shown in Figure 4, average proceeds are

---

[107] *See* Karl Diether, Kuan-Hui Lee & Ingrid Werner, *It's SHO time! Short-Sale Price Tests and Market Quality*, 64 J. FIN. 37 (2009).

[108] *See* Craig G. Doidge, Andrew Karolyi & Rene Stulz, *The U.S. Listing Gap*, 123 J. FIN. ECON. 464 (2017).

[109] *See* Grullon et al., *supra* note 13.

[110] This conclusion is unaffected by whether the number of publicly listed companies excludes IPOs. The tally of public firms includes only those companies that are available through CRSP. Generally, this means that these companies trade on national market exchanges such as the NYSE, Nasdaq and AMEX. The number thus excludes companies that are registered with the SEC but trade in the OTC market and may undercount the number of "public" companies. As a comparison, the number of publicly listed firms in Doidge, Karolyi, and Stulz, *supra* note 108, in 2005 is approximately 5,000 while the Report of the Advisory Committee on Smaller Public companies (https://www.sec.gov/info/smallbus/acspc/acspc-finalreport.pdf) reports 9,428 public companies, many of which trade on the OTC Bulletin Board.

Figure 4: Average IPO Proceeds

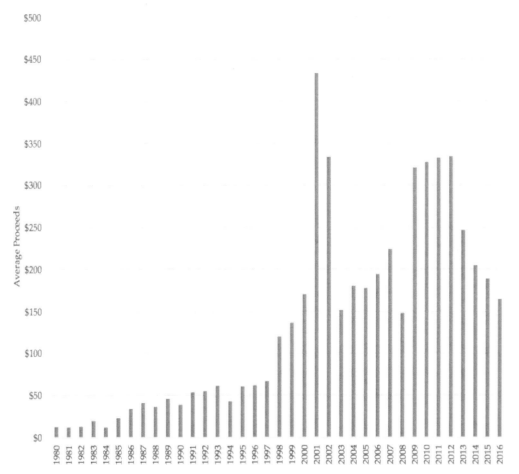

Notes: The figure presents the average IPO proceeds by year from 1980 to 2016 excluding the exercise of the overallotment option. The average proceeds in 2008 exclude Visa's IPO, which raised $19.65 billion. The sample includes IPOs with an offer price of at least $5.00, excluding ADRs, unit offers, closed-end funds, REITs, natural resource limited partnerships, small best efforts offers, banks and S&Ls, and stocks not listed on CRSP (CRSP includes Amex, NYSE, and some NASDAQ stocks). The data are from Jay Ritter's website (https://site.warrington.ufl.edu/ritter/ipo-data/).

significantly higher during the tech IPO bubble, but since 2010 the average proceeds raised (excluding the overallotment option) have grown to over $250 million.

The lack of IPOs has been a subject of discussion by academics, practitioners, and regulators. A plethora of media stories bemoan the lackluster IPO market since 2000 and this lament continues today.[111] A number of explanations have been put forth to account for the decline. Below is a discussion of the main themes.

2.4.1 The Cost of Going Public

The IPO Task Force Report cited the high cost of going public as one of the primary reasons for the decline in the number of IPOs despite the fact that these costs have remained relatively stable over the past 25 years.[112] Going public involves substantial costs, both direct in the form of fees to underwriters, lawyers and accountants, as well as the indirect cost associated with underpricing. Chaplinsky, Hanley, and Moon find that the average proportion of proceeds paid to accountants and lawyers averages almost 2% from 2003 through the first quarter of 2015.[113] The typical gross spread paid to underwriters is 7%[114] for a total of 9% of proceeds paid to all intermediaries. Including average underpricing of 14% means that almost a quarter of the proceeds raised goes to the cost of conducting the offering.[115]

Additional costs include management time and the associated loss in productivity of employees who are involved in the offering process. Given the

---

[111] *See* Noah Smith, *IPOs Are Going Out of Style*, BLOOMBERG VIEW, Sept. 16, 2016, https://www.bloomberg.com/view/articles/2015-09-16/taking-companies-public-is-going-out-of-style.

[112] The IPO Task Force Report is available at https://www.sec.gov/info/smallbus/acsec/rebuilding_the_ipo_on-ramp.pdf

[113] *See* Susan Chaplinsky, Kathleen Weiss Hanley & Katie Moon, *The JOBS Act and the Costs of Going Public*, 55 J. ACCT. RES. 795 (2017).

[114] *See* Hsuan-Chi Chen & Jay R. Ritter, *The Seven Percent Solution*, 55 J. FIN. 1105 (2000). Abrahamson, Jenkinson, and Jones document that the fees charged by investment bankers in European IPOs are roughly three percentage points lower than in the U.S. and that the same investment banks charge significantly lower fees for conducting IPOs in Europe than they do for similar IPOs in the U.S. Gross spreads are also lower for larger U.S. IPOs. Mark Abrahamson, Tim Jenkinson & Howard Jones, *Why Don't U.S. Issuers Demand European Fees for IPOs?*, 66 J. FIN. 2055 (2011).

[115] Chaplinsky et al., *supra* note 113, estimate an average initial return from 2003 to April 2015 of 13.4%, while Jay Ritter, on his website, *see supra* note 30, estimates an average initial return of 14% from 2001-2016.

high cost of conducting an IPO, some issuers may prefer to seek alternative forms of capital that may not entail such a large up-front dead weight loss. As will be discussed later, certain provisions of the JOBS Act seek to reduce the regulatory burden of going public and, thereby, lower the direct costs of going an IPO.

2.4.2 Rigors of the Public Market

It has been argued that the expectations of investors in the public market are unsuited to the technology companies of today. The Nasdaq Private Market states that the "rigors of the public markets are becoming increasingly difficult on companies that are still developing their business models. Investors in the public markets tend to expect their companies to meet expectations and deliver on quarterly guidance. While today's private companies are tackling more challenging problems that require experimentation, iteration and failure, the public markets may not be able to tolerate the volatility."[116]

Similarly, Gao, Ritter, and Zhu hypothesize that for firms in many industries, getting large fast has become more important today than in the past, leaving smaller companies in an uncompetitive position.[117] Ritter documents that the proportion of smaller public companies that are unprofitable continues to trend upward, exceeding 70% in 2017.[118]

Jeff Harris, speaking to the SEC's Advisory Committee on Smaller Public Companies, argues that retail investors were disproportionately burned by the tech IPO bubble, and the IPO scandals that occurred during that time give the perception that the deck is stacked against retail investors.[119] Others note the significant underperformance of smaller company IPOs after going public. The lackluster performance of firms post-IPO may contribute to retail investors' reluctance to buy IPOs, leading to a potential lemons problem in the market.[120]

---

[116] https://www.nasdaqprivatemarket.com/whitepapers.

[117] Xiaohui Gao, Jay R. Ritter & Zhongyan Zhu, *Where Have all the IPOs Gone?*, 48 J. FIN. & QUANT. ANALYSIS 1663 (2014).

[118] *See* Table 9 at https://site.warrington.ufl.edu/ritter/files/2018/01/IPOs2017Statistics_January17_2018.pdf

[119] https://www.sec.gov/info/smallbus/acsec/acsec060812-transcript.pdf

[120] *See* Jay Ritter, *The Long-Run Performance of Initial Public Offers*, 46 J. FIN. 3 (1991); Tim Loughran & Jay Ritter, *The New Issues Puzzle*, 50 J. FIN. 23 (1995); Paul Gompers & Joshua Lerner, *The Really Long-Run Performance of Initial Public Offerings: The Pre-Nasdaq Experience*, 58 J. FIN. 1355 (2003).

Data from Jay Ritter's website[121] indicates that the smallest IPO issuers (those with less than $100 million in sales) have significantly negative average market-adjusted three year buy-and-hold returns of -28% from 1980 to 2015.

2.4.3 Regulation

The IPO Task Force Report argues that securities regulations were "intended to address market issues created exclusively by the behavior of, and risks presented by, the largest companies. While some regulations succeeded in this aim, almost all of them have created unintended adverse effects on emerging growth companies looking to access public capital."[122] The report surveyed CEOs of companies that went public since 2006, and these executives estimate that they spend, on average, $1.5 million per year in compliance costs related to their public company status. Costs associated with compliance with SOX is usually the most mentioned regulatory cost that adversely affects smaller companies.

The SEC Study on Section 404 Internal Control over Financial Reporting estimates that the first year total costs of compliance, including the costs of the audit, outside vendors, and internal labor, average around $785,000 for companies that have a public float of less than $150 million.[123] Iliev confirms the magnitude of these numbers and finds that small firms had average pre-tax audit costs of $697,890.[124] The rise in costs following SOX prompted the SEC to delay the compliance of small firms and to completely exempt them from SOX Section 404(b) in the Dodd-Frank Act of 2010.

Gao, Ritter, and Zhu estimate that the effect of paying SOX compliance costs is not the primary reason that small issuers are unprofitable after going public.[125] Further, Coates and Srinivasan argue that even after regulations exempting smaller companies from compliance with certain provisions of SOX were put in place, IPOs by small firms did not increase as might be expected if regulatory burdens were the reason for the decline in IPOs.[126] Interestingly,

---

[121] *See supra* note 30.

[122] *See supra* note 112

[123] https://www.sec.gov/news/studies/2009/sox-404_study.pdf.

[124] *See* Peter Iliev, *The Effect of SOX Section 404: Costs, Earnings Quality, and Stock Prices*, 65 J. FIN. 1163 (2010).

[125] Xiaohui Gao, Jay R. Ritter & Zhongyan Zhu, *Where Have all the IPOs Gone?*, 48 J. FIN. & QUANT. ANALYSIS 1663 (2014).

[126] John C. Coates & Suraj Srinivasan, *SOX After Ten Years: A Multidisciplinary Review*, 28 ACCT. HORIZONS 627 (2014).

Doidge, Karolyi, and Stulz do not find that the reduction in listed companies is due to firms who decide to delist in order to save compliance costs but rather to mergers and acquisitions.[127]

However, SOX costs are only a small drop in the bucket compared to other compliance costs. Firms must produce quarterly, annual, and current reports as well as proxy statements. Furthermore, insiders must report market transactions of securities in their firm, and firms are obligated to monitor their trading activities. Additional disclosures may be required when the company engages in M&A activity, during capital raising, or when there is a material event that affects the firm. Advice must be sought not to violate prohibitions on communications under Regulation FD or during securities offerings. Reporting and disclosing information on a timely basis requires the advice of in-house compliance staff, legal counsel, and accountants. It is not only the direct costs of producing the necessary filings that are required but also the human capital involved in deciding the information to be disclosed.

Many issuers, such as insurance companies and banks, are overseen by other financial regulators, in addition to the SEC, such as the Federal Reserve, Federal Deposit Insurance Corporation, Office of the Comptroller of the Currency, and state insurance regulators. Each of these regulators has their own rules and requirements and there is little coordination between them to avoid duplication or to promote regulatory efficiency. This may create redundancies that increase the cost of compliance. Despite the importance of understanding the impact of costs on firm behavior and U.S. competitiveness, there has been no comprehensive examination of the costs of compliance across the financial regulatory landscape. An in-depth study that quantifies the amount of productive capital that is tied up in compliance and how the universe of financial regulations collectively work is needed in order to assess how to tailor the regulatory landscape to both larger and smaller public companies.

2.4.4 Trading Ecosystem

The IPO Task Force Report also suggest that changes in the trading environment for smaller public companies make U.S. markets unattractive to companies considering going public. Specifically, the rise of electronic trading and decimalization reduced the compensation and role of full-service brokers, changing their business model and making the market more attractive to high frequency traders. The decline in traditional sources of revenue for brokers, coupled with the implementation of Regulation FD and the Global Analyst Research Settlement in 2003, decreased the profitability of investing in analyst coverage, particularly for smaller companies. The loss of analyst coverage has led

---

[127] Doidge et al., *supra* note 108.

many smaller company stocks to become "orphans," with reduced investor interest and lack of trading.

Whether the charges by the IPO Task Force are true is subject to debate. Gao, Ritter, and Zhu examine the percentage of IPOs that have analyst coverage in the first three years after the IPO and find little evidence that smaller firms are more likely either to not have coverage and/or to have coverage dropped compared to larger firms.[128] They conclude that "the risk of being abandoned by analysts within a few years of going public has not increased."[129]

Weild and Kim cite the move to decimalization and Regulation NMS as a "death star" and claim these regulations lead to a loss of liquidity and aftermarket support for new issues.[130] Changes in the overall market structure for trading from the adoption of Regulation NMS may have led to market fragmentation and the loss of dedicated market makers that benefit small issuers.

Beginning in October 2016, an NMS plan was introduced to implement a Tick Size Pilot Program designed to examine whether rolling back decimalization for a group of small stocks and widening tick sizes may affect the liquidity of the affected securities. Although such a program will likely be useful in understanding the role of tick sizes in trading, it is doubtful that the pilot will be able to determine whether increasing tick sizes will lead to additional analyst coverage for affected stocks. Indeed, O'Hara, Saar, and Zhong argue that increasing the tick size may have the inadvertent consequence of making high frequency traders more aggressive and, depending on the trading environment, could have the opposite of the intended effect on small company trading.[131] Furthermore, widening the tick size may increase the cost of trading and exacerbate the already low liquidity in smaller company stocks. Because high frequency trading is responsible for much of the liquidity provision in the markets today, it is unlikely that any profits from widening the tick size will be dedicated to increasing analyst coverage.

---

[128] Gao et al., *supra* note 125.

[129] *Id.* at 1681.

[130] David DaWeild & Edward Kim, *Market Structure is Causing the IPO Crisis – and More*, Grant Thornton white paper (2010). The JOBS Act refers to decimalization as the "transition to trading and quoting securities in one penny increments." 15 U.S.C. § 78k-1(c)(6)(A) (2017).

[131] Maureen O'Hara, Gideon Saar & Zhuo Zhong, *Relative Tick Size and the Trading Environment* (working paper, 2015), https://papers.ssrn.com/sol3/papers.cfm?abstract_id=2463360.

Figure 5: M&A versus IPO Exits

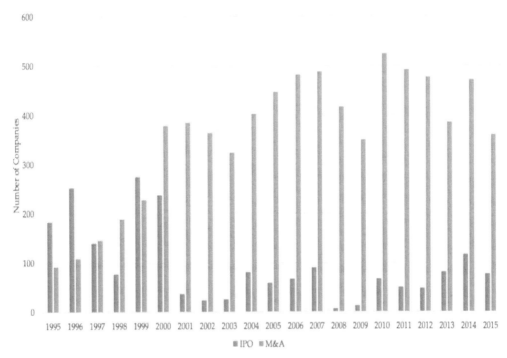

Notes: The figure presents a comparison of M&A and IPO exits using data reported by the National Venture Capital Association 2016 Yearbook. Venture capital IPO exits are those done on U.S. stock exchanges/markets with at least one U.S.-domiciled venture fund investor. Venture capital acquisition exits are completed secondary sales and trade sales where the company was domiciled in the U.S. and had at least one U.S.-domiciled venture capital investor. Write-offs are not included as exits.

2.4.5 Alternate Exits

Alternative exit strategies, such as selling the company through an M&A transaction, may be preferable to conducting an IPO and undertaking the post-IPO burdens of being a public company. Figure 5, using data from the National Venture Capital Association 2016 Yearbook, shows that the number of M&A exits far exceeds those through IPOs. However, many of the larger deals are conducted in the IPO and not the M&A market. In examining the choice of exit strategy, Bayar and Chemmanur find that firms operating in industries without a dominant market player are more likely to go public than be sold to another company.¹³²

Venture capitalists are often the driving force behind the exit strategy of a firm. Despite the growing preference for an M&A exit, a number of papers have documented a valuation premium for IPOs over M&A.¹³³ Chaplinsky and Gupta-Mukherjee, examining venture capital returns, find that an IPO exit results in an average 209.5% return on investment compared to 99.5% for M&A.¹³⁴ While the median return to an IPO is positive, the median return for an M&A transaction is -32.1%, meaning that venture capitalists, on average, are taking winners public and selling losers privately. However, the highest quintile of M&A returns compares favorably to returns from an IPO. The challenge these studies face, however, is overcoming the endogeneity in the choice of exit strategy.

If the public markets are not receptive to smaller, younger companies, then selling the company privately rather than waiting for an IPO may allow the entrepreneur to cash out earlier and move on to a new venture. Consistent with this conjecture, the mean time to exit for an M&A transaction is approximately five years compared to seven for an IPO.¹³⁵

2.4.6 Private Capital

If the entrepreneurs have access to private capital through late stage financing at acceptable terms, they may choose to remain private longer. Figure 6 presents the time-series of the dollar amount of VC financing from 1995 to 2015. As can be seen in the figure, expansion and late stage financing have been on the

---

¹³² Onur Bayar & Thomas Chemmanur, *What Drives the Valuation Premium in IPOs Versus Acquisitions? An Empirical Analysis*, 18 J. CORP. FIN. 451 (2012).

¹³³ *See* Annette Poulsen & Mike Stegemoller, *Moving From Private to Public Ownership: Selling out to Public Firms Versus Initial Public Offerings*, 37 FIN. MGMT. 81 (2008).

¹³⁴ Susan Chaplinsky & Swasti Gupta-Mukherjee, *The Decline in Venture-Backed IPOs: Implications for Capital Recovery*, in HANDBOOK OF RESEARCH ON IPOS (Levis & Vismara eds., 2013). Iliev and Lowry find that venture capitalists often continue to provide capital to newly public firms. *See* Peter Iliev & Michelle Lowry, *Venturing Beyond the IPO: Financing of Newly Public Firms by Pre-IPO Investors* (working paper, 2017), https://papers.ssrn.com/sol3/papers.cfm?abstract_id=2766125.

¹³⁵ *See* NATIONAL VENTURE CAPITAL ASSOCIATION, YEARBOOK 2016 (2016), https://nvca.org/wp-content/uploads/delightful-downloads/2016/11/NVCA-2016_Final.pdf.

Figure 6: VC Financing

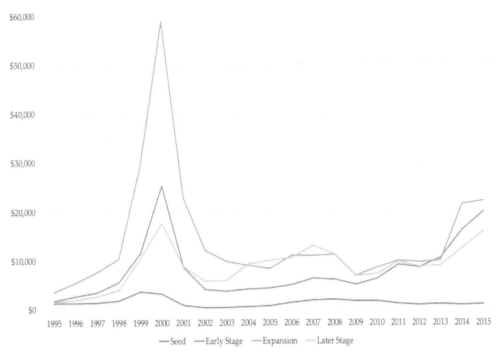

Notes: The figure presents venture capital investments by stage using data reported by the National Venture Capital Association 2016 Yearbook. The stages are defined as follows. Seed stage occurs when the company has just been incorporated and its founders are developing their product or service. Early stage occurs after the seed (formation) stage but before middle stage (generating revenues). Typically, a company in early stage will have a core management team and a proven concept or product, but no positive cash flow. Expansion stage is characterized by a complete management team and a substantial increase in revenues. Later stage occurs when the company has proven its concept, achieved significant revenues compared to its competition, and is approaching cash flow break-even or positive net income. Typically, a later stage company is about 6 to 12 months away from a liquidity event such as an IPO or buyout.

rise over the past few years. However, the amount of venture capital available in later rounds of financing is not nearly as high as during the tech IPO bubble when a significant number of companies went public.

Private capital can also be raised from hedge funds, private equity funds, corporations, and mutual funds. Kwon, Lowry, and Qian find a substantial

Figure 7: Alternative Investment Assets Under Management

Figure: Growth in assets under management by asset class
Total alternative assets under management, $ billions

[Bar chart showing growth from 1999 to 2014 H1, with categories: Other, Private equity, Private equity real estate, Venture capital, Private equity buyouts, Hedge funds]

Source: Preqin, Hedge Fund Research

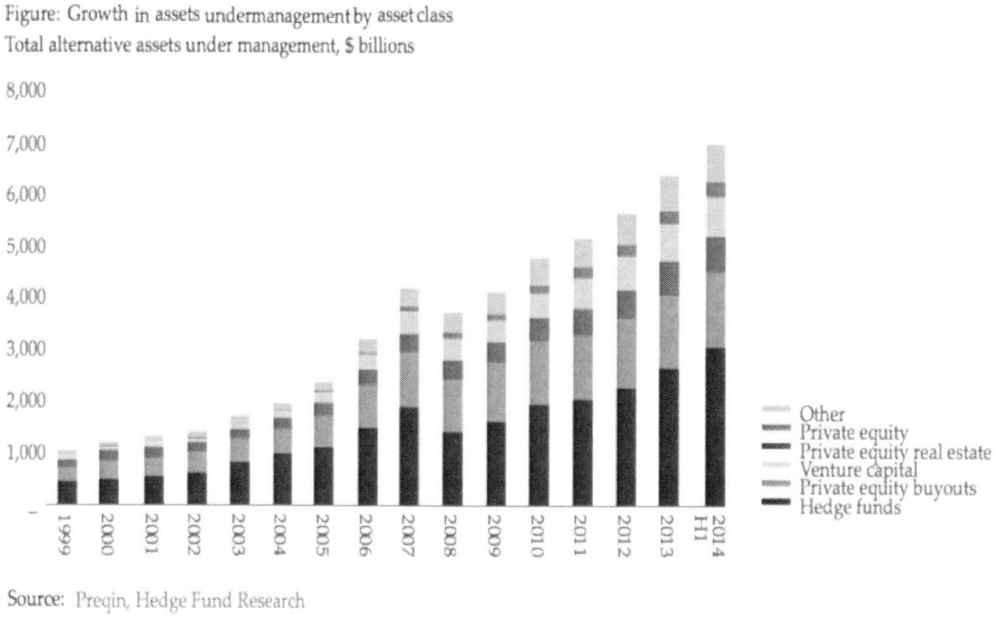

Notes: The figure presents the time-series of assets under management for alternative investments (private equity, venture capital, and hedge funds) from Alternative Investments 2020, published by the World Economic Forum.

increase in mutual fund investment in private, VC-backed firms before an IPO.[136] Prior to 2010, less than 5% of these firms had capital provided by mutual funds. By 2014, the percentage is 19% and more recently, has increased to 36% in 2016. The authors conclude that mutual fund investments allow firms to obtain more capital and to stay private longer.[137]

---

[136] Sungjoung Kwon, Michelle Lowry & Yiming Qian, *Mutual Fund Investments in Private Firms* (working paper, 2017), https://papers.ssrn.com/sol3/papers.cfm?abstract_id=2941203.

[137] Schwartz raises concerns about traditional mutual funds investing in late-stage financing. *See* Jeff Schwartz, *Should Mutual Funds Invest in Startups? A Case Study of Fidelity Magellan Fund's Investments in Unicorns (and other Startups) and the Regulatory Implications*, 95 N.C. L. REV. 1341, 1346 (2017) ("I conclude that, while liquidity does not appear to be a concern, there is reason to suspect that investors fail to realize that their mutual funds are investing in unicorns (and potentially other startups), that mutual-fund investments in these securities are inadequately informed, and that the valuations that mutual funds report publicly and serve as the basis of redemptions and purchases may be inflated.").

Figure 7 from the World Economic Forum shows a dramatic rise in the availability of capital through private investment vehicles. Access to private capital has given rise to the term "unicorn," used to describe a company with over $1 billion in implied market value in its latest financing round.[138] According to CBInsight, there are 185 private unicorn companies as of the beginning of 2017.

Overall, the plethora of reasons as to why smaller companies are not accessing the public markets makes it challenging to identify a regulatory solution to the problem. If the economic environment for product development, industry composition and profitability has changed, then a modification in securities regulation is unlikely to be the mechanism to fix the lack of IPOs. As will be seen in the next subsection, the JOBS Act, an initial attempt to make public markets more attractive to smaller companies, has not been widely successful.

2.5 JOBS Act

In April 2012, the Jumpstart Our Business Startups (JOBS) Act was signed into law in order to reduce the regulatory burden of small firms and facilitate their capital raising in both private and public markets.[139] As noted on the SEC JOBS Act website, "Cost-effective access to capital for companies of all sizes plays a critical role in our national economy, and companies seeking access to capital should not be hindered by unnecessary or overly burdensome regulations."[140] The JOBS Act has its origins in several studies conducted by the U.S. Treasury and the SEC on the capital raising environment for small firms and IPOs. The most important of these was the IPO Task Force Report issued in October 2011. The report made a number of specific recommendations to decrease the initial and ongoing costs of being public, and many of its recommendations were enacted directly through the JOBS Act.

This is not the first time that smaller companies have received regulatory relief. Congress and the SEC have had a long history of permitting scaled disclosure. Beginning with the Securities Act of 1933, small issuers raising capital below a certain threshold ($100,000 in 1933 and later raised to $5 million in the late 1980s) were exempted from registration requirements. In 1992, the SEC adopted Regulation S-B that provided scaled disclosure for issuers whose public

---

[138] *See* Keith Brown & Kenneth Wiles, *In Search of Unicorns: Private IPOs and the Changing Markets for Private Equity Investments and Corporate Control*, 27 J. APPLIED CORP. FIN. 34 (2015).

[139] Much of the discussion in this section is from Chaplinsky et al., *supra* note 113.

[140] https://www.sec.gov/spotlight/jobs-act.shtml.

float was no more than $25 million. As noted in the final rule, the proposal was enthusiastically received by the small business commenters as a significant step to facilitating access to the public market for start-up and developing companies, and reducing the costs for small businesses that have their securities traded in the public markets. More recently, in 2007, the SEC adopted amendments to its disclosure and reporting requirements to expand the benefits of scaled disclosure by increasing the public float cutoff to $75 million for a new category of issuers called smaller reporting companies (SRCs).[141]

Title I of the JOBS Act principally attempts to redress the increased "regulatory cascade" by extending the benefits of scaled disclosure currently enjoyed by SRCs to "emerging growth companies" or EGCs.[142] In addition, the JOBS Act allows the company to test the waters by communicating with investors prior to the offering and to confidentially file its registration statement with the SEC. The testing-the-waters provision eliminates the quiet period restrictions on communications before an offering, enabling issuers to gain important feedback before making the decision to go public. Confidential filing allows an issuer to obtain comments from the SEC before making its registration statement public. If, after completing the registration process, an EGC decides to go public, its registration materials must be made public no later than 21 days before the onset of the roadshow. Thus, an EGC that decides not to pursue an IPO need not disclose any of its information publicly.

The JOBS Act's reduced disclosure during the offering process allows EGCs to provide two rather than three years of audited financial statements; to limit executive compensation disclosure to three rather than five named executive officers; and omit the discussion and analysis of compensation (and continue this more limited disclosure in periodic reports that follow). The JOBS Act also reduces some aspects of ongoing disclosure. After the IPO, EGCs are exempt from auditor attestation of internal controls under SOX Section 404(b) and the Dodd-Frank Act corporate governance requirements. EGCs must begin to comply with SOX 404(b) five years after going public compared to two years before the JOBS Act. EGCs are exempt from Say-on-Pay and advisory votes on golden parachutes, for example, for as long as they remain EGCs. In instances

---

[141] As of this writing, the SEC is proposing to raise the SRC threshold to $250 million in public float.

[142] An issuer qualifies as an EGC if it has less than $1 billion in revenues in its most recent fiscal year-end and otherwise does not qualify as a Well-Known Seasoned Issuer (WKSI). (*See infra* note 170 for the definition of a WKSI.) EGC status lasts until the fifth anniversary of going public or revenues exceed $1 billion.

Figure 8: EGC Qualifying IPOs

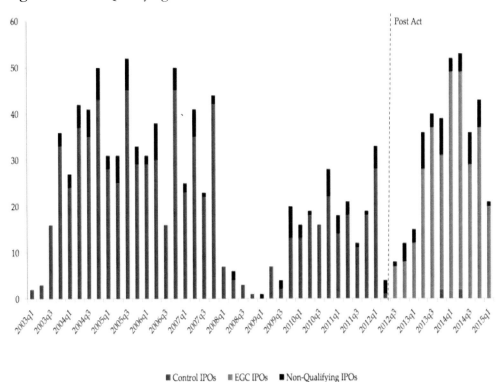

Notes: The figure presents the number of emerging growth company (EGC) qualifying IPOs from 2003 to April 30, 2015 from Chaplinsky et al., *supra* note 113. Prior to the JOBS Act, a control IPO was deemed EGC qualifying if it went public with less than $1 billion in revenue at the most recent fiscal year-end based on 2012 dollars, or after the JOBS Act, it met the EGC criteria but did not select EGC status (5 IPOs). EGCs are IPOs that filed their initial registration statement and went public between April 5, 2012 and April 30, 2015 and self-identified as EGCs in their S-1s.

where the Public Company Accounting Oversight Board establishes new auditing requirements or revises existing ones, the JOBS Act allows EGCs to delay compliance until the rules become effective for private companies, which is typically at a later date than for public companies.

Thus, one of the goals of the JOBS Act is to reduce the costs of going public and subsequent compliance costs. As such, it should increase the number of firms willing to go public and reduce the overall cost of doing so. Dambra, Field, and Gustafson document an increase in the number of firms going public during the first two years after the JOBS Act's enactment, especially those firms with high proprietary information costs, many of which are biotech and pharmaceutical firms.[143] As can be seen in Figure 8, there has been a drop off in EGCs after that time and it is therefore unclear whether the initial increase in IPOs will be sustained over the long-term.

The enactment of the JOBS Act provides a natural experiment to examine the effect of a reduction in disclosure on the pricing of IPOs. If the costs of providing disclosure outweighs the benefits, then firms should have a reduced cost of capital at the time of the offering as measured by underpricing. On the other hand, if disclosure about IPOs is value-relevant to the decision-making of investors, then its absence should increase underpricing and increase the cost of capital.

All of the studies to date document higher underpricing for firms going public after the Act than for those that went public before the Act. Barth, Landsman, and Taylor provide evidence that firms that take greater advantage of the provisions of the JOBS Act to reduce disclosure have greater underpricing.[144] They report additional evidence of increases in post-IPO volatility and bid-ask spreads that are consistent with greater information uncertainty after the JOBS Act. Agarwal, Gupta, and Israelsen analyze the mix of information that issuers disclose and show that the higher underpricing of EGCs is associated with more textual discussion of risk factors and not the disclosure of less accounting information. Furthermore, the content of SEC comment letters becomes more negative in tone, more forceful in the recommendations, and more focused on quantitative information, suggesting that SEC oversight cannot fully reduce the JOBS Act's effect.[145]

The intention of the JOBS Act was to reduce disclosure requirements and therefore, the costs of going public. Chaplinsky, Hanley, and Moon find no evidence that the Act has been effective in decreasing the fees paid to underwriters, accountants and attorneys.[146] Since many of the provisions of the JOBS Act are already available to SRCs, the authors compare the experience of EGCs that would have qualified as SRCs to those of EGCS that would not have qualified. They document that greater underpricing is present only for larger

---

[143] Michael Dambra, Laura Casares Field & Matthew Gustafson, *The JOBS Act and IPO Volume: Evidence that Disclosure Costs Affect the IPO Decision*, 116 J. FIN. ECON. 121 (2015).

[144] Mary Barth, Wayne Landsman & Daniel Taylor, *The JOBS Act and Information Uncertainty in IPO Firms*, 92 ACCT. REV. 25 (2017).

[145] Sumit Agarwal, Sudip Gupta & Ryan Israelsen, *Public and Private Information: Firm Disclosure, SEC Letters, and the JOBS Act* (working paper, 2017), https://papers.ssrn.com/sol3/papers.cfm?abstract_id=2891089.

[146] *See* Chaplinsky et al., supra note 113.

firms (non-SRCs) that are newly eligible for scaled disclosure under the JOBS Act.

Title I of the JOBS Act also allows greater affiliated analyst access to the issuer and offering permitting these analysts to attend road shows and interact with investors prior to the offering. Furthermore, the quiet period moratorium on affiliated analyst coverage has been dropped. Dambra, Field, and Gustafson find no evidence that analyst coverage, either the number of analysts or the days to initiation of coverage for recent IPOs, differs much before and after the introduction of the JOBS Act.[147] In practice, affiliated analysts are not initiating coverage until 25 days after the IPO. In a follow-on paper, Dambra, Field, Gustafson, and Pisciotta examine the relaxation of pre-IPO analyst communication and find that following the Act, affiliated analysts' earnings per share forecasts have become significantly less accurate and more optimistic.[148]

There are, however, some aspects of the JOBS Act that may be beneficial to issuers even if they cannot be quantified. For example, the ability to test-the-waters and confidentially file a registration statement could reduce the probability of a formally withdrawn offering, saving issuers time and money. These provisions, coupled with reduced disclosure, could also lower the costs associated with disclosing proprietary information to competitors. The ability to delay compliance with SOX 404(b) and the Dodd-Frank Act voting requirements could provide cost savings to issuers. Finally, the JOBS Act allows firms to move away from a one-size-fits-all regulatory regime, and thus may lower costs by allowing issuers to tailor their disclosure choices to meet their specific needs.

Figure 8 shows that the vast majority of IPOs would have qualified for EGC status before the Act and that the vast majority of qualifying issuers after the Act have chosen EGC status. Therefore, the JOBS Act extends regulatory relief to the vast majority of IPO issuers. While the Act's intentions are noble, it remains unclear whether its mandate has been achieved. Thus, as the Act matures, regulators should monitor whether the benefits of allowing reduced disclosure to larger issuers have come at the cost of investor protection.

Whether the JOBS Act will result in a sustainable increase in the number of companies going public has yet to be seen. There are other provisions of the Act that may act as a countervailing influence and allow companies to remain private longer, either by increasing the threshold for registration with the SEC or by making access to the private market easier. First, the Act increases the number of shareholders of record that triggers registration and reporting under Section

---

[147] Dambra et al., *supra* note 143.

[148] Michael Dambra, Laura Casares Field, Matthew Gustafson & Kevin Pisciotta, *Pre-IPO Communications and Analyst Research: Evidence Surrounding the JOBS Act* (working paper, 2017).

12(g) of the Securities Act of 1934 for companies with more than $10 million in assets, from 500 to 2000. Second, it permits firms to offer and sell securities when crowdfunding. Third, it permits general solicitation under Regulation D, for Rule 506 offerings and finally, it increases the offering threshold to $50 million for Regulation A offerings. The provisions that apply to private capital raising will be discussed in Section 4.

3 Follow-on Offerings

> These, however, are the issues about which there is most likely to be a reservoir of publicly available information if the issuer is subject to periodic reporting requirements.
>
> Special Study (part 1) at p. 550.

Figure 9 presents the time-series of the number of equity follow-on offerings (or what academics often term "seasoned equity offerings" or SEOs). Interestingly, the issuance of seasoned equity declined during the tech IPO bubble but has since rebounded, unlike the number of IPOs. This section will review the literature on offering methods, issue pricing, and regulatory changes that affect the speed with which these offers come to market.

3.1 Offering Methods

Follow-on offerings are usually brought to market in one of two ways. Traditionally, firms raised additional capital using an offering process similar to an IPO. The firm would file a registration statement (Form S-1) with the SEC that included detailed disclosure about the issuer and the offering. Underwriters would then use bookbuilding to solicit indications of interest from potential investors.

In 1982, the SEC introduced shelf registration (Rule 415), allowing a firm to file a base prospectus on Form S-3. This base prospectus includes information about the issuing firm and the securities the issuer intends to over the next two years. The issuer may conduct multiple offerings off of the shelf registration. Shelf registration also allows "incorporation by reference" meaning that information about the issuer, from both prior and future filings such as 10-Ks, can be incorporated into the filing without having to reiterate the information. Once the shelf registration statement is effective, the issuer is eligible to "take down" or issue securities off the shelf as it sees fit often at very short notice. Bortolotti, Megginson, and Smart document that most shelf-registered offers are conducted using either an accelerated bookbuilding process or the sale of a block

Figure 9: Number of Follow-On Offerings

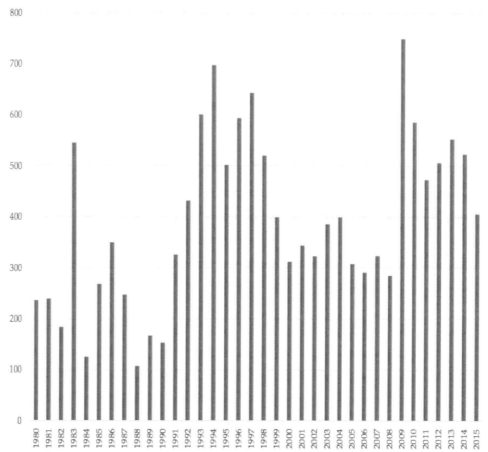

Notes: The figure presents the number of follow-on offers excluding follow-ons that include only secondary shares, ADRs, utilities, and those securities that are not listed within three trading days of the offering. The data is from Jay Ritter's website (https://site.warrington.ufl.edu/ritter/ipo-data/).

of securities to an investment bank at an auction-determined price.[149]

Gao and Ritter document that prior to 2000, the vast majority of follow-on equity capital was raised through a traditional bookbuilt offering.[150] Today,

---

[149] Bernardo Bortolotti, William Megginson & Scott B. Smart, *The Rise of Accelerated Seasoned Equity Underwritings*, 20 J. APPLIED CORP. FIN. 35 (2008). The investment bank then resells the securities, generally overnight, to institutional investors.

accelerated shelf-registered offers are the norm.[151] Furthermore, the speed of issuance has increased significantly. Gao and Ritter document that traditional bookbuilt offers take approximately one month from filing to complete, while shelf registered offers typically take only one to two days.[152] Gustafson finds that between 2000 and 2008, the median time between an equity follow-on announcement and issuance dropped from a month to a single day with 75% of issuers, since 2008, issuing overnight.[153]

In general, the literature finds that the imposition of new rules allowing alternative flotation methods is followed by a sorting out process in which firms choose the issuance process that is best suited to their firm characteristics and informational environment. For example, Smith argues that informational asymmetry between the issuing firm's managers and investors can affect the choice on whether to issue equity using a traditional bookbuilt offer or shelf registration.[154]

Consistent with this view, Denis examines the introduction of shelf registration and shows that its use is limited for equity issues, a relatively high asymmetric information security compared to debt.[155] Bethel and Krigman find that firms with high information asymmetry, even if eligible to use shelf registration, experience large price declines if they register common equity on unallocated shelves.[156] Autore, Hutton, and Kovacs argue that the lack of due diligence available to investors may cause low quality issuers of equity to choose accelerated offers and high quality issuers to prefer bookbuilt offers in order to

---

[150] Xiaohui Gao & Jay Ritter, *The Marketing of Seasoned Equity Offerings*, 97 J. FIN. ECON. 33 33 (2010)

[151] *See* Don Autore, Raman Kumar & Dilip Shome, *The Revival of Shelf-Registered Corporate Equity Offerings*, 14 J. CORP. FIN. 32 (2008); Bortolotti et al., *supra* note 149.

[152] Gao & Ritter, *supra* note 150.

[153] Matthew Gustafson, *Price Pressure and Overnight Seasoned Equity Offerings*, J. FIN. & QUANT. ANALYSIS 837 (2018).

[154] Clifford Smith, *Investment Banking and the Capital Acquisition Process*, 15 J. FIN. ECON. 3 (1986).

[155] David Denis, *Shelf Registrations and the Market for Seasoned Equity Offerings*, 64 J. BUS. 189 (1991).

[156] Jennifer Bethel & Laurie Krigman, *Managing the Costs of Issuing Common Equity: The Role of Registration Choice*, 47 Q. J. FIN. & ACCT. 57 (2008).

allow for information production.[157] Comparing issuers that use both methods, they find that when the same firm uses an accelerated offer to issue equity instead of a bookbuilt offer it has greater overvaluation and poorer post-issue stock and operating performance. As a result, firms faced with high information asymmetry may prefer bookbuilt offers over shelf registered offers when issuing equity because underwriters can lower issuance costs by increasing the elasticity of demand for the firm's shares,[158] provide certification and due diligence on the value of the shares,[159] and market the offer to potential investors.[160]

3.2 Announcement Effects and Offer Pricing

Numerous papers on traditional bookbuilt follow-ons have documented a significant negative market reaction when firms announce they are issuing equity.[161] The decline in value upon announcement is often interpreted to be a signal that the managers of the firm believe the stock is overvalued and are seeking to capitalize on this belief by issuing additional equity at a high price.

In addition to the announcement effect, there is also a subsequent decline in the market value of the shares just prior to issuance.[162] In order to fully subscribe the issue, follow-ons are generally discounted relative to the pre-offer day trading price. Altinkilic and Hanson document an average abnormal announcement return of -2.23% and a discount to the pre-offer trading price of 1.5% for follow-on offerings from 1990 to 1997.[163] Since firms issue new shares at a discount from the market price, investors have an incentive to short sell shares in order to manipulate trading prices downward and thereby, decrease the

---

[157] Don Autore, Irena Hutton & Tunde Kovacs, *Accelerated Equity Offers and Firm Quality*, 17 EURO. FIN. MGMT. 835 (2011).

[158] Gao & Ritter, *supra* note 150.

[159] Ann Sherman, *Underwriter Certification and the Effect of Shelf Registration on Due Diligence*, 28 FIN. MGMT. (1999).

[160] Rongbing Huang & Donghang Zhang, *Managing Underwriters and the Marketing of Seasoned Equity Offerings*, 46 J. FIN. & QUANT. ANALYSIS 141 (2010).

[161] For a review of the literature, see B. Espen Eckbo, Ronald W. Masulis & Oyvind Norli, *Seasoned Public Offerings: Resolution of the "New Issues Puzzle"*, 56 J. FIN. ECON. 251 (2000).

[162] *See* Shane Corwin, *The Determinants of Underpricing for Seasoned Equity Offers*, 58 J. FIN. 2249 (2003).

[163] Oya Altinkilic & Robert Hanson, *Discounting and Underpricing in Seasoned Equity Offers*, 69 J. FIN. ECON. 285 (2003).

expected offer price.[164] Short sellers then cover their short position using their allocation of shares in the offering, pocketing the difference between the short sale price and the offering price. Even absent a manipulative intent, the strategy can result in "free" money because of the discount. Safieddine and Wilhelm, using short interest, and Henry and Koski, using short selling transactions, find that higher levels of short selling prior to an offer are strongly related to larger issue discounts.[165]

Rule 105 of Regulation M is designed to combat short selling in advance of an offer. As amended in 2007, it prohibits an investor from purchasing shares in an offer if they have an open short position in the five days prior to issuance. This prohibition is in effect regardless of whether the investor intends to cover their open short with the allocation of shares. Even after the adoption of the rule, however, Henry and Koski do not find any evidence that the effect of abnormal short selling has been attenuated.[166]

There have been a number of enforcement actions against investors who appear to be trying to take advantage of the decline in price in the period leading up to the offer by short selling or trading options in violation of Rule 105.[167] Despite some high profile cases, the ability of regulators to monitor the behavior of investors across a large number of offerings is hampered by the lack of data. Requiring primary market allocations in follow-on offers to be reported to the CAT can aid regulators in monitoring and identifying potential manipulation and/or violations of Rule 105.

Henry and Koski also note that the relationship between short selling and the offer discount is only present for traditional bookbuilt offers and does not apply to accelerated shelf offers. Thus, the increase in the use of accelerated shelf offerings may be partially due to issuers trying to mitigate the effect of short sellers driving up their cost of capital.[168] Gustafson argues that acceleration of the offering process reduces the pre-offer price pressure and estimates that such accelerated offers save $4 million for the average issuer.[169]

---

[164] Bruno Gerard & Vikram Nanda, *Trading and Manipulation Around Seasoned Equity Offerings*, 48 J. FIN. 213 (1993).

[165] *See* Assem Safieddine & William J. Wilhelm, *An Empirical Investigation of Short-Selling Activity Prior to Seasoned Equity Offerings*, 51 J. FIN. 729 (1996); Tyler R. Henry & Jennifer L Koski, *Short Selling Around Seasoned Equity Offerings*, 23 REV. FIN. STUD. 4389 (2010).

[166] Henry & Koski, *supra* note 165.

[167] https://www.sec.gov/news/pressrelease/2015-239.html.

[168] Henry & Koski, *supra* note 165.

[169] Gustafson, *supra* note 153.

3.3 Securities Offering Reform

The adoption of Securities Offering Reform in 2005 further accelerated the offering process for certain issuers and relaxed rules around pre-offer communication with investors. The regulation allows larger companies, WKSIs, to file a registration statement and immediately effect a take-down off the shelf registration without SEC review.[170] This rule significantly reduced the amount of time investors have to review and process information in the registration documents. As a response to this concern, Securities Offering Reform also allowed WKSIs to engage at any time in oral and written communications with investors, including through the use of a "free writing prospectus," in advance of an offering.[171] Although concern was raised during the rule's comment period about the potential for issuers to hype their security using pre-market communications, this was perceived to be outweighed by the increased need for timelier information flow around security offerings.

Two papers examine the effect of allowing increased communication during the quiet period after the rule's adoption. Shroff, Sun, White, and Zhang document that issuing firms provide more information to the public prior to the follow-on filing date through management earnings forecasts, 8-K filings, earnings announcements, and free writing prospectuses.[172] Examining indicators of information asymmetry such as the adverse selection component of bid-ask spreads, market depth, and analyst forecast accuracy, they show that increased disclosure reduces spreads and increases depth and analyst accuracy. Furthermore, the announcement return is less negative after Securities Offering Reform, consistent with a reduction in the cost of capital.

Clinton, White, and Woidtke, like Shroff, Sun, White, and Zhang, find greater disclosure, both management forecasts and press releases, by WKSIs

---

[170] WKSIs are companies that have a worldwide market value of its outstanding voting and non-voting common stock held by non-affiliates of $700 million or more, or have sold at least $1 billion in aggregate principal amount of registered debt (or other nonconvertible securities) in primary offerings for cash.

[171] A "free writing prospectus" is a written communication deemed to be an offer to sell a security that does not qualify as a prospectus. Such communication may not be inconsistent with the actual prospectus.

[172] Nemit Shroff, Amy X. Sun, Hal D. White & Weining Zhang, *Voluntary Disclosure and Information Asymmetry: Evidence from the 2005 Securities Offering Reform*, 51 J. ACCT. RES. (2013).

prior to an offering after the rule is adopted.[173] The overall frequency of disclosure is 25% greater and the amount of information in a Form 8-K current report during this time is more than double the size prior to Securities Offering Reform. Management earnings forecasts are more accurate as well. They find higher stock returns during the capital formation period with no reversal afterward and conclude that "disclosure during this time, especially 8-K disclosure, is related to a richer information environment with capital formation benefits."

3.4 Unintended Consequences

> Representatives of one member firm state 'flash' secondary distributions, occurring on the same day they were announced, were sold by salesmen who had little time to inform themselves about the securities being offered and who, under the incentive of extra compensation, told customers of 'a wonderful opportunity' without disclosing the fact of the distribution and the payment of a higher than normal rate of compensation.
>
> Special Study (part 1) at p. 567.

Unlike IPOs, investors in follow-on offerings are able to rely on the past disclosures of issuers to value the securities. Although information asymmetry may still exist, the need for careful vetting through the bookbuilding process is reduced. The speed with which these offers come to market can be beneficial because it reduces the impact of pre-market trading on offering prices and allows issuers to take advantage of a window of opportunity when markets may be receptive to new issuance. These benefits, however, come with a potential cost. For example, the use of accelerated shelf offerings raises concerns about the ability of investors and underwriters to conduct appropriate due diligence on the securities sold.

    The consequences of accelerating the offer process using shelf registration became apparent in the issuance of private label residential mortgage-backed securities (RMBS) in the period leading up to the 2008 global financial crisis. When adopting modifications to the shelf registration process for asset-backed securities in 2005, one commenter expressed "reticence in expanding access to the ABS regulatory regime out of concern that it could have certain unintended consequences, such as investment decisions on these additional

---

[173] Sarah B Clinton, Joshua T. White & Tracie Woidtke, *Differences in the Information Environment Prior to Seasoned Equity Offerings Under Relaxed Disclosure Regulation*, 58 J. ACCT. & ECON. 59 (2014).

transactions being made under more compressed time frames and with less access to information through shelf registration."[174]

The rationale for allowing shelf registration, in general, is that an investor can rely on the firm's history of disclosure and past offerings to make an informed decision. While the specific terms of the security being offered may differ (for example, the firm may issue convertible debt instead of straight debt) the underlying fundamentals and the investor's claim to the cash flows of the firm remain relatively transparent. In contrast, the cash flow claim in an RMBS is on a pool of mortgages, the composition of which, its credit quality, and the cash flow stream, can change substantially from one issuance of an RMBS offering to the next even off the same shelf registration. In addition to the complicated nature of these securities, RMBS are often sold very quickly, leaving little time for investors to conduct thorough due diligence. This lack of time to evaluate the offering may have provided an incentive for mortgage lenders to originate poor quality mortgages that were subsequently securitized and offered in a shelf-registered RMBS.

In order to remedy the inability of investors to conduct adequate due diligence, the SEC adopted a number of regulations governing the issuance of asset-backed securities including a required three-day waiting period for the sale of registered ABS and increased disclosure about the underlying assets in the pool.[175] The experience of investors of RMBS in the lead up to the financial crisis provides a cautionary tale of the pitfalls of accelerating the offering process.

4 Unregistered or Private Offerings

> Unregistered distributions can be quite sizable individually, and in the aggregate they are a very significant phenomenon in the securities markets. They are of growing importance because of the increasing participation of institutional investors in the markets. From the point of view of public customers, they are often indistinguishable from registered distributions in respect of disclosure needs.
>
> Special Study (part 1) at pp. 568-69.

The sale of securities in unregistered or private offerings allows young companies to raise capital in advance of an IPO, and provides public companies with an additional source of capital. Firms can obtain capital in private offerings by directly issuing securities to investors or indirectly, through hedge funds,

---

[174] *See* https://www.sec.gov/rules/final/33-8518.pdf at n. 64.

[175] *See* https://www.sec.gov/rules/final/2014/33-9638.pdf.

Figure 10: Capital Raised by Type of Offering

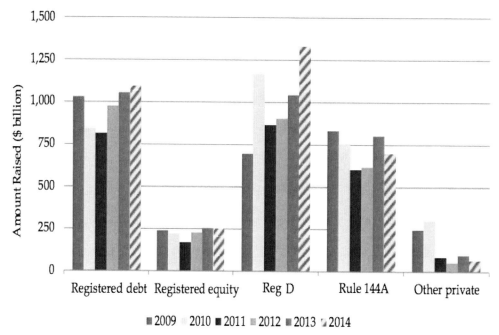

Notes: The figure presents the amount of capital raised by different offering methods and is from Bauguess et al., *supra* note 18. Private offerings (Regulation D, Rule 144A and other) includes both debt and equity securities. Other private includes Regulation S offerings, Section 4(a)(2) offerings, and Regulation A offerings.

private equity firms, and venture capitalists, who use unregistered offerings to raise funds from investors. The private market allows issuers to avoid certain regulatory burdens and the increased scrutiny that comes with a public offering. The intended benefit of a lighter regulatory regime is to reduce both issuance costs and the time required to raise capital.[176] Because disclosure, both at the time of and subsequent to the offering, is often limited in unregistered offerings, participation is generally restricted to sophisticated investors.

As will be seen later in this section, the number of unregistered offerings exceeds public offerings in the amount of capital raised, making the private markets an important venue in capital formation. The literature on the choice between the decision to use private versus public issuance includes both debt and equity and thus, both types of securities will be discussed in this section.

---

[176] *See* Bauguess, et al., *supra* note 18.

4.1 Regulation D and Rule 144A

Regulation D allows firms, both private and public, to issue securities without having to register them with the SEC (although they must file a Form D to report the completion of the offering). As can be seen in Figure 10 from Bauguess, Gullapalli, and Ivanov, *supra* note 18, the amount of capital raised by all types of private offerings (Regulation D, Rule 144A or other private exemptions) rivals that of public issuance.[177] For example, in 2014, private offerings accounted for $2.1 trillion of new capital compared to $1.4 trillion of new capital (both debt and equity) in registered offerings. Furthermore, the amount of issuance in the private market has trended upwards over time.

An examination of the number of offerings paints a much more dramatic picture. In Figure 11, the number of Regulation D offers far exceeds the number of other types of offerings. In 2014 alone, there were over 33,000 Regulation D offers compared to around 3,000 public offerings of debt and equity. Although some exemptions under Regulation D restrict the amount of capital that can be raised (Rule 504 allows issuers to raise $1 million in a year, while Rule 505 allows $5 million in a year), the most popular exemption, Rule 506, has no limit.

Bauguess, Gullapalli, and Ivanov estimate the average amount raised across all issuers in a Rule 506 offering at $25 million, but the median is much smaller at only $1.5 million. The largest issuers under Regulation D are funds (hedge, investment, private equity, and venture capital) but non-financial issuers raised $133 billion in new capital from 20092014. These issuers account for the bulk of the number of Regulation D offerings. Thus, the market appears bifurcated in terms of offering size, with non-financial issuers raising only a median of $1 million in proceeds, compared to much higher proceeds raised by hedge funds ($11 million) and private equity ($30 million).

Bauguess, Gullapalli, and Ivanov also examine the types of investors that are participating in the Regulation D market. Regulation D offerings are primarily targeted to accredited investors although, depending on the exemption, some non-accredited investors may also participate. Alternative investments such as hedge funds and private equity funds have the highest average number of investors compared to non-financial issuers. The mean number of investors in all Regulation D offerings is 14 and the median is 4, indicating that many of these offers are sold to only a few investors even though there are no restrictions on the number of accredited investors that can participate in an offering.

In 2013, the SEC adopted amendments to Regulation D and Rule 144A

---

[177] The statistics reported in Bauguess et al., *supra* note 18, generally do not separately consider equity and debt securities, but the authors note that Rule 144A (discussed later) are predominantly debt offerings while Regulation D offerings are primarily equity offerings.

Figure 11: Number of Offers by Type of Offering

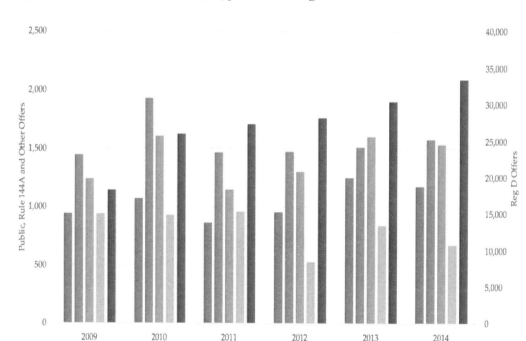

Notes: The figure presents the yearly number of offers by different offering methods and is from Bauguess et al., *supra* note 18. Other private includes Regulation S offerings, Section 4(a)(2) offerings and Regulation A offerings. Regulation D offerings are on the right axis and all other offerings are on the left axis.

to allow general solicitation in the offering of securities as required by the JOBS Act. The SEC defines general solicitation to be advertising or communication in a public media outlet such as a newspaper, television, Internet, radio etc. or at a seminar or meeting, whose attendees have been invited by general solicitation. If an issuer does use general solicitation under Rule 506(c), it may not sell any of the offering to non-accredited investors. As of 2014, only 10% of all Regulation D offerings have used the 506(c) exemption.

Rule 144A allows the resale of restricted securities to large institutional investors or Qualified Institutional Buyers (QIBs). While issuers cannot use Rule 144A directly, the rule allows a financial intermediary to purchase the securities directly from the issuer and resell them to an unlimited number of QIBs. As with Regulation D, general solicitation is permitted in the selling of the securities as long as they are sold only to QIBs. Researchers have studied security placement subject to Rule 144A because often these transactions have registration rights or agreements that the issuer will register the securities with the SEC shortly after issuance. Fenn argues that "by issuing 144A securities and subsequently registering them, issuers combine two of the best features of the private and public markets: speedy issuance (private markets) and maximum liquidity (public markets)."[178]

Much of the research on the pricing of private issues is on private investment in public equity or PIPEs. Chen, Dai, and Schatzberg find that firms are more likely to choose a PIPE when the general market and the firm's stock is performing poorly.[179] They document a median discount relative to the closing price one day before the offering of 12%, which is large compared to a discount of less than 3% for public equity follow-on offers. Chaplinsky and Haushalter also find a substantial discount from the purchase price for PIPEs, and this discount ranges from 15% to 30% depending on the contract provisions and firm characteristics.[180] They argue that the issuance of a PIPE may be a last resort equity alternative for most of these firms. Livingston and Zhou examine bond issuance in the private market. After controlling the characteristics of the bond issue, they find that compared to public issuers, Rule 144A offerings have a 19 basis point greater spread over Treasuries.[181]

The higher cost of capital in private offerings is likely due to both lower liquidity in the market for price placements and reduced disclosure. Researchers have limited access to information on private offerings and therefore, it is difficult to study whether the price impact and decision to issue securities in the private market are driven by the potential costs and benefits of disclosure.[182]

However, a few papers do provide some evidence on this issue. Tang

---

[178] George Fenn, *Speed of Issuance and the Adequacy of Disclosure in the 144A High-Yield Debt Market*, 56 J. FIN. ECON. 383, 388 (2000).

[179] Hsuan-Chi Chen, Na Dai & John D. Schatzberg, *The Choice of Equity Selling Mechanisms: PIPEs versus SEOs*, 16 J. CORP. FIN. 104 (2010).

[180] Susan Chaplinsky & David Haushalter, *Financing Under Extreme Risk: Contract Terms and Returns to Private Investments in Public Equity*, 213 REV. FIN. STUD. 2789 (2010).

[181] Miles Livingston & Lei Zhou, *The Impact of Rule 144A Debt Offerings Upon Bond Yields and Underwriter Fees*, 31 FIN. MGMT. 5 (2002).

[182] Lisowsky and Minnis find that the majority of private firms do not produce audited GAAP financial statements. Characteristics such as growth opportunities, young firm age and greater intangibles are positively related to the presence of audited financial statements. *See* Petro Lisowsky & Michael Minnis, *Accounting Choices and Capital Allocation: Evidence From Large Private U.S. Firms* (working paper, 2016), https://papers.ssrn.com/sol3/papers.cfm?abstract_id=2373498.

uses a difference-in-difference approach to partition issuers into public companies registered with the SEC and private companies.[183] She finds that the offering price is more heavily discounted for private companies even after controlling for the endogeneity of the decision to issue a private placement. Dhaliwal, Khurana, and Pereira examine the decision of firms to issue debt securities in either the public or private market by classifying them based upon their disclosure policy (the frequency and precision of management earnings forecasts and analyst evaluations of the firm's disclosure policy as reported in the Association of Investment Management and Research's Annual Reviews of Corporate Reporting Practices.).[184] They find that firms with poor disclosure policy prior to the offering are more likely to issue private debt even after controlling for the endogeneity of the firm's disclosure policy. Rather than using the private markets to hide information from investors, the authors suggest that firms with strategic information may find it advantageous to raise funds in the private market because it allows private communication between the issuer and investor, thus reducing the public dissemination of information to potential rivals. Gomes and Phillips make a similar observation when examining public firms that issue in both the public and private markets.[185] They suggest that private markets can reduce information asymmetry "because private investors have better information or ability to evaluate firm quality."

Gustafson and Iliev examine an SEC rule change that increased the availability of shelf registration to smaller issuers.[186] They find that after the rule change, smaller firms moved away from PIPEs and toward shelf registration. They state that the "overall observable effect of the new rule on equity issuance transaction costs is equivalent to an economically large reduction in issuance discounts that is not paired with a countervailing increase in fees." Thus, the findings of this and other papers indicate that public market frictions may move issuers to private markets and that reducing such frictions may be beneficial for capital formation in public markets.

---

[183] Vicki Wei Tang, *Economic Consequences of Mandatory Disclosure Regulation: Evidence From Rule 144A Equity Private Placements* (working paper, 2007).

[184] Dan Dhaliwal, Inder Khurana & Raynolde Pereira, *Firm Disclosure Policy and the Choice Between Private and Public Debt*, 28 CONTEMP. ACCT. RES. 293 (2011).

[185] Armando Gomes & Gordon Phillips, *Why Do Public Firms Issue Private and Public Securities?*, 21 J. FIN. INTERMEDIATION 619 (2012)

[186] Gustafson & Iliev, *supra* note 19.

4.2 Regulation A

In the original Special Study, offers using Regulation A to issue securities were almost as popular as registered offers. Initially, the regulation limited the amount of proceeds that could be raised to $300,000 and by 1992, it had been increased to $5 million. There are a number of benefits to Regulation A to issue securities. First, the securities offered under this method are freely tradable in secondary markets, similar to registered offerings. Second, Regulation A offers have reduced disclosure requirements and information required in the financial statements of the offering circular filed with the SEC. These filings are also subject to review by the SEC staff. One of the disincentives to using Regulation A is that such offerings have traditionally been subject to state securities regulation, a process that can be time-consuming for smaller issuers.[187]

A GAO report notes that a staff review of Regulation A offering documents lasted an average of 228 days compared to an average of approximately 130 days in registration for an IPO.[188] Such delays in the ability to begin the offering coupled with the potentially high cost of merit review by the states may have reduced the efficacy of this exemption for capital formation. According to the SEC, between 2009 and 2012, there were only 19 Regulation A offerings raising a total of $73 million.

In 2015, the SEC finalized amendments to Regulation A (Regulation A+) under the JOBS Act that increased the offering size to up to $50 million in a given year. The SEC established two tiers of offerings. Tier 1 offerings may not exceed $20 million and have no ongoing reporting requirements after the offering is complete, but are still subject to state securities regulation. Tier 2 offers may not exceed $50 million, are exempt from state securities laws and have ongoing reporting requirements.

In an SEC white paper, Knyazeva examines the use of Regulation A offerings after the rule change.[189] Between June 19, 2015, and October 31, 2016, there have been 147 offerings that sought to raise almost $2.6 billion. On average, issuers looked to raise $10 million in Tier 1 offerings and $26 million in Tier 2 offerings, well below the maximum but far above the original $5 million

---

[187] *See* U.S. GOVERNMENT ACCOUNTABILITY OFFICE, FACTORS THAT MAY AFFECT TRENDS IN REGULATION A OFFERINGS (2012), https://www.gao.gov/assets/600/592113.pdf.

[188] *See* Chaplinsky et al., *supra* note 113; *id.*

[189] Anzhela Knyazeva, *Regulation A+: What do we Know so Far?*, Securities and Exchange Commission white paper (2016), https://www.sec.gov/files/Knyazeva_RegulationA%20.pdf.

cap. Approximately 29% of issuers across both tiers had maximum offer amounts equal to their tier cap.

Most of these issuers (73%) used a Tier 2 offering and the majority of all Regulation A offerings were equity. Only about a quarter of Tier 2 offers used an underwriter or an investment bank serving as a placement agent but many had other types of intermediaries involved in the issuance. Almost all offerings under Regulation A+ are best efforts offers. Using numbers from the SEC study, Tier 2 issuers have average offering expenses of around 5% of the offering proceeds including legal, auditing, and intermediary fees. In terms of assets, these issuers are very small companies with average total assets of only $50 million and revenues of less than $3 million.

The motivation for the changes to Regulation A is to allow issuers a hybrid alternative for capital raising that stands between a private and a public offering. Although these securities are freely tradable, they are not eligible for exchange trading due to their reduced ongoing reporting requirements and, therefore, most likely trade in the over-the-counter-market.[190] There has been insufficient time to determine whether Regulation A+ will substitute for fully registered offers, particularly for first-time issuers. Thus, it is yet unclear whether the benefits of the regulation, such as reduced disclosure, are outweighed by the potential lack of liquidity and therefore, ongoing monitoring and further analysis is needed.

4.3 Crowdfunding

The JOBS Act's provisions allow early-stage businesses to offer and sell securities through crowdfunding. Typical crowdfunding ventures prior to the enactment of the JOBS Act could only solicit donations and provide goods and services in return. At the time crowdfunding was proposed, concerns were raised about allowing potentially unsophisticated investors to purchase risky securities. Barbara Roper, director of investor protection for the Consumer Federation of America says "you are talking about a market that, by its very nature, brings together inexperienced issuers with unsophisticated investors and harnesses the power of the Internet to hype the stock."[191]

---

[190] Recently, a Wall Street Journal article reported that at least one company that intends to go public using Regulation A+ will be listed on the New York Stock Exchange. *See* Corrie Driebusch, *Here's How to go Public Without Wall St.*, WALL ST. J., June 1, 2017, https://www.wsj.com/articles/heres-how-to-go-public-without-wall-street-1496309403.

[191] *See* https://www.npr.org/2013/11/26/247170871/small-firms-may-soon-turn-to-crowdfunding-to-sell-shares.

The SEC, mindful of its mandate to protect investors while at the same time promote capital formation, set investment limits on the amount of capital an issuer can raise using the crowdfunding exemption and the amount of securities an investor can purchase. Furthermore, the SEC rule requires the issuer to provide some disclosures to investors "about the company, its officers and directors, a description of the business, the planned use for the money raised from the offering, often called the use of proceeds, the target offering amount the deadline for the offering, related-party transactions, risks specific to the company or its business, and financial information about the company."[192] Investors invest in these ventures through portals that are registered with the SEC.

Preliminary evidence on the use of crowdfunding is provided by Ivanov and Knyazeva using data reported on Form C-U. Between May and December 2016, 156 issuers in 163 offerings sought to raise a total of $18 million, not including withdrawn offerings.[193] The authors estimate that 33% of the offerings were successful in meeting their target amount, and that these firms actually raised more than they initially sought. Most of these offerings set a target amount well below the $1 million cap over a 12 month period, with most offers clustered under $100,000. The average duration of crowdfunded offers was 4.5 months and the most popular security was equity.

Many of the companies that engaged in crowdfunding were very young, with a median age of only 18 months and a median of 3 employees. The average issuer had negative net income and 61% had debt in their capital structure. These firms reported very high growth in both assets and sales over the prior fiscal year (on average, 754% and 169% respectively.)

Most of the 21 intermediaries that participated in crowdfunding were portals (13) with the remainder being broker-dealers. The five largest intermediaries accounted for 71% of the offerings. The average intermediary fee was 6% for a completed offering, which is just slightly lower than similarly sized Regulation D offerings. Some portals also take a financial interest in the issuer as part of their compensation.

Further evidence on the feasibility of securities offerings using crowdfunding can be gleaned from the literature on non-security based crowdfunding. Mollick examines 48,500 projects on Kickstarter and finds that the vast majority of founders fulfill their obligations to those who fund them, but

---

[192] https://www.sec.gov/oiea/investor-alerts-bulletins/ib_crowdfunding-.html.

[193] Vladimir Ivanov & Anzhela Knyazeva, *U.S. Securities-Based Crowdfunding Under Title III of the JOBS Act*, Securities and Exchange Commission white paper (2017), https://www.sec.gov/dera/staff-papers/white-papers/RegCF_WhitePaper.pdf.

often not in a timely manner.¹⁹⁴ He uses a number of indicators for the quality of the project and finds that higher quality projects are successful in meeting their funding goals.

Li and Martin, also studying projects funded using Kickstarter, find that entrepreneur reputation is relevant for funding. Prior successful deliveries help to facilitate quicker funding. For first-time entrepreneurs, being well-known through sources such as Wikipedia and having evidence of prior skills, increases the chances of funding success.¹⁹⁵ Both of these papers suggest that crowdfunding investors are not blindly investing in projects and appear to conduct due diligence on the companies for which they provide capital. Indeed, the authors note that out of 40,000 crowdfunded projects on Kickstarter, only one has been subject to litigation in the past four years. (This finding should be treated with caution since it is unclear what damages may have been suffered by the providers of capital since they are not allowed to receive securities in return for their investment.)¹⁹⁶

As with Regulation A+, sufficient time has not passed since the rules have been finalized to analyze the effect of these alternate mechanisms on the ability of issuers to raise capital and whether or not investors have sufficient protection. But it is clear that the funding portal is an important gatekeeper and monitor of these ventures.

4.4 Private Market Trading

Private securities trading platforms offer QIBs and private companies an alternative form of liquidity for holders of unregistered securities. Two of the largest venues are Nasdaq Private Market and SharesPost. Private Market was initially a joint venture between SharesPost and Nasdaq in 2013 but more recently, in 2015, SharesPost sold its stake back to Nasdaq. Nasdaq Private

---

[194] Ethan Mollick, *The Dynamics of Crowdfunding: An Exploratory Study*, 29 J. BUS. VENTURING 1 (2013).

[195] Emma Li & J. Spencer Martin, *Capital Formation and Financial Intermediation: The Role of Entrepreneur Reputation Formation*, J. CORP. FIN. (forthcoming).

[196] Cumming, Hornuf, Karami, and Schweizer also find a low incidence of fraud in crowdfunded ventures and suggest that fraudsters can be detected by certain characteristics. Individuals engaged in fraud are less likely to have had prior experience crowdfunding, lower social media presence and more likely to have poorly worded or confusing campaign pitches. *See* Douglas J. Cumming, Lars Hornuf, Moein Karami & Denis Schweizer, *Disentangling Crowdfunding From Fraudfunding* (working paper, 2016), https://papers.ssrn.com/sol3/papers.cfm?abstract_id=2828919.

Market acquired SecondMarket in late 2015. Details on the volume and type of transactions conducted on these markets are unavailable.[197] A press release announcing the dissolution of the Nasdaq and SharesPost venture states that SharesPost executed over $2 billion in transactions for more than 125 private companies since 2011 with a network of 20,000 institutional investors, family offices, and other accredited investors.[198]

Nasdaq Private Market, in their 2016 Private Company Liquidity Report, notes that many of the transactions conducted on their platform were private tender offers used to facilitate liquidity for employees and shareholders of private companies. In 2016, they partnered with an investment bank specializing in secondary stock transactions, Scenic Advisement. Scenic Advisement estimates that the secondary, private-share market in the U.S. is currently in the neighborhood of $35 billion per year and has grown roughly 26% per year over the last five years.

In addition to these markets, OTC Markets also trade both registered and unregistered securities and have three different tiers depending on the amount of disclosure the company provides. In 2015, OTC Markets traded $196 billion in almost 10,000 securities. Unlike SharesPost and Private Market, which are primarily for transactions between QIBs, OTC Markets is mainly focused on retail transactions.

More recently, the House of Representatives put forth a bill titled "Main Street Growth Act" to allow for the creation of venture exchanges to trade "venture securities".[199] The bill defines "venture securities" as either securities of an early-stage, growth company (market capitalization of $1 million or less) exempt from registration under the Securities Act of 1933 or an EGC. The bill exempts a venture exchange from compliance with: (1) specified National Market System and Alternative Trading System rules, (2) the requirement to submit data to a securities information processor, or (3) mandatory use of decimal pricing.[200]

---

[197] The author requested information on recent trading statistics from both venues but was unsuccessful in obtaining any data.

[198] *See* http://www.prnewswire.com/news-releases/sharespost-sells-interest-in-nasdaq-private-market300164637.html.

[199] https://www.congress.gov/bill/114th-congress/house-bill/4638.

[200] Research focusing on smaller public company exchanges internationally, for example, Toronto Stock Exchange's Venture market and London's AIM, finds that investors have earned low returns by purchasing securities, particularly IPOs, on these exchanges. See Silvio Vismara, Stefano Paleari & Jay R. Ritter, *Europe's Second Markets for Small Companies*, 18 EURO. FIN. MGMT. 352 (2012); Jay R. Ritter, Andres Signori & Silvio Vismara, *Economies of Scope and IPO Activity in*

Whether or not these markets will supplant traditional exchanges in providing liquidity to emerging or private companies is still debatable. The very large valuations of private companies such as Uber and Airbnb keep the spotlight on these secondary markets. Without additional data on the types of companies, investors and market execution in each of these different trading venues, it is difficult to determine whether such markets should be made more widely available, for example, to investors in Regulation A+ or crowdfunding offers.[201] Obtaining and analyzing data from these markets will be necessary to formulate an appropriate recommendation.

5 Conclusion

This chapter provides an overview of primary equity markets with the goal of understanding the economics of capital raising. A number of observations can be made regarding the general findings of the literature. First, access to information plays an important role in the pricing of securities both in the public and private markets. Second, offering methods must balance the investor's need for information against an issuer's cost of raising funds. Third, discretion in the allocation of securities may increase pricing accuracy but leave issuers vulnerable to underwriter conflict of interests. Fourth, both public and private markets are important sources of capital for issuers irrespective of their status as a public company. Finally, regulations that decrease the regulatory burden attract issuers to specific offering methods but not without cost.

The fact that the issues highlighted in the 1963 Special Study remain relevant today is of special interest. While there have been developments in the securities offering process for follow-ons, IPOs are still brought to market by bookbuilding, despite a large body of literature that is critical of this offering method. The New Special Study is an opportunity to delve more deeply into the reasons why bookbuilding has stood the test of time despite its drawbacks before making recommendations for further reform.

It will be challenging to address these issues without access to additional data on IPO allocations, trading in private markets, and financing decisions of private firms. This data may be difficult for regulators to obtain but is a necessary step in understanding the choices available to firms in raising the necessary

---

Europe, in HANDBOOK OF RESEARCH ON IPOs 11-34 (Levis & Vismara eds., 2013).

[201] Bruggemann, Kaul, Leuz, and Werner examine the market quality of 10,000 U.S. OTC stocks. *See* Ulf Bruggemann, Aditya Kaul, Christian Leuz & Ingrid Werner, *The Twilight Zone: OTC Regulatory Regimes and Market Quality* (working paper, 2017), https://papers.ssrn.com/sol3/papers.cfm?abstract_id=2290492.

capital for investment. Much of our knowledge about capital formation has been generated by academic researchers and therefore, it is vital that outside researchers have access to any data that regulatory agencies collect. There are examples of successful collaborations that balance the need for high-quality analysis by academics and the confidentiality of issuers. For example, FINRA has allowed academic researchers access to proprietary TRACE data under controlled circumstances. A similar exchange could occur with the SEC should it be able to obtain data on allocations during bookbuilding and/or on private market trading.

The JOBS Act has made the private markets more attractive for growing companies and blurred the division between public and private markets. Regulators, therefore, should strive to have a comprehensive offering, registration, and disclosure process that allows issuers to balance the costs and benefits of differing offering methods in a way that promotes capital formation and protects investors. It is important to recognize that the choice of the method to issue securities goes hand-in-hand with the choice of how the securities will be traded. Thus, a fulsome examination of the compatibility of offering methods with trading alternatives is important in understanding the future of primary markets.

Chapter 3
THE REGULATION OF PRIMARY MARKETS

Donald C. Langevoort[202]

This chapter on the law of capital-raising and primary markets surveys a large swath of securities regulation—the domain commonly known as "corporation finance"—in search of an agenda for a new Special Study. This territory includes the entirety of the Securities Act of 1933, both in its positive mandate, the intricate regulation of registered public offerings, and its exemptive grace through either statutory or administrative forbearance from registration. Here we see the most direct connection to the goal of allocative capital market efficiency, as issuers ranging from small start-ups to well-known seasoned issuers compete for scarce investor capital. Here, too, we see the most obvious points of tension among the values of investor protection, efficiency, competition and capital formation. But we cannot stop this survey at the capital-raising transaction itself. Investors covet liquidity, the ability to resell what they have bought from issuers, which means that expectations as to secondary trading opportunities will always be integral to primary capital-raising choices and affect the cost of capital.[203] Most initial public offerings today are accompanied by an immediate listing on a national securities exchange. So this chapter extends its scope to on-going disclosure for secondary market trading as well—the subject of much of the Securities Exchange Act of 1934—and the elaborate regulatory infrastructure designed to promote informational integrity throughout the life of a public company.

That is a lot on which to chew.[204] But this is not an occasion to offer concrete reform proposals or resolve any heated policy debates, rather just seek out important but still-unanswered questions that deserve further research via a new Study. My effort here will be to describe briefly the current state of the law and identify notable points of doubt or controversy in the eyes of legal scholars,

---

[202] Thomas Aquinas Reynolds Professor of Law, Georgetown University Law Center. Thanks to commentators and participants at the March 2017 New Special Study of the Securities Markets conference at Columbia Law School for helpful thoughts and suggestions, especially Jay Ritter and Bill Williams.

[203] *See* Merritt B. Fox, *Regulating Public Offerings of Truly New Securities: First Principles*, 66 DUKE L.J. 673, 697-98 (2016).

[204] All the more so if we think of primary capital markets on a global scale. Because there is a separate chapter devoted to internationalization, this chapter has a domestic focus.

practitioners and law-makers. In turn, the companion chapter by Kathleen Hanley focuses on the financial economics of primary capital-raising and secondary trading, giving us a better sense of what existing research already demonstrates and what kind of further empirical work could reasonably be sought in a new project.

The context for this effort to explore the regulatory world of corporation finance is very different from that prevailing in 1963, when the original Special Study of the Securities Markets was submitted to Congress. That was a time of contentment and faith in regulation.[205] To be sure, there was recognition that securities regulation could be done differently and better, not permanently affixed to concerns and beliefs from the Great Depression and the New Deal. But in the early 60s, the United States had reached unmatched hegemony in the global capital markets, for a variety of reasons.[206] Investor protection and the public interest were twinned, faith in which persisted well into the 1970s.[207] Regulatory reform effectively meant regulatory expansion. As to corporate finance, the original Special Study prompted the 1964 Securities Law

---

[205] For much more on the implicit beliefs and attitudes that support securities law-making then and now, see DONALD C. LANGEVOORT, SELLING HOPE, SELLING RISK: CORPORATIONS, WALL STREET AND THE DILEMMAS OF INVESTOR PROTECTION (2016). Thorough historical coverage of the first Special Study can be found in JOEL SELIGMAN, TRANSFORMING WALL STREET: A HISTORY OF THE SECURITIES AND EXCHANGE COMMISSION AND MODERN CORPORATE FINANCE 295-305 (3d ed. 2003). The main focus of the 1963 study was on market structure and the balance between regulation and self-regulation as this played out in the exchange and over-the-counter marketplace. There may have been faith in regulation on the part of the Study's proponents and authors, but not necessarily in bureaucrats or, especially, self-regulators.

[206] See Mark Roe, *Legal Origins and Modern Stock Markets*, 120 HARV. L. REV. 460 (2006).

[207] This was so even in the face of worries throughout this time period that the securities industry had too much control over regulation and the markets. To be clear, self-interest and rent-seeking have never been far below the surface of securities law-making, even in the New Deal era. *See generally* PAUL G. MAHONEY, WASTING A CRISIS: WHY SECURITIES REGULATION FAILS 49-76 (2015). Indeed, the first Special Study was instigated by new SEC Chair William Cary and allies in Congress who were suspicious of Wall Street domination over market structure and trading.

Amendments, enlarging the scope of mandated disclosure to larger issuers traded in the over-the-counter marketplace.[208]

Today, as we contemplate launching a new Special Study, no comparable confidence can be taken for granted.[209] American capital market hegemony is no longer, and with that the recognition that global competition (and arbitrage) undermines any one country's effort to impose either regulatory philosophy or regulatory will. The very idea of public offerings and public companies as dominant solutions to the needs of corporate finance is in doubt,[210] especially as the rapid institutionalization of the holding of both debt and equity enables alternative arrangements for supplying the capital needs of enterprises of all sizes and stages of development without the glaring transparency, short-term pressures and accountability of publicness.[211] Numerous forms of regulation are said to hurt capital-raising, not help. The politics have become self-serving, ideological and often ill-informed.

---

[208] With Milton Cohen's prodding, a long project soon began to integrate the Securities Act and the Securities Exchange Act, eventually bearing much fruit but rethinking the legal foundations of corporate disclosure for seasoned issuers only at the margins, not fundamentally. *See* Milton H. Cohen, *"Truth in Securities" Revisited*, 79 HARV. L. REV. 1340 (1966). Cohen later addressed the agenda for a new Special Study, called for by Congress in 1988 but never funded. *See* Milton H. Cohen, *A Quarter Century of Market Developments—What Should a "Special Study" Study?*, 45 BUS. LAW. 3 (1989).

[209] *See, e.g.*, INTERIM REPORT OF THE COMMITTEE ON CAPITAL MARKETS REGULATION (2006), http://www.capmktsreg.org/wp-content/uploads/2016/10/Committees-November-2006-Interim-Report.pdf.

[210] *See* Xiaohui Gao, Jay Ritter & Zhongyan Zhu, *Where Have All the IPOs Gone?*, 48 J. FIN. & QUANT. ANALYSIS 1663 (2013); Jerold Zimmerman, *The Role of Accounting in the 21st Century Firm*, 45 ACCT. & BUS. RES. 485 (2015). Importantly, this cautions against assuming that drops in public offerings or public listings are mainly caused by regulatory excess, as opposed to these other incentives. An interesting Canadian study traces the comparable drop there even though the regulation of IPOs is less burdensome. Bryce Tingle, J. Ari. Pandes & Michael J. Robinson, *The IPO Market in Canada: What a Comparison with the United States Tells Us About a Global Problem*, 54 CANADIAN BUS. L.J. 321 (2013).

[211] *See* Donald C. Langevoort & Robert B. Thompson, *"Publicness" in Contemporary Securities Regulation After the JOBS Act*, 101 GEO. L.J. 337 (2013); *see also* Hillary A. Sale, *J.P. Morgan: An Anatomy of Corporate Publicness*, 79 BROOK. L. REV. 1629 (2014).

Before we get to the substance of this chapter, a word about its organization. The Securities Act focuses on the public offering of securities, and the Securities Exchange Act on public trading in the secondary markets. But public status is potentially attractive and available to a relatively small (and apparently shrinking) number of firms of considerable size and salience. Arguably, a more realistic survey of the law relating to capital-raising should begin with the options fairly available to start-ups and small businesses, and ascend from there. But because this is a legal discussion, and the non-public capital-raising options under the Securities Act are defined as exemptions from the public offering presumption, we will take the conventional route. Readers should keep in mind, however, that taking publicness as a starting point distorts the reality of what most firms face in the pursuit of needed capital.

1 Initial Public Offerings

The original Special Study understood that the issuance of "truly new securities"[212] poses the quintessential test for the regulation of capital-raising transactions. Almost by definition, a lighter touch is warranted for public offerings by issuers with which the market is already more familiar. So we start with the IPO.

The Securities Act is above all a disclosure statute, famously rejecting the sort of "merit regulation" whereby state securities regulators had passed judgment (and to an extent still do) on the quality of the investment being publicly offered. In that regard, the IPO triggers extensive disclosure obligations, which place a great deal of stress on the ability of potential investors to process the information intelligently. When the Act was passed, there was an assumption that most purchasers in public offerings were ordinary folk, needing the assistance of disclosure—thereby begging the question of how likely they would be, if indeed so unsophisticated, to make good use of the disclosure.[213] Today, by

---

[212] Fox, *supra* note 203.

[213] Early SEC Chairman (and future Supreme Court justice) William O. Douglas made this point before his appointment in criticizing the adoption of the Securities Act. *See* Donald C. Langevoort, *The Politics of Entrepreneurial Capital Raising, in* LAW AND ENTREPRENEURSHIP (Smith & Hurt eds., forthcoming). This point has been a critical theme ever since. *E.g.*, HOMER KRIPKE, THE SEC AND CORPORATE DISCLOSURE: REGULATION IN SEARCH OF A PURPOSE (1979). One answer to this comes via "filtration:" that the disclosure will at least influence those who play a role in advising or soliciting investors, and make the communications more useful and honest. *See* James D. Cox, *Premises for Reforming the Regulation of Public Offerings: An Essay*, 63 LAW & CONTEMP. PROBS. 11, 12-16 (2000).

contrast, initial purchasers are mainly large institutional investors, just one of many changes that justify a hard look at the contemporary efficacy of the statute.

1.1 The Securities Act's Investor Protection Strategies

Although there is little evidence that the drafters of the Securities Act thought in these terms, entrepreneurial capital-raising poses a classic "lemons problem" that arises when rational investors face multiple investment opportunities and the promoters have private information about the quality of their ventures. The cost of capital goes up for all ventures, perhaps prohibitively, unless the investors have some reliable mechanism for telling the difference between the sour lemons and the sweeter fruit. As noted, the Securities Act tries to solve this problem in public offerings via mandatory, credible disclosure.

The mandatory nature of disclosure follows from a number of insights. It elicits presumably useful information, although under the right bargaining conditions rational investors could (and often do) demand what they want and need as a condition for their investment. Issuers thus face disclosure incentives even in the absence of any regulatory mandate.[214] The Act's disclosure requirements are thus better understood to reflect some mix of (1) doubts about the opportunity to bargain and enforce effectively when offerees are unsophisticated and/or widely dispersed; (2) agency costs that arise when there are conflicting interests on the part of those in control of the issuer;[215] (3) a desire to promote uniformity and comparability in presentation and content so as to facilitate comparison shopping; and (4) a recognition that disclosure generates positive externalities by enriching that capital-raising environment generally—offering information that aids in the valuation of other issuers beside the one

---

[214] This is the starting point for a large volume of legal scholarship questioning (or defending) the mandatory disclosure system in light of the incentives for private ordering, whether in primary offerings or secondary trading. *E.g.*, Roberta Romano, *Empowering Investors: A Market Approach to Securities Regulation*, 107 YALE L.J. 2359 (1998); John C. Coffee, Jr., *Market Failure and the Economic Case for Mandatory Disclosure*, 70 VA. L. REV. 717 (1984); Merritt B. Fox, *Retaining Mandatory Securities Disclosure: Why Issuer Choice is Not Investor Empowerment*, 85 VA. L. REV. 1335 (1999); Zohar Goshen & Gideon Parchomovsky, *The Essential Role of Securities Regulation*, 55 DUKE L.J. 711 (2006). Critics of regulation point out that the SEC might do more harm than good even if there is a strong theoretical case for mandates, and that empowering private standard-setters (or more competition in regulation) can better address the market failures that persist.

[215] *See* Paul Mahoney, *Mandatory Disclosure as a Solution to Agency Problems*, 62 U. CHI. L. REV. 1047 (1995).

making the disclosure (e.g., disclosing a product line with a competitive advantage also provides new information about the value of the securities of marketplace incumbents) and facilitating other healthy economic activity. There are many such positive externalities beyond the immediate value of the information for trading purposes, including better corporate governance.[216]

Disclosure content today is massively—perhaps unnecessarily[217]—complex, a product of accretion over nearly eighty-five years. The required disclosure on Form S-1 invokes a catalog of line-items found in Regulation S-K, a mix of both quantitative and narrative about the issuer and its business; the issuer's capital structure; financial performance and risks; management, compensation and governance; and matters relating to the offering itself.

An especially difficult conceptual issue with respect to disclosure content has been with respect to forward-looking information. By and large, mandatory disclosure is a snapshot of the issuer as of the moment of its IPO, largely looking backwards. But the valuation decision made by rational investors is forward-looking: estimates and projections about future financial performance, adjusted for risk and discounted to present value. For many companies making an IPO—especially innovative ones—past performance is not a particularly useful indicator of the future, for better or worse. There have been moves toward some refocusing of attention, most notably in the Management Discussion & Analysis (Item 303) that asks management to assess financial performance by reference to, among other things, those trends and uncertainties affecting reported performance that are known to management and reasonably likely to occur. There is also risk factor disclosure,[218] disclosure of certain pending or threatened lawsuits, etc., plus the residual obligation to volunteer additional material information necessary to make what has been said not misleading. Still—presumably fearing revelation of secrets that could harm the issuer and deter

---

[216] Fox, *supra* note 214; *see also* Marcel Kahan, *Securities Laws and the Social Costs of "Inaccurate" Stock Prices*, 41 DUKE L.J. 997 (1992); Urska Velikonja, *The Cost of Securities Fraud*, 54 WM. & MARY L. REV. 1887 (2013). Also, mandatory disclosure operates as a verification of information voluntarily disclosed previously, thereby constraining opportunism in voluntary disclosure practices.

[217] The SEC is currently engaged in a project to assess the value of the line-item disclosure requirements. See *SEC Solicits Public Comments on Business and Financial Disclosure Requirements in Regulation S-K* (Apr. 15, 2016), https://www.sec.gov/news/pressrelease/2016-70.html. Accretion leads to fear of information overload. *E.g.*, Troy Paredes, *Blinded by the Light: Information Overload and its Consequences for Securities Regulation*, 81 WASH. U. L. Q. 717 (2003).

[218] A.C. Pritchard & Karen Nelson, *Carrot or Stick? The Shift from Voluntary to Mandatory Disclosure of Risk Factors*, 13 J. EMPIRICAL LEGAL STUD. 266 (2016).

innovation[219]—nothing in the required disclosure gives investors anything close to an inside view of the company's future. This is particularly important in assessing the efficacy of the Securities Act, especially if we fear that some IPOs are timed to exploit investor attention before it shifts elsewhere.

Disclosure has no fundamental value unless it is timely, credible, and accurate. To this end, the Securities Act uses a combination of four overlapping strategies.[220] First, using its considerable discretion over whether to accelerate the effective date of a registration and thus enable sales to take place lawfully under Section 5, the SEC has the ability to demand changes and additions to the disclosure in the registration statement filed by the issuer. This can improve clarity and comparability, and probably has the effect of making management and deal participants sense that they are being watched closely, with healthy behavioral consequences. And, of course, a serious or persistent violation of either the rules or the norm of truth-telling can provoke an enforcement action. This oversight function is limited in two respects, however: SEC review is only to the disclosures, not the merits of the offering, and the SEC does not normally investigate the accuracy of what is disclosed, just inclusion and presentation.[221]

Second, in an effort to make disclosure effective, Section 5 of the Securities Act limits the extent to which (and if so how) offers can be made prior to the effective date, and prohibits sales until then.[222] The content of these "gun jumping" rules has evolved over the decades, with major liberalization in 1954 (by statute) and 2005 (by rule-making).[223] Liberalization notwithstanding, the rules are still complicated, with potentially significant adverse consequences for

---

[219] *See* Edmund Kitch, *The Theory and Practice of Securities Disclosure*, 61 BROOK. L. REV. 763 (1995).

[220] For a thorough overview, see CHARLES JOHNSON JR, JOSEPH MCLAUGHLIN & ERIC HAUETER, CORPORATE FINANCE AND THE SECURITIES LAWS (5th ed. 2016).

[221] The staff does review publicly available information in the media and on the internet for purposes of assessing accuracy and completeness.

[222] More precisely, the rules vary based on whether the solicitation efforts occur before the filing of the registration statement, during the waiting period prior to effectiveness, or in the post-effective period. Under the JOBS Act, issuers may "test the waters" prior to deciding whether to commence their IPO by reaching out to certain institutional investors.

[223] *See* Donald C. Langevoort & Robert B. Thompson, *IPOs and the Slow Death of Section 5*, 102 KY. L.J. 891 (2013-14).

slip-ups.[224] For all the complications, in turn, the offering restrictions today mainly assure the availability of the preliminary prospectus at the time of any pre-effective offers so that both those soliciting and those being solicited have access to the most current version of mandated disclosures,[225] and to make other widely used written soliciting materials (free writing prospectuses) available to the SEC staff at the time of their first use. There is still a "quiet period," but not as much as there used to be.

Third, the most visible and notorious mechanism for promoting disclosure accuracy in the Securities Act is a powerful civil liability provision, Section 11, which allows any purchaser of securities issued pursuant to an effective registration statement a rescissionary measure of damages if there was any material misstatement or actionable omission in the registration statement as of the effective date, whether or not the purchaser relied on those disclosures.[226] Liability is strict for the issuer, while others associated with the offering bear liability unless they establish a due diligence defense.[227] Such damages could be catastrophic, and so the threat is assumed to induce a higher level of care in the preparation of the mandatory disclosures. A separate litigation supplement is provided by Section 12(a), which in subsection (1) creates strict rescissionary liability for illegal offers or sales and in subsection (2) creates negligence-based liability as against those who sell securities in a public offering by means of any

---

[224] Illegal offers under Section 5 can trigger a form of strict liability in a suit brought by a purchaser. But most enforcement of the gun-jumping rules is by the SEC staff, invoking its acceleration authority.

[225] The SEC insists that draft prospectus filed with the SEC, even though not final, be widely available during the waiting period when investors are being solicited. The free writing now permitted for such solicitations must ordinarily be linked to the preliminary prospectus then available. The final prospectus and registration statement do not become available until after most or all the selling has taken place, so that the purchaser only receives notice of their availability.

[226] The measure of damages excludes stock price drops unrelated to the misstatements or omissions, but the burden of proof is on the defendants to prove that exclusion.

[227] *See* William Sjostrom, *The Due Diligence Defense Under Section 11 of the Securities Act of 1933*, 44 BRANDEIS L.J. 549 (2006). There is an enumerated list of potential defendants besides the issuer—directors of the issuer, signatories of the registration statement, underwriters and experts who attest to some portion of the registration statement. The list is exclusive, so that those not included (e.g., lawyers, notwithstanding their central role in drafting the registration statement) have no Section 11 exposure.

written or oral communication (e.g., a preliminary prospectus or free writing) that contains a material misstatement or actionable omission. Section 12(a) thus increases the pressure on offering participants to be careful in what they say and do throughout the registration process.

Fourth and finally, the Securities Act causes, and sometimes requires, the involvement of attorneys, investment bankers, auditors and other external experts for there to be a successful IPO. These professionals have reputational incentives to avoid association with a dishonest capital-raising transaction, which itself may be a partial solution to the lemons problem.[228] The Act increases the incentive by making underwriters, accountants and certain other professionals liable under Section 11, subject to proof of due diligence, and potentially under Section 12(a)(2) as well.[229] Investment bankers are also subject to extensive regulation and disciplinary authority by the SEC and FINRA based on their broker-dealer status, creating additional responsibilities and oversight as to sales practices and the pricing and conduct of the public offering.

1.2 Marketplace Changes and the Opportunities for Reform

For all the many statutory and rule-based reforms and revisions to the Securities Act over the last eighty-five years, its foundation remains unchanged. That raises obvious questions about the relative balance of costs and benefits, particularly as we observe a steady drop off in the number of IPOs generally and the near-disappearance of smaller IPOs.[230] The four regulatory strategies described above are very costly to issuers, in terms of legal fees, accounting fees and underwriting spreads, delays and the resulting distraction and uncertainty prior to effectiveness, and (arguably) the extent of underpricing that occurs.[231]

---

[228] On the nature and limits of gatekeeper strategies, see generally JOHN C. COFFEE, JR., GATEKEEPERS: THE ROLE OF THE PROFESSIONS AND CORPORATE GOVERNANCE 55-70 (2006).

[229] Section 12(a)(2) is limited to suits by buyers against sellers, though not necessarily with a privity requirement. A seller includes a person or firm that solicits the purchase with some pecuniary motivation for so doing.

[230] Paul Rose & Steven Davidoff Solomon, *Where Have All the IPOs Gone? The Hard Life of the Small IPO*, 6 HARV. BUS. L. REV. 83 (2016); *see also* Gao et al., *supra* note 210.

[231] Large underwritings today are mainly "firm commitment" fixed price offerings, whereby the underwriters purchase the securities from the issuer and resell them to investors. There remain some "best efforts" underwritings wherein the underwriters do not purchase the securities for resale but rather simply assist

The latter refers to the well-studied economic phenomenon that deals are priced by underwriters below the maximum that the market would be willing to pay, so that there is a predictable near-term market price increase as soon as trading begins. Arguably, the issuer leaves money on the table. The connection between underpricing and regulation is unclear, more fully addressed in the companion economics chapter than this one. One hypothesis—highly debated and not at all resolved—is that a tacit conspiracy exists among investment bankers, lawyers and others to extract rents from the public offering process.[232] To the extent that the fundamentals of Securities Act regulation impede competition and innovation in the methods of offering securities to the public (e.g., by the de facto establishment of fixed price syndicated distributions),[233] reassessing the Act's assumptions may be long overdue.[234] Yet at the same time, there are many observers beside those with skin in the game who find considerable value in the prevailing law and surrounding investment banking practices.[235]

The common practice for IPOs is book-building, whereby underwriters and issuer management spend a great deal of time and effort talking privately with large investors who might be inclined to buy, in what is a two-way

---

the issuer in the sales process, compensated by commissions. The latter are for smaller, riskier public offerings.

[232] Some would include the issuer's own management in the conspiracy. For legal commentary on the risk of collusion, *see, e.g.*, Christine Hurt, *Moral Hazard and the Initial Public Offering*, 21 CARDOZO L. REV. 711 (2005); Jeremy McClane, *The Agency Costs of Teamwork*, 101 CORNELL L. REV. 1229 (2016) (collusive role of lawyers and law firms in IPOs). On the economics at work here see Xiaoding Liu & Jay Ritter, *Local Underwriter Oligopolies and IPO Underpricing*, 102 J. FIN. ECON. 579 (2011). There are many explanations for underpricing, discussed more fully in Kathleen Hanley's chapter. These include, but are not limited to, fear of Section 11 liability by offering participants. *See* Janet Cooper Alexander, *The Lawsuit Avoidance Theory of Why Initial Public Offerings Are Underpriced*, 41 UCLA L. REV. 17 (1993).

[233] *See* Mahoney, *supra* note 207, at 71-76.

[234] This has led many commentators to call for a move away from firm commitment underwritings to auctions and related mechanisms better suited to a high tech investment marketplace. *See* Christine Hurt, *Pricing Disintermediation: Crowdfunding and Online Auction IPOs*, 2015 U. ILL. L. REV. 217 (2015).

[235] *See* Alan D. Morrison & William Wilhelm Jr., *Opacity, Complexity and Self-Regulation in Investment Banking*, GEO. WASH. L. REV. ARGUENDO (2015), http://www.gwlr.org/wp-content/uploads/2015/04/83-Geo.-Wash.-L.-Rev.-Arguendo-1.pdf

conversation. The sellers reveal more about the offering than the legally-mandated documents contain (i.e., forward-looking information); in return, potential buyers reveal their assessments and willingness to buy at different price levels. The collective knowledge learned in these private contacts allows the lead underwriter to price the deal with greater confidence. In other words, a benign explanation for underpricing is that allotments at that lower-than-market price are the quid pro quo for the sharing of otherwise private information.[236]

To the extent that this form of book-building is the norm, we might reasonably ask what useful role SEC supervision and the offering restrictions play at all. Book-building resembles a private placement given the institution-only makeup of the potential buyers consulted. Even if there are others given allotments (e.g., "friends and family" arrangements), the fixed-price nature of the public offering means that the price for everyone has to be set at a level that attracts the smart money. Perhaps, then, there is an opportunity to lower the intensity and costliness of that regulation. (That opportunity is bolstered by the much richer, real-time informational environment in which all economic activity takes place in a wired society,[237] which clearly extends to those private companies with enough promise to qualify for a public offering.)

On a closer look, however, there are two sets of questions still to be answered. One comes from the issuer's perspective: as noted above, can we be confident enough that the underpricing isn't at least partially an agency cost problem? The tech boom scandals at the turn of the last century offered evidence of various anticompetitive and potentially manipulative arrangements whereby underwriters gain at the issuer's expense. Securities Act regulation does little today to deter rent-seeking and weigh in on the side of the issuer. Maybe it should.[238]

Much closer to the traditional concerns of securities regulation are the interests of purchasers in the aftermarket, who buy at prices higher than the

---

[236] *See* Langevoort & Thompson, *supra* note 223, at 909-13 (reviewing arguments in favor of book-building).

[237] *See, e.g.*, Joseph Grundfest, *Regulation FD in the Age of Facebook and Twitter: Should the SEC Sue Netflix?* (working paper, 2013), https://papers.ssrn.com/sol3/papers.cfm?abstract_id=2209525.

[238] *See supra* note 232. On underwriters' compensation as an example of rent-seeking, see William K. Sjostrom, *The Untold Story of Underwriting Compensation Regulation*, 44 U.C. DAVIS L. REV. 605 (2010); on the anticompetitive effects, see Gao et al., *supra* note 210. The anticompetitive potential is exacerbated by the Supreme Court's ruling that securities regulation implicitly displaces antitrust and other lawsuits that might frustrate the SEC's control over securities distribution practices. Credit Suisse Securities LLC v. Billings, 551 U.S. 264 (2007).

official offering price. In the face of a price "pop" after effectiveness, those allotted shares in the initial round will be tempted to flip them quickly to capture a near-guaranteed profit. Because too much short-term reselling would put downward pressure on the market price, there are various restrictions and penalties imposed.[239] But how strong the disincentive is, for whom, and for how long, presumably varies.

Plainly, aftermarket demand can be exuberant, some of which may be deliberately stimulated by underwriter sales practices and issuer publicity, both of which in turn are traditional regulatory worries. The retail investors who may drive some of this demand are not privy to the private book-building discussions that give institutional investors better information, insight and perspective—Reg FD (which otherwise limits the selective disclosure of material non-public information) explicitly exempts such discussions from the norm, and the backwards looking disclosure may be of little help in estimating the future. The loosening of the quiet period in 2005, though conceptually sensible, invites the more aggressive use of channels for publicity that can hype the aftermarket but are difficult to police for candor, even with filing requirements in Rule 433 when free writing is used.[240] This is difficult terrain, because the pressures may not be entirely—or even mainly—from offering participants. The financial media and social media may generate hype well beyond what issuers or underwriters do or say. Whatever its sources, this richer informational environment is neither necessarily unbiased nor one that bespeaks caution.

1.3 The JOBS Act "On-Ramp" Reforms as a Case Study

The JOBS Act of 2012 and the FAST Act extension that followed in 2015 provide a useful case study of deregulation to stimulate economic growth and job creation. So far as registered public offerings are concerned, the main reform was an "on-ramp" for issuers that qualify as emerging growth companies, a category that covers most registrants and ceases to apply only after reaching

---

[239] The SEC's Regulation M sets forth detailed anti-manipulation rules for the conduct of public offerings, which in fact allow substantial stabilization activity to occur. FINRA conduct rules and the antifraud provisions of the securities laws also address efforts by underwriters to control or influence the aftermarket price.

[240] *See* Langevoort & Thompson, *supra* note 223, at 911-12. There are First Amendment limits here, of course. *See* Susan Heyman, *The Quiet Period in a Noisy World: Rethinking Securities Regulation and Corporate Free Speech*, 74 OHIO ST. L.J. 189 (2013); *see also* Grundfest, *supra* note 237.

very high levels of annual revenues ($1 billion) or market capitalization ($700 million).[241]

Most reforms here are far from radical. EGCs may submit their registration statements confidentially with the SEC in order to get initial feedback on disclosure quality outside the gaze of investors and the media, though road shows with potential investors cannot start until fifteen days after the filing becomes public.[242] There is a list of "lightened" disclosure requirements, including only two (rather than three) years of audited financials, less disclosure of executive compensation, and a pass on Sarbanes-Oxley's internal controls auditor attestation regimen. Fear that these relaxations alone allow EGCs to hide sensitive material information from investors would seem to be overblown, however. What remains subject to line-item disclosure is considerable, and the rule that there must be further disclosure of *any* fact necessary to make what is said not misleading (Rule 408) makes nondisclosure of any uncomfortable information from the issuer's past or present legally very risky even in a shortened prospectus. Whether the on-ramp degrades the IPO informational environment—and if so why and by how much—is an open empirical question, discussed more fully in Kathleen Hanley's paper in this volume.

Of all the legal changes in building the on-ramp, perhaps the most interesting is a relaxation on certain rules—many deriving from the sell-side analyst scandals from more than a decade ago—so as to bring "conflicted" analysts (i.e., those working for investment banks who participate in the IPO) back into the informational mix. Though by no means a complete scrapping of the idea of analyst independence, the legal reform here goes to the heart of Section 5's sales practice restrictions: analyst research expressing any information, opinions or recommendations is explicitly excluded from the key words "offer" and "prospectus," which means that the anti-hyping rules no longer apply, nor does the main civil liability provision to protect buyers from false hyping in sales and marketing of the offering outside the registration statement (Section 12(a)(2)).

The motivation for such a change was the fear that smaller companies simply do not get sufficient analyst coverage to sustain investor interest once the issuer goes public, and that given other prophylactic rules and economic incentives promoting candor and objectivity, conflicted research is still better

---

[241] *See* Langevoort & Thompson, *supra* note 211, at 371-74. There is also cut-off based on aggregate non-convertible debt offerings over a three year period ($1 billion). These dispensations extend to on-going disclosure requirements after the public offering, for a period of five years unless the size test is met.

[242] The JOBS Act pegged this at 21 days, which was shortened in the FAST Act.

than no research.[243] But the way the liberalization is drafted seems to go a step or two beyond what was necessary based on that alone, to a re-enlistment of analysts in the process of enticing investors to bid up the aftermarket price.[244] Empirical research on this trade-off, which is only now beginning to appear, will be helpful to shed light not only on the role of sell-side analysts as such, but the bigger question of who wins and who loses in the long run in "hot" or aggressively marketed IPOs.

1.4 Civil Liability Reforms

If disclosure for an IPO is to be as effective as the drafters of the Securities Act hoped, it must be credible; otherwise, investors should rationally lower their bids with the risk that sound capital-raising unravels. Civil liability is the most prominent mechanism to counter this, via the two main overlapping causes of action noted earlier that are available to purchasers of the securities when there is a material misstatement or omission of some fact necessary to make statements made not misleading, Sections 11 and 12(a)(2).

Strict liability for issuers under Section 11 has long been controversial, even as applied to IPOs. As Merritt Fox has shown, there is a strong theoretical case for strict liability as a means to counter adverse selection.[245] A material misstatement or omission as of the effective date results in a distorted transfer of wealth to the issuer and its incumbent owners regardless of who knew what about the matter. Introducing a more demanding state of mind requirement (whether due diligence or intentionality) would bring about factual complications as to what could have been known and how, which takes up judicial resources and creates investor uncertainty.

How well this promise of credibility holds up in practice is open to question, of course. Section 11 cases against issuers are still challenging, even without either a state of mind or a reliance requirement. What is material, and

---

[243] *See* Benjamin J. Catalano, *The Promise of Unfavorable Research: Ramifications of Regulations Separating Research and Investment Banking for IPO Issuers and Investors*, 72 BUS. LAW. 31 (2016-17); *see also* Jill E. Fisch, *Does Analyst Independence Sell Investors Short?*, 55 UCLA L. REV. 39 (2007). In addition, letting analysts play a larger role in the offering may temper the sales enthusiasm of the underwriters.

[244] A well-publicized FINRA enforcement proceeding in December 2014 involving analysts coveting a role in the Toys R Us IPO certainly raised doubts about the efficacy of analyst independence reforms. *See* LANGEVOORT, *supra* note 205, at 122. For a criticism of the enforcement action, see Catalano, *supra* note 243.

[245] Fox, *supra* note 203, at 704-07.

what is a misstatement or actionable omission, are muddled mixed questions of law and fact often not easily resolved, especially against the background of a limited duty to disclose the forward-looking information that investors covet.[246] Quantifying the loss in dollar terms is not easy either, with the issuer allowed to try to separate out the recoverable loss related to the misstatement from other unrelated reasons why the stock price eventually dropped below the offering price. The result is both uncertainty and considerable litigation cost, which lessens the value of the regulatory promise. From the issuer's perspective, this introduces both risk and out-of-pocket cost, which in turn reduces the attractiveness of the IPO vis-à-vis other alternatives.[247] Where the right balance lies—and how much of a role these particular risks and costs play in the larger IPO context—surely invite further study.

Section 11 also employs a gatekeeper strategy, imposing on offering participants beyond the issuer's management team the same liability risk, albeit with a due diligence defense that varies depending on the role and status of the particular participant. Due diligence is two-sided: an affirmative duty to investigate, and a duty to respond reasonably to what is uncovered as the investigation unfolds. As a result, outside directors, underwriters and experts (most notably, auditors) face fearsome liability exposure. They and their insurers also offer a set of deep pockets in the event the issuer is insolvent.

Here again, the mix of costs and benefits is debatable, although there is considerable support in the legal literature for underwriter liability along these lines (and perhaps even stricter liability) given the crucial role underwriters play in the offering process.[248] To be sure, there are substitute incentives for due care and candor for offering participants, including via reputation and the policing of broker-dealer conduct by the SEC and FINRA. But there are major doubts about reputational incentives alone, or whether the resources and will are there for adequate public enforcement.

---

[246] An example here would be disclosure relating to the threat of government litigation, recently addressed in the Securities Act context—with a great deal of uncertainty as to precisely what is expected of issuers—by the Supreme Court. *See* Hillary A. Sale & Donald C. Langevoort, *"We Believe:" Omnicare, Legal Risk Disclosure and Corporate Governance*, 66 DUKE L.J. 763 (2016).

[247] *See* Michael Dooley, *The Effects of Civil Liability on Investment Banking and the New Issues Market*, 58 VA. L. REV. 776 (1972).

[248] *See* COFFEE, *supra* note 228, at 352-54; Fox, *supra* note 203, at 710-15; Frank Partnoy, *Barbarians at the Gatekeepers? A Proposal for a Modified Strict Liability Regime*, 79 WASH. U. L.Q. 491 (2001).

1.5 Summary: Studying the IPO Regulatory Ecology

In many ways (putting aside the increasingly rare small or self-underwritten registered offering[249]), IPOs are effectively private placements made at a fixed price to highly sophisticated institutional buyers, followed by immediate resales into a public trading market. Arguably, the first part of that process by itself—the book-building—gets too much regulatory burden, and could be left much more to private ordering. The harder question is whether the aftermarket has sufficient integrity in light of the apparent incentives to hype, which depends on a better empirical understanding of who wins, who loses, when and why. With that, it becomes possible to then look at the considerable regulatory costs associated with the public offering process and consider which contribute efficiently to investor protection and which might not.

The IPO also squarely poses the question of to what end regulation exists in the modern era of obsession with innovation, growth and job creation. The IPO is a salient "rite of passage" that has been taken by many of the world's most successful companies, which generates the hypothesis that more IPOs would bring more growth.[250] Yet the typical IPO comes later and later in the chronology of the start-up; earlier stage financing comes via exempt offerings of various sorts, as we shall see. So the IPO is commonly viewed as an exit mechanism, by which promoters and funders cash out some or all of their early-stage investments. True, the pay-off is a reward, which presumably incentivizes the risk-taking that occurs earlier in the chronology, but an unanswered question is how essential this particular kind of reward is in light of substitutes (enhanced private equity funding, trade sales) that might offer comparable incentives.[251] A useful first step in any new Special Study would be a far better mapping of the diverse welfare consequences of liberalized access to capital, whatever the stage of entrepreneurship.[252]

---

[249] *See* Rose & Solomon, *supra* note 230.

[250] *See* Shai Bernstein, *Does Going Public Affect Innovation?*, 70 J. FIN. 1365 (2015). To be sure, there are many innovative public companies, though even these often enough out-source the work of innovation to joint venture partners and other affiliates.

[251] On the place of the IPO as an exit mechanism in light of alternatives, see Gao et al., *supra* note 210.

[252] It should be noted that there is no necessary connection between IPOs and net job creation; some IPOs, no doubt, involve companies that substitute technology for human labor and may "creatively" destroy higher-employing marketplace incumbents.

2 Seasoned Equity and Other Public Offerings

2.1 Equity Offerings

The original Special Study largely assumed the need for intense regulation of the IPO, addressing it largely as part of its look at dealer-dominated over-the-counter methods of distribution. But it was fair to ask whether seasoned issuers should necessarily face the same discipline. After all, companies that have made an IPO thereby become registrants under the Securities Exchange Act, and hence subject to on-going disclosure obligations; many of them trade in relatively transparent and now largely institutional markets, the informational efficiency of which increases as the impact of the selling pressure dissipates. As noted, that insight set in motion decades of effort to lessen the severity of the Securities Act strictures on companies at various levels of trading interest and market capitalization. The key initial step came with the regulatory innovations of integrated disclosure (simplified Form S-3) and shelf registration in the 1980s, the latter inviting larger issuers to have a skeletal registration statement go effective with sales occurring pursuant to later-supplied disclosure at the time of take down. Substantial enhancements to integrated disclosure and shelf registration, including creation of well-known seasoned issuer (WKSI) status, came with the 2005 offering reforms, and there was a notable extension of the availability of Form S-3 to smaller issuers a few years later.

The 1980s reforms were informational, and rested on the fairly minimalist insight that information about the issuer that was already available in a 10-K or other Exchange Act filing did not need to be repeated in the registration statement. It could be incorporated by reference, both backwards and forward.[253] Motivated investors purchasing stock of large issuers could handle this easily enough, all the more so as information technology made filings so accessible; any who are motivationally impaired could free ride and probably would not be reading the documents carefully in any event. By contrast, the 2005 reforms mainly addressed sales practices. Especially for seasoned issuers, the ability to communicate with investors—whether in writing or orally—was made easier by

---

[253] Market efficiency was invoked as a justification for integrated disclosure, but need not be assumed in order to make sense of it. *See* Donald C. Langevoort, *Theories, Assumptions and Securities Regulation, Market Efficiency Revisited*, 140 U. PA. L. REV. 851 (1992). Subsequently, there has been a substantial widening of the availability of incorporation by reference, most recently in the FAST Act for forward incorporation by smaller issuers, so that it cannot any longer be said that market efficiency is the theory behind this kind of deregulation.

a series of new safe harbors.[254] This lessened the chilling effect of what heretofore were serious restraints, and any conditions that remained were not hard to navigate once the dense thicket of rules was reasonably well understood. There was also a lessening of the burdens and delays of SEC review for WKSIs via automatic effectiveness for shelf registrations.

As a result of all this, we are much closer to Milton Cohen's ideal of "company registration"—a setting in which seasoned issuers operating within the discipline of the Exchange Act could make public offerings subject to a relatively light set of restrictions on selling practices and without intensive SEC supervision.[255] While there no doubt could be more simplification, what remains in dispute here mainly has to do with liability risks: nothing in the 1980s era or 2005 reforms made significant changes in the Section 11 exposure faced by issuers or underwriters. If anything, Section 12(a)(2) liability was deliberately enhanced as applied to free writing and the preliminary prospectus that is widely distributed during the waiting period.[256]

There are two related controversies here, one of which is whether the threat of issuer strict liability makes sense for seasoned issuers, given the many substitute mechanisms that exist to promote transparency and candor. The other is whether underwriters, independent directors and experts (again, mainly the auditors) should continue to be held to the full level of due diligence expected in an IPO.[257] The 2005 reforms lessened the risk for directors and auditors via a more favorable setting of the effective date of the registration statement when

---

[254] Safe harbors were created for publicity occurring sufficiently before the filing of the registration statement, factual communications and—most importantly, perhaps—free writing prospectuses both before and after effectiveness. *See* Steve Thel, *Free Writing*, 33 J. CORP. L. 941 (2008).

[255] *See* REPORT OF THE ADVISORY COMMITTEE ON CAPITAL FORMATION AND REGULATORY PROCESSES (1996); John C. Coffee, Jr., *Re-engineering Corporate Disclosure: The Coming Debate Over Company Registration*, 52 WASH. & LEE L. REV. 1143 (1995).

[256] Most notably, by new Rule 159A, treating issuers as sellers even when not in privity with the purchaser in questions. Some courts have doubted the viability of this interpretive rule. For a discussion of this and other factors that may limit the effectiveness of Section 12(a)(2) litigation, see Langevoort & Thompson, *supra* note 223, at 916-18.

[257] *See* Merritt B. Fox, *Civil Liability and Mandatory Disclosure*, 109 COLUM. L. REV. 237 (2009). Jack Coffee, Larry Sonsini and Ed Greene issued a separate statement as part of the 1996 Advisory Committee Report, *supra* note 255, raising concerns about its failure to address liability in a satisfactory fashion.

they are sued under Section 11; by contrast, underwriters get the more stringent time of sale date. The impact here for both issuers and underwriters arises mainly in shelf offerings, where takedown and sales occur in an abbreviated time frame with little opportunity for "in the moment" due diligence, thereby forcing them to assume a greater liability risk.[258] The *WorldCom* case highlighted this exposure and led to multi-billion dollar settlements by the underwriters.[259]

The case for a lessening of the liability risk for shelf registrations and other seasoned equity offerings largely turns on how confident one is that other accountability mechanisms in already public companies work well enough to justify such a reduction.[260] Any new Special Study agenda should include Securities Act liability issues as part of a broader inquiry into adequacy of regulation when the issuer is transacting in its own securities.[261] We return to the adequacy of the Exchange Act disclosure apparatus and proposals for improvement in Part 5.

2.2 Debt and Securitization

It is probably a fair point that financial regulation as a discipline failed to address in a timely fashion the issues surrounding the dramatic leveraging of the American economy—corporate, commercial and consumer—that began in earnest in the 1980s, enabled by technological change and marketplace innovation. Major changes occurred in the debt markets, both long term and (especially) short: high-yield bonds, commercial paper, medium-term notes, repos, etc. Meanwhile, shifting economic incentives of various sorts[262] pushed

---

[258] This was recognized early on, with a debate quickly emerging about the efficacy of this. *Compare* Merritt Fox, *Shelf Registration, Integrated Disclosure, and Underwriter Due Diligence: An Economic Analysis*, 70 VA. L. REV. 1005 (1984), *with* Barbara A. Banoff, *Regulatory Subsidies, Efficient Markets and Shelf Registration, An Analysis of Rule 415*, 70 VA. L. REV. 135 (1984). As a practical matter, effective due diligence in the face of a quick takedown has to be of a "continuous" sort.

[259] *In re* WorldCom Inc. Sec. Litig., 346 F. Supp. 2d 628 (S.D.N.Y 2004).

[260] *See, e.g.,* Donald C. Langevoort, *Deconstructing Section 11: Public Offering Liability in a Continuous Disclosure Environment*, 63 LAW & CONTEMP. PROBS. 45 (2000).

[261] Some would suggest that issuer *repurchases* be given more regulatory attention as having comparable conflicts of interest. *See* Jesse Fried, *Insider Trading via the Corporation*, 164 U. PA. L. REV. 801 (2014).

[262] These included corporate governance pressures by institutional investors, the explosion of hostile corporate takeovers and leveraged-buyouts, and equity-based executive compensation.

companies to take advantage of this innovation and leverage all the more, taking on more risk, especially in the financial sector. A significant portion of innovation in debt financing occurred via securitization: the packaging of loans, mortgages and receivables, with sales of interests therein to a largely institutional marketplace. The route to the global financial crisis is by now an oft-told and increasingly well-understood regulatory story, enabled by derivative instruments of many sorts.[263]

Only some of these debt and securitization transactions were registered public offerings, and so we are jumping ahead a bit here.[264] But any new Special Study surely must pay attention to the debt markets, as individual investments and, through correlations among debt instruments throughout the real economy, systemic risk. Here, two subjects are important candidates for study. Some of the relative regulatory indifference to debt offerings was on the assumption that credit ratings were an adequate substitute for individual investor due diligence and the disclosure necessary for such diligence. The incentives to and quality of credit ratings became an issue at the turn of the last century, and became an obsession in the financial crisis and its regulatory aftermath as credit rating agencies profitably expanded the scope of the kinds of financial instruments they were willing (anxious) to rate. In turn, the Dodd-Frank Act addressed the issue through an incoherent set of reforms—mainly a mix of lessened reliance on ratings via regulatory mandate and enhanced oversight and accountability (plus recent high-dollar settlements with the major credit rating agencies). A large literature on credit rating reform in both law and economics in the last decade is largely doubtful that a stable, efficient and sustainable regulatory solution has yet been found.[265] Arguably, for all its imperfections, the existing system of credit

---

[263] *See, e.g.*, DAVID SKEEL, THE NEW FINANCIAL DEAL: UNDERSTANDING THE DODD-FRANK ACT AND ITS UNINTENDED CONSEQUENCES (2011); ERIK GERDING, LAW, BUBBLES AND FINANCIAL REGULATION (2013); CLAIRE HILL & RICHARD PAINTER, BETTER BANKERS, BETTER BANKS (2015).

[264] On the fuzzy line between securities and non-securities in the debt markets that is one part of this overlooked story, see Elizabeth de Fontenay, *Do the Securities Laws Matter? The Rise of the Leveraged Loan Market*, 39 J. CORP. L. 725 (2014).

[265] *See, e.g.*, Robert Rhee, *On Duopoly and Compensation Games in the Credit Rating Industry*, 108 NW. U. L. REV. (2013); Aline Darbellay & Frank Partnoy, *Credit Rating Agencies and Regulatory Reform*, in RESEARCH HANDBOOK ON THE ECONOMICS OF CORPORATE LAW (Hill and McDonnell eds., 2012); Yair Listokin & Benjamin Taibleson, *If You Mis-rate then You Lose: Improving Credit Rating Accuracy through Incentive Compensation*, 27 YALE J. REG. 91 (2010).

ratings works well enough for *common* forms of debt that there was something of an overreaction here.[266]

Securitization has a similar story-line. Again, most securitization transactions were privately offered, but registered offerings—now the subject of Reg AB, upgraded as a result of Dodd-Frank—are not trivial. A number of commentators have suggested that in this context, orthodox disclosure strategies reach the end of usefulness: many financial products are "too complex to depict," as Henry Hu writes.[267] Legal academics have urged two possible directions. On one hand, perhaps there should be mandatory simplification, with government pre-approval for complex add-ons.[268] This is surely costly, and whether a bureaucracy can do this job well under all economic (and political) conditions is disputable. An alternative, which Hu and others espouse, is greater reliance on open source access to the complex, granular mix of portfolio data and to some extent, the issuer's code as well. This would be a massive project, albeit already begun on a much smaller scale as one rulemaking reform within Dodd-Frank.[269] Proponents claim that this open access approach might be useful beyond securitization, extending to any issuer whose balance sheet (and off-balance sheet) assets and liabilities is largely a bundle of hard-to-value financial instruments, e.g., banking institutions. Here, of course, we are edging out of the domain of private corporate finance toward the very different safety-stability norms of prudential regulation.[270]

---

[266] During his commentary on this chapter at the Initiating Conference of the New Special Study, Bill Williams rightly noted that given the many debt financing alternatives issuers have (*see also* De Fontenay, *supra* note 264), overregulation of publicly offered debt has the potential to distort these choices in inefficient ways.

[267] Henry T.C. Hu, *Too Complex to Depict? Innovation, "Pure Information," and the SEC Disclosure Paradigm*, 90 TEX. L. REV. 1601 (2012); Henry T.C. Hu, *Disclosure, Universes and Modes of Information: Banks, Innovation and Divergent Regulatory Quests*, 31 YALE J. REG. 565 (2014) (hereinafter Hu, *Disclosure*).

[268] *See, e.g.*, Eric A. Posner & E. Glen Weyl, *An FDA for Financial Innovation: Applying the Insurable Interest Doctrine to Twenty-First-Century Financial Markets*, 107 NW. U. L. REV. 1307 (2015).

[269] *Asset-Backed Securities Disclosure and Registration*, Securities & Exchange Commission, Release No. 33-9638 (Sept. 4, 2014).

[270] *See* Hu, *Disclosure*, *supra* note 267.

3 Exempt Capital Raising

We started with registered public offerings because that is how the Securities Act is structured: offerings of securities using the facilities of interstate commerce must be registered unless an exemption is available. But that is backwards from a functional perspective: nearly all issuers who engage in real economic activity raise their initial rounds of capital in the private marketplace and only later (if ever) grow to the stage where an IPO is feasible.[271] This statutory presumption is probably unfortunate, though historically understandable given capital-raising practices in the 1930s. Today, private financing dominates the IPO for smaller and start-up issuers,[272] such that the IPO is a graduation exercise for those who wish to go public and a reward for successful product or service innovation, not the antecedent. The JOBS Act (and subsequent, continuing reform efforts) recognizes the importance of this private space. Although the on-ramp for emerging growth company IPOs is important, the political headline was a series of liberalizations for exempt financing.[273]

In this, we confront what is probably the most conceptually interesting subject in securities law, crucial to any new Special Study: is it possible—indeed desirable—that a large segment of economically important firms in the American economy stay private, perhaps indefinitely, yet with easy access to large amounts of capital? If so, what would the consequences be for investors, the public markets, and society generally? And what ring fence, precisely, can or should separate the private from the public?

---

[271] On the many legal preconditions to successful entrepreneurship, see D. Gordon Smith & Darian Ibrahim, *Law and Entrepreneurial Opportunities*, 98 CORNELL L. REV. 1533 (2013).

[272] *See* Scott Bauguess, Rachita Gullapalli & Vladimir Ivanov, *Capital Raising in the U.S.: An Analysis of the Market for Unregistered Securities Offerings*, 2009-2014, SEC White Paper, (2015), https://www.sec.gov/dera/staff-papers/white-papers/30oct15_white_unregistered_offering.html.

[273] For a balanced assessment, see James D. Cox, *Who Can't Raise Capital?: The Scylla and Charybdis of Capital Formation*, 102 KY. L.J. 1 (2013-14). Though outside the scope of this high level overview, certain other hybrid transactions—e.g., confidentially marketed public offerings, PIPE offerings, reverse mergers—straddle the public-private boundary and add to its blurry character. *See* Robert B. Thompson & Donald C. Langevoort, *Redrawing the Public-Private Boundaries in Entrepreneurial Capital Raising*, 98 CORNELL L. REV. 1573, 1588-1604 (2013).

3.1 Conventional Start-Up Financing

The earliest stages of entrepreneurial capital-raising tend to be informal—friends, family and the promoters' own credit cards—and poorly situated within the framework of the Securities Act because of the statutory fixation on the public offering. The statutory exemptions address such early stage financing indirectly. There is an exemption for truly intrastate offerings (and an exclusion from Section 5's registration requirement for those not using the facilities of interstate commerce), which may offer cover to these first steps. There is also an exemption for non-public offerings, which early stage offerings may (or may not) turn out to be, for reasons we are about to see. And ever since the late 1930s there have been rule-based exemptions, never very generous at least until very recently.

The intrastate offering exemption (Section 3(a)(11) and Rules 147 and 147A) has never been central from a policy-standpoint, though it received a boost recently from the SEC.[274] While it has constitutional origins from a time of doubt about Congress' Commerce Clause power, this exemption only makes conceptual sense today as a delegation to state securities administrators to handle transactions wholly or mainly within their jurisdiction. There is a larger issue worthy of study about how much value state blue sky laws add via registration of securities (as opposed to empowering local law enforcers), especially because many carry the legacy of the "merit regulation" that federal securities law disavowed in 1933.[275] That lively debate carries over to a number of other exemptions, and has the attention of the SEC and Congress.

More central to the regulatory story is Section 4(a)(2), for non-public offerings. Congress' failure to define non-public was a striking omission, leaving to the SEC and the courts to work out the borderline between private and public offerings. Famously, useful guidance was long in coming, undermined by the Supreme Court's question-begging suggestion that an offering is private only when the offerees do not need the disclosure and other protections of a registered offering, i.e., can "fend for themselves."[276] Beyond the classic private

---

[274] *Exemptions to Facilitate Intrastate and Regional Securities Offerings*, Securities & Exchange Commission Release No. 33-10238 (Oct. 26, 2016).

[275] *See* Rutheford B. Campbell, Jr., *The Role of Blue Sky Laws after NSMIA and the JOBS Act*, 66 DUKE L.J. 605 (2016); Cox, *supra* note 273.

[276] SEC v. Ralston Purina Co., 346 U.S. 119 (1953). On the subsequent uncertainties, see JAMES D. COX ET AL., SECURITIES REGULATION: CASES AND MATERIALS 254-64 (8th ed. 2016). The SEC rulemaking arguably calls for a new understanding of 4(a)(2) in light of the more modern principles expressed therein. *See* ABA Committee on the Federal Regulation of Securities, *Law of*

placement involving a sophisticated financial institution, or offerings to senior company insiders, navigating this territory was risky for any start-up or small business.

After fits and starts, greater clarity was eventually achieved in the early 1980s, with the SEC's adoption of Regulation D. It offered three safe harbors for making a federally unregistered offering (the middle one of which was recently repealed). One, Rule 504, was for small offerings of no more than what is now $5 million ($1 million for most of its duration), with only minimal additional conditions so long as the offering is registered in at least one state. As with the intrastate exemption, with which it has long been closely coordinated, this is more a form of regulatory delegation to state blue sky regulation than an expression of substantive policy of how very small offerings should be handled.

Most important—then and now—was the Rule 506 safe harbor,[277] which has no cap on how much can be raised. Rule 506 was designed around the relatively new construct of the "accredited investor," defined to include a variety of institutional investors plus natural persons (and members of their household) earning more than $200,000 a year ($300,000 with spouse) or having net assets in excess of $1 million—figures that have not changed in the thirty-five years since adoption.[278] Rule 506 imposes a disclosure requirement if—but only if—there are non-accredited purchasers; it also requires that there be no more than thirty-five non-accredited investors and that these purchasers be "sophisticated" or represented by someone who is. Because of the added burdens of including non-accredited investors, common practice became to make offerings to accredited investors only. The main limitation with respect to Rule 506 was a prohibition on general solicitations that effectively forbade widespread marketing or advertising in search of investors, instead demanding some form of pre-existing relationship that made the use of broker-dealers as placement agents a de facto requirement for any significant outreach. While Reg D was a sea-change in the private offering process, small business and start-up advocates were frustrated by many

---

Private Placements (Non-Public Offerings) Not Entitled to Benefits of Safe Harbors—A Report, 66 BUS. LAW. 85 (2010). *Ralston Purina* involved sales of securities to employees of the issuer, which later emerged as a distinct topic of interest. For non-public companies issuing stock and options for compensatory purposes as opposed to capital-raising, there is now an explicit exemption in Rule 701, with numerous conditions.

[277] On the relative use of Rule 506 vis-à-vis other exemptions, see Bauguess et al., *supra* note 272.

[278] There was a change as a result of the Dodd-Frank Act to exclude the value of the investor's principal residence from the calculation of net worth.

of the lingering conditions for the exemption, particularly the general solicitation ban.[279]

The JOBS Act put all of this in play. Within the Reg D framework, the most notable statutory change was the repeal of the ban on general solicitation for offerings sold only to accredited investors, subject to an arguably heightened obligation to reasonably verify purchaser status (new Rule 506(c)). Issuers remain free to use the older form of the exemption if they wish (now Rule 506(b)),[280] and early data indicated an inclination to stick to those more familiar practices.[281]

To most legal commentators, the ban on general solicitation never made all that much sense in the first place assuming the ability of accredited investors to fend for themselves, such that its repeal seemed logical, if not welcomed.[282] To be sure, there was substantial debate about whether that assumption is correct in the first place, and whether the now long-unchanged metric for accredited investor status was still sound.[283] More aggressive marketing under Rule 506(c) would certainly test those questions.

The issues here are worthy of close study.[284] Disclosure in a private offering made solely to accredited investors is a matter of private bargaining,

---

[279] *See* Stuart Cohn & George Yadley, *Capital Offense: The SEC's Continuing Failure to Address Small Business Financing Concerns*, 4 NYU J. L. & Bus. 1 (2007). The SEC did occasionally make issuer-friendly reforms, including the introduction of a "substantial compliance" defense for inadvertent violations in 1989.

[280] Rule 506(b) insists on the issuer's reasonable belief as to accredited investor status.

[281] Verification in 506(c) offerings is controversial because many potential investors may not be comfortable providing the information (tax returns, bank account statements, etc.) necessary to make such a determination to issuers and their marketing agents. The SEC offered guidance on how verification can occur within the framework of the rule, including a non-exclusive safe harbor for certain practices.

[282] The ban appeared to many to be rent seeking by placement agents and other brokers, imposing extra costs on issuers. *See* William Sjostrom, *Direct Private Placements*, 102 Ky. L.J. 1 (2013-14).

[283] *See* Jennifer Johnson, *Fleecing Grandma: A Regulatory Ponzi Scheme*, 16 Lewis & Clark L. Rev. 993 (2012).

[284] Private equity investments are indirectly available to lower-income public investors via any number of publicly offered or traded intermediaries that, in turn, manage investments or themselves make private investments in portfolio companies. *See* Steven Davidoff Solomon, *Black Market Capital*, 2008 Colum. Bus. L. Rev. 172 (2008). For a useful survey, see Sun Eun (Summer) Kim,

leading to two concerns. One, of course, is whether accredited offerees are likely to bargain well.[285] The other is that even if savvy bargaining occurs at the time of sale, it may not produce a socially optimal level of publicly available information to support an efficient allocation of start-up capital.

The dominance of Rule 506 offerings in the private investment space means that the primary offering space remains quite opaque.[286] Although Form D allows for the collection of certain basic information about exempt offerings by private issuers, it does not provide—nor are there reliable alternative sources for—data that allows us to assess confidently how much risk and return there is for investors.[287] Perhaps, as some suggest, private investments are a source of value in an appropriately diversified portfolio, such that greater access to this marketplace is warranted.[288] Or perhaps it truly is dangerous. We simply don't know enough. Glimpses of the market for alternative-style investments (including some common ones sold via face-to-face marketing) indicate substantial segmentation among investor-types, which is what may also be happening in Rule 506 offerings. Plenty of savvy investors, institutional and individual, do fend for themselves and demand credibility. They seek out reputable brokers and placement agents, who cater to that high-end niche, and get high-quality disclosure from those better issuers anxious to distinguish

---

Typology of Public-Private Equity, FLA. ST. L. REV. (forthcoming). This complication is an important part of the public-private topology, but does not directly affect the question of the public versus private status of the portfolio company.

[285] There is a large body of research today—in the laboratory and in the field—demonstrating flaws and biases in investor decision-making, including among the well-to-do. *See* LANGEVOORT, *supra* note 205, at 15-17, 114-35. It is possible, of course, that wealth-based tests are not predictions that such people will bargain well, but a normative assessment that they should be expected to, and presumably can bear the risk of not doing so.

[286] *See* Jennifer Johnson, *Private Placements: A Regulatory Black Hole*, 35 DEL. J. CORP. L. 151 (2010).

[287] There is sufficient transparency of the over-the-counter secondary trading markets for small issuers to draw an inference that the risk to investors is considerable with respect to thinly-traded stocks. *See* Joshua White, *Outcomes of Investing in OTC Stocks*, SEC White Paper (2016), https://www.sec.gov/dera/staff-papers/white-papers/16dec16_white_outcomes-of-investing-in-otc-stocks.html.

[288] *See* Usha Rodrigues, *Securities Law's Dirty Little Secret*, 81 FORD. L. REV. 3389 (2013) (advocating greater, if indirect, retail investor participation in private offerings). On indirect participation, see *supra* note 284.

themselves from the lemons. As such, their returns are appropriate on a risk-adjusted basis. But because investors vary in their savvy and endowments, the market segments in such a way that, further toward the bottom, salesmanship dominates and returns are poorer.[289] Again, we lack the information to test this thoroughly or estimate the extent of segmentation and the degree of risk in the lower reaches.

The regulatory eclipse here is not total, of course—there is some policing by the SEC, FINRA and/or the states, especially when brokers and investment advisers are involved.[290] But without more transparency, we can't assess the adequacy of that presence, and few think it anywhere near enough. An effort by FINRA (which requires the filing of sales and marketing materials) to create more accountability and shed more light on broker sales practices in private offerings was scaled back under political pressure, but did increase oversight to an extent.[291] Nor should we dwell entirely on the investor risk side of the argument. Start-up financing is crucial to innovation, and it is not unreasonable to trade off some investor protection at the margins for ease of capital formation for small businesses that simply cannot afford heavy costs. But at present, this is policy-making largely in the dark.

These issues are compelling enough, but their significance is compounded going forward. Once again, keep in mind that Rule 506(c) invites a substantial step-up in the tactics that sellers can use to go bottom fishing among the well-off, including older investors.[292] If the test for accredited investor remains static, gradually the substantial majority of active investors will be accredited. Combine that with the never-ceasing institutionalization of the markets and the potential for private offerings to become an acceptable source

---

[289] Matthew D. Cain, Stephen B. McKeon, Steven Davidoff Solomon, *Intermediation in Private Equity: The Role of Placement Agents* (working paper, 2016), https://papers.ssrn.com/sol3/papers.cfm?abstract_id=2586273. Similar segmentation (and rewards to sales pressure) has been observed with respect to PIPE offerings, reverse mergers and broker-sold mutual funds.

[290] Rule 506 offerings (and Reg A offerings, discussed infra) are not available to those "statutorily disqualified" by some bad act or status. On the issues raised by statutory disqualifications and their frequent waiver by the SEC, see Urska Velikonja, *Waiving Disqualification: When Do Securities Violators Receive a Reprieve?*, 103 CAL. L. REV. 1081 (2015).

[291] *See* Jennifer Johnson, *Private Placements: Will FINRA Sink the Sea Change?*, 82 U. CINN. L. REV. 465 (2013).

[292] See Johnson, *supra* note 283 (examining a multi-billion dollar MedCap fraud aimed heavily at accredited but vulnerable investors).

of equity and debt capital for issuers of all sizes and stages of growth. Because this issue requires assumptions about resales and liquidity—the subjects of the next two sections—we will defer further discussion of what Merritt Fox terms the "brave experiment"[293] of the new Rule 506 environment to then. But for now, we can say at the very least that a far better mapping of the private offering terrain is a pressing task for a new Special Study.

3.2 Crowdfunding

In the mainstream media, the headline of the JOBS Act was crowdfunding, a new exemption—which went into effect in mid-2016—to make certain smaller capital raising transactions (capped at $1 million) widely available to investors of all levels of wealth and sophistication on web portals, via an exemption from both federal and state registration requirements. The theory was that mandatory disclosure could be sacrificed to the "wisdom of crowds" to choose early-stage investment projects to fund, with limits on what portion of their wealth or income a given investor could bet on such ventures.[294] In a political compromise, however, the JOBS Act in the end contained additional layers of regulation, including issuer and portal disclosure requirements, marketing restrictions and civil liability. A common assessment is that the compromise made crowdfunding unattractive,[295] regardless of SEC considerable efforts to build a robust regime within those limits. It is too early to tell, although a survey of the earliest crowdfunding offerings shows a fairly sophisticated willingness by portal sponsors to offer templates and other off-the-rack options to make this particular fundraising tool more attractive to issuers and investors.[296] And it may well be that Congress revisits the regulation in the name of easing

---

[293] Fox, *supra* note 203, at 721.

[294] For those with annual income or net worth less than $100,000, the aggregate amount sold to the purchaser in a twelve month period cannot exceed the greater of $2000 or 5% of annual income or net worth. With the removal of the ban on general solicitations under Rule 506(c), it is possible to use crowdfunding techniques directed entirely at accredited investors.

[295] Joan Heminway, *How Congress Killed Investment Crowdfunding: A Tale of Political Pressure, Hasty Decisions and Inexpert Judgment that Begs for a Happy Ending*, 102 KY. L.J. 865 (2013-14).

[296] Exempt or not from the securities laws, crowdfunding also poses challenging corporate law questions, involving voting rights (if any), the ability to sue for breach of fiduciary duty, etc. On solutions proposed by portal sponsors, see Jack Wroldsen, *Crowdfunding Investment Contracts*, 11 VA. L. & BUS. REV. 543 (2017).

burdens; some states have already offered more generous state level crowdfunding plans that take advantage of Securities Act exemptions noted earlier.[297]

There is a considerable legal literature on crowdfunding, starkly split between pro and con.[298] Non-investment crowdsourcing has a mixed record, with some evidence that crowds can be relatively good at funding taste-oriented projects like music and food ventures.[299] How well this is likely to extend to sophisticated technology ventures is less clear, since a promoter cannot afford to reveal much about the project to attract funding because of the risk that the best ideas will be snatched away. However, one positive feature of crowdfunding vis-à-vis private offerings is the level of transparency: projects are publicly visible from inception to after the funding rounds, generating information and accountability that may mitigate some of the risk and educate potential investors tempted to join in the buzz. Regulators can watch. Beyond that, however, the adverse selection problem looms large, and crowdfunding comes to look much like gambling.[300]

3.3 Regulation A

The SEC has long had authority to deregulate smaller offerings even if they were public offerings, and by the time of the first Special Study, it had developed a stepped-down system for very small offerings. Under Regulation A, a small offering by a non-public issuer would be exempt so long as it followed rules much like—but simpler—than those found in registered ones. That is, there would be less intense SEC review, selling restrictions and liability risk. Most

---

[297] *See* Matthew Pei, *Intrastate Crowdfunding*, 2014 COLUM. BUS. L. REV. 854 (2014).

[298] *See, e.g.*, Darian Ibriham, *Equity Crowdfunding: A Market for Lemons?*, 100 MINN. L. REV. 561 (2015); Jason Parsont, *Crowdfunding: The Real and Illusory Exemption*, 4 HARV. BUS. L. REV. 281 (2014); Andrew Schwartz, *Crowdfunding Securities*, 88 NOTRE DAME L. REV. 1457 (2013); Heminway, *supra* note 163; Thompson & Langevoort, *supra* note 273, at 1604-08. On the ideological discord, see LANGEVOORT, *supra* note 205, at 127-31.

[299] It also has an appealing inclusiveness to it, as to geography, gender and racial diversity and other opportunities heretofore blocked to certain entrepreneurs. *See* Andrew Schwartz, *Inclusive Crowdfunding*, 2016 UTAH L. REV. 661, 671-74 (2016).

[300] *See* Fox, *supra* note 203, at 726 (noting the similarities and suggesting that the experience of crowdfunding may be enough reward to overcome low expected returns).

notably, there was no issuer strict liability, as there is in Section 11.[301] Once Reg D was available, especially, Reg A was little-used. The SEC gave it a boost in 1992 by allowing "test-the-waters" solicitations of the sort that were barred in IPOs and most of Reg D, thereby letting issuers get early feedback on whether the offering was feasible. But the cap ($5 million) still made the exemption a doubtful trade-off given all the other regulatory conditions and concurrent state blue sky registration with which to contend.

The JOBS Act makes a considerable change by raising the cap for Reg A offerings to $50 million. The SEC implementing rules went into effect in 2015, creating two alternative offering tiers. Tier 1 offerings are capped at $20 million, and can be made to an unlimited number of investors without any accreditation requirements. State blue sky registration remains. Tier 2 offerings can go to the full $50 million, with blue sky registration preempted. The price of graduation to Tier 2 is that unaccredited investors can purchase the securities only up to a certain portion of their wealth or income,[302] somewhat like the crowdfunding rules. Congress also added an explicit civil liability provision, drawn from Section 12(a)(2)'s negligence-based cause of action.

A fair characterization of the new Reg A regime is "public offering lite" rather than the pass from registration of the sort we see in Rule 506 or even crowdfunding.[303] From a regulatory perspective, presumably, it is now the regulatory route of choice for smaller public offerings. The package of information is smaller, to be sure, but not skeletal, again keeping in mind the obligation of the issuer to volunteer additional material information necessary to make statements made not misleading. From the investor's perspective, the question is whether the combination of diminished information and the loss of issuer strict liability leaves too much to chance. From the issuer's perspective, the question is whether the significant regulatory costs associated with mini-registration makes this a desirable alternative to a less transparent private offering.

---

[301] Section 11 only creates a right of action with respect to false registrations statements that have become effective. Reg A is an exemption from registration, and the relevant filing is an offering statement.

[302] No more than 10% of the greater of annual income or net worth over a twelve-month period.

[303] *See* Thompson & Langevoort, *supra* note 141, at 1608. Not all are impressed, with many arguing that the SEC did not do enough liberalization. *See* Rutheford B. Campbell, Jr., *The SEC's Regulation A+: Small Business Goes under the Bus Again*, 102 KY. L.J. 325 (2013-14). On the other hand, two states sued the SEC for overreaching, especially in granting the blue sky preemption in Tier 2. *See* Lindeen v. SEC, 825 F.3d 646 (D.C. Cir. 2016) (rejecting claim).

4 Resales Under the Securities Act

The drafters of the Securities Act understood that public offerings were commonly conducted by having the issuer sell the securities to underwriters, who in turn sell (at a markup) to the allotted investors, with resales into the aftermarket. Because of the sensitive conduit role they play, underwriters are heavily regulated and face potentially painful liability under Section 11 absent a sufficient showing of due diligence. For registered public offerings, the resale problem is assumed away: the strictures of the Securities Act end, essentially, when the sales pressure of the offering has dissipated.[304] By that time, public company obligations under the Exchange Act have already taken hold, so that the transition is simply from one disclosure-based regime to another.

The definition of underwriter that the drafters created in Section 2(a)(11), however, was put to more use than this, generating some of the most vexing conceptual problems in all Securities Act jurisprudence.[305] With respect to exempt offerings, what if a fully qualified "fend for yourself" purchaser quickly turns around—perhaps by design—and aggressively resells to others who do need protection? It was soon understood that securities issued in private offerings should "come to rest" in the hands of qualified purchasers, with some combination of investment intent and holding period determining if, how and when resales could occur freely. That mandatory lock-up diminished liquidity, creating a costly downside to raising capital via a private offering. In the early 1970s, the SEC adopted Rule 144 to specify the necessary holding period and methods of resale; in subsequent years these holding periods were repeatedly shortened so that today, for private issuers, the lock-up is a simple one year term, with free resales thereafter.[306] There is no guarantee that Exchange Act registration kicks in at that point or ever—that is a matter of the trading venue for the resales and the Section 12(g) metrics for public company status by virtue of size, to which we turn shortly.[307]

---

[304] Issuer and underwriter manipulation concerns during the offering period are addressed comprehensively in Regulation M. *See supra* note 239.

[305] *See* COX ET AL., *supra* note 276, at chap. 6.

[306] Rule 144 also addresses resales by "control persons" (affiliates) of the issuer, which may pose issues comparable to the issuer's own public offering. There are additional "dribble out" requirements here, beyond any holding period arising from a private offering.

[307] To address this, Rule 15c2-11 requires brokers providing liquidity in the over-the-counter market to have a certain quantity of information in their possession. Brokers also have a self-regulatory obligation to "know your security" before making any recommendation.

So far as the Securities Act is concerned, an important question is whether any restriction is necessary if the resale is to those deemed able to fend for themselves. Practitioners and regulators came to an understanding—without explicit textual support in the statute—that such resales could occur (the so-called 4(1½)) exemption, but left the outer limits of that de facto exemption fuzzy. One obvious question was whether any accredited investor should be deemed so qualified. In Rule 144A, the SEC implicitly said no. That safe harbor was designated as a free resale space for large institutional investors (QIBs) only. Why? The reasons were a mix of legal, political and pragmatic.[308] The legal conundrum was that "fending for oneself" was thought to be about both investment sophistication *and* access to information. A second-level purchaser, much less one further down the line, would not necessarily have the ability to extract from the issuer the desired level of current information. That would have to come via either regulation (as, minimally, in 144A) or private contractual covenant, which raises its own set of monitoring and enforcement problems once investor capital is paid-in. If the socially optimal quantity and quality of issuer disclosure are higher than what parties would bargain for privately, the contractual solution is incomplete anyway.

But the question is tantalizing, because to those troubled by the potential for regulatory overreach, the image of large-scale private financing with a high level of resale liquidity but none of the burdens of regulatory "publicness" is something of a nirvana.[309] Getting to that nirvana—or avoiding that terrifying void, depending on one's perspective—is as much a matter of Exchange Act law as Securities Act law, but both pieces are crucial. Thus the importance of the 2015 statutory reform found in the FAST Act, which creates a new Securities Act exemption (4(a)(7)) for resales to accredited investors, so long as there are no special selling efforts that would constitute a general solicitation. This invites the building of accredited-only resale markets that could very easily produce a great deal of liquidity and make private financing of the sort suggested earlier a viable

---

[308] *See* Donald C. Langevoort, *The SEC, Retail Investors and the Institutionalization of the Securities Markets*, 95 VA. L. REV. 1025 (2009); Langevoort & Thompson, *supra* note 211, at 362-65.

[309] Adam Pritchard has advocated abolition of the IPO in favor of requiring emerging issuers to be "seasoned" in the private marketplace before graduating to the public. *See* A.C. Pritchard, *Revisiting "Truth in Securities Revisited": Abolishing IPOs and Harnessing Private Markets for Public Good*, 36 SEATTLE L. REV. 999 (2013). This is somewhat akin to the current policy to reverse mergers, which had been a vibrant backdoor method for issuers (domestic and foreign) to access the public marketplace, particularly Nasdaq. *See* Thompson & Langevoort, *supra* note 273, at 1596-98.

permanent solution for issuers averse to heavy regulation. That is the brave experiment to which Merritt Fox was referring.[310]

5 Secondary Trading and the Securities Exchange Act

As noted at the outset, a legal survey focused on primary capital-raising might be expected to stop at the outer limits of the Securities Act. But it cannot, either conceptually or legally. Conceptually, liquidity affects the cost of capital, and liquidity depends on forward-looking confidence in the integrity of both corporate governance and the secondary trading marketplace. Legally, as we have seen, the Exchange Act plays an important role within the registered public offering, via integration and incorporation by reference in seasoned offerings and the seamless handoff from one statute to the other that usually occurs after a few weeks of post-effective constraints, even in an IPO.

But Exchange Act regulation of public companies is by itself a massive subject that could take us far afield in search of topics for a new Special Study, so that we will have to be even more selective in our attention here. Among other things, this encompasses the content of periodic and continuous reporting via 10-Ks, 10-Qs and 8-Ks, including the optimal frequency of required disclosure, the uneasy line between forward and backward-looking information, scaled-back mandates for smaller issuers and the emergence of social and sustainability-oriented disclosure.[311] It also includes the structural mechanisms and abundance of assigned tasks that have been imposed to generate higher quality disclosure, many of which are products of the Sarbanes-Oxley Act, such as stepped-up

---

[310] Various aspects of this subject have garnered a great deal of attention from legal academics in the last few years, with attention to the law, economics and politics. In addition to articles cited earlier, see Jeff Schwartz, *The Twilight of Equity Liquidity*, 34 CARDOZO L. REV. 531 (2012); Darian Ibrahim, *The New Exit in Venture Capital*, 65 VAND. L. REV. 1 (2012); Elizabeth Pollman, *Information Issues on Wall Street 2.0*, 161 U. PA. L. REV. 179 (2012); Zachary Gubler, *Public Choice Theory and the Private Securities Market*, 91 N.C. L. REV. 745 (2013); Michael Guttentag, *Patching a Hole in the JOBS Act: How and Why to Rewrite the Rules that Require Firms to Make Periodic Disclosures*, 88 IND. L.J. 151 (2013); Usha Rodrigues, *The Once and Future Irrelevancy of Section 12(g)*, 2015 U. ILL. L. REV. 1529 (2015); Elizabeth de Fontenay, *The Deregulation of Private Capital and the Decline of the Public Company*, 68 HASTINGS L.J. 101 (2017).

[311] All this is currently under review. *See supra* note 217; Roberta Karmel, *Disclosure Reform—The SEC Is Riding Off in Two Directions at Once*, 71 BUS. LAW. 781 (2016).

auditor and audit committee regulation, internal controls, executive certifications, whistleblowing and the like.[312]

The threshold legal standard for public company status under the Exchange Act is in three parts.[313] A company that makes a registered public offering under the Securities Act becomes one for that reason alone, guaranteeing the handoff described above.[314] So does a company that is listed on a national securities exchange, whether or not associated with a public offering. By contrast, however, there are many trading venues that are not designated as national securities exchanges. That leaves the third pathway found in Section 12(g), based on issuer size. After the JOBS Act, there is now an awkward standard by which the issuer must register if it has sufficient assets ($10 million) and shareholders of record (2000, no more than 500 of which can be non-accredited investors). As many have stressed, shareholder of record is archaic and dysfunctional as a test, presumably left in place as a political matter precisely because of its plasticity. Currently, 12(g) is not a particularly stable expression of any coherent policy.[315]

---

[312] *See* John Coates IV & Suraj Srinivasan, *SOX after Ten Years: A Multidisciplinary Analysis*, 28 ACCT. HORIZONS 627 (2014). There is much more to that portion of Exchange Act regulation assigned to the Division of Corporation Finance that we are not touching on here, including proxy regulation, large shareholder reporting, tender offers, and statutory insider trading regulation.

[313] The Exchange Act actually uses multiple trigger points for various sorts of regulation. Public company status pursuant to Sections 12(b) and 12(g) predominates, but some regulation depends on listed-company status (directly or through listing standards affected by regulatory mandate). The antifraud provisions apply to all companies, public and private—indeed to all persons. There is also "voluntary filer" status, with a variety of regulatory effects. *See* Robert P. Bartlett III, *Going Private but Staying Public: Reexamining the Effect of Sarbanes-Oxley on Firms' Going-Private Decisions*, 76 U. CHI. L. REV. 7 (2009) (observing incidence of contractual commitments made by private companies to make SEC disclosures).

[314] There are mechanisms for exit from public company status ("going dark") but not necessarily easy to achieve. *See* Edward Rock, *Securities Regulation as a Lobster Trap: A Credible Commitment Theory of Mandatory Disclosure*, 23 CARDOZO L. REV. 675 (2002).

[315] *See* Rodrigues, *supra* note 310; Langevoort & Thompson, *supra* note 211, at 355-61. An SEC staff report offered very little determinate guidance as to when 12(g) applies or not to corporations with more than the requisite number of beneficial owners with shareholder-like stakes. *See Report on Authority to Enforce Exchange Act Rule 12g5-1 and Subsection (b)(3)* (Oct. 15, 2012).

Of all the many questions that could usefully be covered in a new Special Study, four seem especially important:

5.1 Public v. Private

The express lane toward large-scale privatization of corporate finance would be paved by the combination of (1) a continued flourishing and robust primary capital marketplace under Section 4(a)(2) and other exemptions (particularly Rule 506) and (2) a liquid secondary trading market for qualified investors largely free of regulatory burdens on issuers as a result of either the Securities Act or the Exchange Act.[316] Of course, nothing makes this combination inevitable, or even likely. Elsewhere I have written about the political economy of this move and the reticence of the SEC to anything that could threaten the public capital marketplace, the protection of which is the Commission's core mission.[317] But as the JOBS and FAST Acts show, the matter is not entirely within its administrative discretion.[318] Even without regulatory reform, there are signs of growing privatization under the status quo, as sequential private equity arrangements sustain successful start-ups for longer and longer. And there are powerful normative arguments that private equity is the preferable source of capital for "new economy" firms that need the privacy and governance flexibility to be nimble and more consistently innovative.[319]

On the other hand, issuers might hesitate to reject public company status even if the private capital markets offer a sufficiently deep, liquid and deregulated alternative. Perhaps valuable status or branding effects follow from public

---

[316] Trading venues like Second Market and SharesPost emerged to facilitate qualified resales of larger non-public companies like Facebook. *See, e.g.*, Pollman, *supra* note 310. In contrast, OTC Markets Group operates a variety of trading venues encompassing some 10,000 securities (OTCQX, OTCQB and Pink) for resales of the securities of smaller private and public issuers, with varying disclosure obligations. On investor risk in the OTC markets, see *supra* note 287.

[317] *See* Langevoort, *supra* note 308, at 1065-70; for doubts that this is so, see Gubler, *supra* note 310.

[318] Pending legislation in Congress embraces this reform goal.

[319] *See* Zimmerman, *supra* note 210. This is a theme in the "eclipse of the public corporation" genre stimulated many years ago by Peter Drucker and Michael Jensen. *See* Roger L. Martin, *The Public Corporation is Finally in Eclipse*, HARV. BUS. REV. (Apr. 2014), https://hbr.org/2014/04/the-public-corporation-is-finally-in-eclipse.

trading.³²⁰ If public markets continue to become frothy in cycles, there will always be a temptation to exploit noise trader exuberance by going public at an opportune time. We need not predict the future, however, but simply conclude there that this is an immensely promising and important subject for further study along with the better mapping of the private finance terrain suggested earlier. Enough has occurred in this direction to offer data points and invite digging into what has already happened more deeply. Three topics seem particularly crucial.

One is the efficacy of private ordering, which many scholars have advocated as a superior alternative to bureaucratically-imposed disclosure and governance mandates. How well do private capital markets meet informational needs so as to overcome adverse selection when there is a minimalist regulatory infrastructure and only fraud-based liability for enforcement?³²¹ If we gain confidence that there are satisfactory answers, prices in the private secondary markets might be reliable enough to sustain liquidity.³²²

Conversely, even if the level of disclosure is privately negotiated, is there a gap here between what is disclosed and socially optimal disclosure? Many have noted that disclosure benefits a wide variety of economic actors—for example, disclosure about information inside Company X can make both product and capital markets more efficient via the spillover effects on the other companies (private and public) in those same markets. Do mandatory disclosure line-items efficiently address any such gaps? It may be, for example, that robust public disclosures by other firms in a relevant market are essential to the valuation of private equity, such that without a critical mass of public information, both public and private markets might devolve.³²³

---

³²⁰ *See* Victor Fleischer, *Brand New Deal: The Branding Effects of Corporate Deal Structures*, 104 MICH. L. REV. 1581 (2006). Public trading might also be important in using issuer stock as an acquisition currency or for large scale compensation grants.

³²¹ *See* Fox, *supra* note 203. On how institutional investors bargain for credible disclosure, see Howell E. Jackson & Eric Pan, *Regulatory Competition in International Securities Markets: Evidence from Europe, Part II*, 3 VA. L. & BUS. REV. 207 (2008).

³²² For efficient private markets, there must be substantial depth of order flow, and opportunities for short-selling that keep a lid on upward demand pressures. Given the presence of substantial "noise trading" in public markets, the efficiency comparison between public and private is not obvious. As noted earlier, Adam Pritchard has called for greater reliance on accredited-investor only markets as a seasoning mechanism prior to public marketplace trading, thereby effectively abolishing IPOs.

³²³ *See* de Fontenay, *supra* note 310.

This issue of public versus private also helps frame the increasingly heated debate over how tightly coupled SEC disclosure should be to notions of financial materiality, and how much socially-optimal disclosure can veer away from the tasks of investor protection and capital formation.[324] Currently, there are some disclosure items designed (mainly by Congress) to have primarily non-investment consequences, but legitimate ones nonetheless.[325] Of course, there is significant risk that these can be mainly expressive or symbolic, yet very costly. Others, like environmental matters, can readily be material but determining what should be disclosed inevitably invites into the process those whose main ends are social, not just (or for the most part) financial. The work of organizations such as the Sustainability Accounting Standards Board in connecting orthodox materiality to social and sustainability issues is entirely legitimate as an economic matter, notwithstanding the risk of normative bias. There is no clean conceptual separation, and simply declaring that the SEC must be limited to a core mission of investor protection and capital formation is probably futile as a matter of both statutory and administrative law the way the securities statutes are currently written.[326]

So, any new Special Study should consider the costs and benefits of private versus public markets broadly from a social welfare perspective. (This inquiry would presumably include consideration of facilitating new hybrid or quasi-public markets for emerging or smaller issuers, with limited retail access or other structural protections.[327]) Perhaps the outcome would lead to a more sensitive "tiering" of disclosure and governance responsibilities, with the most intensity for those firms with the biggest footprints on the financial markets and

---

[324] *See, e.g.*, Karmel, *supra* note 311. Particularly controversial examples include conflict mineral disclosure and political spending.

[325] A recent study, for example, shows that increased mine safety disclosure for coal and other affected companies reduced accidents. *See* Hans B. Christensen, Eric Floyd, Lisa Yao Liu & Mark Maffett, *The Real Effects of Mandated Information on Social Responsibility in Financial Reports: Evidence from Mine Safety Records* (working paper, 2017), https://papers.ssrn.com/sol3/papers.cfm?abstract_id=2680296.

[326] *See* Yoon Ho (Alex) Lee, *Beyond Agency Core Mission*, 68 ADMIN. L. REV. 551 (2016). On legislative text and history, *see also* Cynthia Williams, *The Securities and Exchange Commission and Social Responsibility*, 112 HARV. L. REV. 1197 (1999).

[327] There is long-standing interest in replicating specialized markets for emerging issuers along the lines of London's Alternative Investment Market (AIM) or Brazil's Novo Mercado.

society generally.[328] To be sure, the idea of a heavily deregulated regulatory regime for all companies that elect to go dark in the new world of private capital is ideologically and normatively seductive. Others consider "publicness" a strong social value.[329] A new Special Study could usefully weigh in on this debate empirically and analytically, rather than in pursuit of some pre-determined resolution.

5.2 Contemporary Corporate Disclosure

A lengthy to-do list could be compiled to better understand the contemporary corporate disclosure environment. There is a strong and plausible impression that many disclosure requirements are outmoded, overly complicated or inefficient, the subject of the SEC's statutorily-mandated Disclosure Effectiveness project.[330] (The same could be said for task overload: too many disclosure and governance-related assignments to directors, auditors and management in the aftermath of Sarbanes-Oxley and Dodd-Frank.) At the same time, new candidates for mandatory disclosure pop up continuously, especially in those related to innovation, sustainability and social responsibility, as just noted. The extraordinary institutionalization of large segments of the financial markets presumably justifies some adjustment to all this in both content and style. Unfortunately, we lack an agreed-upon methodology for confidently assessing the costs and benefits of both disclosure and accountability tools across all markets, whether in terms of investor protection, capital formation or total social welfare. Absent the ability to engage in rigorous regulatory experimentalism, both benefits and costs are too diffuse and dynamic to capture confidently,[331] which quickly shifts the argument to politics and ideology. In practice, there is considerable stubbornness to the precautionary principle[332] and the status quo in the face of all this uncertainty, costly as that may be.

---

[328] *See* Langevoort & Thompson, *supra* note 211, at 379-83; Oonig Dombalagian, *Principles for Publicness*, 67 FLA. L. REV. 649 (2015); Jeff Schwartz, *The Law and Economics of Scaled Equity Market Regulation*, 39 J. CORP. L. 347 (2014).

[329] *See supra* note 211.

[330] *See supra* note 217.

[331] *See, e.g.*, Jeffrey Gordon, *The Empty Call for Benefit-Cost Analysis in Financial Regulation*, 43 J. LEG. STUD. S351 (2014); John C. Coates IV, *Cost-Benefit Analysis of Financial Regulation: Case Studies and Implications*, 114 YALE L.J. (2015).

[332] The precautionary principle is a thumb on the scale in favor of caution in the face of uncertainty. For a criticism, see Troy Paredes, *On the Decision to Regulate Hedge Funds: The SEC's Regulatory, Style and Mission*, 2006 U. ILL. L. REV. 975.

Technological innovation relating to disclosure has both promise and peril. On one hand, technology counters concern about information overload, especially as artificial intelligence and algorithmic trading programs extend beyond anticipating order flow to react almost instantly to corporate news released by formal EDGAR filings or even social media.[333] (XBRL and open source initiatives could enable this all the more.) All this enhances very short-term informational efficiency. Less well understood are the incentive effects on longer-term efficiency—the returns to serious fundamental analysis—as well as the reality and perception of public access to the markets.[334] Maybe the latter is a romantic (or political) illusion in any event, but clearly ties into the future of public markets. As New York's highly-publicized enforcement initiatives show in making fair access to information a building block for "Insider Trading 2.0," there is not yet any coherent assessment of how best to respond to the connections among public access, investment technology and corporate disclosure.[335] This is another place where a new Special Study could help, bridging concerns about corporate finance with market structure issues.

The mechanisms of market efficiency have changed over time, with an increasing recognition that information search is costly and will occur only to the extent that reasonable returns can be expected.[336] Hence, pricing imperfections are persistent, especially with respect to innovative financial products and kinds of information that evolve constantly. Here again, the question of expected returns to fundamental research becomes all the more important and

---

[333] *See* Erik Gerding, *Disclosure 2.0: Can Technology Solve Overload, Complexity and Other Information Failures?*, 90 TULANE L. REV. 1143 (2016).

[334] *See* M. Todd Henderson & Kevin Haeberle, *Information Dissemination Law: The Regulation of How Market Moving Information is Revealed*, 101 CORNELL L. REV. 1373 (2016); Yesha Yadav, *How Algorithmic Trading Undermines Efficiency in Capital Markets*, 68 VAND. L. REV. 1607 (2015).

[335] *See* Chris Brummer, *Disruptive Technology and Securities Regulation*, 81 FORD. L. REV. 977 (2015); LANGEVOORT, *supra* note 205, at 82-84.

[336] Market efficiency has served as justification for deregulation over much of the last decades, perhaps excessively given the persistence of information and transaction costs as markets evolve. *See* Ronald Gilson & Reinier Kraakman, *Market Efficiency after the Financial Crisis: It's Still a Matter of Information Costs*, 100 VA. L. REV. 313 (2013); Robert P. Bartlett III, *Inefficiencies in the Information Thicket: A Case Study of Derivatives Disclosure during the Financial Crisis*, 36 J. CORP. L. 1 (2010).

contestable.[337] The role of the sell-side analyst has changed, with the diminishing returns to public advice-giving and persistent conflicts of interest as other ways are sought to make this activity profitable (another issue connected to debates about insider trading enforcement). Conflicts of interest are problematic well beyond the IPO setting noted earlier, to disputes about insider trading, fair disclosure, broker-dealer recommendations, robo-advisers and many other lively controversies. The information environment for smaller public issuers with little or no analyst coverage (and the means for improving it, as with the recent tick-size experiment) is still only dimly understood.

In the face of all these developments, the old problems of corporate disclosure remain. The right approach to forward-looking disclosure—analyzed by the SEC in multiple reports starting not long after the first Special Study—remains indeterminate,[338] as so many public and private lawsuits still struggle with questions about whether, how and when issuers must reveal developments running the gamut from preliminary government investigations to outright disasters. So, too, with timeliness: what are the virtues and harms associated with leaving most disclosure to quarterly reporting, rather than continuous market alerts? Conversely, what are the adverse effects of immediate disclosures, or of being so insistent on its public release (the costs and benefits of Reg FD[339])?

There are also interesting questions about the real economic effects of mandatory disclosure, beyond informing investors and markets. Notoriously, managers indicate that they will choose different (presumably inferior) projects as to long-term value depending on the accounting and reporting effects—so-called real earnings management.[340] Corporate risk-taking is seemingly affected, too,[341] along with many other behaviors put in the glare of public scrutiny via government-chosen metrics. Some of this is presumably good, but not

---

[337] As is the presence of index investing, purchasing and selling in massive quantities without any analysis at all.

[338] *See supra* note 219.

[339] *See* Jill E. Fisch, *Regulation FD: An Alternative Approach to Addressing Information Asymmetry*, in RESEARCH HANDBOOK ON INSIDER TRADING 112 (Bainbridge ed., 2013).

[340] *See* John Graham, Campbell R. Harvey & Shiva Rajgopal, *The Economic Implications of Financial Reporting*, 40 J. ACCT. & ECON. 3 (2005).

[341] *See* Kate Litvak, *Defensive Management: Does the Sarbanes-Oxley Act Discourage Corporate Risk-taking?*, 2014 U. ILL. L. REV. 1663.

necessarily—hence, the many connections between securities regulation and worries about "short-termism."[342]

5.3 Company Registration Revisited

Whether or not this last cluster of questions is answerable, it seems irresistible for any new Special Study to revisit one of the key issues posed by the first Special Study: how well can the Securities Act and the Exchange Act be knitted together to permit seamless company registration, so that capital-raising transactions by seasoned issuers can take place with the least amount of additional regulatory burden? This was Milton Cohen's campaign, fully vetted in the mid-1990s by an SEC Advisory Committee, with many intermediate steps in between.[343] The 2005 rule-based offering reforms moved in this direction mainly via shelf registration enhancement, especially for WKSIs, but arguably still short of total integration.

The open question is whether there is enough distance between the current system and true integration to make the effort worthwhile, and if so what further steps might be taken. (We might discover the opposite, of course—that reform has gone too far, for some or all levels of issuers.) We covered some possibilities in Part II, particularly ones relating to the impact of Section 11 of the Securities Act on shelf registration and seasoned offerings—clearly the biggest speed bump on the road as currently paved. Alternatively, or in addition to the changes discussed earlier, there could be tweaks on the Exchange Act side beyond the layering of additional tasks. The ill-fated Federal Securities Code drafted under the auspices of the American Law Institute in the 1970s (shepherded by Cohen and Professor Louis Loss) proposed a privately-enforced due diligence liability standard for annual reports, designed to make a careful look into the company's condition and results a yearly exercise. This is costly, however, and depending on periodicity, may miss opportunistically-timed offerings. But proposals like these illustrate the kinds of interventions that might be seriously considered depending on what a closer study of the efficacy of the existing Exchange Act and integrated disclosure system reveals.[344]

---

[342] *See* Mark Roe, *Corporate Short-termism in the Boardroom and the Courtroom*, 68 BUS. LAW. 977 (2013); LANGEVOORT, *supra* note 205, at 105-08.

[343] *See supra* note 255.

[344] For other proposals, see Fox, *supra* note 257 (proposing expert external certification requirement for annual reports, with a "measured" due diligence based liability for the certifier); James D. Cox, *The Fundamentals of an Electronic-based Federal Securities Act*, 75 WASH. U.L.Q. 857 (1997); Cox, *supra* note 213, at

5.4 Enforcement Intensity

The emphasis on civil liability in discussions of disclosure quality under both the Securities Act and the Exchange Act makes clear that such quality is not simply a function of well-articulated disclosure rules but of enforcement intensity, both public and private. Whether the considerable resources devoted to enforcement are well-spent is another source of controversy in need of illumination.[345] We are far from sure how much fraud and financial misreporting by seasoned issuers there is in our financial markets. One often-cited (but unpublished) study estimates roughly that as many as 14.5% of public companies are misleading the market at any given time.[346] If that is anywhere near accurate, there are hard questions about why and what to do about it.

On the public enforcement side, how the SEC enforcement staff picks cases to pursue is opaque.[347] Settlement policy and practices relating to sanction size, enterprise versus individual liability, and whether to impose collateral consequences or insist on admissions of liability, are too. The appropriate degree of criminalization of securities law enforcement is contestable, especially on the highly-contested subject of insider trading. All of these relate to the much bigger question of whether the SEC has the resources and incentives to do its enforcement job well, or whether instead it is impoverished either deliberately or through neglect.[348]

As to corporate disclosure, much of the policing is via private class actions under Rule 10b-5.[349] That rule requires plaintiffs to plead and prove both

---

19-20 (proposals for "redistributing" due diligence obligations for seasoned issuers).

[345] *See* John C. Coffee, Jr., *Law and the Market: The Impact of Enforcement*, 156 U. PA. L. REV. 229 (2007); Howell Jackson & Mark Roe, *Public and Private Enforcement of Securities Laws: Resource Based Evidence*, 93 J. FIN. ECON. 207 (2009); LANGEVOORT, *supra* note 205, at 42-48.

[346] I. J. Alexander Dyck, Adair Morse & Luigi Zingales, *How Pervasive is Corporate Fraud?* (working paper, 2013), https://papers.ssrn.com/sol3/papers.cfm?abstract_id=2222608.

[347] *See* Urska Velikonja, *Reporting Agency Performance: Behind the SEC's Enforcement Statistics*, 101 CORNELL L. REV. 901 (2016).

[348] Though beyond the scope of this chapter, this touches on the long-standing debate about SEC self-funding.

[349] *See, e.g.*, Joseph A. Grundfest, *Damages and Reliance Under Section 10(b) of the Exchange Act*, 67 BUS. LAW. 307 (2014); James D. Cox & Randall Thomas, *Mapping the American Shareholder Litigation Experience; A Survey of Empirical Studies of*

scienter and reliance, thus making Exchange Act civil liability very different from the more potent private remedies found in the Securities Act. This puts a heavier burden of proof on investors, complicates trials and settlement negotiations, and incentivizes ignorance by those whose knowledge would be attributed to the firm. Yet there is immense controversy on whether the litigation threat is nonetheless excessive because of settlement pressures that reward the bringing of claims that would not succeed if tried. As a compensatory matter, moreover, corporate defendants pay judgments and settlements, thus reaching into some shareholders' pockets (or insurance) to shift money to the pockets of others. Whether this "circularity" makes sense—indeed, what its impact on investors even is over time—has been the subject of considerable academic debate, without resolution.[350] Separately, there is a question of how much deterrence these lawsuits provide if, once again, the alleged wrongdoers personally may not suffer the full burden (if any) of their wrongdoing, or if they fail to fully appreciate the legal risks they take.[351]

6 Conclusion

My assignment here was to describe in broad strokes the legal framework for primary and secondary marketplace regulation and identify the knowledge gaps that frustrate rigorous policy-making. Kathleen Hanley's chapter assesses what research in financial economics tells us already and how we might devise an empirical research agenda—a new Special Study—to move both the state of knowledge and policy-making forward, and push back against pure ideology and rent-seeking.

I have suggested quite a few such knowledge gaps as to both the Securities Act and the Exchange Act that make it difficult to decide whether prevailing law is excessive, insufficient or (implausibly) perfectly right, or

---

the U.S. Securities Laws, 6 EUR. CO. & FIN. L. REV. 164 (2009); Merritt B. Fox, *Why Civil Liability for Disclosure Violations When Issuers do not Trade?*, 2009 WISC. L. REV. 297 (2009).

[350] *See, e.g.*, William Bratton & Michael Wachter, *The Political Economy of Fraud on the Market*, 160 U. PA. L. REV. 69 (2011); James Spindler, *We Have a Consensus on Fraud on the Market – And It's Wrong*, 7 HARV. BUS. L. REV. 67 (2017). More generally, see JOHN C. COFFEE, JR., ENTREPRENEURIAL LITIGATION: ITS RISE, FALL, AND FUTURE (2015).

[351] LANGEVOORT, *supra* note 205, at 35-45 (discussing cognitive and cultural biases that distort risk perception). These questions are relevant to public enforcement as well.

precisely how to make it better. One could easily add more. From the regulatory perspective, my priorities would be:

(1) As thorough as possible a mapping of the nature, risks, and rewards to investors and entrepreneurs of the largely unregulated (10b-5 only) private offering marketplace, comparing and contrasting what is observed in terms of behavior and outcomes where sophisticated institutions are the buyers as opposed to retail investors;

(2) A rigorous assessment of trends affecting the long-term balance between private and public markets as sources of corporate financing and liquidity, and the consequences of a strong turn toward the private markets;

(3) An accounting of who wins and who loses in the IPO marketplace, and whether the current system of Securities Act registration addresses the right stress points, including potentially distortive or anticompetitive securities industry practices;

(4) A comparable accounting of the risks to investors in shelf and other seasoned equity offerings, with a view to moving further toward (or away from) more complete company registration, especially as to liability issues;

(5) An examination of the efficacy of periodic and real-time disclosure (e.g., Reg FD and other "prompt" disclosure obligations) in a technology-driven, information rich environment; and

(6) An assessment of enforcement mechanisms and policies under the Exchange Act, both private civil liability and public enforcement actions, and how well they serve goals of compensation and deterrence and reduce the negative consequences of adverse selection.

This is an ambitious agenda, to be sure, and what is on it is politically combustible. But in framing a fruitful Special Study for the 21st century, these truly are things we need to know much better than we currently do, wherever that leads.

Chapter 4
THE ECONOMICS OF TRADING MARKETS

Ryan J. Davies[352] & Erik R. Sirri[353]

1 Introduction

Capital markets are an essential feature of any well-functioning modern economy. These markets link entities with surplus capital to companies and corporations that can put capital to productive use. Markets establish prices that provide important signals for the efficient allocation of capital among corporations and their projects. In the United States, equity markets form an important segment of domestic capital markets. Stock market capitalization of publicly traded companies in the United States is approaching $30 trillion, about one-third greater than the size of domestic bank assets, with average daily trading volume approaching $300 billion. In the United Kingdom, the stock market capitalization is historically only about one-quarter the size of bank assets, with the ratio being roughly the same for Germany and France.

This chapter addresses questions of regulation and design of domestic secondary trading markets. The operation of these markets is subject to comprehensive regulation, primarily by the Securities and Exchange Commission (SEC). Financial Industry Regulatory Authority (FINRA) is the self-regulatory organization (SRO) that oversees broker-dealers, over-the-counter markets, and certain stock exchanges. Many other regulatory organizations also have important roles in trading markets. There are over 40 SROs associated with exchanges and clearing agencies, including specialized SROs such as the Municipal Securities Rulemaking Board (MSRB), which oversees municipal markets. Other regulators that have roles in secondary trading markets include state securities regulators as well as certain federal regulatory bodies such the Federal Reserve Board.

Actual secondary trading markets bear little resemblance to the idealized markets of neoclassical economics. Because trading markets lack complete information, manifest substantial frictions, and exhibit various externalities, it is

---

[352] Associate Professor of Finance and Chair of the Finance Division, Babson College.

[353] Professor of Finance, Babson College. We thank Charles Jones, Carole Comerton-Forde, Steven Gordon, and participants at the New Special Study of the Securities Markets Initiating Conference for helpful comments and suggestions.

generally accepted that regulation is required if they are to effectively perform their basic informational and allocational role. The core framework for the regulation of secondary market trading is embedded in the Securities and Exchange Act of 1934.[354] Crucial amendments to this basic body of law occurred with the passage of the Securities Act Amendments of 1975, which inserted Section 11A into the 1934 Act.[355] Without providing any specific roadmap or requirements, Congress charged the SEC in Section 11A with creating a national market system. The basic goals for this system were: economically efficient execution of transactions; fair competition among broker-dealers, among exchanges, and between exchanges and other markets; ready availability of quotation and transaction information to broker-dealers and investors; the ability of broker-dealers to execute orders in the best market; and an opportunity, consistent with the other goals, for investors to execute orders without the participation of a dealer.

An economically significant change to the core mission of the SEC occurred in 1996 with the signing of the National Securities Markets Improvement Act (NSMIA).[356] Prior to this, the SEC had most often expressed its mission as primarily one of investor protection, with a secondary goal of promoting fair and orderly markets. With the adoption of NSMIA, Congress expressly charge the SEC, when engaged in rulemaking, to also consider "in addition to the protection of investors, whether the action will promote efficiency, competition, and capital formation." The change is important because of the inclusion of capital formation in the SEC's mission. Up to this point, the SEC resembled a policeman, ever vigilant for malfeasance, but paying little attention to either the direct cost or the opportunity cost associated with deterring that malfeasance. By mandating the consideration of capital formation and efficiency, the SEC had to balance its traditional concerns of investor protection with the full economic cost of implementing those policies.

The core principles listed above, as well as the body of rulemaking promulgated over the last 80 years, allows us to extract a series of economic precepts that arise when the SEC, FINRA, and other securities regulators adopt rules governing the participants and institutions of our exchange and over-the-counter markets. While by no means exhaustive, the discussion below serves to provide an economic structure to understand the types of problems faced by securities regulators in matters related to secondary market trading.

---

[354] Securities Exchange Act, Pub. L. No. 73–291, 48 Stat. 881 (1934).

[355] Securities Exchange Act, Pub. L. No. 94-29, 89 Stat. 97 (1975).

[356] National Securities Markets Improvement Act, Pub. L. No. 104-290, 110 Stat. 3416 (1996).

(1) Mandate the production and dissemination of accurate information. Secondary markets manifest significant asymmetric information issues. The value of a firm's securities depends on its future economic prospects, which change constantly as the firm engages in new ventures and realizes the outcomes of previous investments. Investors, who run the gamut from individuals to sophisticated and large financial institutions, have differential access to such information as well as a differential ability to process it. While little can be done about the difference in processing capability, through innovations like EDGAR, the SEC seeks to create a level playing field for core information about public firms and the securities they issue. Even with these and other efforts, asymmetric information remains an important aspect of trading in secondary markets. Not all information that is asymmetric is fundamental, in the sense that it affects firm's cash flows directly. In the case of trading, as we shall see below, some of the most important information concerns orders and trades that either have been, or are about to be, public disseminated through facilities of the national market system. Preferential access to that information, even by fractions of a second, can convey a material advantage to traders. Through its regulatory powers, the SEC seeks, to the extent possible and consistent with its rules, to remove informational disadvantages. Last-sale reporting and the public dissemination of real-time quotes are archetypal examples of this effort.

(2) Alleviate agency problems. Financial markets, and especially trading markets, are fraught with issues of delegation. Investors who wish to deploy their savings in equity and bond markets often retain financial advisors to assist them in making their investment choices. Having made those choices, these same investors cannot on their own find an end counterparty with whom to buy or sell securities. They must retain the services of an intermediary who, in turn, must go to a market center to complete the trade. And even once the trade is completed, investors do not retain ownership and control of their own securities positions. Instead, they generally entrust them to their broker-dealer who, in turn, maintains their position at a clearing corporation or central depositary. Each of the above examples gives rise to a potential principal-agent problem, where the principal has retained the agent to perform some critical function associated with secondary market trading. Left to their own devices and freed from any regulatory constraints, such agents may follow courses of actions inconsistent with the wishes and desires of their principal. Specific examples might include a broker who fails to buy a security at the cheapest price available in the market, or a financial advisor who recommends not the best security for an investor, but one that provides the advisor with the largest sales commission. Even

intermediaries are subject to agency problems, such as when an introducing broker leaves its customers' funds on deposit with a clearing broker. Clearing brokers who hold securities on behalf of introducing brokers have an incentive to use those securities for their own business purposes, for example through rehypothecation. SEC rules seek to mitigate these agency problems where possible. When this cannot be done, regulators often fall back on tools such as disclosure and informed consent.

(3) Constrain market power. To be sure, securities markets are competitive. There are approximately 4,000 registered broker-dealer firms, over 20 registered exchanges (equities and options), and over 50 alternative trading systems (ATSs) at which an instrument may be either bought or sold. While for the most part the SEC tries to stay away from price regulation, it does try to foster environments in which market forces can work to ensure competitive outcomes. For example, throughout the 1970s and 80s, the New York Stock Exchange (NYSE) dominated trade in listed equity securities. Though there were six or eight regional exchanges around the country that had the ability to trade NYSE-listed equities on their local markets, their individual market shares were tiny relative to that of the NYSE. The SEC consciously adopted regulatory policies that allowed these exchanges to remain in existence. By doing so, the SEC created a contestable market for exchange services, and the regional exchanges were responsible for some important innovations in trading over the ensuing decades. Examples of how the SEC accomplished this include the practice of preferencing, whereby individual orders could be preferentially routed to regional exchanges.[357] Once there, the orders traded in an environment where they generally did not interact with the bids and offers from off-exchange participants. Another example is the framework used to regulate broker-dealers. The SEC does not adopt a prudential attitude toward broker-dealers. It fosters an environment where entry and exit costs are low, and individual customers can get quality service from even the smallest firms. In part, it does this because of a regulatory regime that is little concerned with the financial solvency of the broker-dealer, but instead about the safety of customer property. This regime ensures that should a broker-dealer fail, customer property is appropriately segregated and all cash and securities can be returned to customers in short order.

---

[357] For a description of the practice of preferencing, see Mark A. Peterson & Erik R. Sirri, *Order Preferencing and Market Quality on U.S. Equity Exchanges*, 16 REV. FIN. STUD. 385 (2003).

(4) Solve coordination problems. Secondary trading requires the coordination of a host of actors to move securities from order initiation, to trade execution, to confirmation, to clearing, and through settlement. When coordination is absent or insufficient, chaos can result. An oft cited example is the paperwork crisis of the mid-1970s when the exchanges had to shut their doors every Wednesday afternoon simply to get caught up on the processing of paper tickets associated with trades executed over the previous week.[358] The SEC accomplished the required coordination through a myriad of mechanisms. For example, in the United States, market centers are able to jointly synchronize their own clocks to a common time. While the precision of the synchronization may face increasing demands over time, one need only look at attempts in Europe with the Markets in Financial Instruments Directive (MiFID) to see the costs associated with the lack of such a simple coordination tool. Another more recent example is the requirement for private linkages among equity market centers.[359] These private linkages operate at much higher throughput than the channels provided by traditional gateways through which core market data proceed. Though still a work in process, the SEC has improved the speed with which orders and information can move around the various market centers.

(5) Ensure integrity of systems and infrastructure. The SEC has a developed program in place to ensure the integrity and robust operation of key market intermediaries such as exchanges, data providers, and clearing agencies. Regulation SCI, which was promulgated in December 2014, is designed to reduce the occurrence of systems issues; improve resiliency when system problems do occur; and enhance oversight and enforcement of securities market technology infrastructure.[360] Other examples include the examination and inspection process carried out by the staff of the Office of Compliance Inspections and Examinations at the SEC and by the field office staff of FINRA. Among other goals, these examinations seek to improve compliance with securities laws and monitor risk-taking by registered entities.

---

[358] FINRA, WHEN PAPER PARALYZED WALL STREET: REMEMBERING THE 1960S PAPERWORK CRISIS (2015), https://www.finra.org/investors/when-paper-paralyzed-wall-street-remembering-1960s-paperwork-crisis.

[359] *See* Regulation NMS Adopting Release, 70 Fed. Reg. No. 124, at 37497 (June 29, 2005).

[360] *See* Regulation Systems Compliance and Integrity, 79 Fed. Reg. No. 72251 (Dec. 5, 2015).

The examples above are merely illustrative, and represent an attempt to classify various activities of regulators in a traditional economic framework. It should be clear, however, that the SEC is a consummately legal body. It is an organization primarily staffed with lawyers, who in turn are charged with administering and enforcing our nation's securities laws. In the words of Christopher Cox, a recent chairman of the SEC, "First and foremost, the SEC is a law enforcement agency...."[361]

The remainder of the paper is organized as follows. Section 2 provides a brief description of the key participants in market centers involved in secondary trading markets. Section 3 forms the core portion of our paper. It discusses the aspects of secondary trading in equity markets that, in our opinion, are most worthy of additional regulatory attention. These topics include a discussion of market fragmentation, transparency, algorithmic and high-frequency trading, duties and obligations of brokers, system robustness, and secondary market data. The fourth section discusses secondary trading in fixed income markets. The final section briefly concludes.

2 Participants and Market Centers

There are a diverse group of participants in U.S. equity markets. Over the last 50 years, equity ownership has been concentrating in the hands of institutional investors as they intermediate the market for the savings of retail investors. This intermediation comes in the form of retirement plans, such as 401(k) and 403(b) plans, defined benefit plans (though these have been on the decline), and pooled investment vehicles, such as mutual funds and bank-administered collective investment vehicles. Table 1 shows that the share of equity held by households (including non-profit organizations) has fallen from 43.1% in 2001 to 37.3% in 2015.

In terms of broker-dealer intermediaries, FINRA reports that it has 3,816 registered securities firms in February 2017, which is down from 5,005 a decade earlier in 2007.[362] There are likely a host of reasons for this decline, but certainly one of the reasons is the preference of financial advisors to conduct their retail-facing business using the organizational form of a registered investment advisor rather than an introducing broker. There are a number of benefits to this

---

[361] U.S. SENATE, COMMITTEE ON BANKING, HOUSING, AND URBAN AFFAIRS, TURMOIL IN U.S. CREDIT MARKETS: RECENT ACTIONS REGARDING GOVERNMENT SPONSORED ENTITIES, INVESTMENT BANKS AND OTHER FINANCIAL INSTITUTIONS (Sept. 23, 2008) (Testimony of Christopher Cox, Chairman, U.S. Securities and Exchange Commission).

[362] *See* https://www.finra.org/newsroom/statistics.

Table 1: U.S. Holdings of Equities ($ Billions, Market Value)

Year	Value	%	Value	%	Total Value
2001	$6,704.4	43.1	$8,840.3	56.9	$15,544.7
2002	$5,072.6	41.0	$7,314.6	59.0	$12,387.2
2003	$6,662.9	40.2	$9,924.5	59.8	$16,587.4
2004	$7,352.8	38.9	$11,527.5	61.1	$18,880.3
2005	$8,014.0	38.9	$12,586.7	61.1	$20,600.6
2006	$9,931.2	41.2	$14,162.0	58.8	$24,093.2
2007	$9,726.1	38.4	$15,602.9	61.6	$25,329.0
2008	$5,406.9	35.5	$9,830.5	64.5	$15,237.4
2009	$7,034.3	35.5	$12,767.5	64.5	$19,801.8
2010	$8,450.7	36.4	$14,791.7	63.6	$23,242.4
2011	$8,069.9	36.0	$14,376.3	64.0	$22,446.2
2012	$9,401.4	36.4	$16,452.4	63.6	$25,853.8
2013	$12,545.3	37.4	$21,001.3	62.6	$33,546.6
2014	$13,883.1	37.8	$22,887.9	62.2	$36,771.0
2015	$13,310.9	37.3	$22,376.3	62.7	$35,687.2

Source: SIFMA, FACT BOOK (2016), https://www.sifma.org/wp-content/uploads/2017/05/sifma-fact-book-2016.pdf.

Table 2: Average Daily Equity Trading Volumes (Matched Volume for 5 days ended March 14, 2017)

Panel A: Exchange Volume (shares)

Exchange	Tape A	Tape B	Tape C	Total Market	% Market
IEX	82,120,148	20,238,082	39,812,731	142,170,961	2.10%
CHX	12,428,436	12,428,436	4,698,218	29,012,382	0.43%
NYSE (N)	828,539,051			828,539,051	12.23%
NYSE Arca (P)	227,228,365	290,102,387	130,203,073	647,533,825	9.56%
NYSE MKT (A)		13,064,685		13,064,685	0.19%
EDGX (K)	187,149,315	97,019,632	153,584,295	437,753,242	6.46%
BATS BZX (Z)	211,968,076	89,546,514	106,248,730	407,763,320	6.02%
BATS BYX (Y)	161,487,158	67,687,777	81,979,228	311,154,164	4.59%
EDGA (J)	81,714,899	39,020,576	38,513,757	159,249,232	2.35%
Nasdaq (Q)	363,754,710	120,616,142	449,915,452	934,286,303	13.79%
Nasdaq BX	100,673,993	31,452,682	55,690,142	187,816,818	2.77%
Nasdaq PSX	21,771,133	21,101,586	19,606,067	62,478,786	0.92%

Panel B: Trade Reporting Facility (TRF) Volume (shares)

Facility	Tape A	Tape B	Tape C	Total Market	% Market
Nasdaq TRF	1,148,611,147	526,907,736	718,242,565	2,393,761,448	35.33%
NYSE TRF	104,533,901	46,432,750	68,965,564	219,932,215	3.25%

Source: BATS Global Markets, http://www.bats.com/us/equities/market_share/

Table 3: Weekly trading volume of 31 ATS reporting to FINRA (for week ended February 20, 2017)

ATS Name	Total share volume	Total number of trades
QUA AQUA	260,800	43
BCDX BARCLAYS DIRECTEX	24,000	1
BIDS BIDS TRADING	93,169,106	117,574
BLKX BLOCKCROSS	11,436,732	1,065
CBLC CITIBLOC	3,740,544	191
CROS CROSSFINDER	285,513,409	1,602,153
CXCX CITI CROSS	22,061,154	90,803
DBAX SUPERX	201,627,980	1,097,385
DLTA DEALERWEB	26,421,232	81
EBXL LEVEL ATS	115,950,700	595,467
IATS IBKR ATS	22,874,024	76,419
ICBX INSTINET CONTINUOUS BLOCK CROSSING SYSTEM	81,773,936	368,331
ITGP POSIT	75,242,400	273,823
JPMX JPM-X	156,304,206	718,785
KCGM KCG MATCHIT	85,096,689	482,795
LATS BARCLAYS ATS ("LX")	107,455,347	552,078
LMNX LUMINEX TRADING & ANALYTICS LLC	5,269,324	152
LQNA LIQUIDNET H2O	12,315,900	1,196
LQNT LIQUIDNET ATS	22,557,100	567
MLIX INSTINCT X	95,361,619	461,797
MSPL MS POOL (ATS-4)	152,590,410	622,063
MSRP MS RETAIL POOL (ATS-6)	4,810,500	24,949
MSTX MS TRAJECTORY CROSS (ATS-1)	50,942,000	283,909
NYFX MILLENNIUM	29,374,620	90,706
PDQX CODA MARKETS, INC.	14,955,671	75,334
SGMA SIGMA X	85,087,955	439,786
UBSA UBS ATS	458,740,223	2,721,500
USTK USTOCKTRADE SECURITIES, INC.	2,905	66
WDNX XE	2,119,846	1,701
XIST INSTINET CROSSING	13,725,139	2,849
XSTM CROSSSTREAM	52,606,856	149,673

Source: FINRA Alternative Trading System Transparency Data.

organizational form, including the ability to easily charge account wrap fees and the absence of an oversight by an SRO. Smaller advisors need not even register with the SEC if their assets under management are low enough.

Equity trading can occur on any of 12 registered public exchanges, over 30 ATSs,[363] or at off-exchange broker-dealers, including internalizing broker-dealers.[364] Trade conducted on a public exchange is reported to the consolidated tape, and includes an identifier for the market on which the trade occurred. No such identifier is required for trade on ATSs or at off-exchange broker-dealers. SEC and FINRA does require the reporting of these ATS and off-exchange trades, however, and both the NYSE and NASDAQ have created Trade Reporting Facilities (TRFs) for this express purpose. Table 2 provides a snapshot of equity trading volumes across exchanges and the two TRFs for a typical week in 2017. The table does not strictly distinguish between dark and lit order flow, as trade conducted on lit exchanges has the potential to make use of dark orders types. Deutsche Bank reports that the share of high frequency trading appears to have recently plateaued, accounting for approximately 40% of market volume in 2014.[365]

Table 3 provides a weekly snapshot (week of February 20, 2017) of the trading volumes across the ATSs reporting to FINRA. The Tabb Group reports that in Q2-2016, equity market volume was split between 56.9% on lit venues and 43.1% on dark venues. Of the dark volume, Tabb Group finds that 51.4% was through retail wholesalers and single-dealer platforms, 30.0% occurred on dark ATSs, and 18.6% was hidden exchange volume.[366]

Retail investors typically trade through introducing broker-dealers of integrated firms such as Merrill Lynch or Morgan Stanley. Broker-dealers with retail customer orders to execute often send these orders to specialized broker-

---

[363] For a complete current list of ATSs, see SEC, *Alternative Trading Systems*, https://www.sec.gov/foia/docs/atslist.htm.

[364] Angel, Harris, and Spatt provide a nice summary of trends in market quality metrics for equity markets. *See* James J. Angel, Lawrence E. Harris & Chester S. Spatt, *Equity Trading in the 21st Century: An Update*, 5 Q. J. FIN. 1 (2015).

[365] DEUTSCHE BANK, HIGH FREQUENCY TRADING: REACHING THE LIMITS (May 24, 2016), https://www.dbresearch.com/PROD/RPS_EN-PROD/PROD0000000000454703/Research_Briefing%3A_High-frequency_trading.PDF.

[366] Valerie Bogard, *Executive Summary*, TABB EQUITY DIGEST: Q2-2016 (Dec. 8, 2016), https://research.tabbgroup.com/report/v14-071-tabb-equity-digest-q2-2016.

Table 4: Routing venues and routing decisions for an introducing broker for NYSE-listed stocks

Route Venue	Total %	Market %	Limit %	Other %
Citadel Execution Services	28.19	35.87	9.12	32.71
KCG Americas LLC	20.79	30.46	5.47	22.79
NASDAQ	15.89	0.00	47.66	9.81
G1 Execution Services	11.07	15.99	2.90	12.26
BATS (EDGX)	11.02	0.00	31.69	7.38
Two Sigma Securities	7.33	4.64	0.88	11.31
UBS Securities LLC	3.74	6.50	1.16	3.55
Total %	100.00	24.58	22.45	52.97

Source: Scottrade, Inc., SEC Rule 606 Report, 1st Quarter 2017.

dealers, known as wholesale market makers or "internalizers" in return for a compensating payment. Recent data suggests that the vast majority of marketable retail orders are sent to these wholesalers. As an example, Scottrade, an introducing broker that makes use of wholesalers to execute its customer flow, sent a substantial amount of its order flow to wholesalers, as shown in Table 4. Wholesale market makers typically use algorithms to determine whether to execute an order, in whole or in part, as a principal or whether to send it to other trading centers, including exchanges and dark pools.

3 Equity Market Secondary Trading

3.1 Regulation NMS and Market Interaction Rules

When Regulation NMS was adopted in 2005, it was put in place to address a host of perceived shortcomings in U.S. equity markets. The traditional listed market, dominated by the NYSE, was looking increasingly dated in the face of advancing technology. The human specialist was at the center of this floor-based market, while at the same time NASDAQ was operating an order-driven electronic market. Trade-throughs, which are the execution of orders at prices inferior to the current NBBO, were becoming increasingly prevalent. An SEC staff study found that 2.4% of trades on NASDAQ occurred at prices inferior to the NBBO.[367] This tendency was exacerbated by the poor mechanisms in place to link markets around the country, such as the Intermarket Trading System (ITS) plan and Unlisted Trading Privileges (UTP) plan.

Also, registered exchanges were prohibited from charging access fees, while ECNs could and did charge fees up to 0.3 cents per share, and in some cases even higher. These access fees were not reflected in the disseminated public quotes of the ECNs, causing confusion in the marketplace. ECNs also had the ability to pay liquidity rebates for placing limit orders into their order books, which challenged the existing frameworks for brokers' best execution obligations. ECNs could also quote in sub-pennies, while the SIP data feeds prevented the exchanges form doing so.[368] This allowed the ECNs to step ahead of the exchanges by quoting prices that were better by minimis amounts. Finally, because market data was allocated to exchanges based on the number of trades executed, traders engaged in order shredding, cutting single large orders up into large numbers of small orders, in the hopes of driving more market data revenue to their favored exchange.

Regulation NMS attempted to resolve these problems and restoring order to the public markets.[369] Though the adopting release for the rule is over 500 pages long, the essence of the regulation is contained in four of its new rules: (i) Rule 603, which allocates market data revenues among market centers to encourage and reward the dissemination of useful trading and quotation data; (ii) Rule 610, which allows private linkages among market centers, and limits access fees to a maximum of three mils ($.003) per share.; (iii) Rule 611, which protects immediately accessible quotes at automated market centers by requiring incoming orders to interact with the top of their order books; and (iv) Rule 612, which prohibits quoting in less than one-penny increments for stocks priced over one dollar per share.

Not surprisingly, the passage of Regulation NMS engendered a substantial amount of institutional change in secondary trading markets. In this

---

[367] Regulation NMS Adopting Release, 70 Fed. Reg. No. 124, at 37507 & n.74.

[368] Securities Information Processors (SIPs) are industry utilities charged with collecting and disseminating quote and trade data. They are discussed in more detail later in this chapter.

[369] Two of the five sitting SEC Commissioners dissented from the adoption of Regulation NMS because of concerns about its effect on competition and innovation. *See Dissent of Commissioners Cynthia A. Glassman and Paul S. Atkins to the Adoption of Regulation NMS* (June 9, 2005), https://www.sec.gov/rules/final/34-51808-dissent.pdf.

section, we explore the consequences and unresolved issues related to three areas aspects of the regulation: (a) market fragmentation; (b) the order protection rule; and (c) the minimum tick size.

3.1.1 Market Fragmentation

The SEC's framework for regulation of secondary equity markets has sought to balance competition among market centers and competition among individual orders.[370] Competition among market centers can lead to innovation and long-term improvements in trading conditions, while competition among orders can lead to greater price discovery and liquidity. In many ways, current regulation promotes innovation, while attempting to create competition among orders through mandated exchange linkages. Consistent with this view, O'Hara and Ye compare the execution quality and efficiency of stocks with more and less fragmented trading, and conclude that more fragmented stocks have lower transactions costs, faster execution speeds, and greater market efficiency.[371] They conclude that their findings are consistent with U.S. markets being a single virtual market with multiple points of entry.[372]

Issues arise to the extent that linkages between trading venues are not robust or timely.[373] For instance, Rule 611 only protects orders that have been

---

[370] For a survey of the academic market structure literature, see SEC, DIVISION OF TRADING AND MARKETS, EQUITY MARKET STRUCTURE LITERATURE REVIEW – PART I: MARKET FRAGMENTATION (Oct. 7, 2013), https://www.sec.gov/marketstructure/research/fragmentation-lit-review-100713.pdf.

[371] Maureen O'Hara & Mao Ye, *Is Market Fragmentation Harming Market Quality?*, 100 J. FIN. ECON. 459 (2011). Jiang, McInish, and Upson argue that market fragmentation allows uninformed traders to segment their order flow to off-exchange venues, allowing a higher concentration of informed trading on lit exchanges, thereby improving price discovery. *See* Christine Jiang, Thomas McInish & James Upson, *Why Fragmented Markets Have Better Market Quality: The Flight of Liquidity Order Flows to off Exchange Venues* (working paper, 2011), http://utminers.utep.edu/jeupson/pages/Fragmented.pdf.

[372] Aitken, Chen, and Foley show that the introduction of Chi-X in Australia led to the arrival of fee-sensitive liquidity providers. *See* Michael J. Aitken, Haoming Chen & Sean Foley, *The Impact of Fragmentation, Exchange Fees and Liquidity Provision on Market Quality*, 41 J. EMPIRICAL FIN. 140 (2017). Aitken, Chen, and Foley find that quoted and effective spreads fell as Chi-X market share increased.

[373] In the context of ETF trading on the Island ECN, Hendershott and Jones show that less concentration of trading resulted in weaker competition among

visible for at least one second, and automated trading venues are only required to respond to orders within a one second timeframe. But as trading and quote update latency are now measured in milliseconds (or faster), any delay in processing can cause the linkages between trading centers to be economically severed, leading to effective fragmentation and isolation of trading environments.

To better understand the effect of delays in linkages, Bartlett and McCrary examine the latency of the two SIPs in comparison with those of the exchanges' direct data feed.[374] Their results show that there is a low likelihood that liquidity-taking trades receive inferior pricing when priced at the SIP NBBO rather than at an NBBO that is constructed by the authors from the private low-latency direct feeds of each exchange. They find, on average, liquidity-taking trades are more likely to find benefit than harm when priced at stale prices appearing in the SIP NBBO.

Growth in the number of trading venues has increased competition. Some of the public debate concerning market fragmentation has been shaped by the winners and losers of this competition, particularly advocates of the legacy exchange systems that have lost order flow.[375] As well, broker-dealers and other

---

liquidity providers, reflecting imperfect competition due to lack of complete transparency and integration. See Terrence Hendershott & Charles M. Jones, *Island Goes Dark: Transparency, Fragmentation and Regulation*, 18 REV. FIN. STUD. 743 (2005).

[374] Robert P. Bartlett, III & Justin McCrary, *How Rigged are Stock Markets? Evidence From Microsecond Timestamps* (working paper 2016), https://papers.ssrn.com/sol3/papers.cfm?abstract_id=2812123. Ding, Hanna, and Hendershott also study price dislocations between the public NBBO based on consolidated data feeds and prices based on proprietary data feeds. *See* Shengwei Ding, John Hanna & Terrence Hendershott, *How Slow is the NBBO? A Comparison with Direct Exchange Feeds*, 49 FIN. REV. 313 (2014). Similar to Bartlett and McCrary, *supra*, they find that the brevity of dislocations does not pose meaningful costs for infrequent investors, but that the frequency of dislocations can introduce costs for frequent investors.

[375] The debate about market fragmentation was particularly fierce in Europe, as MiFID and then MiFID II, aimed to reduce barriers to competition across national borders. Gomber, Sagade, Theissen, and Weber and Davies describe some of the changes that have resulted. *See* Peter Gomber, Satchit Sagade, Erik Theissen, Moritz C. Weber & Christian Westheide, *Spoilt for Choice: Order Routing Decisions in Fragmented Equity Markets* (working paper 2016), https://papers.ssrn.com/sol3/papers.cfm?abstract_id=2839285; Ryan J. Davies, *MiFID and a Changing Competitive Landscape* (working paper 2008), https://papers.ssrn.com/sol3/papers.cfm?abstract_id=1117232.

market participants have needed to adapt to the additional complexity in the market. This complexity has introduced new trading costs, particularly for institutional traders, and may have made markets more vulnerable to large market moves and technological shocks. As well, best execution and the reference price are more difficult to establish in a fragmented market.

Market fragmentation may be a greater concern for small capitalization issuers, for which their already low transaction volume is potentially spread across too many venues. Some market participants have argued that Regulation NMS should allow for more heterogeneity in rules across firms. For instance, NASDAQ has recently argued that removing UTP obligations for smaller firms would allow liquidity to be concentrated and would reduce volatility. NASDAQ further argues that removing these constraints would create natural opportunities for other market structures (e.g., batch auctions) to develop.[376]

Finally, it is important to distinguish between visible fragmentation (dispersal of volume among lit trading venues) and dark fragmentation (dispersal of volume between lit and dark trading venues).[377] The effects of visible fragmentation can be largely resolved using technology and smart order routing systems. Dark fragmentation, however, can have impacts on price discovery and can cause some orders to be inaccessible to all market participants. In section 3.2, we address issues related to dark trading. Some market participants believe that the order protection rule has promoted the growth of dark venues by "constraining the nature of competition on lit venues to factors such as speed, fees, and exotic order types, in contrast to factors that are more appealing to investors, such as liquidity and stability."[378] We proceed to discuss this rule next.

---

[376] NASDAQ, THE PROMISE OF MARKET REFORM: REIGNITING AMERICA'S ECONOMIC ENGINE (2017), http://business.nasdaq.com/media/Nasdaq%20Blueprint%20to%20Revitalize%20Capital%20Markets_tcm5044-43175.pdf.

[377] Degryse, de Jong, and van Kervel and Gresse examine both types of fragmentation in the context of European markets. *See* Hans Degryse, Frank de Jong & Vincent van Kervel, *The Impact of Dark Trading and Visible Fragmentation on Market Quality*, 19 REV. FIN. 1587 (2015); Carole Gresse, *Effects of Lit and Dark Market Fragmentation on Liquidity*, 35 J. FIN. MKTS. 1 (2017).

[378] *Memorandum (Re: Rule 611 of Regulation NMS) from SEC Division of Trading and Markets to SEC Market Structure Advisory Committee* (Apr. 30, 2015), https://www.sec.gov/spotlight/emsac/memo-rule-611-regulation-nms.pdf, at 17.

3.1.2 Order Protection Rule

Rule 611 of Regulation NMS, the order protection or "trade-through" rule, is designed to promote intermarket price protection by restricting the execution of trades on one venue at prices that are inferior to publicly displayed quotations on another venue. It is fair to say that the rule has been controversial from the onset. Part of the original controversy was due to the fact that the rule only applied to quotes accessible for automated execution, which led to the effective end of manual floor markets on the NYSE and a corresponding dramatic market share loss.[379] Other criticisms of the order protection rule include that it inhibits competition on non-price dimensions, it does not respect time priority across trading venues, and it is difficult to enforce with sub-second trading.[380]

The order protection rule only protects the displayed top-of-book of each protected market center. At the time of implementation, the decision to protect only the top of a market's book was based on a belief that protecting the entire book would be technologically infeasible. Given the advances in computing technology, as well as the massive amount of message traffic already occurring, it may be technologically possible today to protect the entire displayed limit order book. However, many market participants would argue against such a change, as critics have already argued that the existing rule overly complicates the system of interconnections among trading venues.[381]

Closely tied to the order protection rule, is the commonly-used Intermarket Sweep Order (ISO), which allows an institutional trader to access

---

[379] Chung and Chuwonganant provide empirical evidence that market quality, particularly for institutional traders, decreased subsequent to Regulation NMS, in terms of larger trading costs, greater pricing errors, slower order execution speeds, and lower execution probability. *See* Kee H. Chung & Chairat Chuwonganant, *Regulation NMS and Market Quality*, 41 FIN. MGMT. 285 (2012). They argue that these results support concerns about the impact of the order protection rule on market liquidity, by reducing the role of NYSE specialists and floor brokers as the liquidity providers of last resort.

[380] For a critical view of the order protection rule, and Regulation NMS more generally, see Marshall E. Blume, *Competition and Fragmentation in The Equity Markets: The Effects of Regulation NMS* (working paper, 2007), https://papers.ssrn.com/sol3/papers.cfm?abstract_id=959429.

[381] *See, e.g.*, Rick Baert, *Institutions at Odds with Retail Over SEC's Order Protection Rule*, PENSIONS & INVESTMENTS, May 1, 2017, http://www.pionline.com/article/20170501/PRINT/305019978/institutions-at-odds-with-retail-over-secs-order-protection-rule.

the top of the book across all markets.[382] Latency between trading venues helps explain some of the usage of the ISO. The ISO allows a trader to release the market center from the time-consuming tasks of checking other trading venues for possible trade-throughs.

Because only the top of the book is protected for ISOs, there may be an incentive to post limit orders on less liquid exchanges where they may be more likely to be at the top of that venue's book.[383] In this manner, the order protection rule, combined with the high usage of ISOs, may be helping to support exchanges that otherwise would be commercially non-viable. Some market participants have suggested that exchanges satisfy a minimum volume threshold to qualify for order protection. They argue that low volume exchanges force them to incur additional costs, such as paying for direct market feeds and managing routing logic.[384]

The order protection rule allows a trading venue to match the best displayed quote at another venue prior to re-routing the order. Some have argued that this ability discourages displayed liquidity since it allows traders on other venues to trade ahead of existing displayed orders. As well, some market participants are concerned about the growth of dark trading venues. In response to these concerns, a trade-at rule has been proposed as a reform for U.S. markets with the goal of encouraging the public display of orders. In general, a trade-at rule would allow market centers to execute an order against a protected quote up to the amount of its displayed size, with some possible exceptions. Weaver argues that such a trade-at rule would improve the quality of markets, by dramatically reducing the amount of internalization of order flow.[385]

Closely related to a trade-at rule is a minimum price improvement rule. Foley and Putniņš examine the impact of implementing minimum price

---

[382] For an overview of ISOs, see Sugato Chakravarty, Pankaj K. Jain, Robert Wood & James Upson, *Clean Sweep: Informed Trading Through Intermarket Sweep Orders*, 47 J. FIN. & QUANT. ANALYSIS 415 (2012).

[383] It is also possible that market participants may be using exchanges with inverted, taker-maker pricing to extract information from these orders.

[384] *See, e.g.*, BLACKROCK, U.S. EQUITY MARKET STRUCTURE: AN INVESTOR PERSPECTIVE (2014), https://www.blackrock.com/corporate/literature/whitepaper/viewpoint-us-equity-market-structure-april-2014.pdf.

[385] Daniel G. Weaver, *The Trade-at Rule, Internalization, and Market Quality* (working paper, 2014), https://papers.ssrn.com/sol3/papers.cfm?abstract_id=1846470.

improvement rules in Canada in October 2012 and Australia in May 2013.[386] The rules require that dark trades provide price improvement of one full tick (or half a tick if the spread is at one tick). They show that the effect of the rules is different for one-sided dark trading (i.e., midpoint crossing networks) and two-sided dark trading (i.e., markets with fractional price improvement). In both markets, the rule reduced dark trading, as expected. They show that the reduction in two-sided dark trading resulted in higher quoted, effective, and realized spreads, and lower information efficiency.[387] The decrease in trading on midpoint crossing networks did not impact market quality. These findings reinforce the notion that dark traders are not a homogeneous group and that a one-size-fits-all regulatory approach may not be effective. As such, any restrictions on off-market trading, such as a trade-at rule, might need to be applied differentially across trading venues. Comerton-Forde, Malinova, and Park, discussed in more detail below, show that minimum price improvement rules in Canada did not benefit all market participants.[388]

The trade-at rule is being tested in U.S. markets as part of the tick size pilot discussed in the next section. In the pilot, certain exceptions to the trade-at rule are provided for block size orders and for conditions that mirror those already covered by the order protection rule (e.g., crossed markets and orders marked Trade-at-ISO). This pilot is unlikely to provide a definitive answer on the effectiveness of the trade-at rule since it is constrained to small capitalization stocks and it is being implemented in conjunction with an increase in the tick size.

The trade-at rule being tested in the tick size pilot is based on posted prices. These prices do not include market access fees and trading rebates, and as such, do not reflect the true net cost of the transaction. Two possible modifications to the trade-at rule could address this problem. One possible modification is to apply the trade-at rule only to posted orders that have access fees at or below a certain level, which could be zero. Alternatively, the trade-at rule could be changed to apply to prices after including fees and rebates, but this

---

[386] Sean Foley & Tālis J. Putniņš, *Should we be Afraid of the Dark? Dark Trading and Market Quality*, 122 J. FIN. ECON. 456 (2016).

[387] For additional commentary, see CFA INSTITUTE, TRADE-AT RULES IN AUSTRALIA AND CANADA – A MIXED BAG FOR INVESTORS, (2014), https://www.cfainstitute.org/ethics/Documents/Policy%20Brief_Trade-at%20Rules.pdf.

[388] Carole Comerton-Forde, Katya Malinova & Andreas Park, *Regulating Dark Trading: Order Flow Segmentation and Market Quality* (working paper, 2017), https://papers.ssrn.com/sol3/papers.cfm?abstract_id=2755392.

change would require a major change in Regulation NMS and the manner in which prices are quoted and transmitted across venues.

3.1.3 Minimum Tick Size

Rule 612 of Regulation NMS specifies the minimum pricing increments for NMS stocks. The rule prohibits market participants from accepting, ranking, or displaying orders, quotations, or indications of interest in a pricing increment smaller than a cent for stocks with prices exceeding $1.00.[389] Some market participants have argued that decimalization has contributed to poor liquidity in small capitalization stocks, and thereby has led to a loss of aftermarket support for new issues and a dramatic decline in new IPOs.[390] The 2012 Jumpstart Our Business Startups Act (JOBS Act) directed the SEC to run an experiment on the impact of increasing the tick size. In response, the SEC developed the tick size pilot program, which is designed to examine the impact of the minimum quoting and trading increment on the liquidity and trading of small capitalization stocks.[391]

The pilot began on October 3, 2016 and will run for two years. It focuses on companies with market capitalizations less than $3 billion. The pilot has a control group (approximately 1400 stocks), and three test groups (approximately 400 stocks each): the first test group will be quoted at $0.05 increments, but allowed to trade at $0.01 increments; the second test group will be quoted and trade at $0.05 increments, with some exceptions; and the third test group will be quoted and trade at $0.05 increments, as well as subject to a trade-at requirement.

The Capital Markets Cooperative Research Centre (CMCRC) has developed a dashboard that monitors the impact of the pilot study on a day-to-

---

[389] For studies of the impact of decimalization on trading costs see, Charles M. Jones & Marc L. Lipson, *Sixteenths: Direct Evidence on Institutional Execution Costs*, 59 J. FIN. ECON. 253 (2001); Michael A. Goldstein & Kenneth A. Kavajecz, *Eighth, Sixteenth, and Market Depth: Changes in Tick Size and Liquidity Provision on the NYSE*, 56 J. FIN. ECON. 125 (2000); and Hendrik Bessembinder, *Trade Execution Costs and Market Quality after Decimalization*, 38 J. FIN. QUANT. ANALYSIS 747 (2003).

[390] *See, e.g.*, David Weild & Edward Kim, *Market Structure is Causing the IPO Crisis – and More*, Grant Thornton Capital Market Series (2010).

[391] For details, see SEC, INVESTOR ALERT: TICK SIZE PILOT PROGRAM – WHAT INVESTORS NEED TO KNOW (2016), https://www.sec.gov/oiea/investor-alerts-bulletins/ia_ticksize.html.

day basis.[392] Preliminary results show that a wider tick size has led to a more stable quote, with more exchanges quoting at the NBBO for longer periods, thereby making it easier to trade in size. Effective spreads have widened, and market share has shifted from maker-taker venues to inverted (taker-maker) exchanges. The overall welfare effects from changing the minimum tick size have not been fully quantified yet.

The shift to inverted exchanges from widening the minimum tick size appears to be consistent with Yao and Ye.[393] They argue that artificial price constraints caused by the minimum tick size give rise to speed competition, and reduce the ability to compete on price. They argue that the rule has been a factor in driving high-frequency trading and the proliferation of inverted taker-maker markets. Yao and Ye believe that a binding $0.01 tick size led the usage of inverted taker-maker markets; clearly, the $0.05 tick size in the tick size pilot will be even more binding and is likely to increase usage of these venues.

Kwan, Masulis, and McInish provide further evidence of the effects of the minimum tick size.[394] They find a discontinuity in the market share of dark ECNs around the $1.00 price threshold, suggesting that the minimum pricing increment rule provides a competitive advantage to these dark ECNs. They conjecture that when spreads are constrained on major exchanges, traders use dark ECNs to enable them to jump the queue of existing displayed limit orders, reducing their risk of delayed execution.

Harris shows that maker-taker and taker-maker pricing models provide a means for exchanges to provide net quotes in sub-penny increments, thereby undermining the prohibition on sub-penny quotation pricing in Regulation NMS and allowing certain traders to jump ahead of others.[395] Harris argues that these pricing models produce an agency problem between brokers and their clients, since the broker is incentivized to send limit orders to maker-taker exchanges to

---

[392] The dashboard can be found at https://www.mqdashboard.com/tick_size#search/nasdaq,nyse/1,2,4/2016-06-01/2017-02-27/false/false/none/false.

[393] Chen Yao & Mao Ye, *Tick Size Constraints, High Frequency Trading, and Liquidity* (working paper, 2015), https://papers.ssrn.com/sol3/papers.cfm?abstract_id=2359000.

[394] Amy Kwan, Ronald Masulis & Thomas H. McInish, *Trading Rules, Competition for Order Flow and Market Fragmentation*, 115 J. FIN. ECON. 330 (2015).

[395] Larry Harris, *Maker-Taker Pricing Effects on Market Quotations* (working paper, 2013), https://www.marshall.usc.edu/sites/default/files/lharris/intellcont/Maker-taker%20pricing%20v0.91-1.docx.

earn liquidity rebates and avoid access fees. These agency conflicts are discussed further in the discussion on best execution below. Harris also argues that maker-taker pricing models introduce unnecessary complexity and reduce the transparency of bid-ask spreads for retail investors.

Comerton-Forde, Grégoire, and Zhong use the tick size pilot as an exogenous shock to the share of trading on inverted taker-maker fee markets.[396] Trading on venues with inverted pricing models increased following the introduction of the trade-at rule, particularly for stocks that were tick size constrained. They argue that the finer price grid made possible by venues with inverted pricing models encourages competition between liquidity providers and improves market quality, with more orders executed and less orders canceled.

In summary, the effective tick size can be larger or smaller than the minimum tick size because of the presence of maker-taker pricing models and other forms of access fees and liquidity rebates, and payment for order flow arrangements. These fees and rebates are not included in quotations, and confuse the measurement of best execution. To reduce potential conflicts of interest, broker-dealers should be required to disclose how access fees and liquidity rebates affect order routing practices and transaction costs.

Importantly, Rule 612 allowed sub-penny trading under two exceptions: mid-quote executions and execution at a price determined through a VWAP algorithm. These exceptions appear to be used frequently by high frequency traders through dark pools. Buti, Rindi, Wen, and Werner find that approximately 10% of share volume executes at sub-penny increments.[397] They argue that the ability to undercut existing displayed limit / liquidity orders by trivial amounts, can lead to less passive displayed orders, less depth and larger spreads. Bartlett and McCrary use a market discontinuity to show that increasing the incentive to use the exception to the sub-penny quote rule increases the rate of trading at the midpoint of the NBBO on dark venues, thereby offering liquidity takers price improvement equal to the quoted half-spread.[398] They argue that this evidence goes against the belief that sub-penny trading offers little or no price improvement.

---

[396] Carole Comerton-Forde, Vincent Grégoire & Zhuo Zhong, *Inverted Fee Venues and Market Quality* (working paper, 2017), https://papers.ssrn.com/sol3/papers.cfm?abstract_id=2939012.

[397] Sabrina Buti, Francesco Consonni, Barbara Rindi, Yuanji Wen & Ingrid M. Werner, *Sub-Penny and Queue-Jumping* (working paper, 2015), https://papers.ssrn.com/sol3/papers.cfm?abstract_id=2350424.

[398] Robert P. Bartlett, III & Justin McCrary, *Dark Trading at the Midpoint: Pricing Rules, Order Flow and High Frequency Liquidity Provision* (working paper, 2015), https://papers.ssrn.com/sol3/papers.cfm?abstract_id=2621340.

For larger, more active stocks, it is possible that the tick size is no longer relevant in a trading environment in which quotes are only a probabilistic indication of the likely price of a market order. In an environment with flickering and fleeting limit orders, the latency between order submission and order arrival has the effect that posted quotes are only an input into a probabilistic view of the likely execution price.

While the verdict on the SEC Tick Size Pilot is still out, the SEC has announced plans to run an Access Fee Pilot to examine the effect of maker-taker pricing. As pilot studies are more commonly used, we note that the advantages of using a pilot study to obtain information via a controlled experiment must be balanced against the costs such a study imposes on market participants. It is possible that the pilot study period may not be long enough to establish the end state or equilibrium that would arise from a permanent rule change. Market participants, knowing that pilot will end after a certain period of time, may elect to not devote resources towards developing an optimal reaction to the rule change. Rather than develop a process for handling the pilot study rule, these firms may simply elect to avoid certain trades in the pilot study securities. Given the costs of running a pilot study, it is important to determine upfront the goals of the study and set clear guidelines on what it is trying to measure. The pilot study must be well designed, such that it can deliver results that are informative and which could not be obtained through less costly, alternative means.

3.2 Transparency and Dark Pools

Dark liquidity and dark trading have always existed on U.S. equity markets. In prior years, NYSE floor brokers were a source of dark liquidity, either leaving large customer orders with the specialist (passive participation) or working them over time as a member of the trading crowd (active participation).[399] Other floor traders were only partially aware of the magnitude of these orders, and they were not visible to the public outside of the floor. Similarly, dark trading also occurred in the so-called upstairs market as an intermediary or broker searched across brokerage firms to locate a counterparty for a large block trade before sending it to the downstairs market for execution.[400] While some information leakage occurred as the order was shopped, most market participants were unaware of these block trades and were not given the opportunity to participate in the trades.

---

[399] For details, see George Sofianos & Ingrid M. Werner, *The Trades of NYSE Floor Brokers*, 3 J. FIN. MKTS. 139 (2000).

[400] For details, see Donald B. Keim & Ananth Madhavan, *The Upstairs Market for Large-Block Transactions: Analysis and Measurement of Price Effects*, 9 REV. FIN. STUD. (1996).

Today, dark liquidity can be found in the various types of hidden or non-displayed orders available on almost all exchanges.[401] These orders allow traders to hide all, or a portion of, their orders on the book, typically at the cost of lost priority to displayed orders at a given price. These hidden orders constitute an important source of dark liquidity. Non-displayed order types are the most commonly used order types on exchanges, constituting more than 25% of orders on BATS and more than 30% of orders on Nasdaq OMX by a recent estimate.[402] SEC market data show that these order types may account for as much as 11% to 14% of exchange-based volume. Interestingly, Bloomfield et al. use a laboratory experiment to investigate the impact of allowing traders to hide their orders, and they find little effect on overall market outcomes.[403]

Equity trading can occur on traditional exchanges (lit markets) and off-exchange venues (dark markets), such as dark pools, crossing networks, and retail internalizers. In most contexts, dark trading has virtually no pre-trade transparency, but has some post-trade transparency (which may be incomplete, possibly not indicating the venue that executed the trade, and may occur with a lag). Garvey, Huang, and Wu use proprietary data from a direct market access broker to investigate the reasons that orders are sent to dark markets.[404] In their sample, they find that more sophisticated traders tend to participate more in dark markets, particularly when market conditions in lit markets are challenging (wider spreads and higher volatility). They find that more than 80% of dark orders are executed at a price better than the best price available in lit markets at the time of order submission.

Despite having no pre-trade transparency, in some cases the information from dark trading may also be partially reflected in lit market prices. For instance, Nimalendran and Ray use a proprietary dataset of transactions on a crossing network to examine whether information leaks from trading on a dark venue to

---

[401] In addition to hidden orders, another source of dark liquidity is institutional orders that have been sent to agency brokers, such as ITG Inc., but have not yet fully revealed to the market.

[402] Phil Mackintosh, *Demystifying Order Types*, KCG MARKET INSIGHTS (2014), https://www.virtu.com/uploads/documents/KCG_Demystifying-Order-Types_092414.pdf.

[403] Robert Bloomfield, Maureen O'Hara & Gideon Saar, *Hidden Liquidity: Some New Light on Dark Trading*, 70 J. FIN. 2227 (2015).

[404] Ryan Garvey, Tao Huang & Fei Wu, *Why do Traders Choose Dark Markets?* 68 J. BANKING & FIN. 12 (2016).

the trading on the lit venue.⁴⁰⁵ They show that buyer-initiated trades on the crossing network are followed by more net buy signed trades on the lit market, and vice versa. This pattern is suggestive of concurrent informed trading on both dark and lit venues, which means that the potential negative impact of dark pool trading on price discovery might be less than expected.

In the Australian context, Comerton-Forde and Putniņš find that high levels of dark trading impede price discovery and cause prices to become less informationally efficient.⁴⁰⁶ They find that dark trading increases adverse selection risk, bid-ask spreads, and price impact on the transparent exchange. The impact of dark trading on price discovery appears to be driven by smaller trades occurring in the dark, rather than offsetting block trades. While the levels in the Australian market may not apply universally, their findings suggest that there may be a tipping point in U.S. equity markets, and it is important to understand where the tipping point is.

Theoretical work suggests that determining the tipping point is not straightforward, and may differ across securities and market conditions. Zhu develops a model with asymmetric information about the asset value that shows dark pools concentrate price-relevant information on the exchange, improving price discovery but reducing liquidity.⁴⁰⁷ Ye provides a model that shows that the impact of dark pools of price discovery depends critically on traders' information precision.⁴⁰⁸ In her model, dark pools have an amplification effect: price discovery is enhanced by dark trading when information precision is high, and impaired when information precision is low.

When discussing dark pools and their effect on market quality, one should be careful to note that dark pool venues are not all the same.⁴⁰⁹ Some dark pools (e.g., Liquidnet Negotiated, Liquidnet H20, Barclays DirectEx) resemble the old upstairs market with infrequent, large trades (often at negotiated prices or crossed at the NBBO midpoint), while other dark pools automate the execution

---

[405] Mahendrarajah Nimalendran & Sugata Ray, *Information Linkages Between Dark and Lit Trading Venue,* 17 J. FIN. MKTS. 230 (2014).

[406] Carole Comerton-Forde & Tālis J. Putniņš, *Dark Trading and Price Discovery*, 118 J. FIN. ECON. 70 (2015).

[407] Haoxing Zhu, *Do Dark Pools Harm Price Discovery?*, 27 REV. FIN. STUD. 747 (2014).

[408] Linlin Ye, *Understanding The Impacts of Dark Pools on Price Discovery* (working paper, 2016), https://arxiv.org/pdf/1612.08486.pdf.

[409] For a categorization of dark pools, see Hitesh Mittal, *Are you Playing in a Toxic Dark Pool? A Guide to Preventing Information Leakage*, 3 J. TRADING 20 (2008).

of a large number of tiny trades, often used by market makers as retail internalization pools (e.g., Goldman Sachs Sigma-X, KCG Matchit).

It might be tempting to promote dark trading of large blocks, while discouraging venues that execute smaller orders, which may or may not interact directly or indirectly with retail orders. However, the latter venues play an important role in the marketplace as institutions often find it difficult to locate block counterparties of similar size. Menkveld, Yueshen, and Zhu show that the diversity of dark pools provides a valuable range of options for investors facing a tradeoff between price impact and execution uncertainty.[410] They show that as trading needs become more urgent, investors move from low-cost, low immediacy venues to high-cost, high immediacy venues.

Dark trading, in all forms, serves a critical role. Dark pools provide liquidity for orders that would be too large to send to the market fully displayed.[411] Dark pools often advertise that they allow institutions to trade large positions with reduced market impact, lower information leakage, better pricing, and anonymity. On a trade-by-trade basis, these claims may be correct, but it is difficult to assess how dark trading affects overall market quality as there is an endogeneity issue that cannot be easily resolved.[412] To illustrate, consider the impact of a dark pool on bid-ask spreads. On the one hand, wider spreads on lit markets might cause more order flow to be sent to the dark pool. On the other hand, the decision to send the order to the dark pool could lead to wider spreads on the lit market by increasing adverse selection risk. Controlled experiments, such as the tick size pilot combined with the trade-at rule, might help with the identification aspect of this issue.

Importantly, the overall impact of dark trading on market quality cannot be captured solely by examining the percentage of trading volume on lit and dark venues. The characteristics of the trades on lit and dark venues matter. For instance, it is possible that lit markets are becoming dominated by short-term

---

[410] Albert J. Menkveld, Bart Z. Yueshen & Haoxiang Zhu, *Shades of Darkness: A Pecking Order of Trading Venues*, 124 J. FIN. ECON. 503 (2017).

[411] Cheridito and Sepin show in simulation results that the presence of a dark pool lowers the implementation cost of acquiring a large position. *See* Patrick Cheridito & Tardu Sepin, *Optimal Trade Execution with a Dark Pool and Adverse Selection* (working paper, 2014), https://papers.ssrn.com/sol3/papers.cfm?abstract_id=2490234.

[412] Buti, Rindi, and Werner find that increased dark pool activity improves market quality measures such as spread, depths, and short-term volatility, but that the impact on price-efficiency is more complex. *See* Sabrina Buti, Barbara Rindi & Ingrid M. Werner, *Diving into Dark Pools* (working paper, 2011), https://papers.ssrn.com/sol3/papers.cfm?abstract_id=1630499.

trading, while dark markets are being used as the venue of choice for long-term, informed investors. If the majority of informed trading occurs on dark venues, it will likely have a detrimental impact on price discovery.

The opaque nature of some of the automated dark pools is a potential for concern. For these dark pools, is unclear what algorithms are being used to match trades and whether the operators, or a subset of participants, in the pools are able to extract unfair advantages. Recently, Barclays Capital Inc. paid $70 million in fines for, among other things, failing to properly monitor predatory trading on in their LX dark pool, and Credit Suisse paid $84.3 million in fines for, among other things, failing to identify opportunistic traders and executing 117 million illegal sub-penny orders in their Crossfinder dark pool.[413] The SEC may propose a new rule that would require dark pools to publically disclose more information about their procedures and whether some traders receive preferential access to certain functionality.[414] In addition to the new proposed rule, more complete post-trade transparency, in particular more information regarding the counterparties to all of the trades, may help identify similar issues earlier.

Another form of dark trading is retail internalization. Retail internalization refers to the practice by which marketable retail orders in U.S. equity markets are typically routed to wholesale market makers, rather than the exchange. The wholesale market makers pay the retail brokers making these routing decisions a payment for this order flow. The sector is dominated by five wholesale market makers: Citadel Securities (Citadel Execution Services), KCG Americas LLC, G1 Execution Services, UBS Securities, and Two Sigma Securities. At least 10% of consolidated U.S. equity market volumes is in the form of retail internalization.[415]

---

[413] Press Release, SEC, Barclays, Credit Suisse Charged with Dark Pool Violations (Jan. 31, 2016), https://www.sec.gov/news/pressrelease/2016-16.html.

[414] Dave Michaels, *SEC Preparing to Finalize Transparency Rules for Dark Pools, Mary Jo White Says*, WALL ST. J., Sept. 14, 2016, https://www.wsj.com/articles/dark-pools-convince-sec-to-delay-transparency-rules-mary-jo-white-says-1473876535.

[415] Rosenblatt Securities provides its clients monthly statistics on dark liquidity (www.rblt.com). The statistics on retail internalization are reported in U.S. HOUSE OF REPRESENTATIVES, COMMITTEE ON FINANCIAL SERVICES SUBCOMMITTEE ON CAPITAL MARKETS AND GOVERNMENT SPONSORED ENTERPRISES, MARKET STRUCTURE: ENSURING ORDERLY, EFFICIENT, INNOVATIVE AND COMPETITIVE MARKETS FOR ISSUERS AND INVESTORS (June 20, 2012) (Testimony of Joseph C. Gawronski, President & COO, Rosenblatt

Recently, some jurisdictions have attempted to restrict dark trading and retail internalization. Comerton-Forde, Malinova, and Park examine the impact of a rule change in Canada requiring dark venues to provide a minimum price improvement (similar to the trade-at rule proposed by the tick size pilot), which effectively ended intermediation of retail orders in the dark.[416] After the rule change, retail orders were sent primarily to the lit market with the lowest fees for marketable orders, improving liquidity with larger displayed depth and tighter spreads. While liquidity on the lit markets improved, retail traders received less price improvement and institutions had higher implementation shortfall costs. Retail brokers paid higher exchange fees, while high frequency market makers captured larger exchange rebates.

In Europe, when MiFID II rules come into effect in January 2018, each dark pool will be limited to trade no more than four percent of the overall trading volume in an individual security, and total dark trading will be restricted to eight percent of overall trading volume.[417] Based on current dark trading volume statistics, these limits will be binding. Regulators in U.S. markets should watch these developments carefully.

3.3 Algorithmic and High Frequency Trading

While there have been many changes to equity markets over the last 30 years, one of the most important is the transition of trading from a manual to an automated process. This transition has affected not only exchanges and market centers, but brokers and investors as well. Far from being a technical change or merely a step along the way of market evolution, automated trading has reshaped our markets and is almost certainly a permanent fixture of the trading scene.

Traditionally, orders were handled manually from their origination at the desk of a retail or institutional investor to their execution on the floor of an exchange. Over time, technology crept into this chain through devices like the fax machine and later through fixtures of exchanges such as ITS and exchange-based automated execution facilities.[418] The advent of algorithmic trading

---

Securities), http://financialservices.house.gov/uploadedfiles/hhrg-112-ba16-wstate-jgawronski-20120620.pdf.

[416] Comerton-Forde, Malinova & Park, *supra* note 388.

[417] *See, e.g.*, Alistair Cree & Colleen Ruane, *MIFID 2: Impact of Dark Caps on Algorithmic Trading Strategies*, https://www.itg.com/thinking-article/mifid-2-impact-dark-caps-algorithmic-trading-strategies/.

[418] An early example of such an exchange facility was SOES, Nasdaq's small order execution system. ITS was an electronic system that linked exchanges and

brought automation to brokers and public traders for the generation and submission of orders.

The nomenclature in this area is confused, and there is no specific definition of what constitutes computerized, algorithmic, or high frequency trading. Elements of *computerized trading* have been with us for many years. For example, program trading, defined as the simultaneous submission of orders in 15 or more equities, has used automation for years. And clearly, computers have been used in the investment process for decades. Only more recently has automation come to the generation and management of orders on a continuous basis.

While there are no precise definitions, for our purposes we define *algorithmic trading* to be the use of computer-based algorithms to generate, submit, and manage child orders derived from a larger parent order. Examples of such algorithms listed by a major broker-dealer on its website include algorithms based on the VWAP (volume weighted average price), TWAP (time weighted average price), volume in line, price in line, pairs, implementation shortfall, liquidity-seeking strategies, float, hidden DMA, open and close strategies, and bespoke strategies.[419] Of course, in many ways algorithmic trading merely automates a strategy that previously existed in manual form, making it more efficient and customizable.

High frequency trading (HFT) is more difficult to define. The SEC defined the attributes of HFT to include the use of extraordinarily high speed and sophisticated programs for generating, routing, and executing orders; use of co-location services and individual data feeds offered by exchanges and others to minimize network and other latencies; very short time-frames for establishing and liquidating positions; submission of numerous orders that are cancelled shortly after submission; ending the trading day in as close to a flat position as possible.[420] As an illustration of the short-term nature of the HFT business, Menkveld has found that high frequency traders profit only on those positions that are held for less than five seconds.[421]

The speed associated with high frequency trading is truly mind-boggling. Latencies associated with HFT are now well under one millisecond. Data

---

allowed exchange members to execute orders in any market with the best price, not just the one for which they were a member.

[419] *See* http://www.thetradenews.com/GuidesCompany.aspx?id=8589934642.

[420] SEC Concept Release on Equity Market Structure, Release No. 34-61358; File No. S7-02-10 (Jan. 14, 2010).

[421] Albert J. Menkveld, *High Frequency Trading and the New Market Makers*, 16 J. Fin. Mkts. 712 (2013).

produced by the SEC show that order interaction times can be as low as 50 microseconds. That is, once an order is placed on the books of an exchange, it can either be traded against or canceled, in whole or in part, within 50 millionths of a second. Such rapid speeds are only achieved by using ultrafast hardware throughout the trading process. Even the distance between a broker's offices and the exchange's matching engine has become a binding constraint on trading activity. Exchanges now offer colocation services that house traders' analytic hardware in close proximity to the exchange matching engine. The services are available for a fee, but SEC rules require them to be offered on a nondiscriminatory basis. Brogaard, Hagströmer, Nordén, and Riordan examine a colocation upgrade in Stockholm and find that it improves liquidity for the entire market.[422] The reason cited by the authors is that the market making entities who take advantage of the speed upgrade use the advantage to reduce their losses to adverse selection, allowing them to quote tighter markets for all.

High frequency traders generate a tremendous amount of order traffic to accomplish the execution of a single order. Data show the typical trade-to-order submission ratios are between 2% and 4% on the major exchanges. That is, between 25 and 50 orders are generated for every execution. These submission ratios are even lower for exchange traded products such as ETFs, running well under 1%.[423] The lifetime of these orders can be very short as the governing algorithms implementing their designated strategies by continuously canceling and replacing orders. For example, about 8% of orders are fully canceled in 500 microseconds, and almost half of orders are canceled in less than a second.[424] The high number of orders and their attendant cancellations associated with completing a trade is characteristic of the algorithms used by high frequency traders.

The last ten years has seen a wealth of academic research on HFT. It is beyond the scope of this article to summarize all this research here. Jones, Menkveld, and O'Hara each provide reviews of research touching upon algorithmic and high frequency trading and the issues attendant on the

---

[422] Jonathan Brogaard, Björn Hagströmer, Lars Nordén & Ryan Riordan, *Trading Fast and Slow: Colocation and Liquidity*, 28 REV. FIN. STUDS. 3407 (2015).

[423] SEC, TRADE TO ORDER VOLUME RATIOS (2013), https://www.sec.gov/marketstructure/research/highlight-2013-01.html#.WW4NGsbMzxo.

[424] SEC, HAZARD, SURVIVOR AND CUMULATIVE DISTRIBUTION: LARGE STOCKS, https://www.sec.gov/marketstructure/datavis/hazard_survivor_stocks_lg.html #.WW4VUsbMzxo (visited July 17, 2017).

practice.[425] While the articles discussed in these three papers cover a broad range of topics, many of them focus on issues such as information aggregation, pricing efficiency, and the effectiveness of liquidity provision by high frequency traders.

For our purposes, HFT poses some difficulties that must be examined and understood. The bulk of today's regulatory framework was developed long before the advent of computerized trading, let alone HFT. HFT is not just doing the same thing faster, it fundamentally changes the nature of trading and the way participants in the trading process interact with markets and competitors.

3.3.1 HFT and Liquidity

The issue of perhaps greatest concern to regulators is the provision of liquidity to markets. Traditional liquidity providers were exchange market-makers and specialists. These were organizations that held themselves out as providing a liquid and continuous market in the stocks they covered. They received certain regulator-conferred benefits of time and place in the trading process in exchange for both affirmative and negative obligations in their market-making activities. The most well-known of these liquidity providers was the NYSE's specialist, who ran a post on the floor of the exchange and acted as an agent for the book of limit orders left with him, receiving a commission for doing so. Liquidity was also provided by the "upstairs" market, a network of block traders and positioners at major brokerage houses who used proprietary capital to acquire and dispose of large blocks of stocks, profiting on the difference between the purchase and sale prices. Finally, there was also an agency search business in which agency brokers would, for a commission, search for counterparties to large block trades.

The advent of Regulation NMS, and especially its framework of allowing private linkages between exchanges, has led to the replacement of traditional market makers by computer-based and high frequency market-making. These opportunistic market makers are not charged with the same obligations of traditional exchange market makers and specialists. For example, they are not required to continuously quote on both sides of the market, nor are they required to fill gaps in limit order books. This led to a justifiable concern that HFT market makers provide liquidity only episodically and when it is in their economic interest to do so. Under certain conditions, this could lead to highly illiquid markets or the short flash crashes that we have observed. That said, little is

---

[425] Charles M. Jones, *What do we Know About High-Frequency Trading* (working paper, 2013), https://papers.ssrn.com/sol3/papers.cfm?abstract_id=2236201; Albert J. Menkveld, *The Economics of High-Frequency Trading: Taking Stock*, 8 ANN. REV. FIN. ECON. 1 (2016); Maureen O'Hara, *High Frequency Market Microstructure*, 116 J. FIN. ECON. 257 (2015).

known about the algorithms used by these new market-making firms. Algorithms are the core intellectual property possessed by HFT market makers. As such, they zealously guard the confidentiality of this software.

The academic literature, however, has provided some important results for questions associated with algorithmic and high frequency trading. For the most part, this literature has generally established that algorithmic and high frequency trading provide benefits to the marketplace. For example, Hendershott, Jones, and Menkveld examined the introduction of an automated quotation system on the NYSE and its effect on algorithmic trading.[426] This change allows algorithmic traders to effectively make markets via the electronic submission and cancellation of liquidity-providing limit orders. The authors found that algorithmic trading reduced the cost of trading through the narrowing of spreads, which result from a decrease in adverse selection. Algorithmic trading caused price discovery to occur without trading, causing quotes to be more informative and improving pricing efficiency.[427]

Boehmer, Fong, and Wu study ten years of algorithmic trading data across 42 international equity markets.[428] They find that algorithmic trading improves informational efficiency and liquidity, but they also find an accompanying increase in volatility. The authors also find that algorithmic trading harms the market quality of the smallest firms, decreasing their liquidity and increasing their volatility. Hendershott and Riordan use data from the Deutsche Börse that flags orders from algorithmic traders.[429] They find that algorithmic traders primarily submit smaller-sized orders, and provide liquidity through limit orders, thereby narrowing bid-ask spreads when they are wider than average. Algorithmic traders will take liquidity when spreads are sufficiently narrow. Thus, algorithmic traders have the effect of inter-temporally smoothing liquidity.

A number of other papers support the proposition that HFT improves pricing efficiency and decreases adverse selection. Brogaard, Hendershott, and Riordan find that high frequency traders improve market efficiency through their

---

[426] Terrence Hendershott, Charles M. Jones & Albert J. Menkveld, *Does Algorithmic Trading Improve Liquidity?*, 66 J. FIN. 1 (2011).

[427] Notably, these results are found only in large cap and not small cap stocks.

[428] Ekkehart Boehmer, Kingsley Y.L. Fong & Julie Wu, *International Evidence on Algorithmic Trading* (working paper, 2015), https://papers.ssrn.com/sol3/papers.cfm?abstract_id=2022034.

[429] Terrence Hendershott & Ryan Riordan, *Algorithmic Trading and the Market for Liquidity*, 48 J. FIN. & QUANT. ANALYSIS 1001 (2013).

marketable, as opposed to their nonmarketable orders.[430] These traders have short light information whose use cause trading in the direction of permanent price changes and against short-term pricing errors. The authors find that high frequency traders who use nonmarketable orders generally lose to the other informed orders, but these losses are more than offset by spread profits and liquidity rebates. Menkveld examines trading by a single large high frequency trader across two different European equity markets.[431] He finds that most trades by the trader are placed passively, making money on the spread but losing money on inventory positions held longer than five seconds. Interestingly, the author observes that because the central clearing system of the U.S. allows positions acquired on different markets to be netted, thereby reducing capital charges, this may explain why U.S. stock markets are more fragmented than those of Europe.

Brogaard, Hendershott, and Riordan offer a view on how markets may be changing as HFT increases in importance.[432] Using Canadian regulatory data for 15 TSX stocks, the authors show that high frequency traders are responsible for 60% to 80% of price discovery. Most notably, the authors show that high frequency traders react to the trading of others primarily through their use limit orders, not marketable orders. This refutes the notion that high frequency traders behave in a predatory manner by selectively preempting non-HFT trades. However, the authors note that high frequency traders do trade in such a way as to move prices against large non-HFT orders before they can be completed. Of course, this is not necessarily indicative of illegal "front-running" behavior, as some have contended, and may result from high frequency traders extracting information from sequential partial executions of large orders.

Shkilko and Sokolov conduct an interesting analysis that refutes some of the empirical findings above.[433] They examine instances of bad weather disrupting microwave trading networks and reducing the speed advantages of ultralow latency traders. When this occurs, adverse selection falls, trading costs decline, and liquidity improves. Interestingly, the authors show that their results depend on tick size. During periods of bad weather, latent liquidity emerges to narrow spreads when tick sizes are not binding. When tick sizes are binding,

---

[430] Jonathan Brogaard, Terrence Hendershott & Ryan Riordan, *Price Discovery without Trading: Evidence from Limit Orders* (working paper, 2016), https://papers.ssrn.com/sol3/papers.cfm?abstract_id=2655927.

[431] Menkveld, *supra* note 421.

[432] Brogaard et al., *supra* note 430.

[433] Andriy Shkilko & Konstantin Sokolov, *Every Cloud has a Silver Lining: Fast Trading, Microwave Connectivity and Trading Costs* (working paper, 2016), https://papers.ssrn.com/sol3/papers.cfm?abstract_id=2848562.

latent liquidity improves quoted depth. The authors also show that with respect to the use of limit orders by informed traders, when tick sizes bind and queue lengths are long, these traders switch to liquidity-taking marketable orders.

The empirical academic literature is generally consistent with the view that HFT is beneficial to liquidity and pricing efficiency. Though the results are not without exceptions, they are surprisingly consistent across studies and markets. While this is a welcome result from a regulatory perspective, other issues remain. Below we touch upon some of the additional areas of concern with respect to HFT.[434]

3.3.2 Arms Race and Fairness Considerations

Market observers have recently become concerned about an arms race developing among cutting-edge high frequency trading operations. These ultralow latency traders seek to get any advantage they can in the contest to be first to the market to execute or cancel an order. Examples include the 825-mile fiber optic cable installed by Spread Networks between New York and Chicago, at a cost of over $300 million. Fiber-optic linkage already existed between these two cities, and the purpose of this cable was to find the shortest possible path, and hence the least time of travel, between the two cities. Several years later, Anova Technologies, in a game of one-upmanship, bettered this technology by installing yet-faster microwave and millimeter-wave lasers to communicate between these two cities, bypassing optical cable entirely. Hibernia Networks, a global telecommunications firm, has created the Hibernia Express, the 4600-km transatlantic fiber optic cable designed to carry trading and other financial data between market centers in the U.S., London, and Europe.

Exchanges themselves do everything they can to maximize their speed of throughput and minimize their own latency. For example, NASDAQ's matching engine is capable of a sustained 100,000 orders per second at a matching latency of less than 40 microseconds. BATS' exchange-level latency is less than 200 microseconds, which is the time it takes for BATS to accept, process, and fill a member order, as measured from outside the BATS firewall. In addition, BATS can process over 400,000 peak messages per second. Contrast that to execution times of 20 years ago when executions were measured in seconds or even minutes.

Today, exchanges use high-speed private intermarket linkages, but until as recently as 2007, exchanges communicated via the ITS. The ITS Plan restricted the ability of exchange and NASD (now FINRA) members to trade-through the better-priced quotations of other markets. Sometimes described as

---

[434] Flash crashes, whose causes can also be traced, in part, to high frequency trading, are treated separately in Section 3.5.

"two tin cans and a string," this was a linkage mechanism that transmitted quote commitments for a trade. Any receiving exchange was allowed at least 30 seconds to respond to a trading commitment, which in turn could not be canceled during those 30 seconds. That meant that anyone using the ITS granted the receiving trade exchange a 30-second option to trade against their order. Put in place to ensure that regional exchanges were integrated with the primary markets on the East Coast, it should not be surprising that such a system was very unpopular with remote traders.

Today the speed of light has become the binding constraint for many aspects of intermarket communication. This is reflected in the rise of co-location services, whereby exchange seeks to locate their members' servers that house proprietary trading execution systems as close as possible to the matching engine of the exchange. Exchanges charge a tiered fee for doing so, with servers having the closest proximity to the matching engine paying the steepest co-location fees.

In many respects, there is nothing new about this race for greater speed of market access.[435] In the 19th century, a member of the Rothschild family was alleged to have earned a small fortune in London stock market by trading on advanced knowledge of the outcome of the battle of Waterloo. More recently, telegraph, and then telephone, and then handheld electronic communication, has improved access and speed to the floor from outside the exchange. Yet none of these innovations have until now bumped up against the physical limit of communication. Low latency traders desire for the fastest possible access to market centers stems from their desire to be first in the queue for execution. It is doubtful that any social benefits arise from the incremental efficiency of prices over millisecond horizons, and the behavior is seen by many as wasteful.

Per-unit profits of high frequency traders are small as their flow-based business is fundamentally different than the traditional equity trading businesses of decades ago. Brogaard et al. estimate revenues for HFT at about $.04 per $1,000 traded, and cite to public financial data documenting expenses of about two-thirds of trading revenues.[436] The total profitability of the operation arises from the scale and scalability of large high frequency trading operations. The authors document that high frequency traders only make profits on the larger stocks they trade.

Various suggestions have been made to temper this arms race. Budish, Cramton, and Shim argue that a solution can be found in periodic batch

---

[435] For example, see the discussion in Vincent Glode, Richard C. Green & Richard Lowery, *Financial Expertise as an Arms Race*, 67 J. FIN. 1723 (2012).

[436] Jonathan Brogaard, Terrence Hendershott & Ryan Riordan, *High-Frequency Trading and Price Discovery*, 27. REV. FIN. STUD. 2267 (2014).

auctions.[437] The authors suggest that continuous markets be replaced by periodic double auctions, occurring as often as every 100 milliseconds. They argue that short-lived arbitrage opportunities arise from market design and limited processing opportunities, leading to a socially wasteful arms race for speed advantages. By batching auctions, speed advantages would be negated as the first-come first-served characteristic of continuous markets would no longer characterize the allocations of batch auctions. While interesting as a theoretical construction, integrating such a platform into the national market system as a registered exchange would require a substantial rewrite of the rules. Among other consideration, Rule 600 of Regulation NMS states that the quotes of a public exchange are afforded protected status only as long as they are "immediately and automatically" accessible. NMS Rule 611 further requires that trades be executed against the best protected quote, which would likely be problematic for an exchange but pauses to aggregate trades every 100 milliseconds.

A second solution that has been proposed, and in some instances implemented, is the "speed bump," an intentional delay that slows down access and messaging to the market center. The most well-known instance of this occurs on the new U.S. exchange IEX, which was previously organized as an ATS. IEX creates a 350-microsecond delay by running all external communications through a coil of fiber-optic cable. By creating this delay, IEX argues they have created a market ill-suited to the latency arbitrage strategies of high frequency traders and have effectively created a "safe space" for uninformed non-HFT market participants who wish to avoid being adversely selected against. IEX and its founder, Brad Katsuyama, were the protagonists of Michael Lewis's popular book *Flash Boys* [438] when the market center was still an ATS. Since becoming an exchange on June 17, 2016, IEX's market share has remained low at approximately 2.2%.[439] So while the speed bump may be a potential solution to the wasteful arms race, it is too soon to draw any definitive conclusions about its commercial acceptance by the marketplace.[440]

---

[437] Eric Budish, Peter Cramton & John Shim, *The High-Frequency Arms Race: Frequent Batch Auctions as a Market Design Response*, 130 Q. J. ECON. (2015).

[438] MICHAEL LEWIS, FLASH BOYS: A WALL STREET REVOLT (2014).

[439] Data taken from BATS (http://www.bats.com/us/equities/market_statistics/) for the 30 days ending March 10, 2017.

[440] Chen, Foley, and Goldstein study the effects of a speed bump introduced on the TSX Alpha system in Canada and show that the system decreases aggregate liquidity via its effect on other market centers. *See* Haoming Chen, Sean Foley, Michael A. Goldstein & Thomas Ruf, *The Value of a Millisecond: Harnessing*

Perhaps more concerning than the social wasteful aspect of the latency arms race is how such competition alters the public's perception of the fairness of equity markets. Michael Lewis, *Flash Boys* author, made famous the notion that U.S. equity markets are "rigged," when in fact many of the examples he cited were instances of market participants competing according to rules laid out by the SEC. Such confusion is far from harmless, as a loss of faith in the fairness of our capital markets can lead to decreased investment, higher cost of capital, and real effects on public firms. It can also give rise to intervention by Congress in ways that are less than productive. If legislators discover their constituents believe they are not getting a fair shake in U.S. capital markets, history has shown they will not hesitate to act and unilaterally impose legislative solutions where such solutions may not be warranted.

3.3.3 Order Types

One does not have to go too far back in time for the basic trading decision with respect to order type to be between a market and a limit order, with perhaps additional consideration given to a few rarely used modifiers such as immediate-or-cancel, all-or-none, or fill-or-kill. Today, the situation is far more complex. Public exchanges typically have between 25 and 50 different order types, many of them either rarely used or used only by very sophisticated traders such as high frequency traders to accomplish targeted goals.[441] According to KCG, when the number of exchanges is coupled with the number of order types offered by each exchange, a trader has a choice between over 300 order types and exchange destinations. KCG has created an Appendix to describe various order types that runs to 15 pages.[442]

Why are there so many order types? There is likely more than one reason for this. One reason relates to the different demands of the various constituencies that trade in any market center. High-touch traders or traditional algorithmic traders may only make use of a very small number of order types, such as market, limit, ISO, and IOC. High frequency traders, on the other hand, are able to use the other order types tailored for particular situations that the

---

Information in Fast, Fragmented Markets (working paper, 2016), https://papers.ssrn.com/sol3/papers.cfm?abstract_id=2860359.

[441] In a November 2012 Traders magazine article, Chris Concannon, CEO of BATS, is quoted as saying that BATS Global Markets itself has more than 2,000 order types. It is not clear how he arrives at this high a number, and it may be the result of computing the permutations that result from the various input parameters that define an order.

[442] *See* Mackintosh, *supra* note 402.

HFT strategies are designed to address. Second, a number of these order types arise because of the complex working of Regulation NMS and its protected quotes. For example, orders linked to price sliding generally stem from Regulation NMS's prohibition on displaying orders that lock or cross markets. The liquidity seeking order that wishes to avoid paying take fees would normally immediately execute if, when it was placed, it was immediately marketable. Price sliding algorithms reprice the order a minimum variation below the contra side of the market and continuously adjust the limit price so as to avoid crossing the market and paying take fees, while still preserving market display at the allowable minimum variation price. There are many variations on the price sliding algorithms.

There are two primary concerns with the large number of order types. First, they add substantial complexity to the marketplace, making it difficult to understand how all these orders interact. A case in point is the BATS error in allowing its own price-sliding orders to trade-through the protected quotes in the current NBBO, in violation of Rule 611 of Regulation NMS.[443] While the economic magnitude of this mistake was small, it is representative of the complexity in today's marketplace. The second concern is the advantage that a large array of complex order types affords to sophisticated traders and institutions over less skilled market participants. The more sophisticated traders can make greater use of these various order types and, in conjunction with their low latency trading systems, gain a meaningful advantage over less adept traders.

Note that in such a world it is not enough for a non-HFT market participant to merely content itself with a small set of order types. As an example, consider the case of a "hide not slide" order.[444] It works similarly to the price sliding order described above with one important exception. Whereas the price sliding order will initially reprice the displayed portion of the order to be one minimum variation below the contra side of the NBBO, "hide not slide" orders will simply go dark and not display at all when the order locks or crosses the market. When the NBBO moves so that the original order no longer locks or crosses, it will not only be redisplayed, but will move to the front of the queue at the display price, achieving an advantage over other orders that were active in the market and tracking the spread through price sliding over the ensuing period. A less sophisticated trader making use of simpler order types, including the simple

---

[443] *See BATS Jan. 9 Notification of System Issue - Revised Jan. 25* (2013), http://www.bats.com/us/equities/notices/41072/status/.

[444] For a description of how this order type works, see Scott Patterson & Jenny Strasburg, *How "Hide not Slide" Orders Work*, WALL ST. J., Sept. 19, 2012, https://www.wsj.com/articles/SB10000872396390444481270457760584026315 0860.

price sliding order, would not be aware that they were sacrificing their queue positions to these "hide not slide" orders.

It also appears that some market center operators were less than clear with their market's participants about available order types. For example, in 2015 the SEC charged UBS with failing to disclose to all subscribers of one of its ATSs the existence of an order type called the PrimaryPegPlus, which allowed certain subscribers to buy and sell securities by placing orders priced in increments of less than one penny. The SEC stated the UBS was prohibited from accepting such orders under Regulation NMS. By doing so, UBS allowed users of the PrimaryPegPlus order to jump ahead of other orders placed in conformance with Regulation NMS rules at whole penny increments. In another example, Direct Edge Holdings, which operates the EDGEA and EDGEX exchange markets, settled charges with the SEC that they had failed to disclose the operation of price-sliding orders on their exchanges.[445] The SEC charged that while exchange rules described a single price-sliding order, there were in fact three different types of price-sliding orders in place including a Price Adjust, a Single Re-Price, and the Hide Not Slide order type. The exchanges were alleged to have selectively disclosed information about order types to a subset of members, creating a risk that not all markets in a participant would understand how exchange order types operated.

In June 2014, SEC Chairman Mary Jo White gave a speech entitled "Enhancing Our Market Equity Structure," in which she requested that the equity exchanges conduct a comprehensive review of their order types and how they operate in practice, and as part of this review, consider appropriate rule changes to help clarify the nature of their order types.[446] Though many of these order types exist to facilitate compliance with the various strictures of Regulation NMS, it may also be possible to comprehensively reduce collective complexity of the array of order types. While some of these types may serve to reduce message traffic by, for example, automating cancel and replace functions induced by the order protection rule, others may be easier to eliminate. IEX, which only began operation to year ago, has on its rulebooks only five types of orders.[447] Perhaps other exchanges and ATSs can be induced to follow suit.

---

[445] In the Matter of EDGA Exchange, Inc., and EDGX Exchange, Inc., Respondents, Administrative Proceeding, Release No. 74032, File No. 3-16332 (Jan. 12, 2015).

[446] Mary Jo White, *Enhancing Our Equity Market Structure*, June 5, 2014, www.sec.gov/News/Speech/Detail/Speech/1370542004312#.U5HI-fmwJiw.

[447] IEX order types are Market, Limit, Midpoint Peg, Primary Peg, and Discretionary Peg. *See* IEX Rule 11.190, *Investors Exchange Rulebook*, https://iextrading.com/docs/Investors%20Exchange%20Rule%20Book.pdf.

3.4 Best Execution Considerations

Broker-dealers who handle customer orders have an obligation to obtain best execution for the orders. Though not precisely defined in any SEC rules, the obligation derives from a common law agency duty obligating an agent to act exclusively in the principal's best interest. This is true regardless of whether the broker-dealer trades the customer order in an agency or principal capacity. FINRA Rule 5310 on Best Execution provides that "[i]n any transaction for or with a customer or a customer of another broker-dealer, a member and persons associated with a member shall use reasonable diligence to ascertain the best market for the subject security and buy or sell in such market so that the resultant price to the customer is as favorable as possible under prevailing market conditions."[448]

While obtaining the best price for the customer is of paramount importance, the rule also contemplates consideration of other factors including the possibility of price dis-improvement, execution speed, likelihood of execution of limit orders, and customer needs and expectations. In addition, the SEC requires that "broker-dealers deciding where to route or execute small customer orders in listed or OTC securities must carefully evaluate the extent to which this order flow would be afforded better terms if executed in a market or with a market maker offering price improvement opportunities. In conducting the requisite evaluation of its internal order handling procedures, a broker-dealer must *regularly and rigorously examine execution quality likely to be obtained from the different markets or market makers* trading a security."[449] Thus, though the number and type of trading venues and market centers change, speed increases, and technology evolves, the obligation of a broker-dealer for best execution of customer orders remains a constant.

Certain institutional features of present-day U.S. equity markets pose challenges for the consistent application of best execution principles. Many of these features arise from legacy practices that began years or even decades ago

---

[448] *See* FINRA Rule 5310 (Best Execution and Interpositioning), http://finra.complinet.com/en/display/display_main.html?rbid=2403&element_id=10455.

[449] Securities Exchange Act Release No. 37619A (Sept. 6, 1996), 61 Fed. Reg. 48290, ("Order Handling Rules"), at section III.C.2 (emphasis added); *see also Best Execution*, NASD Notice to Members 01-22, at 205 (Apr. 2001) ("At a minimum, firms should conduct such [regular and rigorous] reviews on a quarterly basis; however, members should consider, based on the firm's business, whether more frequent reviews are needed, particularlty [sic] in light of the monthly market center statistics made available").

when the structure of equity markets was quite different than it is today. Yet these institutional practices persist and are allowed under securities laws and current interpretations of best execution. We detail two of these institutional features below.

3.4.1 Payment for Order Flow

Payment for order flow is a long-standing practice whereby a market center offers to pay a routing broker compensation in exchange for sending orders to the venue. One of the earliest practitioners of payment for order flow was third-market firm Madoff Securities. When stocks traded in increments of 1/8th of a dollar, Madoff offered to pay firms with large amounts of customer orders, such as Charles Schwab and Fidelity, $.01-$.02 per share in exchange for sending their customer orders to Madoff. Firms such as Madoff were interested in purchasing such flow because retail customer order flow is uninformed, allowing market makers to avoid adverse selection and profitably trade at quotes determined in the exchange market.[450] Though the practice raised concerns about conflicts of interest, it was allowed by the SEC because it reasoned that such payments didn't necessarily violate best execution obligations since customers obtained prices at least as good as they would have obtained in exchange markets. Furthermore, if the market for order flow payments was competitive, customers of retail brokerages might expect to see the benefits of such payments in either in the form of lower trading commissions or improved services at the introducing brokers. The SEC required these payments to be disclosed to investors on confirmation statements, account statements, and new account opening forms.[451]

Today, some of the largest firms that "internalize" retail orders include Citadel Securities, KCG Holdings, and UBS Securities. These are sophisticated firms that internally trade against purchased customer orders, taking the opposite side of the customer when possible, and routing out to market centers in other instances. The firms use sophisticated computer algorithms and monitor multiple market centers in an effort to discharge the duties of best execution that they inherit from the introducing brokers who route their order flow to them. The

---

[450] For examples of the effects of informed trading on market prices and quotations, see Lawrence R. Glosten & Paul R. Milgrom, *Bid, Ask and Transaction Prices in a Specialist Market With Heterogeneously Informed Traders*, 14 J. FIN. ECON. 71 (1985) and David Easley & Maureen O'Hara, *Price, Trade Size, and Information in Securities Market*, 19 J. FIN. ECON. 69 (1987).

[451] Payment for Order Flow, Final Rule, Release No. 34-34902, File No. S7-29-93 (Apr. 3, 1995).

SEC has made it clear that such firms do not discharge their best execution duties merely by guaranteeing to fill customer orders at the NBBO. The internalizing broker-dealers must offer customers a chance of price improvement or execution at prices superior to the best bid and offer in the national market.

Of course, inferring what these prices are is a difficult exercise. For example, prices referenced in such calculations require determination of the NBBO, which comes from the SIP data feeds. This is assembled by these data processing utilities, who aggregate data from exchange venues, compute the best prices across all markets, and disseminate these data in a uniform nondiscriminatory manner. The SIP prices generally form the basis for determining the best prices in the market for most internalizers. However, proprietary firms that trade against incoming order flow are not limited to obtaining only SIP data--they are free to subscribe to private linkages from various market centers. SIP data contain only top of book prices and depth at each market center. Private linkage direct feeds, however, can contain detailed depth of book information and are generally disseminated with lower latency than the SIP data feeds.

Because the determination of what constitutes the best prices available in the market must be made on a continuous basis, the actual obligations of the broker-dealer with respect to best execution are not well-defined. The industry has generally interpreted the SIP NBBO to define the best prices available in the market, but it is not clear the regulator shares this view. Uncertainty around the benchmark for determining a broker-dealer's best execution obligations is unproductive and should be clarified by the SEC or FINRA. Conflict around this situation was made clear in the recent administrative action against an internalizing broker-dealer. The SEC charged that the broker-dealer made misleading statements to its introducing broker-dealer clients about the manner by which it would seek to obtain the best price for customer orders, either through internalization or via routing to other market centers.[452]

The situation is further complicated because of how the market data are priced. The SIP data are priced through a process that is regulated by the SEC. For enhanced market data that contain depth of book and other information, however, the SEC has taken a lighter hand with respect to pricing and has generally left it to market forces to determine these prices. As such, OTC market makers and internalizers may not consume direct feed data from all market centers, leading different internalizers to compute different contemporaneous market prices.

While the SEC could act to prohibit the practice of payment for order flow and the attendant practice of internalization, given that it has been allowed

---

[452] In the Matter of Citadel Securities LLC, Administrative Proceeding, File No. 3-17772 (Jan. 13, 2017).

for over 20 years, an outright prohibition seems unlikely at this point. A possible solution is to more precisely define the obligations of the various parties to these transactions. First are the obligations of the introducing broker that receives the payment for order flow and routes customer orders to the internalizing dealer. Such brokers do not merely transfer their obligation of best execution to the executing broker-- they retain responsibility for the original order. The terms of trade offered by the internalizing broker are usually spelled out in a precisely written contract between the two parties. Appropriate disclosures to end investors, including disclosures about the economics of the payment arrangements, seem a likely place to begin the improvement.

With respect to the executing broker, the situation is more difficult. These firms have large scale internalization execution processes. They are difficult for a regulator to audit, and thus assurances that a customer's order received appropriate treatment are difficult to substantiate, and often come down to question of what an order would have received under some counterfactual execution practice. Ultimately, the answer may lie in more refined disclosures of execution quality. At present, execution quality data in the form of Rule 605 reports for market centers, and Rule 606 reports on broker routing, are produced on a highly aggregated basis. Data are produced monthly and are binned relatively coarsely. If more detailed and precise execution quality reporting is produced, this may facilitate both better audits of executing brokers and enhance competition between internalizers. This was the original purpose of the predecessor execution quality reports,[453] but given the changes in the technology of trading, the Rule 605 and 606 reports no longer effectively serve this purpose.

3.4.2 Maker-Taker Fees

Another form of payment for order flow that occurs on market centers such as exchanges and ATSs is a maker-taker fee. This fee model is a pricing structure whereby market centers charge traders a "take" fee for removing liquidity by trading against a resting order, and rebate to traders a "make" fee for placing liquidity on the market's limit order book that subsequently gets executed.[454] Rule 610 of Regulation NMS requires these fees to be no more than 0.3 cents per-share. However, maker-taker pricing is not a consequence of Regulation NMS, as the practice predated the rule by at least a decade when the Island ECN used a maker-taker pricing model to attract order flow to its book.

---

[453] *See* Disclosure of Order Execution and Routing Practices, SEC Release No. 34-43590, File No. S7-16-00, creating the 11Ac1-5 and 11Ac1-6 ("Dash 5" and "Dash 6") reports.

[454] There are also venues that use an inverted fee schedule, charging for "making" liquidity and paying rebates for "taking" liquidity.

Maker-taker pricing in today's market is a dynamic process, and traders with order flow to route pay careful attention to the pricing charges and rebates. Maker-taker pricing is of concern for a number of reasons, and a complete treatment of the subject is far beyond the space pages that can be allotted to the topic in this chapter. However, one of the most important concerns is that these payments create a conflict for brokers who have an obligation to seek best execution for their customers' orders. Instead of routing orders to the markets with the best expected outcome, brokers might seek to maximize the value of the rebates they receive, while minimizing the cost of the fees they pay. This is true for both marketable and nonmarketable orders. Battalio et al. examined the routing decisions for nonmarketable orders by a group of brokers and found that a number of brokers routed these nonmarketable orders to the market centers that paid the highest rebates.[455] The authors felt that the data indicated that these routing decisions were inconsistent with the brokers' duty of best execution. At a Senate hearing in 2014, a senior executive of one of the routing firms, TD Ameritrade, testified that the firm had a policy of sending its nonmarketable orders to market centers that paid the highest rebate. While there has been some industry critique of the Battalio study, it seems clear that the potential for such a conflict is very real.

Proponents of maker-taker pricing argued that it is a competitive reality of today's marketplace and that exchanges compete vigorously along these dimensions. Were maker-taker pricing to be prohibited for public exchanges, they would be at a disadvantage relative to unregistered (as an exchange) venues such as broker-dealers and ATSs that do not have prohibitions against paying inducements or charging fees. If maker-taker payments were prohibited, volume might migrate to internalizers and dark ATS venues, which, as discussed earlier in the section, would be concerning to regulators and other market participants.

Finally, critics have observed that because of Regulation NMS prohibitions against displaying sub-penny quotations, maker-taker fees are not reflected in market quotations, harming pricing transparency and violating the spirit of the firm quote rule. The price you see at a given market may not be the net price you will pay if you trade that market. They argue that either prices should be inclusive of these fees, if they are to be allowed at all.

If the SEC decides that maker-taker pricing is a problem they need to resolve, there are a number of paths that could be taken. First, there could be a requirement that fees paid and rebates received be passed through to the ultimate investor. Second, the 0.3 cents per share limit could be reduced or set to zero, eliminating maker-taker pricing. Finally, the requirements against quoting sub-

---

[455] Robert Battalio, Shane A. Corwin & Robert Jennings, *Can Brokers Have it all? On the Relation Between Make-Take Fees and Limit Order Execution Quality* (working paper, 2015), https://papers.ssrn.com/sol3/papers.cfm?abstract_id=2367462.

penny increments could be relaxed and the maker-taker fees could be reflected in displayed quotes. These solutions have been previously discussed and have been found wanting for various reasons.

More realistic perhaps is to approach the problem from the perspective of disclosure. Executing brokers, and the introducing brokers that route to them, could be required to disclose their routing policies with respect to maker-taker fees. Executing brokers would be required to disclose how they factor the existence and size of rebates and fees into their routing decisions. Because this routing is automated and is encoded into software, the disclosure should be readily verifiable. The introducing brokers would be required to disclose how the maker-taker routing practices of the various potential executing brokers affect their choice of executing broker. This disclosure could be further enhanced by quantification of the per-share rebates earned and taker fees paid by the executing broker. In addition, introducing brokers could be required to disclose how their policy toward executing broker selection is affected by payment for order flow fees received.

Regardless of which solution, if any, is taken, brokers retain the responsibility for best execution toward customer orders. FINRA and the SEC could consider issuing additional guidance with respect to best execution obligations as they relate to maker-taker fees. It is not clear what form such guidance would take, but such disclosure would allow exchanges to retain the competitive benefits of maker-taker pricing vis-à-vis the less regulated ATS and dealer markets centers.

*　　*　　*　　*　　*　　*

As the above discussion shows, there are a number of challenges concerning the application of the duty of best execution to today's markets. Yet the very flexibility of the agency duty may in fact be its most valuable trait. The obligation to seek the best terms of trade for the order is, by its very definition, flexible and adaptable to the current market environment. Brokers, and especially brokers who route high volumes of retail orders, are the market participants most able to make judgments about which venues are best for customer orders at any one moment in time. Rather than viewing best execution as a problem for today's environment that needs to be solved, it may be better to view it as the solution to the thornier market structure problems. A renewed and vigorous approach on the part of the SEC and FINRA to best execution oversight may cause introducing and executing brokers to be increasingly vigilant of their routing decisions for retail orders. Regulators could make it clear that they expect such brokers to be fully informed on issues such as current maker-taker pricing structures, order forms, adverse selection intensity, and other features that determine how well a given retail order will fare in at any particular market center.

Such an approach may require reconsideration of a basic aspect of the application of best execution principles. To date regulators have not generally looked at the best execution on an order-by-order basis, but have simply required that brokers periodically "regularly and rigorously" assess their routing decisions, considering both venues to which orders were routed and those to which they did not route. Given the advances in routing technology and the fact that routing decisions are now made on an order-by-order basis, perhaps best execution requirement should also begin to reflect this order-by-order feature. FINRA has already contemplated such standards for larger-sized orders, but has yet to bring such standards to smaller retail orders.[456] Were such a proposal to be made by regulators, it would surely raise substantial concern among industry participants. Great care would need to be taken to avoid creating an environment where executing brokers are judged on an *ex-post* basis and held responsible for statistically unfavorable outcomes for retail orders.

3.5 System Robustness

The success of our equity markets depends on a belief that trading venues will operate in a reliable and fair manner. In recent years, however, there have been numerous widely reported events that have raised concerns, such as: the May 6, 2010 flash crash; system shutdowns at NYSE, NASDAQ, BATS and other venues; and fines levied against high frequency traders, trading venues, and other market participants for improper behavior. As well, technological advances have increased the likelihood that a seemingly minor operational problem at a single entity can spread rapidly across the entire system and cause harm to a wide range of market participants.

These concerns should be taken seriously. In today's highly charged, populist political environment, the public's perception of market robustness and fairness may matter more than the reality. If the tide of public opinion decides that the market is rigged or unfair, then there is the risk that market rules and regulations will be set based on political calculations, rather than based on objective evidence and careful deliberations.

To address concerns about system disruptions and other technological failures, in 2014 the SEC adopted the Regulation Systems Compliance and Integrity (Regulation SCI). This regulation is designed to: (i) reduce the occurrence of systems issues; (ii) improve resiliency when systems problems do

---

[456] *See* NASD Notice to Members, 01-22, Best Execution, April 2001, at n. 13. Also, see the discussion in FINRA Regulatory Notice 15-46, Best Execution, November 2015, at 3.

occur; and (iii) enhance the SEC's oversight and enforcement of securities market technology infrastructure.[457] A large component of Regulation SCI is requiring certain entities to have written policies and procedures to deal with issues related to the capacity, integrity, resiliency, availability, and security of their systems.[458] In addition to the prevention of system issues, Regulation SCI considers how to contain and minimize problems should they occur.

Regulation SCI applies to "SCI entities" which include SROs, alternative trading systems with trading volumes exceeding specified volume thresholds, disseminators of consolidated market data, and certain exempt clearing agencies. Since each system disruption has unique causes, it is a challenge for the regulation to define what constitutes a "major SCI event" requiring the SCI entity to disseminate information about the disruption. Risk management after an event can be slow relative to the speed of the overall market.

Importantly, Regulation SCI would not apply to HFT market makers and broker-dealers. As such, had the rule been in effect in 2012, it would not have protected the market from the severe adverse effects of the accidental inclusion of obsolete code in the automated routing system at Knight Capital. In that incident, while handling just 212 small retail orders, the system routed millions of orders into the market over a 45-minute period, obtaining 4 million executions in 154 stocks for more than 397 million shares.[459] The resulting unwanted long and short positions in these shares led to over $460 million in losses for Knight Capital, and perhaps more importantly, caused severe price dislocations in many securities.[460]

The scope of Regulation SCI is limited and does not cover many of the most pressing concerns about system robustness and integrity in U.S. trading markets. In this section, we consider five additional areas of potential concern: (a) flash events; (b) episodic liquidity and the role of designated market makers; (c) potential breakdowns in the creation and destruction mechanism for exchange traded funds; (d) quote stuffing and latency arbitrage; and (e) cybersecurity. We conclude by examining the potential implications of using blockchain technology in trading markets.

---

[457] SEC, REGULATION SCI, https://www.sec.gov/spotlight/regulation-sci.shtml.

[458] *See* SEC Release No. 34-73639, File No. 67-01-13 (Feb. 3, 2015).

[459] In the Matter of Knight Capital Americas LLC Respondent, SEC Administrative Proceeding File No. 3-15570, https://www.sec.gov/litigation/admin/2013/34-70694.pdf.

[460] For 75 of the stocks, Knight's executions comprised more than 20 percent of the trading volume and contributed to price moves of greater than five percent. *Id.* at 6.

3.5.1 Flash Events

Market breaks are not a new phenomenon. An entire chapter (Chapter XIII) of the original Special Study focused on the market break of May 28, 1962. As these two passages from the study illustrate, many of the issues in 1962 are still relevant today:

> The avalanche of orders which came into the market during this period subjected the market mechanisms to extraordinary strain, and in many respects they did not function in a normal way. Particularly significant were the lateness of the tape and the consequent inability of investors to predict accurately the prices at which market orders would be executed.
> [...]
> The history of the May 28 market break reveals that a complex interaction of causes and effects--including rational and emotional motivations as well as a variety of mechanisms and pressures--may suddenly create a downward spiral of great velocity and force.[461]

In today's markets, one area of concern has been whether high frequency trading promotes sudden and unexpected price dislocations, which are popularly referred to as "flash crashes." Public attention first focused on flash crashes with the events of May 6, 2010, when an algorithm rapidly sold 75,000 S&P500 e-mini futures contracts. The index was already down 4% by the time the large sell order hit at 2:30 PM. The index fell a further 5 to 6% and then recovered most of the decline within the space of about a half hour. In the initial joint report of the CFTC and SEC,[462] these price movements were attributed to a sequence of events including the exhaustion of the liquidity supply high frequency traders, traditional buyers, and cross market arbitrageurs who spread the price pressure to other markets. Eventually a "hot potato" effect developed where blocks of futures contracts rapidly moved among the same set of traders. Depth fell, liquidity vanished, and prices crashed. When a five second pause was triggered on the CME, prices began to recover and within minutes they had risen to almost their previous levels. In a follow-on report several months later, the SEC

---

[461] Special Study (part 4) at pp. 859, 861.

[462] REPORT OF THE STAFFS OF THE CFTC AND SEC TO THE JOINT ADVISORY COMMITTEE ON EMERGING REGULATORY ISSUES, FINDINGS REGARDING THE MARKET EVENTS OF MAY 6, 2010 (2010), https://www.sec.gov/news/studies/2010/marketevents-report.pdf

made a set of recommendations including the implementation and coordination of "limit up/limit down" trading halts,[463] pre-trade risk safeguards to prevent access the markets without appropriate risk controls, and improved controls over algorithmic trading strategies.[464]

On October 15, 2014, the U.S. Treasury market severely dislocated in a "melt-up" during which over a 13-minute period the yield of the 10-year government bond experienced a 16 basis point drop and subsequent rebound. According to a subsequent joint regulatory report,[465] HFT firms withdrew from their market-making function as the dislocation proceeded, causing liquidity to fall. This in turn caused different business units of individual high frequency trading firms to unintentionally engage in self-trading. This higher trading volume slowed the pace of trading. The report cited no single factor as the cause of the event.

On August 24, 2015, broad-based exchange traded funds (ETFs) declined sharply before and at the 9:30 a.m. opening of the market. The $65 billion iShares Core S&P 500 ETF fell by over 25% in the opening minutes of the session,[466] and the equity of KKR fell by almost 60% from its previous close before recovering. Though the exact causes of this dislocation are still being debated, the operation of "limit up/limit down" halts put in place after the May 2010 flash crash appear to have played a role.[467,468]

---

[463] SEC Release 34-67091, File No. 4-631 (May 31, 2012).

[464] The SEC also alleged in a civil complaint that spoofing activity of a U.K. based trader caused artificial prices to exist. *See* Complaint, CFTC v. Sarao, Case 1:15-cv-03398 (N.D. Ill. 2015) at ¶¶ 1-2.

[465] U.S. DEPARTMENT OF THE TREASURY, BOARD OF GOVERNORS OF THE FEDERAL RESERVE SYSTEM, FEDERAL RESERVE BANK OF NEW YORK, U.S. SECURITIES AND EXCHANGE COMMISSION, U.S. COMMODITY FUTURES TRADING COMMISSION, JOINT STAFF REPORT: THE U.S. TREASURY MARKET ON OCTOBER 15, 2014 (2015), https://www.treasury.gov/press-center/press-releases/Documents/Joint_Staff_Report_Treasury_10-15-2015.pdf.

[466] We consider the role of ETFs in more detail in a later section.

[467] The October 7, 2016 UK Sterling flash event is another example of a sudden market dislocation. For details, see BANK OF INTERNATIONAL SETTLEMENTS, THE STERLING 'FLASH EVENT' OF 7 OCTOBER 2016 (2017), https://www.bis.org/publ/mktc09.pdf

[468] Trading halts may be a problematic solution to flash events. As an alternative, Bethel, Leinweber, Rubel, and Wu explore the feasibility of an early warning system to predict flash crashes. *See* Wes Bethel, David Leinweber, Oliver Rubel & Kesheng Wu, *Federal Market Information Technology in the Post Flash Crash Era:*

Here, too, there is an academic literature on the subject, but unlike the topics of liquidity and pricing efficiency, the evidence is somewhat more mixed. Kirilenko, Kyle, Samadi, and Tuzun show that the trading patterns of high frequency traders did not change as prices fell during the May 6, 2010 event.[469] Aldrich, Grundfest, and Laughlin conclude that instability of the market data infrastructure contributed to the May 2010 flash crash, and emphasize that in a market dominated by algorithmic and high frequency trading, data integrity becomes a paramount issue.[470] Menkveld and Yueshen attribute the cause of the 2010 flash crash to the breakdown of cross-market arbitrage mechanisms.[471] Because the seller was forced to find sellers only in the E-mini market, this concentrated the effect of the decline. They point out that failed intermarket linkages can be costly for investors in highly fragmented markets. Easley, López de Prado, and O'Hara attribute the 2010 flash crash to the combination of automated market makers and increased order flow toxicity, which combined to cause market makers to withdraw their quotes and liquidate positions.[472] Interestingly, the authors propose contracting around liquidity provision conditional on times of high adverse selection.

Roles for Supercomputing (working paper, 2011), https://papers.ssrn.com/sol3/papers.cfm?abstract_id=1939522. When a flash crash is likely, a mechanism could be used to "slow" the market down, rather than using an abrupt trading halt.

[469] Andrei A. Kirilenko, Albert S. Kyle, Mehrdad Samadi & Tugkan Tuzun, *The Flash Crash: High-Frequency Trading in an Electronic Market*, 72 J. FIN. 967 (2017).

[470] Eric M. Aldrich, Joseph Grundfest & Gregory Laughlin, *The Flash Crash: A New Deconstruction* (working paper, 2017), https://papers.ssrn.com/sol3/papers.cfm?abstract_id=2721922.

[471] Albert J. Menkveld & Bart Z. Yueshen, *The Flash Crash: A Cautionary Tale About Highly Fragmented Markets*, MGMT. SCI. (forthcoming).

[472] David Easley, Marcos M. Lopez de Prado & Maureen O'Hara, *Flow Toxicity and Liquidity in a High-Frequency World*, 25 REV. FIN. STUD. 1457 (2012). Easley, Lopez de Prado, and O'Hara develop a measure of the toxicity of order flow, which captures the extent to which (algorithmic) market makers may be unknowingly providing liquidity at a loss. The measure is calculated by grouping consecutive trades across time according to the time required to trade an exogenous level of order flow. Within each group, the sign of price changes over one-minute periods is used to infer buyer- versus seller-oriented trades, which is then used to create a high frequency analog of the popular PIN measure. Easley, Lopez de Prado, and O'Hara show that this measure (VPIN) is a useful indicator of short-term volatility.

A notable contrast to the above papers is the study by Golub, Keane, and Poon.[473] The authors study four months of volatile prices over a period of six years and find that there were over 4,500 mini flash crashes in individual stocks over this period. They attribute the cause of these mini crashes to the use of intermarket sweep orders that scrape liquidity from the top-of-book market centers. Once these protected quotes are taken out, NMS rules permit traders to execute against the remaining unprotected orders of individual market centers, eating into the limit order book and ignoring superior prices available on other exchanges. They attribute these mini crashes to HFT and fragmented markets.

The lack of clear consensus by both regulators and academics as to the root causes of the various flash crashes suggests more work needs to be done. This should not be surprising given the tightly-coupled nature of the systems depend so integrally on data feeds, order types, and the pre-programmed behavior of automated trading systems. A potentially complicating aspect of flash crashes is the ability of SROs and regulators to break previously agreed-upon trades based on the notion that these trades were done at "clearly erroneous" prices.[474] If high frequency traders and their algorithms believe they have entered a period in which there is an increased probability that consummated transactions will, on an *ex-post* basis be negated on the basis of such a regulatory finding, they will not be able to appropriately manage the risk of their trading operations and hedge their positions. They can logically be expected to pull back from their market-making function, exacerbating liquidity issues at a time when market depth is most critically needed. That the infrequency of the major flash crashes makes their study more challenging should not dissuade regulators and researchers from seeking to better understand these complex interactions.

3.5.2 Episodic Liquidity and Designated Market Makers

Flash crashes, both market wide and stock specific), are a dramatic manifestation of episodic liquidity.[475] But even in the absence of flash crashes,

---

[473] Anton Golub, John Keane & Ser-Huang Poon, *High Frequency Trading and Mini Flash Crashes* (working paper, 2012), https://papers.ssrn.com/sol3/papers.cfm?abstract_id=2182097.

[474] *See, e.g.*, NASDAQ Rule 11890. Jurich, Maslar, and Roseman examine the effect of uncertainty regarding the possible cancellation of erroneous executions in U.S. markets. *See* Stephen N. Jurich, David A. Maslar & Brian S. Roseman, *Clearly Erroneous Executions*, 34 J. FIN. MKTS. 16 (2017).

[475] Carlin, Lobo, and Viswanathan provide a theoretic model of episodic liquidity. *See* Bruce I. Carlin, Miguel S. Lobo & S. Viswanathan, *Episodic Liquidity Crises: Cooperative and Predatory Trading*, 62 J. FIN. 2235 (2007).

liquidity can be fleeting in an environment in which its provision is primarily via high frequency traders, who can enter and exit the market as market conditions change. For this reason, it is important that market quality measures are considered in the time series, not only in averages.

The measurement of liquidity itself can be challenging in modern markets. Quote-based measures of liquidity, such as bid-ask spreads, effective spreads, inside depth, and round-trip costs, are less relevant to institutional traders in a world with fleeting quotes that have tiny spreads and little depth. To address this, Barardehi, Bernhardt, and Davies develop a new measure of liquidity based on the average per-dollar price impact of trading a fixed-dollar position of institutional trading size.[476] Using this measure in an asset pricing framework, they show that liquidity premia have risen somewhat in recent years, suggesting that institutional traders are pricing in higher liquidity risk.

Prior to the changes triggered by Regulation NMS, liquidity and price stability were provided by NYSE specialists and NASDAQ dealers. Those roles have been supplanted by high frequency traders acting as market makers. Most of these market makers have no formal obligations or designations, although the NYSE has designated certain Supplemental Liquidity Providers (SLPs) that are given monetary incentives to provide liquidity in assigned securities.[477] These market makers, however, do not have an affirmative obligation to provide liquidity and as a consequence, they may stop providing liquidity under certain market conditions. In such an environment, it is worthwhile asking whether human market makers can still play a role.

On the NYSE, the former specialist role has been effectively replaced by designated market makers (DMMs) that have mild obligations to maintain a fair and orderly market.[478] Their obligations are so loosely defined that the obligations are unlikely to have substantial impact. Clark-Joseph, Ye, and Zi, however, use an exogenous shock to the NYSE system to show that even with relatively weak obligations, these DMMs improve the overall market quality.[479] Clark-Joseph et al. do not have a conclusive explanation for why the DMMs

---

[476] Yashar H. Barardehi, Dan Bernhardt & Ryan J. Davies, *Trade-Time Based Measures of Liquidity* (working paper, 2016), https://papers.ssrn.com/sol3/papers.cfm?abstract_id=2749732.

[477] NYSE, SUPPLEMENTAL LIQUIDITY PROVIDERS, https://www.nyse.com/publicdocs/nyse/listing/fact_sheet_slps.pdf.

[478] NYSE, DESIGNATED MARKET MAKERS, https://www.nyse.com/publicdocs/nyse/listing/fact_sheet_dmm.pdf.

[479] Adam D. Clark-Joseph, Mao Ye & Chao Zi, *Designated Market Makers Still Matter: Evidence From Two Natural Experiments*, 126 J. FIN. ECON. 652 (2017).

provide liquidity under such weak obligations, but conjecture that the DMMs compete with each other on reputation for preferred stock allocations.

DMMs appear to play a valuable role in Canada as well. Anand and Venkataraman compare liquidity provision by endogenous liquidity providers and designated market makers on the Toronto Stock Exchange, and show that the DMMs reduce execution uncertainty by participating in undesirable trades.[480]

Some European markets have DMMs that are required, by contract, to keep the spread within certain binding limits. These DMMs receive compensation for providing this service. Anand et al. find that, on balance, firms contracting with designated liquidity providers on the Stockholm Stock Exchange experience a decreased cost of capital and significant improvements in market quality and price discovery.[481]

Until recently, issuers in U.S. markets have not been able to enter into a contract arrangement with a DMM to support the liquidity of their stock. In 2013, the SEC approved programs on a pilot basis to allow issuers of exchange-traded products to compensate market makers in those securities.[482] It is unclear whether these programs have been successful, as one of the largest ETF providers, BlackRock, announced in July 2016 that it was withdrawing from the program.[483] In light of this decision and other evidence on episodic liquidity, regulators and trading venues must decide what role designated market makers, with an affirmative obligation to provide liquidity, have in modern financial markets.

3.5.3 Exchange Traded Funds

Exchange Traded Funds (ETFs), and more generally, Exchange Traded Products (ETPs) are enormously popular. ETFs now have more than $2.614 trillion in assets.[484] Credit Suisse estimates that ETFs account for 30% of all U.S.

---

[480] Amber Anand & Kumar Venkataraman, *Market Conditions, Fragility, and the Economics of Market Making*, 121 J. FIN. ECON. 327 (2016).

[481] Amber Anand, Carsten Tanggaard & Daniel G. Weaver, *Paying for Market Quality*, 44 J. FIN. QUANT. ANALYSIS 1427 (2009).

[482] Dolgopolov provides an overview of the regulatory framework prohibiting issuer-to-market maker compensation, and the motivation for the pilot ETF programs. *See* Stanislav Dolgopolov, *Linking the Securities Market Structure and Capital Formation: Incentives for Market Makers?*, 16 U. PENN. J. BUS. L. 1 (2013).

[483] Jackie Noblett, *BlackRock Quits ETF Liquidity Pools*, FIN. TIMES., July 4, 2016, https://www.ft.com/content/e3257e1c-41dd-11e6-9b66-0712b3873ae1.

[484] *See* https://www.ici.org/research/stats/etf/etfs_01_17.

trading by value, and 23% by share volume.[485] More and more retail investors are electing to buy ETFs rather than have direct ownership of individual stocks or owning open-end mutual funds. Notably, the vast majority of ETFs, by assets under management, are issued by only four firms (Blackrock, Vanguard, State Street Global Advisors, and Invesco Powershares).[486] The magnitude of trading in ETFs, combined with their special features, have led to them being a potential source of stress for overall market conditions.

Authorized participants ensure that the price of an ETF tracks that of its constituents through a complex process of creation and redemption. This arbitrage process can break down when there are trading halts or other dislocations in the market. The magnitude of ETFs combined with breakdowns in the arbitrage relationship have introduced an important potential source of fragility in trading markets. Ben-David et al. find that during turbulent market episodes, arbitrage is limited and ETF prices diverge from those of the underlying securities.[487]

On August 24, 2015, delays in the opening of trading for many stocks, combined with a trading pause in S&P 500 Index futures, lead to a breakdown of the arbitrage relationship between ETFs and their constituents. Over the next 30 minutes, there was a crash in the prices of many ETFs, resulting in prices that were far below those of their no arbitrage values. Limit Up-Limit Down (LULD) trading halts appear to have compounded the problem. 327 ETFs were hit with five-minute trading halts that morning, with 11 ETFs halted 10 or more times.[488] Notably, many of the LULD halts occurred in smaller ETFs with lower

---

[485] Robin Wigglesworth, *ETFs are Eating the U.S. Stock Market*, FIN. TIMES, Jan. 24, 2017, https://www.ft.com/content/6dabad28-e19c-11e6-9645-c9357a75844a.

[486] *ETF League Table as of March 14, 2017* (Mar. 15, 2017), http://www.etf.com/sections/etf-league-tables/etf-league-table-2017-03-14.

[487] Itzhak Ben-David, Francesco A. Franzoni & Rabih Moussawi, *Exchange Traded Funds*, 9 ANN. REV. FIN. ECON. 169 (2017). In the context of bond ETFs, Pan and Zeng show that the arbitrage relationship can breakdown further when there is a liquidity mismatch between the ETF and the underlying bonds, and the ETF's authorized participants have the incentive to use ETF creations and redemptions to manage their own bond inventory imbalances. *See* Kevin Pan & Yao Zeng, *ETF Arbitrage Under Liquidity Mismatch* (working paper, 2017), https://papers.ssrn.com/sol3/papers.cfm?abstract_id=2895478.

[488] BLACKROCK, VIEWPOINT – U.S. EQUITY MARKET STRUCTURE: LESSONS FROM AUGUST 24 (2015), https://www.sec.gov/comments/265-29/26529-52.pdf.

turnovers. Gerig and Murphy find that ETFs in the bottom quartile of turnover were three time more likely to pause than those in the top quartile.[489] Furthermore, Gerig and Murphy find that ETFs with high correlations with the S&P 500 index were much more likely to pause, and that ETFs within the top quartile of S&P 500 correlations 21 times more likely to pause, than those in the bottom quartile. These ETFs with high S&P 500 correlations experienced both large volume spikes and large liquidity drops.

The events of August 24th suggest that regulators need to think carefully about the impact of trading halts on ETFs, and about the breadth and diversity of holdings of an ETF. Of the ETFs focused on domestic equity, the ICI classifies 397 as broad-based and 388 as sector/industry based.[490] Some of the sector/industry ETFs are highly specialized, with a small number of constituent holdings. For a narrow ETF, a breakdown of the creation/destruction arbitrage relationship is more likely to occur when some of the underlying securities are halted.

ETFs raise other issues that impact market integrity and performance. For instance, narrowly defined ETFs can be used to engage in manipulation and insider trading, in a practice known as ETF-stripping, by which a trader buys the ETF that includes the stock of interest and then short sells all of the other stocks in the ETF, or vice versa.[491] Also, ETFs tend to increase stock return co-movement,[492] which reduces the ability of liquidity providers to diversify their stock specific risks, and thereby increases volatility across stocks.

3.5.4 Quote Stuffing

Quote stuffing refers to a high frequency trading strategy in which a very large number of orders to buy or sell securities are placed in quick succession and

---

[489] Austin Gerig & Keegan Murphy, *The Determinants of ETF Trading Pauses on August 24th, 2015* (working paper, 2016), https://www.sec.gov/files/feb2016-white-paper-determinants-etf-trading-pauses.pdf.

[490] *See* https://www.ici.org/research/stats/etf/etfs_01_17.

[491] *See, e.g.*, Abigail Rubenstein, LAW360, *SEC to Probe Use of ETFs for Insider Trading*, Feb. 10, 2011, https://www.law360.com/articles/224950/sec-to-probe-use-of-etfs-for-insider-trading.

[492] *See* Lawrence R. Glosten, Suresh Nallareddy & Yuan Zou, *ETF Activity and Informational Efficiency of Underlying Securities* (working paper, 2016) https://papers.ssrn.com/sol3/papers.cfm?abstract_id=2846157.

then canceled almost immediately. As described in two Credit Suisse reports,[493] quote stuffing can be done for three reasons: (i) it can be used to game other orders, such as peg-to-mid orders, that base their pricing on the best bid and ask prices, and subsequently take advantage of these orders; (ii) it can be used to create false mid-points near the prior bid or ask, which are then used to trade in a dark pool that uses the mid-point as its reference price; (iii) it can be used to create stale prices and slow market data, which allow the quote stuffer to take advantage of other market participants' slower connections and create opportunities for latency arbitrage. Latency arbitrage refers to a practice whereby high frequency traders profit by simultaneously buying at the ask on one market and sell at the bid on the other market during short instances when the best quotes on those two venues are crossed. While quote stuffing could be a form of manipulation, it is also important to note that it could be a natural by-product of two algorithms interacting with each other but failing to converge to a stable equilibrium. Regardless of the cause, quote stuffing impacts market integrity by clogging message traffic and preventing other traders from updating or submitting their orders.

Quote stuffing is challenging to identify empirically, since it is unclear whether episodic spikes in quoting activity are the consequence of manipulation or a natural response to higher volatility. Gai, Yao, and Ye develop a clever identification strategy based on the fact that NASDAQ stocks are randomly grouped into six identical but independent data feed channels.[494] They find that stocks in the same channel have an abnormal correlation in message flow, which is consistent with quote stuffing. Egginton, Van Ness, and Van Ness find that over 74% of U.S. exchange-listed securities experienced at least one episode of quote stuffing during 2010.[495] They also show that such episodes have a negative impact on market quality, with targeted stocks suffering decreased liquidity, higher trading costs, and increased short-term volatility.

---

[493] *See* CREDIT SUISSE AES ANALYSIS, HIGH FREQUENCY TRADING – THE GOOD, THE BAD, AND THE REGULATION (2012); CREDIT SUISSE AES ANALYSIS, HIGH FREQUENCY TRADING – MEASUREMENT, DETECTION AND RESPONSE (2012).

[494] Jiading Gai, Chen Yao & Mao Ye, *The Externalities of High-Frequency Trading* (working paper, 2013), https://papers.ssrn.com/sol3/papers.cfm?abstract_id=2066839.

[495] Jared F. Egginton, Bonnie F. Van Ness & Robert A. Van Ness, *Quote Stuffing*, 45 FIN. MGMT. 583 (2016).

Despite evidence that quote stuffing is a relatively common occurrence, it appears that only one broker-dealer has been fined to date.[496] Quote stuffing is related to other forms of market manipulation often associated with HFT, such as layering, spoofing, price and venue fade, and momentum ignition. Regulatory proposals designed to limit quote stuffing and other related forms of manipulation include: (a) fines for exceeding a specified order-to-trade ratio; (b) fees to update quotes or a limit on the number of quote updates within a certain time period; and (c) a minimum resting time for orders.[497] All of these proposals come with the risk that they will harm long-term investors and have other unintended consequences. More research is needed to establish whether the apparent costs of quote stuffing are sufficient to warrant these measures.

3.5.5 Cybersecurity

The frequency and sophistication of cybersecurity attacks is a major concern for trading venues and broker-dealers. Fortunately, major U.S. trading systems do not appear to have been directly compromised thus far. There have been some concerns, such as when NASDAQ announced in February 2011 that suspicious files had been found on its servers, although the files appeared to have only affected its web applications and did not compromise its trading systems.[498]

In a recent FINRA survey on cybersecurity[499], the top threat according to respondents was "Cyber risk of hackers penetrating systems for the purpose of account manipulation, defacement or data destruction, for example." A hacker could shut down an exchange, tamper with critical market data, or use a financial intermediary to execute unauthorized trades. Direct market access by non-brokers, without proper risk management controls, may increase the likelihood of a successful attack. SEC Commissioner Aguilar has noted that U.S. markets

---

[496] *See* June 16, 2014 Letter from NASDAQ to Citadel Securities LLC, The Nasdaq Stock Market Notice of Acceptance, Waiver and Consent No. 20100223345-02, *available at* http://www.nasdaqtrader.com/content/marketregulation/NASDAQ/DisciplinaryActions/CDRG_NQ_2014.pdf.

[497] For additional details, see CREDIT SUISSE AES ANALYSIS, HIGH FREQUENCY TRADING – THE GOOD, THE BAD, AND THE REGULATION (2012).

[498] *See* Announcement by Nasdaq OMX (February 5, 2011), http://www.nasdaq.com/includes/announcement-2-5-11.aspx.

[499] FINRA, REPORT ON CYBERSECURITY PRACTICES (2015), https://www.finra.org/sites/default/files/p602363%20Report%20on%20Cybersecurity%20Practices_0.pdf.

lack a market-wide risk management system that would deal with computer generated chaos in real time.[500]

The large number of trading venues adds to the cost and complexity of managing security and responding to a cyber-attack. At the same time, the existence of multiple trading venues provides a useful redundancy; if one trading venue is unable to operate due to a cyber-attack, malfunction, natural disaster, or terrorist event, another trading venue can serve in its place. Regulation SCI recognizes the issues with interconnected systems, and requires that written notice be provided to the SEC within 24 hours of any responsible personnel becoming aware of a systems intrusion. As well, SCI firms are required to develop a coordinated response to a breach, in which a process is established for the information security, technology, legal and compliance teams.

Much of the issues with cybersecurity come from the enormous complexity of the financial trading systems. Kirilenko and Lo argue that financial regulation should be designed with this complexity in mind, and adhere to four basic design principles: (i) regulation should promote best practices in systems design and complexity management, viewing automated markets as complex systems composed of software applications, hardware devices, and human personnel; (ii) effective risk safeguards should be consistent with machine-readable communication protocols, in addition to human oversight; (iii) financial regulation should make the design and operation of financial products and services more transparent and accessible to automated audits; and (iv) financial regulation should encourage innovation to be platform-neutral, helping to avoid locking-in old technology and practices.[501]

The risks of a cyber-attack are more than that of bringing down the trading system for a few days; there is also the long-term risk of corrupt records in the system. Distributed ledger technology, discussed below, appears to show great promise as a means to provide redundancy of trading records and thereby reduce the potential negative consequences of cyber-attacks.

3.5.6 Blockchain

Distributed ledger technology, commonly referred to as blockchain, has the potential to transform the payment, clearing, and settlement processes for

---

[500] Luis A. Aguilar, *U.S. Equity Market Structure: Making Our Markets Work Better for Investors* (2015), https://www.sec.gov/news/statement/us-equity-market-structure.html.

[501] Andrei A. Kirilenko & Andrew W. Lo, *Moore's Law Versus Murphy's Law: Algorithmic Trading and its Discontents*, 27 J. ECON. PERSP. 51 (2013).

securities trading.[502] It can enable direct peer-to-peer trading, without the need for clearing intermediaries, and it can allow for settlement on a nearly instantaneous basis. The management consulting firm Oliver Wyman estimates revenue from clearing and securities services (settlement, custody, collateral management) alone to be $45 - $55 billion per year, so the potential cost savings from using blockchain technology to reduce market frictions are substantial.[503]

Blockchain is best known as the technology behind Bitcoin, a virtual currency.[504] A blockchain is a distributed ledger or database that contains a list of ordered records, called blocks. Each block contains a record of a transaction and a link to the previous block. The entire database is stored across all of the computers (or nodes) in a peer-to-peer network. The distributed network helps protect the system against hacking, since changes to the blockchain must be verified using a decentralized protocol based on the entire network of nodes. By design, blockchain has a built-in redundancy, and blocks cannot be modified once they are created and verified.

Because blockchain transactions occur in a peer-to-peer fashion, every transaction requires signature verification to prove its source. From a security perspective, this process is a potential weak link in the blockchain since there needs to be a consensus mechanism for verifying these signatures. Policies need to be established to handle these "virtual identities" and how much information they should reveal about the actual participants in the transaction.

Applications of blockchain technology in securities trading are already starting to emerge. For instance, blockchain technology was used for the recent

---

[502] Lee provides an overview of the potential of blockchain technology in securities trading. *See* Larissa Lee, *New Kids on the Blockchain: How Bitcoin's Technology Could Reinvent the Stock Market*, 12 HASTINGS BUS. L J. 81 (2016).

[503] OLIVER WYMAN, THE CAPITAL MARKETS INDUSTRY: THE TIMES THEY ARE A-CHANGIN (2014), http://www.oliverwyman.com/content/dam/oliver-wyman/global/en/files/insights/financial-services/2015/March/The_Capital_Markets_Industry.pdf.

[504] The Federal Reserve is studying distributed ledger technology applications in payment, clearing, and settlement processes. *See* David Mills, Kathy Wang, Brendan Malone, Anjana Ravi, Jeff Marquardt, Clinton Chen, Anton Badev, Timothy Brezinski, Linda Fahy, Kimberley Liao, Vanessa Kargenian, Max Ellithorpe, Wendy Ng & Maria Baird, *Distributed Ledger Technology in Payments, Clearing and Settlement*, Finance and Economics Discussion Series 2016-095 (2016),
https://www.federalreserve.gov/econresdata/feds/2016/files/2016095pap.pdf.

preferred stock issuance by Overstock.com.[505] DTCC will use blockchain technology to process credit default swaps.[506] Nasdaq Linq uses blockchain technology to allow private-market securities issuers to complete and record private securities transactions.[507] The Australian Stock Exchange has announced plans to use blockchain technology in a new post-trade system to replace the existing CHESS system for clearing, settlement and asset registration for equity cash markets.[508] Lykke has developed a peer-to-peer foreign exchange trading platform based on blockchain.[509] The Japan Exchange Group has established an internal working group to explore the pros and cons of using blockchain technology.[510] A fintech company, R3, is leading a consortium of 80 of the world's largest financial institutions to develop a new distributed ledger platform, Corda, for the banking industry, designed to provide privacy and limit duplication of records.[511] Another platform, known as Hyperledger, is being led by the Linux Foundation.[512]

A core feature of the traditional blockchain is that it is based on an open, permissionless network. In a public blockchain, there is a distributed network,

---

[505] Press Release, *Overstock.com Announces Rights Offering Including Blockchain Shares on t0 Platform* (Oct. 25, 2016), http://investors.overstock.com/mobile.view?c=131091&v=203&d=1&id=2215653.

[506] Anna Irrera, *DTCC to rebuild credit default swaps processing platform with blockchain*, REUTERS, Jan. 9, 2017, http://www.reuters.com/article/us-blockchain-dtcc-cds-idUSKBN14T1EA.

[507] Press Release, *Nasdaq Linq Enables First-Ever Private Securities Issuance Documented With Blockchain Technology* (Dec. 30, 2015), http://ir.nasdaq.com/releasedetail.cfm?releaseid=948326.

[508] AUSTRALIAN STOCK EXCHANGE, ASX'S REPLACEMENT OF CHESS FOR EQUITY POST-TRADE SERVICES: BUSINESS REQUIREMENTS (2016), http://www.asx.com.au/documents/public-consultations/ASX-Consultation-Paper-CHESS-Replacement-19-September-2016.pdf.

[509] *See* https://www.lykke.com/exchange.

[510] *See* Atsushi Santo, Ikuo Minowa, Go Hosaka, Satoshi Hayakawa, Masafumi Kondo, Shingo Ichiki & Yuki Kaneko, *Applicability of Distributed Ledger Technology to Capital Market Infrastructure* (working paper, 2016), https://www.jpx.co.jp/english/corporate/research-study/working-paper/b5b4pj000000i468-att/E_JPX_working_paper_No15.pdf

[511] *See* http://www.r3.com/.

[512] *See* https://www.hyperledger.org/about.

with open access and irreversible blocks. The entire ledger is public, so while a user's public key (or identifier) may not be easily connected to their real-world identity, it may be possible to identify patterns in the usage of a given public key in the transaction history which might allow one to infer information about ownership.[513] The distributed network makes a public blockchain more secure since the information is stored across a potentially unlimited number of nodes and, in theory, an attacker would need to gain control of more than half of the network nodes to corrupt the ledger. An alternative form of blockchain is based on a closed, private network in which verification is authorized or permissioned by a central authority. In a private blockchain, the network has a select number of nodes, with filtered access and blocks that can be changed. In a private blockchain, ownership information can be public or private. A closed network is less secure, but there is more control on entrants. Importantly, signature verification in an open network can be a time-consuming process (at least in the context of high frequency trading), whereas in a closed network signature verification may not be necessary.

In the context of trading markets, Malinova and Park develop a model that illustrates the trade-offs between open and private blockchains.[514] In their model, the key issue is whether the public identifier allows other traders to know the identity and size of their counterparty. As is true in trading markets today, in some situations, too much transparency can be detrimental to liquidity and the execution of large institutional sized positions, as other investors will trade ahead of this information. But despite this consideration, Malinova and Park show that the highest welfare occurs in environments with full transparency, in part because it enables large investors to contact other large investors directly.

Blockchain and related technologies are still in their infancy. In its current form, the decentralized nature of distributed ledger technology does not appear to be well-suited for aggregating orders in real-time due to the massive amount of information generated by the high speed of equity trading. As such, some market participants are already concerned about potential costs from having only some securities and only some parts of the trade lifecycle on blockchain. In particular, the payment system can prove to be a bottleneck in settlement process, unless a blockchain-based currency such as Bitcoin is also used.

---

[513] A market participant could reduce this risk by using a new public key after just a few transactions.

[514] Katya Malinova & Andreas Park, *Market Design with Blockchain Technology* (working paper, 2016), https://papers.ssrn.com/sol3/papers.cfm?abstract_id=2785626.

Despite these concerns, there is genuine excitement about the potential uses of blockchain technology across diverse areas of finance and commerce. At the 2017 World Economic Forum Annual Meeting in Davos, there were a dozen formal and informal sessions on blockchain.[515] Blockchain technology has the potential to transform the organization and regulation of trading by enabling direct "end-investor" to "end-investor" transactions. It is worth noting that one of the attractions of Bitcoin was the perception that its decentralized nature made the currency beyond the control of government. In this light, regulators may want to be proactive in establishing a framework for the control and access of information on distributed ledgers used for trading securities. To this end, the SEC has already formed a working group to build expertise, identify risk areas, and coordinate efforts on distributed ledger technology.[516]

3.6 Market Data Environment

Market data are the trade and quotation information associated with trade in equities.[517] Core trade data consist of a time-stamped real-time record of the price and number of shares associated with each stock trade (i.e., the "ticker tape.") Core quotation data consist of the top-of-book prices and depth of each registered public exchange, as well as the NBBO. These data are provided pursuant to several SEC-approved market data plans, which are administered by a securities information processor (SIP). The exchanges provide the core data to the SIPs, who then compute an NBBO and distribute the consolidated data to the public. Currently, NYSE Euronext and Nasdaq OMX Group each run a SIP on behalf of the public exchanges.

Trade in securities both produces and consumes market data. The data are *produced* when orders are placed on the exchange, which produces quotation information, and when trades occur on the exchange, which produces last sale information. Market data are *consumed* during the process broker-dealers follow

---

[515] Don Tapscott, *Blockchain Transformations at Davos*, HUFFINGTON POST, Jan. 19, 2017, http://www.huffingtonpost.com/don-tapscott/blockchain-transformation_b_14268140.html.

[516] At this stage, it is unclear whether some existing SEC regulations, such as those for transfer agents and clearing agencies, require registration for blockchain applications.

[517] For more comprehensive discussion of the institutional and legal framework around the provision, use, and pricing of market data, see REPORT OF THE ADVISORY COMMITTEE ON MARKET INFORMATION: A BLUEPRINT FOR RESPONSIBLE CHANGE (SELIGMAN REPORT) (2001), https://www.sec.gov/divisions/marketreg/marketinfo/finalreport.htm.

when accepting orders from customers. A broker-dealer wishing to trade would need to know, at a minimum, what the bids and offers are at the various exchanges. In crafting its order placement strategy, the broker may very well also like to know the prices and quantities of recent trades. In addition, Exchange Act Rule 11Ac1-2, also known as the "Display Rule," requires that any broker-dealer using quotation data be provided data that at a minimum contains either (a) the NBBO for the stock, or (b) a quotation montage for the stock from all reporting market centers. Similarly, a broker-dealer using last sale data must at a minimum be provided the price and volume of the most recent transaction in that stock from any reporting market center, as well as an identification of that market center. This means that if a broker-dealer is in the business of executing orders for customers, they must purchase and use the consolidated SIP data in transacting their business.

The effect of the above is to create an inelastic demand for core market data on the part of broker-dealers and other market participants. To ensure that such data are reasonably priced, the collection and pricing of these data must occur in a manner that is consistent with the requirements of Exchange Act and its various rules, following a process overseen by the SEC. This process insures that core data prices are reasonable. For example, for Network A (NYSE) securities, current monthly charges for core market data include price points at $0.0075 per quote, $1.00 for a non-professional user, and $1,250 for professional electronic access to quotations.[518] The SEC has stated that fees for core market data "need to be tied to some type of cost-based standard in order to preclude excessive profits if fees are too high or underfunding or subsidization if fees are too low."[519]

In addition to core data, market centers that route and execute orders produced a host of other enhanced market data products. These market centers recognize that market data is a key input for their trading constituency. The sale of data has become an important revenue source for the exchanges. For example, for BATS Global Markets, while transaction revenue net of liquidity payments was $164.4 million, market data fees were $99.4 million.[520] Nasdaq OMX data products revenue was $399 million for 2015.[521]

---

[518] *See* CTA Pricing Schedule, https://www.nyse.com/publicdocs/ctaplan/notifications/trader-update/CTA%20Network%20A%20Pricing%20-%20Jan%201%202015.pdf

[519] Market Data Concept Release, Release No. 34-42208, 64 Fed. Reg. 70613, 70627, Dec. 17, 1999.

[520] BATS Global Markets, Inc., Registration Statement (Form S-1) (Dec. 15, 2015).

[521] Nasdaq Inc., Annual Report (Form 10-K) (Dec. 31, 2015).

Enhanced market data contain detailed information about the state of the market's order book, including the price and share quantity of every displayed order on the book, broadcast in a variety of formats. These data are available at various degrees of latency, with higher costs associated with the lower latency products. For example, the NYSE Integrated Feed provides a microsecond precision order-by-order view of events in the NYSE equities market. Its pricing for non-display use (algorithmic and high frequency trading) can run to $20,000 per month.[522] There is no SEC or FINRA imposed regulatory requirement that broker-dealers accepting customer orders obtain or use such non-core data. Accordingly, the SEC has taken a much more hands-off approach to oversight of the pricing of non-core data products. This pricing approach has not been without controversy, however. In 2009, the SEC was sued by NetCoalition, a public policy corporation representing approximately 20 internet companies (including Google and Yahoo!) and SIFMA (a trade association representing more than 600 securities firms and banks) over the approval of NYSE ARCA data fees that NetCoalition deemed excessive.[523]

While the environment around market data may seem quiescent, this is not the case. Though a complete treatment of market data questions is beyond the scope of this chapter, we highlight below several key issues that we feel should be examined in any comprehensive reform of U.S. equity market structure.

3.6.1 Market Data Plan Governance

Each of the NMS plans associated with the individual pools of market data are governed by an operating committee that has one representative from each SRO participant. There are no broker-dealer or bank committee members, nor are there any data vendors or members of the public on the operating committees of these plans. This is notable because market data are an essential input for equity trading, yet the trading public are not exchange members and thus have no direct representation in plan governance. The current market data regime was established when exchanges were closer to public utilities than they are now, before they became public for-profit entities. The SRO members of the

---

[522] Market Data Pricing, https://www.nyse.com/publicdocs/nyse/data/NYSE_Market_Data_Pricing.pdf.

[523] While the ultimate disposition of this litigation is still pending, NetCoalition prevailed over the SEC in objecting to the fees and the decision by the DC circuit court. NetCoalition v. SEC, 615 F.3d 525 (D.C. Cir. 2010). The matter is currently before an SEC administrative law judge.

operating committee, as producers of market data, stand to benefit from approving higher fees. Somewhat surprising from a governance perspective are the voting requirements of the plans. Making changes to the existing plans, including any changes to the fee structure of the plans, requires a unanimous vote of all participants. The SEC has issued a concept release in 1999 touching upon these issues, but as yet, little has changed in plan governance.[524]

Concerns go beyond simply the voting protocols of the plan operating committees. Some critics have observed that the exchange personnel who are responsible for marketing consolidated core data are also responsible for the marketing of non-core proprietary data.[525] This provides little incentive to improve core data, for which pricing is tightly regulated, when market participants may be willing to substitute more expensive non-core data in its place. Others are concerned with the reliability of the SIPs, the quality of data they produce, and the lack of transparency around the investigation of certain SIP shortcomings.[526] Regardless of the details, it would seem that a quasi-utility responsible for the provision of an input as essential to our secondary markets as market data should, as a part of its formal governance process, incorporate input from the public and other core constituencies of their markets.

3.6.2 Market Data and the Oversight Function

Market data are important not only for the trading decision but also for the ex-post regulatory oversight function. Today, use of core and even most non-core data are insufficient to properly surveil technologically advanced trading firms. Market data identify transactions that occurred and quotations for orders that were placed, but do not attribute these trades or quotations to any particular party. More importantly, they cannot be used to identify where a particular order has been routed on its way to an eventual fill or cancellation. Regulators have the ability to access internal records of firms, but firms do not have an obligation to make and retain the type of detailed audit trails necessary to reconstruct the trading process. Without such ability to reconstruct trading, surveillance of

---

[524] *See* Securities Exchange Act Release No. 42208 (Dec. 9, 2000), 64 Fed. Reg. 70613 (Dec. 17, 1999).

[525] *See* December 10, 2014 letter from IEX to Securities and Exchange Commission Chair Mary Jo White, Governance of the NMS Plans Concerning Securities Information Processors and the Consolidated Audit Trail, https://iextrading.com/policy/sec/02/.

[526] *See* October 14, 2014 letter from SIFMA to NASDAQ/UTP Plan Operating Committee, NASDAQ/UTP Plan: Selection of Processor for the NASDAQ SIP.

broker-dealers for enforcement or examination purposes is lacking. The ability to enforce and examine is essential for deterring bad actors and for fostering compliance by the regulated entity with applicable rules and regulations.

As a remedy to the situation, the SEC has approved a plan for the creation of a Consolidated Audit Trail (CAT).[527] The CAT would allow tracking of order information and executions throughout the lifecycle of the order, including origination, routing, modification or cancellation, and execution. The audit trail would identify not only the broker submitting the order, but also would contain a unique identifier for each customer as well. Timely submission of such information would be required of broker-dealers. This information would markedly improve regulators' ability to surveil for improper trading practices.

While this is an important piece of the solution to the oversight problem, it is not by itself likely to be enough. Because most trading today is algorithmic, the logic for actions taken on orders is embedded in the code resident at the broker-dealer. The code is the intellectual property of the broker-dealer, and these firms are very reticent to part with their intellectual property when regulators make investigative requests. Because secondary trading is so competitive, if any proprietary knowledge is leaked outside of their firms, it could easily become valueless since knowledge or use by other traders competes away any advantages conferred by the code. When the Commodity Futures Trading Commission (CFTC) proposed its new Regulation AT, which among other things allowed the regulator access the algorithmic trading code of its traders, the industry strenuously objected to overreaching by the CFTC and the potential compromising of valuable intellectual property.[528] Yet without access to such code, it becomes problematic for a regulator such as the SEC to perform some of its basic oversight functions, including the deterrence of market manipulation, front-running, spoofing, or layering, most of which are based on the concept of fraud. Finally, it is worth noting that there are no requirements for broker-dealers to make and retain records of the operational versions of the order-routing and execution software. Because this software often evolves on a nearly continuous basis, as a practical matter it makes ex-post auditing of firm behavior a problematic exercise.

---

[527] Joint Industry Plan; Order Approving the National Market System Plan Governing the Consolidated Audit Trail, SEC Release No. 34-79318 (Nov. 15, 2016).

[528] Regulation Automated Trading, 80 Fed. Reg. 78824 (Dec. 17, 2015).

3.6.3 Validity of Market Data for Best Execution Purposes

As discussed above, broker-dealers owe customers a duty of best execution when handling and routing customer orders. Most broker-dealers conceive of best execution as a process that seeks to obtain the best terms of trade for their customers. If conceived solely as a process, best execution obligations are relatively easy to describe and to surveil. As a hypothetical example, the best execution process for a particular broker-dealer for executing marketable customer orders may be to route the order to the market that shows the best price for the stock. In cases where there is a tie for best price, the broker-dealer would route to the market with the best price and greatest depth. This best execution process is easy to describe and relatively easy to audit on an ex-post basis. An examiner can, in principle, forensically rely on public quotation data to confirm that all outbound routes by the broker-dealer were to markets at the NBBO.[529]

More nuanced than the question of whether the broker-dealer followed their own prescribed best execution process is the question of whether the prescribed process was likely to obtain best execution for the client orders. This question is much more difficult to answer. We know the prints the broker received from customer orders, but what we would most like to have to judge the efficacy of the broker's best execution process are prints the broker would have received had the orders been routed in another manner, knowledge that is impossible to ascertain with precision. This lies at the heart of FINRA's requirement that broker-dealers "regularly and rigorously examine execution quality likely to be obtained from the different markets trading a security."[530] In conducting such an analysis, and even in routing orders for actual execution, broker-dealers must form judgments about the reliability of market quotations and the degree to which a customer order routed to a particular market center can be reasonably assured of executing at a favorable price. Publicly disseminated quotations are noisy signals of prices that would be obtained upon routing, not previews of the actual execution price itself. Prices may be better than, equal to, or worse than the quoted price at a given market center at the moment an order is routed. The differences can arise for a number of reasons. There may be hidden liquidity that would improve the execution of the marketable order. Or as discussed by O'Hara, the quote may be flickering and be canceled before the

---

[529] Even a simple exercise such as this may be challenging in a world of microsecond routing sequences, time-varying latencies, and imperfect clock synchronization.

[530] Best Execution, FINRA Regulatory Notice 15-46 (Nov. 2015).

order arrives at the market, which would harm execution quality.[531] Or the state of the market may change with the arrival of a new better-priced order or the execution against the current quote of a quicker order. Sophisticated traders build complex proprietary models that assign probabilities to the likelihood of such events.

In establishing a benchmark for analyzing best execution, regulators must make judgments about the reliability of information in the quote record when assessing a broker-dealer's performance. The record is often insufficient to reliably conduct such assessments. For example, suppose a broker-dealer internalizes an order for execution based on the price of a market whose quote at the time of in execution is inferior to the NBBO. The broker does so because they consider the superior NBBO quote short-lived and not reachable. Can such a broker be deemed to have violated their duty of best execution by not internalizing the customer order at the NBBO prevailing at the time the order was executed? Similarly, suppose a broker-dealer has the opportunity to route a customer buy order to a venue that will execute the order at a price of $10.00 with certainty. They also have the opportunity to route to another venue that has a 60% probability of executing at a price of $9.99, in a 40% chance of executing at a price of $10.01. If the broker-dealer internalizes the order at $10.00 per share, selling the customer shares out of its own inventory, and simultaneously routes its own offsetting order to the 60/40 market and happens to buy the shares at price of $9.99, can the broker-dealer be judged to have violated its duty of best execution on an order-by-order basis for not internalizing the original customer order at a price of $9.99? The answer in part lies in the regulators' beliefs about the reliability of signals contained in market data and, we believe, remains an open question.

3.6.4 The Obligation of Broker-Dealers to Purchase Non-Core Data

As discussed in the best execution section above, broker-dealers who execute or route customer orders have an obligation to purchase core market data consisting of trades and quotations from all public exchanges. The same obligations do not apply to the use of enhanced non-core market data delivered via low latency direct feeds. As shown by Ding et al., latencies between core and non-core market data can run up to 2 milliseconds.[532] During times of high traffic volume, these latencies can be even larger and demonstrate considerable variation. Given that exchanges have latencies measured in the hundreds of

---

[531] *See* O'Hara, *supra* note 425.

[532] Shengwei Ding, John Hanna & Terrence Hendershott, *How Slow is the NBBO? A Comparison With Direct Exchange Feeds*, 49 FIN. REV. 313 (2014).

microseconds, the best representation of what price a trader would get at a particular public exchange is probably more accurately represented by the direct feeds rather than by SIP data.

This causes a problem for a broker-dealer seeking to fulfill their obligation of best execution. If the broker uses only SIP data, they can expect they will be routing sub-optimally and will lose out to better informed traders making use of direct feeds. If they feel compelled to buy direct feed data, exchanges that understand the inelastic demand on the part of broker-dealers may raise prices on proprietary data knowing that broker-dealers will be forced to buy the data regardless of its cost. Broker-dealers are sensitive to this issue since they feel the exchanges selling market data are charging them for a compilation of their own past trading history. To date, the SEC has sidestepped this issue by not requiring purchase of non-core data, but this is less likely to remain the case as data from SIPs lose their relevance in the domain of high-frequency traders and market makers.

Perhaps the problem can in part be addressed through disclosure. Executing broker-dealers can be required to disclose their policies for obtaining and using the various types of market data. In this way, customers can make informed choices about whether they want to pay the additional costs that may be charged by broker-dealers who consume non-core data. In principle, this same logic could apply to the relationship between introducing brokers and internalizing broker-dealers who execute their orders. If the internalizing brokers must disclose in their contracts their policies toward obtaining and using the various types of market data, introducing brokers, who retain their obligations of best execution, can make informed judgments about whether they will fully discharge their best execution obligations when they route to brokers who consume only a subset of available market data. The ultimate solution remains unclear, but what is certain is that there will continue to be friction between exchanges who charge for market data and broker-dealers who must pay for the right to use data that they feel should belong to them.

4 Fixed Income Secondary Trading Markets

Though the focus of this chapter is on equity markets, the domestic fixed income markets are both larger and in more need of market structure reform than their equity counterparts. Whereas the market capitalization of listed equity markets is about $26.5 billion, the corporate, asset-backed, mortgage, treasury, agency, and municipal bond market in aggregate totaled $37.1 billion.[533] U.S. equities trade in an integrated system of 12 public exchanges, more than 30

---

[533] SIFMA, U.S. FACT BOOK 33-34 (2016), https://www.sifma.org/wp-content/uploads/2017/05/sifma-fact-book-2016.pdf.

ATSs, and a substantial number of broker-dealers, all integrated by low latency high-capacity data linkages and a uniform system of both pre-and post-trade transparency. In addition, U.S. exchange-traded equities have the benefit of being publicly registered firms for which all fundamental information is available freely in a timely manner on the SEC's EDGAR system. Spreads in equities are measured in pennies and in many cases stocks trade in increments of less than a cent.

Contrast this with the corporate and municipal bond markets. Here, trade occurs in an over-the-counter dealer market. Pre-trade transparency is very limited, provided only by a few private systems and a growing number of bond ATSs.[534] There is no integrated public display of dealer bids and offers, only a collection of private subscription-based systems. When a subscriber to one of these systems wishes to sell a bond, the system disseminates a "bid wanted" list to other subscribers, who are given a 1- to 2-hour window to post bids for the CUSIPs advertised for sale. There are also internal systems used by broker-dealers who have retail clients. These private systems display a select inventory of bonds for sale to the broker-dealer's own customers, and typically only advertise bonds that the dealer already has in inventory.

Over the last decade, post-trade transparency has much improved. FINRA has created the TRACE system for corporate bonds, and the Municipal Securities Rulemaking Board (MSRB) has created the EMMA system for municipal bonds.[535] Both systems are public last-sale trade reporting systems that disseminate time, price, and quantity of bonds traded in near real time. While these systems are applauded by small investors and their advocates, both dealers and large institutional investors generally opposed their creation. The likely reason for this opposition is that TRACE and EMMA dissipated the information advantages of large and sophisticated traders in the previously opaque market.

Even with these improvements, trading costs in corporate and municipal bond markets far exceed those in equity markets.[536] Harris and Piwowar show that municipal bond trading costs decrease with trade size and are substantially more expensive than comparable dollar amounts of equity securities.[537] They also

---

[534] There are now 23 TRACE-eligible ATSs.

[535] TRACE has also been expanded to include certain mortgage and agency debt, and in July 2017 FINRA members will be required to report their Treasury trades to TRACE.

[536] There is a large and growing literature on secondary market trading in fixed income instruments. The authors apologize for the space constraints that prevent us from appropriately citing to all the relevant work is this space.

[537] Lawrence E. Harris & Michael S. Piwowar, *Secondary Trading Costs in the Municipal Bond Market*, 61 J. FIN. 1361 (2006).

show that trading costs rise with time to maturity and instrument complexity. Green et al. show that dealers earn their greatest profit in the municipal bond market on the smallest trades, and attribute this profit to the exercise of market power, which they show decreases in trade size.[538] Using MSRB regulatory data, Sirri studies the manner by which dealers intermediate trades between customers and shows that trading costs fall with increasing trade size and rise with the complexity of intermediation required.[539] The study also shows that it can take many days to fully intermediate a large trade, and that costs are lower if the dealer can lay off their principal risk position quickly.

Goldstein, Hotchkiss, and Sirri study the effect of increased transparency in the corporate bond markets and find it has either a neutral or positive effect on liquidity.[540] They show that spreads decline on bonds that trade in regimes of greater post-trade transparency, which they attribute to investors' ability to negotiate better terms of trade once they have access to such data. Edwards et al. show that transaction costs in the corporate bond market decrease with trade size, and increase with the complexity of the bond, such as nonstandard payment, call, and maturity features.[541] Bessembinder et al. find that corporate bond execution costs fell one-half when an early version of the TRACE reporting system was introduced.[542]

There are several fundamental factors that contribute to the high cost of trading in fixed income instruments described above.[543] One is the large number

---

[538] Richard C. Green, Burton Hollified & Norman Schuerhoff, *Dealer Intermediation and Price Behavior in the Aftermarket for New Issues*, 86 J. FIN. ECON. 643 (2007).

[539] Erik R. Sirri, *Report on Secondary Market Trading in the Municipal Securities Market* (2014), http://www.msrb.org/msrb1/pdfs/MSRB-Report-on-Secondary-Market-Trading-in-the-Municipal-Securities-Market.pdf.

[540] Michael A. Goldstein, Edith S. Hotchkiss & Erik R. Sirri, *Transparency and Liquidity: A Controlled Experiment on Corporate Bonds*, 20 REV. FIN. STUD. 235 (2007).

[541] Amy K, Edwards, Lawrence E. Harris & Michael S. Piwowar, *Corporate Bond Market Transaction Costs and Transparency*, 62, J. FIN. 1421 (2007).

[542] Hendrik Bessembinder, William Maxwell & Kumar Venkataraman, *Market Transparency, Liquidity Externalities, and Institutional Trading Costs in Corporate Bond*, 82 J. FIN. ECON. 251 (2006).

[543] U.S. Treasury markets are notable exception to the high cost of domestic bond trading. Fleming, Mizrach, and Nguyen find that Treasury bonds trade in a basis point or less, and two electronic ETSs, BrokerTec in eSpeed, have substantial market shares of Treasury volume. Michael J. Fleming, Bruce Mizrach

of separate offerings in each of these markets. Municipal bond markets alone have over one million different bond issues outstanding. Many of these bonds go weeks or months without a single trade, and the odds of a natural buyer and seller having coincident interest to transact is low. Contrast this to the equity market with less than ten thousand publicly-traded equities. Also, because bonds trade only in dealer markets, and there are hundreds of different dealers asynchronously trading the bonds, it can be hard for two investors to find each other even if they do have simultaneous demand for trade unless they are customers of the same dealer. Finally, the information environment for fixed income is very different than it is for publicly-traded equities. Municipal issuers are not required to file public offering documents, such as prospectuses, with the federal government,[544] and what limited obligations there are for disclosure arise indirectly through SEC rules imposed on brokers who trade or offer these bonds.[545]

    Although there has been progress in improving fixed income market structure, much more can and needs to be accomplished. As described above, post-trade transparency has improved for both corporate and municipal securities. In addition, the SEC and FINRA have recently improved trade disclosure for both municipal and corporate bond trades.[546] These new rules will require disclosure of the dealer's mark-up or mark-down on the customer's confirmation statement if the dealer both trades as principal with a retail investor and engages in one or more offsetting transactions on the same day. The mark-up/mark-down confirmation disclosure must be expressed both as a total dollar amount and as a percentage amount. Regulators hope that such disclosure will make investors more sensitive to trading costs and increase cost-based competition among dealers.

    Bond market participants are quick to point out that bonds are not equities, and it is incorrect to presume that the same market structures are optimal for both. That said, it is highly likely that some meaningful improvements can still be made to fixed income market structure. One suggestion by the Financial Economists Roundtables, described in Harris et al. is an enhancement to pre-trade transparency by requiring the development facilities

---

& Giang Nguyen, *The Microstructure of a U.S. Treasury ECN: The BrokerTec Platform*, J. FIN. MKTS. (forthcoming).

[544] *See* Securities Exchange Act of 1934, §15B(d).

[545] *See, e.g.*, 17 C.F.R. §240.15c2-12.

[546] For a more detailed description, *see* FINRA Regulatory Notice 17-24 (describing changes to FINRA Rule 2232) and MSRB Regulatory Notice 2016-28 (describing changes to MSRB Rule G-15 and Rule G-30).

that would allow for the display and execution of priced customer orders.[547] Creation of the facility would be mandated either by the SEC or by FINRA. Broker-dealers who accept or execute customer orders could be required to place such orders into these display and execution systems. In this way, dealers and their customers at other firms would more easily be able to interact with what had previously been captive order flow of investors' broker-dealer. As broker obligations with respect to best execution evolve in the presence of such systems, retail investors would have a chance to transact at much better prices than in a pure dealer market. Coupled with a requirement against inter-positioning, such a system might increase the likelihood that two customers come together for a natural trade without the involvement of an intermediary dealer. Improving markets by fostering investor transactions without the involvement of a dealer is one of the basic precepts behind the creation of the National Market System for equities.

Other improvements may arise by rethinking the obligations on brokers and advisers with respect to the bonds they recommend to retail investors. Best execution only addresses the terms of trade with respect to the bond under consideration for trade. Municipal securities and high-grade corporate bonds have very low probabilities of default, and thus with respect to credit risk show a great degree of fungibility. Most retail investors, when buying a municipal bond, classify their purchase desires in terms of general characteristics of the bond, such as the credit rating, tenor, and traits such as callability and type of obligation (general obligation vs. revenue). Few investors would walk into their broker's office armed with the specificity to demand purchase of a Scarsdale, New York 7-year non-callable water bond. Given the enhanced disclosures around bond costs, and with the future availability of agency platforms as suggested by the Financial Economists Roundtable, regulators may be able to encourage financial advisors to take greater consideration of the all-in-costs associated with bonds currently displayed in the various agency execution platforms when making initial purchase recommendations to their investors. Such a practice would lead to better after-cost yields for investors.

Ang and Green offer a completely different approach to the fixed income market structure issue by focusing on mechanisms to lower the borrowing costs for states and municipalities.[548] They observe that both issuers

---

[547] Larry Harris, Albert S. Kyle & Erik R. Sirri, *Statement of the Financial Economists Roundtable, April 2015: The Structure of Trading in Bond Markets*, 71 FIN. ANALYSTS J. 5 (2015).

[548] Andrew Ang & Richard C. Green, *Lowering Borrowing Costs for States and Municipalities Through CommonMuni* (working paper, 2011), https://www.brookings.edu/wp-content/uploads/2016/07/02_municipal_bond_ang_green_paper.pdf.

and investors pay unnecessary fees and transactions cost because of the poor liquidity and transparency in municipal markets. Tax considerations cause the market for municipal bonds to be dominated by retail investors. The Tower Amendment prohibits the federal government from compelling the production and disclosure of core information from bond issuers, such as annual reports and offering documents, leaving investors largely in the dark about the bonds they are buying.[549] The authors propose the establishment of a not-for-profit platform, which they call CommonMuni, that would centralize the production and dissemination of information about issuers and offerings. It would also offer advice to issuers to help lower their financing costs. The authors observe that because bond complexity reduces market competition, it is in the interests of issuers to work together to standardize and harmonize the types of municipal bonds they offer. With larger and more homogenous offerings, market liquidity should improve and bond ownership should broaden. This is consistent with the findings of Harris and Piwowar, who find that trading costs of more complex bonds are higher than those with simpler terms.[550] Ang and Green estimate that the CommonMuni platform could be developed for about $25 million.

Doubtless there are other sound proposals for improvements to corporate, municipal, and other fixed income markets. Relative to domestic equity markets, improvements should come with relative ease. We would encourage regulators to refocus attention on fixed income markets and continue the trend of the last decade in improving the structure of these markets and the quality of information surrounding them. Especially for the municipal markets, the primary beneficiaries for such improvements are the retail investors who are at the heart of the SEC's traditional mission.

5 Conclusion

The primary purpose of trading markets is to provide a mechanism whereby investors can allocate their monies among productive firms. Such investment simultaneously allows investors to save for various life-cycle needs while facilitating capital formation on the real side of the economy. As such, any regulatory system for secondary trading must jointly serve the needs of both investors and issuers. Corporations receive their monies in primary market transactions involving the issuance of securities. What subsequently occurs in secondary markets primarily serves the needs of investors, though through the informational role of markets, the aggregation of information reflected in prices is a valuable signal in the capital allocation process.

---

[549] *See* Securities Exchange Act of 1934, §15B(d).

[550] Harris & Piwowar, *supra* note 537.

All regulations and market rules involve potential trade-offs, such as between pricing efficiency and considerations of fairness. Thus, any regulator is put in the position of making trade-offs between various stakeholders and constituents in the trading process. Striking the correct balance in making these trade-offs is essential, and certainly one of the key requirements to achieve an appropriate balance requires the collection and analysis of high-quality empirical data. On this dimension, there is good reason to be optimistic about future rulemakings. Over the last 10 years, the SEC has shown an increased proclivity to use financial economics as an organic part of the rulemaking process. In the not too distant past, use of economics was relegated to the so-called "back end" of rule releases. Here, economics was often used on a *post hoc* basis to justify rules that were crafted without the benefit of economic insight. Whether because of several high-profile losses in appellate courts, or pressure from Congress, the SEC seems to have changed their rulemaking processes. The old Office of Economic Analysis, typically staffed by 20 to 30 professionals, has evolved into the Division of Economic Risk and Analysis, whose 110+ professionals form an important group within the Commission. Although it is too soon to judge, we should be hopeful that this change is permanent and not merely a reaction to pressures from the courts or the Hill.

With respect to equity markets, retail investors have never before had such low trading costs or such access to markets. Not only are spreads for small trades extremely low, but commissions charged by discount brokers are often under $10. And for this low cost, the service received by retail investors is far from rock-bottom. By most metrics, U.S. equity markets are liquid, transparent, efficient, and competitive. Yet at the same time, there is a perception, whether correct or not, by some market participants that the market is unfair or rigged, as highlighted in Michael Lewis' bestselling book *Flash Boys*. Even if the unfairness is far less severe than portrayed in this book, perceptions of unfairness can do lasting damage to markets. Whether through the unwarranted involvement of Congress to cure the perceived unfairness, or the withdrawal of skeptical investors from market participation, perceptions of fairness and integrity must be carefully managed.

As we discussed, for some issues the data seem relatively clear, even if counterintuitive. For example, with respect to high-frequency trading, academic studies generally indicate that this activity improves liquidity and pricing efficiency. But that does not mean it does so in every situation and at all times. Though the evidence generally indicates that high-frequency traders transact against temporary price movements, there is still a legitimate concern about whether a market substantially composed of high-speed computer-driven traders is as robust and resilient to shocks as a market intermediated by humans. One thing is certain--we will not be going back to the days of human traders walking the floors of physical exchanges and carrying paper tickets in their hands as they search for a contraside for their order. By 2008, the NYSE was forced to admit that the traditional market model, with a human specialist on the exchange floor charged with both positive and negative obligations, was no longer viable in the face of competition from off-exchange electronic market makers. When the NYSE migrated their market model away from their traditional form, and the floor specialist gave up their agency obligation to the limit order book, it was clear we had reached the point where humans were largely out of the market making business.

The Committee on Capital Markets Regulation (CCMR) has produced a report containing a list of suggested changes to regulations governing secondary trading equity markets.[551] We concur with the authors of that study in their support of the use of pilot programs and independent studies as the basis for sound regulatory proposals. Recently, the SEC has made greater use of pilot programs to investigate the effect of rule changes on measures of market quality. This is a positive change, and one that should be encouraged. Pilots have been used to study the effects of the uptick rule, equity tick sizes, securities lending, option penny trading, and options position limits. The SEC has even discussed a pilot for maker-taker pricing. Whether these pilots will provide useful data for future rulemaking is a difficult question.

Notable in the CCMR report is the incremental nature of the regulatory changes suggested by the Committee. That is not to say these changes are unimportant, but it is interesting to note that this group did not call for wholesale changes into our market structure, such as the repeal of large components of Regulation NMS, or the return to secondary markets intermediated by humans. Nor did the Committee ask for trading to be forced out of dark venues and away from dark order forms. Rather, their recommendations revolved around promulgating and enhancing policies that foster competition. This, too, is a framework with which we agree. The choices the U.S. has made to encourage intermarket competition, at times even at the expense of intra-market competition, have served us well. We feel regulators should continue along this general course. At times, it does demand certain compromises that favor one business model over another, such as in the case of allowing payment for order flow, or permitting exchanges to pay maker-taker fees. But we believe the benefits of robust competition, and the innovation that comes with it, will stand secondary trading markets in good stead in the decades to come.

---

[551] COMMITTEE ON CAPITAL MARKETS REGULATION, THE U.S. EQUITY MARKETS: A PLAN FOR REGULATORY REFORM (2016), https://www.sec.gov/comments/s7-21-16/s72116-1.pdf.

Chapter 5
THE REGULATION OF TRADING MARKETS

Paul G. Mahoney[552] & Gabriel V. Rauterberg[553]

1 Introduction

The U.S. equity markets have undergone profound changes in the past 15 years. The manual creation of contracts to buy and sell shares, either face to face on a trading floor or by telephone with a securities dealer, has been mostly replaced by the automated matching of buy and sell orders by electronic communications and information processing systems. Trading in listed stocks, which used to be heavily concentrated on the listing exchange, is now widely dispersed among multiple automated trading venues.[554] Exchange specialists and over-the-counter market makers have been eclipsed by proprietary traders that offer liquidity to the automated markets by executing algorithmic trading strategies. Those strategies often rely on a menu of new and complex order types that trading venues create to supplement the traditional market and limit orders.[555]

Technological advances made these developments possible. The cost of creating a trading platform has fallen as computers replace trading floors, allowing investors, exchanges, and brokers to solve old problems in new ways.[556] In place of market makers who manually update quotations to reflect information and their own inventory management needs, proprietary traders use automated systems to obtain market data and execute transactions pursuant to predetermined strategies in milliseconds or less. Rather than giving large orders to brokers who can "work" the order, large institutional investors split up their

---

[552] David and Mary Harrison Distinguished Professor of Law, University of Virginia School of Law.

[553] Assistant Professor of Law, University of Michigan School of Law.

[554] *See* Securities and Exchange Commission, Concept Release on Equity Market Structure 6 (January 14, 2010), https://www.sec.gov/rules/concept/2010/34-61358.pdf (hereinafter Market Structure Release) (NYSE's share of trading volume in its listed stocks fell from 79% in 2005 to 25% in 2009).

[555] *See* Phil Mackintosh, *Demystifying Order Types*, KCG TRADING STRATEGIES & MKT. ANALYTICS (Sept. 2014).

[556] *See* James J. Angel, Lawrence E. Harris & Chester S. Spatt, *Equity Trading in the 21st Century*, 1 Q. J. FIN. 1 (2011).

orders into many pieces routed to different trading venues. The technologies themselves and the way market participants use them differ in detail but not in kind from past technological breakthroughs. Throughout history, securities traders have been among the earliest adopters of new communications technologies, always seeking to profit from faster execution and access to information.

The changes are also a product of Congress's and the SEC's regulatory policies.[557] Both consider technology a tool for bringing greater competition to the securities markets. Moreover, each has a vision of how that competition should operate. As we will discuss in more detail below, Congress saw the automation of securities markets as a way to promote its longstanding goal of a market in which investors would trade directly with one another without the intermediation of an exchange specialist or market maker. For its part, the SEC encouraged a structure in which markets compete for trading volume in each individual stock rather than for listings.

On objective measures, the current equity market structure is a great success. A retail investor today can trade with greater convenience and speed, and with lower commissions and spreads, than ever before.[558] Nevertheless, numerous commentators, most notably Michael Lewis, argue that the new stock market is rigged against the average investor.[559] The argument, in summary, is that exchanges and other trading centers collude with "high-frequency" proprietary traders to help those traders identify changes in market prices, order volumes, and other market information before the rest of the trading public has access to it, to the ultimate detriment of other investors.[560] Other commentators

---

[557] *See* Lawrence Harris, *The Homogenization of U.S. Equity Trading* 2 (2011), https://www.bankofcanada.ca/wp-content/uploads/2012/11/Larry-Harris.pdf ("decisions made by the SEC have effectively determined market structure for all U.S. equities"). Harris is a former SEC Chief Economist.

[558] *See infra* Section 6.

[559] *See* MICHAEL LEWIS, FLASH BOYS: A WALL STREET REVOLT (2014); *see also* Jay Somaney, *Is Our Stock Market Rigged?*, FORBES, Aug. 24, 2015, http://www.forbes.com/sites/jaysomaney/2015/08/24/is-our-stock-market-rigged/#731a33291b15 ("Of late the most common question I get asked whether on the golf course or at dinner with friends is whether our markets are rigged?").

[560] Yesha Yadav refers to high-frequency traders as "structural insiders" and argues that their trading harms other investors similarly to traditional insider trading. *See* Yesha Yadav, *Insider Trading and Market Structure*, 63 UCLA L. REV. 968 (2016).

decry the growth of so-called "dark pools," trading platforms that do not publicly display their quotations.[561] Commentators also criticize the fee structures that exchanges have implemented to attract order flow in a highly competitive market.

It is a safe bet that neither Congress nor the SEC foresaw how technology-based competition would unfold in practice. The number and importance of traditional intermediaries has in fact declined, but they have been replaced by high-frequency and other proprietary traders, not by a trading environment catering exclusively to long-term investors. The SEC required the traditional exchanges to open up their quotations to the public, but traders still hide their trading interest using dark trading venues and non-displayed order types. Competition among public trading markets is no longer based on different methods of bringing together buyers and sellers, like the old competition between the NYSE and Nasdaq, but on different incentive structures for attracting order flow.[562] The SEC appears to be having second thoughts about some aspects of the equity trading markets.[563]

This chapter was prepared for a conference exploring the desirability and structure of a new special study of the securities markets.[564] A companion chapter by separate authors addresses the financial economics literature, and we accordingly focus on the regulatory and legal aspects of trading markets.[565] Our objective is not to resolve all of the questions that commentators have raised

---

[561] *See* Scott Patterson, DARK POOLS: THE RISE OF THE MACHINE TRADERS AND THE RIGGING OF THE U.S. STOCK MARKET (2012); Yesha Yadav, *Dark Pools and the Decline of Market Governance* (working paper, 2017).

[562] *Id.* at 2.

[563] *See* Market Structure Release, *supra* note 554; U.S. Securities and Exchange Commission, Securities Exchange Act Release No. 60997 (November 13, 2009) (hereafter "Non-Public Trading Interest Release") (proposing changes to rules regulating non-exchange trading platforms); U.S. Securities and Exchange Commission, Securities Exchange Act Release No. 60684 (September 18, 2009) (hereafter "Flash Order Release") (proposing rule changes to remove certain exemptions for orders that are canceled if not immediately executed).

[564] In 1961, Congress by joint resolution directed the SEC to "make a study and investigation of the adequacy, for the protection of investors, of the rules of national securities exchanges and national securities associations. . . ." *See* Pub. L. No. 87-196, 75 Stat. 465 (1961). The SEC delivered its report in 1963. *See* U.S. Securities and Exchange Commission, Report of Special Study of Securities Markets, House Doc. 95, 88th Cong., 1st Sess. (1963).

[565] Ryan Davis & Erik R. Sirri, *The Economics of Trading Markets*, *supra*.

about the new equity markets, but to lay the groundwork for a new special study by surveying the state of market regulation, identifying issues, and offering preliminary evaluations.

Section 2 of the paper briefly describes existing trading markets and their functions. Sections 3, 4, and 5 survey the regulatory landscape, with Section 3 focused on the statutory scheme, Section 4 on the SEC's implementing regulations, and Section 5 on the largely judge-made regulation of fraudulent or manipulative trading. Section 6 identifies aspects of equity market structure that have generated criticism and merit further study. Section 7 discusses proposals for alternative market structures. Section 8 concludes.

2 The U.S. Equity Markets

A well-functioning secondary market for securities is essential to the health of the primary market in which businesses raise needed capital. Investors will more eagerly purchase shares in a company if they know they can sell the shares when desired on an efficient and low-cost secondary market. We describe the key operational features of the trading markets for equities, both conceptually and as they currently exist in the United States.

2.1 Nature and Functions

It is tempting to think of a stock market as a facility, physical or virtual, but it is better described as a set of rules and procedures pursuant to which investors buy and sell securities. Through those rules and procedures, the market attempts to attract enough trading interest to provide liquidity. Liquidity implies that there is only a small trade-off between speed and price. In a liquid market, someone wishing to trade can find a counterparty with minimal delay and the resulting trade will be at a price that is attractive to both parties, meaning that it reflects a consensus value of the security at the time of the trade.

A market may create the price dimension of liquidity by bringing together a sufficiently large and informed group of traders to offer both competition and effective price discovery. Alternatively, it may offer the opportunity to trade at prices derived from the primary market, meaning the market in which price discovery takes place. Trading markets typically attract both long-term investors and securities professionals who continuously gather information about traded companies and the trading interest of investors. Securities professionals may have a formal relationship with the market that imposes an obligation to quote prices or trade in order to provide liquidity to other traders. Alternatively, they may provide liquidity simply as a by-product of their attempt to earn trading profits.

Stock markets have generated liquidity in various ways at different times and places. Perhaps the easiest to understand, because it is analogous to markets in many other goods, is a dealer market. In a dealer market, intermediaries known as market makers or dealers continuously quote two-way prices—a "bid" price at which they are willing to buy, and an "ask" or offer price at which they are willing to sell. The difference, or spread, is their compensation for providing liquidity through their willingness to trade. Customers wishing to buy at the market price contact a dealer, either directly or through a broker, and purchase at the dealer's ask price or buy at its bid price. A dealer market is often referred to as "quote-driven" because the dealer's posting of bid and ask prices, or quotations, initiates the transaction process.

Virtually every dealer market throughout history, whether in grain, spices, jewels, foreign exchange, or any other tangible or intangible good, has attracted criticism because the dealers appear to make money for nothing; they neither manufacture nor improve the good being bought or sold. Stock markets are no different. As we will see, securities regulation is sometimes driven by the desire to maintain liquidity but avoid the spread.

A floor-based exchange is a different and somewhat more complex market. It is often referred to as "order-driven" because the transaction process originates with a customer's request to a broker to buy or sell, either at the market price (a "market" order) or a designated price (a "limit" order). Brokers holding buy and sell orders in a particular stock meet on the trading floor and participate in a two-way auction.

If the auction results in a price that both a buyer and seller are willing to accept, the trade can be agreed directly between the brokers acting as their agents. However, in case that does not occur, floor-based exchanges often incorporate dealers known as specialists. The specialist assigned to a stock is expected to quote two-way prices at all times to accommodate market orders that do not find a counterparty in the trading crowd.

In the continuous-auction model, limit orders supply liquidity apart from the specialist. Auctions on a stock exchange, like auctions at Sotheby's or eBay, generally follow rules of price and time priority. Imagine that since the time of the last trade in the stock of XYZ Corp. a potential trader—a broker holding a customer order, a dealer trading for its own account, or a specialist—has bid $25.00 for XYZ; no one has yet agreed to sell at that price nor bid as much. Shortly thereafter, a broker arrives at the trading post with a customer limit order to buy at $25.10. The limit order now has priority, meaning that the next market order to sell will be matched with that limit order and execute at $25.10. Should there be multiple bids at $25.10, the one first in time will be matched with an incoming market order up to the number of shares subject to that bid.

A newer, and now dominant, form of market is an electronic limit order book, in which limit orders are entered and displayed electronically to attract trading interest. In both a traditional dealer market and a floor-based exchange, executions are done manually by telephonic or face-to-face interaction between the buying and selling broker. Electronic limit order books, by contrast, are automated. Marketable orders (market orders or limit orders that can be matched against a contra-side order at the same or a superior price) are executed electronically. These systems blur the distinction between a (professional) dealer and a (nonprofessional) investor and between an order-driven and quote-driven market. They also emphasize that ultimately a stock market is a set of rules that determine how potential buyers and sellers interact, now mostly implemented electronically by what is often called a "matching engine."

2.2 Institutions

The specific institutions that make up the current U.S. equity market fall into four broad categories, which we will describe briefly in turn.

2.2.1 Registered Exchanges

There are twelve securities exchanges registered with and regulated by the Securities and Exchange Commission (SEC) that trade common stocks and related products and seven that trade options.[566] The oldest and most prominent, the New York Stock Exchange (NYSE) was for most of its existence a traditional, floor-based exchange as described above. In response to technological, competitive, and regulatory developments, however, the NYSE now refers to itself as a "hybrid" between an automated and a manual market. It offers automated access to its publicly displayed quotations. It still, however, incorporates "designated market makers," the successors of the specialists, who trade to smooth order imbalances. Brokers overwhelmingly place orders and trade through its electronic trading system.

The second most prominent exchange, Nasdaq, was not registered with the SEC as an exchange until 2006. It began as a decentralized dealer market that used computers to display quotations but not to match customer orders with those quotations. But today, Nasdaq is an entirely automated, electronic matching system.

As markets rely on software to match buy and sell orders automatically, the difference between an exchange and the other markets we will describe is

---

[566] Several of these are affiliated with other exchanges and operate under a single brand, such as the four exchanges owned by the NYSE parent company, Intercontinental Exchange (NYSE, NYSE MKT, NYSE Arca, and NSX), the 4 BATS exchanges, and the three Nasdaq exchanges.

increasingly a matter of the degree of organization and regulatory responsibility rather than the trading process itself.

2.2.2 Alternative Trading Systems

A significant portion of U.S. equity trading takes place through electronic limit order books owned and operated by broker-dealers. Historically, some display their limit orders publicly through a consolidated quotation system operated by the regulated exchanges. They are known formally as "electronic communication networks" or ECNs. Together with the registered securities exchanges, they make up what is popularly known as the "lit" market. Other proprietary systems do not publicly disseminate their orders and are known as "dark pools."

The distinction between lit and dark markets, however, is a matter of degree. Lit markets hold non-displayed orders. For example, a broker may hold a customer order but not make it public until it chooses to execute a trade. Lit markets also may permit non-displayed order types or display a smaller trading size than the actual order. Dark pools may communicate trading interest in the system to selected subscribers either as a formal offer or an indication of interest.

From a regulatory perspective, trading systems, whether lit or dark, that are not regulated as exchanges are known as "alternative trading systems" (ATSs). As of December 1, 2016, there are 82 ATSs registered with the SEC, although only around 30 are active in equities.[567]

2.2.3 Internalization

Broker-dealers also internalize orders. That is, they either match orders they hold as agent or take the other side of the trade as principal. A few dealers do a very large internalization business by paying retail brokers to route customer orders to the dealer. Retail orders are highly attractive because the dealer can earn a spread with little adverse selection risk. A substantial portion of retail orders are internalized through payment for order flow arrangements.[568] Internalization is a type of dark liquidity, in the sense that broker-dealers do not publicly quote the prices and quantities at which they are willing to internalize orders.

---

[567] The list is available at *Alternative Trading Systems with Form ATS on File with the SEC* (November 4, 2016), https://www.sec.gov/foia/ats/atslist1116.pdf; *see also* FINRA, *OTC Transparency Data, ATS Data*, https://otctransparency.finra.org/TradingParticipants (ATSs reporting equity executions to FINRA).

[568] *See* Market Structure Release, *supra* note 554, at 21.

The regulatory definition of an ATS excludes broker-dealer internalization. However, by SEC rule, dealers who execute trades must generally disclose information about execution quality.[569] At the end of 2016, 206 broker-dealers reported executions as internalizers and/or operators of ATSs.[570]

2.2.4 OTC

Equities that are not listed on a registered exchange are defined as over-the-counter (OTC) stocks. Some companies, mostly smaller and less-established ones, are not listed on an exchange. Their shares trade in a dealer market in which one or more dealers quote prices and customers or brokers bring market orders to a dealer for execution.

Dealers may also execute trades in listed stocks off the exchange. In the era of manual markets, institutional trades in listed stocks negotiated and executed with an OTC dealer were known as the "third market," while direct institution-to-institution trading was called the "fourth market." These terms have become less prevalent in the era of electronic trading.

2.3 Selection Among Trading Venues

Different markets may offer different non-price advantages or disadvantages to a would-be buyer or seller. These include commissions and fees and other transaction costs. A persistent issue for institutional investors is that their orders are relatively large and accordingly have market impact. Market (or price) impact refers to the tendency for prices to move in the direction of order flow, an effect that increases with order size.

One reason for this tendency is that large orders are more likely to be informed than small orders. Market makers and other traders move prices when attempting to protect themselves against adverse selection. Facing a potentially informed trader, they widen the spread.[571]

Empirically, however, even large uninformed trades (such as an index fund buying in response to cash inflows) produce temporary market impact. This is often described, tautologically, as a consequence of other traders buying (selling) in anticipation of the price rise (fall) created by a large order. A non-

---

[569] *See* Rule 605 of Regulation NMS, 17 C.F.R. §242.605 (2016).

[570] The list is available at http://www.finra.org/industry/market-centers.

[571] *See* Lawrence R. Glosten & Paul R. Milgrom, *Bid, Ask and Transaction Prices in a Specialist Market with Heterogeneously Informed Traders*, 14 J. FIN. ECON. 71 (1985); Albert S. Kyle, *Continuous Auctions and Insider Trading*, 53 ECONOMETRICA 1315 (1985).

tautological explanation relies on the assumption that market makers do not like to hold large net long or short positions. If a large trader begins making purchases, the market makers who sell to it accumulate short positions. They may then increase their bid and ask prices to induce investors to sell to them and thereby get back to a neutral position. The large purchaser perceives itself being front run by the market makers, who perceive themselves as short covering.[572] However produced as a matter of theory, market impact is an important practical problem for institutional investors. Much of their trading strategy is designed to minimize it.

With this brief introduction to market structure, we turn to the regulatory system.

3. The Statutory Environment

3.1 Pre-1975

As initially enacted, the Securities Exchange Act of 1934 was concerned principally with securities exchanges, defined then and now as organizations that make available "a market place or facilities for bringing together purchasers and sellers of securities."[573] Most of its substantive provisions covered registered exchanges, their member broker-dealers, and listed securities and their issuers.

Section 12(a) of the statute bars brokers and dealers from transacting in any security on any exchange unless the security is registered on that specific exchange. In theory, this gives the listing exchange a monopoly on trading a listed stock. However, Section 12(f) originally gave the SEC the authority, upon application by an exchange, to afford unlisted trading privileges to a stock listed elsewhere. In the Unlisted Trading Privileges Act of 1994, Congress amended Section 12(f) to generally allow exchanges to trade unlisted stocks without SEC approval.[574]

The Exchange Act also reflects the New Deal Congress's skepticism that specialists and other securities dealers add value.[575] Section 11 of the statute instructed the newly-created SEC to consider whether to ban principal trading by

---

[572] *See* Phil Mackintosh, *The Need for Speed: It's Important, Even for VWAP Strategies*, KNIGHT CAPITAL GROUP NEWS & PERSPECTIVES, https://www.kcg.com/news-perspectives/article/the-need-for-speed-its-important-even-for-vwap-strategies.

[573] Securities Exchange Act 15 U.S.C. 78a-78kk (hereinafter SEA) § 3(a)(1).

[574] *See* Pub. L. No. 103-389, 108 Stat. 4081 (1994).

[575] For a more thorough description of this issue, see Paul G. Mahoney, *The Stock Pools and the Securities Exchange Act*, 51 J. FIN. ECON. 343 (1999).

exchange members, either on or off the floor of the exchange.[576] Exercised to the fullest, the provision could have meant the end of the specialist. The SEC ultimately chose not to make such a fundamental change to the NYSE's structure.

In 1936, Congress amended Section 15 of the Exchange Act to mandate registration of broker-dealers operating in the over-the-counter (OTC) market.[577] Previously, the statute gave the SEC the authority to regulate OTC brokers if it chose. The Maloney Act of 1938 added Section 15A, authorizing any association of OTC broker-dealers to register with the SEC and gain regulatory power over its members similar to those of a registered exchange.[578] The National Association of Securities Dealers, Inc. (NASD) registered as the sole self-regulatory organization for OTC broker-dealers. In 2007, the NASD and NYSE merged their self-regulatory, enforcement, and arbitration arms to create the Financial Industry Regulatory Authority (FINRA), which regulates exchange and OTC trading markets and broker-dealers.

The Securities Acts Amendments of 1964 took a large step toward harmonizing treatment of the exchange and OTC markets by requiring large, widely-held companies whose equity securities were not traded on a regulated exchange to register those securities and become subject to periodic reporting and other requirements already imposed on exchange-traded companies.[579] The statute further required the NASD to adopt rules "governing the form and content of quotations" disseminated by its members.[580]

The timing of these amendments was significant because the development of minicomputers and related peripherals was about to make it possible for OTC market makers to disseminate quotes by screen rather than by paper and telephone. In the late 1960s, the NASD began work on an inter-dealer quotation network, Nasdaq, that began operation in 1971.

---

[576] *See* Act of June 6, 1934, § 11(a), 47 Stat. 891 (since repealed).

[577] Act of May 27, 1936, § 3, 49 Stat. 1377, codified as amended at SEA § 15.

[578] Act of June 25, 1938, 52 Stat. 1070, codified as amended at SEA § 15A.

[579] Pub. L. 88-467, § 3(c), 78 Stat. 566, codified as amended at SEA § 12(g).

[580] *Id.* at § 7(a)(7), 78 Stat. 577, codified as amended at SEA § 15A(b)(11).

3.2 Structural Change and the Paperwork Crisis

The rise of institutional investors during the 1960s put pressure on the NYSE's floor-based, continuous auction model. Institutions' share of trading volume on the NYSE nearly doubled from 28% in 1960 to 52% in 1969.[581]

Institutions typically trade in larger sizes than retail investors. The floor-based model did not entirely suit the needs of large traders, particularly their desire to minimize market impact. In the late 1960s, exchanges and their member brokers created new procedures for handling block trades, defined as trades of 10,000 shares or $200,000, whichever is less.[582]

Under those procedures, a broker holding an order of block size may solicit contra-side interest from other brokers or investors "upstairs," or off the trading floor. The broker, either acting as agent for both parties or taking the other side of the trade as principal, may then take the pre-negotiated "cross" to the floor for execution. The trade is executed under special rules of priority that generally permit the trading crowd or specialist to trade with the original order only if offering a better price than the crossed trade.[583] This block trading was accordingly a hybrid between over-the-counter and exchange trading and between dark and lit orders.

Institutions were also highly attentive to transaction costs, putting substantial pressure on the NYSE's fixed commission model. Institutions sometimes looked to the third market for less expensive execution of trades in listed stocks. They also demanded other services, including equipment and research, from their brokers. Mutual funds used brokerage commissions to reward brokers who sold the funds' products.

The NYSE, although forced to accommodate these changes, was uneasy with them. It argued that the securities laws should be amended to eliminate third-market and other off-exchange trading to prevent market fragmentation.

---

[581] SEC, INSTITUTIONAL INVESTOR STUDY OF THE SECURITIES AND EXCHANGE COMMISSION (1971) at 2168.

[582] NYSE Rule 127.10. For a description of the history of the NYSE's rules on block trading, see Division of Market Regulation, U.S. Securities and Exchange Commission, *Market 2000: An Examination of Current Equity Market Developments II-7* (1994).

[583] A detailed description of block trading and other crossed trades on the NYSE appears in Joel Hasbrouck, George Sofianos & Deborah Sosebee, *New York Stock Exchange Systems and Trading Procedures* (working paper, 1993), http://people.stern.nyu.edu/jhasbrou/Research/Working%20Papers/NYSE.PDF.

Less sympathetic observers argued that the NYSE was simply trying to hamper competition and protect its commission structure.

A market crash at the end of the decade ensured that the NYSE would lose the argument. The Dow Jones Industrial Average fell by a third from early 1969 to mid-1970. Unprecedented trading volumes overwhelmed the cumbersome physical clearance and settlement process and caused further damage. The combination of falling prices and paperwork backlogs led to the failure of many smaller brokerage firms.

Congress responded by creating the Securities Investor Protection Corporation to protect customer accounts in the event of a broker's failure. It also began the process of amending the securities laws with the stated purpose of preventing a recurrence of the paperwork crisis. To set the stage for legislation, Congress instructed the SEC to study the role of institutional investors and report back its conclusions.

The SEC took this opportunity to pursue its own views about market structure. Contrary to the NYSE's desire to concentrate trading in listed stocks on the exchange, the SEC wanted to encourage competition among trading venues. But the mere existence of multiple trading venues was not, in the SEC's view, sufficient to produce effective competition. Each trading venue separately reported transaction prices and volumes in the stocks it traded. Dealer transactions off an organized market were not necessarily reported at all. There was even less pre-trade transparency because exchanges viewed their specialists' quotations as proprietary information. NYSE rules also limited member brokers' ability to buy or sell a listed stock off the floor of the exchange. A broker holding a customer market order and wanting to execute it at the best available price accordingly faced substantial hurdles.

In its report to Congress and a separate statement on the future of the trading markets, the SEC urged the creation of a central market, including links between venues trading listed stocks. It also raised concerns about the trading of unlisted securities in dealer markets, including the new Nasdaq market. The SEC suggested that interposing a dealer between the buyer and seller was not always necessary and might be unfair to customers. Dealer markets could be improved by introducing auction principles allowing customer orders to interact directly with one another.

Even before Congress acted, the SEC began to use its statutory authority over stock exchange rules to force changes at the NYSE. It adopted Rule 19b-3, banning fixed commissions on stock exchanges effective May 1, 1975.

3.3 The 1975 Securities Acts Amendments

Congress responded to the SEC's report with the Securities Acts Amendments of 1975.[584] They added Section 11A to the Exchange Act, giving the SEC new regulatory authority to spur the creation of a "national market system" (NMS).[585] Section 11A suggested that a broker holding a customer order to buy or sell a stock should be able to see the quotations in every market in which that stock traded and route the order to the market offering the best price.[586] It also called for SEC registration and regulation of securities information processors, or companies disseminating trade reports and quotations.[587]

Section 11A(a)(2) instructs the SEC to designate by rule the securities that will be eligible for trading in the national market system, termed "qualified securities" in the statute and "NMS securities" in the SEC's rules.[588] Congress did not, however, mandate any particular institutional structure for the trading markets but left it to the SEC to define and create the NMS.

The statute also changed the relationship between exchanges, clearing agencies, and the NASD, on the one hand, and the SEC, on the other.[589] It for the first time referred to the former entities as "self-regulatory organizations" (SROs)[590] but simultaneously inserted the SEC more deeply into their regulatory role. The SROs must submit most proposed internal rule changes to the SEC for approval after public notice and comment.[591] The SEC gained more authority to rescind or amend SRO rules.[592] The statute also codified the abolition of fixed brokerage commissions.[593]

---

[584] Pub. L. 94-29, 89 Stat. 97.

[585] SEA §11A.

[586] *Id.* §11A(a)(1)(C)(iv).

[587] *Id.* §11A(b). The term "securities information processor" is defined in Section 3(a)(22).

[588] *See* Rule 600 of Regulation NMS, 17 C.F.R. §242.600.

[589] The statute also gave the SEC regulatory authority over municipal securities broker-dealers and expanded the regulation of the clearance and settlement process.

[590] *Id.* §3(6), 89 Stat. 100, codified at SEA §3(a)(26).

[591] *Id.* §16, 89 Stat. 147, codified as amended at SEA §19(b).

[592] *Id.* §16, 89 Stat. 150, codified as amended at SEA §19(c).

[593] *Id.* §4, 89 Stat. 107, codified as amended at SEA §6(e)(1).

The 1975 amendments authorized the SEC to pursue changes it had contemplated since at least the early 1970s. The next section describes how it used that authority.

4 Regulatory Implementation of the 1975 Amendments

4.1 Information Links

The SEC's early efforts to create a national market system focused on information linkages.[594] It took tentative steps in 1972 with the adoption of Rule 17a-15, which introduced consolidated reporting of transactions in listed stocks, whether taking place on the principal exchange, a regional exchange, or the third market. In particular, the rule required each securities exchange and securities association to adopt a transaction reporting plan to provide last-sale information for all transactions on its trading platform. Brokers and dealers were barred from transacting on a market unless the SEC declared its reporting plan effective. As a condition of effectiveness, the plan had to require any vendor purchasing transaction information to consolidate the information from all reporting markets into a single, real-time composite tape.

The 1975 amendments gave the SEC additional tools to require a consolidated system of transaction and quotation reporting, including direct regulatory power over securities information processors. The SEC accordingly amended and designated Rule 17a-15 as Rule 11Aa3-1 (the rules adopted under Section 11A have since been moved to Regulation NMS).[595] The amended rule continued to require effective transaction reporting plans but broadened the requirement to large-cap Nasdaq stocks as well as listed stocks. It also authorized SROs to act jointly to create transaction reporting plans.

The SEC also adopted Rule 11Ac1-1, requiring SROs to make the best bids and offers in their trading systems continuously available to quotation vendors.[596] A complementary provision, Rule 11Ac1-2, required that a securities

---

[594] For further background and an insightful overview of secondary market issues at the turn of the millennium, see Laura Nyantung Beny, *U.S. Secondary Stock Markets: A Survey of Current Regulatory and Structural Issues and a Reform Proposal to Enhance Competition*, 2 COLUM. BUS. L. REV. 399 (2002).

[595] The rule is adopted under the provision of Exchange Act §11A(a)(3) authorizing the SEC to permit or require SROs to act jointly with respect to creating an NMS. The rule, as amended, has since been redesignated Rule 601 of Regulation NMS, 17 C.F.R. §242.601 (2016).

[596] Rule 11Ac1-1, as amended, has been redesignated Rule 602 of Regulation NMS, 17 C.F.R. §242.602 (2016).

information processor (SIP) display transaction and quote information on a consolidated basis.[597]

Pursuant to Rule 11Aa3-1, the NYSE, Amex, regional exchanges, and Nasdaq cooperated to create four separate transaction and quotation reporting plans: one for NYSE-listed securities, one for securities listed on other exchanges, one for Nasdaq and certain OTC securities, and one for listed options. The Consolidated Tape Association, owned by the exchanges, is the SIP for transaction and quote data for listed securities; Nasdaq is its own information processor. Brokers operating alternative trading systems report trades executed in the system to an SRO-operated market where they "print," or are publicly identified, as trades on the relevant venue. The SIP accordingly consolidates across all exchanges "core data" consisting of last-trade reports and each exchange's current highest bids and lowest offers for each security.[598] For each stock, the overall highest bid and lowest offer provided to the SIP and disseminated by it pursuant to a national market system transaction reporting plan are known as the national best bid (NBB) and national best offer (NBO), collectively called the NBBO.[599]

As the national market system developed, a broker holding a customer order had many options for executing that order. The SEC accordingly adopted rules designed to give customers information about executions and order routing that could help them monitor their brokers. Rule 11Ac1-3 required brokers opening a new customer account to give the customer information about the broker's policies regarding payment for order flow.[600] Rule 11Ac1-5 required execution venues to provide summary information about the quality of executions, including information about execution speeds, prices relative to the NBBO, and average effective and realized spreads on orders of different sizes.[601]

---

[597] Rule 11Ac1-2, as amended, has been redesignated Rule 603 of Regulation NMS, 17 C.F.R. §242.603 (2016).

[598] *See* 17 C.F.R. §§ 242.601, 242.602 (2015) (requiring exchanges to report last sales—price and size of the most recent trades—and current best bids and offers); NetCoalition v. SEC, 615 F.3d 525, 529 (D.C. Cir. 2010) (discussing the core data regime).

[599] *See* Rule 600(b)(42) of Regulation NMS, 17 C.F.R. §242.600(b)(42) (2016).

[600] Rule 11Ac1-3, as amended, has been redesignated Rule 607 of Regulation NMS, 17 C.F.R. §242.602 (2016).

[601] Rule 11Ac1-5, as amended, has been redesignated Rule 605 of Regulation NMS, 17 C.F.R. §242.605 (2016).

Rule 11Ac1-6 required broker-dealers to disclose summary information about their order routing decisions.[602]

4.2 Order Handling and Execution

4.2.1 ITS

In the 1975 amendments, Congress encouraged the SEC to remove barriers to competition between markets. The SEC interpreted the statutory language not merely to give it authority to require information linkages, but to regulate order handling and execution within each trading platform—in short, to shape the institutional structure of the markets by rule.[603]

Its first exercise of this authority came in 1978. The SEC encouraged the NYSE, Amex, and several regional exchanges to create an Intermarket Trading System (ITS).[604] The ITS created an electronic link between the exchanges allowing brokers to route market orders to the exchange offering the best price at the time of the order.

The rules of the participating exchanges were amended to discourage trade-throughs, or executions in one market at a price inferior to that available in another linked market. In general, those rules gave a broker a right of redress when an order it publicly displayed was traded through.[605] The ITS reflected the SEC's view that it could and should change the rules and procedures of individual trading venues to require member brokers to take market orders to the market offering the best price regardless of the broker's or even the customer's preferences.

---

[602] Rule 11Ac1-6, as amended, has been redesignated Rule 606 of Regulation NMS, 17 C.F.R. §242.606 (2016).

[603] This was not an uncontroversial reading of the statute. *See* Dale A. Oesterle, *Congress's 1975 Directions to the SEC for the Creation of a National Market System: Is the SEC Operating Outside the Mandate?*, American Enterprise Institute Monograph (May 2003).

[604] *See* Securities Exchange Act Release No. 14416, 43 Fed. Reg. 4354, 4357 (1978).

[605] *See* Order Approving Proposed Rule Changes, Midwest Stock Exchange, Inc. et al., Exchange Act Release No. 17704, 46 Fed. Reg. 22520 (1981).

4.2.2 NYSE Rule 390

The ITS integrated the regional exchanges with the principal exchanges. Bringing the third market fully into the ITS took another two decades. The NYSE's Rule 390, which (with some exceptions) required that any NYSE member firm's principal trades in listed stocks take place on the exchange, stood in the way of complete integration.

In 1980, the SEC adopted Rule 19c-3, which made Rule 390 inapplicable to any stock listed after April 26, 1979. In 1982, the SEC required the exchanges and the NASD to extend the ITS to third market makers with respect to "Rule 19c-3" stocks not grandfathered into Rule 390. It was not until the end of 1999, however, that the NYSE, under SEC pressure, proposed to eliminate Rule 390 altogether.[606]

4.2.3 The Order Handling Rules

In the early 1990s, an academic study of the Nasdaq market created momentum for new and consequential market structure regulations. The study found that Nasdaq market makers rarely quoted prices in odd eighths.[607] In other words, the typical spread was at least 25 cents even though the minimum price increment at the time was 12.5 cents. Although there were potentially innocent explanations for the practice, the SEC concluded that Nasdaq's rules and procedures did not provide competitive pricing to retail investors.

Market makers at that time were under no obligation to display customer limit orders. A market maker might accordingly quote $20 bid, $20.25 ask and receive a customer limit order to sell at $20.125. The market maker might or might not choose to "price improve" and fill the customer order at the limit price. If it chose not to do so, the order remained on its books, to be executed only when the market maker's bid price reached $20.125. In the meantime, incoming market orders to buy would execute at the market maker's $20.25 ask rather than at the customer limit price.

From Nasdaq's perspective, this was a fundamental design feature of the competing market-maker model. The NYSE assigns a single specialist to a stock,

---

[606] *See* Securities Exchange Act Release No. 42758, https://www.sec.gov/rules/sro/ny9948o.htm.

[607] *See* William G. Christie & Paul H. Schultz, *Why do NASDAQ Market Makers Avoid Odd-Eighth Quotes?*, 49 J. FIN. 1813 (1994). Specifically, Christie and Schultz studied 100 actively traded Nasdaq-listed stocks and found that 70 almost never traded at an odd eighth. For the remaining stocks, odd eighth quotes were observed, although even eighths were more common.

but that specialist maintains a central limit order book containing limit orders that brokers have left with the specialist. Orders on the book are executed under auction principles offering price/time priority. Customer orders on an exchange accordingly interact with one another and thereby compete with the specialist's quotations. In a market-maker system, the market maker internalizes orders, executing them against its own public quotes rather than against limit orders it or another dealer holds. It therefore captures the spread on most or all trades. Competition comes from the existence of multiple market makers in a stock, not from direct interaction of customer orders.

The SEC, however, concluded that requiring market makers to display price-improving customer limit orders would reduce spreads, reviving a concept it had first floated in the 1970s. It accordingly adopted the so-called Order Handling Rules in 1996 to take effect in 1997.[608] New rule 11Ac1-4 required a market maker, with certain exceptions, to publish the price and size of any customer limit order that either improved the market maker's quotation or increased size at the quoted price.[609]

The Order Handling Rules also included an amendment to Rule 11Ac1-1 requiring a market maker that posts a quotation in an electronic communications network to make the same price available, in at least the minimum quote size, in the primary market. The ECN itself may meet the market maker's obligation by including its best bid and offer in the consolidated quotation system and providing all broker-dealers the ability to execute a trade against its public quote.

The number and trading volumes of ECNs increased after adoption of the Order Handling Rules. There is ample reason to think there is a causal link. Rule 11Ac1-4 ensured that orders submitted to an ECN could appear on Nasdaq screens in direct competition with market maker quotes. While prior rules mandating communication linkages indirectly affected market structure, the Order Handling Rules directly mandated a new type of competition among trading platforms.

It is also worth noting that the Order Handling Rules did *not* require that public orders take priority over securities professionals trading for their own account, a policy goal the SEC suggested as far back as 1973.[610] For a time, the Nasdaq market remained a decentralized dealer market based principally on

---

[608] *See* Order Execution Obligations (Rules 11Ac1-4 and 11Ac1-1), Securities Exchange Act Release No. 37619A, https://www.sec.gov/rules/final/37619a.txt.

[609] Rule 11Ac1-4, as amended, has been redesignated as Rule 604 of Regulation NMS, 17 C.F.R. § 242.604.

[610] *See* Securities and Exchange Commission, Policy Statement on the Structure of a Central Market System (1973).

internalization of customer orders. A dealer willing to match the best bid or offer in the system could execute a customer market order as principal even though another dealer held a customer limit order at the same price.

4.3 Regulations ATS and NMS

After adoption of the Order Handling Rules, the SEC accelerated the pace of regulating market structure. In addition to the final abolition of NYSE Rule 390, discussed above, the most important developments were the adoption of Regulations ATS and NMS, which together exert a substantial influence on how equity markets operate today.

4.3.1 Regulation ATS

In 1969, Institutional Networks Corp. (later Instinet) began operation as an electronic trading system. Unlike Nasdaq, which gave dealers the opportunity to update and display their quotations on-screen, Instinet catered to institutional investors, allowing them to trade directly with one another without a dealer. Investors could enter limit orders and indications of interest into the system. Initially handling listed stocks in competition with the third market, Instinet and other proprietary trading systems would later become a major presence in Nasdaq stocks.

The question naturally arose whether these systems are exchanges. Both Nasdaq and Instinet operate facilities for bringing together buyers and sellers and therefore meet the statutory definition of an exchange. But the definition itself is overbroad. A telephone system brings together buyers and sellers of securities, but it was never thought necessary to register AT&T as a securities exchange. The SEC did not push the regulatory definition to its limit, but applied the term only to organizations that centralized quotations on a continuous basis and executed trades.[611]

It was not terribly consequential whether Nasdaq was required to register as an exchange. The market was operated by the NASD, an organization with regulatory powers similar to those of an exchange and subject to similar SEC oversight. Soon the SEC would begin adding the term "or interdealer quotation system" alongside the term "exchange" in many of its regulations.

Instinet, however, was not initially a regulated entity. In 1969, the SEC accordingly proposed a rule regulating "automated trading information systems," defined as automated systems for communicating indications of interest or offers

---

[611] *See* Securities Exchange Act Release No. 27611, 55 Fed. Reg. 1890, 1900 (1990).

to buy or sell securities.[612] The proposed regulation, Rule 15c2-10, would have required such systems to file and have the SEC declare effective a plan describing the system and its rules and agreeing to maintain certain records.

As the SEC considered the proposed rule, however, Instinet sought to register as a broker-dealer, offering a different solution to the regulatory gap. As a registered broker-dealer, Instinet would be subject to SEC and NASD oversight. Moreover, by becoming a member of one or more exchanges, Instinet could access the order book of those exchanges. Eventually, it would offer its institutional subscribers "direct market access," or the ability to look through the broker-dealer and interact directly with the exchange's order book.

Instinet registered as a broker-dealer and became a member of several regional exchanges, and the SEC did not adopt proposed rule 15c2-10. Instinet and other proprietary computer-based trading systems expanded and competed with the primary markets—the NYSE, Amex, and Nasdaq—for institutional and broker-dealer order flow. They offered investors the opportunity to enter orders and have them matched automatically and rapidly by computer algorithm.

Although initially conceived as a way to facilitate block-size trades in listed stocks, this did not become the mainstay of the ECNs' business. When limit orders did not match internally, the ECNs needed a way to access other sources of liquidity. Accessing manual orders on the floor of an exchange was cumbersome compared to accessing market maker quotations through a Nasdaq terminal. The ECNs therefore came to specialize in trading Nasdaq stocks until the NYSE's transformation into a largely electronic market.

As ECNs grew, they became unwilling to rely solely on informal guidance from the SEC staff and sought formal assurance that the Division of Market Regulation would not recommend enforcement action should a system not register as an exchange. In the mid-1980s, the Division issued several no-action letters to electronic trading systems conditioned on their providing various ongoing data to the SEC.[613] The SEC would later formalize the reporting conditions in these no-action letters by adopting Rule 17a-23.[614] The rule required any registered broker-dealer operating an automated trading system to report information about participants, orders, trades, and other data to the SEC on a quarterly basis.

Traditional stock exchanges complained that the SEC's use of the no-action approach rather than formal rulemaking kept the exchanges from

---

[612] *See* Securities Exchange Act Release No. 8661, 34 Fed. Reg. 12952 (1969).

[613] A list of no-action letters appears in Securities Exchange Act Release No. 26708, 54 Fed. Reg. 15429, 15430 n. 3 (1989).

[614] Rule 17a-23 was repealed by the Regulation ATS adopting release cited *infra* note 618.

participating in the regulatory process. They argued, moreover, that the proprietary networks would likely be fair-weather markets. During times of substantial volatility, liquidity might disappear on the electronic markets, leaving the slack to be picked up by stock exchange specialists, who are required to maintain orderly markets, and Nasdaq market makers, who are required to quote continuous two-way prices.

At the same time, the SEC became concerned about market fragmentation. In particular, it worried that orders in the public markets did not necessarily interact with those in the proprietary systems. Retail investors might therefore receive inferior prices to those available to institutions trading in the automated systems. The concern was not hypothetical; the SEC found that some Nasdaq market makers quoted prices on Instinet that were better than their quotes in the Nasdaq system.[615]

Ironically, however, the 1975 National Market System amendments complicated the SEC's attempts to bring proprietary trading systems into the national market system. The amendments were drafted under the assumption that a stock exchange would be a membership organization and that its members would all be registered broker-dealers.[616] ECNs operated on a different business model; they were proprietary and allowed direct access to institutional investors. They could not maintain that business model and comply with the Exchange Act's requirements for registered exchanges. Any integration of those systems into the national market system, accordingly, would have to take place under the rubric of broker-dealer regulation.

In 1996, as part of the Order Handling Rules, the SEC required stock exchange specialists and Nasdaq market makers to make publicly available any price quoted on a proprietary system representing an improvement on their displayed prices.[617] Shortly thereafter, Congress gave the SEC general exemptive authority, making it possible for the SEC to expand its interpretation of the term "exchange" while applying different regulatory standards to different types of exchanges.

---

[615] *See* Securities Exchange Act Release No. 38672, 62 Fed. Reg. 30485, 30492 (1997).

[616] *See, e.g.*, Securities Exchange Act §6(b) (regulating the relationship between an exchange and its members); §6(c) (requiring that members be registered broker-dealers).

[617] *See* Securities Exchange Act Release No. 37619A, 61 Fed. Reg. 48290 (1996) (adopting the so-called "Order Handling Rules").

The SEC accordingly overhauled its rules relating to exchanges and other markets in 1998.[618] The new rules define an "exchange" to include any organization that brings together the orders of multiple buyers and sellers and uses non-discretionary rules or processes to execute trades.[619] The definition excludes broker-dealer internalization. In the adopting release, the SEC also declared that it had no objection to a registered exchange demutualizing and operating as a for-profit organization, which the registered exchanges have subsequently done.[620]

Not every entity meeting the broad definition of "exchange" must register as such. An "alternative trading system" (ATS), defined as an exchange that does not operate as a self-regulatory body (that is, does not seek to regulate the conduct of its subscribers apart from their use of the system) may instead operate under Regulation ATS.[621]

Regulation ATS keeps in place the longstanding practice under which ATSs register as broker-dealers. As the adopting release summarizes, any ATS handling less than five percent of the aggregate trading volume in each security it trades need only "(1) file with the Commission a notice of operation and quarterly reports; (2) maintain records, including an audit trail of transactions; and (3) refrain from using the words 'exchange', 'stock market', or similar terms in its name."[622]

However, any ATS that handles at least 5% of the trading volume in any national market system security is potentially subject to two forms of integration into the national market system under the "order display" rule and the "fair access" rule of Regulation ATS. The order display rule requires an ATS that displays subscriber orders to potential counterparties to create a link to an exchange or securities association to display the best bid and offer in its system for any such security. It must also allow any member broker-dealer of the linked exchange or association to execute trades using the same rules of priority as the linked exchange or association.

The "fair access" rule applies at the same volume threshold but does not apply to an ATS that uses strictly passive pricing (that is, pricing derived from public last-sale prices) and that does not display orders. It requires an ATS to

---

[618] *See Regulation of Exchanges and Alternative Trading Systems*, Securities Exchange Act Release No. 40760, 63 Fed. Reg. 70844 (1998) ("ATS adopting release").

[619] 17 C.F.R. § 242.3b-16(a) (2016).

[620] *See* ATS adopting release, *supra* note 618, at 70848.

[621] 17 C.F.R. §§ 242.300-303 (2016).

[622] ATS adopting release, *supra* note 618, at 70847.

establish written standards for subscriber access and permit any person meeting those standards to subscribe.

In principle, then, Regulation ATS inaugurated a process of bringing ATSs into the national market system by bringing their best bids and offers into the public quote stream and giving the public the ability to execute against them. But the regulation has not been the primary driver of integration. Individual ATSs have generally not accounted for a sufficient portion of trading in individual stocks to trigger the order display and fair access requirements.[623] Individual ATSs choose to be a "lit" ECN or a dark pool for reasons of business strategy rather than regulatory requirement. Moreover, even a large dark pool could avoid triggering the order display rule by not displaying system orders to other subscribers, but instead communicating only indications of interest.

In 2009, the SEC proposed to amend Regulation ATS to broaden application of the order display rule. The proposed amendments would lower the threshold for public display of ATS best bid and offer quotations dramatically, to 0.25% of trading volume.[624] They would also define certain indications of interest as orders. Operators of ATSs argued that the existence of non-displayed pools of liquidity was not a new phenomenon and was not detrimental to public investors.[625] At the time of this writing, the amendments have not been adopted.

4.3.2 Regulation NMS

In 2005, the SEC reorganized existing regulations adopted pursuant to the 1975 national market system amendments and added significant new regulations. Rules previously adopted under Section 11A and described above were moved to a new Regulation NMS.

The most notable and controversial of the new rules was the so-called trade-through rule, or in the SEC's terminology the order protection rule, Rule 611.[626] Recall that the ITS Plan requires the participating exchanges to take certain steps to discourage trade-throughs in listed stocks. By contrast, the order protection rule imposes a mandatory requirement that every exchange, securities association, and ATS adopt rules reasonably designed to prevent trade-throughs

---

[623] *See Regulation of Non-Public Trading Interest*, Securities Exchange Act Release No. 60997, at 24 ("Few if any dark pool ATSs exceed the 5% threshold for any NMS stocks").

[624] *Id.*

[625] *See* Goldman Sachs Group, *Market Structure Overview* (Sept. 2009), https://www.sec.gov/comments/s7-21-09/s72109-53.pdf.

[626] Rule 611 of Regulation NMS, 17 C.F.R. §242.611.

of "protected quotations" in NMS stocks.[627] Protected quotations are the best publicly displayed bid and offer on the exchanges or OTC market, but only to the extent those quotations can be automatically accessed. An order on a floor-based exchange that would require manual execution is not a protected quotation.

Rule 611 is designed in part to protect investors entering market orders from receiving inferior prices. This is not, however, the principal objective. A broker acting as the customer's agent owes a duty of best execution that would usually (although not always) lead the broker to route the order to the trading venue offering the best price even without a trade-through rule. Exceptions would occur when the customer instructs the broker to trade in a particular venue or when the customer or broker believes trading through the best bid or offer could reduce market impact. In short, trade-through protection is not principally for the benefit of market orders.

Instead, the rule was justified as an attempt to reward and thereby encourage the provision of liquidity through limit orders. If a trader knows that any limit order he or she enters will be protected against a trade-through when it is the best-priced bid or offer, traders will be more likely to enter limit orders, all other things equal.

There is room for debate, however, about whether the order protection rule was necessary for this purpose. The two dissenting commissioners argued that there was little evidence that trade-throughs were a problem on Nasdaq (which was not subject to the ITS trade-through rules) or that traders were discouraged from entering limit orders there. Some commentators had argued in favor of an opt-out provision that would have permitted the trader entering a market order to ignore the best-priced order, presumably pursuant to a trading strategy designed to reduce market impact. The final rule did not include an opt-out, consistent with the view that the principal beneficiaries of trade-through protection are those who enter limit orders.

A related provision, Rule 610(d), requires SROs to prohibit a trading venue from displaying quotations that lock or cross protected quotations. A bid price in one market that equals the (previously entered) ask price in another "locks" that quotation, while a bid price that exceeds that ask price "crosses" the quotation. Similarly, an ask price that is the same or less than a previously entered bid locks or crosses that quote, respectively.

The logic behind the rule is that submitting a locking or crossing quotation is a way to avoid trading with the best bid or offer without violating the trade-through rule. Imagine, for example, that a trader prefers to trade in

---

[627] At the time of Regulation NMS's adoption, Nasdaq was not yet a registered exchange. Rule 611 accordingly extended trade-through protection for the first time to Nasdaq NMS stocks.

Venue A rather than Venue B, perhaps because the former typically has better depth, resulting in less price impact. At some point in time, Venue B displays an ask price of $20.01 for a particular stock, while Venue A displays an ask price of $20.02. Absent the trade-through rule, the trader would simply ignore the quote in Venue B and purchase the shares offered at $20.02 in Venue A. But the trade-through rule prohibits this.

An alternative strategy to execute the trade in Venue A is to post a bid at $20.01 there in hopes that the bid will attract trading interest. Note that this strategy locks the ask price in Venue B and is inconsistent with the spirit of the trade-through rule, which aims to reward the person posting the best ask. Rule 610(d) comes to the rescue of Venue B by forbidding Venue A to display the $20.01 bid.

Regulation NMS also regulates execution access to quotations displayed by various markets. Effective trade-through protection requires that brokers be able to route customer orders quickly to the venue providing the best price. As described above, the SEC spurred the creation of the ITS that facilitated routing among exchanges. However, Regulation NMS does not mandate the use of the ITS or any other specific link between trading centers. In practice, exchanges and ATSs typically offer brokers private links to their systems, giving those willing to pay for such links rapid execution access to displayed quotations. Rule 610(a) prohibits SROs from imposing unfairly discriminatory terms that inhibit customer access, through member brokers, to trading facilities regulated by the SRO.

Rule 610(c) caps fees for access to quotations. In particular, no trading center can charge more than $0.003/share for execution access to a protected quotation or to certain other displayed quotations. The rule effectively limits the amount of the "take" fee imposed pursuant to a maker-taker fee structure, described in more detail in Section 6.2.2 below.

Finally, Regulation NMS added a new "sub-penny" provision, Rule 612, restricting trading venues from quoting or accepting quotations in increments of less than one penny so long as the stock price is at least $1.00. The rule was designed to prevent traders from stepping ahead, or making an economically inconsequential improvement to the best quotation in order to obtain priority over it. In effect, the practice of stepping ahead is inconsistent with the spirit of the price/time priority system, which gives priority to the first-in-time order at a given price until an economically superior price is quoted. Rule 612 does not, however, forbid executing trades in sub-penny increments. A crossing network that executes trades at the midpoint of the quoted spread can execute in a half-penny increment. Similarly, a broker-dealer internalizing an order can price improve by less than a penny.

Adoption of Regulation NMS, like adoption of the order handling rules, was followed by significant changes in market structure that are likely due, at least in part, to the regulatory change. Shortly before the final adoption of the rule, both the NYSE and Nasdaq acquired ECNs and prepared to transform themselves into mostly electronic markets allowing for automated execution against publicly displayed quotations. New exchanges and ATSs quickly began operation. In particular, the number of ATSs operating as dark pools increased from 10 in 2002 to 29 in 2009.[628]

5 The Regulation of Trading Practices

The centerpiece of the Securities Exchange Act, for the purposes of regulating misconduct by traders, is § 10(b) and Rule 10b-5 promulgated thereunder. Section 10(b) broadly prohibits any "manipulative or deceptive device[s] or contrivance[s] in contravention of" rules and regulations prescribed by the SEC "as necessary or appropriate in the public interest or for the protection of investors."[629] Rule 10b-5, adopted without fanfare in 1943, has served for more than eighty years as the workhorse of federal securities enforcement.[630] It prohibits, *inter alia*, "in connection with the purchase or sale of any security," employing "any device, scheme, or artifice to defraud" and engaging "in any act, practice, or course of business which operates or would operate as a fraud or deceit upon any person." The most important forms of trader misconduct proscribed under § 10(b) are insider trading and manipulation.

5.1 Insider Trading

Alongside the rise of high-frequency trading, perhaps no aspect of securities law has ignited the popular imagination as much as insider trading law, which generally prohibits individuals from trading while in possession of material nonpublic information in violation of a duty owed to their employer. The modern story of insider trading law begins with the Supreme Court's decision in *Chiarella v. United States*,[631] which held that an insider has no duty to disclose

---

[628] *See Regulation of Non-Public Trading Interest*, *supra* note 623, at 6 (increase from 2002 to 2009).

[629] 15 U.S.C. § 78j(b).

[630] 17 C.F.R. § 240.10b-5.

[631] 445 U.S. 222, 235 (1980). The origins of federal insider trading law begin with the SEC's opinion in *Cady, Roberts & Co.*, 40 S.E.C. 907 (1961), finding that a person with a special relationship with a company violates Rule 10b-5 if that person trades the company's stock while in possession of material nonpublic information without first disclosing it. The Second Circuit, in *SEC v. Texas Gulf Sulphur Co.*, 401 F.2d 833 (2d. Cir. 1968), radicalized *Cady, Roberts* by dispensing

material, nonpublic information or abstain from trading under § 10(b) based on "the mere possession of nonpublic information."[632] *Chiarella* articulated the "classical" theory of insider trading that a trade based on material nonpublic information violates Rule 10b-5 if alongside possession of material nonpublic information there was "a relationship of trust and confidence between the parties to a transaction."[633] The Supreme Court subsequently supplemented it with the "misappropriation" theory of insider trading in the *O'Hagan* case,[634] which held that transactions based on material nonpublic information violate Rule 10b-5 when the trade "was in breach of a duty [of loyalty and confidentiality] owed to the source of the information."[635] While the classical theory would only seem to reach corporate insiders of an issuer of securities, who plausibly owe a duty to all the shareholders of that firm who own its securities, the misappropriation theory reaches beyond insiders of the issuer to insiders within other institutions who possess material nonpublic information about the issuer, and may owe their own institution a duty of loyalty. In other words, the "relationship of trust and confidence" need no longer exist "between the parties to a transaction" for the purposes of insider trading law.

The source of additional complications—and an issue recently ruled upon by the U.S. Supreme Court—is the applicability of Rule 10b-5 to persons who directly or indirectly learn of (and trade on) material nonpublic information ("tippees") from a person who, if he traded on that information himself, would be acting unlawfully ("tippers").[636] Tippees will often owe no duty of loyalty or confidence to either an issuer or an institution holding material information about the issuer, but the Supreme Court inventively found a way to apply insider trading laws to both tippers and tippees. In *Dirks v. SEC,* the Court held that "a tippee assumes a fiduciary duty to the shareholders of a corporation not to trade on material nonpublic information [] when the insider has breached his fiduciary

---

with the special relationship requirement and holding that "*anyone* in possession of material inside information must either disclose it to the investing public or . . . must abstain from trading . . . while such inside information remains undisclosed." *Id.* at 848 (emphasis added).

[632] 445 U.S. 222, 235 (1980).

[633] *Id.* at 230.

[634] United States v. O'Hagan, 521 U.S. 642 (1997).

[635] *Id.* at 652.

[636] For a fuller discussion of these issues, see Merritt B. Fox, Lawrence R. Glosten & Gabriel V. Rauterberg, *Informed Trading and its Regulation*, J. Corp. L. (forthcoming), and the literature discussed there.

duty to the shareholders by disclosing his information to the tippee and the tippee knows or should know that there has been a breach,"[637] and, in addition, for the tipper to breach her duty to the shareholders, the source must "personally . . . benefit, directly or indirectly, from [her] disclosure."[638] A tippee, effectively, is deemed to have become a "participant after the fact" in the tipper's breach of her relationship of trust and confidence to an issuer when the tipper provided information to someone likely to trade on it. Further downstream tippees, who receive information from a predecessor tippee, can also violate Rule 10b-5, either through awareness of the breach by the original source, including her personal benefit,[639] or where the downstream tippee is breaching her own duty of confidentiality to the person providing her with the information.[640]

The issue of tipper liability recently returned to the Supreme Court in *United States v. Salman*,[641] where the Court analyzed the gift prong of the personal benefit test as applied to a remote tippee. In *Salman*, the tipper and initial tippee had clearly violated Rule 10b-5. The dispute concerned the defendant, who had received information from the initial tippee and knew the improper origin of the information, but argued that there was no evidence that the tippee had received a personal benefit from communicating the information, as the Second Circuit's decision in *United States v. Newman*,[642] supposedly required. The Court clarified that the tipper need not receive a pecuniary benefit, and that a close familial relationship or friendship was sufficient to infer that the defendant receiver a personal benefit from making a gift.

---

[637] 463 U.S. 646, 660 (1983) (citation omitted).

[638] *Id.* at 662. Where an insider provides a gift of information to a relative or friend, the personal benefit requirement is also satisfied. *See Dirks*, 463 U.S. at 664; *see also* Adam C. Pritchard, *Dirks and the Genesis of Personal Benefit*, 68 SMU L. REV. 857 (2015) (discussing the origins of the personal benefit test).

[639] *See, e.g.*, SEC v. Musella, 678 F.Supp. 1060, 1062-64 (S.D.N.Y. 1988) (defendants "should have known that fiduciary duties were being breached with respect to confidential, non-public information"); *In re* Motel 6 Sec. Litig., 161 F. Supp. 2d 227, 242 (S.D.N.Y. 2001) ("a defendant's subjective belief that information received 'was obtained in breach of a fiduciary duty . . . may . . . be shown by circumstantial evidence'").

[640] In each of these two cases, if someone who himself is prohibited from trading instead, or in addition, tips someone else, he would violate Rule 10b-5 as a tipper.

[641] Salman v. United States, 580 U.S. __ (2016).

[642] 773 F.3d 438 (2d Cir. 2014).

The tipping situations above involved information originating within an issuer. The law differs for information originating within an institution other than the issuer and importantly discriminates between two distinct scenarios. In the first, a source with a duty of confidentiality to an institution willingly provides material nonpublic information to a tippee who has no duty to that institution. The tipper had no authorization to disclose the information, and the tippee trades based on it. Here, the tipper violates Rule 10b-5 under the misappropriation theory by breaching a duty of confidentiality in providing information to an individual likely to trade based on it.[643] The tippee violates Rule 10b-5 if he was aware of the breach by the source when trading due to the information.[644] In the second scenario, a tippee owes a duty of confidentiality to the tipper and/or her employer institution and does not know the tip to be authorized. Here, the tippee violates the misappropriation theory quite clearly. Further downstream tippees can also violate Rule 10b-5 under applicable versions of the "participant after the fact" and misappropriation theories.

While the academic debate regarding the desirability of insider trading law continues,[645] the law remains politically popular and vigorously enforced. In light of this reality, practically open questions largely concern how an optimal anti-insider trading regime should work. Here, a series of separate issues appear, including whether we should replace our current common law approach with a statutory one, and how to resolve ongoing debates regarding the scope of tippee liability. In particular, *Salman* fails to provide precise answers regarding fact patterns in which material nonpublic information is provided as a gift among

---

[643] *See, e.g.*, SEC v. Yun, 327 F.3d 1263, 1274-75 (11th Cir. 2003); SEC v. Gansman, 657 F.3d 85, 92 (2d Cir. 2011); 18 DONALD C. LANGEVOORT, INSIDER TRADING REGULATION, ENFORCEMENT AND PREVENTION § 6:13 (2015).

[644] *See, e.g.*, United States v. Falcone, 257 F.3d 226, 234 (2d Cir. 2001) ("the government was simply required to prove a breach by Salvage, the tipper, of a duty owed to the owner of the misappropriated information, and defendant's knowledge that the tipper had breached the duty").

[645] The range of classic papers on insider trading is far too vast to summarize, but for two recent analyses reflecting the current state of debate, see, e.g., Stephen Bainbridge, *An Overview of Insider Trading Law and Policy*, in RESEARCH HANDBOOK ON INSIDER TRADING 1 (Bainbridge ed., 2013) and Laura Nyantung Beny, *Insider Trading Laws and Stock Markets Around the World: An Empirical Contribution to the Theoretical Law and Economics Debate*, 32 J. CORP. L. 237 (2007) (hereinafter Beny, *Insider Trading Laws*), and the sources cited therein, e.g., *id.* at 239-244, n.1-3, 6-13, 32, and elsewhere.

acquaintances in social contexts in the financial world. Careful analysis could provide clarity for courts in this regard.

5.2 Manipulation

Securities manipulation is expressly prohibited by statute, but notoriously difficult to define, analyze, or prosecute. There are two express prohibitions. Section 10(b) prohibits the use of "any manipulative or deceptive device" in connection with trading a security in contravention of rules promulgated by the SEC.[646] Section 9(a)(2) proscribes effecting "a series of transactions" in a security (i) that "creat[e] actual or apparent active trading" or affect its price, (ii) "for the purpose of inducing the purchase or sale of such security by others."[647] While § 9(a)(2)'s language may seem clearly applicable to manipulation, its jurisprudence has failed to robustly develop for a number of reasons,[648] leaving § 10(b) as the basis of most manipulation enforcement.

Scholarship has identified three principal forms of manipulative activity: manipulations involving misrepresentations, such as driving up a stock's price by making false statements about its value, which is ambiguously similar to fraud; transaction-based manipulations, based on trading a security to affect its price, where the manipulation's profitability arises from a distinct transaction referring to that price; and market manipulation (also known as "trade-based"

---

[646] *See* 15 U.S.C. § 78j(b). Neither the statute, nor subsequent rulemaking has further defined "manipulative," however. Further, despite the explicit reference to manipulation, rules promulgated pursuant to Section 10(b) have made no mention of manipulation except for Rule 10b-1, which simply refers back to Section 9 to the effect that an act or omission that would violate Section 9 if made in connection with an exchange-listed security is a violation of Section 10(b) whether registered or not.

[647] *See* 15 U.S.C. § 78i(a)(2).

[648] Perhaps foremost among these is that until 2010, § 9(a)(2) could only apply to securities traded on exchanges, which due to their volume and liquidity are less likely to be manipulated than OTC securities. Indeed, until 2006, NASDAQ was not even an exchange. Some courts have also interpreted § 9(a)'s scienter requirement to be more demanding than Rule 10b-5. *See, e.g.*, Chemetron Corp. v. Bus. Funds, Inc., 682 F.2d 1149, 1162 (5th Cir. 1982).

manipulation),[649] where the manipulation consists solely of a trading strategy in the securities markets.[650]

The law applying § 10(b) to the various types of manipulation is significantly confused with a split among the federal circuit courts as to central questions in manipulation jurisprudence.[651] The circuit split involves whether market manipulation, without an additional act that is itself unlawful, can be proscribed by § 10(b).[652] The Third and Seventh Circuit hold that a manipulation cannot consist of actual trades without some further improper act, i.e., that market manipulation is *not* unlawful under Rule 10b-5.[653]

---

[649] *See* Franklin Allen & Douglas Gale, *Stock Price Manipulation*, 5 REV. FIN. STUD. 503 (1992) (providing seminal model of manipulation executed exclusively through actual transactions).

[650] On transaction-based manipulation, see Steve Thel, *$850,000 in Six Minutes – The Mechanics of Securities Manipulation*, 79 CORNELL L. REV. 219, 251-55 (1994). On market manipulation, there is a large literature, but some prominent sources include Albert S. Kyle & S. Viswanathan, *How to Define Illegal Price Manipulation*, 98 AM. ECON. REV. PAP. & PROC. 274, 274 (2008), and the well-known critique of the possibility of profitable market manipulation, Daniel R. Fischel & David Ross, *Should the Law Prohibit "Manipulation" in Financial Markets?*, 105 HARV. L. REV. 503 (1991).

[651] This confusion as to what manipulation is and when it might be unlawful is at least in part a legacy of the Supreme Court's repeated emphasis on fraud and deceit in interpreting § 10(b). *See, e.g.*, Ernst & Ernst v. Hochfelder, 425 U.S. 185, 198 (1976) ("the word 'manipulative' . . . is and was virtually a term of art when used in connection with securities markets. It connotes intentional or willful conduct designed to deceive or defraud investors by controlling or artificially affecting the price of securities.") (citations omitted); Santa Fe Industries, Inc. v. Green, 430 U.S. 462, 476 (1977) (manipulation "refers generally to practices, such as wash sales, matched orders, or rigged prices, that are intended to mislead investors by artificially affecting market activity."); Schreiber v. Burlington Northern, Inc., 472 U.S. 1, 8 n.6 (1985); Chiarella v. United States, 445 U.S. 222, 234-35 (1980).

[652] Louisiana Corp. v. Merrill Lynch & Co., 571 F. App'x 8, 10 (2d Cir. 2014) (discussing the general elements of an open market manipulation claim), *citing* ATSI Commc'ns, Inc. v. Shaar Fund, Ltd., 493 F.3d 87, 101 (2d Cir. 2007).

[653] GFL Advantage Fund, Ltd. v. Colkitt, 272 F.3d 189, 205 (3d Cir. 2001) ("the essential element of the [market manipulation] claim is that *inaccurate* information is being injected into the marketplace."); Foss v. Bear, Stearns & Co., 394 F.3d 540, 541 (7th Cir. 2005) ("There is no violation of Section 10(b) without fraud").

On the other side, are the D.C. Circuit,[654] and as of 2015, the Second Circuit,[655] holding that lawful trading alone, when done with the wrong intent, can be a form of market manipulation prohibited by § 10(b). This split was the subject of a petition to the Supreme Court in 2016.[656] More scholarly attention is merited in assessing how the law should address manipulation.

5.3 Short Selling

Short selling is a trading practice in which a trader borrows a security from a third party, sells that security, and later "covers" by acquiring an identical security and returning it to the third party.[657] While short selling has been intermittently controversial, especially during times of financial crisis, it is generally permitted, although scrutinized, by current regulation, and there appears to be widespread academic support for this position.[658]

6 Current Issues in Equity Market Structure

On high-level measures of liquidity and transaction costs, the U.S. equity markets are remarkably healthy. Commissions and spreads have dropped dramatically in the past two decades.[659] Retail investors can trade conveniently

---

[654] Markowski v. SEC, 274 F.3d 525, 528-29 (D.C. Cir. 2001) (interpreting Congress, through Section 9(a)(2) of the Securities Exchange Act, to have proscribed manipulations exclusively involving trades based "solely because of the actor's purpose" when that purpose was improper, without necessitating any further unlawful act).

[655] Fezzani v. Bear, Stearns & Co. Inc., 777 F.3d 566, 571 (2d Cir. 2015) (Section 10(b) does *not* require "reliance by a victim on direct oral or written communications by a defendant.").

[656] Koch v. SEC, No. 15-781 (S. Ct. Mar. 28, 2016).

[657] There are a number of short selling structures, not all of which involve borrowing a security.

[658] Regulation SHO and Rule 10a-1, Securities Exchange Act Release No. 34-55970, 72 Fed. Reg. 36,348 (July 3, 2007) (codified at 17 C.F.R. pts. 240, 242); *see also* Exchange Act Release No. 50103 (July 28, 2004), 69 Fed. Reg. 48008, 48011 (Aug. 6, 2004); Exchange Act Release No. 48795 (Nov. 17, 2003), 68 Fed. Reg. 65820 (Nov. 21, 2003).

[659] *See* James J. Angel, Lawrence E. Harris & Chester S. Spatt, *Equity Trading in the 21st Century: An Update*, 5 Q. J. FIN. 1 (2015) (documenting improvements in

online for commissions of $10 per trade (10 cents per share for a round lot) or less.

At a more detailed level, however, several recent equity market developments have generated criticism and concern. The number of trading venues has proliferated. The structural and functional differences among them have diminished, but the regulatory system continues to treat exchanges, ATSs, and broker-dealer internalization differently. Registered exchanges and ATSs both operate automated matching systems. Competition among trading venues has led most to adopt pricing structures designed to attract order flow. It does not make obvious sense for trading platforms offering similar services using similar technologies and matching procedures to fit into different regulatory boxes.

Another important question is whether trading venues' pricing structures lead brokers to provide less than optimal executions for their customers. There are two dominant pricing models, described in more detail below, that provide brokers a financial incentive to execute orders in a particular market.

The trading practices of securities professionals are another source of concern. The replacement of traditional manual markets by automated matching engines has, as commentators expected, reduced the number and importance of traditional specialists and market makers. But contrary to some expectations, it has not resulted in a market in which long-term investors' trades are mostly made directly with one another. Instead, so-called high-frequency traders (HFTs) have stepped in as an important category of liquidity provider.

In this section, we explore each of these structural issues.

6.1 Venue Types

6.1.1 Regulatory Categories

All exchanges and most other organized trading venues now operate electronic limit order books that automatically match marketable and nonmarketable order flow. However, for regulatory purposes, these trading venues are put into separate buckets labeled "exchange," "ATS," or "broker-dealer internalization." These distinctions were initially driven by the need to accommodate new electronic trading venues that neither maintained the volume, nor regulated their members in a manner reminiscent of, a traditional exchange. The technological differences, however, have largely disappeared and the operational differences are becoming blurred. Broker-dealer trading platforms may mimic the exchanges' matching procedures. Exchanges offer a variety of

---

speed of execution, bid-ask spread, commissions, and number of quotes per minute); *see also* Angel, Harris & Spatt, *supra* note 556.

order types that can mimic the way a broker-dealer traditionally "works" a large order.

As a result of these technological and operational developments, the governing regulatory regime is largely a choice variable for the trading venue. BATS began operation as an ATS but converted to a registered exchange. Citadel Execution Services, an automated trading system that is one of the largest trading venues for retail orders, has chosen to be regulated as a broker-dealer that internalizes order flow and not as an ATS.

The choice whether to be an exchange, an ATS, or a broker-dealer has a number of consequences:

- exchanges engage in market surveillance and otherwise regulate their members; ATSs do not[660]
- unlike an ATS, the rules of an exchange must meet a public interest standard and changes to those rules are subject to SEC approval[661]
- exchanges must make membership available to any registered broker-dealer; ATSs are subject to the fair access requirement only if they exceed the 5% trading volume threshold; broker-dealers may offer to internalize an order or not at their discretion
- exchange quotations are included in the consolidated quotation system, whereas ATSs may choose to include their quotations or not unless they exceed the 5% trading volume threshold and broker-dealers need not publicly display the prices at which they intend to internalize orders.

The difference between an exchange, an ATS, and a broker-dealer is in part a difference in the rules of internal governance that provide the terms of explicit and implicit contracts between the trading venue and its members or customers. In that respect, the choice to be one type of regulated entity or another is analogous to a business's choice to be a corporation, a partnership, or an LLC. While legislators or regulators provide the menu of options, they have little reason to care which one a particular trading venue selects.

However, the choice of regulatory type has external effects as well. Most notably, it affects other market participants' access to quotations. While insisting on linked markets, Congress and the SEC have permitted a degree of competition among different trading platforms with respect to transparency and order types. An important question for a new special study is whether to rethink the regulatory categories.

---

[660] *See* 15 U.S.C. §§ 78f(a), 78c(a)(26); Lanier v. Bats Exch., Inc., 838 F.3d 139 (2d Cir. 2016).

[661] 15 U.S.C. § 78f(b).

6.1.2 Liability Rules

Distinctive liability rules currently apply to different kinds of trading venues. Broker-dealers, whether internalizers or ATSs, are subject to the same liability rules as any other private financial institution. In contrast, exchanges and their officers enjoy "absolute immunity" from suits for monetary damages when they are acting pursuant to their regulatory and oversight functions as self-regulatory organizations.[662] The policy and legal foundation for this immunity is that as SROs, the exchanges perform regulatory functions that would otherwise be performed by the SEC—an agency afforded sovereign immunity from any monetary liability.[663] As a result, an exchange is immune to suits for fraud, incompetence, or other forms of misconduct when engaged in interpretation, discipline, or enforcement, or other activities necessary or critical to its quasi-governmental regulatory functions.[664]

The sharp discontinuity between the regulatory burdens and immunity benefits of exchange status and the burdens and liabilities of ATSs highlights the importance of revisiting whether the current structure for categorizing trading

---

[662] A "self-regulatory organization 'when acting in its capacity as a SRO, is entitled to immunity from suit when it engages in conduct consistent with the quasi-governmental powers delegated to it pursuant to the Exchange Act and the regulations and rules promulgated thereunder.'" DL Capital Grp., LLC v. Nasdaq Stock Mkt., Inc., 409 F.3d 93, 97 (2d Cir. 2005) (citations omitted), citing D'Alessio v. N.Y. Stock Exch., Inc., 258 F.3d 93, 106 (2d Cir. 2001); Barbara v. N.Y. Stock Exch., Inc., 99 F.3d 49, 59 (2d Cir. 1996) abrogated on other grounds by Merrill Lynch, Pierce, Fenner & Smith Inc. v. Manning, 136 S. Ct. 1562 (2016); Weissman v. Nat'l Ass'n of Sec. Dealers, Inc., 500 F.3d 1293, 1296 (11th Cir. 2007) ("SROs are protected by absolute immunity when they perform their statutorily delegated adjudicatory, regulatory, and prosecutorial functions"); Sparta Surgical Corp. v. Nat'l Ass'n of Sec. Dealers, Inc., 159 F.3d 1209, 1214 (9th Cir. 1998); Austin Mun. Sec., Inc. v. Nat'l Ass'n of Sec. Dealers, Inc., 757 F.2d 676, 692 (5th Cir. 1985) ("the NASD . . . requires absolute immunity from civil liability for actions connected with the disciplining of its members.") (citations omitted).

[663] DL Capital, 409 F.3d at 97; *id.* ("the NYSE should, in light of its 'special status and connection to the SEC,' out of fairness be accorded full immunity from suits for money damages, as well."); *id.* (when "alleged misconduct falls within the scope of quasi-governmental powers delegated to the NYSE pursuant to the Exchange Act . . . absolute immunity precludes [any plaintiff] from recovering money damages in connection with his claims.").

[664] *Id.* at 98-99.

venues makes sense. Does immunity from liability still make sense for SROs, at least when read as broadly as it is by, for example, the Second Circuit? Does the lack of regulatory scrutiny applied to internalizers, like Citadel, make sense given that their share of equity market volume exceeds that of many exchanges and any ATS?

6.2 Broker-Dealer Routing Decisions

Broker-dealers are pivotal actors in the equity marketplace. The term "broker-dealer" is a regulatory status created pursuant to the Exchange Act. The SEC mandates that any individual or institution that acts as either a broker or dealer register as a "broker-dealer" with Form BD.[665] A broker is defined as "any person engaged in the business of effecting transactions in securities for the account of others," and a dealer as "any person engaged in the business of buying and selling securities . . . for such person's own account through a broker or otherwise."[666] While capacious, these definitions are expressly crafted to exclude investors who simply actively trade equities, while capturing those participants whose business is intermediating trade, whether as principal or agent.

6.2.1 The Duty of Best Execution

The main legal framework relevant for assessing agency functions of broker-dealers, such as handling the execution of customer orders, is the duty of best execution. Brokers owe customers a duty of best execution as a matter of state common law, self-regulatory organization rules, and arguably federal securities law. The seminal discussion of best execution is *Newton v. Merrill Lynch*,[667] a class action stemming from the Nasdaq odd-eighths scandal. As defined by the *Newton* court, the duty of best execution "requires a broker-dealer to 'use reasonable efforts to maximize the economic benefit to the client in each transaction.'"[668] This duty is multi-dimensional, requiring a broker to take into account best price, but also "order size, trading characteristics of the security,

---

[665] *See* Securities Exchange Act of 1934 § 15(b); 15 U.S.C. § 78o(b).

[666] *See* Securities Exchange Act of 1934 §§ 3(4)(A), 3(5)(A), 15 U.S.C. § 78c.

[667] Newton v. Merrill Lynch, Pierce, Fenner & Smith, Inc., 259 F.3d 154, 162 (3d Cir. 2001) (hereinafter *Newton II*), *as amended* (Oct. 16, 2001); Newton v. Merrill, Lynch, Pierce, Fenner & Smith, Inc., 135 F.3d 266, 271 (3d Cir. 1998) (hereinafter *Newton I*).

[668] *Newton II* at 173.

speed of execution, clearing costs, and the cost and difficulty of executing an order in a particular market."[669]

FINRA Rule 5310 similarly defines a broad standard, requiring a broker to use *reasonable diligence* to ascertain the best market for a security in any transaction for or with a customer, and to provide an execution such that the resultant price for the customer is "as favorable as possible under prevailing market conditions."[670] Reasonable diligence includes considering: "the character of the market for the security (e.g., price, volatility, relative liquidity, and pressure on available communications)"; "the size and type of transaction"; "the number of markets checked"; the "accessibility of the quotation"; and "the terms and conditions of the order which result in the transaction."[671]

Perhaps because of the standard's complexity, the SEC has opted for a combined "rules and standards" approach. As described above, the best execution standard applicable to brokerage executions is supplemented by Rule 611 of Regulation NMS, the trade-through rule, which is in part designed to provide a minimum floor for "best price" execution for small orders.[672] The broader "best execution" standard does most of the work regulating the execution of larger and more complicated orders and strategies.

Although Rule 611 forces brokers to recognize price priority across markets, it does not recognize time (or any other non-price) priority across markets. Thus, when multiple markets display the same best bid or offer, a broker can route a customer order to any one of those venues. It can also route the order to a venue that does not display quotations, so long as that venue executes the trade at the NBBO or better. Trading venues attempt to influence this exercise of discretion through their pricing systems. There are two common pricing practices: "maker-taker" fees and "payment for order flow." From the perspective of a retail investor, the first is relevant primarily to non-marketable limit orders and the second to marketable orders, as will be explained below.

6.2.2 Maker-Taker Fees

In a maker-taker model, a trading venue pays a rebate for each non-marketable limit order posted to it that executes on the venue. The theory is that

---

[669] *Newton I* at 271. For a more recent opinion fundamentally applying the analysis of *Newton*, see Gurfein v. Ameritrade, Inc., No. 04 CIV. 9526(LLS), 2007 WL 2049771, at *3 (S.D.N.Y. July 17, 2007), *aff'd*, 312 F. App'x 410 (2d Cir. 2009).

[670] FINRA Rule 5310 "Best Execution and Interpositioning" (emphasis added).

[671] *Id.* at Rule 5310(a)(1)(A)-(E).

[672] *See supra* subsection 4.3.2.

the trader who submitted a resting limit order added liquidity to the trading venue. The subsequent trader who "takes" that liquidity by submitting a contra-side marketable order pays a fee that is typically slightly larger than the liquidity rebate, with the difference representing revenue to the exchange. This is a common fee structure on ATSs and exchanges, although some have experimented with an inverted "taker-maker" fee structure.[673] Rule 610(c) of Regulation NMS caps the "take" fee at $0.003/share to the extent the resting order is a protected order or the best bid or offer in a displayed market.

Brokers do not typically pass along the liquidity rebate directly to retail customers who submit non-marketable limit orders.[674] There is evidence that the rebates lead brokers to send those orders to venues that may be inferior with respect to fill rates and other indicia of execution quality.[675] It is more difficult to determine whether competition leads brokers to pass on the resulting revenue to customers in the form of lower commissions. In any event, the SEC's position is clear that these maker-taker fee structures are legally permissible and that broker-dealers do not necessarily violate their fiduciary duties simply by directing orders to such venues.

A separate concern with this fee structure is that it adds a layer of complexity for traders attempting to determine the best available price.[676] Displayed prices do not reflect the actual price paid or received net of the rebate or fee. Regulation NMS defines the "best" bid or offer without reference to the actual cost of accessing that bid or offer.

---

[673] Inverted "taker-maker" fee arrangements impose the opposite fee structure on incoming orders. Typically, maker-taker arrangements award $.0020-$.0025 per share for executed nonmarketable orders and charge $.0025-$.0030 per share for executed marketable orders. These arrangements must be publicly available on an exchange's website. *See* Securities Exchange Act of 1934 § 19(b)(3)(A)(ii)(4), 15 U.S.C. § 78s(b)(3)(A)(ii) (2012); 17 C.F.R. § 240.19b-4(f)(2) (2013).

[674] *See* Larry E. Harris, *Maker-Taker Pricing Effects on Market Quotations* (working paper, 2013).

[675] *See* Robert Battalio, Shane A. Corwin & Robert Jennings, *Can Brokers Have It All? On the Relation Between Make-Take Fees and Limit Order Execution Quality*, 71 J. FIN. 2193 (2016).

[676] *See* SEC Market Structure Advisory Committee, *Maker-Taker Fees on Equities Exchanges* (2015), https://www.sec.gov/spotlight/emsac/memo-maker-taker-fees-on-equities-exchanges.pdf.

6.2.3 Payment for Order Flow

Dealers who internalize orders often pay third party brokers to direct orders to them for execution rather than to an exchange or ATS, a practice known as "payment for order flow" (PFOF).[677] As part of the arrangement, the internalizer typically commits to execute trades at a price that is at least a slight improvement over the NBBO.[678] The broker can therefore argue that it has met its best execution obligation to the customer while pocketing the incentive payment from the dealer, an argument the SEC has accepted.[679]

Retail customer orders are extremely desirable because they are assumed to be uninformed and therefore to create no adverse selection risk for the dealer. Accordingly, retail brokers route nearly all of their customer market orders to internalizers pursuant to PFOF arrangements.[680] Payments to large retail brokerages for order flow in 2014 ranged from $92 million to $304 million, with the rate per share ranging from $0.0010 to $0.0031.[681]

A small number of firms dominate internalization, with Citadel, KCG Americas, and G1 accounting for around 28%, 20%, and 10% of non-ATS OTC volume and the ten largest non-ATS venues accounting for over 80% of volume.[682] This means that by parent company, Citadel and KCG are some of

---

[677] SEC, *Certain Issues Affecting Customers in the Current Equity Market Structure*, Jan. 26, 2016.

[678] *Id.* at 6.

[679] *See* Payment for Order Flow Proposing Release, Securities Exchange Act Release No. 33026 (Oct. 7, 1993) 58 Fed. Reg. 52934, 52936 (Oct. 13, 1993) ("Payment for Order Flow Proposing Release"). The principal regulatory strategy toward PFOF has been disclosure. *Id.* at 59 FR 55006. For an overview of the relevant distinct disclosure requirements, *see* 17 CFR 240.10b-10; 17 CFR 240.606; and 17 CFR 240.607(a)(1)-(2).

[680] SEC, *Certain Issues Affecting Customers in the Current Equity Market Structure*, Jan. 26, 2016, at 2 n.2 ("Internalization is believed to account for almost 100% of all retail marketable order flow.")

[681] *Id.* at 6.

[682] All statistics are derived from data from FINRA's OTC Transparency Data facility. *See OTC Transparency Data*, https://otctransparency.finra.org/ (calculations for the months of September 2016 and April 2017).

the largest execution forums for U.S. equities, after the NYSE, BATS, and Nasdaq exchange groups.[683]

Although brokers receive the PFOF, competition among brokers should lead them to reduce retail commissions to attract more customers in order to have more retail orders to sell. Certainly the level of retail commissions has declined in recent years. At least one online broker has taken advantage of PFOF (among other revenue sources) to offer commission-free trading.[684] Empirically, the effects of PFOF, like maker-taker fees, on customer welfare is a topic for further study.

Internalization is controversial apart from concerns about retail brokerage customers.[685] Dealers' willingness to internalize is another form of non-displayed liquidity that has attracted the same criticism as dark pools and non-displayed order types. A separate criticism is that internalizers "skim" the uninformed (usually retail) order flow. Thus, the relative proportion of informed order flow arriving at the primary exchanges, where price discovery takes place, is necessarily greater than would be the case absent internalization and PFOF.[686]

Because market makers respond to adverse selection risk by increasing the bid-ask spread, PFOF might cause an increase in market-wide spreads. The counterargument is that the aggregate amount of adverse selection risk that liquidity providers face should not depend on how it is distributed. It is always in the best interests of retail investors to have a separating equilibrium where the lit markets have all the informed traders and wider spreads to compensate, while retail investors trade exclusively OTC with dealers inside the spread. Thus, it is again an empirical question whether concentrating adverse selection risk in the lit markets has adverse welfare consequences.

---

[683] Data on exchange volume in U.S. equities is available on BATS's website. *See U.S. Equities Market Volume Summary*, http://www.bats.com/us/equities/market_statistics/current_most_active/.

[684] *See, e.g.*, http://www.robinhood.com; *see also* Jane Morrissey, *With No Frills and No Commissions, Robinhood App Takes On Big Brokerages*, N.Y. TIMES, Feb. 18, 2017, https://www.nytimes.com/2017/02/18/business/robinhood-stock-trading-app.html.

[685] For a sample of important analyses, *see, e.g.*, Allen Ferrell, *A Proposal for Solving the "Payment for Order Flow" Problem*, 74 S. CAL. L. REV. 1027 (2001); John C. Coffee, Jr., *Order-Flow Payments Get New Scrutiny*, NAT'L L.J., July 19, 1993.

[686] *See* Beny, *supra* note 594, at 432-33 (discussing empirical evidence addressing whether internalization has actually increased the proportion of informed trade on exchanges).

The SEC has suggested that it might consider a "trade at" rule that would prohibit a trading center from executing an order at the NBBO unless it was already displaying that price when the order arrived.[687] The rule would reduce broker discretion over order routing, particularly to internalizers. But it would also have significant distributional consequences for trading venues. The requirement that the venue "display" the NBBO would mean that dark ATSs and internalizers would always have to price improve in order to execute a trade. The rule would accordingly have to define a "meaningful" price improvement in order to prevent internalizers from "stepping ahead" of the NBBO by trivial amounts. Not surprisingly, the concept of a trade at rule is popular among lit venues and unpopular among dark venues. It is also unpopular among large traders, who fear that being forced into lit venues would increase the price impact of their trades.

An alternative approach to addressing PFOF is for regulators to clarify the requirements of best execution. FINRA's recent best execution guidance provides that the duty applies to a FINRA member executing transactions as principal where the member accepts order flow "for the purpose of facilitating the handling and execution of such orders," but not where "the member is acting solely as the buyer or seller in connection with orders presented by a broker-dealer against the member's quote."[688] This guidance plausibly requires that broker-dealers paying for order flow are under a duty of best execution when transacting with that order flow.[689] The SEC and/or FINRA may wish to provide further guidance as to how that duty of best execution applies to an internalizer's order routing decisions.

6.2.4 Dark Pool Agency Problems

A significant portion of executed volume involves non-displayed orders. Dark pools, like broker-dealer internalization, raise concerns about whether uninformed order flow is overwhelmingly being executed off-exchange, resulting

---

[687] *See* Market Structure Release, *supra* note 554, at 70.

[688] FINRA Rule 5310 Supplementary Material .04.

[689] *See also* FINRA Regulatory Notice 15-46 *Best Execution: Guidance on Best Execution Obligations in Equity, Options and Fixed Income Markets* 3 (2015), http://www.finra.org/sites/default/files/notice_doc_file_ref/Notice_Regulatory_15-46.pdf (firms "cannot transfer to another person their obligations to provide best execution to their customers' orders, although other firms may also acquire that best execution obligation.... [A] broker-dealer that routes all of its order flow to another broker-dealer without conducting an independent review of execution quality would violate the duty of best execution.").

in higher spreads on exchanges due to correspondingly greater adverse selection concerns. Dark pools raise other concerns as well.

Large broker-dealer firms run many of the high-volume dark pools, creating a potential agency problem. The broker has an interest in routing orders to its own dark pool, both because it receives execution fees and because it may offer its own trading desk or other favored traders opportunities to transact with its customer orders. These interests may conflict with the customer's interest in best execution. At least one recent settlement suggests that these conflicts of interest may have led a dark pool operator to put its own interests ahead of its customers. Two other settlements involve dark pools that made material misrepresentations to customers in marketing materials. In aggregate, Credit Suisse, Barclays Capital, and Deutsche Bank were fined over $200 million for violations of the Exchange Act in connection with their dark pools. At various times, these firms operated the first, second, and fourth largest equity ATSs, respectively.[690]

Credit Suisse owns and operates the dark pool Crossfinder. The Commission found that Crossfinder communicated confidential subscriber trading information to affiliated entities.[691] This violated Rule 301(b)(10) of Reg. ATS, which requires protection of confidential trading information. The ATS adopting release also stated that brokers should separate their ATS and brokerage functions.[692] More importantly, the Commission found that Credit Suisse misrepresented to clients that its smart order router did not preference Crossfinder (or any other venue) although the router systematically privileged Crossfinder.[693] In particular, certain router default settings automatically routed orders to Crossfinder.

---

[690] In the Matter of Barclays Capital Inc., Securities Exchange Act Release No. 77001, https://www.sec.gov/-litigation/admin/2016/33-10010.pdf (hereinafter Barclays Order); In the Matter of Credit Suisse Securities (USA) LLC, Securities Exchange Act Release No. 77002, https://www.sec.gov/litigation/admin/2016/33-10013.pdf (hereinafter Credit Suisse Order); In the Matter of Deutsche Bank Securities Inc., Securities Exchange Act Release No. 79576, https://www.sec.gov/litigation/-admin/2016/33-10272.pdf (hereinafter Deutsche Bank Order).

[691] Credit Suisse Order, *supra* note 690. Credit Suisse neither admitted nor denied the findings in the Commission's Order. *Id.* at 1. Crossfinder also violated the subpenny quote prohibition, *see supra* subsection 4.3.2, by permitting customers to submit almost 500 million orders at subpenny prices.

[692] 17 C.F.R. § 242.301(b)(10); ATS Adopting Release at 70879.

[693] Credit Suisse Order, *supra* note 690, at 11.

Barclays admitted making material misrepresentations in marketing and operating its dark pool, Barclays LX ("LX").[694] In particular, Barclays misrepresented LX's Liquidity Profiling function and its related surveillance tools for policing LX trading activity.[695] Liquidity Profiling was a program designed to categorize LX users as more or less aggressive depending on particular aspects of their order flow and then to allow users generally to block the most aggressive traders from interacting with them. In fact, Barclays conducted very little surveillance of LX trading activity and would sometimes override the Liquidity Profiling tool's categorization of participants, including manually moving users from the most to the least aggressive categories. This resulted in other users trading with them after having opted to block such trades.

The action against Deutsche Bank ("DB") involves a possibly inadvertent failure to operate its order router in the manner it represented to customers.[696] DB developed an order router, SuperX+, primarily for routing equity orders to dark pools. DB marketed SuperX+ as based on a routing algorithm called the "Dark Pool Ranking Model" ("DPRM"), which was described as SuperX+'s "quantitative core." DPRM was designed to rank venues based on execution quality, and then to route orders to eligible venues that historically had offered the best liquidity. However, SuperX+ largely failed to update DPRM due to a coding error, and DB's personnel sometimes supplemented DPRM with their subjective assessments. DB's marketing materials accordingly failed to reflect the actual operation of SuperX+.

6.3 High-Frequency Trading

HFTs are proprietary trading firms or desks that enter and cancel orders and make trades in high volume and at great speed.[697] Like traditional market

---

[694] Barclays Order, *supra* note 690.

[695] *Id.* at 3-5. Barclays also misrepresented to customers that it relied on market data feeds generally to calculate its internal NBBO, while it relied on a combination of the SIP and direct feeds from some exchanges, but not NYSE.

[696] Deutsche Bank Order, *supra* note 690. That DB's errors were largely inadvertent is underlined by the fact that due to a coding error, its own dark pool was erroneously placed among the worst venues by its algorithm, which rendered the venue incapable of receiving almost any orders. *Id.* at 4. Subsequently, Deutsche Bank manually overrode the ranking and placed its dark pool in the highest ranking.

[697] For a review of recent academic research on high-frequency trading, see Charles M. Jones, *What Do We Know About High-Frequency Trading* 10, 26 (working paper, 2013), https://papers.ssrn.com/sol3/papers.cfm?abstract_id=2236201.

makers, they seek to earn a spread on their trades, but not to establish large long or short positions. Unlike traditional market makers, they need have no formal connection to the market and no corresponding obligation to quote continuous prices or smooth order imbalances. However, many HFTs have taken on institutional market making roles at exchanges. For instance, prominent HFTs, such as Virtu, Citadel, and GTS are among the few Designated Market Makers (DMM) at NYSE.[698] HFTs have become an important class of market professional.[699]

Although there is no single accepted definition of HFTs, they are typically described as using high-speed communications, private data feeds from trading venues, and algorithmic trading strategies to rapidly and frequently enter, cancel, and update quotations at trading venues.[700] As a result, they play substantial roles in both market making and arbitrage activities. Research indicates that they supply a majority of the limit orders against which marketable orders transact.[701]

HFTs argue that they face the same challenges as traditional market makers—to earn a spread on as many trades as possible while managing adverse selection and inventory risk. Because they do so in a highly dispersed electronic market, they necessarily use algorithms rather than the continuous manual updating of quotations that characterized traditional market makers. Critics claim that they exploit their speed advantage over other traders to earn nearly riskless

---

[698] NYSE Membership, NYSE Designated Market Maker Firms, https://www.nyse.com/markets/nyse/membership.

[699] Another fact suggestive of HFTs' increasing prominence is GTS's purchase of Barclay's DMM business at NYSE. With this development, all NYSE DMMs are now operated by automated, algorithmic trading firms, which have crowded out all of the traditional brokerages that were once common market makers. *See* NYSE Membership, *Designated Market Makers*, https://www.nyse.com/markets/nyse/membership; *see also* Annie Massa, *High-Speed Firms Now Oversee Almost All Stocks at NYSE Floor*, BLOOMBERG, Jan. 26, 2016.

[700] *See* Charles R. Korsmo, *High-Frequency Trading: A Regulatory Strategy*, 48 U. RICH. L. REV. 523, 540 (2014) (defining attributes of HFTs).

[701] Jonathan A. Brogaard, *High Frequency Trading and its Impact on Market Quality* 2, 11 (July 16, 2010) (unpublished manuscript), http://www.futuresindustry.org/ptg/downloads/HFT_Trading.pdf (finding HFTs supply limit orders for 51% of trades and provide market quotes 50% of the time, based on NASDAQ data set); *see generally* Albert J. Menkveld, *High Frequency Trading and the New Market Makers*, 16 J. FIN. MKTS. 712 (2013).

profits through superior access to information about transactions and quotations. We will examine some of the practices that have generated criticism.

6.3.1 Latency Arbitrage

Media commentators, industry insiders, and academics all worry about the prevalence of "latency arbitrage" by HFTs. The term refers to a family of trading practices that can differ considerably in their economics, riskiness, and desirability from a welfare standpoint, but all use information asymmetries generated by speed differences to exploit potential profit-making opportunities.[702] We will briefly consider three different types.

The first is inter-venue order cancellation, or simply "order cancellation" as we will refer to it.[703] The term refers to a liquidity provider cancelling quotes for a given security at one or more venues on which it has posted orders after detecting trading activity at another venue or venues. In a highly competitive market, inter-venue order cancellation is to be expected and is unlikely to be problematic.[704] Quote removal often represents defensive risk management by liquidity providers. They may be concerned that large transactions on one venue are informationally motivated and that current orders posted on other venues thus face a significant adverse selection risk.[705] Alternatively, they may accumulate positions in one market and therefore need to quote less aggressively in another.

---

[702] Robert P. Bartlett, III & Justin McCrary, *How Rigged Are Stock Markets? Evidence from Microsecond Timestamps* (working paper, 2016), https://papers.ssrn.com/sol3/papers.cfm?abstract_id=2812123.

[703] *See* Vincent van Kervel, *Liquidity: What You See Is What You Get?*, 2–6 (2012) (unpublished Ph.D. dissertation, Tilburg University), http://www.rsm.nl/fileadmin/home/Department_of_Finance__VG5_/LQ5/VanKervel.pdf. Michael Lewis refers to inter-venue order cancelation as "electronic front-running" in *Flash Boys*. *See* Lewis, *supra* note 559. The nomenclature of "slow market arbitrage" and "midpoint order exploitation" are similarly taken from Lewis's book.

[704] *See* van Kervel, *supra* note 703 (showing that trades on venues are followed by cancellations of limit orders on competing venues and would be expected based on adverse selection dynamics).

[705] Under non-competitive market dynamics, the possibility of a liquidity provider canceling its quotes and replacing them with quotes providing marketable orders with inferior executions may represent a socially undesirable increase in transaction costs for traders.

Lewis identifies two other forms of latency arbitrage and argues that they are ethically similar to front-running, or the improper use of information about another trader's intentions. In traditional forms of front-running, the use is improper because the trader owes a duty to the source of the information, as when a broker or investment advisor trades ahead of a large customer order. That is not the case with latency arbitrage. Instead, the use is argued to be improper because the HFT obtains information about changes in quotations or last-transaction prices through a private data feed more rapidly than other traders.

"Slow market arbitrage" involves an HFT with a limit order at the NBB or NBO on one exchange which then learns of a new quote at another venue that improves on that quote. If a marketable order then arrives at the first venue and transacts against the HFT's now-stale quote, that HFT could make a riskless profit by transacting against the improved quote standing on the alternative venue (if it is still there).

"Midpoint order exploitation" involves a "midpoint" limit order resting on a dark pool that will transact against the next incoming marketable contra-side order at the current midpoint of the NBBO. An HFT could potentially detect a quote improving on the current NBB or NBO at a lit venue and then rapidly transact with that improving quote, while sending an opposite order to a dark pool with a contra-side midpoint limit order still based on the stale NBB/NBO, resulting in riskless profit (if there was such an order). So-called slow market arbitrage and midpoint order exploitation both depend on the same reality, which is an order transacting against (or being based on) a kind of "stale quote" – a quote that was, but no longer is, the best bid or offer.

6.3.2 Latency Arbitrage and Regulation NMS

The NBBO as defined for regulatory purposes consists of the best quotations disseminated by the SIP. Trading venues provide their quotations to the SIP pursuant to a national market system plan. At the same time, they offer private feeds of the same data to market participants willing to pay for the private link. Co-location, or putting the market professional's servers in close physical proximity to the exchange's servers, assures the minimum possible delay in receipt of the data. Traders can use this data to privately construct the NBBO some milliseconds before the NBBO is available from the SIP.[706]

A trader can exploit the resulting time difference because of the SEC's interpretation of Rule 603(a)(2) of Regulation NMS. The rule prohibits

---

[706] *See* Market Structure Release, *supra* note 554.

exchanges from "unreasonably discriminatory" distribution of market data.[707] The SEC's interpretation of the provision has been that "distributed data could not be made available on a more timely basis [to private clients] than core data is made available to a Network processor [the SIP]."[708] Thus, "Rule 603(a) prohibits an SRO or broker-dealer from transmitting data to a vendor or user any sooner than it transmits the data to a Network processor."[709]

In short, the SEC's interpretation of "unreasonably discriminatory" is based on when the market center sends a signal, not when traders actually receive it. Traders who get core data from the SIP will generally receive it with a slight delay compared to those who get it directly from the trading center even though the trading center sends them to private clients and the SIP simultaneously. The usefulness of private data feeds and co-location is partly predicated on this interpretation.[710]

Critics dispute the SEC's interpretation of Rule 603(a)(2), arguing that the simultaneous distribution of information to private data feeds and the SIP—knowing private data feeds will arrive before the SIP's data—is "unreasonably discriminatory."[711] They offer an alternative interpretation under which it would be "unreasonably discriminatory" to send a signal that will reach private customers before the SIP core data are publicly available.[712] The SEC has adopted analogous interpretations, emphasizing when information reaches end

---

[707] *See* 17 C.F.R. § 242.603(a)(2) (2015). Section 11A(c)(1) of the Exchange Act authorizes the Commission to regulate market data. 15 U.S.C. § 78k-1(b) (2012).

[708] *See* Regulation NMS, 70 Fed. Reg. 37,496, 37,567 & 37,569 (June 29, 2005) (adopting release for Regulation NMS).

[709] *Id.*

[710] In fact, the Market Structure Release, *supra* note 554, at 3601, confirmed this interpretation by acknowledging these arrangements. *Id.* (consolidation processing time of the SIP "means that [private] data feeds can reach end-users faster than the consolidated data feeds.").

[711] *See Direct vs. SIP Data Feed*, Nanex (Apr. 4, 2014), http://www.nanex.net/aqck2/4599.html.

[712] For instance, the market research firm Nanex views exchange private data feeds as violating Regulation NMS. *See HFT Front Running, All The Time*, Nanex (Sept. 30, 2013), http://www.nanex.net/aqck2/4442.html.

users rather than the time it is sent, in other contexts, including for when information is no longer nonpublic for insider trading purposes.[713]

There is a tension with the principle behind the trade-through rule when a trader can execute a trade at a particular price knowing that in a millisecond or so the SIP may show that it is no longer the best available price. However, Rule 611(b)(8) of Regulation NMS permits a trade-through when "[t]he trading center displaying the protected quotation that was traded through had displayed, within one second prior to execution of the transaction that constituted the trade-through, a best bid or best offer, as applicable, for the NMS stock with a price that was equal or inferior to the price of the trade-through transaction."[714]

Put simply, a trading venue may permit an order to transact against a quote that is no longer best if the now-best quote is on a venue which, within one second prior, had displayed as its best bid or offer a price equal or inferior to the price of the transaction.[715] A new, price-improving quote thus only becomes protected after being in force for one second, far more time than trading venues

---

[713] *See, e.g.*, SEC v. Texas Gulf Sulphur, 401 F.2d 833, 854 (2d Cir. 1968); Investors Mgmt. Co., Exchange Act Release No. 9207, 1971 WL 120502, at *8 (July 29, 1971).

[714] 17 C.F.R. § 242.611(b)(8).

[715] *See also* Regulation NMS, 70 Fed. Reg. 37,496, 37,522 (June 29, 2005) (adopting release for Reg. NMS) ("pursuant to Rule 611(b)(8) trading centers would be entitled to trade at any price equal to or better than the least aggressive best bid or best offer, as applicable, displayed by the other trading center during that one-second window. For example, if the best bid price displayed by another trading center has flickered between $10.00 and $10.01 during the one-second window, the trading center that received the order could execute a trade at $10.00 without violating Rule 611."). The SEC's motivation for adopting this exception was a concern that rapid changes in trading center quotes would "create the impression that a quotation was traded-through, when in fact the trade was effected nearly simultaneously with display of the quotation," and that the SEC did "not believe that the benefits would justify the costs imposed on trading centers of attempting to implement an intermarket price priority rule at the level of sub-second time increments." *Id.* at 37,523. However, even at the time of the exception's adoption, critical commentators alleged that its use would "create arbitrage opportunities for computerized market participants." *See* Letter from Meyer S. Frucher, Chairman and Chief Executive Officer, Philadelphia Stock Exchange, Inc., to Jonathan G. Katz, Secretary, Commission, dated January 31, 2005 at 3, *cited by* Regulation NMS, 70 Fed. Reg. 37,496, 37,522 (June 29, 2005).

generally need to register a new quote at another venue and update their own systems accordingly.

From a customer welfare perspective, the question is whether venues deliberately use the one-second exception to attract HFTs with risk-free profits at the cost of providing customers inferior executions. This is in principle subject to empirical testing. If trading venues allow HFTs to use the one second exception to execute trades at stale prices, there should be many transactions occurring "outside the quote," or inferior to the best available prices in the market. To gain a sense of their magnitude, one would analyze how often trades occur on trading venues at prices that were outside the best quote for that security at the time of trade.[716] A breakdown of this data by venue would be vital as certain ATSs are likely to be the principal suspects, if the one second rule is in fact exploited.

7 Alternative Market Structures

Several of the issues identified above arise from differences in the speed with which various market participants receive updated core data. A number of commentators have proposed changes to market structure to reduce the advantages associated with speed. We survey the most prominent ones in this section.

7.1 Batched Auctions

One of the best developed ideas for major market structure reform is Budish, Cramton, and Shim's proposal to replace the current structure of continuous trading on exchanges with frequent batched auctions.[717] All thirteen active stock exchanges presently share the same structure, in which displayed orders receive execution priority based on time of arrival within a continuous sequence. Orders are processed serially, however small the difference in their arrival times.

---

[716] Intermarket sweet orders are another source of outside the quote transactions, but should not be included in any estimate of the possibilities of latency arbitrage, given that they are deliberately ordered by investors.

[717] *See* Eric Budish, Peter Cramton & John Shim, *The High-Frequency Trading Arms Race: Frequent Batch Auctions as a Market Design Response*, 130 Q. J. ECON. 1547, 1548 (2015); *see also* Michael S. Barr, Howell E. Jackson & Margaret E. Tahyar, FINANCIAL REGULATION: LAW AND POLICY 547 (2016) (discussing various proposed responses to the rise of high-frequency trading).

This structure, Budish et al. suggest, bakes in opportunities for latency arbitrage. New information results in frequent revaluation of individual securities resulting from the revaluation of other instruments with which those securities' prices are correlated. Under current market structure, each of these changes triggers a race to react, whether to withdraw now-stale quotes by liquidity providers or to "pick off" stale quotes in order to make a profit. Because the liquidity provider is just one among a large N of traders, and orders are processed serially in continuous time based on order of arrival, getting picked off becomes a pervasive fact of liquidity providers' lives.[718] This pervasive phenomenon has at least two pernicious consequences. First, it makes liquidity costlier because losses to speedier snipers acts as a kind of tax on the business of liquidity provision. Second, it triggers an arms race for speed that consumes resources in the real economy but has no tangible welfare consequences given the near-zero time differences at which modern trading occurs.[719]

Their proposal is to replace continuous time trading with discrete but frequently repeated batched auctions, say every one millisecond. Rather than processing orders serially as they arrive, incoming orders would be aggregated in a uniform-price double auction. As a result, minute differences in speed would cease to confer a competitive advantage, heightening incentives for price competition.[720] Essentially, they propose a "tick for time," analogous to the "tick" or minimum price variation in which quoting is permitted in equity markets.

7.2 Speed Bumps: IEX

Perhaps the most important, and certainly the most controversial, market structure development of 2016 was the application of the ATS IEX to become a stock exchange. The application generated extensive comments, but the SEC ultimately approved it.[721] While providing a familiar electronic limit order book

---

[718] Eric Budish, Peter Cramton & John Shim, *Implementation Details for Frequent Batch Auctions: Slowing Down Markets to the Blink of an Eye*, 104 AM. ECON. REV. 418 (2015) (a liquidity provider's "request to adjust their stale quotes would have to reach the exchange before *all* of the requests to pick off their stale quotes."). Importantly, the proposed auction involves "sealed-bids," so none of the orders submitted are displayed until the auction outcome is reported. *Id.* at 419.

[719] Budish et al., *supra* note 717, at 1576-1608.

[720] *See also* SEC, Letter from Eric Budish to Brent J. Fields, Secretary (Feb. 5, 2016), https://www.sec.gov/comments/10-222/10222-371.pdf.

[721] SEC, In the Matter of the Application of Investors' Exchange, LLC for Registration as a National Securities Exchange Findings, Opinion, and Order of

structure, IEX adopted a series of innovative practices, some of which it will continue as an exchange.

Most famously, as an ATS, IEX imposed a "speed bump," largely intended to address the perceived problem of inter-exchange order cancelation, noted above. The speed bump applies to communications arriving at and departing the IEX matching engine, and it means that when an order arrives at IEX, IEX's systems will wait 350 microseconds to post and/or execute it, and that when an execution occurs on IEX, the counterparties are only notified after a 350 microsecond delay. Because those involved in an order do not find out about the execution for a delayed period of time, a large trader has sufficient time for its orders to arrive at other exchanges or for IEX to route the remainder of an order to other exchanges, before other market participants discover the IEX execution and can react. During its exchange application process, IEX adjusted its structure so that IEX's own order routing technology was also subject to the 350 microsecond speed bump after the router's exemption from the speed bump came under fierce attack.[722]

7.3 Eliminating the NMS

IEX's application to become a registered exchange raised an interpretive issue under Regulation NMS. To qualify as a "protected" quotation that may not be traded through, the quotation has to be "immediately" executable.[723] An essential design principle behind IEX was the "speed bump," or physical delay of approximately 350 microseconds between receipt of a message at the point of connection and delivery to the matching engine.[724] Approval of the application therefore required that the SEC conclude that access to IEX's quotations is "immediate" despite the delay. Ultimately, it issued interpretive guidance

---

the Commission, June 17, 2016, Release No. 34-78101, https://www.sec.gov/rules/other/2016/34-78101.pdf.

[722] Letter from Sophia Lee, General Counsel, IEX to Brent Fields, Secretary, SEC, Re: Investors' Exchange LLC Form 1 Application, Release No. 34-75925, https://www.sec.gov/comments/10-222/10222-421.pdf ("The Router will interact with the IEX matching system over a 350 microsecond speed-bump in the same way an independent third party broker would be subject to a speed bump.").

[723] 17 C.F.R. §600(b)(3), (57).

[724] *See* Securities and Exchange Commission, In the Matter of the Application of Investors' Exchange, LLC for Registration as a National Securities Exchange, Exchange Act Rel. No. 78101, at 47-52 (June 17, 2016).

permitting an intentional *de minimis* delay but did not provide a bright-line rule for what is *de minimis*.[725]

Any attempt to create a new exchange based on batched auction principles would also require interpretive or exemptive relief. The point of a batched auction is to do away with time priority within the time frame of each auction, thus avoiding a microsecond-scale race to get in line at a particular price. The batch auction would be permissible only if the entrepreneur could persuade the SEC that the interval between auctions is *de minimis*.

These examples illustrate a fundamental point: although the national market system was intended to permit competition among trading venues, Regulation NMS channels that competition into particular, and arguably narrow, forms. The SEC has concluded that the only permissible market structure (1) permits any stock to trade on any venue that wishes to trade it, and (2) requires that brokers route marketable orders to a venue offering the best price. Regulation NMS rules out any form of competition among exchanges that would concentrate trading in listed stocks on the listing exchange.[726] Such a system could conceivably result in competition among entirely different types of trading platforms—some manual, some electronic, some continuous, some batched, some trading 24 hours a day and others during limited periods, and so on. It is not obvious how or why that form of competition would be less desirable than the current competition among fairly homogeneous linked electronic limit order books.

A bit of history helps to explain the SEC's adherence to its position. Prior to the 1975 National Market System amendments, the NYSE was unapologetic in contending that the market functioned best when all liquidity in a particular stock was consolidated in a single location, and for NYSE-listed stocks that single location should be the NYSE. Its rules and procedures attempted to maintain its market share in trading of listed stocks. Rule 390 limited brokers' ability to trade off the exchange. Specialists' quotations and limit order books were not publicly disseminated.

---

[725] The SEC staff did offer guidance that an intentional delay of one millisecond or less is acceptable. Staff Guidance on Automated Quotations under Regulation NMS (June 2016), https://www.sec.gov/divisions/marketreg/automated-quotations-under-regulation-nms.htm.

[726] Beny, *supra* note 594, at 465, argues for a listings-focused approach. Beny's argument is to prohibit transactions in a firm's shares on any venue on which that issuer has chosen not to list, with the ambition of moving market centers away from competition for order flow and toward competition for corporate listings.

The SEC and Congress were united in their disagreement with the NYSE's view. In particular, they were concerned that allowing the NYSE to continue doing business in the traditional way would impede the growth of electronic markets that could match buyers and sellers more rapidly and at lower cost. In their view, the markets had to be forced into a world of high-tech trading and competition.

But this belief at least requires some explanation. We ordinarily assume that when the cost of entry into a business falls, the number of competitors will increase. In the business of operating trading markets, technology substantially reduced the non-regulatory costs of entry. The result should have been more trading platforms and more competition without the need for regulatory encouragement. Although the NYSE can write a rule requiring its member brokers to trade listed stocks exclusively on the exchange, it cannot force companies to list there if competing markets are better.

The current regulatory design may lack a compelling account of the externality being solved. Without it, it is not clear why competition for liquidity provision in each traded stock is good and competition for (exclusive) listings is bad. Because liquidity attracts liquidity, one might argue that securities trading is subject to network externalities. But while this is true of the trading in any given stock, there is little reason to think that it is true of listings. Technology has dramatically decreased the cost of creating a new electronic market, meaning that companies would have substantial choice among listing venues.

The strongest argument in favor of the SEC's stance may be empirical, not theoretical. The period since the implementation of the Order Handling Rules in 1997 has seen continuous improvement in basic measures of market quality. The U.S. equity markets perform well in comparison both to equity markets in other countries and in comparison to the fixed income markets, which are not subject to the same regulatory regime. This makes a powerful case for the current structure.

A speculative counterargument is that in the 20th century, for a variety of historical reasons, the NYSE obtained a dominant market position. Once Congress and the SEC had achieved the stock market equivalent of the AT&T breakup, competition flourished and the need to oversee that competition at such a detailed level vanished along with the NYSE's dominant position. A key question for a new special study is whether less intrusive regulations could provide the same competitive benefits.

7.4 Venue Innovation

Provided there is sufficient regulatory flexibility, innovation by trading venues is likely to also mean that market structure continues to evolve in sometimes dramatic ways. IEX's exchange application seems to have ignited a spate of new proposals.

For instance, Nasdaq has proposed an innovative new order type.[727] Named the "Extended Life Priority Order Attribute," this change would give displayed orders that commit to remaining on the order book for one second or more a higher priority than other displayed orders on Nasdaq's limit order book.[728] While not framed by Nasdaq in this way, the rule seems designed to address a widely shared concern about today's market structure, which is that it features an excessive amount of intermediation. The worry is that professional dealers' market making capabilities have in some way "crowded out" liquidity provision by "natural" end-users or investors interested in actually owning firms' stock. More straightforwardly, the order type would also serve to provide incentives for non-fading liquidity. Whether changes to intellectual property law are necessary to promote the emergence of further innovations is an open question worth consideration by legal scholars.

New types of exchanges may emerge to supplement innovation at existing stock exchanges. For instance, there have been recent calls for something like a venture exchange in which listed firms could have their stock traded among a limited set of investors, free of the disclosure requirements federal securities law currently imposes on public corporations.[729] In a somewhat similar vein, the exchange operator BATS has called for the concentration of liquidity for thinly-traded securities at the primary listing exchange for that security.[730] As part of that ambition, BATS expressed interest in no longer offering trading on BATS in illiquid securities listed on other exchanges.[731]

---

[727] Notice of Filing of Proposed Rule Change to Adopt a New Extended Life Priority Order Attribute under Rule 4703, Nov. 30, 2016, Release No. 34-79428, SR-NASDAQ-2016-161.

[728] *Id.* at 40.

[729] *See* A. C. Pritchard, *Revisiting "Truth in Securities" Revisited: Abolishing IPOs and Harnessing Private Markets in the Public Good*, 36 SEATTLE U. L. REV. 999 (2013).

[730] Chris Concannon, *Letter to BATS Customers and Trading Community*, http://cdn.batstrading.com/resources/newsletters/CEO-Newsletter-April-2015.pdf.

[731] *Id.* (arguing that "concentrating displayed liquidity in thinly-traded stocks at a single venue will enable market participants to more efficiently form prices, and that one venue also will be better able to innovate their markets specifically for thinly traded stocks (i.e., tick size, auctions, etc.).").

Increasing pressure on how securities law currently conceives of the "public" corporation could have other implications for equity market structure.[732]

7.5 EMSAC's Proposed Reforms

In early 2015, the SEC formed an Equity Market Structure Advisory Committee (EMSAC). Its members are tasked with studying the structure and functioning of the U.S. equity markets and providing advice and recommendations for market reform. The EMSAC has made a number of notable recommendations:

- An Access Fee Pilot proposal that would study the effects of altering access fee caps on rebates, order routing, liquidity, and other market quality outcomes[733]
- Reforms to liability limits of SROs, whereby rule-based liability limits are increased and regulatory capital potentially required. EMSAC also suggested reforms to the governance structure of NMS plans, involving a greater role for non-exchange constituents[734]
- Recommendations involving volatility, including price band mechanisms to address flaws regarding re-openings auctions after volatility halts[735]

All of these efforts would produce highly valuable data, particularly concerning the interaction between access fee caps, maker-taker fees, and off-exchange trade, but some may also increase market complexity.

---

[732] *See* Donald C. Langevoort & Robert B. Thompson, *"Publicness" in Contemporary Securities Regulation After the Jobs Act*, 101 GEO. L.J. 337, 339 (2013).

[733] EMSAC, *Regulation NMS Subcommittee Recommendation for an Access Fee Pilot*, June 10, 2016, https://www.sec.gov/spotlight/emsac/emsac-regulation-nms-recommendation-61016.pdf.

[734] EMSAC, RECOMMENDATIONS REGARDING ENHANCED INDUSTRY PARTICIPATION IN SRO REGULATORY MATTERS (2016), https://www.sec.gov/spotlight/emsac/emsac-trading-venues-regulation-subcommittee-recomendation-61016.pdf.

[735] EMSAC, RECOMMENDATIONS FOR RULE-MAKING ON ISSUES OF MARKET QUALITY (2016), https://www.sec.gov/spotlight/emsac/emsac-market-quality-subcommittee-final-recommendations-1116.pdf.

7.6 The Tick Size Pilot

Beginning in October 2016, the SEC implemented a pilot project to adjust the tick size or minimum increment in which a displayed order can price a bid or ask quote for a stock.[736] In the early 2000s, the U.S. stock market went through decimalization, or the process of reducing the tick size to one cent.[737] Since then, some have argued that this reduced tick size has had adverse effects on market quality. The essential argument is that a large tick size rewards liquidity provision, and that because IPO underwriters often make markets in the company's stock, increasing market makers' return on liquidity provision can arguably make investment banks more eager to underwrite IPOs, with positive effects for capital formation and job creation.[738] This argument was influential in initiating the tick size pilot.

The pilot program, which spans two years, involves a control group and three test groups, each consisting of around 400 small capitalization issuers, and will allow for a five-cent tick size for those issuers' securities. During the pilot, the SEC will gather and make available market quality data in order to test whether a widening tick size for small capitalization companies improves or harms liquidity, volume, and market quality. While the tick size will produce market data for research purposes, various critics, including the SEC's Investor Advisory Committee, argue that increasing the tick size will harm investors.[739] They contend that in the past, market making has increased even as the tick size decreased; a larger tick size means costlier liquidity for the smallest investors for whom the spread is a good measure of liquidity; and the current spread

---

[736] FINRA, TICK SIZE PILOT PROGRAM, http://www.finra.org/industry/tick-size-pilot-program (providing extensive details on rationale and function of pilot).

[737] Decimalization was codified in Rule 612 of Reg. NMS. *See* 17 C.F.R. §242.612 ("No national securities exchange, national securities association, alternative trading system, vendor, or broker or dealer shall display, rank, or accept from any person a bid or offer, an order, or an indication of interest in any NMS stock priced in an increment smaller than $0.01 if that bid or offer, order, or indication of interest is priced equal to or greater than $1.00 per share.").

[738] *See, e.g.*, David Weild, Edward Kim & Lisa Newport, *The Trouble with Small Tick Sizes: Larger Tick Sizes Will Bring Back Capital Formation, Jobs and Investor Confidence*, Grant Thornton Capital Markets Series (2012).

[739] *Recommendation of the Investor Advisory Committee Decimalization and Tick Sizes*, https://www.sec.gov/-spotlight/investor-advisory-committee-2012/investment-adviser-decimilization-recommendation.pdf.

represents the efficient equilibrium of a competitive market.[740] Indeed, one might argue that the tick size should be made *smaller* for actively-traded, large capitalization stocks that typically trade with a one-penny spread. Critics also point out that underwriters are typically no longer actively involved in market making.

8 Conclusion and Implications for Future Research

Equity trading markets changed dramatically in the past two decades, while the regulatory architecture has undergone far less updating. Considering which aspects of that architecture should be revised, and if so how, constitutes the foundation of a future research agenda for those invested in the regulation of trading markets. As a starting point for this research, we conclude by summarizing major pressure points placed on the current regulatory system.

First, there are a series of overlapping concerns about the current categorization system for trading venues as well as the structure of SROs and status of exchanges. Should there be multiple different regulatory statuses for trading venues that are becoming increasingly functionally similar? Should exchanges remain individual SROs with the absolute immunity from private suit that accompanies that status? Should the exchanges retain their low rule-book liability limits?

Second, the current system relies heavily on broker-dealers as gatekeepers. Accordingly, the regulatory system should be attentive to whether competition sufficiently mediates the conflicting interests of broker-dealers and their customers. Areas for particular study include monetary inducements in the form of maker/taker fees or payment for order flow.

Third, there are significant drawbacks to the predominantly common law approach to trader misconduct on which the SEC and Department of Justice currently rely. Insider trading law may have more coherency than some commentators appreciate, but significant uncertainties remain under current law regarding important issues. Manipulation law is the subject of considerable disagreement among the federal circuit courts on foundational questions. Section 9(a)(2) of the Exchange Act, because of the very limited case law addressing it, may offer courts and regulators a fresh start for conceptualizing and prosecuting manipulation. Both the law of insider trading and of manipulation might also benefit from well-crafted statutory enactments defining their precise contours.

Fourth, important open empirical questions could have a significant impact on policy if answered in specific ways. For instance, the conceptual case for the negative externality imposed on lit liquidity by dark liquidity is plausible, but its actual economic significance is unknown. Using data from IEX's

---

[740] *Id.* at 7-9.

transition to an exchange, or from an SEC-mandated experiment, empiricists should study whether increased dark liquidity has a negative effect on the lit market and market quality overall.

Chapter 6
THE ECONOMICS OF INTERMEDIARIES

Jonathan B. Berk[741] & Jules H. van Binsbergen[742]

1 Introduction

Equity markets have undergone several important changes in the past 70 years. Arguably, one of the most important is how individuals hold equity. While in 1945 almost all corporate equities were held directly by households and non-profits, today direct holdings by individuals make up less than 40% of holdings. In fact, some studies argue that this number is closer to 20%. At the same time, the market has witnessed enormous growth in the open-end mutual fund sector. From almost no presence at all in 1945, these funds now make up 25% of the market or more. In short, in the last 70 years there has been a large trend away from direct investing into delegated fund management. We view this trend as the single most important change in how investors use financial intermediaries. In 1945, when investors invested directly, the intermediary was a broker who was most likely paid as a function of the number of trades he made. Today, investors give their money to fund managers or financial advisors, who then invest this money on investors' behalf in equity (and sometimes other) funds. These intermediaries are compensated based on the amount of assets under management (AUM). The move away from trade based compensation to AUM based compensation represents important progress. As we will argue, AUM based compensation contracts much better align the incentives of the money manager and her investors and is likely a primary factor in driving the trend from direct investing through brokers to indirect investing.

The invention of the mutual fund has made diversified investing accessible to essentially all investors. Previously, each individual investor had to construct diversified portfolios themselves, which involved an inefficient amount of trade given the amounts invested. Compared to that counterfactual, the mutual fund industry in all its diversity adds large amounts of value to investors.

Because of the rise in delegated money management, the bulk of this chapter will be devoted to that sector of the investment intermediary space. We believe the importance of delegated money managers is likely to keep rising as investors keep moving from direct investing into indirect investing. As we will

---

[741] A.P. Giannini Professor of Finance, Stanford Graduate School of Business.

[742] Nippon Life Associate Professor of Finance, the Wharton School, University of Pennsylvania.

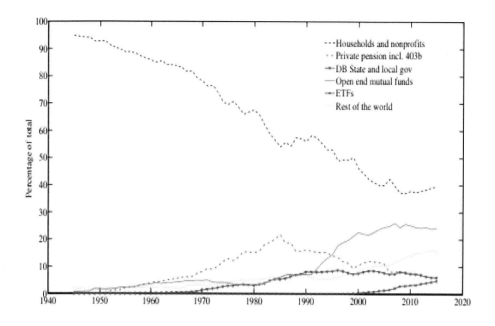

Figure 1: **Who Holds Corporate Equities?**
The graph shows the fraction of US corporate equity held by its largest investor groups.

argue in this chapter, the future regulation of equity markets relies on an in-depth understanding of the delegated money management equilibrium. Consequently, a large fraction of our report will focus on describing the equilibrium, and its implications for competition in the sector. We begin by first summarizing the important trends in the last 70 years.

2 The Last 70 Years

As we pointed out in the introduction, the single most important trend in the last 70 years is the secular decline of direct investing in equity markets and the concomitant rise of several other important players who hold equity on behalf of investors. Table L.223 of the Flow of Funds Accounts of the United States published by the Federal Reserve provides an overview of the amounts of corporate equity held by various types of investors. We compute how much each of these investors holds as a fraction of the total and plot these fractions for the six groups with the largest relative holdings in Figure 1. As we have already noted, the fraction held directly by households and non-profits has decreased from over 90% to about 40%. This downward trend is reflective of an equally important concomitant trend: rather than investing directly in markets, individual investors have increasingly chosen to allocate their money to investment

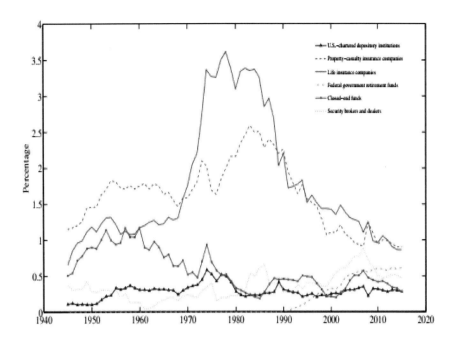

Figure 2: **Who Holds Corporate Equities? Continued**
The graph shows the fraction of US corporate equity held by various smaller investor groups.

managers. The fraction of equity held by open end mutual funds has increased to about 25%. The remainder can be explained by the rise of pension plan holdings (both defined contribution and defined benefit), as well as the rise of exchange traded funds (ETFs). Finally, holdings by foreigners have also increased.

French argues that the Fed uses the household and nonprofit sector as a residual.[743] Its allocation is the aggregate value of corporate equity minus the combined values of the other sectors, implying that the household and nonprofit sector includes not only the publicly traded common equity held by households and nonprofits, but also preferred stock and closely held corporations. French uses various other data sources to separate these pieces, and argues that the fraction of public equity held by households is substantially lower than 40% and closer to 20% in 2007. The downward trend for these adjusted numbers up until 2007 is the same as the computations we present here. Based on these computations, it is therefore not unreasonable to assume that since 2007, the fraction of equity held by households has not changed much.

---

[743] Kenneth R. French, *The Cost of Active Investing*, 63 J. FIN. 1537 (2008).

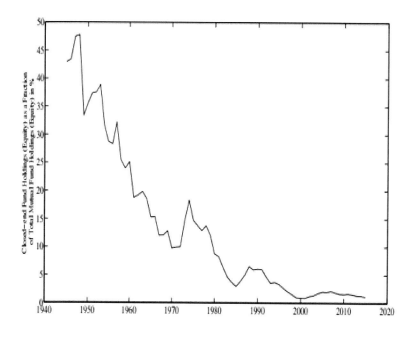

Figure 3: **Disappearing Closed End Funds**
The graph shows the value of equity holdings of closed-end funds as a fraction of the total equity holdings of open and closed-end mutual funds.

In Figure 2 we show the holdings of the remaining 6 groups. All of these groups, which includes (among others) life insurance companies, properties/casualty insurance companies, and broker-dealers all have very small holdings of equity and by 2015 all these holdings are below 1%. Note also that over the entire sample, closed-end funds only hold a very small fraction of the total. To gauge the trend in closed-end investing, we plot in Figure 3 the equity holdings of closed-end funds as a fraction of the total mutual fund holdings (including open-end and closed-end funds). The graph shows a marked decline in closed-end fund holdings, particularly in the seventies. In relative terms, closed-end funds have all but disappeared.

Finally, in Figure 4 we plot the corporate equity holdings of ETFs as a fraction of the total corporate equity holdings of open-end mutual funds, closed-end mutual funds and ETFs. The graph shows a clear upward trend. While ETFs were essentially non-existent in the early nineties, their fraction has increased to over 16% in 2015.

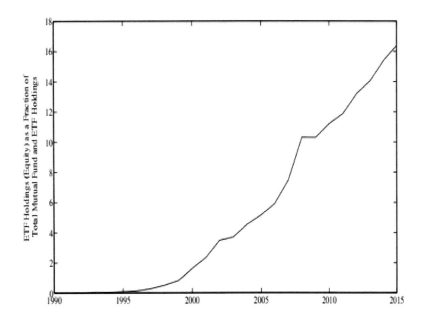

Figure 4: **The Rise of ETFs**
The graph shows the AUM invested with ETFs as a fraction of the total corporate equity holdings of open-end mutual funds, closed-end mutual funds and ETFs.

3 Money Management Firms

The explosive growth of the money management industry spurred a very large academic literature that studies this sector. The literature has largely been focused on answering two important questions: (1) whether investors are better off investing directly themselves or indirectly through a money manager, and (2) whether money managers add value by selecting stocks on behalf of investors. Until recently, the consensus view was that the answer to the first question is a qualified yes: investors are better off so long as they avoid active managers and invest in passive index funds. Further, the consensus is that the answer to the second question is no: money managers are no better at picking stocks than monkeys throwing darts at a dartboard.

In fact, both these conclusions are not correct. They are a result of inconsistently applying the rational expectations equilibrium concept (commonly referred to as "efficient markets") to delegated money management. In a series of research articles, we have demonstrated that when the rational expectations equilibrium is consistently applied to both direct and indirect investing, a different picture emerges.[744] Specifically, the answer to the first question is that market competition implies that in equilibrium investors are indifferent between active and passive investing and the answer to the second question is yes. Active mutual fund managers add considerable value, but competition between investors ensures that this value accrues to the intermediaries rather than to investors. Because of the importance of these results, we will describe them in detail.

3.1 Competition and Rational Expectations

The primary question we have been asked to address is the competitiveness of the money management industry. To answer this question it is essential to first understand the nature of the competition in this industry. So far, financial economists have viewed investors who invest in stocks directly as fundamentally different from investors that invest in stocks through money managers. When investors invest in stocks directly, it is broadly accepted that the rational expectations equilibrium paradigm provides a very good description of how investors (and therefore prices) behave in practice. In fact, today, the rational expectations view is so common that when stock prices adjust in response to a piece of news, the change in the price in response to that news can be used as legal evidence of how valuable that piece of information is. On the other hand, when investors invest in stocks through money managers, a very common view is that they irrationally invest almost exclusively in investments that underperform their next best alternative.[745] Further, because of this assumed investor irrationality, returns are informative about the (lack of) investment skill of investment managers, as opposed to just risk. Also, because abnormal returns to investors have no persistence, financial economists labeled investors that acted upon outperformance as naive return chasers. This line of thinking took the lack of persistence as an exogenous fact unrelated to investor actions. The possibility that the flow performance relationship (the rational term for return chasing) is in

---

[744] Jonathan B. Berk & Richard C. Green, *Mutual Fund Flows and Performance in Rational Markets*, 112 J. POL. ECON. 1269 (2004); Jonathan B. Berk & Jules H. van Binsbergen, *Measuring Skill in the Mutual Fund Industry*, 118 J. FIN. ECON. 1 (2015); Jonathan B. Berk, Jules H. van Binsbergen & Binying Liu, *Matching Capital and Labor*, 72 J. FIN. 2467 (2017).

[745] Burton G. Malkiel, *Returns from Investing in Equity Mutual Funds 1971 to 1991*, 50 J. FIN. 549 (1995); Mark M. Carhart, *On Persistence in Mutual Fund Performance*, 52 J. FIN. 57 (1997); Eugene F. Fama & Kenneth R. French, *Multifactor Explanations of Asset Pricing Anomalies*, 51 J. FIN. 55 (1996).

fact what causes the lack of persistence was never considered. What is arguably most surprising about this fundamentally different view of these two groups of investors is the significant amount of overlap between the two groups. Unfortunately, this perspective of money management is still very pervasive today and continues to shape policymaking. As we illustrate in this chapter, there is in fact little support for this view. We show that under the standard rational expectations assumption, many of the documented empirical findings can be explained. In fact, we show that the documented empirical patterns are exactly what we should expect to see in a competitive mutual fund market.

Applying the rational expectations equilibrium correctly goes a long way to better understanding the nature of competition in money management. Even though the paradigm was first presented in Muth,[746] it gained traction in finance in papers by Eugene Fama who labeled it the efficient market hypothesis.[747] A key insight of the framework is that the expected return on a firm's stock is solely a reflection of the risk (appropriately measured) of that stock rather than of the quality of that firm's management. The high (low) quality of the firm's management is already reflected in the current high (low) stock (and bond) price of the firm, and thus leaves expected returns going forward unaffected. Put differently, firms with successful managers therefore already have a high market capitalization today, not a high expected return going forward.

Even though the literature has heavily debated whether prices incorporate all available information, there is little doubt that they reflect a large majority of it. Consequently, the cross-sectional distribution of firms' market capitalizations better measures the cross-sectional distribution of firm quality than the cross-sectional distribution of expected returns. As argued before, this idea is so widespread that when new information is released, it is common (including in our courts of law) to measure the value of that new information by simply looking at the response of stock prices immediately upon the release of the information. The expected return subsequent to the release is never used for this purpose.

Surprisingly, in the money management literature the exact opposite way of thinking was widely adopted. Instead of focusing on the total value of the fund as being reflective of the skill of a mutual fund manager (the mutual fund counterpart to market capitalization), the literature focused on return-based

---

[746] John F. Muth, *Rational Expectations and the Theory of Price Movements*, 29 ECONOMETRICA 315 (1961).

[747] Eugene F. Fama, *The Behavior of Stock Market Prices*, 38 J. BUS. 34 (1965); Eugene F. Fama, *Efficient Capital Markets: A Review of Theory and Empirical Work*, 25 J. FIN. 383 (1970); Eugene F. Fama, *Efficient Capital Markets: Reply*, 31 J. FIN. 143 (1976).

measures such as the abnormal return before or after management fees (the so-called gross and net alpha). By not appropriately applying the rational expectations framework, several important insights from that framework were missed. Changes in the size of mutual funds were seen as random and even irrational. However, once the rational expectations framework is applied correctly, it becomes clear that just as stock price changes happen as a rational response to new information regarding the quality of a firm, changes in total fund size happen in response to new information regarding the quality of a mutual fund manager. Perhaps even more importantly, the lack of an abnormal return to investors (a net alpha of zero) was erroneously seen as evidence of managers lacking skill, instead of what it really is: evidence of rational investors competing for managerial skill. Once the rational expectations framework is applied correctly, it becomes clear that the return to investors is unrelated to the skill of a manager in the same way that the expected return on a stock is unrelated to the quality of a company.

One may wonder why in two so closely related literatures two such different paradigms prevailed. One potential explanation is the way the original efficient markets papers were presented.[748] The idea those papers put forward was that if stock prices reflect all available information, then no investor should be able to benefit from picking stocks. The fact that mutual fund managers deliver a zero net alpha to their investors was interpreted as evidence that not even people that are specialized in stock picking could pick stocks. This fact was seen as the ultimate evidence that stock markets are highly efficient. What this line of thinking misses, however, is that it inconsistently applies the rational expectations framework. Once this discrepancy between the two literatures was put in place, it continued for several decades.

So how far does the analogy between stock markets and mutual funds go? The answer is very far. In both markets, investors compete with each other for positive net present value investment opportunities and by doing so eliminate them. For stocks, on seeing a mispricing, investors compete to invest in the stock and this competition drives stock prices to the right level. As a consequence, the expected return on the stock is solely driven by risk. For mutual funds, the mechanism is the same save for one difference: the price for a mutual fund is fixed—it is always equal to the value of the underlying securities. As a consequence, the market for mutual funds cannot equilibrate through prices. Instead, it equilibrates through quantities, that is, the AUM of the fund. The expected return to investors in both cases is only reflective of the risk of the investment and is unrelated to quality or skill.

---

[748] Eugene F. Fama, *The Behavior of Stock Market Prices*, 38 J. BUS. 34 (1965); Burton G. Malkiel, *Returns from Investing in Equity Mutual Funds 1971 to 1991*, 50 J. FIN. 549 (1995).

Most readers will be familiar with how attractive investment opportunities in stock markets are rapidly competed away. If the price of the stock is too low relative to the expected future cash flows, investors will all want to buy the stock, thereby increasing the price of the stock. This adjustment will stop when the price of the stock has risen so much that investors no longer view it as an attractive deal, and the price equals the present value of the cash flows. How does this work for mutual funds? We have argued that mutual funds also become less of an attractive investment opportunity as more and more investors compete for the skill of the manager. But why does a larger investor base decrease the attractiveness of the investment opportunity? The answer is decreasing returns to scale: as the fund size grows, it becomes harder and harder for a mutual fund manager to fund attractive investment opportunities for these new inflows. As the fund size (the assets-under-management) grows, the expected return on the fund will decrease. It will keep increasing until the abnormal expected return to investors (the net alpha) is 0. Similarly, if the net alpha is negative, funds will flow out, and the net alpha will increase until it is zero.

Applying the rational expectations framework correctly to mutual funds thus provides two important insights. The first insight is that the average abnormal return (or net alpha) that investors make by investing in a mutual fund does not teach us anything about the skill of the manager. Instead it teaches us something about the rationality of investors and/or the competition that they face. If net alphas are positive then the market for mutual funds is not very competitive as investors are leaving money on the table. If net alphas are negative, then investors are irrational as they are investing too much money with active managers and thus invest in negative net present value investment opportunities. The second insight is that just as the quality of a firm is reflected in the market capitalization of the firm, the skill of a mutual fund manager is reflected in the size of the fund that manager manages. If the fund size is large, the manager is highly skilled. If the fund size is small, the manager is much less skilled.

To further illustrate how rational expectations work in mutual funds, consider the following simple example based on Berk and Green.[749] Take a manager, let's call her manager 1, who can earn a 1.5% gross alpha (the abnormal return before fees are taken out) on a $5 billion fund. Because the manager does not have an infinite number of ideas and implements the ideas with the highest returns first, the fund's alpha deteriorates as the fund grows. Due to these decreasing returns to scale, the manager makes a 1% alpha when the fund's AUM is $10 billion and a 0:5% gross alpha when the fund size equals $15 billion.

---

[749] Berk & Green, *supra* note 744.

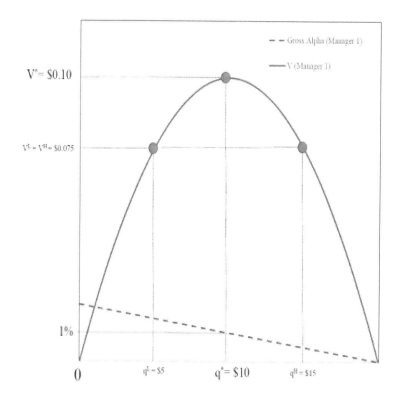

Figure 5: **Size, Value Added and Gross Alpha**
The graph shows the relationship between size and value added/gross alpha. This graph is an adjusted version of Figure 1 in Berk and van Binsbergen (2017).

How much money does the manager extract from financial markets (what we term value added) for each of these three fund sizes? When the fund size is small and equal to $5 billion, the manager extracts $5 0:015 = $0:075 billion, or $75 million. For the intermediate fund size, the value added equals $100 million (1% of $10 billion), and for the large fund size it equals $75 million (1:5% of $15 billion). These numbers are plotted in Figure 5, where the solid line represents the value extracted from financial markets (or value added) and the dashed line represents the gross alpha.

Looking at Figure 5, it is clear that the maximum value added occurs when the fund size equals $10 billion. For this size, the gross alpha is 1%. Before we turn to the problem that investors are solving, let us compare the manager above to another manager that is less talented. Manager 2 is also very good at delivering high gross alpha for small fund sizes, but is not nearly as talented in generating additional trading ideas as the fund size grows. That is, on a $5 billion fund, manager 2 can only generate a 1% gross alpha, leading to a value added of $50 million. We plot the value added and the gross alpha of both managers in

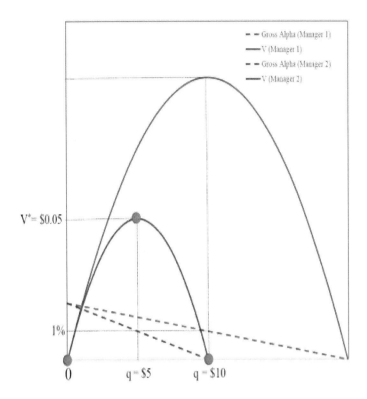

Figure 6: **Size, Value Added and Gross Alpha**
The graph shows the relationship between size and value added/gross alpha for two managers. Manager 1 is more skilled than Manager 2 while both make the same gross alpha on the first cent they invest. Manager 2 runs out of ideas more quickly than manager 1. That is, manager 2 is more affected by the decreasing returns to scale than manager 1 is. This graph is an adjusted version of Figure 2 in Berk and van Binsbergen (2017).

Figure 6. The graph shows that the gross alpha for both managers at the optimal amount of money is the same and equal to 1%. This implies that gross alpha is not a good measure of skill. After all, manager 2 is running out of ideas more quickly than manager 1, and is therefore less skilled. Where does this skill difference show up if not in gross alpha? It shows up in the amount of money the managers can handle, which is twice as large for manager 1 compared to manager 2. Because the gross alpha at the optimal amount of money is the same, but the optimal amount of money is twice as large for manager 1, this implies that manager 1's value added (the product of the size of the fund and the gross alpha) is twice as large for manager 1. That is, manager 1 is able to extract twice as much money from financial markets compared to manager 2.

The conclusion that value added measures skill while gross alpha does not, follows only from the notion that both managers eventually run out of ideas, that is, they have decreasing returns to scale. Whether or not the rational expectations paradigm holds is irrelevant for this argument.

What about investors? Suppose that investors have rational expectations. This implies that if an attractive (positive NPV) investment opportunity presents itself, investors will pursue it until it is competed away. As a consequence, in equilibrium, the return that the investment delivers is solely a function of its risk. Put differently, investors in each fund must all earn a risk-adjusted expected return (or net alpha) of 0. If the risk-adjusted expected return is not 0, the equilibrium hasn't been reached yet. When the managers choose their percentage fee, f, to be equal to

$$f = 1\%,$$

investors invest $10 billion with manager 1 and $5 billion with manager 2. The net alpha, which is the difference between the gross alpha and the fee, will be zero for both managers and the mutual fund market equilibrates: investors have no incentive to either give money to or take money away from either fund. Although the net and gross alpha of the two managers is the same, the AUM of manager 1 is twice as large as that of manager 2, in equilibrium.

Before we proceed, let us summarize the important insights that the rational equilibrium paradigm has delivered. First, because investors compete with each other for attractive investment opportunities, the net alphas are zero, always. This implies that net alphas cannot be informative on managerial ability as it does not differentiate across managers. Similarly, the gross alpha is also not informative. As argued above, the reason for why gross alpha, which is a return-based measure, does not measure managerial skill and value added does, is the same as the reason why present value measures dominate internal rate of return (IRR) measures when choosing between investment projects. Return-based measures simply fail to take into account the scale of the project. Only when there are constant returns to scale (an unreasonable assumption in investment management) can scale be ignored.

For ease of exposition, the framework we have presented is a static one where all players know the gross alpha that the manager delivers at each potential fund size. In reality, investors (and managers) need to learn about this. This learning process implies that each time the manager does better than expected, investors will update their beliefs positively on the alpha the manager will deliver. As soon as investors update positively, there is a positive net alpha opportunity at the current fund size. As we have already seen, such an opportunity cannot survive in equilibrium. After all, as soon as the opportunity presents itself, investable money (that is in very large supply) will find its way there. The fund size will grow, and due to the decreasing returns to scale, the net alpha will be driven back down to zero. In summary, the fund size will change as the investors learn about the skill of the manager.

In addition to the fund size adjusting as investors learn, there is another potential equilibration mechanism: the fee the manager charges. If the manager increases (decreases) her percentage fee every time investors update positively (negatively) on the gross alpha she can deliver, the net alpha can be kept at zero while keeping the fund size constant over time. Even though this mechanism could also work, it is not the mechanism that we observe in the data: managers very rarely change their fees, implying that nearly all of the equilibration happens through the adjustment of the fund size.

So how can managers ensure that they extract the maximum amount of money from markets without changing their fee? From the point of view of the manager, the optimal amount to invest in active management (i.e. where the value added graph peaks) remains the same regardless of the level of the fee. So what does the manager do if fees are too low and thus investors invest more than the optimal amount? The answer is he indexes the remaining money. This indexed money by definition earns a gross alpha of zero, and thus as the fraction of indexed money grows, the gross alpha of the fund as a whole decreases. Following the same logic as before, this process will continue until the gross alpha equals the fees and thus the net alpha is zero.

That brings us to the next important insight. The gross alpha and the size of the fund cannot be meaningfully interpreted in isolation and should be studied jointly. Let us illustrate this point with a simple example. Suppose there is an investment manager, call her manager A, whose optimal amount of money to manage is $1 billion, at which point the gross alpha is 1%. So, at the peak of the value added graph, value added equals $10 million. Suppose next that this manager is already managing the optimal amount of money and that the fee is 1%. The net alpha is 1%-1% = 0, and thus the fund is in equilibrium. Now consider another manager, manager B who is the twin sister of manager A. The only difference between her and her sister is that she chooses to charge a fee of 0.5%. At a fund size of $1 billion, this would imply that the net alpha is 1%-0.5% = 0.5%. This is not an equilibrium. Investors want in on this opportunity and the fund size grows. Because the manager's optimal amount to actively invest is $1 billion, the new inflows cannot be put to productive use. The manager therefore indexes the new inflows. When the fund size reaches $2 billion, half of the money is indexed. Given that the indexed money does not earn a gross alpha (by definition), the gross alpha of the whole fund is 0.5 x 1% + 0.5 x 0% = 0.5%, the net alpha is zero, the fund is in equilibrium and like her twin sister her value added is $10 million. Note that even though the managers are identical in their skill level, to a naive spectator the two managers may look very different: they have a different fund size and a different gross alpha. Only when we take the product of these two quantities does it become clear that we are dealing with two equally skilled managers.

This delivers yet another important insight: the percentage fee is irrelevant. Because the fund size adjusts to ensure that the net alpha is zero (i.e. the gross alpha is sufficiently high to cover the fees), it does not matter whether manager A and B choose a fee of 1% or 0.5%. With low fees, the fund is big and with high fees the fund is small but the money extracted from financial markets remains unchanged. It is often argued that the increase in AUM of mutual funds that charge a low fee is a result of the success of those funds in comparison with their high fee competitors. What the arguments above imply is that in equilibrium, low-fee funds will automatically be larger, even if without any difference between the skill level of the managers and/or the net alpha that investors receive. Finally, because the fund size adjusts in response to fee changes to ensure that the net alpha is always zero, regulating fees without also regulating the size of the fund is ineffective.

In the next section, we will illustrate how well the framework presented above performs in the data. However, before we do so, we wish to address an often-heard argument for why the active mutual fund sector as a whole cannot add value. This argument is often referred to as Sharpe's arithmetic[750] and goes as follows. Suppose we split up the universe of investors in two groups, passive investors that invest in the market portfolio and all other investors which Sharpe labeled active investors. Because the first group earns the market return and because the two groups together must also hold the market, the active investors must by definition also earn the market return, and hence will not be able to beat it.

As it turns out, the reasoning above is flawed for two reasons. First, when defining "active" investors, Sharpe takes all investors that do not passively hold the market. In addition to active mutual funds, that also includes individual investors and investors in specialized index funds that do not exactly hold the market. So, if active mutual fund managers trade against these other groups of investors, then active mutual funds can make trading profits at the expense of these investors. This does of course raise the question of why these investors are not indexing their money in a fund that holds the market.

What is perhaps more surprising is that the arguments in Sharpe[751] leave open the possibility that active managers as a group can beat the market even if all investors are assumed to be fully rational. The reason is that even a passive investor must trade at least twice, once to get into the passive position and once to get out of the position. If we assume that active investors are better informed than passive, then whenever these liquidity trades are made with an active

---

[750] William F. Sharpe, *The Arithmetic of Active Management*, 47 FIN. ANALYSIS J. 7 (1991).

[751] *Id.*

investor, in expectation, the passive investor must lose and the active must gain. Hence, the expected return to active investors must exceed the return to passive investors, that is, active investors earn a liquidity premium.

3.2 Empirical Evidence

In this subsection, we will demonstrate that the simple dynamic rational expectations equilibrium derived above is able to explain the important empirical regularities documented in the mutual fund literature, as well as resolve the most important puzzles. We will focus exclusively on the mutual fund sector because that is the only place in the money management space where the data is of very high quality. All mutual funds are required to report their results to the SEC, and these numbers must be verified by independent auditors. Other money managers are not subject to these strict reporting requirements, and so the resulting datasets are subject to self-reporting biases.

We use the data set in Berk and van Binsbergen.[752] That data set, which covers the period from January 1962 to March 2011 is comprised of monthly observations compiled from combining two databases, the CRSP survivorship bias free mutual fund database and the Morningstar Principia database.

Our first objective is to test the implications of the rational expectations paradigm on investors. The equilibrium has two main implications. First, we should see net alphas of zero and second, there should be no easy way to predict which funds will deliver positive net alphas to investors going forward. The main roadblock to testing these two predictions is constructing an estimate of the funds' net alpha. Generally, financial economists have used two methods to convert the fund's returns into abnormal returns (net alphas) relative to the alternative investment opportunities investors have. The standard practice is not to construct the alternative investment opportunity itself, but rather to simply adjust for risk using a risk model. The problem with this approach is that the extent to which these risk models in fact appropriately correct for risk has been fiercely debated. As a consequence, researchers often choose to construct the alternative investment opportunity set after all. Even though, in principle, this addresses the problem of not knowing the appropriate risk model, the way researchers implement this in practice replaces one shortcoming with another. What researchers have typically done is assume that investors' next best investment opportunity is spanned by the factor mimicking portfolios in the Fama-French-Carhart factor specification.[753] That is, they have interpreted the factor mimicking portfolios in these factor specifications as investment opportunities available to investors, rather than risk factors.

---

[752] Berk & van Binsbergen, *supra* note 744.

[753] Fama & French, *supra* note 745; Carhart, *supra* note 745.

Fund Name	Ticker	Asset Class	Inception Date
S&P 500 Index	VFINX	Large-Cap Blend	08/31/1976
Extended Market Index	VEXMX	Mid-Cap Blend	12/21/1987
Small-Cap Index	NAESX	Small-Cap Blend	01/01/1990*
European Stock Index	VEURX	International	06/18/1990
Pacific Stock Index	VPACX	International	06/18/1990
Value Index	VVIAX	Large-Cap Value	11/02/1992
Balanced Index	VBINX	Balanced	11/02/1992
Emerging Markets Stock Index	VEIEX	International	05/04/1994
Mid-Cap Index	VIMSX	Mid-Cap Blend	05/21/1998
Small-Cap Growth Index	VISGX	Small-Cap Growth	05/21/1998
Small-Cap Value Index	VISVX	Small-Cap Value	05/21/1998

Table 1: **Benchmark Vanguard Index Funds:** This table lists the set of Vanguard Index Funds used to calculate the Vanguard benchmark. The listed ticker is for the Investor class shares which we use until Vanguard introduced an Admiral class for the fund, and thereafter we use the return on the Admiral class shares (Admiral class shares have lower fees but require a higher minimum investment). Source: Berk and van Binsbergen (2015), Table 1

*NAESX was introduced earlier but was originally not an index fund. It was converted to an index fund in late 1989, so the date in the table reflects the first date we included the fund in the benchmark set.

There are at least two arguments for why these often-used factor portfolios are not opportunities investors can actually invest in.[754] First, the portfolios ignore transaction costs. The performance of a fund that incurs transaction costs cannot be compared to the performance of a theoretical alternative that does not. The second reason is more subtle and relates to the hindsight bias of the portfolios that are used. The typical factors researchers used were discovered in the late 1980's and 1990's and popularized by Fama and French and Carhart.[755] However, it is common to include data for these factors that start many years before their discovery date. If, in those earlier years, investors did not know about these portfolios, they do not represent a true alternative investment opportunity. By using these portfolios to benchmark managers, academics are essentially evaluating managers in 1970 using 1990's knowledge. Any manager who, in 1970, had discovered the trading strategies explored in these factors should be credited for this knowledge in the performance evaluation.

In summary, by evaluating fund performance against non-investable benchmarks, the academic literature has potentially biased the results against finding managerial skill. To assess the importance of this issue, we next evaluate

---

[754] Berk & van Binsbergen, *supra* note 744.

[755] Fama & French, *supra* note 745; Carhart, *supra* note 745.

	MKT	SMB	HML	UMD
Alpha (b.p./month)	2	22	35	70
t-Statistic	0.83	2.80	3.37	3.38
Adjusted R^2	99%	74%	52%	15%

Table 2: **Net Alpha of FFC Portfolios:** We regress each FFC factor portfolio on the Vanguard Benchmark portfolios. The table lists the estimate (in b.p./month) and t-statistic of the constant term (Alpha) of each regression, as well as the R^2 of each regression. Source: Berk and van Binsbergen (2015), Table 2.

the "performance" of the most commonly-used factor portfolios against the set of index funds offered by Vanguard. These index funds are by definition investable alternatives for investors. The reason why we choose the funds offered by the Vanguard company is that these index funds have the purpose of giving investors access to diversification at the lowest cost. Other often-used benchmarks provided by Morningstar, for example, do not share this objective. Moreover, not only is Vanguard the market leader, it is also the pioneer in the space of index investing. For example, the 11 funds listed in Table 1 span the set of all index funds offered by the firm between 1977 and 2011. In each case, the Vanguard fund was the first index fund to offer that particular strategy. As such, the introduction dates of these funds can be used to infer when these strategies became widely known to investors

Table 2 shows the results of evaluating the performance of each factor mimicking portfolio using the set of passively managed available index funds offered by Vanguard over the period 1977-2011.[756] The only portfolio with an insignificant positive alpha is the market. The alpha for all the other factors is positive and statistically significant. The numbers vary between 22 b.p. per month (for the size portfolio) and 70 b.p. (for momentum). As momentum is also the trading strategy with the highest transaction costs, it is perhaps not surprising that the "outperformance" measure is the largest. We can thus conclude that the factor mimicking portfolios represents a much better (theoretical) investment opportunity set than what was actually available to investors. We therefore argue that the correct way to benchmark mutual funds is to use the available Vanguard index funds.

In particular, to evaluate mutual fund performance, we construct each fund's benchmark as the closest portfolio spanned by the set of Vanguard index funds. Let R_t^j denote the excess return (over the risk free rate) earned by investors in the jth Vanguard index fund at time t, then the benchmark return

---

[756] We start in 1977 because that was when Vanguard introduced its first index fund. Details of how the benchmarks are constructed can be found in Berk & van Binsbergen, *supra* note 744.

for fund *i* is given by:

$$R_{it}^B = \sum_{j=1}^{n(t)} \beta_i^j R_t^j,$$

where *n(t)* is the total number of index funds offered by Vanguard at time *t* and β_i^j is obtained from the appropriate linear projection of the *i*'th active mutual fund onto the set of Vanguard index funds.[757] As argued above, these benchmarks have two major advantages. First, they account for the industrial organization of the mutual fund sector through the dynamic discovery of various trading strategies. Second, the Vanguard returns are the actual returns that investors receive and thus are net of all transaction costs. We can thus be confident that these benchmarks represent actual investable alternative investment opportunities for investors.

Further, note that when we employ the benchmark above to measure the value added of one of the Vanguard index funds itself, it will be equal to the dollar fees that fund charges. The reason why Vanguard funds add value is that they give investors the lowest cost access to diversification services. Therefore, when we use as the benchmark the net returns of the Vanguard index funds, we explicitly account for the value added through such diversification services. Because active funds also provide diversification services, our measure credits them with this value added. We can also separate these diversification services from other skills by using gross returns on the Vanguard benchmarks.

Using this benchmark, we can now construct an empirical estimate of net alpha. If R_{it}^n is the return investors in fund *i* earn (i.e., the return after all fees are taken out) at time t, then define

$$\varepsilon_{it} \equiv R_{it}^n - R_{it}^B.$$

The average across time of ε_{it} is an estimate of fund *i*'s net alpha.

3.2.1 Net Alpha

Many researchers have argued that by investing in active mutual funds, investors underperform in the sense that their net alpha is negative.[758] Berk and

---

[757] *See id.* for a detailed description of the methodology used.

[758] Eugene F. Fama, *Luck versus Skill in the Cross Section of Mutual Fund Returns*, 65 J. FIN. 1915 (2010).

Equally Weighted	2.74
t-statistic	0.73
Value Weighted	-0.95
t-statistic	-0.31
Number of Funds	5974

Table 3: **Net Alpha (in b.p./month)**: The table reports the net alpha of two investment strategies: Investing $1 every month by equally weighting over all existing funds (*Equally Weighted*) and investing $1 every month by value weighting (based on AUM) over all existing funds (*Value Weighted*). Source: Berk and van Binsbergen (2015), Table 6.

van Binsbergen argue that this finding is largely driven by two very common empirical implementation choices.[759] The first of these choices we have already discussed above. By using non-investable benchmarks, researchers have biased the performance measurement against finding skill. The second choice relates to sample selection. It has become common in mutual fund research to exclude from the sample mutual funds that hold foreign stocks. Further, most studies start the sample in the mid-eighties while earlier data is readily available. Because of these two data sample restrictions, researchers have dropped more than half of the observations. More importantly, the fraction of total mutual fund AUM that is in funds that exclusively hold U.S. stocks is strongly decreasing over our sample period and represents less than 25% of it by the end of our sample (in 2011). Put differently, academic researchers have focused on a fast-shrinking part of the industry. We can think of no reason for either of these two data selection choices.

In Table 3, we report both the equal-weighted and value-weighted alpha over our data sample. The table shows that they are not statistically different from zero.

Once we have corrected the literature's implementation choices by using the right data sample and by using the Vanguard benchmark, the numbers in Table 3 are consistent with the predictions of the rational expectations paradigm. Importantly, however, the rational expectations equilibrium has additional predictions. It implies that net alphas are not predictable. To test the validity of this prediction, we sort firms into decile portfolios based on their historical net alpha and assess to what extent funds that have outperformed in the past will continue this outperformance in the future. Berk and van Binsbergen show (see

---

[759] Berk & van Binsbergen, *supra* note 744.

their Figure 5) that this is indeed the case.[760] There is no relation between past and future net alphas.

3.2.2 Skill

If active mutual funds have a net alpha of 0 and yet charge a fee, this must imply that they have skill. This skill is measured by the value added of the fund. So, the next question we need to address is how we estimate value added. To construct this measure, we first adjust the gross realized return of the fund by the realized return of the benchmark, $R_{it}^g - R_{it}^B$. This quantity is then multiplied by the real size of the fund (assets under management adjusted by inflation) at the end of the previous period, $q_{i,t-1}$, to obtain the realized value added between times $t-1$ and t:

$$V_{it} \equiv q_{i,t-1}\left(R_{it}^g - R_{it}^B\right).$$

The time series average of V_{it} measures a fund's value added.

As we have already argued, under the rational expectations paradigm, the only way to measure skill is value added. However, even when the rational expectations paradigm does not hold, this by no means implies that alpha measures can be used as a measure of skill. The observation that return measures do not appropriately adjust for scale holds whether or not the rational expectations paradigm is true. Further, value added always measures the amount of money extracted from markets. It is a consequence of the following simple adding-up constraint:

$$V_t = q_t \alpha_t^g(q_t) = q_t \alpha_t^n(q_t) + q_t f$$

where $\alpha_t^n(q_t)$ is the net alpha of the fund at time t as a function of the fund's size.

The first term in the above equation is the amount of money the manager either gives to or takes from investors. The second term is the amount of money the manager takes for himself. Notice that there is *no other source of funds*. What this observation implies is that the money the manager takes in compensation (dollar fees) can only come from one of two places, either from skill (through stock picking) or from investors (by underperforming). So the sum of these two terms must equal the amount of money the manager makes from his stock picks. This observation relies on no assumption other than this adding up constraint.

We begin by measuring the average value added of mutual fund managers

---

[760] Berk, van Binsbergen & Liu, *supra* note 744.

Cross-Sectional Mean	0.14
Standard Error of the Mean	0.03
t-Statistic	4.57
1st Percentile	-3.60
5th Percentile	-1.15
10th Percentile	-0.59
50th Percentile	-0.02
90th Percentile	0.75
95th Percentile	1.80
99th Percentile	7.82
Percent with less than zero	57.01%
Overall Mean	0.27
Standard Error of the Overall Mean	0.05
t-Statistic	5.74
No. of Funds	5974

Table 4: **Value Added:** For every fund in our database, we estimate the monthly value added. The *Cross-Sectional* mean, standard error, *t*-statistic and percentiles are the statistical properties of this distribution. *Percent with less than zero* is the fraction of the distribution that has value added estimates less than zero. The *Overall* mean, standard error and *t*-statistic are computed by computing the average value added in the data set. The numbers are reported in Y2000 $ millions per month. This table is based on Table 3 in Berk and van Binsbergen (2015).

over the period 1977-2011 in January 1, 2000 dollars.[761] The results in Table 4 show that mutual fund managers have skill. The average fund adds an economically significant $140,000 per month (in Y2000 dollars). There is also large variation across funds. The fund at the 99th percentile cutoff generated $7.82 million per month and the fund at the 90th percentile cutoff generated $750,000 a month on average. The median fund lost an average of $20,000/month, and only 43% of funds had positive estimated value added. The main insight is that most managers destroyed value but because most of the capital is controlled by skilled managers, as a group, active mutual funds added considerable value.

Well-performing funds have a higher likelihood of surviving compared to their less-performing counterparts. Therefore, first averaging by fund and then averaging across funds leads to estimates of what we call the ex-ante distribution

---

[761] The data is available from 1962, but the analysis begins in 1977 because that is the year Vanguard offered its first index fund.

of skill. If we compute an average without first averaging by fund, the estimate is different because surviving funds make up a larger part of the sample in this case (i.e. they are overrepresented). In that case, the resulting average is an estimate of the ex-post distribution of skill. It is the average skill level of the set of funds actually managing money. As expected, ex-post mean is higher than the ex-ante mean: the average fund added $270,000/month.

If managers are skilled, one would expect this skill to persist. Berk and van Binsbergen test for this persistence.[762] In Figure 3 of that paper they demonstrate strong evidence of this persistence for horizons up to ten years. The paper shows (Table 4) that the Null Hypothesis that skill is not persistent can be rejected at the 95% confidence level at almost all horizons between 3 and 10 years. It also documents that managers in the top 10% control 25% of all invested capital implying that investors reward skilled managers by providing them with more capital.

Berk and van Binsbergen also demonstrate how competitive mutual fund markets are. They show that if funds are ranked by the managerial compensation—the current size of the fund multiplied by the fee charged, performance is even more predictable. Because investors determine compensation (by determining the size of the fund) these results indicate that investors reward better managers with higher compensation. That means that investors are able to identify better managers ex ante. Investors appear to use more information to make this inference than what is contained in past returns.

In the past few decades financial economists have come to view mutual fund investors as naive, dumb and prone to the irrational "chasing" of past returns. The collective evidence we have presented here suggests quite the opposite. Investors use past returns to infer the skill of managers and rationally reallocate capital from bad managers to good managers. Because investors so fiercely compete with each other for skilled managers, they end up deriving no benefit from identifying this skill (i.e. the net alpha is zero), and the managers, because they have a skill in short supply, collect all the rents from their skill.

We can conclude that overall the data is consistent with the rational expectations frame-work. Markets are highly competitive and because investors do not bring anything to the table that is in short supply—after all, investable money is in very large supply—they do not earn abnormal returns. Given that net alphas are not statistically significantly negative, there is also little evidence that too much capital is allocated to active managers. Our findings also suggest that there is very large cross-sectional variation in the level of skill. This cross-sectional variation can only be observed by using value added (fund size) to measure skill. Put differently, because the cross-sectional variation in fees is so low, the cross-sectional variation in gross alpha is low, and thus the large

---

[762] Berk & van Binsbergen, *supra* note 744.

majority of the cross-sectional variation in skill is reflected in fund size, not gross alpha. Good managers manage large funds and bad managers manage (very) small funds. Because compensation is also primarily determined by fund size, good managers earn the highest compensation, which in turn is a good predictor of future dollar performance (value added).

3.3 Why Do Mutual Fund Firms Exist?

Next, we address the question of whether the framework above is consistent with and/or can help shed light on the question of why mutual fund firms exist. If investors can allocate money to mutual funds (and thus managers) directly, is there a need for mutual fund firms to intermediate in this process? Berk, van Binsbergen, and Liu find that firms indeed play an important role in this intermediation process.[763] The reason why there is room for intermediation is that executives in mutual fund firms seem better informed about managerial skill than investors are, and that they use this information to improve upon the capital allocation done by investors. Firms thus help investors allocate capital better.

More specifically, Berk, van Binsbergen, and Liu find that when a mutual fund firm decides to increase a manager's AUM by giving that manager an additional fund (a promotion), this increases that manager's value added. Similarly, the decision to take away a fund from a manager (a demotion) also leads to increases in subsequent value added. These capital reallocation decisions add at least $474,000 per manager per month compared to the counterfactual where managers would have kept their original capital allocation done by investors. This number represents about 30% of the total value that the industry adds.

Berk, van Binsbergen, and Liu further provide evidence that the improved capital allocation results from a unique informational advantage that insiders of the firm have relative to outsiders. If indeed only the insiders of the firm are privy to this informational advantage then capital reallocations that happen as a consequence of managers switching firms should not lead to increases in value added. This is indeed what Berk, van Binsbergen, and Liu find. Secondly, if promotions are based on private information of the firm, then they should not be predictable by variables easily observable to outsiders of the firm. After all, investors themselves can already observe those variables and thus can already adjust the allocated capital accordingly. This is also confirmed in Berk, van Binsbergen, and Liu. They find that past performance and past flows, which are both observable to outside investors, have very little predictive power for firms' promotion and demotion decisions. Finally, investors appear to be paying

---

[763] Berk, van Binsbergen & Liu, *supra* note 744.

strong attention to these personnel decisions, as they are followed by inflows into the firm's funds. These inflows also allow the firm to capture the rents from these allocation decisions, as the total fee revenue goes up because of these additional invested funds.

One interesting finding in Berk, van Binsbergen, and Liu is that value added goes up after a demotion. As we have argued above, as long as the manager indexes all money above the optimal amount of capital, the value added should not change when the fund is larger than the optimal amount. One interpretation of this finding is therefore that mutual fund executives know the ability of fund managers better than they do themselves.

Finally, the idea that firm executives have unique information regarding the level of skill of managers can also shed light on the empirical finding that compensation better predicts future performance than past performance does. By successfully intermediating between mutual fund managers and the fund's investors, firms achieve a better capital allocation than investors would without such intermediation. As argued above, investors seem to recognize this advantage of the firm and invest more money in the firm's funds. Because of this improved capital allocation, fund size (and thereby fees in dollars) are a better predictor of future performance than the information in past performance.

3.4 Compensation Contract

Viewed from a high level, the trend from direct investing to indirect investing is fundamentally a change in the compensation contract under which intermediaries work, more than a change in how investors invest. In 1945, investors hired a broker who executed trades and provided investment advice. Because most investors lacked any investment skill, they relied on such advice, and thus, one could view the broker as effectively managing the investors' portfolio. Viewed in that light, there is not much difference in the role of the intermediary today and in 1945. Instead of a broker managing an investor's equity investments, today a money manager or financial advisor performs the same role. What has fundamentally changed is how these intermediaries are compensated. In 1945, they were paid as a function of the number of trades they executed. Today, they are largely paid as a function of the amount of assets under management (and in some cases they also have a performance based component). We view this change as beneficial because, as we will argue, it more closely aligns incentives.

It is hard to understand how a compensation contract that is based on the number of trades could be optimal. Because trading incurs costs, from a manager whose objective is to maximize the amount of money she can extract from markets, the amount of trading should be minimized. But when such a manager is compensated in the number of trades, the compensation contract induces a conflict between maximizing the value she can add and her own compensation. In such an equilibrium, an optimizing manager will trade too much, reducing the total value added. In a fully competitive market these costs will be borne by the manager, and so we would expect better managers to eschew such contracts. This observation is likely one reason for why the sector has moved away from such contracts.

In contrast, Berk and Green demonstrate the surprising result that a compensation contract that rewards managers as a function of AUM is optimal.[764] At first glance, one would expect an optimal contract to depend on the manager's performance. But in the rational expectations equilibrium net alphas are zero. On average, regardless of their skill level, managers are expected to deliver the same abnormal return to investors. In contrast, compensating based on fund size does compensate for performance because investors react to returns by investing funds to ensure that net alpha is zero. Thus, compensating a manager based on fund size implies that that compensation will be a function of the market's perception of her skill level.

The crucial assumption in Berk and Green that delivers the above result is that managers are no better informed about their own ability as investors. There is evidence in Berk, van Binsbergen, and Liu that supports this assumption—that paper shows that when a manager is demoted (the firm lowers her AUM), her value added goes up. That means the manager must have been actively managing too much money. Since she could have chosen to index this capital, this result is consistent with the assumption that she does not know her own ability better than investors. When the assumption is not true it is unlikely that a contract that rewards managers in only AUM will be optimal. The reason is that a manager who is aware that she has more skill than the market is giving her credit for, will desire a performance-based contract. That is, she will prefer a contract that is at least partly a function of how she performs. Such a contract is ubiquitous in hedge funds and private equity, and we return to this issue below.

3.5 Index Funds

An important trend that is not visible in Figure 1 is the recent rise in index and/or passive investing. While index investing was close to non-existent 70 years ago, today the fraction of assets managed by open-end funds that designate themselves as index funds exceeds 20%. While this trend is notable in its magnitude, caution is in order when interpreting it. The lines between active and passive management have gradually blurred. For example, there are index funds that offer value or growth strategies at low fees. Take, for example, the Vanguard Value Index fund. Vanguard writes about this fund: "This fund invests

---

[764] Berk & Green, *supra* note 744.

in stocks of large U.S. companies in market sectors that tend to grow at a slower pace than the broad market; these stocks may be temporarily undervalued by investors." Given that such funds offer diversified strategies in specific sectors, investing in such a fund is not necessarily a passive strategy (especially if investors actively switch between such funds). Furthermore, as these strategies are based on sorting criteria such as the book-to-market ratios of the underlying stocks that change over time, substantial turnover is still required for such strategies. It is thus not obvious that these strategies should be classified as passive buy-and-hold strategies, what the profession usually associates with index investing. These days, Standard and Poor's (S&P) proudly advertises that they keep track of over 170,000 different indices, the vast majority of which are not proxies for or representative of the aggregate market portfolio. Because the costs to implement these strategies vary widely depending on the strategy, one should not expect the value different index funds add to be the same.

Even the funds that closely replicate a market index, such as the S&P 500, have important differences between them. For example, some index funds hold more cash than others to accommodate in and outflows, some S&P 500 index funds do not hold the full set of stocks in their portfolio to minimize on trading costs, and some funds engage in securities lending while others do not. In other words, even S&P 500 index funds are far from a homogeneous product.

An important issue to keep in mind for all mutual funds, but particularly for index funds, is that different investors in the same fund do not necessarily earn the same net return because all investors do not necessarily pay the same fee. Consider Vanguard's S&P 500 index fund, which features two classes, the so-called "Investor" class and the so-called "Admiral" class. There are substantial differences in fees between these two products. The Admiral class only charges 5bp per year, whereas the Investor class charges 16bp, a difference of 11bp. There are, however, good reasons for these differences to exist. The Admiral class is only available to investors who invest an amount bigger or equal than $10,000. Because there are fixed costs to running an account, it is not surprising that percentage fees are higher for smaller accounts. It is hard to believe that Vanguard can actually cover the fixed expenses associated with things like customer service for an investor who merely invests $1000 and thus pays $1.60 in fees annually.

Berk and van Binsbergen show that about half the value added of active funds is attributable to diversification services.[765] This implies that the value added of funds that just provide these services is significant. Fund size adjusts in equilibrium to the level of the fees. Because index funds charge low fees, we should expect these funds to be large, and thus we should expect to see these funds make up a large fraction of the market capitalization of mutual fund

---

[765] Berk & van Binsbergen, *supra* note 744.

investments.

3.6 Other Sectors of the Money Management Industry

Thus far we have concentrated on the mutual fund sector because of the availability of high quality data. The other important sectors of the money management industry include hedge funds, private equity funds and venture capital funds. All investors in these sectors must satisfy the requirement to be classed as "qualified" investors. Because these requirements impose high net wealth and income constraints, investors in these sectors are either rich individuals or institutions. Given these facts, we think a legitimate question that any policy maker should answer before imposing any regulation on these sectors is why these investors should be protected. We do not take a stand on this issue, other than emphasizing the importance of answering the question before any policy is put in place.

Almost all the datasets researchers use to analyze these sectors suffer from one of two drawbacks. Either the data set is made up of data self-reported by the management company, or it comes from investors investing in that management company. In the former case there are serious reliability concerns. Bad performing funds might choose not to report at all, funds might time their reporting based on their performance and funds might choose to report some funds (the successful ones) and not others (the unsuccessful ones). A common problem in early mutual fund studies is that companies would seed funds, see how they do, and then report the results for only the successful funds (quietly shutting down the others). Today, this problem is largely solved in the mutual fund space because researchers have been careful to make sure that all funds that represented an investable strategy are included in the database. However, there is no equivalent process in other sectors of the money management industry.

Databases that have been put together based on information from investors do not suffer from these biases because the investor received the data by making investments in the funds. However, because no one investor can invest in all funds in the sector, these databases represent a subset of the data. It is also likely that the subset contains selection biases. Clearly, ex-post successful investors are more likely to part with their data, which implies that the data will contain a bias in favor of ex-post successful funds.

Another important limitation is that even if the returns to investors are deemed of sufficient quality, no reliable data on gross returns are available. The reason for this is that both the fees and performance component are often negotiated per client. Even though most funds report that they charge a 2 and 20 fee schedule, many investors do not in fact pay this amount. This complicates the computation of returns and as a consequence our value added measure. It is therefore hard to assess the level and cross-sectional differences in skill across managers in this sector.

Finally, a last important difference is that hedge funds are not restricted by regulation to lever their investment strategies. This allows them to take aggressive bets even with little AUM. Mutual funds on the other hand usually do not take leverage, although a type of specialty mutual fund called a 30/130 fund is gaining popularity. Such funds go short 30% and extra long 130% in the strategy the fund is implementing.

Next, we discuss how well the framework we have laid out so far can be applied to hedge funds. Overall, the literature has found that hedge fund performance to investors is similar or somewhat better than that of mutual funds.[766] Given the data selection issues discussed above, better performance should not be unexpected. Whether this actually translates to better risk adjusted returns to investors is not clear.

In other dimensions, the literature on hedge funds also finds results that are consistent with the framework we have discussed in this chapter. Fung, Hsieh, Naik, and Ramadorai study funds-of-funds of hedge funds and find that alpha producing funds-of-funds experience far greater and steadier capital inflows than their less fortunate counterparts.[767] In turn, these capital inflows adversely affect their ability to produce alpha in the future. These findings are in line with the rational expectations framework and decreasing returns to scale discussed above. Lim, Sensoy, and Weisbach find that younger and more scalable hedge funds have stronger flow-performance relations.[768] This is also fully consistent with a world where rational investors learn about the ability of hedge funds over time. As the speed of learning slows with the age of the fund, so does the flow-performance relationship.[769] Furthermore, if hedge funds employ highly scalable strategies, then a given outperformance warrants a larger adjustment to the size of the fund, relative to a strategy that is less scalable. Fung and Hsieh find that hedge funds follow strategies that are dramatically different from mutual funds, and support the claim that these strategies are highly dynamic,

---

[766] For an overview of the literature, see Vikas Agarwal, Kevin Mullally & Narayan Y. Naik, *Hedge Funds: A Survey of the Academic Literature*, 10 FOUNDATIONS AND TRENDS IN FIN. 1 (2015).

[767] William Fung, David A. Hsieh, Narayan Y. Naik & Tarun Ramadorai, *Hedge Funds: Performance, Risk, and Capital Formation*, 63 J. FIN. 1777 (2008).

[768] Jongha Lim, Berk A. Sensoy & Michael S. Weisbach, *Indirect Incentives of Hedge Fund Managers*, 71 J. FIN. 871 (2016).

[769] *See* Berk & Green, *supra* note 744.

suggesting that hedge funds are more active than mutual funds.[770] This could imply that the value added of hedge funds is larger than that of mutual funds, though measurement of value added is complicated by a lack of fee data, as argued above.

The one question that the special study proposal raises that remains largely unanswered is the extent to which differences in the fee structure of mutual funds and hedge funds are justified by the differences in those vehicles. The existence of a different contract in the other sectors points towards examining the assumptions that underlie the optimality of the mutual fund contract. In our opinion, the assumption in Berk and Green that is most likely violated in the other sectors is the assumption of symmetric information between investors and managers.[771] That is, managers have as much information about their own ability as investors. When managers know more about their own ability than investors, they have an incentive, using the contract, to signal their ability. Because lesser ability managers can always mimic the contract of better managers, the resulting equilibrium will likely feature pooling, which limits the ability of better quality managers to separate from lower quality managers. In such an equilibrium it therefore becomes optimal to offer a contract that rewards outperformance. That is, although the contract is the same across all managers, better managers are paid more because they do better. Viewed from this perspective, the fact that the contract in the other sectors is performance-based is evidence that managers in these sectors likely know their own abilities better. However, why the contract would feature an asymmetric payoff is unclear. Further research is required before any policy recommendations can be made.

3.7 Frictions

It is common in finance and economics to first study the properties of markets and equilibria in a frictionless setting, as this provides a useful benchmark. Once the frictionless benchmark is well understood, various frictions, if empirically relevant, can then be added to obtain a model that is closer to the data. A very illustrative example of such a framework is the seminal work by Modigliani and Miller, who evaluate capital structure and dividend decisions by firms. Even if such a frictionless framework ends up being far removed from the data, this by no means implies that the framework is not a useful benchmark to start with.

The important insight that our paper has delivered is that the neoclassical

---

[770] William Fung & David A. Hsieh, *Empirical Characteristics of Dynamic Trading Strategies: The Case of Hedge Funds*, 10 REV. FIN. STUD. 275 (1997).

[771] Berk & Green, *supra* note 744.

frictionless framework (with learning) actually provides a surprisingly accurate description of the behavior of the mutual fund market in the data. That is not to say that frictions could not be important, and could potentially make the t of the model even better. One example of such a friction is taxes. Investors should care about after-tax returns, not pre-tax returns. As we do not observe the marginal tax rate of the marginal mutual fund investor, it is hard to ad-just returns for taxes, but future work could focus on such adjustments. Other frictions that could be interesting to evaluate are settings where the adjustment in fund size is inhibited for one reason or another. If the size of the fund cannot freely adjust, this implies that the equilibrating mechanism described in this chapter cannot do its work. This could potentially change the predictions of the model and the excess rents that investors could earn.

4 Broker Dealers

As we have already discussed, the role of broker-dealers has changed dramatically in the last 50 years. The rise of discount brokers and delegated money management has meant that broker-dealers pay a much less important role as investment advisors. Today, their primary responsibility is to intermediate trading, rather than also provide investment advice. We view this development as positive, because it is hard to see, given the compensation contract, how broker-dealers could avoid the conflict of interest that incentivizes them to trade too much.

With the declining role of broker-dealers as investment advisors, the question of whether they should be subject to a fiduciary standard is less pressing. With that said, there is very little evidence on whether such a standard would be beneficial. At first glance, imposing such a standard would seem to be very low cost and since one would expect that customers benefit when broker-dealers act in their interests, the argument not to impose the standard appears week. But, in reality, there is very little empirical or theoretical work that provides much insight beyond this observation. The work that does exist does not provide support for imposing this standard. Egan, Matvos, and Seru find no evidence of a difference in misconduct violations between broker-dealers and financial advisors, even though financial advisors are subject to a fiduciary standard already.[772]

We can think of two reasons to proceed with caution. First, requiring somebody to act as a fiduciary does not mean they will in fact act that way. As we have already mentioned, the compensation contract that compensates dealers

---

[772] Mark Egan, Gregor Matvos & Amit Seru, *The Market for Financial Adviser Misconduct*, J. POL. ECON. (forthcoming), https://papers.ssrn.com/sol3/papers.cfm?abstract_id=2739170.

in the number of trades sets up a conflict of interest that we believe is more likely to influence behavior than a law imposing a fiduciary standard. Broker-dealers are also subject to other incentives that conflict with many of their clients. Second, imposing such a standard could be detrimental if it leads clients to believe that their brokers are representing their interests when in reality the conflict of interest means that they are not. One could argue that setting a "buyer beware" standard might better serve client interests. In summary, given the lack of evidence and uncertainty on whether a fiduciary standard would be beneficial, we think further investigation is needed before any policy determination can be made.

Unfortunately, we can provide no insight on the question of whether the relationship between a broker dealer and its customer is competitive or monopolistic.

5 Policy

This chapter suggests a number of topics that policy makers might consider. First, we discuss issues related to regulations on fees and fund size. Second, we discuss the need for better quality data sources for the non-mutual fund sectors of money management.

5.1 Regulation on Fees and Fund Size

All of our conclusions rely on the assumption that the rational expectations equilibrium closely approximates the equilibrium in money management. We believe we have presented convincing evidence suggesting that this is indeed the case. In the case that a policy maker finds this assumption objectionable, we simply point out that such a position be consistent. That is, if one is to take the position that the rational expectations equilibrium does not describe the equilibrium in money management, then we believe one cannot also maintain the position that the rational expectation equilibrium does closely approximate the equilibrium in the stock market.

If indeed the rational expectations paradigm is an accurate description of the equilibrium in the money management industry, then the following statements are true:

1. Regulating the percentage fees charged by funds does not change the surplus (or absence thereof) that consumers extract from investing with those funds.
2. Regulating the fund size without regulating fees does not change the surplus (or absence thereof) that consumers extract from investing with those funds.

3. When fees and fund size are jointly regulated consumer surplus can be affected.

Perhaps the first question that should be answered is under what circumstances it is desirable to increase consumer surplus. However, even if we take as given that consumer surplus should be increased, our framework shows that regulating fees without regulating fund size is ineffective. As we showed in Section 3.1, if a regulation is imposed that puts an upper limit on the fee, fund size simply adjusts to the new level of the fee, once again driving the consumer surplus to zero.

What the framework shows is that it is not the level of fees that sets the return to investors equal to zero. It is competition between investors for good investment opportunities. This also means that managerial compensation (aggregate fees) is determined in equilibrium by this same competition, not by managers trying to fleece their investors. Importantly, even in the case when consumer surplus to investors is negative, this unfortunate state of the world does not derive from managers fleecing their investors. Instead, it derives from decisions investors themselves make—investors are investing too much money with active managers. In this case regulating fees is unlikely to address the problem. A better approach might be to educate investors.

In summary, the only way to change managerial compensation through regulation would be to limit competition between investors in some way. One obvious method would be to limit the size of funds based on the fee they charge. Leaving aside that such regulation would favor existing investors over new investors, it is not obvious whether such interference in resource allocation is desirable from an economy wide perspective. Given the restrictions that regulation imposes on the leverage that mutual funds can take, the relation between size and value added plotted in Figure 5 shows that if size is restricted below the optimal size, the manager will not be able to extract the optimal amount of money from financial markets. That will likely negatively impact the informativeness of market prices. So it is not clear whether such policies are desirable. We leave this question for future research.

5.2 Data

As we have argued above, the current data sources for hedge funds, private equity and venture capital have several important limitations. Policy makers should consider implementing regulations to improve the quality of this data. Specifically, policy makers should consider requiring funds to report returns-to-investors, fees charged and fund size.

Chapter 7
THE REGULATION OF INTERMEDIARIES

Allen Ferrell[773] & John D. Morley[774]

1 Introduction and Summary

Institutional intermediaries have grown massively in American capital markets since the mid-20th century. Where investors used to buy and sell stocks and bonds directly, they now overwhelmingly invest through mutual funds, hedge funds, private equity funds and similar vehicles. Fully three quarters of the common stock of America's public companies now belongs to institutional intermediaries. Broker-dealers and credit rating agencies have changed as well as they have weathered the financial crisis and searched out new opportunities in markets dominated by intermediaries. This chapter, written for the Conference on the New Special Study of Securities Markets at Columbia Law School, identifies the key regulatory challenges posed by the changing role of America's institutional intermediaries. We survey existing legal and economic research in the area and suggest new areas for regulatory reform and scholarly inquiry. We cover registered investment companies, such as mutual funds, private investment funds, such as hedge funds and private equity funds, and credit-rating agencies and broker-dealers.

2 Registered Investment Companies

We begin with registered investment companies. Registered investment companies, or "RICs," consist mostly of the open-end mutual funds that dominate household investing and are publicly registered and regulated under the Investment Company Act of 1940. America's system for regulating these vehicles has been, by almost any measure, an enormous success. Since Congress adopted the Investment Company Act (the "ICA") and its sister statute, the Investment Advisers Act (the "IAA") in 1940, the mutual fund industry has grown massively, progressing from its origins as a niche industry for wealthy northeasterners to a vast behemoth. Investment funds publicly registered under the ICA now reach 43% of American households and comprise some $18 trillion in assets.[775] Even

---

[773] Greenfield Professor of Securities Law, Harvard Law School.

[774] Professor of Law, Yale Law School.

[775] INVESTMENT COMPANY INSTITUTE, INVESTMENT COMPANY FACT BOOK 112 (2016).

more remarkable is that the investment fund industry's growth has brought with it remarkably few problems. Though the 1920s and 1930s witnessed extensive fraud and abuse and saw the dramatic bankruptcy of dozens of large publicly traded investment funds, the years since the ICA and IAA began regulating investment funds in 1940 have been impressively quiet. Even during the once-in-a-generation catastrophe of the financial crisis of 2008 and 2009, remarkably few publicly registered investment funds collapsed from debt or illiquidity. Fraud, though an ever-present challenge, has never been pervasive or widespread. The ICA and IAA have become models for regulatory statutes around the world.

Despite their enormous success, however, the ICA and IAA are now significantly out of date. Drafted when the investment fund industry was only about 15 years old, the ICA and IAA reflect only a rough understanding of what an investment fund was and what the investment management industry would become. The main targets of the ICA's detailed provisions were closed-end funds, but in the years since 1940, the industry has become overwhelmingly dominated by open-end funds. And the statute's drafters had no inkling of the future rise of private funds, such as hedge funds and private equity funds. The ICA was written before modern law and economics and even before modern portfolio theory, and it reflects little awareness of some of the foundational principles of organizational economics.

The Securities and Exchange Commission has dealt with the weaknesses of the ICA and IAA admirably, but there have always been limits to the SEC's authority. The ICA permits the SEC enormous power to grant exemptions from the statute[776] and the SEC has often used this exemption power to effectively rewrite many portions of the statute. But rewriting is not the same as reimagining, and there yet remain many innovations that Congress and the SEC could pursue. Our goal here is to consider those possibilities and how we might learn more about them.

2.1 Definition of an Investment Company

The first task is to define what exactly an investment company is. The challenge here is not to distinguish between a public investment company and a private investment company, but to distinguish between an investment company and an operating company. Instead of probing the difference between the Vanguard S&P 500 index mutual fund and a hedge fund, in other words, we wish here to probe the difference between the Vanguard S&P 500 index mutual fund and Microsoft. The line between an investment company and an operating company matters, because it determines who has to comply with the ICA (either

---

[776] Investment Company Act of 1940 § 6(c), 15 U.S.C. §80a-6(c) (2012) (hereinafter ICA).

by registering under the ICA or by staying private and issuing securities only to a limited class of investors). For a public company that does not think of itself as an investment fund, having to comply with the ICA can be disastrous.

Though the dividing line between an investment company and an operating company may seem obvious, it has been surprisingly difficult to draw in practice.[777] Intuition tells us that an investment fund is a business that *invests*. But every business invests in some sort of asset, whether factories, brands or human capital, and so the ICA has to say more. The ICA thus defines an investment company not just as a business that invests, but a business that invests in a particular kind of asset, namely *securities*. Section 3 of the statute says that an investment fund, among other things, is an issuer that "is . . . engaged primarily . . . in the business of investing, reinvesting, or trading in securities," or which "owns . . . investment securities having a value exceeding 40 per centum of the value of such issuer's total assets."[778]

This focus on securities ownership seems intuitive at first, but it often produces strange results that bump awkwardly against a deeper sense of what an investment fund is. Consider, for instance, PepsiCo. Everyone would agree that PepsiCo is an operating business, not an investment fund, but it is hard to say exactly why. Though it would seem that most of Pepsi's assets consist of factories and brand names, in fact most of its assets are securities. The reason is that PepsiCo does not actually own the factories and brands directly—instead it owns securities in operating subsidiaries that own the factories and brands directly. If securities ownership is the defining essence of an investment fund, therefore, it is hard to see why PepsiCo is not an investment fund.

The ICA's solution to this conundrum is to say that PepsiCo is not an investment fund, because its securities in the operating subsidiaries represent control stakes, rather than minority stakes, and this makes PepsiCo's securities different from an investment company's securities.[779] This makes sense, until we

---

[777] The term "investment company" has never been popular in common usage. Prior to Congress' adoption of the ICA in 1940, investment vehicles were commonly known as "investment trusts" See John D. Morley, *The Common Law Corporation: The Power of the Trust in Anglo-American Business History*, 116 COLUM. L. R. 2145 (2016). The term "investment company" was thus a neologism invented by the ICA's drafters to satisfy the industry's desire for a term that was neutral as to entity form. The term never stuck in popular usage, however, and nowadays people commonly use the word "fund," rather than company. We will often follow this practice in this chapter except when referring specifically to the statutory definition of an investment company in section 3 of the ICA.

[778] ICA §§ 3(a)(1)(A), (C).

[779] ICA § 3(b).

compare PepsiCo to a private equity fund. Just like PepsiCo, a private equity fund also holds securities that represent control stakes. And yet a private equity fund is clearly an "investment company" within the meaning and intent of the ICA (though it avoids having to comply with the ICA by remaining private). So if a private equity fund is an investment company, why not PepsiCo? Though we can go on to find legal details in section 3 of the ICA that permit us to distinguish between PepsiCo and a private equity fund, it is not clear whether any of these details truly matter, or whether they are just bandages added on to the ICA to cover an obvious hole.[780]

Consider also Yahoo!, the internet search and technology company. As the value of Yahoo!'s internet search business has declined, the company's main asset has become its large and valuable stakes in other companies, such as Alibaba, the Chinese online retailer. Though Yahoo! thinks of itself as an operating business, under section 3 of the ICA, Yahoo! technically qualifies as an investment company, because its securities in other companies now comprise more than 40% of its assets).[781] Yahoo! has not actually had to comply with the ICA, because it received a special exemption from the SEC early in its life. But there is no real principle behind this exemption, just the SEC's discretionary decision to let Yahoo! go because of a vague intuition that Yahoo! is an operating company for reasons that no one can clearly articulate.

Think also about Microsoft. Early in its history, Microsoft raised cash to fund research and development operations and then invested the cash in securities as it waited for the research and development program to use the cash up. Microsoft clearly intended to operate a real business, but because none of Microsoft's intellectual property had any significant accounting value, the investment securities in which Microsoft had parked its cash quickly became the only significant item on the company's balance sheet. From the perspective of

---

[780] The deciding detail is the fact that a private equity fund, unlike PepsiCo is "engaged in the business of investing, reinvesting, or trading in securities," whereas PepsiCo is engaged in the business of making snack foods and soft drinks. ICA § 3(a)(1)(A). But this just begs the question, which is what exactly it means to "invest, reinvest, or trade in securities" and how this differs from carrying on an operating business through the ownership of securities.

[781] ICA § 3(a)(1)(C); William Gorta, *Pension Suit Over Yahoo Investment In Alibaba Again Tossed*, LAW360, Feb. 10, 2017, https://www.law360.com/articles/891085/pension-suit-over-yahoo-investment-in-alibaba-again-tossed.

assets, Microsoft was indistinguishable from a closed-end bond fund.[782] Like Yahoo!, Microsoft also received a special exemption from the SEC, again with no discernible principle behind it.

And what about a pension fund? Just like an investment company, a pension fund's main business is to invest in securities. So why is a pension fund not an investment company under the ICA? The answer, obviously, is that a pension fund is subject to a different regulatory regime, the Employment Retirement Income Security Act, or ERISA. But if we believe that the primary and essential characteristic of an investment fund is its tendency to invest in securities, then it is not obvious why this different regulatory regime should exist. A pension fund and an investment company are surely different—but not in terms of the one key characteristic that the ICA singles out as the defining essence of an investment company. So why should we regulate them differently? It must be because of one of the many differences that the ICA does not single out.

The ICA and SEC have employed a number of patches to address each of these problems, so that neither PepsiCo, Yahoo!, Microsoft, nor the nation's many pension funds have had to comply with the ICA. Still, the need for patches and fixes in such obvious cases suggests that there is something deeply wrong with the ICA definition. The core features of the ICA definition do not match our intuition about what an investment fund truly is. To make up for the ICA definition's basic incoherence, the patches and fixes have grown so numerous and complex that the definition of an investment company in section 3 of the ICA now spans nearly 3,000 words and 94 separately numbered subsections, paragraphs and subparagraphs. And even then, the SEC has only been able to spare some companies, such as Yahoo! and Microsoft, by granting them special one-off exemptions, without any attempt to ground the exemptions in principle, regulation or statute. The definition of an investment fund has become a Rube Goldberg contraption, covered in duct tape and Elmer's glue.

The result is a system of often incoherent differences in treatment. To deal with future iterations of the Microsoft problem, for example, the SEC adopted Investment Company Act Rule 3a-8, which exempts certain companies from the Investment Company Act if they invest large amounts of cash in securities and then quickly spend the cash on research and development activities. This rule works fine as far as it goes, but its logic is unclear and its effects are unfair. If indeed a company exempted by the rule holds large amounts of securities, which is the sine qua non of an investment company under ICA section 3, then why should the company be exempted? And why is the

---

[782] Microsoft Corp., Release No. IC-16,467, 41 SEC Docket 472 (July 5, 1988) (order granting exemption); Microsoft Corp., Investment Company Act Release No. 16,467, 41 SEC Docket 205 (June 10, 1988) (notice of application for order).

exemption limited to companies that spend money on research and development, rather than on other activities? What if a company raises cash to explore for diamonds or develop video content for a web site? Neither of these activities qualifies as "research and development" and so neither would get the exemption in Rule 3a-8. But there is no obvious reason why.

This confusion forces companies to live with frustrating levels of uncertainty. As recently as February 2017, Yahoo! fought off a shareholder suit in federal district court alleging that the company was an investment company under the ICA. Though the company had received a special one-off exemption from the SEC early in the company's life, the plaintiffs argued that the company lost the exemption as more and more of its balance sheet became devoted to securities. Since there is now no discernible legal reason why Yahoo! should not be an investment company other than the SEC's unprincipled discretionary grant of an exemption, Yahoo!'s status under the statute has become precarious.

Future research should search for a more elegant and principled solution. The persistent difficulties with the section 3 definition suggest that securities ownership is not, in fact, the sole essential feature of an investment fund, and so perhaps we ought to look more deeply. One possibility, identified by Morley,[783] is to focus on organizational structure. Morley argues that the most salient feature of an investment fund is not its tendency to invest in securities, but its tendency to separate its investment holdings from its management structure. Almost everything we commonly think of as an investment fund in the ICA regime has a unique tendency to combine two distinct enterprises: a *fund* holding investment assets, and a *management company* or *adviser* holding workers, computers, office space and other managerial assets. These two distinct enterprises are not merely different entities in the same parent-subsidiary family—they are distinct businesses with distinct owners. This pattern of bifurcated organization creates an array of unique contractual and regulatory challenges, such as the possibility that a manager can face conflicts of interest by simultaneously working for multiple clients at the same time. It is perhaps these organizational challenges, more than any unique characteristic of securities ownership, that demand the special regulatory attention of the ICA.

When coupled with a focus on securities ownership, this bifurcated pattern of organization may do better job of identifying investment companies than securities ownership alone. The thing that makes PepsiCo, Microsoft, Yahoo! and a pension fund different from an investment company is that none of these businesses divides its investments from its management like an investment company. Though some of these businesses employ multiple entities, all of their entities exist in the same parent-subsidiary structure under common

---

[783] John D. Morley, *The Separation of Funds and Managers: A Theory of Investment Fund Structure and Regulation*, 123 YALE L.J. 1228 (2014).

ownership. None of these businesses could be said to have a truly external adviser like a hedge fund or mutual fund.

In future study, the Commission might examine how this pattern of bifurcated organization maps onto the existing investment company definition and how useful it would be in close cases, such as Yahoo!. Researchers might also search for other, more elegant ways of defining an investment company in addition to this method focused on organization.

2.2 Management Fees

Once we define what an investment company is, we next have to figure out how to regulate it. And no issue in investment company regulation has been more hotly debated than the fees charged by managers. Though management fees have declined profoundly since the ICA's adoption in 1940, many commentators nevertheless argue that fees must decline even further before they fairly reflect the value of the services that investment companies provide.

Financial economists have assembled a mountain of theory and evidence on the fees charged by open-end mutual funds and there is still a robust debate about whether fees are too high. In this chapter, however, we will try to avoid this debate. Rather than staking out a position on whether the mutual fund market is competitive or not, we will focus instead on the legal details of how to craft effective fee regulation. Though people may disagree about the big question of whether the market is competitive, we believe that almost everyone can agree that if the government is going to implement fee regulation, it ought to do so in a way that is maximally effective and minimally intrusive. We will thus ignore the grand economic question of whether fees are excessive and focus instead on the technical legal question of how exactly one might build an effective fee regulatory system in practice, assuming such a system is thought to be necessary.

The first task is to learn more about the *least competitive* segments of the mutual fund market. It seems fair to say, based on the last twenty years of economic research, that although most mutual fund managers charge reasonably competitive fees, at least some do not. We need not march into the center of the battlefield over fees by expressing an opinion on just how numerous the uncompetitive managers are. It is enough to say merely that the inability of investors to understand and rationally react to fees in experimental settings suggests that even if large management complexes such as Vanguard, Fidelity, State Street and Blackrock charge highly competitive fees (as indeed they almost certainly do), there nevertheless may be some significant number of managers who do not charge highly competitive fees.[784] Carhart's famous paper provides

---

[784] *See* James J. Choi, David Laibson & Brigitte C. Madrian, *Why Does the Law of One Price Fail? An Experiment on Index Mutual Funds*, 23 REV. FIN. STUD. 1405

support for this view.⁷⁸⁵ Though Carhart found that very few managers could *overperform* year after year, a distressing number of managers tended to *underperform* year after year.

More knowledge about the worst funds would be useful, because although researchers such as Coates and Hubbard have taught us a tremendous amount about the competitiveness of the mutual fund market *overall*, we still know too little about what lies in the market's darkest corners.⁷⁸⁶ And these dark corners are where regulation is most urgently needed.

There is still much we could learn about the worst funds. Research has already taught us, for example, that funds in the highest decile of fees tend to be concentrated among management companies in the lowest decile of size.⁷⁸⁷ But we do not yet know what investors in these high-fee funds are like. Did they initially understand and accept the high fees in exchange for elaborate add-on services? Or did they initially invest with low fees and then lethargically stay put as the fees crept slowly higher? Do the highest-fee funds have institutional share classes with large institutional investors? Do extremely high-fee funds tend to be older than other funds or younger? Is performance more likely to persist at the high end of the fee distribution than in the middle? And do high-fee funds tend to provide additional services beyond mere portfolio management that independently warrant the high fees?

Beyond understanding the worst-performing and highest-fee funds, a second task will be to learn more about the precise details of how exactly investors respond to fee disclosures. Even if there are sound theoretical reasons not to worry about the weak correlation between past and future returns, as Berk

---

(2009); Molly Mercer, Alan R. Palmiter & Ahmed E. Taha, *Worthless Warnings? Testing the Effectiveness of Disclaimers in Mutual Fund Advertisements*, 7 J. EMPIRICAL L. STUD. 429 (2010); John Beshears, James J. Choi, David Laibson & Brigitte C. Madrian, *How Does Simplified Disclosure Affect Individuals' Mutual Fund Choices?* (working paper, 2009), https://papers.ssrn.com/sol3/papers.cfm?abstract_id=1400943; John Kozup, Elizabeth Howlett & Michael Pagano, *The Effects of Summary Information on Consumer Perceptions of Mutual Fund Characteristics*, 42 J. CONSUMER AFFAIRS 37 (2008).

⁷⁸⁵ Carhart, *supra* note 745.

⁷⁸⁶ John C. Coates & R. Glenn Hubbard, *Competition in the Mutual Fund Industry: Evidence and Implications for Policy*, 33 J. CORP. L. 151 (2007).

⁷⁸⁷ Quinn Curtis & John D. Morley, *An Empirical Study of Mutual Fund Excessive Fee Litigation: Do the Merits Matter?*, 30 J. L. ECON & ORG. 275 (2014).

and Green have argued,[788] everyone can surely agree that there is dysfunction lurking in investors' tendency to misunderstand disclosures, because experimental evidence strongly indicates that many investors do not understand fees or their importance.[789]

One way to improve fee regulation, therefore, would be to experimentally test different forms of disclosure. There is still much to be learned here, because although experimental researchers have already taught us which sorts of disclosures *do not* work, they have not much explored which sorts of disclosures *do* work. We know that existing forms of disclosure do a bad job of pushing investors to low-fee funds, but we do not know whether other forms of disclosure would do a better job. The SEC or private researchers should therefore test different forms of disclosure by presenting experimental subjects with a variety of different forms. Insights from cognitive psychology could be used to theorize how different forms of disclosures might affect investors, and then the effect of the disclosures could be tested by seeing how investors respond to them. A good template for this kind of research would be the work of Bertrand and Morse, who identified potential borrowers from payday lenders and assessed how different disclosures forms affected a borrower's likelihood of taking out a payday loan in the future.[790] Another template is the work of Beshears, Choi, Laibson, and Madrian, who randomly gave experimental subjects either a standard mutual fund prospectus or the new summary mutual fund prospectus mandated by the SEC in 2009 and then compared how the two documents influenced investors' choices (with sadly disappointing results).[791] Researchers could take a step beyond the Beshears, Choi, Laibson, and Madrian work by imagining entirely new forms of disclosure and seeing how they work.

A third task will be to revise and repair the excessive fee liability provisions of section 36(b) of the ICA. Congress added section 36(b) to the ICA in 1970 by saying that a fund's adviser has a fiduciary duty to the fund regarding fees the adviser receives from the fund. Congress left the content of this fiduciary duty unexplained, but the courts subsequently supplied the content, most recently in *Jones v. Harris Associates*, a 2010 case in which the Supreme Court

---

[788] Jonathan B. Berk & Richard C. Green, *Mutual Fund Flows and Performance in Rational Markets*, 112 J. POL. ECON. 1269 (2004).

[789] *See supra* note 784.

[790] Marianne Bertrand & Adair Morse, *Information Disclosure, Cognitive Biases, and Payday Borrowing*, 66 J. FIN. 1865 (2011).

[791] Beshears et al., *supra* note 784.

formally adopted a standard that had long prevailed among the circuit courts.[792] *Jones* said that a fee violates an adviser's fiduciary duty if it is "so disproportionately large that it bears no reasonable relationship to the services rendered and could not have been the product of arm's length bargaining." Prior judicial opinions in the circuit courts developed a list of six factors to aid judges in their assessment of this general standard.[793]

Section 36(b) may be the single most written-about topic in all of investment management regulation—Curtis and Morley collect the literature in a two-page long footnote.[794] Most of this literature tends to focus on the grand economic question of whether the mutual fund market is competitive and whether excessive fee liability is therefore desirable.[795] But in this chapter, we will

---

[792] Jones v. Harris Assocs. L.P., 559 U.S. 335 (2010); Gartenberg v. Merrill Lynch Asset Mgmt., Inc., 694 F.2d 923, 928 (2d Cir. 1982).

[793] These include: (a) the nature and quality of services provided to fund shareholders; (b) the profitability of the fund to the adviser-manager; (c) fall-out benefits; (d) economies of scale; (e) comparative fee structures; and (f) the independence and conscientiousness of the trustees. Krinsk v. Fund Asset Mgmt., Inc., 875 F.2d 404, 409 (2d Cir. 1989).

[794] *See* Quinn Curtis & John D. Morley, *The Flawed Mechanics of Mutual Fund Fee Litigation* (working paper version, 2014), https://papers.ssrn.com/sol3/papers.cfm?abstract_id=2405307, at 3-4 n.2. Johnson also provides a nice summary. *See* Lyman Johnson, *A Fresh Look at Director Independence: Mutual Fund Fee Litigation and Gartenberg at Twenty-Five*, 61 VAND. L. REV. 497 (2008).

[795] For a sample, see the recent articles by William A. Birdthistle, *Investment Indiscipline: A Behavioral Approach to Mutual Fund Jurisprudence*, 2010 U. ILL. L. REV. 61 (2010); John C. Coates, *The Downside of Judicial Restraint: The (Non-)Effect of Jones v. Harris*, 6 DUKE J. CON. L. & PUB. POL'Y 58 (2010); John C. Coates & R. Glenn Hubbard, *Competition in the Mutual Fund Industry: Evidence and Implications for Policy*, 33 J. CORP. LAW 151 (2007); James D. Cox & John W. Payne, *Mutual Fund Expense Disclosures: A Behavioral Perspective*, 83 WASH. U. L. Q. 907 (2005); Jill E. Fisch. *Rethinking the Regulation of Securities Intermediaries*, 158 U. PENN. L. REV. 1961 (2010); John P. Freeman, Stewart L. Brown & Steve Pomerantz, *Mutual Fund Advisory Fees: New Evidence and a Fair Fiduciary Duty Test*, 61 OKLA. L. REV. 83 (2008); John P. Freeman & Stewart L. Brown, *Mutual Fund Advisory Fees: The Cost of Conflicts of Interest*, 26 J. CORP. L. 609 (2000); M. Todd Henderson, *Justifying Jones*, 77 U. CHICAGO L. REV. 1027 (2010); D. Bruce Johnsen, *Myths About Mutual Fund Fees: Economic Insights on Jones v. Harris*, 35 J. CORP. L. 561 (2009); Donald C. Langevoort, *Private Litigation to Enforce Fiduciary Duties in Mutual Funds: Derivative Suits, Disinterested Directors and the Ideology of Investor Sovereignty*, 83 WASH. U. L. Q.

steer clear of this grand debate, focusing on the more practical—and in many ways more important—question of how exactly excessive fee liability should be crafted, assuming it is thought to be necessary.

The clearest empirical picture of section 36(b)'s present functioning comes from a 2014 study by Curtis and Morley.[796] The picture is not encouraging. Curtis and Morley statistically examined every section 36(b) case filed between 2000 and 2009 and found that although there is some positive correlation between fees and the likelihood that a fund would be targeted for a suit, the correlation was fairly weak. Ultimately the strongest predictor of whether a fund would be targeted was not its fees, but the size of its adviser. Lawyers tended to go after the biggest advisers, rather than the most expensive funds. Indeed, almost no funds managed by the smallest one third of advisers were ever targeted, even though these were the funds that tended to charge the highest fees.

There were other troubling findings as well. One was that funds targeted for excessive fee lawsuits did not tend to reduce their fees after being targeted. Another was that the rate of settlements bore no discernible relationship to the level of fees. Overall, the results were consistent with a pattern of scattershot filing of complaints observed by the study's authors. Plaintiffs' law firms tended to pursue excessive fee suits by filing standard-form complaints against dozens of fund managers at a time, suggesting that targeting decisions were guided more by access to plaintiffs with standing to bring suit than by careful assessments of actual fee levels.

Besides its poor functioning in practice, there are others reasons to worry about how section 36(b) operates in its mechanical details. In a legal analysis of section 36(b) published separately from their empirical analysis, Curtis and Morley identified a number of mechanical flaws in the statute and judicial doctrine.[797] These flaws seemed to involve unwitting mistakes of drafting and construction, rather than deliberate policy choices. One problem was that the judicial standard for assessing liability provides little space for an obviously low-fee fund to avoid a protracted lawsuit. The Supreme Court's standard in *Jones* emphasizes that comparisons to other funds are not dispositive, meaning that a defendant advisor cannot resolve a case on a motion for summary judgment by showing that its fees are lower than those of its competitors—even if this is indisputably true. The problem with this standard is that it makes even low-fee

---

1017 (2005); Larry E. Ribstein, *Federal Misgovernance of Mutual Funds*, 2010 CATO SUP. CT. REV. 301 (2009).

[796] Curtis & Morley, *supra* note 787.

[797] Quinn Curtis & John D. Morley, *The Flawed Mechanics of Mutual Fund Fee Litigation*, 32 YALE J. REG. 1 (2015).

funds vulnerable to the risk that a suit will proceed beyond a motion for summary judgment. Fidelity, for example, tends to charge very low fees, but was recently mired in section 36(b) litigation for years. The vulnerability of low-fee funds to suits is distressing not just because it is unfair, but also because it undermines the purposes of section 36(b) by diminishing the incentive to reduce fees. If an adviser cannot reduce its odds of getting sued by reducing its fees, then why then should it reduce its fees?

A further problem is the remedies. Section 36(b) restricts recoveries to the excessive portion of fees paid by a fund during the period beginning one year prior to the commencement of a suit and continuing to the suit's termination.[798] This recovery provides too little incentive for lawyers to pursue the most meritorious lawsuits. As noted, the highest-fee funds tend to be affiliated with the smallest advisers, and yet the smallest advisers were almost never targeted during the period of Curtis and Morley's empirical study, probably because the potential recoveries on the highest-fee funds—and thus the potential rewards to plaintiffs' attorneys — were too small. The only way to encourage lawyers to go after the highest-fee funds would thus be to increase the recoveries or the attorneys' fees. The statute's prohibition on punitive damages is also a problem, because it undercuts deterrence. The worst that can happen to an adviser that charges excessive fees is that the adviser has to give the excessive fees back. So why should the adviser not at least try to charge excessive fees?

Yet another problem is that when a recovery is finally paid, section 36(b) pays it to the wrong investors. By statute, an adviser who loses a section 36(b) suit must pay the recovery to the *fund*, rather than to the *investors*.[799] But by the time the adviser pays the recovery to the fund, many of the investors who paid the fees will already have redeemed and left the fund, leaving behind new investors who did not pay the fees. Since fees accrue and are taken out of a fund on a daily basis, only an investor who holds shares at the moment a fee is charged actually ends up paying the fee. An investor who invests later cannot be said to have paid the fee. Hence, when a manager pays a 36(b) recovery directly to a fund, the payment benefits only investors who hold shares at the moment the recovery is paid—not the investors who held shares at the time the fees were paid. Put bluntly, the recoveries go to the wrong people. This problem was almost certainly not foreseen or understood by the statute's drafters, because the problem results from the quirky way in which mutual funds are bought and sold. In an operating company, the mismatch in share ownership between the time of an alleged wrong and the time of a resulting recovery poses no problems,

---

[798] ICA § 36(b)(3).

[799] Section 36(b) requires this by providing that a suit may be brought by an investor "on behalf of" a fund, rather than on behalf of investors. ICA § 36(b).

because the expected value of a recovery is baked into the share price. An outgoing shareholder can share in a recovery even if she sells before the recovery is received, because she will be able to sell at a price that reflects the recovery's expected value. This neat solution disappears in a mutual fund, however, because a mutual fund's share price does not reflect expectations about events that will happen in the future.[800] The fund's share price is mechanically tied to net asset value, and net asset value does not include the expected value of future litigation recoveries. Section 36(b) should therefore be amended to give recoveries not to a fund, but to the investors who held shares at the time an excessive fee was paid. Other class action recoveries in mutual funds are already paid this way.

A further mechanical flaw is the statute's awkward treatment of sales loads. Section 36(b) exempts sales loads from liability,[801] apparently on the logic that sales loads are regulated by FINRA.[802] This distorts the analysis of a fund's annual management fees, however, since an annual management fee is impossible to understand without first considering the sales load that preceded it. An annual fee that was preceded by a massive sales load is more likely to be unreasonable than an annual fee that was preceded by a small sales load. The exclusion of sales loads is also inconsistent with the inclusion of Rule 12b-1 fees. Rule 12b-1 fees are widely understood to be substitutes for sales loads, since, like sales loads, they can be used to pay commissions to brokers and other distribution expenses. Unlike sales loads, however, Rule 12b-1 fees are not exempt from section 36(b). The only way to explain this inconsistency is that Rule 12b-1 did not exist in 1970, when Congress added section 36(b) to the ICA, and Congress has simply failed to update the statute in the years since.

Beyond tweaking disclosure and fine-tuning section 36(b), a final area of research for fee regulation might be to consider some grander reform. It may well be that no amount of mandatory disclosure or fiduciary fee liability can adequately stamp out high fees. And so perhaps researchers and the SEC ought

---

[800] In the worst-case scenario, a savvy investor could steal much of a fund's recovery by investing one day before the recovery is received and redeeming one day after. Since the stock price the day before the recovery is received will not go up in expectation of the recovery, the investor can net a large chunk of the recovery, by just redeeming at the higher value after the recovery has been received.

[801] ICA § 36(b)(4) ("This subsection shall not apply . . . to sales loads for the acquisition of any security issued by a registered investment company.")

[802]. At the same time Congress added Section 36(b) to the ICA, it also added section 22(b)(1), empowering FINRA to regulate sales loads. Act of Dec. 14, 1970, Pub. L. No. 91-547, §§ 12, 22, 84 Stat. 1413, 1422-23 (hereinafter 1970 Act).

to imagine some more ambitious scheme of price regulation. Perhaps, for instance, the law could impose "smart" fee caps that adjust as a function of the fees of similar funds (e.g., any fee more than two standard deviations for funds in the same style category could be inherently suspect). Or perhaps extremely aggressive disclosures, akin to the surgeon general's warnings on cigarette packs, could be appended to the prospectuses of unusually high-fee funds. In any case, if one seriously believes fees to be a problem, there may be more imaginative ways of limiting them than the law has imagined so far.

2.3 Capital Structure

Another area of interest is the regulation of investment company capital structure. Roughly speaking, the ICA regulates capital structure along three dimensions: (1) the *sources*; (2) *form*; and (3) *amount*.[803] The ICA regulates *sources* of capital by prohibiting open-end mutual funds from taking on debt obligations to anyone other than banks.[804] The ICA also regulates the *form* of debt capital by specifying that the only kind of security an open-end fund can issue is a single layer of common stock.[805] The ICA further regulates the *amount* of debt capital by saying that in an open-end mutual fund, the ratio of total assets to bank-loan principal must always equal or exceed 3/1.[806] The statute has separate rules for borrowing by closed-end funds.[807]

One of the more important consequences of these capital structure regulations is to prevent a mutual fund from ever issuing a debt security. Though few people tend even to notice, it is a striking fact of American capital markets that one cannot buy a bond in a mutual fund.

The first question to ask is whether these restrictions even make sense. Though the rules might seem at first to be basically sensible, it turns out to be very difficult to come up with a satisfying explanation why. We could imagine many plausible rationales for regulating mutual fund capital structure. But the real-life details of mutual fund regulation are not actually consistent with any of them. The ICA is internally inconsistent. Morley explores the various rationales for capital structure regulation and their limitations.[808]

---

[803] John D. Morley, *The Regulation of Mutual Fund Debt*, 30 YALE J. REG. 343 (2013).

[804] ICA § 18(f)(1).

[805] ICA § 18(a).

[806] ICA § 18(f)(1).

[807] *E.g.*, ICA §§ 18(a)(1)(A); (a)(2)(A).

[808] *See supra* note 803.

One plausible rationale for the capital structure restrictions is that they guard against systemic risk. But this argument does not tell us why the restrictions apply only to publicly registered funds, such as mutual funds, and not to private funds, such as hedge funds. If borrowing generates systemic risk, then it does so just as surely in a hedge fund as in a mutual fund. The world already saw the evidence of this in the debt-driven collapse of the hedge fund Long Term Capital Management.[809] So why exempt hedge funds from borrowing restrictions? The answer the law gives is that section 3 of the ICA says that an investment company can choose to stay private so long as it has only a small number of wealthy and sophisticated investors. But the number and wealth of investors are only important if our concern is the welfare of the *investors*, not if our concern is the welfare of the *financial system*. A fund with a small number of wealthy investors can spill just as much risk into the financial system as a fund with a large number of middle class investors. Systemic risk is often compared to environmental pollution in its tendency to spill out market externalities. And what we have in ICA capital regulation, essentially, is a rule that says only rich people can dump sludge into rivers.

Another possible rationale for the capital structure regulations is to protect mutual fund investors from excessive risk in their portfolios. The ICA diminishes the riskiness of mutual fund investments for mom-and-pop investors by reducing the risks of leverage. But this, too, is inconsistent with the overall design of the ICA, because the ICA permits every other imaginable form of portfolio risk. The ICA places essentially no limits on the riskiness of portfolio assets other than the limits on borrowing. A fund can put all of its assets in lottery tickets and penny stocks if it so wishes. It can bet everything on out-of-the-money call options on the common stock of a single bankrupt issuer. In the grander scheme of investment management regulation, therefore, the distinction between leverage and the myriad other sources of investment risk is arbitrary.

Yet another potential rationale for the capital structure rules is that open-end mutual funds are mechanically incapable of issuing debt. Perhaps, one might argue, the redeemability of open-end fund shares prevents an open-end fund from issuing senior securities for reasons having to do with accounting difficulties or other technical problems. But this is plainly not true. Several open-end mutual funds issued debt securities before the ICA was passed in 1940 and industry leaders at the time saw no problem with their doing so[810] And even today, mutual funds still maintain debt obligations other than securities, including loans from banks. Hedge funds, which are also open-ended, incur debt obligations in elaborate variety.

---

[809] ROGER LOWENSTEIN, WHEN GENIUS FAILED: THE RISE AND FALL OF LONG-TERM CAPITAL MANAGEMENT (2000).

[810] *See* Morley, *supra* note 803.

Given the weakness of the various rationales we might imagine to support the mutual fund capital structure rules, it may be worth exploring whether the rules should be changed, perhaps even by permitting open-end mutual funds to issue debt securities. We know that people already buy debt securities from closed-end funds and operating companies, and we also know that people buy common stock in money market funds in large part because they believe it to be similar to debt securities. Why then should we not permit mutual funds to experiment with a single class of a simple kind of debt security? Though mutual funds do not often borrow money from banks,[811] they might see in debt securities an opportunity for profits through underwriting and sales fees.

Permitting mutual funds to issue debt might offer the possibility of a less fragile alternative to money market funds. Part of what makes a money market fund so fragile is that, like every other type of open-end mutual fund, a money market fund can issue only a single kind of security under the ICA. And since money market funds try to structure their common stock to functionally resemble debt, the capital structure restrictions in the ICA have the perverse effect of forcing money market funds to become effectively 100% leveraged—the only security they can issue is a common stock that functionally resembles debt. This strategy of total leverage has no parallel in any other financial institution (or operating business, for that matter), and it naturally makes money market funds extremely fragile. A business with no real equity is a house made of very thin glass. If the ICA were reformed to permit a money market fund to adopt a more rational capital structure that combined a layer of debt with a layer equity, money market funds might become more stable, since the equity could cushion the debt.

Another problem of practical importance is the regulation of leveraged derivative instruments, for which the SEC has recently proposed new rules (whose status in the early days of the Trump administration is now uncertain).[812] It is unclear what exactly the derivatives rules hope to accomplish. If the answer is that derivatives pose special risks to investors, then this is hard to square with the ICA's permissiveness toward other risky investments. Remember that under the ICA, a mutual fund can invest in basically anything, no matter the risk. So why obsess over the risk of derivatives? And if the reason for regulating derivatives is that they pose risks to the financial system, then this, too, is hard to square with the existing regulatory scheme, since other open-end funds—namely

---

[811] A. Joseph Warburton, *Mutual Fund Capital Structure*, 100 MARQUETTE L. REV. 670 (2017).

[812] SEC Release No. IC-31933, Use of Derivatives by Registered Investment Companies and Business Development Companies (2015), https://www.sec.gov/rules/proposed/2015/ic-31933.pdf.

hedge funds—can still use derivatives indiscriminately. Mutual funds have managed to use their freedom to invest in risky securities remarkably responsibly over the past 90 years. They have had very few bankruptcies or liquidity crises, even during the once-in-a-generation havoc of the financial crisis of 2008. It is hard, then, to see why mutual funds should not be trusted to invest in derivatives with the same sober responsibility with which they have long invested in other risky assets—and with which hedge funds are freely permitted to invest.

Of course, more research on the riskiness of derivatives in mutual funds would be helpful. There is some useful research already,[813] but the challenge, as in so much of economic research, is to develop a study that avoids the pervasive problem of endogeneity.

2.4 Voting

Another area of concern is shareholder voting. Prior to Congress' passage of the ICA in 1940, shareholder voting was common in closed-end funds, but not in open-end funds.[814] Open-end funds generally offered their shareholders no right to vote on any matter, including the election of directors. The ICA then imposed a system of mandatory shareholder voting in director elections and other matters for both types of funds.[815] Our view is that although the shareholder voting requirements continue to make sense for closed-end funds, they should be eliminated for open-end funds.

The case for eliminating shareholder voting in open-end funds has been made by Morley and Curtis,[816] who argue that the problem with the right to vote in an open-end fund is simply that no investor will ever use it. Drawing on the analytical framework of exit, voice and loyalty proposed by Albert Hirschman,[817] Morley and Curtis argue that since mutual fund investors have an unusually strong form of exit, they will almost never tend to use their right to voice. Indeed, they are *even less interested* in voice than the highly passive shareholders of

---

[813] Jennifer L. Koski & Jeffrey Pontiff, *How are Derivatives Used? Evidence from the Mutual Fund Industry*, 54 J. FIN. 791 (1999).

[814] John D. Morley & Quinn Curtis, *Taking Exit Rights Seriously: Why Governance and Fee Litigation Don't Work in Mutual Funds*, 120 YALE L.J. 84 (2010).

[815] ICA § 16.

[816] *See* Morley & Curtis, *supra* note 814.

[817] ALBERT O. HIRSCHMAN, EXIT, VOICE, AND LOYALTY: RESPONSES TO DECLINE IN FIRMS, ORGANIZATIONS, AND STATES (1970).

ordinary public companies are. A similar point has also been made by Fama and Jensen.[818]

Open-end shareholders' disinterest in voice stems from the fact that an investor in an open-end fund has a much stronger right of exit than an investor in an ordinary operating company. Unlike an operating company investor, a mutual fund investor does not sell her shares—she redeems them from the issuing fund for cash. When a shareholder in an open-end fund redeems, the fund pays the shareholder a cash amount equal to the net asset value, or NAV, which is the value of the portion of the fund's assets that corresponds to each share. The upshot is that an open-end fund shareholder can basically pull her money out of the fund. She can demand that the fund give her back what she originally contributed, with the result that the fund will no longer own it. This stands an open-end fund shareholder in contrast to an operating company shareholder. An ordinary company shareholder can sell her shares, but she cannot remove the assets that underlie the shares from the company's possession and control. When a shareholder in General Electric sells to another shareholder, the shares may change hands, but the factories, cash and brand names all remain locked inside the company. General Electric pays out nothing.

Morley and Curtis walk through a technical analysis that shows why the redemption in open-end funds discourages shareholders from voting.[819] We need not work through this technical analysis here, however, because we can see the basic intuition by simply thinking about how a mutual fund shareholder might choose between exit and voice when the shareholder believes her fund to be in decline. Imagine that an open-end fund shareholder decides that her fund's management is bad and ought to be fired. The shareholder has two options. She can either (1) run a proxy contest and rally other shareholders to vote the managers out, or (2) fire the managers on her own by just redeeming her shares unilaterally. The two options are substitutes for one another, because the ultimate result is similar—either way, the current managers will no longer have control of the shareholder's money. Because redeeming removes the shareholder's money from the fund—the fund has to liquidate the portion of its assets that corresponds to the shares and pay out the cash—redemption will terminate the managers' control over the shareholder's assets just as surely as firing the managers.

Given that voting and redeeming tend to produce very similar outcomes, which option will a shareholder tend to choose? The answer is that the shareholder will almost always choose redemption, because it is *much, much*

---

[818] Eugene F. Fama & Michael C. Jensen, *Separation of Ownership and Control*, 26 J. L. & ECON. 301 (1983).

[819] Morley & Curtis, *supra* note 814.

cheaper. As the last eighty years of corporate law scholarship have taught us, firing a manager is costly, because voting is costly. Winning a proxy contest requires a company's shareholders to act collectively through voting, and rallying shareholders to collective action takes huge amounts of time and money. Proxy forms have to be prepared and mailed and minds have to be persuaded. Few shareholders are willing to spend all of this money, not only because the amount of money necessary is so large, but also because any shareholder who does incur all of these costs will end up reaping only the small portion of the gains that corresponds to her shares. She might foot the entire bill for a proxy contest but own only 10 percent of the fund's shares.

A mutual fund shareholder will thus rarely choose to pay the costs of activism, because redemption will offer a much cheaper alternative. As we have seen, redemption achieves the same basic result of removing a shareholder's money from a manager's control, but unlike voting, redemption does not require collective action. Redemption is a choice each investor can make unilaterally, without any need to coordinate with others. There is no collective action problem in a mutual fund, because redemption requires no collective action. As a result, proxy contests in mutual funds are virtually unheard-of. To our knowledge, no director election has ever been contested by shareholders in the 90-year history of the open-end mutual fund industry.[820]

The availability of redemption thus stands a mutual fund investor in stark contrast to an ordinary company. Ordinary company investors rarely use their right to vote, because of the costs we have already seen. But unlike in mutual funds, in ordinary companies, shareholder activism is not unheard-of; it is merely unusual. Sometimes when the circumstances are right in an ordinary company, the vote becomes a serious tool for change. Every now and again, an activist hedge fund or other investor will spend the costs necessary to run a proxy contest and force a change. And the reason is that there is no alternative. Even though collective action is costly, there is no option for unilateral action. An activist hedge fund that wants to get rid of the management cannot withdraw its money from the management's control by redeeming. It must get control of the board. And since the costs of bad management sometimes exceed even the high costs of collective action, shareholders in ordinary companies occasionally pay the costs of collective action and use the shareholder vote.

One might argue that redemption is not obviously better than voting, because redemption is costly. Redemption requires time, knowledge, and sometimes the premature realization of tax liabilities. All of this is surely true, but

---

[820] The handful of proxy contests in open-end funds in the last ninety years have all originated in internal struggles inside of management firms or between boards and management firms. Shareholders have never initiated these contests and have never been materially involved in waging them.

this does make the vote appealing in a mutual fund, because the judgment here is comparative, rather than absolute. Redemption may be costly, but voting is even costlier. If getting on the web and opening an account with Vanguard sounds costly, imagine paying Kirkland & Ellis to run a proxy campaign.[821] A shareholder may fail to redeem because the costs of redemption are too high. But that shareholder will also fail to vote for the very same reasons.

Mutual fund shareholders thus exhibit an extreme of passivity that exceeds even the much-discussed passivity of ordinary public company investors. In an ordinary public company, small and unsophisticated investors tend to find it rational not to vote. But in a mutual fund, even the large and sophisticated investors will fail to vote, because they will always find it easier instead to redeem. This is why proxy contests in mutual funds are not just rare, as they are in ordinary companies, but completely unheard-of.

The experience of other types of funds illustrates how redemption undercuts incentives to vote. Compare an open-end mutual fund to a closed-end fund. A closed-end fund is subject to the same governance and voting requirements under the ICA as an open-end fund, and it tends to attract the same kinds of small investors.[822] But unlike open-end funds, closed-end funds are beehives of shareholder voting activity.[823] There is so much shareholder activism in closed-end funds that published newsletters chronicle the activism in daily detail. The incredible vivacity of shareholder governance in closed-end funds is directly attributable to the closed-end funds' refusal to permit redemptions. Because closed-end funds do not permit redemptions, their shares trade on stock exchanges at prices that reflect expectations about how managers will use their

---

[821] Taxes pose a more interesting problem, but as Morley and Curtis, *supra* note 814, show, taxes affect so few people that when an investor who cannot redeem for tax reasons tries to lead a proxy contest, most of the other investors who might have supported her will already have redeemed and left before the vote is held. At any given time, a mutual fund's shareholder base tends to include only people who are (1) satisfied, (2) apathetic, or (3) locked in for tax reasons. Everyone who was unsatisfied, attentive and free to move will already have redeemed. Thus, unless the investors who are locked in by taxes comprise a majority all on their own, they will never be able to cobble together a critical mass for change from among the other investors, because all of the other investors will either be satisfied or apathetic.

[822] Kathleen Weiss Hanley, Charles M.C. Lee & Paul L. Seguin, *The Marketing of Closed-end Fund IPOs: Evidence from Transactions Data*, 5 J. FIN. INTERMEDIATION 127 (1996).

[823] Michael Bradley, Alon Brav, Italy Goldstein & Wei Jiang, *Activist Arbitrage: A Study of Open-ending Attempts of Closed-end Funds*, 95 J. FIN. ECON. 1 (2010).

assets in the future. These prices naturally diverge from NAV and it is precisely this divergence that motivates shareholder activism.[824]

Further support comes from the experience of hedge funds. Like mutual funds, hedge funds also permit redemptions. And so, like mutual funds, hedge funds also experience no significant shareholder voting. A standard hedge fund operating agreement prohibits shareholder voting altogether. This is not because hedge fund investors tend to be sophisticated and few in number, because if anything, sophistication and small numbers ought to render the vote *more* valuable in hedge funds, not *less*. Sophistication and small numbers ought to diminish the collective action problem that plagues shareholder voting in public companies, seemingly making shareholder voting even more useful in hedge funds than in ordinary companies. And yet, the only conditions under which hedge funds commonly permit shareholder voting are when redemptions have been suspended, presumably because when redemptions are available, voting is just not very useful.

One might argue that we should not eliminate voting, because some small investors might lack the sophistication or awareness to redeem their shares efficiently. But we have already seen the answer to this objection above: though small shareholders may not redeem, they also will not vote for the very same reasons. Voting presupposes even more sophistication than redemption. And so if one believes that small shareholders need protection, voting is a terrible way to provide it. The suggestion that we eliminate voting is thus not an argument that we should stop regulating mutual funds. Indeed, it is precisely the opposite. The implication of this understanding of voting is that regulation is quite urgent, precisely because we cannot step back and let investors protect themselves by voting.

The reason voting made its way into the ICA initially is because at the time of the ICA's adoption in 1940, the investment fund industry was dominated by closed-end funds, rather than open-end funds. In the late 1930s, when the ICA was being drafted, there were only a handful of open-end funds in existence, and the experience of the industry had been dominated by scandals among closed-end funds in the early 1930s.[825] And, of course, in these closed-end funds, voting made sense, because closed-end funds did not offer redemption rights. It should therefore come as no surprise that when the SEC proposed the voting requirements in 1940, it had its eyes mainly on the closed-end funds. And while

---

[824] The idea is to buy at a price below NAV and then later force the fund to liquidate at a value close to NAV.

[825] Natalie R. Grow, The "Boston-Type Open-End Fund"—Development of a National Financial Institution: 1924-1940 (1977) (unpublished Ph.D. dissertation, Harvard University).

the closed-end funds supported the requirements, the open-end funds opposed them.[826] Indeed, the only reason the open-end funds agreed to drop their opposition was that the SEC promised to include a grandfather provision in the statute that exempted all open-end funds then in existence out of the voting rules.[827] The grandfather exemption still appears in the ICA today.[828]

The voting requirements in open-end funds generate significant costs. One cost is the tremendous expense of proxy solicitation. Because shareholders in open-end funds are so extraordinarily apathetic, getting enough shareholders to return their proxies to form a quorum is very challenging. This is why the open-end mutual fund industry lobbied so hard for an exemption from the new NYSE rule prohibiting broker voting in uncontested director elections.[829] Shareholder voting also often does more harm to shareholders than good. The ICA says, for example, that a board cannot fire a fund's adviser unless the shareholders approve. But this greatly weakens a board's leverage over the adviser by dramatically increasing the costs of firing the adviser. Imagine if the board of a company like Microsoft had to get a shareholder vote every time it wanted to fire the CEO.[830] A further cost of shareholder voting is that it provides an unhelpful distraction. The belief that shareholder voting meaningfully protects shareholders in mutual funds may lull Congress and the SEC into a false sense of security that shields the industry against more meaningful regulation.

Much of shareholder voting has already been eliminated in mutual funds by clever lawyering and industry lobbying. Directors, for instance, tend to be able to appoint most of their own successors and rarely have to stand for annual elections. The little shareholder voting that remains is thus unhelpful, confusing and unnecessary.

---

[826] John D. Morley, *Collective Branding and the Origins of Investment Fund Regulation*, 6 VA. L & BUS. REV. 341 (2011).

[827] Morley & Curtis, *supra* note 814.

[828] ICA § 16(c).

[829] Order Approving Proposed Rule Change, as Modified by Amendment No. 4, To Amend NYSE Rule 452 and Corresponding Listed Company Manual Section 402.08, 74 Fed. Reg. 33,293 (July 1, 2009), http://www.sec.gov/rules/sro/nyse/2009/34-60215.pdf.

[830] The effect is even worse in a mutual fund than in Microsoft, since any shareholder who is unhappy with the management of a mutual fund will tend to redeem before the vote takes place, depriving the fund of a critical mass of investors who would vote for change.

2.5 Directors

Mutual fund shareholders' extraordinary disinterest in shareholder voting raises deep questions about another aspect of mutual fund governance: boards of directors. Given that shareholders never meaningfully participate in mutual fund director elections, is it appropriate to think of mutual fund directors as shareholder representatives? If it is not appropriate to think of directors as shareholder representatives, then where do directors derive their legitimacy? Why should they have the authority to make important decisions?

Given their extreme distance from any meaningful chance of shareholder voting, mutual fund directors are perhaps best regarded as being similar to the directors of autonomous nonprofits. Many commercial nonprofits, such as hospitals, operate without any system of member voting, and their directors appoint successors in perpetuity without election by constituents. This is essentially how mutual fund boards operate. One sensible reform might thus be to openly acknowledge the reality of mutual fund board autonomy by eliminating the fiction of shareholder elections, just as nonprofit hospitals do.

Another reasonable reform might be to eliminate boards of directors altogether. Boards have come under serious attack by a number of legal scholars.[831] And there is ample precedent for open-end funds operating without boards. Open-end funds generally did not have boards of directors before the ICA required them, and open-end funds that are not regulated by the ICA, such as hedge funds and certain categories of exchange-traded funds, often operate without boards even now.

To be sure, the case for eliminating boards is not nearly as strong as the case for eliminating shareholder voting, because boards of directors arguably serve some useful functions. Still, even these functions deserve serious scrutiny, because they may well be better served in other ways. For example, the ICA and its administrative rules give directors a major compliance function by requiring them to make certain technical decisions and to oversee a fund's adherence to certain aspects of regulation. This compliance role might be filled more effectively, however, by dedicated compliance professionals. The SEC already implicitly acknowledged as much after the market-timing and late-trading scandals of the early 2000's when it began requiring all funds and advisers to hire Chief Compliance Officers.[832] These CCOs may well be more competent, more

---

[831] Fisch, *supra* note 795; Anita K. Krug, *Investment Company as Instrument: The Limitations of the Corporate Governance Regulatory Paradigm*, 86 S. CAL. L. REV. 263 (2013); Langevoort, *supra* note 795; Morley & Curtis, *supra* note 814; Ribstein, *supra* note 795.

[832] Compliance Programs of Investment Companies and Investment Advisers, Release No. IC-26299, (Feb. 5, 2004).

focused, and more diligent than directors in handling the complex details of compliance, because directors usually serve only part-time and often lack the expertise and inclination to grapple with the details of accounting and portfolio valuation that make up the bulk of compliance monitoring. Perhaps the SEC could further empower CCOs by letting them function independently, without the ostensible oversight of a board of directors that has no real claim to being a shareholder representative. This is how hedge funds operate now, and it works reasonably well. Further research into the role and effectiveness of CCOs in both hedge funds and mutual funds would be tremendously useful.

Another function boards arguably serve is the negotiation of fees. Section 15(c) of the ICA, which was added by Congress in 1970, requires a board to re-approve a management contract every year. Ostensibly, this process of re-approval offers a board a chance to renegotiate and reduce management fees. In practice, however, the 15(c) process probably offers little benefit. Mutual fund boards almost never use the 15(c) process to fire their managers, in part because the shareholder voting requirement would make it almost impossible to do. As a consequence, a board's bargaining leverage with its managers in the 15(c) process is extremely limited. Additionally, there is a distressing ambiguity about whose interests the 15(c) process actually serves. Perhaps the main output of the 15(c) process is a written record that an adviser can later use in litigation under section 36(b).[833] The *Gartenberg/Jones* standard that governs excessive fee liability under section 36(b) says that one factor in determining a fee's excessiveness is whether the fee was established by a strong bargaining process between a fund's board and adviser. A board that extensively documents its bargaining with its adviser thus provides the adviser with evidence that the adviser can later use in litigation against shareholders. Ironically, therefore, the main effect of a board's diligence in the 15(c) process is to cut off the rights of the very shareholders the board is supposed to protect.

Mutual funds could easily live without the 15(c) process. Section 15(c) was not part of the ICA until 1970, and the 15(c) process has no analogue today in hedge funds, even though hedge fund investors' size and sophistication ought to make board governance even more useful for them than for mutual fund investors. The 15(c) process also has no parallel in markets for other products and services that are also characterized by strong exit. Mutual fund advisers are much like other professionals, such as lawyers and accountants, and in the markets for the services of these other professionals, consumers tend to be protected by direct regulation of ethics, prices, and quality, rather than by boards of directors. No one would ever argue that the customers of H&R Block should be represented in price negotiations by a board of directors whom they elected,

---

[833] H. Norman Knickle, *The Mutual Fund's Section 15(C) Process: Jones v. Harris, the SEC and Fiduciary Duties of Directors*, 31 REV. BANKING & FIN. L. 265 (2011).

even though the customers of H&R Block are basically the same demographic we worry about in mutual funds.

2.6 Performance Compensation

The time is perhaps also ripe to reconsider the restrictions on performance compensation. In the nearly eighty years since the ICA and IAA were adopted, the popularity of performance compensation has exploded. Performance compensation is now ubiquitous in all manner of contracts, including executive employment contracts and private investment funds. And yet performance compensation remains very difficult for registered investment companies.

The ICA and IAA impose two sets of restrictions. One includes provisions added to the IAA by Congress in 1970, which say an adviser can only charge a performance-based fee if (1) the performance is measured relative to a benchmark and (2) the fee is symmetric in the sense that the adviser loses from underperforming the benchmark as much as it gains from overperforming the benchmark.[834] These restrictions have received significant attention from researchers.[835]

The second restriction is less well-known. Section 22(g) of the ICA, which Congress passed as part of the original statute in 1940, prohibits a mutual fund from issuing shares as compensation for services. The practical effect is to prevent a fund from paying the adviser with shares of the fund. For reasons that are unclear, this restriction applies only to open-end funds and not to closed-end funds.

Both of these restrictions ought to be re-examined. The main reason is the frequency with which private funds adopt performance-fee schemes that would violate these restrictions. Private equity and hedge funds are not subject to the restrictions in the IAA, and so they almost always pay fees on a performance basis and often pay them in the form of equity interests equivalent to shares. If the sophisticated investors in private tend to prefer performance-based compensation, then perhaps the unsophisticated investors in mutual funds should, too. The example of private funds is especially forceful, because with

---

[834] Investment Advisers Act § 205(b)(2), 15 U.S.C. §80b-5(b)(2) (2012).

[835] Danilo Drago, Valter Lazzari & Marco Navone, *Mutual Fund Incentive Fees: Determinants and Effects*, 39 FIN. MGMT. 365 (2010); Edwin J. Elton, Martin J. Gruber & Christopher R. Blake, *Incentive Fees and Mutual Funds*, 58 J. FIN. 779 (2003); Sanjiv R. Das & Rangarajan K. Sundaram, *Fee Speech: Signaling, Risk-sharing, and the Impact of Fee Structures on Investor Welfare*, 15 REV. FIN. STUD. 1465 (2002).

several decades now separating us from Congress' adoption of the performance compensation restrictions, it is hard to see what the original logic of the restrictions was.

Another reason to doubt the value of these restrictions is that they can be avoided fairly easily. The downside risk that a symmetric performance fee so assiduously imposes can mostly be hedged away with derivatives. And the restriction on paying shares as compensation can be gotten around by just paying a manager in cash and then requiring the manager to spend the cash on shares.[836]

Of course, there may be reasons to think that asset-based fees are more efficient in mutual funds than performance fees. This is largely what the research noted above tries to explore. But showing why a performance fee might be unwise or inefficient is not the same as showing why it ought to be *illegal*. And there is little high-quality empirical evidence on the efficiency of performance fees, because of the profound and unavoidable problem of endogeneity and self-selection. In any case, further attempts at empirical evidence and theoretical modeling would be most helpful.

2.7 Inter-Client Conflicts

As noted above, one of the features that distinguishes an investment fund from an operating company is the investment fund's tendency to employ an external manager. Instead of hiring a CEO directly, an investment fund receives its management from a different company with a different set of owners. One consequence of this tendency toward external management is that a manager can have other clients in addition to a particular fund. In a large advisory complex, a manager might have hundreds or even thousands of different clients, ranging from hedge funds, private equity funds, mutual funds and closed-end funds to myriad un-pooled accounts for individual investors. The trouble with this managerial promiscuity is that all of these many clients can come into conflict with one another. Since a manager has a separate fiduciary duty to each client, favoring one client over another in the allocation of any resource raises thorny problems of fiduciary duty. Already, much has been written about these conflicts.[837]

---

[836] This practice appears to be fairly common for fund directors and individual portfolio managers. *See* Martin Cremers, Joost Driessen, Pascal Maenhout & David Weinbaum, *Does Skin in The Game Matter? Director Incentives and Governance in The Mutual Fund Industry*, 44 J. FIN. & QUANT. ANALYSIS 1345 (2009).

[837] *See* Utpal Bhattacharya, Jung H. Lee & Veronika K. Pool, *Conflicting Family Values in Mutual Fund Families*, 68 J. FIN. 173 (2013) (conflicts arising when a manager uses a "fund of funds" to invest in and subsidize the family's other funds); William A. Birdthistle & M. Todd Henderson, *One Hat Too Many?*

At first, each of these conflicts can seem deeply alarming. How could a mutual fund be getting a fair deal when, for example, its adviser also operates a hedge fund that pays a performance fee that gives the adviser greater incentive to favor the hedge with investment opportunities and other resources? On further examination, though, these conflicts seem less worrying. Though it is tempting to pluck out one conflict at a time and express alarm about its risks, the truth is that conflicts are pervasive. Virtually everything an investment manager does raises a conflict among its clients. The most obvious conflicts involve investment opportunities, but clients can collide in myriad other ways as well. Every time a manager assigns an employee to serve one client, decides the order in which to execute trades, or chooses whether to make a purchase for one client that would trigger 13D filing obligations for other clients, the manager is facing a conflict of interest. Even the allocation of computer equipment and office space involves a conflict among clients, since a computer allocated to one client is a computer not allocated to another client. Conflicts are everywhere, and there is no escaping them.

Rather than picking out one conflict at a time and wringing our hands about it, therefore, we ought to think more holistically about why investors so willingly permit all of these conflicts in the first place. It cannot be the case that all inter-client conflicts are bad, because even sophisticated institutional clients routinely permit them. And so there must be some deeper logic that renders all of these conflicts acceptable.

To date, however, we lack a fully fleshed-out theory to tell us what that logic might be. Morley offers a preliminary account by identifying some reasons why inter-client conflicts might be more efficient in investment advisory

---

Investment Desegregation in Private Equity, 76 U. Chicago L. Rev. 45 (2009) (conflicts arising when a manager's different funds or proprietary trading strategies invest at different levels of the same portfolio company's capital structure); Gerald F. Davis & E. Han Kim, *Business Ties and Proxy Voting by Mutual Funds*, 85 J. Fin. Econ. 552 (2007) (conflicts arising when mutual fund managers seek pension management business from operating companies in which the fund managers' mutual funds invest); José-Miguel Gaspar, Massimo Massa & Pedro Matos, *Favoritism in Mutual Fund Families? Evidence on Strategic Cross-Fund Subsidization*, 61 J. Fin. 73 (2006) (conflicts arising from strategic shifting of performance between various funds); Tom Nohel, Z. Jay Wang & Lu Zheng, *Side-by-Side Management of Hedge funds and Mutual Funds*, 23 Rev. Fin. Stud. 2342 (2010) (conflicts arising when mutual fund management companies also operate hedge funds); Gjergji Cici, Scott Gibson & Rabih Moussawi, *For Better or Worse? Mutual Funds in Side-by-Side Management Relationships With Hedge Funds* (working paper, 2006), https://papers.ssrn.com/sol3/papers.cfm?abstract_id=905600 (same).

complexes than ordinary companies.[838] Morley argues that elements of fund organization, including exit rights and the limits on fund investors' control over managers, render inter-client conflicts less problematic in investment funds than ordinary companies. Still, Morley's account is short on details, and researchers might make major progress by trying to model them.

The absence of a clear theory of inter-client conflicts has often rendered regulation incoherent. The ICA and IAA and their administrative rules tend to grab onto particular kinds of conflicts without a discernible rationale for why some of them are worse than others, producing confusion and unfairness. Section 17 of the ICA, for example, prohibits a manager from investing jointly in a transaction alongside a registered fund, but permits an unlimited number of the manager's other clients to do so. And in 2004, the SEC began requiring a fund to disclose the number of other clients the fund's portfolio managers work for, as well as whether the other clients paid the manager performance fees.[839] But the SEC did not require a fund to disclose whether the other clients had the same investment objectives as the fund in question, even though this is critical to knowing whether there could be a conflict.

One especially valuable place to look for guidance might be the inter-client conflict restrictions that prevail by contract in private funds. Restrictions on inter-client conflicts vary significantly between hedge funds on the one hand and private equity funds on the other (Morley 2014), but among each type of fund the restrictions tend to be highly standardized. Hedge funds tend to be extremely permissive towards inter-client conflicts. Their operating agreements almost always waive the corporate opportunity doctrine, technically permitting an adviser and its other clients to invest in anything without regard to whether something might be an investment opportunities of the fund. Private equity funds, by contrast, are much more restrictive. They typically prohibit a manager from actively investing the assets of more than one private equity fund in a particular investment objective at any given time. Private equity funds also adopt elaborate restrictions on the ability of managers and their other clients to invest alongside the funds. The width and clarity of the divergences between private equity and hedge funds suggest that there may be a deep structural logic to the regulation of inter-client conflicts, and that it depends on many aspects of a fund's structure and investing objectives that may or may not be present in mutual funds.

---

[838] Morley, *supra* note 783.

[839] Disclosure Regarding Portfolio Managers of Registered Investment Companies, Investment Company Act Release 17 C.F.R. §§239, 249, 270, 274 Release No. IC-26533 (2004).

Conflicts among clients are likely to intensify in the future. The investment management industry is consolidating and growing more concentrated,[840] which may mean that the biggest investment management complexes will have more clients and thus more conflicts among them. Additionally, the client bases of investment managers are fragmenting as more and more investors opt out of pooling arrangements and choose instead to have their money be managed individually.[841] More than ever, regulators will need a clear understanding of when to intervene and when to let the market find an equilibrium on its own.

2.8 The Long Shadow of Closed-End Funds

So far, we have focused almost entirely on open-end funds, since they hold the vast bulk of the registered fund industry's assets. But closed-end funds are worth thinking about, too, in large part because they cast a long shadow over open-end funds. When the SEC drafted the ICA in the late 1930s, it focused overwhelmingly on closed-end funds. Until the very end of the 1930s, closed-end funds were vastly larger in both number and assets than open-end funds.[842] Open-end funds were a niche business centered in a handful of small management firms in Boston, while closed-end funds were a big business centered in large investment banks in New York. Size was not the only reason the SEC obsessed over closed-end funds. Closed-end funds had also piled up a horrific record of abuse during the bull market of the late 1920s and the bust of the early 1930s, and it was the SEC's years-long investigation into these misdeeds in the late 1930s that became the basis of the ICA.

Because the open-end fund industry was so small in the late 1930s, and because the experience with the closed-end fund industry was so much more salient, the SEC and other industry observers overwhelmingly saw the statute's purposes as having to do with closed-end funds.[843] Today, the core of the regulatory scheme is identical for both types of funds, with a slant toward the needs of closed-end funds.

This is unfortunate, because the industry is now composed overwhelmingly of open-end funds. Indeed, open-end funds hold about 70 times

---

[840] Einer Elhauge, *Horizontal Shareholding*, 129 HARV. L. REV. 1267 (2016).

[841] William Clayton, *Preferential Treatment and the Rise of Individualized Investing in Private Equity*, 11 VA. L. & BUS. REV. 249 (2017).

[842] Grow, *supra* note 825; Morley, *supra* note 826.

[843] MATTHEW P. FINK, THE RISE OF MUTUAL FUNDS: AN INSIDER'S VIEW (2008); Morley, *supra* note 826.

more assets than closed-end funds.[844] The differences between closed- and open-end funds thus warrant serious scrutiny. The ICA was written decades before the work of Henry Hansmann, Oliver Hart, Albert Hirschman, Oliver Williamson and others who demonstrated the importance of exit rights in contractual relationships, and so perhaps the drafters of the ICA might be forgiven for failing to understand the profound significance of redemption rights in open-end funds. But the time has now come for a sweeping reassessment. It is unclear how exactly regulation ought to differentiate between open- and closed-end funds, but researchers should set themselves the task of figuring it out.

One obvious area of interest is shareholder voting and board governance. As noted above, voting makes much less sense in an open-end fund than a closed-end fund. Another area of interest is the role of boards in defending closed-end fund managers against shareholder activism. In closed-end funds, boards tend to exercise very little supervisory oversight, since the funds are dominated by their external advisers. But boards nevertheless play a major role in building and defending the anti-takeover fortifications that make it difficult for shareholder activists to hold fund advisers accountable. Is this a useful function for boards to serve? That is a hard question that deserves a serious answer.

Taxation also requires serious scrutiny. Though in this chapter we have generally avoided taxation, the differences in taxation between open- and closed-end funds are too glaring to ignore. Tax law treats open- and closed-end funds identically, but it has radically different consequences for each. In order to avoid entity-level income taxation, tax law requires a RIC to distribute all of its income every year. This creates some very weird problems, which manifest in open- and closed-end funds in different (though equally weird) ways. In an open-end fund, taxation creates a problem of *tax overhang*, in which the failure of open-end fund share prices to adjust to expectations means that the expected value of tax liabilities is not reflected in share prices.[845] Closed-end funds face a different problem. In a closed-end fund, the income distribution requirement gradually bleeds the fund of its assets by requiring the fund to pay out its income, even though a fund that trades at a discount at NAV can't easily recover the distributed income by issuing new shares.[846] The distribution requirement thus works as a kind of ratchet, forcing the fund to pay out all of its income in good years even as it suffers losses in bad years. The differences between open-end

---

[844] INVESTMENT COMPANY FACT BOOK, *supra* note 775.

[845] Michael J. Barclay, Neil D. Pearson & Michael S. Weisbach, *Open-end Mutual Funds and Capital-Gains Taxes*, 49 J. FIN. ECON. 3 (1998).

[846] Morley, *supra* note 826.

and closed-end funds were never seriously considered when Congress first adopted the tax system in the late-1930s and early 1940s.[847]

Another area of possible difference is disclosure. Disclosure works better in closed-end funds than in open-end funds, because closed-end fund shares tend to be traded on securities exchanges. Closed-end funds' tendency to trade on exchanges means that their shares can be bought and sold at prices that reflect efficient market estimates of value even if only a small number of investors actually read and understand the fund's disclosures.[848] One can rely on the market price of an exchange-traded security as an accurate estimation of the security's value, even if one did not personally read the fund's annual report. This is the logic, for example, of the fraud-on-the-market theory of reliance in securities class actions. Open-end fund shares, by contrast, are not traded on exchanges, and their prices thus do not automatically adjust to efficient levels to reflect supply and demand conditions. This is a consequence of redemption rights. A fund's NAV stays fixed regardless of how many people buy or sell shares on a given day and a fund's fees only adjust when a board and adviser make a decision to change them, not when demand increases or declines. Unlike the shares of closed-end funds and other exchange-traded securities, there is no price quotation scheme by which mutual fund fees and NAV automatically update to reflect the opinions of sophisticated investors. This means that the efforts of a few investors to read and understand an open-end fund's disclosures do not generate the same positive externalities in an open-end fund as they do in a closed-end fund. One cannot rely on an open-end fund's share price as an accurate estimate of the fund's expected value, because the price does not necessarily reflect sophisticated investors' estimations of expected value. Every investor in an open-end fund has to form an opinion for himself. In this regard, an open-end fund is like a consumer product, which also requires individual consumers to form their own estimates of a product's value.[849] And just as with a

---

[847] *See id.*

[848] Of course, some economists doubt whether closed-end fund share prices reflect the valuations of sophisticated investors. *See* Charles Lee, Andrei Shleifer & Richard H. Thaler, *Investor Sentiment and The Closed-End Fund Puzzle*, 46 J. FIN. 75 (1991). But at least in theory, there is a possibility that a few sophisticated investors could move prices in an inefficient direction in a closed-end fund.

[849] Of course, Schwartz argues that not every consumer has to be comprehend a disclosure in order for the disclosure to produce efficient outcomes in a product market. *See* Alan Schwartz, *Proposals for Products Liability Reform: A Theoretical Synthesis*, 97 YALE L.J. 353 (1988). But the percentage of buyers who have to comprehend the disclosure is no doubt much higher in a product market than a securities market.

consumer product, with a mutual fund, disclosure often demands too much sophistication from purchasers, rendering it deeply problematic as a tool for regulation.

In addition to exploring how regulation could better accommodate open-end funds, researchers should also explore whether regulation could better address the problems of closed-end funds. Though the puzzle of closed-end fund *share pricing* has endlessly fascinated financial economists, we know of no academic paper specifically devoted to the challenges of closed-end fund *regulation*. Research on the unique regulatory problems of closed-end funds is urgently necessary, because the nature of the closed-end fund business has changed since 1940. In 1940, everyone still expected that closed-end funds would continue to dominate the industry they had started and would one day return to trading at premiums to NAV—as they did before 1929. Now that closed-end funds overwhelmingly trade at discounts to NAV, however, there are deep questions about how closed-end funds should be regulated and about whether they should even be permitted to exist at all. Because closed-end funds commonly trade at discounts to NAV, an IPO of a closed-end fund is generally a terrible investment. An IPO investor buys at NAV, with a virtual guarantee that the stock will quickly trade below NAV. Evidence indicates that a distressing share of IPO investors tend to be individuals who are directed to purchase the closed-end fund IPOs by their brokers.[850] Closed-end funds also have a tendency to coerce investors through the use of dilutive rights offerings, in which they sell shares to existing investors at prices below NAV. These rights offerings operate much like poison pills by forcing investors to buy or else be diluted. Closed-end funds may have many other regulatory challenges, and they present a deep vein for legal researchers to mine.

3 Private Funds

So far we have focused entirely on publicly registered investment funds. But the big story in investment management in the last several decades, of course, has been the rise of private funds, such as hedge funds, private equity funds, and venture capital funds. The important fact about these funds for regulation is that the drafters of the ICA never foresaw them.[851] The prospect that a large industry of private funds might someday challenge the dominance of registered funds never entered the debates about the ICA. The dramatic rise of private funds thus raises fundamental questions about whether the law ought to change.

---

[850] *See* Hanley et al., *supra* note 822.

[851] *See* Grow, *supra* note 825; Morley, *supra* note 826.

3.1 The Public/Private Distinction

The natural starting point is the set of exemptions that permits private funds to stay private. The key dividing line between public and private appears in section 3(c) of the ICA, which, among other things, exempts a fund from registration under the ICA if the fund has fewer than 100 investors or if its investors are all large enough to satisfy the definition of a "qualified purchaser" in section 2(a)(51).[852]

The main question is whether the exemptions for private funds should be expanded. The reasons to consider expansion are several. First, there are tremendous tax advantages to remaining private. The taxation of registered investment companies in the United States is almost always less favorable than the taxation of private funds, for both investors and managers.[853] Private funds are taxed as partnerships, even as registered investment companies are taxed under their own unique system. And given the choice between partnership and RIC taxation, almost no rational investor would ever choose RIC taxation. We therefore ought to consider expanding the range of funds that can qualify as private funds as a way of broadening access to the favorable tax treatment of private funds.

Another reason to doubt the line between public and private in the ICA is that it differs from the line between public and private in the other securities laws, and there is no obvious reason why. The ICA and the other securities laws employ similar concepts for distinguishing public and private funds, but they establish the threshold dollar and number amounts differently. Under the Exchange Act, for example, an individual can qualify as an "accredited investor" with just one million dollars in assets. But under the ICA, an individual can only become a "qualified purchaser" with at least five million dollars in assets. Similarly, the Exchange Act permits a company to remain private with as many 500 "non-accredited" investors; the ICA draws the line at just 100 "non-qualified purchasers."[854] We know of no effort, historical or modern, to justify the differences.

---

[852] ICA §§ 2(a)(51) (defining "Qualified Purchaser"); 3(c)(1), (7) (exempting funds with fewer than 100 investors and funds with only qualified purchasers).

[853] Samuel D. Brunson, *The Taxation of RICs: Replicating Portfolio Investment or Eliminating Double Taxation*, 20 STAN. J. L. BUS. & FIN. 222 (2014); Samuel D. Brunson, *Mutual Funds, Fairness, and the Income Gap*, 65 ALA. L. REV. 139 (2013); John C. Coates, *Reforming the Taxation and Regulation of Mutual Funds: A Comparative Legal and Economic Analysis*, 1 J. LEG. ANALYSIS 591 (2009).

[854] Both an ICA and an operating company will become public under the Exchange Act if it exceeds 2,000 investors of any kind. 15 U.S.C. §78l(g)(1).

It is also unclear why the number of investors in a fund should matter if the fund offers redemption rights like an open-end fund. In an operating company, where investors are locked in and cannot redeem, the number of investors matters because it affects the collective action problem. As the number of investors increases, so does the investors' tendency to become rationally apathetic, heightening the need for regulation to protect the investors' collective interests. In an open-end fund with redemption rights, however, the collective action problem does not matter, because there is no such thing as collective action. An open-end fund investor can withdraw her money unilaterally, and so, as observed above, open-end fund shareholders have very little reason ever to vote collectively. So then why should it matter whether an open-end fund has a hundred investors or a thousand?

Permitting more funds to stay private might also offer small investors the prospect of better investment returns. Many aspects of RIC regulation, such as the restrictions on leverage, the requirements for frequent and costly redemptions, and the prohibition on incentive fees arguably prevent RICs from achieving the same investment returns as private funds. Even if we do not have any faith in private fund managers' ability to outperform the market by skill, we might nevertheless think they could outperform RICs simply by virtue of being free of the burdens of regulation. The drain some regulations place on investment returns creates a real tension between *protecting* public fund investors and *impoverishing* them.

3.2 Inter-Client Conflicts of Interest

Like publicly registered funds, private funds also pose serious problems of inter-client conflicts of interest. When a manager simultaneously operates many different private funds and client accounts, the interests of all these funds and accounts inevitably clash. As observed above, the issue is growing more important because of the increasing fragmentation of pooled vehicles into unpooled individually managed accounts. The fragmentation is intensified in private funds by the growing popularity of side letters, which require a manager to give special treatment to one investor over others in a pooled fund. The most sustained academic treatment of this challenge comes from Clayton,[855] who describes the fragmentation and explores the conditions that might be required for it to be efficient. More research on the empirical extent and theoretical risks of inter-client conflicts would be valuable.

---

[855] Clayton, *supra* note 841.

4 Investment Funds as Investors

We have focused so far mostly on investment funds as *issuers* of securities, but investment funds also play an important role as *investors* in securities. A great deal has been written about how well investment funds function as investors in other companies, but the most urgent academic research at the moment involves the recent discovery of astonishing statistics about the concentration of holdings in the hands of the largest investment management companies. Work by a number of authors has shown that the investment management industry has grown both much larger and much more concentrated in recent years, causing the biggest investment managers to control astoundingly large stakes in American public companies.[856]

Some of this research suggests that the largest managers' stakes are so vast and so widespread that they might be tilting toward monopolization. In one paper, José Azar, Martin Schmalz, and Isabel Tecu show that as a handful of large investment managers came to control increasingly large stakes in every major airline, the intensity of price competition among the airlines decreased.[857] Labeling this phenomenon "horizontal ownership," a number of legal scholars have argued that although the declines in competition likely do not reflect direct collusion by investment managers, overlapping ownership by investment managers should nevertheless be regulated as an antitrust problem.[858]

---

[856] Miguel Antón, Florian Ederer, Mireia Giné & Martin C. Schmalz, *Common Ownership, Competition, and Top Management Incentives* (working paper, 2016), https://papers.ssrn.com/sol3/papers.cfm?abstract_id=2802332; José Azar, *Portfolio Diversification, Market Power, and the Theory of the Firm* (working paper, 2016), https://papers.ssrn.com/sol3/papers.cfm?abstract_id=2811221; José Azar, Sahil Raina & Martin C. Schmalz, *Ultimate Ownership and Bank Competition* (working paper, 2016) https://papers.ssrn.com/sol3/papers.cfm?abstract_id=2710252; José Azar, Martin C. Schmalz & Isabel Tecu, *Anti-Competitive Effects of Common Ownership*, J. Fin. (forthcoming), https://papers.ssrn.com/sol3/papers.cfm?abstract_id=2427345; Jan Fichtner, Elke M. Heemskerk & Javier Garcia-Bernardo, *Hidden Power of the Big Three? Passive Index Funds, Re-Concentration of Corporate Ownership, and New Financial Risk*, 19 Bus. & Pol. 298 (2017).

[857] Azar et al., *supra* note 856.

[858] Elhauge, *supra* note 840; Eric A. Posner, Fiona M. S. Morton & E. Glenn Weyl, *A Proposal to Limit the Anti-Competitive Power of Institutional Investors*, Antitrust L.J. (forthcoming), https://papers.ssrn.com/sol3/papers.cfm?abstract_id=2872754.

The investment management industry, understandably, tends to believe there is nothing to worry about. And even many academics argue that there are yet reasons to remain skeptical of the academic evidence. Still, even if one feels inclined to accept the investment management industry's skepticism, it is important to take the issue of horizontal ownership seriously. Though no one can tell the future, the potential impact of concentrated ownership is vast. It is now possible to foresee a day when the clients of two or three large investment managers might hold thirty percent of the shares of a majority of America's large public companies. Though the intentions of investment managers may be entirely benign, the power that these growing stakes will bring is too significant to ignore.

Researchers should thus continue to describe the concentration of ownership and seek out new ways to draw causal inferences about its consequences. Researchers should also continue exploring the antitrust aspects of the issue, as many authors have already done. And beyond the antitrust law, researchers should explore the implications of corporate and securities law. Morley, for example, argues that the power of large investment managers is inherently limited, because conflicts among clients make it difficult for an adviser to convert holdings into direct control.[859] Activism by one client inevitably generates costs and headaches for other clients, and this creates persistent and often unmanageable fiduciary conflicts. And some of these costs come from securities regulation, such as the way in which one client's activism can increase the Form 13D filing obligations of other clients. The tendency of the costs of activism to spill across different clients may be one reason why activist hedge funds tend always to be managed by small advisors with only a handful of clients. Large advisers, such as Goldman Sachs and Fidelity, have never managed activist hedge funds, for example, and probably never will. These complications and many others warrant exploration as we try to understand what a future of growing ownership concentration will bring.

5 Credit Rating Agencies

A topic of extensive public debate, academic study, and market commentary has been the role played by credit rating agencies (CRAs) in the fixed income markets. Concerns over the quality of credit ratings first received widespread attention in 2001 when Enron bonds still had investment grade ratings from the three major CRAs (Moody's, S&P and Fitch) just five days before Enron's bankruptcy filing.[860] However, the far more powerful impetus for

---

[859] John D. Morley, *Too Big to Be Active* (working paper, 2017).

[860] Lawrence J. White, *Credit Rating Agencies: An Overview*, 5 ANN. REV. FIN. ECON. 93 (2013).

this interest in CRAs has been the credit ratings provided to structured finance securities (mortgage-backed securities (MBS), asset-backed securities (ABS), and collateralized debt obligations (CDO)) in the lead up to the financial crisis of 2007-2008 by the dominant CRAs (Moody's, S&P's, and to a lesser extent, Fitch) and the subsequent very poor performance of many of these securities during the crisis. For instance, some 95% of all credit rating downgrades over the 2007-2008 period were of MBS, ABS, or CDOs. ABS CDOs constituted over 40% of the total write-downs of financial institutions during this period.

Importantly, these downgrades of structured finance securities and their poor performance included a substantial number of triple-A rated obligations. The following is a figure from Benmelech and Dlugosz[861] reflecting the number of downgrades of structured finance securities and the percent that were triple-A:

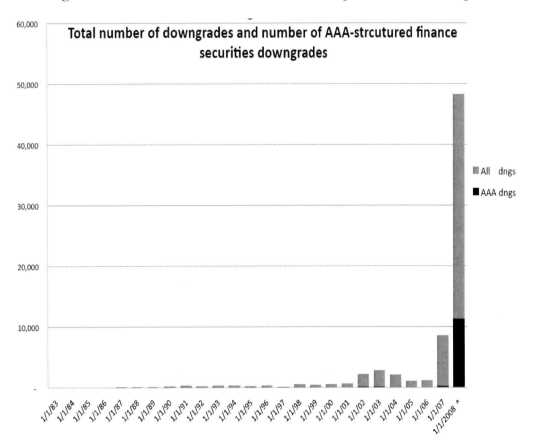

---

[861] Efraim Benmelech & Jennifer Dlugosz, *The Credit Rating Crisis*, 24 NBER MACROECONOMICS ANN. 161 (2010) at Figure 4a.

The ratings on corporate debt by contrast have by comparison fared far better historically, despite the experience of the Enron bonds. As a general matter corporate debt ratings over the 1985-2009 period have become *more* conservative and in fact are arguably too conservative (in light of market pricing).[862] During the 2001-2002 recession, a period that was especially trying for corporate bonds with a wave of corporate bankruptcies occurring during this time, there were a significant number of corporate bonds downgraded at the time. However, virtually none were triple-A rated corporate debt. Moreover, for those corporate bonds that were downgraded, the number of downgrade notches (how far the bond was downgraded) during the 2001-2002 recession were far smaller than that experienced by structured finance securities during the financial crisis of 2007-2008. Benmelech and Dlugosz conclude during this time that "corporate bond ratings were well calibrated to the underlying economic risk of the issuer." [863] As for the financial crisis, significantly fewer triple-A corporate bonds were downgraded during the financial crisis relative to structured finance instruments.

Given all this, it is not surprising that public debate, academic study, and market commentary concerning the CRAs have tended to focus on ratings of structured finance securities, rather than corporate debt securities. Also not surprisingly, much of the empirical work (although certainly not all) has tended to focus on the ratings of structured finance securities and their performance during the financial crisis. The policy debate over CRAs has therefore generally focused on whether investors, and the market more generally, relied to their detriment on flawed credit ratings of structured finance instruments. In unpacking this general debate, several issues present themselves.

First, to what extent did the market in fact rely on CRAs' ratings, perhaps most importantly in pricing debt securities such as MBS, ABS, and CDOs? The answer to this question is of interest regardless of the ultimate answer. If the market did rely to some significant extent on ratings and, moreover, the ratings were somehow flawed this raises an obvious policy concern in terms of the market being misled and capital being misallocated. But even if the market did not actually rely on these ratings (or, equivalently, ignored these ratings when they are inconsistent with other evidence) this merely raises a different set of policy concerns: how well are the CRAs serving their role as information intermediaries if the market views the ratings as superfluous? And if CRAs are not playing a valuable information intermediary role for whatever reason then

---

[862] Ramin P. Baghai, Henri Servaes & Ane Tamayo, *Have Rating Agencies Become More Conservative?*, 69 J. FIN. 1961 (2014).

[863] Benmelech & Dlugosz, *supra* note 861, at 175.

why should one use these ratings for a wide variety of regulatory purposes as was in fact the case historically (and to some significant extent still today)?

Second, assuming the market does rely to some significant on ratings, to what extent were the credit ratings flawed (measured from an ex ante perspective, rather than using the benefit of hindsight)? The focal point in the literature and public debate here has been on ratings accuracy. One additional issue of particular importance can be folded into this discussion and that is of systematic risk. To the extent that CRAs made the same (mistaken) judgments for a variety of structured finance securities does this create a source of systematic risk? In other words, does uniformity in ratings judgment turn a mistaken ratings judgment in a particular case into a systematic issue for the marketplace?

Third, if the market has relied on flawed ratings, what is the proper regulatory/policy response? Obviously first understanding what problems exist and why is the necessary predicate for any potential regulatory changes. Before discussing (at a general level) these three issues, we will first briefly discuss at a basic level the function of CRAs in the marketplace and in the regulatory scheme.

5.1 Credit Rating Agencies: Function and Regulation

CRAs produce ratings that are designed to reflect credit risk of debt securities (default risk and/or expected loss). While credit risk is obviously an important source of risk for debt securities, it is not the only one (such as liquidity and duration risk). In providing information concerning credit risk, CRAs can serve a valuable information intermediary role for debt markets. Debt markets are both enormous and heterogeneous[864] which speaks to the potential economies of scale and scope enjoyed by such an information intermediary. Given the repeated game nature of debt ratings, the reputational capital of CRAs is one potentially important market mechanism that can help ensure ratings quality[865] Importantly, CRAs, such as Moody's, existed long before the regulatory use of credit ratings indicative of a market-based role for these entities. During this time (up until the late 1960s/early 1970s), investors would purchase these ratings from CRAs. Presumably clients of CRAs wished to purchase ratings given their informational content, i.e. CRAs were valued information intermediaries.

But any consideration of the role of CRAs in the modern era must also reflect the fact that credit ratings are used extensively by regulators for a wide

---

[864] Robert J. Rhee, *Why Credit Rating Agencies Exist*, 44 ECON. NOTES 161 (2015).

[865] *See, e.g.*, Robert W. Holthausen & Richard W. Leftwich, *The Effect of Bond Rating Changes on Common Stock Prices*, 17 J. FIN. ECON. 57 (1986).

variety of purposes, i.e. the regulatory treatment of a particular debt issuance might well be a function of its rating.[866] In short, favorable ratings can help ensure favorable regulatory treatment. This effect is potentially quite separate and apart from these ratings providing valuable information to the debt markets concerning credit risk, even though favorable regulatory treatment might itself have real pricing effects. The regulatory issue of credit ratings had its origins in the 1930s when regulators first used them in regulating commercial banks[867] but truly blossomed in the 1970s, roughly contemporaneous with the move from investors paying for ratings to those ratings being paid for by the debt issuers. Perhaps most importantly, in 1975, the regulatory category of "nationally recognized statistical rating organization" (NRSRO) was created with the credit ratings of CRAs receiving the NRSRO designation being used for a variety of regulatory purposes.

The regulatory uses of credit ratings include the calculation of minimum capital requirements for a variety of financial institutions (insurance, banking and broker-dealers), pension fund asset allocations, and Basel II bank capital requirements. Also, money market mutual funds have been required by the Investment Company of 1940 to hold highly rated assets. Hunt identifies 44 SEC rules and forms that incorporate credit ratings. The regulatory use of ratings is not confined to federal law.[868] State regulators also often use ratings for investment limits on regulated entities, such as insurance companies, as do international bodies as well.

Concern over CRAs and their regulatory use has triggered two legislative responses. In 2006, Congress passed the Credit Rating Agency Reform Act mandating transparency and ensuring procedural regularity in the SEC's designation of NRSROs. Ultimately, seven new CRAs received NRSRO designation, in addition to Moody's, S&P and Fitch. The second legislative response is contained in the Dodd-Frank Wall Street Reform and Consumer Protection Act of 2010 (Dodd-Frank), which mandated the cessation of regulatory use of credit ratings in federal law.

Ratings have been used not only for regulatory purposes but also for contractual purposes in the marketplace. This is yet another role that can be

---

[866] Frank Partnoy, *How and Why Credit Rating Agencies Are Not Like Other Gatekeepers*, in FINANCIAL GATEKEEPERS: CAN THEY PROTECT INVESTORS? (Fuchita & Litan eds., 2006).

[867] Lawrence J. White, *Credit Rating Agencies: An Overview*, 5 ANN. REV. FIN. ECON. 93 (2013).

[868] John P. Hunt, *Credit Rating Agencies and the "Worldwide Credit Crisis": The Limits of Reputation, the Insufficiency of Reform and a Proposal for Improvement*, 2009 COLUM. BUS. L. REV. 109 (2009).

played by an information intermediary: distilling information into clear signals of credit risk that market actors, if they so choose, can use in contracting. Consider three examples. First, the need for institutions to post additional collateral can result from changes in the ratings of the collateral. These ratings-based triggers for posting of additional collateral is an important issue in considering the role of CRAs during the financial crisis of 2007-2008. Second, asset managers often rely on ratings in managing their portfolios with ratings of portfolio securities often being explicitly incorporated into the investment management agreements that govern the construction of these portfolios. For instance, a survey of pension plan sponsors reported that 75% have minimum rating requirements and 50% limits on portfolio distribution by credit rating.[869] Third, ratings can play an important role in determining whether a debt covenant has been violated.

5.2 Do the Markets Rely?

Adelino finds that the yields on MBS issued in the lead-up to the financial crisis did in fact contain important information predicting future downgrades and defaults above and beyond that reflected in the credit rating.[870] Interestingly, yields were more effective at predicting downgrades than credit ratings for MBS rated below AA, i.e. the market appears to rely on information beyond that reflected in the credit rating. This complements the finding of Ashcraft, Goldsmith-Pinkham and Vickrey who find that credit ratings did not reflect all available (negative) information concerning the risk of default.[871]

Importantly, however, Adelino's findings do not hold true for triple-A MBS tranches. Here, Adelino finds that the market did to a significant extent rely just on the credit rating. The market emphasis on triple-A ratings as a determinant of pricing is consistent with a number of other papers in the literature that argue that triple-A MBS investors were generally passive and/or less informed. These investors often had a preference to purchase securities believed to be information insensitive making triple-A rated securities a natural

---

[869] Richard Cantor, Owain A. Gwilym & Stephen Thomas, *The Use of Credit Ratings in Investment Management in the U.S. and Europe* (working paper, 2007), https://papers.ssrn.com/sol3/papers.cfm?abstract_id=996133.

[870] Manuel Adelino, Do Investors Rely only on Ratings? (2009) (unpublished Ph.D. dissertation, MIT).

[871] Adam Ashcraft, Paul Goldsmith-Pinkham & James Vickery, *MBS Ratings and the Mortgage Credit Boom*, (working paper, 2010), https://papers.ssrn.com/sol3/papers.cfm?abstract_id=1615613.

fit.[872] On a related note, Coval, Jurek and Stafford document that the many senior (triple-A rated) CDO tranches were in fact more risky than that implied by either their credit rating or their pricing.[873] The argument that triple-A investors to some significant degree were generally passive and/or less informed is also consistent with Ashcraft, Goldsmith-Pinkham and Vickrey, who find that MBS ratings inaccuracy was most severe during the height of the market i.e. the time at which investors (or least a segment of investors) were arguably most likely to be passive and/or less informed.[874] In other words, there is some evidence that the market relied on the triple-A ratings of structured finance instruments potentially at the expense of additional (negative) information relevant to pricing. The role that the extensive regulatory usage of ratings potentially plays in this connection is an interesting one: to what extent (if any) did the regulatory importance placed on the triple-A rated designation result in increased investor passivity? If regulations suggest that a triple-A designation is sufficient to establish that the security is information insensitive, to what extent does this substitute for investor due diligence?

In thinking about potential investor clientele effects of highly rated securities, it is worth noting that significant purchasers of non-agency triple-A MBS during the 2007-2008 period were overseas investors (25.2%), Fannie Mae, Freddie Mac and the Federal Home Loan Bank (18.8%), money market managers (13.8%), and insurance companies (7.6%)[875] Triple-A securities were also commonly used in the repo markets, arguably because the parties to these transaction wanted to use an information insensitive asset for collateral (an asset for which the parties to the repo transaction generally did not need to worry about the fundamental value so as to minimize transaction costs). It is also worth noting that outside the context of the financial crisis, it is more challenging to empirically study the informational content of credit ratings with respect to triple-A securities given the very low level of downgrades and default for these securities historically (combined with the relatively recent development of the structured finance market). This raises the general issue of how generalizable are the results from the multiple studies of one particular, albeit important, historical episode: the rating and performance of structured finance instruments before and during the financial crisis.

---

[872] *See* Marco Pagano, Paolo F. Volpin & Wolf Wagner, *Credit Ratings Failures and Policy Options*, 25 ECON. POL'Y 401 (2010).

[873] Joshua Coval, Jakub Jurek & Erik Stafford, *The Economics of Structured Finance*, 23 J. ECON. PERSP. 3 (2009).

[874] Ashcraft et al., *supra* note 871.

[875] LEHMAN BROTHERS SECURITIZED PRODUCTS RESEARCH, RESIDENTIAL CREDIT LOSSES (2008).

Turning to corporate debt, there have been a long series of papers, starting with Katz,[876] generally finding that corporate debt reacts negatively to negative credit rating events such as downgrades, i.e. ratings are viewed as having informational content.[877] Whether the market views the credit rating as having information because it reveals new negative information concerning the firm's prospects ("information channel") or, alternatively because of the regulatory and contractual effects of a change in credit rating ("non-information channels") is not always addressed in these papers. One interesting paper that does is Kisgen and Strahan, which finds a meaningful pricing effect on corporate debt due to non-information channels.[878] On a similar note, Sangiorgi and Spatt discuss the fact that Moody's recalibration of its municipal bond ratings had real effects on municipal bond pricing even though the recalibration was not based on a new evaluation of information concerning default/expected losses.[879] In other words, municipal debt ratings appear to have pricing effects outside the informational channel.

From a policy perspective it can be important to separate out the two potential pricing effects of ratings: the information channel would be consistent with CRAs providing new value-relevant information to the market filling a valuable information intermediary role to the debt markets, whereas the non-informational channels would reflect a choice to have the credit rating trigger certain real effects for the firm (or the municipality in the case of municipal bonds). If the pricing effects are a function of the latter, then one could ask the question whether this choice, particularly if it is a regulatory choice, is a wise one.

5.3 Competition and Revenues

One important set of policy issues concerns how the industrial organization of the CRA market impacts ratings quality along two related dimensions: competition (meaningful choice among CRAs) and the nature of that competition (competing for business from debt issuers).

---

[876] Steven Katz, *The Price and Adjustment Process of Bonds to Rating Reclassifications: A Test of Bond Market Efficiency*, 29 J. FIN. 551 (1974).

[877] *See, e.g.*, James W. Wansley, John L. Glascock & Terence M. Clauretie, *Bond Pricing and Information Arrival: The Case of Bond Rating Changes*, 19 J. BUS. FIN. & ACCT. 733 (1992).

[878] Darren J. Kisgen & Philip E. Strahan, *Do Regulations Based on Credit Ratings Affect a Firm's Cost of Capital?*, 23 REV. FIN. STUD. 4324 (2010).

[879] Francesco Sangiorgi & Chester S. Spatt, *The Economics of Credit Rating Agencies*, 12 FOUNDATIONS & TRENDS IN FIN. 1 (2017).

Turning first to competition, while there have been a total of ten CRAs that are NRSROs, approximately 96% of all ratings are provided by just three CRAs: Moody's Investor Services, Standard & Poor's, and Fitch Rating (with Fitch Rating being significantly smaller than the other two). Providing ratings, along with ancillary services such as consulting, was quite profitable for these entities, with Moody's profits tripling between 2002 and 2006. As of 2006, 44% of its profits came from structured finance.

Whether this apparent lack of choice among CRAs (given the largely duopoly structure of the CRA market) should raise policy concerns is a complicated policy question with no obvious answer: more competition could (i) result in greater concern by a CRA for its reputational capital as a source of competitive advantage (positive for ratings accuracy); (ii) reduce the value of a CRA's reputation capital because the business is itself less profitable (negative for ratings accuracy); and (iii) create more opportunities for "rate shopping" by debt issuers (negative for ratings accuracy). Some of the empirical evidence on shopping will be reviewed later (in the section entitled Ratings Shopping).[880]

Even assuming the relative lack of CRA choice reduces ratings accuracy, this hardly ends the analysis. At least two further difficult questions present themselves: First, what accounts for the concentrated nature of the industry and, second, assuming a concentrated CRA industry how can (if at all) regulation improve the situation? The answer to the first question is nonobvious. Is the relative lack of competition due to: (i) the benefit of being designated a NRSRO and the resulting regulatory treatment as some have argued; (ii) the reputational capital of the dominant CRAs which cannot be easily replicated; and/or (iii) economies of scale and scope for information intermediaries? As for (i), the NRSRO designation by itself cannot explain the dominant positions of Moody's and S&P among the ten NRSROs. As for (ii), both Moody's and S&P have been heavily criticized for the accuracy of their credit ratings for structured finance securities up to and during the financial crisis, but nevertheless continue to retain their dominant position.[881] As for (iii) merely invoking the notion of economies of scale and scope, while certainly plausible in the context of a centralized information intermediary serving a large and heterogeneous market, hardly provides the level of elucidation needed to understand exactly the nature of the barriers of entry limiting competition. Sangiorgi and Spatt point out that the Dodd-Frank Act might have increased barriers to entry and reduced competition by imposing costly regulations on CRAs that might be difficult for a new entrant to bear and amortize.[882] As for the second question, regulation as a substitute for

---

[880] *See also* generally *id.* on this topic.

[881] *See id.*

[882] *See id.*

the disciplining effect of competition (or perhaps regulation encouraging competition), one needs to examine in more detail the potential areas arguably necessitating consideration of regulatory intervention.

The nature of CRA competition is an important issue as well: CRAs compete with each other for the ratings business of debt issuers. Generally, the issue here is traditionally thought of as CRA conflicts of interest. Simply put, debt issuers generally want higher ratings for their securities assuming that they can credibly communicate those ratings to the market. In terms of conflicts of interest, all else being equal, CRAs would have an incentive to cater to issuers and particularly to large issuers that control significant ratings business.

Here it is important to emphasize a fundamental difference in the nature of issuers in the structured finance market relative to the corporate and municipal debt markets: there is far more concentration among issuers of structured finance instruments than there is in these other markets. For instance, the top five issuers of private MBS in 2006 constituted approximately 40% of the market.[883] This literature documents that debt issuers are more likely to go back to the same CRA if they received a positive rating. They report that large issuers of triple-A securities had significantly less subordination for those securities (i.e. those securities were more risky holding all else constant) than triple-A securities issued by smaller issuers. Moreover, they find that a CRA is less likely to downgrade a security than a different CRA if that CRA has rated more securities by that issuer. He, Qian, and Strahan document that structured securities receive more favorable ratings if the issuer is large, i.e. a more important potential source of revenues to the rating agency.[884] And, moreover, MBS sold by large issuers performed significantly worse during the financial crisis than did similarly rated securities of smaller issuers.

The tradeoff a CRA faces between avoiding reputational harm due to inaccurate/noisy ratings and generating ratings business from issuers can vary not only based on the ratings business controlled by the issuer but also over the course of the business cycle. Bar-Isaac and Shapiro argue that CRAs face higher potential short-term profits from providing inaccurate ratings during good economic times as revenues from providing ratings (and ancillary services) are

---

[883] *See* Jie He, Jun Qian & Philip E. Strahan, *Credit Ratings and the Evolution of Mortgage-backed Securities*, 101 AM. ECON. REV. PAPERS & PROC. 231 (2011); *see also* Sivan Frenkel, *Repeated Interaction and Rating Inflation: A Model of Double Reputation*, 7 AM. ECON. J.: MICROECONOMICS 250 (2015); Oliver Faltin-Traeger, Kathleen W. Johnson & Christopher Mayer, *Issuer Credit Quality and the Price of Asset Backed Securities*, 100 AM. ECON. REV. 501 (2010).

[884] He et al., *supra* note 883.

greater at this point.⁸⁸⁵ And, as was mentioned previously, the dominant CRAs became far more profitable between 2002-2006, with a very large percentage of those profits derived from the structured finance business. Moreover, detecting inaccurate/noisy ratings are more difficult during good economic times given the low default rates. Finally, the cost of human capital to perform the analysis necessarily to provide accurate ratings is likely to be more costly during good economic times. In short, good economic times might be the right moment for CRAs to draw down on their reputational capital. A number of the papers we cite in the following sections look at precisely this issue: rating accuracy during the years of good economic performance and performance during the financial crisis.

5.4 Complexity and Ratings Quality

The more complex a security is to model, the more likely there is to be "noise" in the rating. This obvious observation is simply a reflection of the fact that complexity can increase the range of reasonable judgments that underlie a rating decision and, hence, increases the likelihood that different CRAs come to different conclusions. Even without a conflict of interest, differences in ratings due to genuine differences can create an incentive for rate shopping (which we will discuss in the next section). Moreover, Mathis, McAndrews, and Rochet modeling predicts that a CRA may decide to assign inflated ratings when the CRA derives a large percentage of its income from rating securities with high complexity.⁸⁸⁶

Complexity and extensive regulatory use of ratings can interact in a way that could also result in rating inaccuracy. In the model of Opp, Opp, and Harris, CRAs might rationally decide not to incur the expense of actually figuring out complex securities but rather just sell a high rating to an issuer for its regulatory benefit. In this model, investors and the market are not fooled as to the informational value of the rating, but the rating nevertheless has value due to regulatory usage.⁸⁸⁷ Consistent with this model, Stanton and Wallace document ratings inflation in the commercial MBS market for triple-A securities in

---

[885] Heski Bar-Isaac & Joel Shapiro, *Ratings Quality over the Business Cycle* (working paper, 2010), https://papers.ssrn.com/sol3/papers.cfm?abstract_id=1723259.

[886] Jérôme Mathis, James McAndrews & Jean-Charles Rochet, *Rating the Raters: Are Reputation Concerns Powerful Enough to Discipline Rating Agencies?*, 56 J. MONETARY ECON. 657 (2009).

[887] Christian C. Opp, Marcus M. Opp & Milton Harris, *Rating Agencies in the Face of Regulation: Ratings Inflation and Regulatory Arbitrage*, 108 J. FIN. ECON. 46 (2013).

response to changes in the regulatory treatment of triple-A commercial MBS.[888] When triple-A commercial MBS received significantly more favorable regulatory treatment, the value of these securities increased (yields decreased) substantially.

The issue of complexity suggests yet another difference between the structured finance and the corporate debt markets. Mark Adelson, Director of Structured Finance Research at Nomura Securities, testified before Congress: "The complexity of a typical securitization is far above that of traditional bonds. It is above the level at which the creation of the methodology can rely solely on mathematical manipulations. Despite the outward simplicity of credit-ratings, the inherent complexity of credit risk in many securitizations means that reasonable professionals starting with the same facts can reasonably reach different conclusions."[889] In other words, complexity can be more of an issue for the structured finance market.

One particular form of complexity is the lack of sufficient historical data to calibrate the parameters used for generating a rating. The ABS CDO market which performed very poorly during the financial crisis of 2007-2008 was a new market with the first ABS CDO only being issued in 1999. Calomiris discusses the limited data available on the performance subprime mortgages in a severe downtown.[890] Ashcraft, Goldsmith-Pinkham, and Vickery document that securitizations with more interest-only loans, for which historical performance data was limited, tended to perform worse during the financial crisis.[891] Benmelech and Dlugosz document that while a far smaller market, structured finance securities performed quite poorly during the 2001-2002 recession.[892]

5.5 Ratings Shopping

One widely expressed concern that could lead to ratings inaccuracy is the ability of issuers to shop for favorable ratings from different CRAs. The extent of this phenomenon could theoretically depend, among other factors, on: (i) the number of CRAs that an issuer could go to if the issuer did not like the initial rating (i.e. competition increasing the number of places to shop thereby reducing

---

[888] Richard Stanton & Nancy Wallace, *CMBS Subordination, Ratings Inflation, and Regulatory-Capital Arbitrage*, 47 FIN. MGMT. 175 (2017).

[889] Quoted in Vasiliki Skreta & Laura Veldkamp, *Ratings Shopping and Asset Complexity: A Theory of Ratings Inflation*, 56 J. MONETARY ECON. 678 (2009).

[890] Charles W. Calomiris, *The Subprime Turmoil: What's Old, What's New, and What's Next*, 15 J. STRUCTURED FIN. 6 (2009).

[891] Ashcraft et al., *supra* note 871.

[892] Benmelech & Dlugosz, *supra* note 861.

rating accuracy); (ii) likelihood of rating inaccuracy/noise at a particular CRA; and (iii) the degree to which the market uncritically relies on ratings (or in Bolton, Freixas, and Shapiro's parlance the existence of "trusting investors"[893]). As for (ii), the incentive to shop might increase if there is likely to be variation in ratings due to rating inaccuracy/noise due to factors such as complexity. As for (iii), rating shopping for an inaccurate rating presumably has more value to the shopper the extent to which the resulting rating will be accepted by the relevant investors. Importantly, Bolton, Freixas, and Shapiro model CRA rating incentives and predict outcomes in line with these three factors.[894] Their modeling assumes a duopoly CRA market structure and, moreover, that there is a segment of investors who are passive and/or uninformed investors and rely on credit ratings. In this model, these investors do not have Socratic knowledge: they don't know they don't know and just accept the rating at face value. It is worth noting that this concern with ratings shopping could still exist even if all CRAs were solely focused on providing the most accurate rating possible, i.e. there were no conflicts of interest. Different CRAs might genuinely have different views.

These three factors collectively suggest that rating shopping might be a particular issue in the structured finance market relative to other debt markets. For instance, factor (i) suggests that the issue of shopping in debt markets is less likely to be an issue as most corporate debt is routinely rated by both the dominant CRAs: Moody's and S&P. The same pattern of dual ratings does not hold as strongly for structured finance securities (although dual rating is common).

Factor (ii) indicates that to the extent there is rating inaccuracy or rating noise already, rating shopping is likely to be more of a concern. Complexity as a source of CRA disagreement will arguably be less severe for the debt than the structured finance market. As Skreta and Veldkamp model, security complexity can be an endogenous response. Issuers knowing they can rate shop more effectively with complex securities have an incentive to increase complexity for that reason.[895] Municipal bonds are an interesting example in terms of complexity. Municipal bonds tend to be quite heterogeneous giving rise to some potential complexity. If there is rating noise or inaccuracy for other reasons, perhaps due to conflicts of interest, this could also give rise to an incentive for ratings shopping.

---

[893] Patrick Bolton, Xavier Freixas & Joel Shapiro, *The Credit Ratings Game*, 67 J. FIN. 85 (2012).

[894] *See id.*

[895] Vasiliki Skreta & Laura Veldkamp, *Ratings Shopping and Asset Complexity: A Theory of Ratings Inflation*, 56 J. MONETARY ECON. 678 (2009).

Whether factor (iii) cuts in favor of being more concerned about ratings shopping in the structured finance market depends on whether one views the investor clientele effects (discussed earlier) in the structured finance market stronger than in other markets. This is not to suggest rating shopping is not possible in the corporate debt market. Indeed, Becker and Milbourn find that CRA competition (Fitch entering the market to compete with Moody's and S&P for ratings business) in the corporate debt market appears to reduce ratings quality.[896]

There have been several empirical papers on the topic of ratings shopping. Benmelech and Dlugosz found that ABS CDOs that had a single rating were more likely to be downgraded and have more severe downgrades than dual rated ABS CDOs.[897] That being said, most ABS CDOs have more than one rating (80% of the total) and it is this market that experienced the worst ratings downgrades and performance during the financial crisis. A potential counter-consideration to this observation is that even for dual rated ABS CDOs, ratings quality is impaired given that CRAs know that issuers could rate shop, thereby inducing them to provide more favorable ratings than would otherwise be the case. If this were true, then a comparison of single versus dual-rated securities would not necessarily capture the full impact of rating shopping. Adelson, Sun, Nikoulis and Manzi found that ABS rated by S&P alone were more likely to be downgraded than dual rated ABS during the 2001-2002 recession.[898] Griffin and Tang on the other hand failed to find evidence that CDOs with more than one rating performed better.[899]

5.6 Non-Model Adjustments to Ratings

The SEC report investigating credit ratings of MBS and CDOs found, among other things, that the rating agencies "made out of model adjustments and did not document the rationale for the adjustment."[900] On a related note,

---

[896] Bo Becker & Todd Milbourn, *How Did Increased Competition Affect Credit Ratings?*, 101 J. FIN. ECON. 493 (2011).

[897] Benmelech & Dlugosz, *supra* note 861.

[898] Mark Adelson, Yu Sun, Panos Nikoulis & James Manzi, *ABS Credit Migrations*, Nomura Fixed Income Research (2002).

[899] John Griffin & Dragon Y. Tang, *Did Subjectivity Play a Role in CDO Credit Ratings?* 67 J. FIN. 1293 (2012).

[900] SEC, SUMMARY REPORT OF ISSUES IDENTIFIED IN THE COMMISSION STAFF'S EXAMINATIONS OF SELECT CREDIT RATING AGENCIES 14 (2008), https://www.sec.gov/files/craexamination070808.pdf.

the SEC also found that "None of the rating agencies had specific written procedures for rating RMBS and CDOs."[901] Griffen and Tang found that for CDOs, the CRAs would regularly make a positive adjustment to its main model, resulting in a larger AAA tranche size with larger positive adjustments correlated with higher subsequent downgrades.[902] These findings suggest that the discretion created by the ability to make non-model based adjustments was problematic for these securities during this time period. One interpretation might be that there should have been more reliance on models, rather than less. Of course, the tradeoff between discretionary non-model adjustments versus more reliance on models is likely to be a complicated one, including the fact that applying a model to a particular situation might itself require judgment and hence the use of discretion.

5.7 Systematic Risk

One particular source of concern is the interaction of rating inaccuracy/noise and systematic risk. If highly rated (such as triple-A securities) of structured finance instruments, such as CDOs, are held by passive and uninformed investors who might also be risk-averse, then having these highly rated securities being substantially downgraded and falling in price all at the same time could create a systematic problem for the market. Benmelech and Dlugosz document that for CLOs, a popular type of CDO, the structures exhibited a high degree of similarity.[903] They further note that the models CRAs would use to rate CDO securities was easily available to debt issuers potentially enabling them all to arrive at similar structures that would ensure the desired rating outcome. Benmelech and Dlugosz speculate that "the uniformity of CLO structures is driven by a boiler-plate model."[904]

All this implies that if the CRA modeling is inaccurate (or for that matter the modeling is ex ante accurate but ex post ratings have to be downgraded due to unexpected states of the world), this inaccuracy will not be a one-off but rather will be reflected across CDO structures generally. So when one fails there will be many more likely to follow. This has consequences for a wide range of institutions, such as financial institutions posting these securities as collateral. It is in this context that the extensive regulatory and contractual use of ratings rears

---

[901] *Id.* at 16.

[902] Griffin & Tang, *supra* note 899.

[903] Efraim Benmelech & Jennifer Dlugosz, *The Alchemy of CDO Credit Ratings*, 56 J. MONETARY ECON. 617 (2009).

[904] *Id.* at 618.

its head again. If institutions have to dispose of their downgraded triple-A securities for regulatory or contractual reasons, if debt covenants are violated as a result of ratings downgrades, and so on, then the failure of structured finance structures due to common mistakes in ratings modeling will have additional negative knock-on, and potentially systematic, effects.

5.8 Regulatory Menu

Pulling together several major strands in the literature on CRA incentives and behavior reviewed above, it appears that concerns over ratings quality should be heightened during good economic times for complex structured instruments, especially when the securities are highly rated, given potential investor clientele effects, and when the instruments are issued by larger debt issuers. Of course one could largely surmise this by looking at the performance of highly rated structured products during the financial crisis. This is not to suggest the theoretical and empirical literature is not valuable, it is in fact crucial, but rather to note that the empirical literature is drawing broad lessons largely (although certainly not exclusively) in terms of what can go wrong from an in-depth investigation of one particular historical episode. This raises the question of whether future problems in this space are likely to be sufficiently similar. For instance, to the extent that the problem with rating accuracy for structured finance instruments was a function of limited historical data on how pools of subprime mortgages that were being structured would perform in a severe downturn (and the willingness of some investors to take those ratings at face value), this would obviously not hold true in the future.

Two further aspects of the literature are worth highlighting: the first observation is that the evidence for systematic problems with CRA ratings is far weaker with respect to the corporate and municipal debt markets.[905] The second observation is the importance of ratings for triple-A securities in the context of structured finance. These securities are of particular interest given: (1) the apparent market reliance on these ratings (presumably reflecting the nature of the investors in this marketplace); (2) the substantial academic literature questioning the accuracy of these ratings; (3) the potential implications for systematic risk arising from the similar structuring of these securities; (4) the concentrated nature of the issuers in this market; and (5) the large percentage of MBS and CDO structures (often in excess of 60% of the overall structure) that have historically been rated triple-A.

In terms of potential regulatory changes/issues, any number of possibilities have been proposed, including (but certainly not limited to):

---

[905] *See generally* Baghai et al., *supra* note 862.

(i) Upfront disclosure of any ratings received so as to combat ratings shopping;
(ii) Full removal of all regulatory uses of ratings (not just under federal law), perhaps replaced with more market-based measures;
(iii) Increased liability for CRA;
(iv) Regulatory oversight of CRA analytical methods used to generate ratings;
(v) Greater disclosure of CRA internal processes;
(vi) Movement away from the existing issuer-pays (and issuer-chooses) model, perhaps to an investor-pay model.

With respect to all these proposals as formulated above, one question is whether they are overbroad in covering the debt and municipal markets (and other debt markets serviced by the CRAs) and not just structured finance. In other words, is the evidence for credit ratings problems in these markets sufficiently severe to justify regulatory intervention? A few brief comments (offered in seriatim) on the above regulatory proposals might be helpful in demonstrating the complexity of the choice.

(i) One important set of issues here is implementation. How would "soft" conversations exploring the possibility of a rating between an issuer and a CRA be addressed? Moreover, the literature indicates that one potential issue with ratings shopping is selection of a CRA that is known to have a view that is favorable for a particular debt instrument. If this is known in advance of any actual rating being provided, then rating shopping could still occur without even "soft" conversations. Moreover, to the extent that CRAs disclose their ratings processes (see proposal (v)), this could improve the ability of issuers to select a CRA without having any interaction. Finally, in terms of the importance of such a change, one would obviously have to form a judgment as to how important overall rating shopping is as an empirical matter.

(ii) The removal of the regulatory use of ratings (as is now required under federal law) itself raises a set of important questions. First, the removal of the required use of ratings does not imply that ratings would not be used in conjunction with other evidence by regulators in forming judgments, such as in the area of prudential regulation.[906] To this extent, there would still remain a potentially important regulatory impact of ratings, as a *de facto* if not a *de jure* matter. Also, assuming decreased regulatory reliance on ratings, what implications does this have for the appropriate level of regulation of CRAs (such as proposals (iv) and (v))? Does this imply that they should be viewed as private

---

[906] *See* Lawrence J. White, *Markets: The Credit Rating Agencies*, 24 J. ECON. PERSP. 211 (2010).

market actors providing a business service or is regulation still needed given their continuing impact in the marketplace?

(iii) Putting aside any first amendment questions, increased liability (such as Section 11 liability for ratings provided in a registration statement) also raises a host of issues, including all the standard ones concerning the ability of the legal system to assess on an ex ante basis the reasonableness/appropriateness of a particular rating decision. Depending on how and when liability was imposed, increased liability could be argued to have the effect of increasing accuracy (more information) or, alternatively, reducing the willingness of CRAs to provide ratings at the margin (less information) and perhaps a bias towards lower ratings than would otherwise be the case (less information) in order to reduce disappointment ex post that could lead to litigation. So far, CRAs have successfully avoided incurring Section 11 liability despite the Dodd-Frank Act.

(iv) & (v): One important question that would need to be considered is whether regulatory imposition of a similar set of "best practices" and/or disclosure of techniques could induce greater conformity in the rating processes. This could ensure that any mistake is compounded throughout the system. Moreover, greater conformity might reduce the incentive for a firm to enter the CRA market as a new competitor if such an entrant would merely be replicating what is already currently on offer. Whether such an impact on competition is a positive or a negative is itself another difficult question as the earlier discussion on competition emphasized. One particular comment in terms of (v) is the widely expressed view that CRAs were "too" model-based at the expensive of seeing the bigger picture. The work of Griffen and Tang, however, suggests that qualitative (and perhaps ad hoc) adjustments to models were an issue. Of course no one could object to having "better" models, but this is hardly a helpful observation as a basis for policy.[907]

(vi) In terms of the investor-pays model, it is entirely possible that an investor-pays model could also suffer from conflicts of interest. If a large investor has significant stakes in a particular debt instrument a ratings downgrade might not be in the investor's interest (or a rating downgrade for a group of debt instruments that the investor owns). Or an investor might desire, in the spirit of Opp, Opp, and Harris,[908] an inflated rating for regulatory or contractual purposes (such as avoiding limits placed on the investor in terms of their holdings). On a separate note, what would be the impact of selective disclosure of ratings (disclosure to just paying investors) on price discovery in the debt markets? Obviously, investors would not pay for ratings if they are publicly disclosed

---

[907] Griffin & Tang, *supra* note 899.

[908] Opp et al., *supra* note 887.

anyway.[909] One proposal is for the SEC or some other governmental body to choose the CRA to do a particular rating with the issuer still paying. Obvious questions with this proposal are the standard ones concerning the incentives and information capacity of governmental actors and how fees in such a system would be set. One could also imagine a regulatory capture scenario with such a structure.

6 Broker-Dealers

Broker-dealers are clearly important intermediaries in the financial markets. In particular, they are important intermediaries in terms of how households and retail investors participate in the financial markets, including retirement savings, direct ownership of stock and as an important source of financial advice. There are approximately 4,000 registered-broker-dealers with some 100 million investor accounts.[910]

The central role played by broker-dealers as a financial intermediary for households and retail investors directly implicates important issues of investor protection which in turn is a core mission of both the Securities and Exchange Commission and the Financial Industry Regulatory Authority ("FINRA"), the self-regulatory organization which overseas broker-dealers subject to SEC oversight. The centrality of investor protection issues as a focal point of broker-dealer regulation is further heightened by the dual roles that broker-dealers often play as a financial intermediary: broker-dealers act as both the agent for retail investors (hence the "broker" portion of broker-dealer) and as a potential trading counterparty for retail investors' orders (hence the "dealer" portion of broker-dealer). To be sure, there are other issues besides investor protection raised by broker-dealers' role in the financial markets, such as the issue of systemic risk,[911] but these will not be covered in this section.

Not surprisingly, the original Special Study spent a considerable amount of time, resources, and ink on the topic of broker-dealers. Chapter III of the original Special Study is entitled: "Broker-dealers, Investment Advisors and their Customers – Activities and Responsibilities" and extensively covers broker-dealer sales practices. Broker-dealer sales practices are still very much relevant

---

[909] *See generally* Lawrence J. White, *Credit Rating Agencies: An Overview*, 5 ANN. REV. FIN. ECON. 93 (2013); John C. Coffee, *Ratings Reform: the Good, the Bad, and the Ugly*, 1 HARV. BUS. L. REV. 231 (2011).

[910] SIFMA, FACT BOOK (2016), https://www.sifma.org/wp-content/uploads/2017/05/sifma-fact-book-2016.pdf.

[911] *See, e.g.*, Darrel Duffie, *Failure Mechanics of Dealer Banks*, Bank of International Settlements Working Paper (2010), https://www.bis.org/publ/work301.pdf.

regulatory topics such as: the training and oversight of broker-dealers that interact with the investing public; the contours of the "suitability" requirement (the general requirement that broker-dealers only recommend securities that are suited for investors being solicited); and (mis)incentives resulting from broker-dealer commission-based compensation. Naturally, some broker-dealer issues addressed in the original Special Study are no longer relevant, most notably those arising from the fixed broker-dealer commission schedule of the day (abolished in 1975).

It is fair to say that while an important and longstanding regulatory topic, broker-dealer sales practices as a general matter have not received significant academic attention (unlike, for example, other topics we have discussed such as mutual funds and CRAs). This raises an important point concerning any future Special Study: if broker-dealer sales practices are going to be covered, as was the case before, it is likely that a significant additional amount of work would have to be undertaken to do so given the relative dearth of academic work which traditionally would serve as a starting point. That being said, there are a few areas where academic work has been done, particularly in recent years, shedding light on the interface between broker-dealers and the investing public, perhaps most notably on the important topic of the market for financial advice for retail investors.

6.1 Suitability Versus Fiduciary Obligations

The formulation and scope of the legal responsibilities owed by a broker-dealer to the investing public is just as topical today as it was at the time of the original Special Study. The original Special Study found that "some segments of the [broker-dealer] industry appear to be earnestly promoting high standards of selling while others seem only to be earnestly promoting sales" and recommended (among other things) that "greater emphasis should be given by the Commission and the self-regulatory bodies to the concept of suitability of particular securities for particular customers."[912] There have recently been a number of proposals to move from a suitability standard to a fiduciary standard for broker-dealers. For instance, the SEC in its 2011 *Study on Investment Advisors and Broker-Dealers* ("SEC Broker-Dealer Study") recommended that:

> The standard of conduct for all brokers, dealers, and investment advisers, when providing personalized investment advice about securities to retail customers (and such other customers as the Commission may by rule provide), shall be to act in the best interest of the consumer without regard to the financial or other

---

[912] Special Study (part 1) at p. 323.

interest of the broker, dealer, or investment adviser providing the advice.[913]

The SEC Broker-Dealer Study also recommended that the Commission promulgate rules and provide interpretive guidance on what this standard actually entails. The Department of Labor proposed regulations (now suspended) that impose fiduciary obligations on broker-dealers offering investment advice for assets held in IRAs.

A natural starting point before discussing proposals like this is an understanding of the current governing standards in this area. The Supreme Court's decision in *SEC v. Capital Gains*, 375 U.S. 180 (1963), decided around the same time that the original Special Study came out, held that "investment advisors" pursuant to the Investment Advisors Act have fiduciary obligations that run to their clients. This fiduciary obligation creates both a duty of care and a duty of loyalty. Under the duty of care, investment advisors must provide investors only recommendations that serve their clients' best interests. Under the duty of loyalty, investment advisors must disclose to clients any potential conflicts of interest, such potential conflicts resulting from the firm's compensation arrangements.

In contrast, broker-dealers that are not considered "investment advisors," while not having a fiduciary obligation under the *Capital Gains* decision, nevertheless have numerous legal obligations. The SEC in summarizing the regulatory purpose behind these obligations has consistently emphasized the goal of investor protection:

> The broker-dealer registration and associated regulatory requirements of the Act, as well as those of the self-regulatory organizations, provide important safeguards to investors. Investors are assured that registered broker-dealers and their associated persons have the requisite professional training and that they must conduct their business according to regulatory standards. Registered broker-dealers are subject to a comprehensive regulatory scheme designed to ensure that customers are treated fairly, that they receive adequate disclosure and that the broker-dealer is financially capable of transacting business.[914]

---

[913] SEC, STUDY ON INVESTMENT ADVISORS AND BROKER-DEALERS vi (2011), https://www.sec.gov/news/studies/2011/913studyfinal.pdf.

[914] *See* SEC, *Persons Deemed Not to Be Brokers*, SEC Release No. 34-20943 (May 9, 1984).

These broker-dealer requirements include: (1) providing only recommendations that are "suitable" for the customer; (2) complying with FINRA's "know your security" requirements; (3) ensuring that customers' orders receive "best execution"; (4) complying with broker-dealer rules governing "markups" on securities[915]; (5) acting consistent with an implied representation of fair dealing (sometimes referred to as the "shingle theory"); (6) comporting with FINRA's rules requiring broker-dealers to "observe high standards of commercial honor and just and equitable principles of trade"; (7) complying with the nontrivial registration and qualification requirements of Section 15 of the Exchange Act of 1934;[916] and (8) complying with various affirmative obligations to disclose information in conjunction with a broker-dealer recommendation.

The distinct regulatory regimes for investment advisors and broker-dealers raises two immediate questions: (1) when are broker-dealers deemed "investment advisors" and hence have a fiduciary duty under *Capital Gains*; and (2) given the host of rules that broker-dealers currently face, what conduct exactly is permitted under existing broker-dealer regulation that would be barred under a fiduciary obligation? In other words, how much of a practical difference would a move towards imposing on broker-dealers a fiduciary obligation represent? A surprising amount of the discussion swirling around various proposals to extend fiduciary obligations to broker-dealers are silent on exactly how existing broker-dealer legal obligations would be altered.

As to the first question, there are various scenarios where broker-dealers are currently deemed to have a fiduciary obligation. To generalize and simplify existing law, these include situations where the broker-dealer: (1) specifically charges separately for investment advice (as opposed to a general wrap/fee on

---

[915] See Allen Ferrell, *The Law and Finance of Broker-Dealer Mark-Ups*, (working paper, 2008), https://papers.ssrn.com/sol3/papers.cfm?abstract_id=1805131.

[916] Under Section 15, registered broker-dealers are subject to a host of compliance requirements and obligations such as "meeting certain standards of operational capability and standards of training, experience, competence, and other qualifications established by the SEC; becoming a member of a self-regulatory organization; being subject to investigations, inspections, and disciplinary actions by the SEC; complying with minimum net capital requirements, customer protection rules, specific recordkeeping, financial compliance, and financial reporting requirements. Registered Broker-Dealers are also subject to the general antifraud and anti-manipulation provisions of the federal securities laws and implementing rules, as well as specific antifraud requirements." Robert L.D. Colby, Lanny A. Schwartz & Zachary J. Zweihorn, *What is a Broker-Dealer?*, Practising Law Institute (2015).

the account) and by virtue of this fact are deemed an "investment advisor"; (2) is considered a fiduciary under state law (such as California); or (3) has investment control over a discretionary account (sometimes these take the form of a wrap account that combine brokerage and discretionary management with fees being based on assets under management). Approximately 18% of all broker-dealers are in fact registered as "investment advisors."

As to the second question, Langevoort points out that disclosure of broker compensation arrangements that give rise to conflict of interests concerns, and other information on broker-dealers' potential conflicts of interest, is the most likely candidate for situations where the existence of a fiduciary obligation might make a practical difference.[917] Consistent with this, the Investment Advisors Association letter to the SEC on fiduciary obligations identifies the following as broker-dealer obligations that do not presently exist but would under a fiduciary obligation: "Brokers recommending and selling investment products to customers would have to disclose all fees, compensation, and other incentives they earn from the advice . . . Brokers would have to disclose not only information about investment products they recommend, but also information about themselves, including conflicts of interest."[918] To take an often discussed example, a broker-dealer could arguably recommend to a customer a high-load mutual fund for which they receive undisclosed payments from the fund despite there being a more attractive alternative investment, perhaps a no-load mutual fund. In other words, the broker-dealer, perhaps out of self-interest, might recommend a high-load mutual fund that could be considered a "suitable investment" but may not be the "best investment." The high-load mutual fund type example is a scenario that has loomed large in the Department of Labor's proposed (and now suspended) fiduciary rule.

That being said, the broker-dealer suitability requirement does ensure some meaningful degree of consistency between the interests of a customer and the security being recommended. FINRA in its 2012 suitability guidance explained that the suitability rule "prohibits a broker from placing his or her interests ahead of the customer's interests" such as a "broker whose motivation for recommending one product over another was to receive larger commissions."[919] This guidance is in line with enforcement cases over the years that have repeatedly found broker-dealer recommendations to be unsuitable

---

[917] Donald C. Langevoort, *Brokers as Fiduciaries*, 71 U. PITT. L. REV. 439 (2009).

[918] Investment Advisor Association, Letter to SEC (Aug. 30, 2010) https://higherlogicdownload.s3.amazonaws.com/INVESTMENTADVISER/aa03843e-7981-46b2-aa49-c572f2ddb7e8/UploadedImages/publications/100830cmnt_BDIA.pdf.

[919] FINRA, Regulatory Notice 12-25, at 3–4 (May 2012).

because of a failure to properly factor in costs.[920] One question given this articulation of the suitability requirement (and others like it) concerns the likelihood of a divergence between the suitability requirement and what is in a customer's "best interests" under a fiduciary standard in any given set of circumstances.[921] How important are these "gaps" as a practical matter?

In terms of the overlap between broker-dealer regulation and fiduciary obligations, one could approach the question by starting with a focus on what broker-dealer's fiduciary obligations might look like. The Supreme Court long ago observed long that:

> To say that a man is a fiduciary only begins analysis. To whom is he a fiduciary? What obligations does he owe as a fiduciary? In what respect has he failed to discharge these obligations?[922]

What exactly does it mean to say that broker-dealers have a fiduciary obligation? To take an important example, how would the answer to this question be affected by the ability of a broker-dealer to act as principal in a customer's trade? The ability of a broker-dealer to act as principal gives rise to a potential conflict of interest/disclosure issues in terms of execution quality. Importantly, the Dodd-Frank Act does not appear (at least explicitly) to authorize the SEC to impose section 206(3) of the Investment Advisors Act, the provision of the Act that requires investment advisors acting as a principal to provide disclosure and customer consent for each and every transaction, on broker-dealers.[923] Presumably then, extension of fiduciary obligations to broker-

---

[920] *See, e.g.*, National Adjudicatory Council (NAC), FINRA *Department of Enforcement v. Belden* (2002), https://www.finra.org/sites/default/files/NACDecision/p006984.pdf ("We find that [the broker-dealer] made an unsuitable recommendation to his customer. [The customer's] purchase of Class B shares, instead of Class A shares, resulted in significantly higher commission costs . . .").

[921] *See* Benjamin Edwards, *Fiduciary Duty and Investment Advice: Will a Uniform Fiduciary Duty Make a Material Difference?* 14 J. BUS. & SEC. L. 105 (2014); Thomas L. Hazen, *Are Existing Stock Broker Standards Sufficient? Principles, Rules, and Fiduciary Duties*, 10 COL. BUS. L. REV. 710 (2010).

[922] SEC v. Chenery, 318 U.S. 80 (1943).

[923] *See generally* James S. Wrona, *The Best of both Worlds: A Fact-Based Analysis of the Legal Obligations of Investment Advisors and Broker-Dealers and a Framework for Enhanced Investor* Protection, 68 BUS. LAWYER 1 (2012).

dealers would not include Section 206(3) investment advisor restrictions on principal trading.

In determining the possible content of broker-dealer fiduciary obligations, the question is complicated by the tremendous variation in the size of broker-dealers (from one local office to multinational operations); the variation in the range of services provided by broker-dealers (from full-service to execution services only); the sophistication of the customers (from retail to highly sophisticated institutional actors); and the range of compensation arrangements employed (from solely commission-based to assets under management fee-based). Tellingly, the SEC Broker-Dealer Study recommends alongside an extension of the fiduciary obligation to broker-dealers that the "Commission should engage in rulemaking and/or issue interpretive guidance addressing the components of the uniform fiduciary duty." But the meaning and impact of extending fiduciary duties turns on the content of this future rulemaking/interpretative guidance making it difficult to evaluate the merits and demerits of that Study's recommendations.

The upshot of this discussion is that an important issue for a new Special Study in the area of broker-dealer regulation would be to document and identify areas where existing broker-dealer regulation and fiduciary law would likely diverge as a practical matter and then assess whether these areas of divergence are problematic and best addressed via imposition of a fiduciary obligation.

6.2 Compensation and Financial Advice

A recurring and longstanding concern with the current state of affairs is the incentive effects of commission-based brokerage compensation (the dominant form of brokerage compensation). Commission-based compensation will be defined for these purposes to include side payments from financial product providers to broker-dealers for marketing and selling their product. Concerns over brokerage compensation arrangements appear prominently in the original Special Study. The Special Study stated the concern this way:

> The general rule of commission compensation for sales efforts creates two problems: the salesman is economically motivated to persuade customers to enter into as many transactions as possible, thereby creating the danger of excessive trading or churning; he also benefits most from sales of those securities for which the rate of commission i.e. highest, and is thus motivated to recommend purchases of securities without sufficient regard for their merit or suitability for a particular customer.[924]

---

[924] Special Study (part 1) at p. 254.

Concerns over brokerage commission-based compensation has continued unabated in the fifty plus years following the Special Study. While there is still the traditional concern with the "churning" of investors' accounts induced by commission-based compensation, a broader concern is that the financial advice provided by broker-dealers might be biased as a result of compensation arrangements, such as side payments from financial product providers. The CFA Institute in a survey of its membership reported that 64% believed that the "fee structures of investment products drive their sales to customers rather than their suitability requirements."[925] (CFA 2009).

There have been from time to time over the years various proposals for moving towards a compensation regime based on fees as a percentage of assets under management, as is the case with investment advisors – approximately 95% of investment advisors are compensated based on assets under management[926] – rather than commissions and side payments for particular transactions. For example, in 2009 the UK Financial Services Authority considered a proposal requiring that "advisor firms to be paid by advisor charges: the rules do not allow advisor firms to receive commissions offered by service providers."[927] Concerns over the incentive effects of commission-based brokerage compensation became a particular focal point for the SEC during the 1990s. In particular, the Tully Committee Report of 1995 took the view that fee-based, rather commission-based brokerage compensation better aligned broker-dealer incentives.[928] These concerns led the Commission to exclude from the category of "investment advisor" many broker-dealers that used fee-based, rather than commission-based, brokerage compensation. This exclusion was motivated to a significant extent by a desire to encourage broker-dealers to adopt fee-based compensation

---

[925] CFA INSTITUTE, EUROPEAN UNION MEMBER POLL ON RETAIL INVESTMENT PRODUCTS (2009).

[926] INVESTMENT ADVISOR ASSOCIATION, EVOLUTION REVOLUTION (2014), https://www.investmentadviser.org/publications/evolution-revolution.

[927] FINANCIAL SERVICES AUTHORITY, DISTRIBUTION OF RETAIL INVESTMENTS: DELIVERING THE RDR 26 (2009), https://www.fca.org.uk/publication/consultation/fsa-cp09-18.pdf.

[928] COMMITTEE ON COMPENSATION PRACTICES, REPORT OF THE COMMITTEE ON COMPENSATION PRACTICES (1995), https://www.sec.gov/news/studies/bkrcomp.txt.

arrangements by excluding these broker-dealers from the category of "investment advisor" and therefore fiduciary obligations.[929]

Interestingly, some commentators take the opposite approach, arguing that an across-the-board imposition of fiduciary duties on broker-dealers would help address the type of undesirable incentive effects identified by the original Special Study. This approach raises several questions: first, to what extent should the focus be squarely on brokerage compensation arrangements (and/or disclosure of these compensation arrangements), rather than tackling these particular issues indirectly through the imposition of a fiduciary duty? In this connection, it is worth noting that the Dodd-Frank Act poses a potential constraint on such a backdoor approach: the Act states that a broker's commission "shall not, in and of itself, be considered a violation of [any fiduciary duty] applied to a broker-dealer." And, indeed, it has long been possible for investment advisors to charge commissions consistent with the Investment Advisors Act, although this is infrequent.

Putting aside the general policy debate over extending fiduciary obligations to broker-dealers, there has been academic work, particularly in recent years, relevant to considering broker compensation arrangements and broker-dealer provision of financial advice. The following identifies some strands of that literature:

First, there has been empirical work investigating how retail investors interact with broker-dealers and investment advisors. It appears as if investors do in fact commonly receive financial advice. Hung, Clancy, Dominitz, Talley, Berrebi, and Suvankulov report that 73% of investors in their sample consulted a financial adviser before purchasing shares or mutual funds.[930] Chater, Huck, and Inderst report in a survey that most investors in their sample were essentially ignorant of financial advisors' conflicts of interest.[931] Finally, there is some empirical evidence that investors most in need of financial advice often do not

---

[929] The SEC's rule was later vacated in 2007 by the United States Court of Appeals for the D.C. Circuit in *Financial Planning v. SEC*, 482 F.3d 4181 (D.C. Cir. 2007).

[930] Angela A. Hung, Noreen Clancy, Jeff Dominitz, Eric Talley, Claude Berrebi & Farrukh Suvankulov, *Investor and Industry Perspectives on Investment Advisors and Broker-Dealers*, RAND Institute for Civil Justice (2008), https://www.sec.gov/news/press/2008/2008-1_randiabdreport.pdf.

[931] Nick Chater, Steffen Huck & Roman Inderst, *Consumer Decision-Making in Retail Investment Services: A Behavioral Economics Perspective*, Report to the European Commission Directorate-General Health and Consumers (2010).

actually follow the investment advice actually given.⁹³² In short, while investors often receive financial advice, there are questions as to the extent to which they evaluate that financial advice in light of potential biases or necessarily even follow the advice proffered.

Second, there is evidence that financial advice can in fact be biased due to conflicts of interest. For instance, Hackethal, Inderst, and Meyer find that using a financial advisor was associated with increased turnover/churning of investor accounts.⁹³³ Interestingly, this study thus implies that investors do rely on their financial advisor, even if not necessarily to their benefit. Other papers on this topic include Anagol, Core, and Sarkar and Mullainathan, Noeth, and Schoar.⁹³⁴ Noteworthy for present purposes is the fact that these studies typically do not separately analyze broker-dealers and investment advisors.⁹³⁵

Third, there has been interesting work done analyzing the incentive effects of various compensation arrangements on financial advisors. Inderset and Ottaviani model broker-dealers' incentives to sell unsuitable financial products and find that this incentive can significantly increase when employees at a broker-dealer are paid both for finding new customers and selling financial products to customers, rather than having these tasks undertaken by different individuals at the firm.⁹³⁶ Among the most important work in this area has been that of Gabaix and Laibson, who present a model in which "myopic" customers do not realize that a financial advisor can have an incentive to sell high-priced

---

⁹³² *See* Utpal Bhattacharya, Andreas Hackethal, Simon Kaesler, Benjamin Loos & Steffen Meyer, *Is Unbiased Financial Advice to Retail Investors Sufficient? Answers from a Large Field Study*, 25 REV. FIN. STUD. 975 (2012).

⁹³³ Andreas Hackethal, Roman Inderst & Steffen Meyer, *Trading on Advice* (working paper, 2011), https://papers.ssrn.com/sol3/papers.cfm?abstract_id=1701777.

⁹³⁴ Santosh Anagol, Shawn Cole & Shayak Sarkar, *Understanding the Incentives of Commissions Motivated Agents: Theory and Evidence from the Indian Life Insurance Market* (working paper, 2013), https://papers.ssrn.com/sol3/papers.cfm?abstract_id=1978876; Sendhil Mullainathan, Markus Noth & Antoinette Schoar, *The Market for Financial Advice: An Audit Study* (working paper, 2012), https://papers.ssrn.com/sol3/papers.cfm?abstract_id=2028263.

⁹³⁵ *See e.g.*, Mullainathan et al., *supra* note 934 at 2 ("The specific advisers we are looking at in this study are retail advisers whom the average citizen can access via their bank, independent brokerages, or investment advisory firms.").

⁹³⁶ Roman Inderst & Marco Ottaviani, *Misselling Through Agents*, 99 AM. ECON. REV. 883 (2009).

financial products even though the financial advisor benefits from the high prices charged (such as through the provision of a side payment from the product seller to the broker-dealer).[937] As a result, firms will have an incentive to lower the prices that myopic customers actually observe while "shrouding" the high fees these customers actually pay. In this model, competition does not necessarily result in myopic customers being better served. Essentially, competitors who might educate the myopic customers will not benefit from these customers defecting to their firm as these customers will now know how to avoid unnecessarily high fees. In a similar vein, Inderset and Ottaviania find that when customers are naive about broker-dealer conflicts of interest, there is an incentive to increase the unobserved prices and fees charged these customers for a financial product.[938]

Interestingly, in this literature, if customers are not naive, which is to say that they understand that broker-dealers have an incentive to sell high-priced products, broker-dealers receiving side payments from financial product providers can in fact be efficiency-enhancing. Commissions based on selling a financial product can provide an incentive to broker-dealers to learn more about the financial product that they might market and sell. The possibility of earning a commission provides a financial motivation to work hard in contrast to earning a guaranteed fee based on assets under management which could induce shirking.

Putting aside incentive effects, commission-based compensation can simply be more cost-effective for some investors than a fee-based account, for example for investors that do not trade very often. Indeed, there have been enforcement cases against broker-dealers for inappropriately recommending fee-based accounts given the added expense such accounts can entail for some customers. It is also possible that commission-based accounts are not only the best choice but the only choice for some investors of more modest means. If a customer's assets under management are modest, then a fee-based account (assuming one is applying a typical percentage of assets) might not provide sufficient compensation for services rendered. Consistent with this, empirical evidence indicates that lower-wealth individuals tend to have commission-based accounts, including those with investment advisors.[939] This fact dovetails with the concern that a legal regime that makes commission-based arrangements less

---

[937] Xavier Gabaix & David Laibson, *Shrouded Attributes, Consumer Myopia, and Information Suppression in Competitive Markets*, 121 Q. J. ECON. 505 (2006).

[938] Roman Inderst & Marco Ottaviani, *How (not) to Pay for Advice: A Framework for Consumer Financial Protection,* 105 J. FIN. ECON. 393 (2012).

[939] *See* Luke Dean & Michael S. Finke, *Compensation and Client Wealth Among U.S. Investment Advisors*, 21 FIN. SERVS. REV. 81 (2012).

available could reduce the availability of needed financial advice for investors with more limited means.

In both the Gabaix and Laibson and Inderst and Ottaviania models, a critical factor in terms of the impact of a broker-dealers' potential conflicts of interest on customers is how sophisticated those customers are with respect to understanding the incentives of the broker-dealer.[940] The importance of this factor could argue for a regulatory distinction between sophisticated and unsophisticated investors (and raise the question of how well this distinction is captured by the commonly drawn regulatory distinction between institutional and retail customers). Consistent with the implications of these models, and the importance of focusing on customer sophistication, are the findings of Bergstresser and Beshears, who document that less financially sophisticated borrowers tended to purchase adjustable-rate mortgages at a higher rate, mortgages which then went on to have higher rates of foreclosure.[941]

Fourth, there has been interesting research on complexity and embedded fees in financial products relevant to broker-dealer marketing and selling practices. Consider two papers from this literature. Celerier and Vallee analyze 55,000 structured products marketed to retail investors over the 2002-2010 period.[942] They report that the more complex the structured product is, the more profitable that structured product is to the financial institution selling it and the worse it tends to perform *ex post*. Henderson and Pearson find significant overpricing of a sample of popular structured products.[943] This raises the general investor protection concern over fees being embedded in these structures.[944]

---

[940] Xavier Gabaix & David Laibson, *Shrouded Attributes, Consumer Myopia, and Information Suppression in Competitive Markets*, 121 Q. J. ECON. 505 (2006); Inderst & Ottaviani, *supra* note 936.

[941] Daniel Bergstresser & John Beshears, *Who Selected Adjustable-Rate Mortgages? Evidence from the 1989-2007 Surveys of Consumer Finances* (working paper, 2010), https://papers.ssrn.com/sol3/papers.cfm?abstract_id=1573625.

[942] Claire Celerier & Boris Vallee, *Catering to Investors through Product Complexity*, Q. J. ECON. (forthcoming).

[943] Brian J. Henderson & Neil D. Pearson, *The Dark Side of Financial Innovation: A Case Study of the Pricing of a Retail Financial Product*, 100 J. FIN. ECON. 227 (2011).

[944] *See* Jennifer E. Bethel & Allen Ferrell, *Policy Issues Raised by Structured Products*, in BROOKINGS-NOMURA PAPERS ON FINANCIAL SERVICES (Fuchita & Litan eds., 2007).

6.3 Proposals and Regulatory Menu Besides Fiduciary Duties

6.3.1 Enhanced Disclosures

One could image any number of disclosure enhancements to the existing regulatory regime. One interesting proposal was presented in a 2010 FINRA concept release. The proposal here was to require broker-dealers to make publicly available disclosures concerning potential conflicts of interest at the very outset of any advisor-customer relationship, much as investment advisors currently do on Form ADV. Imposition of such disclosures would arguably represent removing an important area of divergence between current broker-dealer and investment advisors' obligations that motivate arguments for imposition of fiduciary duties.

In the Inderst and Ottaviania model, mandatory disclosure of potential broker conflicts of interest (such as receipt of side payments) can improve investor outcomes if the disclosure turns naive investors into "wary" or sophisticated investors (investors that take into account the incentive effect these conflicts create).[945] But whether enhanced disclosure will have this salutary result (or to what extent) is non-obvious. There is room for skepticism.[946] On a behavioral note, Loewenstein, Cain and Sah show that disclosure of conflicts of interest in some circumstances could perversely actually increase the bias in financial advice with customers being more willing to follow that advice.[947] One additional consideration that bears on assessing the ability of some retail customers to become more sophisticated in light of new information is the failure of retail investors who actively trade to learn from their mistakes, such as the need for diversification. On the other extreme, it is also possible to imagine a customer reaction that overemphasizes the importance of the disclosure, such as broker-dealer receipt of side payments, at the expense of other relevant dimensions of the decision.[948]

Even with disclosures, broker-dealers could simply vertically integrate by providing both financial advice and the financial product, thereby rendering unnecessary the transfer of a side-payment. Indeed, as discussed, one of the defining features of broker-dealers is the ability to engage in transactions as a

---

[945] Inderst & Ottaviani, *supra* note 938.

[946] *See, e.g.*, Beshears et al., *supra* note 784.

[947] George Loewenstein, Daylian M. Cain & Sunita Sah, *The Limits of Transparency: Pitfalls and Potential of Disclosing Conflicts of Interest*, 101 AM. ECON. REV. 423 (2011).

[948] *See* ANDREAS HACKETHAL & ROMAN INDERST, HOW TO MAKE THE MARKET FOR FINANCIAL ADVICE WORK (2013).

principal. This observation calls into question the effectiveness of a more stringent prohibition such as a bar or limits on side-payments even if one were to put aside efficiency-enhancing reasons for such payments. Consideration of more substantive non-disclosure based regulation of broker compensation arrangements leads naturally into consideration of best execution and markup requirements as a potential regulatory tool to address potential conflicts of interest.

6.3.2 Uniformity and Investor Confusion

A common critique of existing broker-dealer regulation is the need for equal treatment of broker-dealers and investment advisors insofar as they are engaged in the same activity, i.e. providing financial advice. The SEC Broker-Dealer Study, for instance, states that its recommendations, including the proposed extension of fiduciary obligations, are "intended to make consistent the standards of conduct applying when retail customers receive personalized investment advice about securities from broker-dealers or investment advisors." But, once again, a threshold question is the actual extent of divergence between these two bodies of law as a practical matter.

Given that one is not creating a regulatory regime on a blank slate, but rather dealing with long-standing existing structures, one would need to consider whether pursuing uniformity for its own sake is worth the costs in terms of disruption and transition. And it is at least an open question as to how much uniformity can be achieved even with across-the-board fiduciary obligations given the differences between broker-dealers and investment advisors that are likely to remain, such as on the issue of principal trading and enforcement mechanisms (more of which later). It is interesting to note in this connection that SIFMA supported the adoption of a uniform standard of conduct but then stated that what conduct served the "best interest of the customer" should be based on existing case law and guidance developed under Section 206 only for investment advisors, not broker-dealers.

Related to the common argument for the need for uniformity is the argument that the existing distinction between broker-dealers and investment advisors generates investor confusion over the responsibilities of broker-dealers. Indeed, this appears to be the main empirical foundation for the SEC Broker-Dealer Study's recommendation to extend fiduciary duties. But it is hardly surprising that there is investor confusion over complex legal rules, a confusion that would surely exist regardless of whether fiduciary obligations are extended or not. The more relevant question is how regulation can be substantively improved so as to ensure better investor outcomes.

6.3.3 Enforcement

A critical component of any regulatory regime focused on financial intermediaries is examination and enforcement. Here, the differences between broker-dealers and investment advisors might be as important as any differences between existing broker-dealer obligations and the investment advisor fiduciary obligation. Interestingly, these differences can be used to argue that broker-dealer regulation is actually more demanding than that of investment advisors.

Broker-dealer examinations largely occur under the umbrella of its self-regulatory organization (SRO) FINRA. Broker-dealers are also occasionally examined by the Commission. FINRA examinations of broker-dealers can and often do lead to disciplinary action ranging from deficiency letters to loss of FINRA membership. Investment advisors, on the other hand, are examined by the SEC's Office of Compliance Inspections and Examinations. This results in significant differences in the frequency of examinations of broker-dealers relative to investment advisors. Over half of all broker-dealers are examined every year by FINRA whereas approximately 9% of investment advisors are examined by the SEC. Indeed, the ratio of assets under management by investment advisors per SEC examiner has increased from $42 billion in 2004 to $83 billion per examiner in 2010.

In terms of enforcement, there are also disparities. The SEC regularly brings enforcement actions against both broker-dealers and investment advisors. But on top of this, FINRA also regularly brings enforcement actions against broker-dealers. Wrona estimates for 2009 the total number of disciplinary actions against broker-dealers at 1,102 (SEC plus FINRA) and for investment advisors a total of 76 (SEC actions).[949] In 2016 FINRA brought a total of 1,434 disciplinary actions against registered broker-dealers and individuals. While comparing the mere number of disciplinary actions ignores important information such as the value of those actions or the resources incurred in bringing them, there does appear to be a significant gap between broker-dealers and investment advisors along the dimension of enforcement.

In considering the level of examinations and enforcement for investment advisors, it is worth bearing in mind that the size of the investment advisor universe (which includes broker-dealers registered as investment advisors) is enormous: there are approximately 11,000 firms registered as investment advisors with over $61 trillion in client assets and 27.8 million clients.[950] The nature of the clients served varies widely from pensions funds to high-net worth individuals to more typical retail investors.

---

[949] Wrona, *supra* note 923.

[950] *See* INVESTMENT ADVISOR ASSOCIATION, EVOLUTION REVOLUTION, *supra* note 926.

A potential issue for a new Special Study therefore is whether these disparities between broker-dealers and investment advisors along the dimensions of examination and enforcement are cause for concern. There have been repeated calls, starting with the Special Study itself, for investment advisors to form their own SRO with similar enforcement and examination functions that are now played by FINRA for broker-dealers. The U.S. Treasury Department in its Treasury Blueprint for a Modernized Financial Regulatory Structure likewise recommended a SRO for investment advisors.[951] The Dodd-Frank Act required the SEC to consider whether such an investment advisor SRO would improve the examination and enforcement process with the resulting SEC study arguing for augmenting resources at the SEC's Office of Compliance Inspections and Examinations.

---

[951] DEPARTMENT OF THE TREASURY, BLUEPRINT FOR A MODERNIZED FINANCIAL REGULATORY STRUCTURE (2008), https://www.treasury.gov/press-center/press-releases/Documents/Blueprint.pdf.

Chapter 8
GLOBALIZATION

John Armour,[952] Martin Bengtzen[953] & Luca Enriques[954]

1 Introduction

This chapter explores how globalization has affected the operation of securities markets and the challenges this poses for their regulation. We review the current state of the law and practice of international securities transactions and services, with a view to identifying issues where further research may usefully inform the future design of U.S. securities regulation. In so doing, we offer a framework for understanding cross-border issues in securities regulation policymaking and consider some of the most salient phenomena debated by legal scholars and financial economists, and addressed by policymakers, in recent decades. We also zoom in, by way of contrast, on some issues on which other countries have taken a notably different regulatory approach from the U.S. Our focus, in keeping with the general orientation of the New Special Study ("NSS"), is on equity markets.

We begin in Section 2 by outlining macro-level issues. Securities markets have experienced unprecedented levels of cross-border activity over the past 30 years. Three secular trends have contributed to this phenomenon of "globalization." First, liberalization: the removal of national foreign exchange controls and barriers to trade and investment. Second, the growth of collective investment, encouraged by favorable tax treatment of retirement saving. This has fostered a shift away from retail, and toward institutional, participation in securities markets. Professional asset managers have the skills and the scale to invest beyond national borders. They are also in a better position to access less

---

[952] Hogan Lovells Professor of Law and Finance, University of Oxford and Research Fellow, ECGI.

[953] DPhil Candidate, University of Oxford and Fellow in Law, London School of Economics and Political Science.

[954] Allen & Overy Professor of Corporate Law, University of Oxford and Research Fellow, ECGI. We thank Chris Bates, Edward Greene, Howell Jackson, Kate O'Rourke, Eric Pan and Joanna Perkins for valuable comments and suggestions, as well as other participants at the Initiating Conference for the New Special Study of the Securities Markets at Columbia Law School, a Sydney Law School/ASIC Law & Business Seminar and a Hebrew University Law and Finance Seminar.

liquid asset classes, such as non-publicly traded securities. The third trend has been technological: advances in information and communications technology (ICT) have enabled the digitization of business processes, increased connectivity that seamlessly links market participants regardless of their location, and allowed for the automation of processes and services. This has facilitated new order-driven markets and precipitated a gradual decline in the role of exchanges as pools of liquidity.

Together, these factors have broken the link between listing on a particular exchange and having access to the capital base originating in the country where that exchange is located. At the same time, they have increased the attractiveness of using alternative (private) forums for capital-raising. We suggest that a framework to understand international competition and coordination issues in securities law can usefully be introduced by the slogan of "investor choice." Thanks to the removal of barriers to free movement of capital, the intermediation of professional managers who have the skills and the scale to invest internationally, and the digital interconnection of markets across the globe, investors can reach all markets and issuers, regardless of where the issuers raise capital and have their securities traded, or which securities laws apply on the issuers' side.

The two subsequent Sections discuss the regulatory dynamics of international securities transactions. Section 3 considers (unilateral) rules governing market access and Section 4 looks at (bilateral and multilateral) regulatory coordination. Formerly, the well-understood dilemma in international capital-raising was that regulatory competition might pressure states to compromise domestic investor protection goals. To avoid this, international coordination was used to encourage states to align their regulatory requirements and cooperate in enforcement. Initiatives for regulatory coordination were spearheaded at the global level by the U.S. SEC (through international institutions such as IOSCO) and, on a regional level, by the EU.

However, the trends toward collectivization and connectivity have changed this picture. If domestic retail investors' funds are channeled into investment funds, international issues need no longer affect the position of these investors. Cross-border investment and capital-raising can become a dynamic between issuers and sophisticated investors—primarily the collective investment funds themselves. Sophisticated investors don't need extensive protection, and so the former trade-off with regulatory competition is lessened. Funds are consequently channeled instead through private or "wholesale" markets, relying on exemptions from ordinary securities laws for transactions with sophisticated investors. Growing global competition for listing and liquidity services is paradoxically paired with a waning significance, in policy terms, of regulatory competition. As a result, regulatory coordination seems likely to engender less enthusiasm in the future.

The remaining substantive Sections mirror topics covered by the other papers in the New Special Study. As regards primary markets, we consider in Section 5 the state of the international "market for IPOs," including case studies of the UK's Alternative Investment Market ('AIM') and U.S. private placements, the London Stock Exchange's experiments with different listing segments catering to foreign issuers of differing quality, and Asian primary markets.

In Section 6, we turn to global issues in the regulation of trading venues. We provide an overview of the trading venue options available in the U.S. and in Europe, explore three areas where EU regulation differs significantly from the U.S. (dark pools, the new concentration rule for EU broker-dealers, and high frequency trading) and reflect upon how these differences impact international markets. This segues into a discussion, in Section 7, of global regulatory issues in relation to intermediaries. Here we focus on a comparative overview of the U.S. and EU regulation of cross-border investment services relating to equity markets, the U.S. regulation of foreign broker-dealers, the implications of Brexit, and EU-style fiduciary duties for broker-dealers. A key policy question is whether and to what extent restrictions on the freedom of institutional investors to execute their trades wherever it is suitable to them and through their preferred broker-dealer wherever it is based and regulated are justified. Section 8 then considers issues of enforcement. Section 9 concludes with a discussion of implications and an agenda for future research.

Part I
The Global Dimension of Securities Markets

2 Macro-Level Issues

Global securities markets have experienced unprecedented levels of cross-border activity over the past 30 years. Three secular trends have contributed to this phenomenon of (financial) globalization: (1) *Liberalization*: in most economies, capital controls and national barriers to trade have been removed or considerably reduced; (2) *Institutionalization*: encouraged by favorable tax treatment of retirement savings, collective investment has become the dominant mode of investment in publicly traded securities; and (3) *Technologization*: advances in information and communications technology (ICT) have enabled its deployment to digitize business processes, to improve connectivity by seamlessly linking market participants, wherever located, and to automate processes and services, with corresponding reductions in transaction costs. We consider each of these in turn.

Figure 1: Global net inflows of portfolio equity, 1970-2015, $bn.

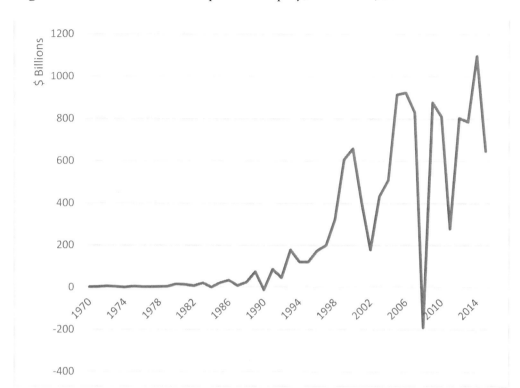

Notes: Data are from World Bank, *World Development Indicators*. Portfolio equity includes net cross-border inflows from equity securities other than those recorded as direct investment and including shares, stocks, depository receipts (American or global), and direct purchases of shares in local stock markets by foreign investors. Data are in current U.S. dollars.

2.1 Liberalization

The progressive dismantling of national barriers to capital flows since the demise of the Bretton Woods system in the early 1970s has facilitated global capital flows.[955] Figure 1 reports World Bank data on aggregate global net inflows

---

[955] For a discussion of capital account liberalization, see, e.g., MAURICE OBSTFELD & ALAN M. TAYLOR, GLOBAL CAPITAL MARKETS: INTEGRATION, CRISIS, AND GROWTH 164-68 (2004). While many barriers to cross-border investment have been dismantled, important emerging markets still deploy various tools to control capital flows and limit cross-border investment. For example, China and India both maintain capital account restrictions and limits foreign investments in certain industries.

of portfolio equity (that is, investments in liquid securities) for the period 1970-2015. Inflows for each country represent capital that is invested from abroad.[956] The global aggregate of such investment gives a rough-and-ready indication of the degree of "globalization" in relation to equity investment. As can be seen, the period from 1985-2015 was one of enormous growth in this indicator.[957]

A first channel for international activity in securities markets is for *firms* to raise capital in foreign countries. An obvious motivation for doing this is to access additional liquidity from foreign investors—the so-called "liquidity" rationale. A second goal may be for firms to opt into the disclosure and liability regimes of the "host" country in which capital is raised. Where the host country's regulation is of higher quality, or more intensely enforced, than that in the issuer's home country, this can be understood as "bonding": the firm committing itself to higher standards in order to signal that the managers have positive information about its likely performance and do not intend to expropriate investors.[958] While the bonding rationale is widely discussed in the literature, it is relevant only for a subset of cross-border capital-raising. It requires the firm to opt into a legal or enforcement regime that is clearly superior to that in the issuer's home jurisdiction. As we shall see, however, much international capital-raising is done by private placements, utilizing exemptions from regular securities laws.[959]

---

[956] The World Bank sources this data from the IMF, which defines "portfolio investment" as "cross-border transactions and positions involving debt or equity securities, other than those included in direct investment or reserve assets." *See* IMF, BALANCE OF PAYMENTS AND INTERNATIONAL INVESTMENT POSITION MANUAL ¶ 6.54 (6th ed. 2009).

[957] As can also be seen in the figure, this measure experienced tremendous volatility during the global financial crisis. This experience led the IMF to explicitly acknowledge that "[t]here is no presumption that full liberalization [of countries' capital accounts] is an appropriate goal for all countries at all times." IMF, THE LIBERALIZATION AND MANAGEMENT OF CAPITAL FLOWS: AN INSTITUTIONAL VIEW (2012), http://www.imf.org/external/np/pp/eng/2012/111412.pdf.

[958] *See, e.g.*, Craig Doidge, G. Andrew Karolyi & René M. Stulz, *Why are Foreign Firms Listed in the U.S. Worth More?*, 71 J. FIN. ECON. 205 (2004); Craig Doidge, G. Andrew Karolyi, Karl V. Lins, Darius P. Miller & René M. Stulz, *Private Benefits of Control, Ownership, and the Cross-Listing Decision*, 64 J. FIN. 425 (2009).

[959] *See, e.g.*, Howell E. Jackson & Eric J. Pan, *Regulatory Competition in International Securities Markets: Evidence from Europe in 1999—Part I*, 56 BUS. LAW. 653 (2001); Howell E. Jackson & Eric J. Pan, *Regulatory Competition in International Securities*

A second channel for international securities market activity is for *investors* to send their capital abroad, investing in firms that have issued securities under the legal and regulatory structures operative in foreign countries. Third, some sort of *international intermediation* can be offered by financial institutions. Many types of intermediation facilitate the bringing together of issuers in one country and investors in another, including international investment funds (investment funds that raise capital from domestic investors with a view to investing in foreign securities) and depositary receipts (foreign securities are purchased by an institution that then makes a market to domestic investors in claims backed by these securities). These intermediation techniques have historically often been deployed by countries to achieve some *de facto* liberalization of equity markets before official *de jure* deregulation allowed foreign investors to invest in domestic stock markets and domestic investors to invest abroad.[960] As will be further discussed in Sections 3 and 4 below, developments in securities regulation have also facilitated globalization by reducing regulatory barriers. In addition to facilitating cross-border investment for their domestic clients, intermediaries have increasingly engaged in international competition over the provision of intermediary services. In this area, U.S. global players in the broker-dealer services markets have reached a dominant position in all major financial centers.[961]

2.2 Institutionalization

The second secular trend has been the continued rise of collective investment. Figure 2 illustrates this from the standpoint of the U.S. The lines, respectively, show the ratio of the assets under management by insurance companies and mutual funds to national GDP over the period 1980-2014. Insurance company assets have more than doubled, as a proportion of GDP,

---

Markets: Evidence from Europe—Part II, 3 VA. L. & BUS. REV. 207 (2008) (collectively hereinafter Jackson & Pan, Parts I & II).

[960] *See, e.g.,* Christian Lundblad, *Measurement and Impact of Equity Market Liberalization, in* THE EVIDENCE AND IMPACT OF FINANCIAL GLOBALIZATION 35 (Beck, Claessens & Schmukler eds., 2013) (presenting data by country of their "official liberalization date," the date of the first ADR issuance from a firm in that country, and the date of introduction of the first closed-end mutual fund focused on issuers from that country).

[961] *See* Charles Goodhart & Dirk Schoenmaker, *The United States Dominates Global Investment Banking: Does It Matter for Europe?*, Bruegel Policy Contribution (2016), http://bruegel.org/2016/03/the-united-states-dominates-global-investment-banking-does-it-matter-for-europe/.

Figure 2: Growth of assets held by institutional investors in the U.S., 1980-2014.

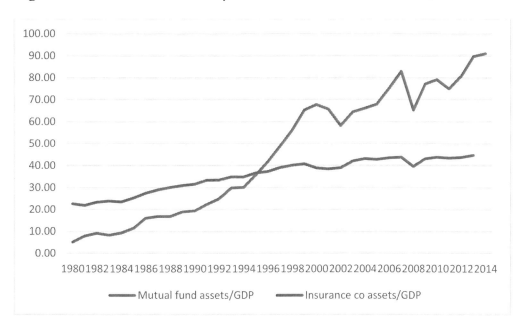

Notes: Data are from the World Bank's Global Financial Development database.

during this period. However, this increase is dwarfed by the rise in mutual fund assets, from around five per cent of GDP in 1980 to 90 per cent by 2014. Pension fund assets are only available in the World Bank time series from 1990, and so are not shown alongside, but add a further 70-80 percent of GDP.[962] Thus, assets held by these three core institutional investor types together amount to nearly twice the size of U.S. GDP. A similar long-term growth in institutional investment is also apparent in European financial systems, where the proportion of financial intermediation that takes place other than through banks has also been steadily rising, albeit starting from a smaller base.[963]

This growth in the scale of institutional investors is matched by a growth

---

[962] Institutional investors are gaining importance globally. For example, pension funds in the OECD have grown their assets from 51.8% of GDP in 2001 to 61.9% of GDP, or $30.2 trillion, in 2014. *See* OECD, ANNUAL SURVEY OF LARGE PENSION FUNDS AND PUBLIC PENSION RESERVE FUNDS 10 (2016).

[963] JAKOB DE HAAN, SANDER OOSTERLOO & DIRK SCHOENMAKER, FINANCIAL MARKETS AND INSTITUTIONS: A EUROPEAN PERSPECTIVE 283-98 (3rd ed. 2015).

Figure 3: Distribution of ownership of U.S. corporate equities, 1945-2015.

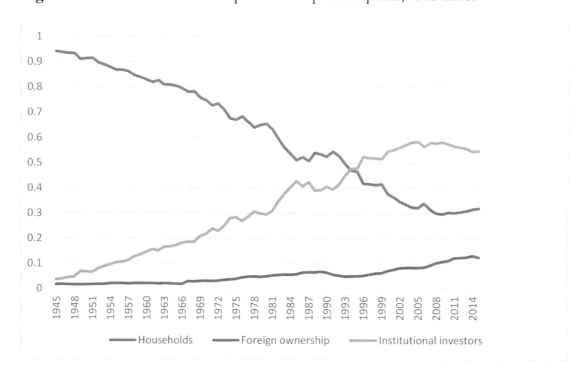

Notes: Data are taken from Federal Reserve, Financial Accounts of the United States, Table 223 (Corporate Equities), 1945-2015. Data are scaled to sum to the total value of U.S. equities outstanding.

in their significance as holders of equities in U.S. corporations. Figure 3 shows the proportion of the total value of U.S. corporations' equity stock held by different types of investor over the period 1945-2015. As can be seen, households held almost all U.S. equities at the beginning of this period, a proportion which declined to a low of 29.5 per cent in 2009. Conversely, the proportion held by institutional investors (comprising all types of investment company, pension fund, and insurance company) grew from almost nothing in 1945 to a peak of 58 per cent in 2009. Foreign ownership of U.S. equities has long been low, rising only since the financial crisis to a high of 13 per cent in 2014.

2.3 Technologization

Advances in ICT, including developments in digitization, connectivity and automation, have fundamentally reshaped international capital markets. ICT

Figure 4: Global Internet Bandwidth and its Distribution, 2008-2015.

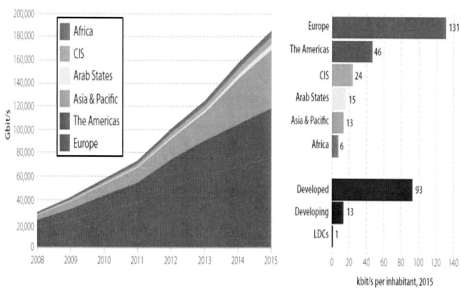

Notes: Charts are taken from ITU Facts and Figures 2016. "CIS" refers to Commonwealth of Independent States. "LDCs" refer to the world's Least Developed Countries, as defined by the United Nations.

Figure 5: Percentage of individuals using the Internet in selected countries.

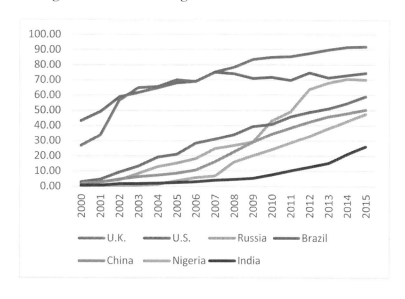

Source: ITU.

Figure 6: Mobile network coverage (estimated), by technology.

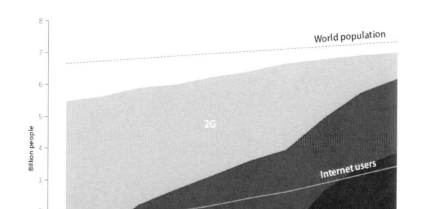

Source: ITU Facts and Figures 2016

has allowed information and capital to flow seamlessly across borders, fostering international integration.[964] As an example of the evolution in the infrastructure supporting international interconnectedness, Figure 4 shows the growth of global internet bandwidth in recent years. Total global bandwidth reached 185,000 Gigabits per second at the end of 2015, a six-fold increase on 2008, although it is distributed unevenly around the world.

Countries outside of the Americas and Europe are nevertheless catching up. Figure 5 compares internet penetration of selected countries. While Nigeria, the most populous country in Africa, had almost no internet penetration at the turn of the century, this had mushroomed to 47 per cent by 2015, equivalent to the U.S. level in 2001. Mobile broadband is growing particularly rapidly

---

[964] For early analyses of the impact of technology on securities regulation, see Donald C. Langevoort, *Information Technology and the Structure of Securities Regulation*, 98 HARV. L. REV. 747 (1985) and John C. Coffee, *Brave New World? The Impact(s) of the Internet on Modern Securities Regulation*, 52 BUS. LAW. 1195 (1997).

throughout the world,[965] such that 95 per cent of the global population now live in an area covered by a mobile network, as shown in Figure 6.[966]

As the level and speed of connectivity increases, geographical proximity decreases in importance. This allows for decentralization of existing market functions and higher levels of market participation, as new countries and investors get cheap access to international markets. Technological advances allow issuers to have their securities trading on venues abroad and investors to gain access to an increasingly international set of investment opportunities.

Automation, in turn, has dramatically changed the day-to-day operation of capital markets. Machines have replaced human beings in fundamental market functions such as market making and inter-market price arbitrage (via high frequency trading) and trading on newly available information (via algo-trading). This process is now extending its reach to investment services such as financial advice (via robo-advisors). The cost of processing data and information have plummeted, making it easier for analysts and professional investors to use big data to identify price discrepancies that human beings would have been unable to gauge.

In short, technology has increased the markets' liquidity and informational efficiency and made new trading venues competitive.[967] More specifically, it has lowered the costs of international trading by (amongst other things) allowing for instant transmission of data, automating processes to reduce the need for human involvement, improving execution quality, reducing the need for physical facilities, and increasing transparency to facilitate competition. These factors have contributed to the commoditization of trading services and allowed new entrants into markets.[968] Consequently the costs of trading international

---

[965] ITU, ICT FACTS AND FIGURES: THE WORLD IN 2015 (mobile broadband penetration grew twelve-fold between 2007 and 2015 and covered 47% of the world's population in 2015).

[966] Of course, connection speeds differ: in the U.S., the average broadband connection is at 16.3 Megabits per second ('Mbps'), with 39 per cent of connections above 15 Mbps. This compares to average connection speeds in China of 5.7 Mbps (with 1 per cent above 15Mbps), Brazil of 5.5 Mbps (with 3 per cent above 15Mbps) and world leader South Korea at 26.3 Mbps (with 61 per cent above 15Mbps). AKAMAI, Q3 2016 STATE OF THE INTERNET REPORT (2016).

[967] *See, e.g.*, Chris Brummer, *Stock Exchanges and the New Markets for Securities Laws*, 75 U. CHI. L. REV. 1435, 1464-65 (2008).

[968] *Id.*, at 1459-66; STEPHANIE HAMMER, ARCHITECTS OF ELECTRONIC TRADING: TECHNOLOGY LEADERS WHO ARE SHAPING TODAY'S FINANCIAL MARKETS 69-73 (2013).

equities have declined over time, to the point where trading in some emerging markets is reportedly cheaper than in certain established markets.[969] Nevertheless, institutional trading costs for large-cap U.S. stocks remain among the lowest in the world.[970]

At the same time, increased connectivity reinforces the trend towards collective investment and has stimulated the creation of new models for pooled investments.[971] The combination of connectivity and collective investment has made listing on a stock exchange just one of many alternative channels through which issuers can raise capital. Significant amounts of equity capital are now raised privately,[972] and shares sold in such offerings can be traded on electronic ATSs.[973]

2.4 Limits to Securities Markets Globalization

Securities markets globalization can be thought of as the process of integration of such markets across countries. While the secular trends outlined above have arguably contributed to increased integration of markets across the world, there is no single measure that allows for a definitive assessment of the extent of securities markets globalization.[974] There are, however, various metrics

---

[969] INTERNATIONAL MONETARY FUND, GLOBAL FINANCIAL STABILITY REPORT: MOVING FROM LIQUIDITY- TO GROWTH-DRIVEN MARKETS 73 (2014) (the average cost of a one-way global equity trade declined by approximately half between 2000 and 2013).

[970] James J. Angel, Lawrence E. Harris & Chester S. Spatt, *Equity Trading in the 21st Century: An Update*, 5 Q. J. FIN. 1, 19 (2015) (also providing a comparison of institutional trading costs for different markets across the world).

[971] *See, e.g.*, IOSCO, RESEARCH REPORT ON FINANCIAL TECHNOLOGIES 68 (2017) (describing how technological advances have facilitated the creation of cross-border investment platforms in Asia).

[972] *See, e.g.*, Chris Brummer, *Disruptive Technology and Securities Regulation*, 84 FORDHAM L. REV. 977, 1020-24 (2015).

[973] *See, e.g.*, Elizabeth Pollman, *Information Issues on Wall Street 2.0*, U. PA. L. REV. 179 (2012).

[974] Merritt Fox characterises "full globalization" of securities markets as involving two distinct dimensions: a price dimension (the extent to which the "law of one price" holds true between countries) and a stock ownership dimension (the extent to which investors hold globally diversified portfolios). Fox concluded in 1997 that markets were not 'fully global', particularly as regards stock ownership, but predicted a move toward full globalization if national regulators did not

that can be used to assess different aspects of the phenomenon, such as cross-border asset price correlation, international portfolio diversification (or its inverse: investment "home bias"), cross-border capital flows, as well as indices that aim to measure a country's level of openness to cross-border investment.[975] Some of these metrics have been discussed above; here, we will next briefly review the home bias phenomenon to illustrate the limits to globalization.

Across the world, investors persistently direct a larger amount of their funds to investments in their home country than is warranted by its share of the global investment portfolio. Such home bias is not easily explained by standard finance theory, which would suggest that investors should form global portfolios to invest in the most profitable projects worldwide and benefit from international diversification.[976] Measurements of home bias in recent decades suggest that although globalization has increased—reflected in a reduction in home bias over time—enough home bias remains to suggest we are still far from full globalization.[977] For example, a recent study found that U.S. investors allocated 77 per cent of their equity investments to domestic stocks, even though the U.S. only represents 33 per cent of global market capitalization.[978]

Various factors help explain why home bias persists, pointing up the current limits of securities markets globalization.[979] First, while technologization has increased the interconnectedness of countries and markets, information markets are not yet fully global, meaning local investors may find it easier to procure accurate information, understand the language of issuers' disclosures, or

---

obstruct market participants. *See* Merritt B. Fox, *Securities Disclosure in a Globalizing Market: Who Should Regulate Whom*, 95 MICH. L. REV. 2498 (1997) (hereinafter Fox, *Securities Disclosure*). For an updated discussion, *see* Merritt B. Fox, *The Rise of Foreign Ownership and Corporate Governance*, *in* THE OXFORD HANDBOOK OF CORPORATE LAW AND GOVERNANCE (Gordon & Ringe eds., forthcoming).

[975] HAL S. SCOTT & ANNA GELPERN, INTERNATIONAL FINANCE: TRANSACTIONS, POLICY AND REGULATION 22-25 (2016).

[976] *See, e.g.*, Fox, *Securities Disclosure*, *supra* note 974, at 2508-12.

[977] Nicolas Coeurdacier & Hélène Rey, *Home Bias in Open Economy Financial Macroeconomics*, 51 J. ECON. LIT. 63 (2013). Whether full globalization is desirable is a separate question that we do not attempt to answer.

[978] *Id.*

[979] The factors discussed in this paragraph are analyzed in more detailed in, e.g., Fox, *Securities Disclosure*, *supra* note 974; Coeurdacier & Rey, *supra* note 977; and Piet Sercu & Rosanne Vanpée, *The Home Bias Puzzle in Equity Portfolios*, *in* INTERNATIONAL FINANCE: A SURVEY (Baker & Riddick eds., 2012).

assess the reputation and credibility of directors and officers who write such disclosures.[980] Secondly, less-than-full liberalization may prevent foreign investors from entering certain equity markets, make entry more expensive through tax laws, or deny full exit from a domestic regime by way of prudential regulation.[981] Relatedly, national laws requiring securities to be cleared, settled, or held with local organizations may also make the administration of a global portfolio expensive, although institutionalization responds to and mitigates this concern. Fourth, investors may want to avoid the exchange rate exposure that foreign equity investment brings, or prefer local securities for their superior ability to hedge against local risk factors. Fifth, cultural factors, for example the acceptance of egalitarianism, may influence the extent to which investors confidently invest overseas.[982] Familiarity is a sixth factor: individuals invest more internationally as they get older (and presumably gain experience) and those who live in areas with a higher proportion of residents born abroad have less home bias.[983] Corporate

---

[980] This may have real effects. *See, e.g.*, Bok Baik, Jun-Koo Jang & Jin-Mo Kim, *Local Institutional Investors, Information Asymmetries, and Equity Returns*, 97 J. FIN. ECON. 81 (2010) (finding, based only on intra-US data, that local institutional investors have a significant information advantage over non-local investors and execute more profitable trades).

[981] *See* Zsolt Darvas & Dirk Schoenmaker, *Institutional Investors and Home Bias in Europe's Capital Markets Union* (working paper, 2017), http://bruegel.org/2017/03/institutional-investors-and-home-bias-in-europes-capital-markets-union/ (finding that home bias is positively related to prudential restrictions on pension funds' foreign investment as measured by the OECD, and that larger pension funds display less home bias). For recent data on the state of foreign ownership restrictions, see UNCTAD, WORLD INVESTMENT REPORT 2016, Chapter IV (presenting data that 78 per cent of countries globally have at least one industry where foreign equity ownership is limited below 50 per cent, while the figure is 100 per cent in Europe and 64 per cent in Africa). *See also* OECD, IS INVESTMENT PROTECTIONISM ON THE RISE? EVIDENCE FROM THE OECD FDI REGULATORY RESTRICTIVENESS INDEX (2017), http://www.oecd.org/investment/fdiindex.htm.

[982] Jordan I. Siegel, Amir N. Licht & Shalom H. Schwartz, *Egalitarianism and International Investment*, 102 J. FIN. ECON. 621 (2011); Jordan I. Siegel, Amir N. Licht & Shalom H. Schwartz, *Egalitarianism, Cultural Distance, and Foreign Direct Investment: A New Approach*, 24 ORG. SCIENCE 1174 (2013).

[983] Geert Bekaert, Kenton Hoyem, Wei-Yin Hu & Enrichetta Ravina, *Who is Internationally Diversified? Evidence from the 401(k) Plans of 296 Firms*, 124 J. FIN. ECON. 86 (2017).

law and governance rules may present another factor of significance: in countries where corporate insiders or the government can appropriate value from outside investors, large local shareholders may be the optimal way to control agency costs.[984] Finally, it is not necessarily the case that investors suffering from home bias are suffering at all. An empirical study found that investors with more concentrated holdings earned higher risk-adjusted returns—a finding that supports the proposition that investors have an information advantage in their local markets and thus rationally prefer to invest there.[985]

It may be helpful to keep these various frictions in mind, as we later note other phenomena that might not be expected under full globalization. For example, depositary receipts and cross-listings on foreign stock exchanges, which are frequently observed, would not add value in a world of full globalization, but they presumably provide relatively efficient solutions to reduce frictions in international securities markets today.

3 Market Access and Unilateralist Approaches to Cross-Border Securities Regulation

Cross-border capital-raising, investment, and investment services pose questions of regulatory interface. We can characterize the core question for regulatory policy as a jurisdiction's approach to *market access*. In this section, we focus on unilateral approaches to cross-border securities regulation, that is, how an individual jurisdiction may set its own rules in isolation from others, while in Section 4 we turn to bilateral and multilateral approaches, based on international cooperation.

Countries are free in principle to make their rules about international securities market access as liberal or restrictive as they wish. Public-interest minded policymakers tend to prioritize concerns related to investor protection and capital formation. As regards investors, policymakers may wish to avoid exposing domestic investors to international investment risks from which local regulation would protect them vis-a-vis domestic securities. On the other hand, policymakers may also care that domestic investors have available to them as large a pool of potential investment opportunities as possible. Turning to capital formation concerns, there may be a desire to stimulate inward investment from foreign investors, if domestic savings are insufficient to meet domestic firms' demands for finance.

---

[984] Rene M. Stulz, *The Limits of Financial Globalization*, 60 J. FIN. 1595 (2006).

[985] Nicole Choi, Mark Fedenia, Hilla Skiba & Tatyana Sokolyk, *Portfolio Concentration and Performance of Institutional Investors Worldwide*, 123 J. FIN. ECON. 189 (2017).

However, policymakers may also cater to special interests: they may seek to channel domestic investment to domestic firms, to which cause national securities law rules may be conscripted to serve. While capital constraints of this latter type were largely abandoned in the last quarter of the twentieth century, they may yet enjoy renewed interest given the recent resurgence of economic nationalism. Similarly, policymakers may take the financial services industry's interests to heart. Although it is in society's interests to have a competitive financial sector, if attracting foreign business for the domestic securities industry becomes a goal in itself, then the main concern becomes the maximization of the finance industry's profits—and the associated tax revenues. That may well be at odds with the goal of protecting domestic investors, and even with the goal of facilitating capital formation for domestic issuers.[986] It therefore tends to be pursued most aggressively in "finance hubs": jurisdictions for which the scale of the finance industry is large relative to the economy at large. Such financial centers compete internationally in markets for listings on stock exchanges and for liquidity services—whether on stock exchanges or other trading venues.

The trend towards institutionalization of investment enables a new sort of balance to be struck between the interests of the real economy and those of the financial sector. Investment institutionalization means investor protection can be focused on the point at which investors' funds enter collective vehicles. Investments *by* such funds are then made as sophisticated investors, who do not need the protections provided for retail investors. This implies that the quality of the legal regime under which issuers operate becomes less important, as institutions are better able to do their own due diligence and insist on appropriate protections.[987] Moreover, increasingly large pools of liquidity can be tapped through exemptions available only to sophisticated investors, giving rise

---

[986] A striking recent example is the UK FCA's proposal for a new subcategory of premium listings for "sovereign controlled companies," which would involve disapplying rules requiring a shareholder vote for related party transactions as between such a company and its sovereign controlling shareholder. *See* FINANCIAL CONDUCT AUTHORITY, PROPOSAL TO CREATE A NEW PREMIUM LISTING CATEGORY FOR SOVEREIGN CONTROLLED COMPANIES, Consultation Paper CP17/21 (2017), https://www.fca.org.uk/publications/consultation-papers/cp17-21-proposal-create-new-premium-listing-category-sovereign. This seems quite transparently directed towards encouraging Saudi Aramco to list in London. *See, e.g.*, Caroline Binham, Dan McCrum & Hannah Murphy, *London Reforms Set to Open Door for Saudi Aramco Listing*, FIN. TIMES, Jul. 13, 2017.

[987] *See* Craig Doidge, G. Andrew Karolyi & René M Stulz, *The U.S. Left Behind? Financial Globalization and the Rise of IPOs Outside the U.S.*, 110 J. FIN. ECON. 546, 548 (2013).

Figure 7: Inbound and outbound capital market access

Outbound market access: domestic investors buying securities abroad; domestic issuers raising funds abroad.

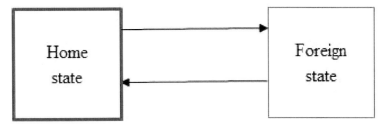

Inbound market access: foreign issuers raising funds from domestic investors; foreign investors buying domestic securities.

International intermediation: intermediary raises funds from domestic investors and buys securities from foreign issuers.

to a whole range of "private capital markets." Facilitating the operation of such private markets provides a parallel channel through which larger countries can pursue business for their domestic securities industry, without harming domestic retail investors. Such private markets carry few regulatory compliance obligations, making them a low-cost option for foreign issuers. At the same time, if more foreign firms tap a country's private markets, there is less need for sophisticated investors from that country to make investments abroad, as opposed to through domestic private markets.

In the following sections, we discuss regulatory choices on market access by distinguishing between *inbound* and *outbound* market access, as illustrated in Figure 7. Inbound market access is concerned with the extent to which foreign firms are permitted to raise capital from, or to provide investment services to, domestic investors. Outbound market access is concerned with the extent to which, on the one hand, domestic investors are permitted to invest in securities that are only traded abroad and, on the other, domestic issuers are permitted to raise capital abroad without triggering the application of their own domestic rules. While this twofold distinction is necessarily an over-simplification—the role of intermediaries blurs the line between the two categories—we offer it here as an organizing heuristic for expositional purposes.

3.1 Inbound Capital-Raising and Local Compliance

A simple position to take for inbound market access is that foreign issuers and intermediaries wishing to offer securities and investment services to domestic investors must comply with the entire body of domestic securities regulation. This *local compliance* model, better-known as "national treatment,"[988] ensures that domestic investors receive seamless protection, independent of the origin of the securities and the investment services they are offered. With due qualifications, most countries—including the U.S.—have traditionally taken this approach.[989]

Local compliance is costly for foreign firms: if they are also raising capital in their own jurisdiction or are subject to their own state broker-dealer rules, they must comply with two sets of regulatory requirements.[990] This cost may cause foreign firms to forego capital-raising and business opportunities in jurisdictions enforcing local compliance, reducing the range of investment opportunities for those jurisdictions' domestic investors. Where the domestic economy is large, this approach may be readily justifiable. It is reasonable to assume that the amount of domestic capital for investment, and the number of domestic investment opportunities, are both increasing functions of the overall size of the economy.[991] In this case, the marginal gain to domestic investors from permitting capital to be raised by foreign firms is only a modest increase in diversification. At the same time, a large pool of domestic capital for investment will make the

---

[988] Hal S. Scott, *International Finance: Rule Choices for Global Financial Markets*, in RESEARCH HANDBOOK IN INTERNATIONAL ECONOMIC LAW 361, 370-86 (Guzman & Sykes eds., 2007); IOSCO, TASK FORCE ON CROSS-BORDER REGULATION, FINAL REPORT 6 (2015), http://www.iosco.org/library/pubdocs/pdf/IOSCOPD507.pdf.

[989] *See, e.g.*, Chris Brummer, *Territoriality as a Regulatory Technique: Notes from the Financial Crisis*, 79 U. CIN. L. REV. 499, 502-3 (2010).

[990] Of course, foreign entrepreneurs may decide simply to found and grow their firms in the market where the largest pool of capital is available. For discussion of this in relation to innovative start-up firms, see Edward B. Rock, *Greenhorns, Yankees, and Cosmopolitans: Venture Capital, IPOs, Foreign Firms, and U.S. Markets*, 2 THEO. ENQ. L. 711 (2001).

[991] For countries that have relatively large financial services sectors (that is, finance hubs), the trade-off is rather different. Finance hubs are likely to be more concerned to attract foreign firms as a way of generating business for their financial sectors, and less concerned about the welfare of their domestic investors.

potential gains to foreign firms from inbound market access relatively large. Consequently, they will be willing to incur compliance costs to do so.

In any event, where the domestic regime has high-quality rules and/or enforcement, then compliance can allow foreign firms from jurisdictions with weaker securities regimes to "bond" themselves to high standards of behavior vis-à-vis their investors.[992] Consequently, for well-designed and enforced securities regimes, local compliance may be expected to *attract* high-quality foreign issuers for which the additional regulatory costs are more than offset by the reduction in cost of capital obtained by credibly signaling their quality to investors. This is also consistent with protecting domestic investors.

Local compliance regimes are subject to various exemptions, to which we now turn.

Exemptions specifically for foreign firms. Where regulators provide exemptions specifically to foreign firms, this seems hard to explain in investor-facing terms. Were the goal the broadening of investment opportunities, there would be no reason to treat foreign issuers—the monitoring of which by domestic investors is intuitively more difficult—more leniently than domestic ones. Nevertheless, many jurisdictions offer such exemptions. For example, in the U.S., companies qualifying as "foreign private issuers" (FPIs) that have securities registered with the SEC are granted several exemptions from domestic securities regulation, including the proxy rules, the requirement to file quarterly reports, and Regulation Fair Disclosure.[993] In the UK, the practice until 2010 was to have a special market segment for foreign firms known as "secondary listing," to which corporate governance and related party transaction provisions did not apply.[994]

Exemptions for transactions with sophisticated investors. Another important set of exemptions relate to transactions with investors sophisticated enough to fend for themselves. Such investors (that is, institutional investors and high net-worth individuals), enjoy economies of scale in purchasing investment advice and can make investments in a much more informed way. Similarly, sophisticated investors' large asset portfolios mean that access to foreign investments is significantly more valuable to them than to retail investors. Such exemptions permit a jurisdiction to attract foreign issuers consistently with investor protection at home. The rise of institutional investors makes these exemptions of growing significance in practice.

Exemptions for particular jurisdictions. Another way to condition waivers of local compliance obligations is by reference to the quality of foreign regulation

---

[992] *See also infra* Section 5.2.

[993] Rule 3a12-3 under the Exchange Act (proxy rules), Rule 101(b), 17 CFR 243.101 (Regulation FD).

[994] *See infra* Section 5.3.

applying to issuers or intermediaries. This approach is known as "substituted compliance" in the U.S.,[995] and "equivalence" in the EU.[996] This involves domestic authorities performing an assessment of the quality of foreign regulatory environments, and granting exemptions where they are comparable to the local regime. The idea is that local investors can then be confident that the foreign regime provides equivalent, or substituted, protection. If the regimes really are equivalent, then purchasing securities or services in the foreign jurisdiction should expose local investors to no higher risks of fraud or misbehavior than if they dealt with domestic issuers and intermediaries. This approach has been applied quite widely by the EU since the financial crisis, including, for example, in relation to prospectuses for securities offers.[997] However, examples can also be found in U.S. securities laws[998] and elsewhere.[999]

3.2 Outbound Capital-Raising

Issuers may tap domestic capital markets, foreign ones, or both. They may engage in domestic and/or in foreign offerings and, relatedly, may list on a domestic and/or a foreign trading venue. In doing so, they usually choose the applicable securities law as well. This introduces an element of regulatory

---

[995] *See e.g.*, Ethiopis Tafara & Robert J. Peterson, *A Blueprint for Cross-Border Access to U.S. Investors: A New International Framework*, 48 HARV. INT'L L.J. 31 (2007); Howell E. Jackson, *A System of Selective Substitute Compliance*, 48 HARV. INT'L L.J. 105 (2007); Howell E. Jackson, *Substituted Compliance: The Emergence, Challenges, and Evolution of a New Regulatory Paradigm*, 1 J. FIN. REG. 169 (2015).

[996] John Armour, *Brexit and Financial Services*, 33 OXFORD REV. ECON. POL'Y S54 (2017); Eilís Ferran, *The UK as a Third Country Actor in EU Financial Services Regulation*, 3 J. FIN. REG. 40 (2017).

[997] Prospectus Directive 2003/71/EC, Art. 20; Proposed Prospectus Regulation COM (2015) 583 final, Art. 27.

[998] These include the concept of a "designated offshore securities market," a status accorded to a foreign market by the SEC based on various substantive regulatory and oversight requirements: SEC Regulation S, 17 CFR § 230.902(b).

[999] For instance, Israeli regulations allow Israeli and foreign companies listed on Nasdaq, NYSE, and the London Stock Exchange to dual list and conduct offerings in Israel without subjecting to Israeli securities law. *See* ISA, *Dual Listing*, http://www.isa.gov.il/sites/ISAEng/Supervised%20Departments/Public%20Companies/Dual_Listing/Pages/default.aspx.

arbitrage,[1000] which the macro trends we have highlighted in Section 2 only make more salient: liquidity pools are more mobile, and ICT makes foreign listing cheaper. Nevertheless, policymakers may subject domestic firms that choose to list abroad to local compliance—even firms that do not enter the domestic primary market—whenever a given number of domestic investors come to hold those firms' securities.[1001] This may act as a curb to outbound capital raising when, as was the case in the U.S. until recently, it is impossible for a firm to stay below the relevant thresholds without sacrificing key governance arrangements, such as broad-based equity compensation policies.[1002]

3.3 Cross-Border Investment

Ever since capital controls were abandoned in the late twentieth century, there has been little restriction on outbound market access for capital, that is, on the ability of domestic investors to invest abroad: most jurisdictions, including the U.S. and the EU, take the view that if investors wish to pursue opportunities abroad, then it is disproportionate to try to prevent them from doing so.[1003] The traditional justification for this was that retail domestic investors were unlikely to purchase foreign securities: the search costs and generally the transaction costs were simply too high to make this a common phenomenon worthy of policymakers' attention.

The rise of institutional investment and of connectivity has profoundly changed the dynamics of offshore investing. Thanks to the size and scope of their investment business, sophisticated institutions can make offshore

---

[1000] Brummer, *supra* note 967, at 1449.

[1001] Registration with the SEC is triggered, under section 12(g)(1) of the Securities Exchange Act, when a firm has more than $10 million in assets and its shares are held of record by either 2,000 persons or 500 persons who are not accredited investors. Note that subjecting domestic issuers to securities regulation even when they only tap foreign markets may be justified, if its rationale is to ensure efficiency through better allocation of capital and reduced intra-firm agency costs. *See* Fox, *Securities Disclosure*, *supra* note 974 at 2582.

[1002] In May 2016, the SEC amended its Rule 12g5-1 to exclude from the calculation of the number of holders of record (which mandates Exchange Act registration when exceeding specified thresholds) employees that hold securities received under an employee compensation plan. 17 CFR § 240.12g5-1.

[1003] This is provided that securities of foreign firms and related services are not marketed to domestic investors within domestic territory, which would otherwise prompt local compliance.

Figure 8: U.S. mutual fund inflows and net equity portfolio inflows in the U.S. and EU, 1980-2014

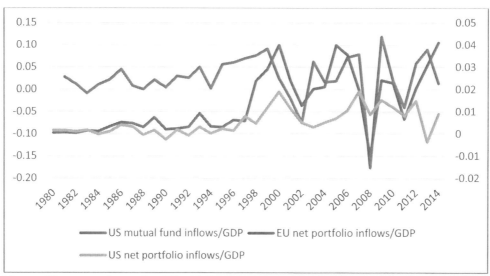

Notes: Data are from the World Bank's Global Development Indicators (GDP and net portfolio inflows) and Global Financial Development (mutual fund holdings).

investments at a relatively low cost and—thanks to ICT—at a low informational disadvantage to foreign investors and traders.[1004] Correspondingly, in primary markets, U.S. institutions can invest in foreign-issued securities with no U.S. listing by participating in private placements of securities admitted to trading on foreign trading venues: liquidity will be ensured on the foreign venues that issuers have chosen. This means that the traditional picture described in relation to inbound access for public markets—whereby a large economy such as the U.S. can rely on the size of its domestic pool of liquidity to make it worthwhile for foreign firms to list on its exchanges and therefore to comply with local regulation—has been undermined. Foreign firms can tap U.S. capital markets without engaging in a U.S. public offering and without listing on a U.S. exchange. And even in the absence of a private placement in the U.S., foreign firms' securities will be accessible to U.S. institutional investors via secondary trading on any main stock exchange or trading venue.

Figure 8 illustrates some interesting apparent implications of this trend. It shows (blue line) the net annual inflows of assets under management by U.S. mutual funds, scaled for U.S. GDP. The orange and grey lines, respectively, show annual inflows of portfolio equity in the EU and U.S., also scaled for GDP.

[1004] Brummer, *supra* note 967, at 1461.

What is interesting is the correlation, since the turn of the century, between the inflows to the U.S. mutual fund sector and to EU portfolio equity.[1005] This is consistent with U.S. mutual funds having become an increasingly important source of equity investment for the EU.

3.4 Extraterritorial Financial Regulation and Systemic Risk

Especially since the financial crisis, the U.S. and the EU have made certain aspects of financial regulation applicable on an extraterritorial basis. This means that the rules apply to the activity in question wherever located in the world, and not just in U.S. or EU territories, respectively. Extraterritoriality, which goes against principles of international comity, has been justified in these instances by the need to maintain *financial stability*. These rules apply to aspects of the activity of firms that could have a systemic impact in the U.S. or the EU. Extraterritoriality is deployed in particular for rules governing to OTC derivatives, except where the relevant authorities satisfy themselves of the equivalence of another jurisdiction's regime.[1006] However, given the focus of the New Special Study on equity markets, we do not here consider the implications of extraterritoriality in OTC derivatives markets.[1007]

Core securities laws aimed at "investor protection" and focused on equity and other securities markets have a much less direct connection with systemic risk. One consequence of this is that securities regulators did not focus as much on systemic risk before the global financial crisis as did prudential regulators. As legislators and regulators drew lessons from the crisis, however, the need to reduce systemic risk became an important rationale for new initiatives also in securities regulation. IOSCO, for example, revised its "Objectives and Principles

---

[1005] The correlation coefficient for U.S. mutual fund inflows and EU portfolio equity inflows for 1981-2014 is 0.42, rising to 0.66 for 2000-2014.

[1006] *See* § 722(d), Dodd Frank Act (Commodity Exchange Act provisions relating to swaps have extraterritorial reach); Articles 4, 9, 10 and 11, Regulation (EU) No 648/2012 of the European Parliament and of the Council of 4 July 2012 on OTC derivatives, central counterparties and trade repositories, O.J.E.U. L201/1 (2012) (known as the European Markets Infrastructure Regulation or "EMIR") (similarly applying OTC derivatives rules to transactions involving non-EU counterparties).

[1007] For discussion of such matters, see, e.g., Alexey Artamonov, *Cross-Border Application of OTC Derivatives Rules: Revisiting the Substituted Compliance Approach*, 1 J. FIN. REG. 206 (2015).

of Securities Regulation" to increase the focus on systemic risk reduction.[1008] Building on joint work by the FSB, IMF, and BIS,[1009] IOSCO documented sources of systemic risk in securities markets, highlighted factors that securities regulators should monitor, and reviewed regulatory tools that may be useful in combating systemic risk.[1010] In the U.S., systemic risk was a key rationale for the introduction under the Dodd-Frank Act of 2010 of new frameworks for financial market utilities (systems for transfer, clearing, and settlement), disclosure requirements on investment advisers to private funds, the orderly liquidation of systemically important broker-dealers, and the Volcker rule that prohibits banks from engaging in proprietary trading.[1011]

The need to mitigate systemic risk is arguably a strong rationale for extraterritorial regulation, but it has not historically been a prominent justification in the U.S. Until 2010, most U.S. courts applied a conduct and an effects test to determine whether the U.S. prohibition of securities fraud applied

---

[1008] *See* Press Release, IOSCO, Global Securities Regulators Adopt New Principles and Increase Focus on Systemic Risk (June 10, 2010), https://www.iosco.org/news/pdf/IOSCONEWS188.pdf. IOSCO also created a research department tasked with establishing a methodology for securities regulators to monitor and mitigate systemic risk, and now publishes annual reports assessing risks in the securities markets. *See* Werner Bijkerk, *Systemic Risk Research at IOSCO* (2011), https://www.iosco.org/research/pdf/Introduction_to_Research_at_IOSCO.pdf.

[1009] FINANCIAL STABILITY BOARD, INTERNATIONAL MONETARY FUND & BANK FOR INTERNATIONAL SETTLEMENTS, REPORT TO G20 FINANCE MINISTERS AND GOVERNORS: GUIDANCE TO ASSESS THE SYSTEMIC IMPORTANCE OF FINANCIAL INSTITUTIONS, MARKETS AND INSTRUMENTS: INITIAL CONSIDERATIONS (2009), http://www.bis.org/publ/othp07.pdf.

[1010] IOSCO, MITIGATING SYSTEMIC RISK: A ROLE FOR SECURITIES REGULATORS (2011), http://www.iosco.org/library/pubdocs/pdf/IOSCOPD347.pdf. IOSCO subsequently mapped the various practices employed by securities regulators to identify and assess systemic risk. *See* IOSCO, RISK IDENTIFICATION AND ASSESSMENT METHODOLOGIES FOR SECURITIES REGULATIONS (2014).

[1011] For an overview of the SEC's work on systemic risk reduction and its role under the Dodd-Frank Act, see TESTIMONY OF MARY JO WHITE ON MITIGATING SYSTEMIC RISK IN THE FINANCIAL MARKETS THROUGH WALL STREET REFORMS, UNITED STATES. CONG. SENATE. COMMITTEE ON BANKING, HOUSING, AND URBAN AFFAIRS. (July 30, 2013), https://www.sec.gov/news/testimony/2013-ts073013mjw#_ftn6.

to transactions carried out beyond U.S. territory.[1012] While that interpretation was quashed by the Supreme Court in *Morrison*,[1013] a provision was added to the Dodd-Frank Act, late in the legislative process, that attempted to revive the antifraud rule's extraterritorial reach. Section 929P(b) of the Dodd-Frank Act purports to extend U.S. courts' jurisdiction to actions brought by the SEC or the Department of Justice for extraterritorial violations that have a connection with the U.S. according to a conduct or an effects test, in line with the case law prior to *Morrison*, but its extraterritorial reach is subject to uncertainty and debate.[1014] Further, the transactional approach in *Morrison* may be inadequate or insufficient from the perspective of preventing systemic risk – an issue to which we will return in Section 9, where we propose a research agenda.

4 Regulatory Coordination in Securities Regulation

Regulatory coordination in securities regulation can take a variety of forms, ranging from relatively modest cooperation in enforcement among securities regulators to full-scale convergence in substantive rules. The grant of exemptions from local compliance conditional on foreign regimes demonstrating equivalent levels of regulation and oversight can be used as a means of encouraging such coordination, especially in the hands of larger players.

A number of steps have been made towards cross-jurisdictional cooperation in securities regulation over the past 40 years, often at the initiative

---

[1012] For references to prior case law, see *Morrison v. National Australia Bank*, 561 U.S. 247, 255-61 (2010).

[1013] *Id.*

[1014] This uncertainty relates to the new provision's potential failure to address the actual issue in the *Morrison* holding. In *Morrison*, the Supreme Court declined to apply the 1934 Act extraterritorially because of a lack of Congressional intent for extraterritorial application – a merits issue, while § 929P, read literally, grants subject-matter jurisdiction, which *Morrison* had explicitly recognized. 561 U.S. at 253-4. Consequently, it has been suggested that § 929P might be "'stillborn' in that it conferred jurisdiction that could not be used for anything substantive—in cases without a U.S. securities transaction—until a further statute were enacted." Richard W. Painter, *The Dodd-Frank Extraterritorial Jurisdiction Provision: Was it Effective, Needed or Sufficient?*, 1 HARV. BUS. L. REV. 195, 208 (2011); see also Edward Greene & Arpan Patel, *Consequences of* Morrison v. NAB, *Securities Litigation and Beyond*, 11 CAPITAL MKTS. L.J. 145 (2016). *But see* SEC v. Traffic Monsoon, LLC, No. 2:16-cv-00832-JNP, 2017 WL 1166333 (D. Utah Mar. 28, 2017) (interpreting § 929P to provide congressional intent for extraterritorial application).

of the U.S. SEC. Nevertheless, such cooperation has delivered fewer meaningful achievements in the field of securities regulation than in other segments of financial regulation. The simple explanation is that the inter-jurisdictional externalities that may derive from securities regulation, at least as far as equity markets are concerned, are far less dramatic than those stemming from failures in prudential regulation. States' incentives to compromise and to adapt to other regulatory frameworks in multilateral negotiations are correspondingly weaker.

Historically, what prompted international cooperation in securities regulation was the need for assistance from foreign regulators in enforcement: the detection and investigation of securities fraud—more specifically, insider trading—on U.S. markets.[1015] The realization that there would be no way to find out who lay behind trades originating from anonymous Swiss bank accounts unless Swiss authorities agreed to cooperate led the U.S. SEC to push for such agreements. That, in turn, required at least a minimum degree of convergence in substantive rules: without it, and specifically, without the global adoption of insider trading prohibitions, cooperation in enforcement would have been much harder to achieve.

In fact, the criminalization of insider trading is perhaps the most visible attainment in the quest for regulatory convergence that started in the 1980s.[1016] Of course, the nitty-gritty details of securities laws still diverge widely, as reflected by the general vagueness of multilateral codes of conduct and best practices such as IOSCO's,[1017] not to mention the gap in enforcement intensity between the U.S. and virtually all other jurisdictions.[1018] Even so, most jurisdictions now have laws on their books that reflect the core pillars of U.S. securities regulation: a ban on insider trading and securities fraud, mandatory disclosures in the case of public offerings and, on an ongoing basis, for corporations with publicly traded securities, and rules on broker-dealers and mutual funds.[1019]

[1015] *See, e.g.*, James D. Cox, *Coping in a Global Marketplace: Survival Strategies for a 75-Year-Old SEC*, 95 VA. L. REV. 941, 984 (2009).

[1016] *See, e.g.*, Utpal Bhattacharya & Hazem Daouk, *The World Price of Insider Trading*, 57 J. FIN. 75 (2002).

[1017] Pierre-Hugues Verdier, *The Political Economy of International Financial Regulation*, 88 INDIANA L.J. 1405, 1451 (2013).

[1018] Howell E. Jackson & Mark J. Roe, *Public and Private Enforcement of Securities Laws: Resource-Based Evidence*, 93 J. FIN. ECON. 207 (2009); John C. Coffee, Jr., *Law and the Market: The Impact of Enforcement*, 156 U. PENN. L. REV. 229 (2007).

[1019] *See generally*, Laura Nyantung Beny, *Do Insider Trading Laws Matter? Some Preliminary Comparative Evidence*, 7 AM. L. & ECON. REV. 144 (2005); Rafael La

A number of factors have contributed to this convergence. First, many jurisdictions—in Europe and elsewhere—saw this as a route to boost their equity markets and attract investment from abroad. In other words, regulatory emulation was at play.[1020] Second, the World Bank and the IMF prompted East Asian countries to overhaul their financial regulations and corporate laws following the 1997 crisis,[1021] and more generally insisted on the adoption of core common principles in their regular consultations with member states.[1022] Finally, the U.S. SEC used international fora, such as IOSCO, to press for convergence.[1023]

In fact, one important impetus for such convergence has been the work of international financial institutions and standard setters. An additional driver of convergence has been reciprocal arrangements over market access. The most ambitious experiment to date is the multilateral "passporting" facilitated within the EU, but reciprocal arrangements also exist outside the EU. In the subsections that follow, we consider international institutions and reciprocal arrangements, including within the EU, and then reflect on the prospects for further international coordination.

Porta, Florencio Lopes-de-Silanes & Andrei Shleifer, *What Works in Securities Laws?*, 61 J. FIN. 1 (2006).

[1020] *See, e.g.*, Luca Enriques, *EC Company Law Directives and Regulations: How Trivial Are They?*, U. PA. J. INT'L ECON. L. 1, 22 (2006) (discussing Europe).

[1021] *See, e.g.*, Verdier, *supra* note 1017, at 1419.

[1022] *See infra* Section 4.3.

[1023] *See, e.g.*, Chris Brummer, *Post-American Securities Regulation*, 98 CAL. L. REV. 329-30 (2010). In going beyond what might have been sufficient to ensure cooperation in the enforcement of its own securities laws, the SEC appears to have been motivated by a number of rationales. First, it sought to protect the interests of U.S. domestic investors making investments abroad. *Id.* at 334. A second reason is that regulatory convergence lowers domestic firms' costs of providing intermediary services or raising capital abroad—reducing risks of conflicting duties and lowering the costs of setting up shop abroad. Third, international approximation to the U.S. securities law paradigm enhanced the prestige of the SEC and its officers. *See id.* at 335. And fourth, in an environment where the U.S. financial sector competes internationally to attract issuers, having foreign securities laws approximate to those of the U.S. reduces the possibilities for other jurisdictions to pursue a "race to the bottom" to attract (lower-quality) issuers.

4.1 International Institutions and Convergence

The international institutions active in financial regulation may be characterized as "agenda setters," "standard setters," and financial institutions.[1024] International agenda setters are intergovernmental organizations that facilitate high-level policy coordination amongst their members. International standard setters are inter-agency organizations that share information and coordinate standards between domestic regulators. International financial institutions, established under international treaties to provide direct investment in public finance projects, in some cases also encourage compliance with international financial standards.

4.1.1 Agenda-Setting Institutions

The FSB. In the period since the financial crisis, the most influential agenda-setter for financial regulation at the international level has been the G20 group, a forum for finance ministers and central bankers of the world's 20 largest economies, and its offshoot, the Financial Stability Board (FSB). The FSB (formerly the Financial Stability Forum) was established in 2009 and charged with responsibility for coordinating the design and implementation of the G20's post-crisis policy agenda for ensuring financial stability.[1025] The FSB has no formal enforcement powers,[1026] but FSB member states must submit themselves

---

[1024] Chris Brummer, *How International Financial Law Works (and How It Doesn't)*, 99 GEO. L.J. 257 (2011).

[1025] The FSB's mandate includes: (1) assessing vulnerabilities affecting the global financial system and reviewing the regulatory, supervisory, and other actions needed to address them; (2) promoting coordination and information exchange among authorities responsible for financial stability; (3) monitoring and advising on market developments and their implications for regulatory policy; (4) coordinating the policy development work of international standard setters, and (5) promoting member states implementation of agreed upon commitments, standards, and policy recommendations through monitoring, peer review, and disclosure. The FSB is also responsible for coordinating cross-border contingency planning in connection with the failure of systemically important financial institutions.

[1026] Simultaneously, however, the eligibility of members must be reviewed periodically by the plenary board in light of the FSB's objectives; FSB Charter, Art. 5. Theoretically, this could lead to the discharge of members which consistently fail to implement FSB policy initiatives.

to periodic peer reviews.[1027] As financial stability is not generally a core concern for securities regulation, the FSB has made relatively few statements relevant to the current enquiry.[1028]

The U.S.-EU Joint Financial Regulatory Forum. The U.S. and EU have also since 2002 maintained a bilateral regulatory dialogue on financial regulation. Initially known as the Financial Markets Regulatory Dialogue, this has recently been re-branded as the "U.S.-EU Joint Financial Regulatory Forum" as part of an effort to "enhance the dialogue."[1029] The Forum is intended to meet twice per year, with a view to identifying and solving potential issues at an early stage.[1030] A particular goal is to expedite the completion of equivalence or substituted compliance assessments.[1031]

4.1.2 Standard-Setting for Securities

The most influential international standard-setting body for securities is the International Organization of Securities Commissions (IOSCO). Also important, however, are the International Accounting Standards Board (IASB) and the Committee on Payment and Settlement Systems (CPSS).

IOSCO. Established in 1983, IOSCO is the premier global venue for cross-country interaction among securities regulators. Its objectives are (i) to promote *cooperation* among its members in the development and implementation of regulation, supervision and enforcement; (ii) to enhance *investor protection* and

---

[1027] Financial Stability Board, *Framework for Strengthening Adherence to International Standards* (2010), www.financialstabilityboard.org/publications/r_100109a.pdf; Financial Stability Board, *Handbook for Peer Reviews*, www.financialstabilityboard.org/publications/r_120201.pdf (2011).

[1028] These include statements on OTC derivatives and beneficial ownership transparency.

[1029] *See* Press Release, U.S. Treasury, Joint U.S.-EU Financial Regulatory Forum Joint Statement, (July 25, 2016), https://www.treasury.gov/press-center/press-releases/Pages/jl0528.aspx (hereinafter U.S. Treasury Press Release).

[1030] *See* Press Release, European Union, Upgrading EU financial regulatory cooperation with the United States (July 28, 2016), http://ec.europa.eu/newsroom/fisma/itemlongdetail.cfm?item_id=33100.
Participants include representatives of, on the EU side, the Commission, the European Supervisory Authorities ('ESAs') and the Single Resolution Board and Single Supervisory Mechanism; and on the U.S. side, the Treasury, the CFTC, the SEC, the PCAOB, the Federal Reserve.

[1031] U.S. Treasury Press Release, *supra* note 1029.

promote investor confidence in the integrity of securities markets; and (iii) to *exchange information* about members' experiences. IOSCO has 214 members, of which 126 are ordinary members.[1032]

In order to join IOSCO, a securities regulator must sign the Multilateral Memorandum of Understanding concerning consultation and cooperation and the exchange of information (MMoU).[1033] This is a framework for mutual assistance and exchange of information.[1034] The SEC, the CFTC and the UK's FCA are among the current 109 MMoU signatories.[1035] The volume of information requests among international regulators under the MMoU has grown from 56 requests in 2003 to 3,203 requests in 2015.[1036]

IOSCO conducts policy work through eight subject-matter committees.[1037] It also sets up task forces and working groups; some of these cooperate with other international standard setters such as the CPMI or the BCBS.[1038] IOSCO issues standards and recommendations which are not legally binding on its members but still influential. IOSCO has established *Objectives and*

[1032] See https://www.iosco.org/about/?subsection=membership&memid=1. Associate members include the European Commission, ESMA, and the IMF. *See* https://www.iosco.org/about/?subsection=membership&memid=2.

[1033] *See* https://www.iosco.org/about/?subsection=becoming_a_member. For the MmoU, see IOSCO, MULTILATERAL MEMORANDUM OF UNDERSTANDING CONCERNING CONSULTATION AND COOPERATION AND THE EXCHANGE OF INFORMATION (2012), https://www.iosco.org/library/pubdocs/pdf/IOSCOPD386.pdf.

[1034] *Id.* at clause 7.

[1035] *See* https://www.iosco.org/about/?subSection=mmou&subSection1=signatories. Not all IOSCO members have yet signed the MMoU, and IOSCO are working on getting the remainder signed up. IOSCO maintains a public list of the members that have not signed up, which currently includes 19 countries such as Algeria, Bolivia, Chile and the Philippines, and is available at https://www.iosco.org/about/?subSection=mmou&subSection1=2013_list.

[1036] *See* https://www.iosco.org/about/?subsection=mmou.

[1037] These cover, respectively: (1) issuer accounting, audit, and disclosure; (2) regulation of secondary markets; (3) regulation of market intermediaries; (4) enforcement and information exchange; (5) investment management; (6) credit rating agencies; (7) commodities futures markets, and (8) retail investors.

[1038] Stavros Gadinis, *Three Pathways to Global Standards: Private, Regulator, and Ministry Networks*, 109 AMER. J. INT'L. L. 125-28 (2015).

Principles of Securities Regulation, which have been endorsed by the G20 and the FSB. They form the basis for the evaluation of the securities sector for the Financial Sector Assessment Programs (FSAPs) of the IMF and the World Bank.

IOSCO's work stream has traditionally been heavily influenced by the U.S.,[1039] with the SEC having initiated early IOSCO work towards cross-border cooperation between securities regulators.[1040] Moreover, a number of IOSCO's standards owe their format to U.S. norms.[1041] However, when the U.S. was evaluated by the IMF in 2015, and the report recommended a detailed plan of actions as regards IOSCO's *Objectives and Principles*,[1042] the U.S. authorities responded that they "disagreed with certain of the conclusions, recommendations, ratings, and interpretations of the IOSCO principles."[1043] While IOSCO has established a "Strategic Direction to 2020," which includes reinforcing IOSCO's position as the key global reference point for markets regulation,[1044] some commentators suggest it has become subservient to the work of the FSB.[1045]

IASB. Established in 2001, the IASB is the independent standard setting body of the International Financial Reporting Standards (IFRS) Foundation.[1046]

[1039] *See, e.g.*, CALLY JORDAN, INTERNATIONAL CAPITAL MARKETS 32-36 (2014).

[1040] Roberta S. Karmel & Claire R. Kelly, *The Hardening of Soft Law in International Securities Regulation*, 34 BROOK. J. INT'L L. 883, 913-15 (2009).

[1041] For example, its International Disclosure Standards, which were rolled into the EU Prospectus Directive, were based on U.S. standards. *See* JORDAN, *supra* note 1039, at 36.

[1042] INTERNATIONAL MONETARY FUND, DETAILED ASSESSMENT OF IMPLEMENTATION OF THE IOSCO OBJECTIVES AND PRINCIPLES OF SECURITIES REGULATION – UNITED STATES 31-33 (2015), http://www.imf.org/en/Publications/CR/Issues/2016/12/31/United-States-Financial-Sector-Assessment-Program-Detailed-Assessment-of-Implementation-on-42827.

[1043] *Id.* at 34.

[1044] *See generally* Janet Austin, *The Power and Influence of IOSCO in Formulating and Enforcing Securities Regulations*, 15 ASPER REV. INT'L BUS. & TRADE L. 1 (2015).

[1045] Roberta Karmel, *IOSCO's Response to the Global Financial Crisis*, 37 J. CORP. L. 849, 901 (2012) (stating that IOSCO has become "to some extent subservient to the G-20" and is not among the most important international financial regulators).

[1046] The objectives of the IFRS Foundation are to: (1) develop a single set of high quality, understandable, enforceable, and globally accepted international financial

Uniquely amongst international financial standard setters, IASB members are not representatives of the governments or regulatory authorities of the states which adopt its standards.[1047] Rather, the IASB is composed of 16 independent experts specifically drawn from around the world,[1048] and funded by private contributions.[1049] Monitoring of compliance with IFRS is the responsibility of its Interpretations Committee.[1050] The primary monitoring objective is to identify divergences in national accounting practices with a view to determining whether it is necessary to issue an official Interpretation of IFRS in relation to the point in question.

To ensure accountability, the IASB members are selected by the IFRS Foundation Trustees, whose own appointments are subject to approval from a Monitoring Board of representatives of the European Commission, IOSCO, Japan's Financial Services Agency, the U.S. SEC, and the BCBS.[1051] Despite its formal independence, the relationship between the IASB and politics is contested. On the one hand, the EU has sought to exert greater influence over its standard-setting since the financial crisis;[1052] on the other hand, concerns have

---

reporting standards (IFRS); (2) promote the use and rigorous application of those standards; (3) to take account of the financial reporting needs of emerging economies and small and medium-sized entities (SMEs), and (4) promote and facilitate the adoption of IFRS through the convergence of national accounting standards and IFRS. IFRS Constitution, §. 2.

[1047] Karmel & Kelly, *supra* note 1040, at 901-03; TIM BÜTHE & WALTER MATTLI, THE NEW GLOBAL RULERS: THE PRIVATIZATION OF REGULATION IN THE GLOBAL ECONOMY (2011); Gadinis, *supra* note 1038, at 21-25.

[1048] They are drawn from the following regions: Asia Oceania (4 members), Europe (4 members), North America (4 members), Africa (1 member), and South America (1 member). IFRS Constitution, §. 26. The remaining two members can be appointed from any area, subject to maintaining an overall geographical balance.

[1049] The big four accounting firms are the largest donors ($2.5m each in 2015). *See* http://www.ifrs.org/About-us/Documents/2015-financial-supporters.pdf.

[1050] The Interpretations Committee is composed of 14 members appointed by the Trustees for renewable 3-year terms: IFRS Constitution, §. 39.

[1051] IFRS Constitution, §. 21.

[1052] Elias Bengtsson, *Repoliticalization of Accounting Standard Setting*, 22 CRIT. PERSP. ON ACCT. 567 (2011).

been raised that the process is open to influence by the agendas of business and accounting firms.[1053]

The question whether IFRS and U.S. GAAP would merge into one global accounting standard appears to have decreased in salience as they converged. The two accounting standards are broadly similar in philosophy, and reconciliation is no longer needed for U.S. listings. This appears to have reduced frictions enough so that the issue no longer is a significant bottleneck for international transactions.

CPSS. The CPSS, which operates under the aegis of the Bank for International Settlements (BIS), is an international standard-setting body for payment, clearing, and securities settlement systems. It undertakes studies and spearheads policy initiatives at the request of the BIS, or at its own discretion. It also serves as a forum for central banks to monitor and analyze developments in domestic payment, clearing, and settlement systems as well as in cross-border and multicurrency settlement systems. Its most significant recent policy initiative has been the joint CPSS-IOSCO *Principles for Financial Market Infrastructure*. The CPSS has no formal enforcement powers. However, the *Principles* will form the basis of future IMF/World Bank FSAP assessments.[1054]

4.1.3 Financial Institutions: The IMF and World Bank

International financial institutions include global organizations such as the International Monetary Fund (IMF) and World Bank, along with various regional development banks.[1055] While the IMF does not play a direct role in the design of international financial standards, it does play a frontline role in conducting surveillance of member states' compliance with these standards, both individually and jointly with the World Bank under the auspices of the Financial Sector Assistance Program (FSAP).

The World Bank and the IMF prompted East Asian countries to overhaul their financial regulations and corporate laws following the 1997

[1053] KARTHIK RAMANNA, POLITICAL STANDARDS: CORPORATE INTEREST, IDEOLOGY, AND LEADERSHIP IN THE SHAPING OF ACCOUNTING RULES FOR THE MARKET ECONOMY (2015).

[1054] *See* CPSS, STANDARD SETTING ACTIVITIES, http://www.bis.org/cpss/cpssinfo02.htm.

[1055] These include the European Bank for Reconstruction and Development (EBRD), the Asian Development Bank (ADB) and the more recently-established New Development Bank (NDB, formerly the BRICS Bank) and Asian Infrastructure Investment Bank (AIIB).

crisis,[1056] and have more generally insisted on the adoption of core common principles in their regular consultations with member states. The World Bank has also, since then, sponsored an influential comparative ranking of the quality of the legal environment—the *Doing Business* survey—the results of which have (controversially) been associated with outcomes in securities markets.[1057]

4.2 The European Union: Harmonization and Passporting

The European Union is perhaps the most ambitious voluntarily-adopted international legal order in global history. Its legislative process is deliberately designed to give precedence to a strong technocratic civil service, in the form of the European Commission. This is intended to foster the pursuit of common aims and de-emphasize the potential for domestic politics.

The EU is also an outlier when it comes to the use of reciprocal market access within its borders, having in place a broad-scope scheme of mutual recognition for issuers and intermediaries: with due qualifications, they need only comply with regulation in their home country to offer their securities or services to investors throughout the EU. The driver for the project has been as much market forces as politics: financial services exporter countries such as the UK, Ireland and Luxembourg leveraged a strong political push toward the creation of a single market to obtain mutual recognition in many areas of financial regulation.[1058] This freedom to approach investors throughout the EU is known as "passporting" the firm's compliance with their local regulations.[1059] In the EU, a precondition for agreement on passporting was the requirement for jurisdictions to align their regulations, a process known as "harmonization." But

---

[1056] *See, e.g.*, Thomas Carothers, *The Rule of Law Revival*, 77 FOREIGN AFF. 95 (1998); Peter Boone, Alasdair Breach & Eric Friedman, *Corporate Governance in the Asian Financial Crisis*, 58 J. FIN. ECON. 141 (2000).

[1057] *See* La Porta et al., *supra* note 1019. For critical responses, see KENNETH W. DAM, THE LAW-GROWTH NEXUS: THE RULE OF LAW AND ECONOMIC DEVELOPMENT (2007); John Armour, Simon Deakin, Priya Lele & Mathias Siems, *How Do Legal Rules Evolve? Evidence from a Crosscountry Comparison of Shareholder, Creditor, and Worker Protection*, 57 AM. J. COMP. L. 579, 582-92 (2009); and Holger Spamann, *The "Antidirector Rights Index" Revisited*, 23 REV. FIN. STUD. 467 (2010).

[1058] *See* John Armour & Wolf-Georg Ringe, *European Company Law 1999-2000: Renaissance and Crisis*, 48 COMMON MKT. L. REV. 125, 154-7 (2011).

[1059] *See generally* NIAMH MOLONEY, EU SECURITIES AND FINANCIAL MARKETS REGULATION (2014).

Figure 9: Percentage of EU-wide activity occurring in the UK, by sector (2015).

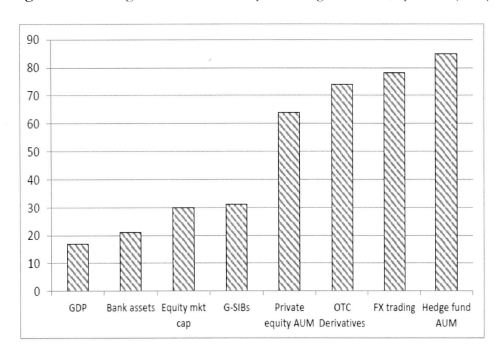

Notes: GDP and equity market data are from World Bank. Bank asset data are from ECB and PRA. G-SIB data are from FSB. Data on private equity assets under management, OTC derivatives transactions, FX trading and hedge fund assets under management from TheCityUK. Source: John Armour, *Brexit and Financial Services*, 33 OXFORD REV. ECON. POL'Y S54, S55 (2017).

passporting still requires mutual trust in the quality of local supervision and enforcement. Mutual trust also has to extend to local regulation, insofar as harmonization is incomplete—as it still is in many areas—or where negative synergies exist with other components of a given legal system.

Harmonization in the EU was traditionally achieved through the means of a type of legislation known as a "Directive," which specifies to states the general goals to be achieved but leaves the precise format to be implemented in national law in accordance with the local regime. This permits some degree of cross-sectional variation, which is problematic in areas where mutual trust is crucial. Moreover, legislators lack the time and expertise to produce rules of sufficient detail, and to update them with sufficient speed, to provide a workable regime. Consequently the EU financial markets regime has seen the evolution of a specialist delegated legislation mechanism, whereby "implementing" measures produced by specialist committees buttress general securities legislation.[1060] Since

---

[1060] *See* EILÍS FERRAN, BUILDING AN EU SECURITIES MARKET (2004); *id.*

the financial crisis, the alignment has been tightened even further by the establishment of the European Securities Market Authority (ESMA), to which jurisdiction to make the most detailed implementing measures – the so-called "single rule book"—has been transferred from national securities regulators.[1061] However, with few exceptions,[1062] enforcement is still generally a matter of national competence. Given the differences in resources allocated to national securities authorities,[1063] this likely leaves considerable variation in the extent to which the rules affect firms' behavior.[1064]

The persistent role of national regulators in the enforcement of securities laws can be more easily understood in the light of the very UK-centric nature of EU capital markets. Figure 9 shows the proportion of various types of EU economic and financial activity based in the UK. As can be seen, the UK's GDP accounts for 17 per cent of the EU's aggregate GDP. This is closely tracked by the fraction of EU bank assets held by UK banks (21 per cent). However, the UK's share of total EU activity grows as we move to the right of Figure 9, encompassing 30 per cent of equity market capitalization, and very high proportions of wholesale market activities such as OTC derivatives and hedge fund assets under management. The UK's outsize representation in financial markets meant that, in effect, the rest of Europe could rely on the City of London for the supply of financial services (especially wholesale ones) to the entire area. Given London's success as the regional financial hub and the political clout that the British government derived from it, the centralization of securities law enforcement within an EU-level supervisory authority on the lines of the U.S. SEC has until very recently been a political non-starter. With the UK imminently departing from the EU, this division of labor is likely to be revisited very rapidly, and a centralized supervisory framework may well be the outcome.[1065]

[1061] *See* HIGH-LEVEL GROUP ON FINANCIAL SUPERVISION IN THE EU, REPORT OF THE HIGH-LEVEL GROUP ON FINANCIAL SUPERVISION IN THE EU (the "de Larosière Report") (2009).

[1062] ESMA has direct supervisory powers in respect of CRAs and Trade Repositories. *See generally* MOLONEY, *supra* note 1059, at 973-1009.

[1063] *See infra* Section 8.

[1064] *See* Luca Enriques & Matteo Gatti, *Is There a Uniform European Securities Law After the Financial Services Action Plan?*, 14 STAN. J. LAW BUS. & FIN. 43 (2008).

[1065] *See* André Sapir, Dirk Schoenmaker & Nicolas Véron, *Making the Best of Brexit for the EU-27 Financial System*, Peterson Institute for International Economics Policy Brief 17-8 (2017).

4.3 Reciprocal Market Access More Generally

Reciprocal market access can in principle be used as a lever towards convergence more generally.[1066] Where a foreign regulatory regime is of similar quality to the domestic one, such agreement will be relatively easy to achieve: potential losses to domestic investors, and costs to domestic firms, are relatively modest. This is consistent with the pattern observed in the EU, discussed in Section 4.2.

However, performing an assessment of the functional equivalence of securities laws is extremely complex, requiring the local authority to evaluate not only the applicable foreign rules, but also the quality of the relevant supervisory agencies and the intensity of enforcement. Each of these features is hard to observe. Consequently, such assessments are a potential minefield: they are both politically sensitive and prone to errors. For these reasons, the U.S. has generally fought shy of such assessments.

The U.S.: Substituted compliance. In the U.S., reciprocal access arrangements are known as 'substituted compliance'. Although the idea showed great promise in the pre-crisis era, the SEC only managed to implement a couple of instances before post-crisis political realities put paid to further moves.[1067] Although the U.S. reached a mutual recognition agreement with Australia in 2008, which provides a framework for stock exchanges and broker-dealers to operate in both countries,[1068] it has not resulted in the granting of any actual exemptive relief.[1069] This means that the only current mutual recognition arrangement of practical importance is the SEC's Multijurisdictional Disclosure System (MJDS) with Canada, which allows Canadian issuers that meet certain eligibility criteria to

---

[1066] *See, e.g.*, EUROPEAN COMMISSION, EU EQUIVALENCE DECISIONS IN FINANCIAL SERVICES POLICY: AN ASSESSMENT, SWD(2017) 102 final, 4 ("A possible equivalence finding by the EU is one of the major incentives for third-country regulators to enhance supervisory co-operation and to seek closer regulatory convergence with the EU.")

[1067] Tafara & Peterson, *supra* note 995, at 53, 56.

[1068] Press Release, SEC, SEC, Australian Authorities sign Mutual Recognition Agreement (Aug. 25, 2008). A schedule for the completion of a process agreement with Canada aimed at a similar mutual recognition agreement was also announced, *see* Press Release, SEC, Schedule Announced for Completion of U.S.-Canadian Mutual Recognition Process Agreement (May 29, 2008), but was never followed by the actual agreement.

[1069] Howell E. Jackson, *Substituted Compliance: The Emergence, Challenges, and Evolution of a New Regulatory Paradigm*, 1 J. FIN. REG.169, 180 (2015).

conduct securities offerings in the U.S. based on their compliance with Canadian law and without SEC review.[1070]

The EU: Third country equivalence. Central to the EU's emerging approach to market access arrangements with third countries are "equivalence" determinations. These are legislatively-sanctioned assessments of third country regulations and regulators, delivered by the European Commission, acting on guidance from ESMA. While many of the equivalence frameworks in place are—at least facially—unilateral in their operation, there is an increasing trend toward making their application depend expressly on reciprocity. This includes most significantly the MiFIR/MiFID II regime, whereby the potential for a determination regarding regulatory equivalence is conditioned expressly on the need for reciprocity of treatment.[1071] This shifts the determination of "equivalence" away from what is facially an enquiry as to the relative quality of the foreign regulatory regime in favor of the sort of horse-trading negotiations that might encompass a bilateral reciprocal access arrangement.

4.4 Prospects for Future International Cooperation

We conclude this Section with some conjectures as to the likely future trajectory of international regulatory coordination. While there are obvious political contingencies,[1072] our focus here is on the implications of the secular trends in global equity markets we have highlighted.

First, technological advances push down the cost of direct investment abroad by U.S. retail investors. While this might be expected to stimulate demand for better local rules aimed at investor protection in foreign jurisdictions, the massive parallel shift away from individuals' direct investment in securities to their delegation to specialized institutions makes the need for convergence in

---

[1070] The agreement is mutual and could also be used by U.S. companies to raise capital in Canada, but its main use has been for Canadian capital raisings in the U.S. *See, e.g.*, CHRIS BRUMMER, SOFT LAW AND THE GLOBAL FINANCIAL SYSTEM 55 (2015).

[1071] Markets in Financial Instruments Regulation (EU) No 600/2014, Art. 47(1).

[1072] Not only the resurgence of U.S. isolationist tendencies, but also the displacement of democratic governments by semi-dictatorial regimes in various countries. Such regimes raise the risk that governmental power, including those related to securities regulation, may be used against citizens and organizations who happen to fall out with the ruling majority. This may erode the trust that underlies cooperation among securities regulators: they may rightly be reluctant to share information with another country's supervisor, if they can fear that information thereby exchanged may be used to quash political opponents.

investor protection regulation—such as conduct of business rules for broker-dealers—less salient.

Second, the international dominance of U.S. investment banks reduces incentives for U.S. regulators to encourage regulatory coordination as a means of facilitating export of investment services. U.S. firms have already conquered the main global markets and are now powerful incumbents wherever they are present. Regulatory idiosyncrasies in those markets raise new entrants' costs and therefore actually favor the U.S. incumbents.

Third, stronger competition in the markets for listings and liquidity services may increase the demand for special, more lenient rules for foreign private issuers, but is unlikely also to lead to any push for international coordination, because the U.S. markets no longer enjoy a dominant position globally, making it more difficult for U.S. regulators to impose their solutions on other jurisdictions.[1073]

Fourth, institutionalization and the global reach of the major asset manager companies—with the ability to invest and purchase broker-dealer services in every relevant market—make agreements aimed at lifting domestic compliance burdens for foreign issuers and broker-dealers—such as the MJDS or the mutual recognition agreement between the U.S. and Australia—obsolete.

Nevertheless, the institutionalization of savings and the increased tendency of U.S. institutional investors to invest abroad may still generate pressure for the U.S. government to seek improvements in foreign securities and corporate governance regulations. Giant U.S. institutional investors may feel that the political risks of lobbying local policymakers directly for enhanced investor protection are too high. They may prefer to lobby the U.S. government, via the SEC, to seek better investor protection rules in the usual fora, such as IOSCO.

To conclude, the combination of (1) technological progress, (2) global dominance of U.S. players in the investment banking sector, (3) a more decentralized market for listings and liquidity services, and (4) institutionalization seems to imply a reduced impetus for international coordination in securities regulation. The first three factors greatly reduce the incentives for the U.S. to take a leadership role in regulatory coordination, and the fourth reduces demand for substitute compliance or equivalence regimes for broker-dealers. That said, a U.S. government push towards better issuer-facing securities laws around the world may still be prompted by pressures from institutional investors holding ever more internationally-diversified equity portfolios.

[1073] Brummer, *supra* note 1023; Stavros Gadinis, *The Politics of Competition in International Financial Regulation*, 49 HARV. INT'L L.J. 447 (2008).

Part II
Regulation of Cross-Border Securities Transactions

In Part II, we consider aspects of securities market regulation that are of particular relevance to cross-border equity investment. The discussion has a comparative orientation, contrasting regulatory strategies in major non-U.S. jurisdictions—especially the EU—with those in the U.S., which are more fully described in the other chapters of the *New Special Study*. Such a comparative approach is valuable for at least two reasons. First, for descriptive analysis, it enables a better understanding of actual market practices in cross-border transactions, which are a function of triangulation between various relevant regulatory regimes. Second, from a normative perspective, it may provide insights as to the relative functionality of different regulatory choices.

Part II begins in Section 5 with cross-border capital raising (primary markets). Next, in Section 6, we turn to cross-border trading (secondary markets), while Section 7 focuses on the regulation of cross-border investment intermediation. Finally, Section 8 discusses supervision and enforcement.

5 Primary Markets and Cross-Listings

As regards *primary markets*, we consider first inbound market access to the U.S. and the EU (and in particular the UK)—that is, domestic rules governing how foreign issuers may raise capital from local investors. After establishing these "rules of the game" and potential frictions with cross-border capital raising, we discuss the state of the international "market for IPOs," including case studies of competition between the UK's Alternative Investment Market ('AIM') and U.S. private placements, the London Stock Exchange's experiments with different listing segments catering to foreign firms of differing quality, and Asian primary markets.

5.1 Capital Raising and Market Access

5.1.1 Foreign Firms Raising Capital in the U.S.

Foreign issuers seeking to raise funds from U.S. investors may (a) pursue a U.S. public offer, necessitating full local compliance with U.S. securities laws, (b) make a U.S. private offering, relying on one or more exemptions from U.S. securities laws, or (c) raise capital from U.S. investors offshore.[1074] In addition,

---

[1074] Offshore transactions could be categorised as "outbound" access, but we discuss Regulation S offerings by foreign issuers under this heading, since they can approach U.S. investors for an offshore transaction.

Canadian issuers may rely on their domestic offering materials based on the substituted compliance approach of the MJDS.[1075]

Capital-raising in the form of a public offering would involve registration with the SEC and periodic reporting requirements.[1076] However, there are several relevant exemptions that may be used to avoid making a public offering in the U.S.[1077] The most important of these are (i) Regulation D; (ii) Rule 144A; and (iii) Regulation S. At the beginning of the twenty-first century, foreign firms raised approximately two-thirds of their U.S. equity through private offerings, a figure which has since risen steadily to 95 per cent in 2015.[1078]

Regulation D provides the most important set of exemptions through which private offers to sophisticated investors are made in the U.S.[1079] Over the period 2009-2014, an average of $660 billion per annum in fresh equity was issued using Regulation D offers, nearly three times as much as was raised each year using public (registered) equity offers.[1080] Of this, approximately twenty per cent was raised by foreign issuers.[1081] Regulation D offers tend to be very small in comparison to offers via public markets, with the mean capital-raising being only $28 million.[1082]

[1075] *See* text accompanying note 1070.

[1076] Securities Act, § 5, Exchange Act § 15(d) requires ongoing reporting following a registered offering under the Securities Act.

[1077] Notably, the exemptions introduced in Regulation A+ in 2015 are not available to non-Canadian FPIs (since the SEC preferred to first evaluate the impact of the regulation on a smaller set of issuers). *See* SEC, Final Rule: Amendments for Small and Additional Issues Exemptions Under the Securities Act (Regulation A), 80 Fed Regulation 21806 (Apr. 20, 2015).

[1078] Press Release, Committee on Capital Markets Regulation, Continuing Competitive Weakness in U.S. Public Capital Markets (Oct. 28, 2016) (presenting data for initial offerings of foreign equity in the U.S.). We note that while FINRA now collects and disseminates data on Rule 144A debt transactions, there is no official source for data regarding the Rule 144A equity market.

[1079] Securities Act of 1933, §§ 3(b) and 4(a)(2); SEC Regulation D, Rules 504-506, 17 CFR 230.504-506.

[1080] Scott Bauguess, Rachite Gullapalli & Vladimir Ivanov, *Capital Raising in the U.S.: An Analysis of the Market for Unregistered Securities Offerings, 2009-2014* 7-11, SEC Division of Economic and Risk Analysis Working Paper (2015).

[1081] *Id.* at 18-19.

[1082] *Id.* at 9.

Rule 144A is a sophisticated investor exemption for private placements that allows both domestic and foreign issuers to avoid various restrictions that apply to other types of exempt offerings. Rule 144A is technically a resale rule, under which purchasers must be "qualified institutional buyers" (QIBs),[1083] but private offerings are made to an "initial purchaser" who may resell the securities to other QIBs. To fall within Rule 144A, the securities offered must not be fungible with securities listed on a U.S. exchange.[1084] Once issued, Rule 144A securities can be traded among QIBs, but are otherwise 'restricted', meaning they cannot be resold for at least six months.[1085] Unlike Regulation D offerings, however, almost all (over 99%) Rule 144A transactions involve debt securities.[1086]

Regulation S provides a safe harbor from registration for offshore offerings, where the *sale* occurs outside the U.S., without any prior directed selling efforts in the U.S.[1087] Regulation S also contains a safe harbor for resales, which for foreign issuers is available for offshore transactions without directed selling efforts in the U.S.[1088] However, securities issued under Regulation S may be resold to U.S. QIBs under Rule 144A.[1089] The annual amount of capital (both debt and equity) raised by using Regulation S over the period 2009-2014 was

---

[1083] QIBs are typically institutions with a securities investment portfolio above $100 million. *See* Rule 144A(a)(1).

[1084] The securities must, further, not be "quoted on a U.S. automated inter-dealer quotation system," but there are currently no systems designated as such. GREENE ET AL., *infra* note 1101 at 5-21. This appears to mean that securities issued under Rule 144A may be fungible with securities traded off-exchange.

[1085] Six months if the issuer is SEC reporting, otherwise one year. Rules 144(a)(3), 144(d).

[1086] Bauguess et al., *supra* note 1080, at 11.

[1087] Regulation S stipulates different requirements for the availability of the safe harbor depending on the type of security offered. If the FPI does not have "substantial U.S. market interest" (SUSMI) in the particular class of equity security offered, the offering is "Category 1" and only the requirements of an offshore transaction and no directed selling efforts apply. However, if there is "substantial U.S. market interest" (SUSMI) in the particular class of equity offered, further requirements will apply. SUSMI requires, however, that the U.S. is either the largest trading market for the securities, or constitutes at least 20% of trading while less than 55% of trading took place in, on or through another country's markets. 17 CFR § 230.902(j)(1).

[1088] 17 CFR § 230.904.

[1089] *See* Bauguess et al., *supra* note 1080, at 6.

approximately $140 billion,[1090] slightly less than the total of $200 billion per year raised by foreign issuers using Regulation D over the same period.[1091]

5.1.2 Non-EU Firms Raising Capital in the EU

Foreign firms wishing to raise capital through a public offer in the EU face a similar regulatory starting point to that in the U.S. They must in principle comply with the local rules applicable to primary offers, set out in the Prospectus Directive,[1092] and—once listed—with continuing disclosure obligations set out in the Transparency Directive.[1093] However, the enforcement of securities law obligations is—for the present time at least—a matter for Member States' national competent authorities (NCAs), as opposed to an EU-level agency. Supervision and enforcement jurisdiction is allocated to the country in which the third country firm first offers securities to the public, or is admitted to trading on a regulated market.[1094] In other words, third country issuers can choose which individual securities law and enforcement apparatus will apply to them. Variation in the quality of enforcement, as well as in key aspects of related substantive law (for example, the liability regime for misrepresentations), means that there is significant scope for regulatory arbitrage.[1095]

There is a general exemption from the EU prospectus obligations for issues offered solely to sophisticated investors, analogous to Regulation D in the U.S. A typical EU capital-raising transaction then consists of a listing in the issuer's home jurisdiction coupled with capital-raising on wholesale markets across the EU, as well in the U.S.[1096]

There are, however, significant aspects without analogues in the U.S. rules. One is that, unlike the U.S., no effective resale restrictions apply to those

---

[1090] *Id.* at 7.

[1091] This figure includes both debt and equity issuances. *Id.*

[1092] Directive 2003/71/EC, as amended.

[1093] Directive 2004/109/EC, as amended.

[1094] Prospectus Directive, Art. 2(m)(iii).

[1095] EU domestic issuers can make a similar choice, provided they incorporate in their desired jurisdiction. *See* Luca Enriques & Tobias Tröger, *Issuer Choice in Europe*, 67 CAMBRIDGE L.J. 521 (2008). Despite attempts to curb regulatory arbitrage, this will continue to be the case under the Prospectus Regulation, which will shortly replace the Prospectus Directive. *See* Article 2(1)(m)(i), Prospectus Regulation Proposal, as approved by the Council and the Parliament.

[1096] Jackson & Pan, *supra* note 959.

who purchase securities in an EU private placement.[1097] A second is that the EU regime has an exception to local compliance where a third country issuer has complied with rules in the (non-EU) country of the issuer's registered office, which are equivalent to those applicable under the EU regime. "Equivalence" denotes not only substantive equivalence of disclosure obligations with those set out in the Prospectus Directive itself, but also in accordance with the IOSCO disclosure standards.[1098] The Prospectus Directive contains perhaps the earliest example of a third country equivalence framework in EU financial markets law. In contrast to later legislative instruments, the determination of equivalence is a matter for the NCAs in the Member State in which the issuer wishes to first make the offer. This is then deemed to be the issuer's home state for the purposes of application of the Directive. Delegating the matter to NCAs in this way of course creates an incentive to take a relaxed approach to equivalence determinations: the revenues from the issue and associated trading will be local to the country of listing, but the investors who might buy the securities are dispersed throughout the EU. To ensure greater uniformity, ESMA has taken to issuing guidance on equivalence.[1099] However, the framework is set to be centralized in the hands of the European Commission under the forthcoming Prospectus Regulation.[1100]

For U.S. issuers—that is firms that have already issued securities in the US—there may also be outbound obligations with which to comply when raising capital abroad. Such firms can make use of Regulation S to conduct an offshore offering that is exempt from the Securities Act. This would be a "Category 3" offering, meaning that more restrictions apply than for an FPI. In particular, a "distribution compliance period" of six months (one year if the issuer is a non-

---

[1097] *See* Prospectus Directive, Art. 3(2), second para; *see also* Luca Enriques, *A Proportionate Approach to Disclosure Regulation for Securities Offerings Within the EU* (working paper, 2017).

[1098] Prospectus Directive, Art. 20.

[1099] To date, such an assessment has been offered in favour of two countries: Israel and Turkey. *See* ESMA OPINION, FRAMEWORK FOR THE ASSESSMENT OF THIRD COUNTRY PROSPECTUSES UNDER ARTICLE 20 OF THE PROSPECTUS DIRECTIVE (Mar. 20, 2013).

[1100] Proposed Regulation on the Prospectus to be Published when Securities are Offered to the Public or Admitted to Trading, COM (2015) 583 final, Articles 26-28.

reporting company) will apply, during which (among other things) Regulation S securities may not be sold to U.S. persons.[1101]

5.2 International Primary Markets

The traditional explanation for cross-border listings was to see them as a way for issuers to overcome investment barriers, to reach investors who were otherwise practically prevented from supplying capital.[1102] This explanation is often labeled the "market segmentation" hypothesis. However, it looks increasingly implausible given the liberalization of cross-border investment barriers and consequent interconnection of markets. The collectivization of investment means that much liquidity is available through private placements. Consequently, it is no longer necessary for firms to establish listings in multiple countries to deliver liquidity. Issuers can rather select their preferred jurisdiction for listing—whether for bonding reasons, to ensure access to analyst coverage, or to exploit or build brand recognition among retail investors—and tap into

---

[1101] Other requirements include that the securities of a U.S. issuer must contain a legend to the effect that transfer is prohibited except in accordance with Regulation S. *See* 17 CFR § 230.903(b)(iii)(B)(3). This, and other technical aspects of the rule such as a requirement to send a notice of Regulation S requirements to the purchaser, has caused problems for U.S. issuers that wished to offer and list securities abroad, since modern trading systems do not provide for share certificates with legends or notices to be sent. *See* EDWARD F. GREENE, ALAN L. BELLER, EDWARD J. ROSEN, LESLIE N. SILVERMAN, DANIEL A. BRAVERMAN, SEBASTIAN R. SPERBER, NICOLAR GRABAR & ADAM E. FLEISHER, U.S. REGULATION OF THE INTERNATIONAL SECURITIES AND DERIVATIVES MARKETS §6.27 et seq. (2014). While the London Stock Exchange and Euroclear have provided a technical solution, its legal status is uncertain. *See* Travers Smith, *One Year On: Electronic Settlement of Category 3, Regulation S Securities* (2017), http://www.traverssmith.com/assets/pdf/legal-briefings/One_Year_On_Electronic_Settlement_of_Category_3_Regulation_S_Securities.pdf.

[1102] *See, e.g.*, G. Andrew Karolyi, *Why Do Companies List Shares Abroad? A Survey of the Evidence and Its Managerial Implications*, 7 FIN. MARKETS, INSTITUTIONS AND INSTRUMENTS 1, 19 (1998) (dividing investment barriers into "direct costs," which includes foreign exchange controls, withholding taxes, and limits on foreign ownership, and "indirect costs," which arise from higher monitoring costs of firms in low-disclosure regimes).

Figure 11: Change in number of listed companies for selected exchanges (2003-2017)

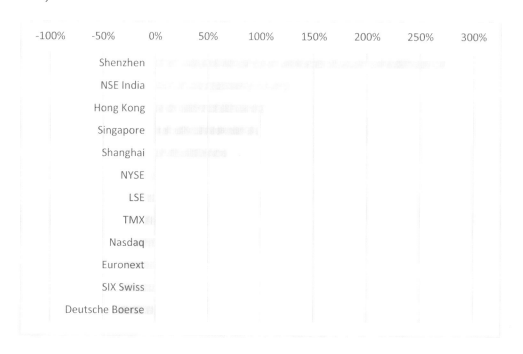

Notes: Data are from World Federation of Exchanges.

liquidity elsewhere using private placements.[1103]

An alternative explanation for cross-listings is known as the "bonding" hypothesis.[1104] This characterizes cross-listing as a commitment device that allows firms from jurisdictions with weak substantive securities laws and/or enforcement to signal their quality by subjecting themselves to a regulatory regime with strong substantive rules and/or high-intensity enforcement—such as the U.S. Rendering themselves open to enforcement action either by the SEC or private plaintiffs in securities class actions is something that is credibly more costly for a low-quality than for a high-quality issuer, hence making cross-listing a

---

[1103] As can be seen in Figure 12, issuers appear to overwhelmingly prefer to list in their home country.

[1104] René M. Stulz, *Globalization, Corporate Finance, and the Cost of Capital*, 12 J. APPLIED CORP. FIN. 8 (1999); John C. Coffee, Jr., *The Future as History: The Prospects for Global Convergence in Corporate Governance and its Implications*, 93 NW. U. L. REV. 641 (1999); G. Andrew Karolyi, *Corporate Governance, Agency Problems and International Cross-listings: A Defense of the Bonding Hypothesis*, 13 EMERGING MKTS. REV. 516 (2012).

plausible signal of quality. The differential may be expected to persist over time, generating significant costs for issuers who mistreat investors and consequently serving as a bond of good behavior. Low levels of SEC enforcement against foreign firms in the early 2000s led some to question how much work was done by bonding to legal rules (as opposed, perhaps, to a contemporaneous reputational bond).[1105] More recent evidence suggests, however, that the SEC has subsequently increased its enforcement activity in relation to foreign firms.[1106]

When measured by total market capitalization, the largest stock markets in the world are still in the U.S. However, if we focus instead on changes in the number of listed firms, captured in Figure 11, U.S. exchanges show less dynamism.[1107] For example, Nasdaq has 717 (or 20 per cent) fewer firms listed today than in 2003. By contrast, the Hong Kong Stock Exchange has more than doubled its number of listed firms over the same period. Consistently with the picture in Figure 11, many of the world's largest IPOs no longer take place in the U.S. markets. Of the ten largest IPOs in 2016, six were in Asia and four in Europe.[1108] Figure 12 ranks by offer size the 15 largest IPOs worldwide in the last five years. In 14 of these 15 offerings, issuers listed on an exchange in their home country, which indicates that investor mobility is high.

The trend to raising capital through local IPOs is also reflected in Figures 13 and 14, showing the regions and exchanges that raised the most IPO funds. While the NYSE was the exchange on which most IPO funds were raised in 2013 and 2014, and the Americas the number one region, Asia-Pacific IPOs received the most IPO funds in 2015 and 2016, with Hong Kong the world's largest exchange in terms of money channeled to IPOs in the two most recent years.

Figure 15 shows World Federation of Exchanges data on the development of the number of foreign companies listed on NYSE and Nasdaq, as well as for selected other major exchanges. Although the numbers of cross-listings on the major U.S. exchanges have been relatively stable in recent years,

---

[1105] Jordan Siegel, *Can Foreign Firms Bond Themselves Effectively by Renting U.S. Securities Laws?*, 75 J. FIN. ECON. 319 (2005).

[1106] Roger Silvers, *The Valuation Impact of SEC Enforcement Actions on Nontarget Foreign Firms*, 54 J. ACCT. RES. 187 (2016).

[1107] *See* Craig Doidge, G. Andrew Karolyi & René M. Stulz, *The U.S. Listing Gap*, 123 J. FIN. ECON. 464 (2017).

[1108] DEALOGIC, INVESTMENT BANKING SCORECARD, http://graphics.wsj.com/investment-banking-scorecard/.

Figure 12: 15 Largest IPOs worldwide since 2012

Rank	Issuer	Listing Venue	Offer Size ($ m)	Market Cap at Offer	Industry	Issuer Domicile
1	Alibaba Group Holding Ltd	NYSE	$25,032	$167.6 bn	Internet	China
2	Facebook Inc	NASDAQ	$16,007	$24.1 bn	Internet	US
3	Japan Post Holdings Co Ltd	Tokyo	$8,855	$80.5 bn	Insurance	Japan
4	Japan Airlines Co Ltd	Tokyo	$8,437	$8.7bn	Airlines	Japan
5	Postal Savings Bank of China Co Ltd	Hong Kong	$7,624	$12.2bn	Banks	China
6	National Commercial Bank	Saudi Arabia	$6,000	N/A	Banks	Saudi Arabia
7	BB Seguridade Participacoes	BM&F Bovespa	$5,669	N/A	Insurance	Brazil
8	Innogy SE	Xetra	$5,179	$22.3bn	Energy	Germany
9	Medibank Pvt	ASE	$4,986	$4.99bn	Insurance	Australia
10	Japan Post Bank Co Ltd	Tokyo	$4,959	$54.1bn	Banks	Japan
11	Guotai Junan Securities Co Ltd	Shanghai	$4,852	$24.3bn	Diversified Financial	China
12	Aena SA	Soc.Bol SIBE	$4,798	$9.8bn	Engineering	Spain
13	ABN Amro Group NV	Euronext Amsterdam	$4,213	$18.3bn	Banks	Netherlands
14	Kyushu Railway	Tokyo	$4,068	$4.1bn	Transportation	Japan
15	Dalian Wanda Commercial Properties Co Ltd	Hong Kong	$4,039	$27.7bn	Real Estate	China

Source: Bloomberg (IPOs completed between 1 January 2012 and 30 June 2017).

Figure 13: IPO funds raised 2012-2016, by geographic area ($ bn)

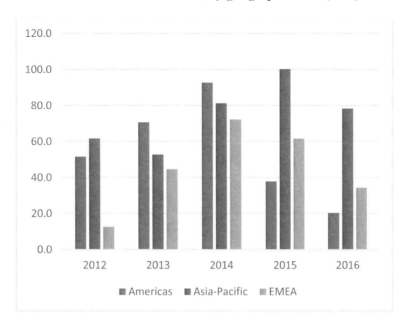

Source: Data from World Federation of Exchanges

Figure 14: IPO funds raised 2012-2016, selected exchanges ($ bn)

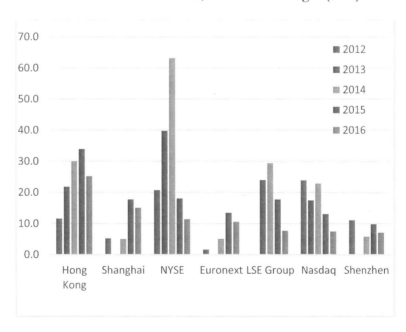

Source: Data from World Federation of Exchanges

Figure 15: Number of foreign companies listed on selected exchanges (2003-2017)

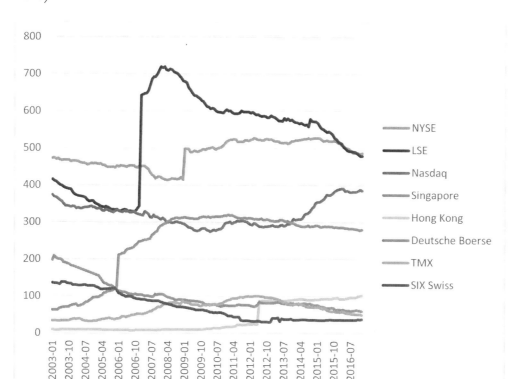

Note: Data are from World Federation of Exchanges.

the U.S. cross-listings market peaked at around the turn of the millennium.[1109] However, the time series data used for this figure suffer from a lack of consistency, with sudden jumps owing to recategorization of which companies count as "foreign" by various exchanges at various points in time.[1110]

To verify the downward trend in U.S. cross-listings, we also hand-collected data from the SEC on foreign issuers, which are reported in Table 1.

[1109] Doidge et al, *supra* note 108, at 258.

[1110] The increase for the London Stock Exchange in January 2007 appears to relate to a recategorization, where issuers that in effect were UK "topcos" of overseas companies were designated as foreign issuers. The increase for NYSE in January 2009 appears to relate to the addition of ARCA and AMEX to the data.

Table 1: Number of foreign-incorporated issuers registered and reporting with the SEC, 2000-2015

	2001	2002	2003	2004	2005	2006	2007
Start of year	1,310	1,344	1,323	1,235	1,245	1,237	1,146
New entrants	198	106	93	112	116	76	102
Leavers	164	127	181	102	124	167	187
End of year	**1,344**	**1,323**	**1,235**	**1,245**	**1,237**	**1,146**	**1,061**

	2008	2009	2010	2011	2012	2013	2014	2015
Start of year	1,061	1,028	968	974	965	947	940	906
New entrants	57	57	102	72	58	56	69	76
Leavers	90	117	96	81	76	63	103	56
End of year	**1,028**	**968**	**974**	**965**	**947**	**940**	**906**	**926**

Notes: Data for foreign-incorporated issuers from 2000 to 2015 made available by the SEC at https://www.sec.gov/divisions/corpfin/internatl/companies.shtml. The SEC presents this issuer data by year. We collated it and reviewed it for changes of issuers' registered names during the period, to avoid counting a name change as a combined exit from the U.S. by one issuer and an entry by another. Our totals may differ slightly from those of the SEC as we sought to remove duplicate records and made other minor adjustments.

There were approximately 1,310 foreign issuers registered with the SEC at the end of 2000, which had declined steadily to only 926 foreign issuers by the end of 2015. However, there has been significant turnover in the composition of foreign issuers each year, also presented in Table 1 to add a sense of the dynamics. In the last 15 years, we estimate that 1,350 foreign issuers have become SEC registrants (mean 90 per year) while 1,734 (mean 116 per year) have left the U.S. regime. Of the 1,310 foreign issuers registered with the SEC at the end of 2000, only 300 remained at the end of 2015.

A variety of (potentially complementary) explanations exist for the decline in U.S. cross-listings. Some focus on U.S.-specific factors, such as the perceived increased cost of U.S. regulation, in particular the Sarbanes-Oxley Act of 2002.[1111] Another perspective is that the U.S. had a competitive advantage in capital markets after World War II since its economic infrastructure was

---

[1111] COMMITTEE ON CAPITAL MARKETS REGULATION, INTERIM REPORT (2006).

undamaged, and it did not face real competition until the 1980s.[1112] A third possibility is the considerably higher IPO fees typically charged in the U.S. than elsewhere.[1113] However, for present purposes the most interesting explanations are those that relate to the macro trends described in Section 2. On this view, it is less important to bring listings to the U.S. to access capital from U.S. investors: they can be reached through a private placement or invest offshore in a foreign issue.[1114]

The attraction of cross-listing as a bonding mechanism may also have been damped. Bonding depends on differences in the practical intensity of securities laws. Efforts at international regulatory coordination, discussed in Section 4, have reduced these differences, at least amongst developed countries.[1115] Moreover, the growth in institutional investment may mean that the protections offered to investors by regulation may be less important, as they are better able to assess protection at the firm-level than retail investors.[1116] Consistently with this view, a recent study reports that the Supreme Court's 2010 decision in *Morrison*, which geographically limited the reach of private enforcement of U.S. securities law, triggered indifferent or even positive market reactions for affected firms.[1117] This suggests that the majority of such firms had received no valuation benefit from legal bonding.

Nevertheless, it seems likely that bonding continues to play a role. Convergence in securities law has reduced, but not eliminated, differences in substantive securities laws, and there remain substantial differences in

---

[1112] Donald C. Langevoort, *U.S. Securities Regulation and Global Competition*, 3 VA. L. & BUS. REV. 191, 193-96 (2008).

[1113] Mark Abrahamson, Tim Jenkinson & Howard Jones, *Why Don't U.S. Issuers Demand European Fees for IPOs?*, 66 J. FIN. 2055 (2011) (documenting U.S. IPO fees typically at 7% whereas European IPO fees typically at 4%, and falling).

[1114] Jackson, *supra* note 995.

[1115] *See* Andreas Wöller, *How the Globalization of Capital Markets Has Affected the Listing Behavior of Foreign Issuers - The Case of Daimler's Listing on the NYSE (Part II)*, 38 DAJV News. 54 (2013) (studying Daimler's 1993 listing on, and 2010 delisting from, the NYSE and arguing that bonding effects have been dissipated by refinements in German securities laws).

[1116] Doidge et al., *supra* note 108.

[1117] Amir N. Licht, Christopher Poliquin, Jordan I. Siegel & Xi Li, *What Makes the Bonding Stick? A Natural Experiment Involving the U.S. Supreme Court and Cross-Listed Firms*, forthcoming J. FIN. ECON. (2018). The *Morrison* decision is discussed *infra* Sections 5.5 and 8.

enforcement styles and intensity.[1118] Empirical support for a continued role for bonding comes from a study of foreign issuers that elected to terminate their U.S. registration and associated reporting obligations following the introduction of SEC Rule 12h-6 in 2007, which made termination easier.[1119] The firms that consequently de-registered generally had lower funding requirements than the foreign issuers that remained. This is consistent with bonding, as the benefits of a more credible commitment to investor protection should be more pronounced for firms with an ongoing need to raise capital.[1120] Another study found that the value of a U.S. cross-listing was significantly reduced following the introduction of Rule 12h-6; a finding that is consistent with both the legal and the reputational versions of the bonding hypothesis.[1121] It thus appears that, as U.S. disclosure regulation became less of a "lobster trap" (easy to enter, hard to leave) after the introduction of Rule 12h-6, foreign issuers were no longer able to make credible

---

[1118] Coffee, *supra* note 1018; s*ee also* Howell E. Jackson, *The Impact of Enforcement: A Reflection*, 156 U. PA. L. REV. PENNUMBRA 400 (2008), http://www.pennumbra.corn/responses/02-2008/Jackson.pdf; *infra* Section 8.

[1119] Rule 12h-6 made de-registration easier for foreign issuers whose securities were comparatively thinly traded in the U.S. market. *See* SEC, Termination of a Foreign Private Issuer's Registration of a Class of Securities Under Section 12(g) and Duty to File Reports Under Section 13(a) or 15(d) of the Securities Exchange Act of 1934, 72 Fed. Reg. 16,934 (Apr. 5, 2007).

[1120] Craig Doidge, G. Andrew Karolyi & René M. Stulz, *Why do Foreign Firms Leave U.S. Equity Markets?*, 65 J. FIN. 1507 (2010).

[1121] Chinmoy Ghosh & Fan He, *The Diminishing Benefits of U.S. Cross-Listing: Economic Consequences of SEC Rule 12h-6*, 52 J. FIN. & QUANTITATIVE ANALYSIS 1143 (2017). Using the voting premium in dual-class firms as a proxy for agency costs, the authors found (with a difference-in-difference approach) that the voting premium had declined significantly in U.S. cross-listed firms relative to their not cross-listed peers, and that the overall "cross-listing premium" had declined from 29% to 8% following the introduction of Rule 12h-6. This decline was most significant for firms from countries with weak disclosure rules and weak investor protection, indicating a reduction in the value of legal bonding mechanisms. Interestingly, the authors also found that reputational bonding mechanisms (proxied by analyst coverage and institutional ownership) were associated with a higher cross-listing premium, and that issuers with higher levels of analyst coverage (but not institutional ownership) suffered less of a decline in cross-listing premium following the introduction of Rule 12h-6.

commitments to the U.S. disclosure regime for an indefinite period of time and their valuation suffered.[1122]

5.3 Case Study: Primary Markets in the UK

While the literature on bonding reported measurable valuation and cost of capital benefits associated with foreign firms listing in the U.S.,[1123] there were no equivalent results in relation to listing in the UK.[1124] However, the UK listing regime in place at the time of these studies relegated most foreign issuers to a junior segment of the market. Until 2005, foreign firms were required to list in a "Secondary" segment, which imposed only the EU minimum rules. It seems likely such a listing would have proved most appealing to liquidity-seeking firms, rather than those wishing to bond, as it was significantly more lenient to issuers than the "Primary" segment, which was reserved for domestic issuers. However, foreign companies could obtain a Primary listing if they were willing to incorporate a new "topco" in the UK, which it appears from Figure 15 was done quite frequently.[1125]

Following a three-year review, the UK amended its listing regime in 2010 to divide issuers—both domestic and foreign—into "Premium" and a "Standard" listings.[1126] A Standard listing, like the former Secondary listing, entails only compliance with the minimum requirements of EU rules, whereas a Premium listing—like the former Primary listing—contains various super-

---

[1122] *See generally* Edward Rock, *Securities Regulation as Lobster Trap: A Credible Commitment Theory of Mandatory Disclosure*, 23 CARDOZO L. REV. 675 (2002).

[1123] Luzi Hail & Christian Leuz, *Cost of Capital Effects and Changes in Growth Expectations Around U.S. Cross-Listings*, 93 J. FIN. ECON. 428 (2009); *see also* sources cited in *supra* note 958.

[1124] Craig Doidge, G. Andrew Karolyi & René M. Stulz, *Has New York Become Less Competitive than London in Global Markets? Evaluating Foreign Listing Choices Over Time*, 91 J. FIN. ECON. 253 (2009).

[1125] *See supra* note 1109.

[1126] Until 2010, the UK listing regime was divided into "primary" and "secondary" listings. Primary listings were for IPOs, and were consequently largely UK companies. The secondary listing segment, in contrast, was only open to overseas companies. However, the term "secondary" became a misnomer after 2005, from when foreign firms were permitted to have this listing type in London without a primary listing in their home jurisdictions. *See* FINANCIAL SERVICES AUTHORITY, A REVIEW OF THE STRUCTURE OF THE LISTING REGIME, DP08/1, 12 (2008).

equivalent provisions. A Premium listing requires issuers to establish a three-year financial track record, to apply rules on shareholder approval for significant transactions and pre-emption rights for seasoned equity offerings, and to comply with the UK Corporate Governance Code (or explain non-compliance).[1127] The rationale was to seek to establish a separating equilibrium for cross-listing firms: bonding for high-quality firms, using the more onerous Premium listing; and the pursuit of liquidity at lower cost, using the Standard listing, for lower-quality firms. The 2010 changes permit cross-listing firms to distinguish themselves more clearly. However, we are aware of no studies specifically investigating the performance of foreign firms that have opted into the Premium regime. This is an interesting avenue for future research.

Of course, the extent to which such bonding can occur depends on how effective the rules and their associated enforcement are in dealing with corporate governance problems. Cheffins argues that the UK corporate governance model, aimed primarily at tackling managerial agency costs, rather than abuse by dominant shareholders, is ineffective when it comes to policing the blockholder-controlled firms that have tended to cross-list in the UK, often obtaining Premium listing status.[1128] For example, the cornerstone of the UK's Corporate Governance Code – the "comply or explain" model – is undermined when there is a dominant shareholder who declines to take action.[1129] For that reason, the FCA recently amended its Listing Rules to insert provisions that tackle companies with a dominant shareholder. They do so mainly by strengthening directors' independence and, subject to one director alleging abuse of power by the dominant shareholder, by widening the scope of related party transaction provisions.[1130]

However, the changes described in this chapter have meant that cross-listing is in decline in the UK as well. In February 2017, the UK Financial Conduct Authority (FCA) announced another review of the regulation of

---

[1127] Only companies with a Premium listing are eligible for inclusion in the LSE's main FTSE indices, however. *See* FTSE RUSSELL, GROUND RULES FOR THE FTSE UK INDEX SERIES, v12.8 (2016).

[1128] Brian Cheffins, *The Undermining of UK Corporate Governance(?)*, 33 OXFORD J. LEG. STUD. 503 (2013).

[1129] *Id.* at 509-13; *see also* Eilís Ferran, *Corporate Mobility and Company Law*, 79 MODERN L. REV. 813 (2016).

[1130] *See* Roger Barker & Iris H-Y Chiu, *Protecting Minority Shareholders in Blockholder-Controlled Companies – Critically Evaluating the UK's Enhanced Listing Regime*, 10 CAP. MARKETS L.J. 98 (2015).

primary markets.[1131] The FCA is concerned that cross-listings are in long-term decline and that stakeholders have informed it that this is due to the increasing ease with which institutional investors can transact in overseas stock markets using Global Depositary Receipts (GDRs).[1132] The FCA has floated the question whether an "international segment" could better serve issuers and investors by providing a more prestigious form of listing than the current Standard listing, while still being less stringent than the Premium listing.[1133]

As we have seen, however, there are routes to tap liquidity that have even lower costs than cross-listing on a "Standard" segment. These consist of private placements to institutional investors that are undertaken without any associated listing. In the U.S., this has traditionally occurred using private placements to institutional buyers. This mechanism also underpins London's much-touted Alternative Investment Market (AIM), launched in 1995. AIM is actually only a secondary market, with the primary market component operating as a private placement. However, unlike U.S. private placements, thanks to the absence of meaningful resale restrictions, retail as well as sophisticated investors can participate in AIM's secondary market. It was deliberately structured in this way to take advantage of then-EU rules that exempted a "multilateral trading facility" (MTF) from compliance with issuer securities law rules. Empirical studies suggest that firms that list on AIM are typically smaller and younger than those listing on the Main Market, and that they join AIM to take advantage of its lower costs.[1134] AIM-listing firms are not, however distinguishable from Main Market firms in terms of market valuation or risk of failure.[1135]

In its first decade, AIM was highly successful in attracting issuers, so much so that in 2006, its "IPOs" raised more funds than those on Nasdaq.[1136] In

---

[1131] FINANCIAL CONDUCT AUTHORITY, DISCUSSION PAPER: REVIEW OF THE EFFECTIVENESS OF PRIMARY MARKETS: THE UK PRIMARY MARKETS LANDSCAPE (2017).

[1132] *Id.* at 22.

[1133] *Id.* at 21-23. The FCA is at the same time apparently content to relax certain Premium listing rules in favour of sovereign-controlled issuers. *See supra* note 986.

[1134] John A. Doukas & Hafiz Hoque, *Why Firms Favour the AIM When They can List on Main Market?*, 60 J. INT'L MONEY & FIN. 378 (2016).

[1135] Ulf Nielsson, *Do Less Regulated Markets Attract Lower Quality Firms? Evidence from the London AIM Market*, 22 J. FIN. INTERMEDIATION 335 (2013).

[1136] Joseph Gerakos, Mark Lang & Mark Maffett, *Post-Listing Performance and Private Sector Regulation: The Experience of London's Alternative Investment Market*, 56 J. ACCT. & ECON. 189 (2013).

so doing, it drew the ire of U.S. regulators, with an SEC commissioner labelling it a "casino" where 30 per cent of new listings were "gone in a year"[1137] and the then-head of the NYSE saying AIM "did not have any standards at all."[1138] Subsequent empirical research reports that AIM-listed firms have underperformed those listed on traditional regulated exchanges. Firms with a higher proportion of retail investors were particularly badly affected,[1139] suggesting investor protection concerns are a real issue. Another study found that firms switching from AIM to the London Main Market saw positive announcement returns, whereas those moving in the opposite direction had negative announcement returns.[1140]

After peaking in 2007 with 1,694 issuers (347 of which were international),[1141] AIM's size has steadily declined, today having only 973 issuers (171 of which are international). Many firms on AIM are small and, as such, unlikely to list on a regulated exchange; only 36 per cent have a market capitalization above £50m ($62m). Part of AIM's decline is attributable to changes in EU laws that partially assimilated MTFs to regular exchanges,[1142] making AIM access costlier. The London Stock Exchange has recently begun a

---

[1137] Jeremy Grant, Norma Cohen & David Blackwell, *SEC Official Sparks Row Over Aim "Casino,"* FIN. TIMES, Mar 8, 2007 (also noting that Commissioner Campos explained that his comments were taken out of context).

[1138] John Gapper, *Thain Lambasts AIM Standards*, FIN. TIMES, Jan. 26, 2007. In his chapter, *supra*, Donald Langevoort describes "large-scale private financing with a high level of resale liquidity but none of the burdens of regulatory 'publicness'" as either "nirvana or … a terrifying void, depending on one's perspective," a description that seems to suit the AIM market well.

[1139] Gerakos et al., *supra* note 1136.

[1140] Tim Jenkinson & Tarun Ramadorai, *Does One Size Fit All? The Consequences of Switching Markets with Different Regulatory Standards*, 19 EUR. FIN. MGMT. 852 (2013). However, these authors also found positive cumulative abnormal returns of 25 per cent in the year after a switch to the AIM market, implying that these firms had used the flexibility to opt into a regime more suitable to their needs, in the ultimate interest of shareholders.

[1141] LONDON STOCK EXCHANGE, AIM FACTSHEET (2017).

[1142] As a recent example, the EU Market Abuse Regulation that came into effect in July 2016 extended the framework to cover instruments trading on MTFs, including AIM.

review of the AIM Rules.[1143]

5.4 Primary Markets in Asia

In addition to being the region channeling the most IPO funds to issuers in 2015 and 2016,[1144] exchanges in Asia also have significant amounts of trading and new listings, as shown in Figures 16 and 17.[1145] More than half of all listed companies in the world are listed in Asia, but they represent only a third of the world's market capitalization.[1146] Singapore is a financial hub whose main exchange has the fourth highest number of cross-listed firms in the world, serving many of the developing countries of Asia.[1147] In contrast, the Stock Exchange of Hong Kong (SEHK) is focused on China. Since December 2016, SEHK operates two links to Chinese mainland markets – the "Shanghai-Hong Kong Stock Connect" which was introduced in 2014 and the more recent "Shenzhen-Hong Kong Stock Connect" in December 2016. These links allow international investors to trade stocks listed in Shanghai or Shenzhen in mainland China, with clearing through the local Hong Kong system.

In 2014, HKEX (the SEHK's parent company) launched a public consultation regarding safeguards to permit dual-class share listings.[1148] The exchange concluded from the responses that it had support for a proposal which would include various safeguards for firms listing with a non-one-share-one-vote structure. Contemplated safeguards included only allowing such structures for very high expected market cap firms and tougher rules for independent non-executive directors.[1149] However, the Hong Kong Securities and Futures

---

[1143] *See, e.g.*, London Stock Exchange Group, *Discussion Paper: AIM Rules Review* (2017).

[1144] *See supra* Section 5.2.

[1145] Note that the statistics from WFE are based on data from its member exchanges. For the U.S., only data from Nasdaq and NYSE are included.

[1146] According to data from the World Federation of Exchanges as of the end of January 2017, Asia had 26,959 listings out of a global total of 51,651.

[1147] David C. Donald, *Bridging Finance without Fragmentation: A Comparative Look at Market Connectivity in the U.S., Europe and Asia*, 16 EUR. BUS. ORG. L. REV. 173 (2015).

[1148] HKEX, CONCEPT PAPER: WEIGHTED VOTING RIGHTS (2014).

[1149] HKEX, CONSULTATION CONCLUSIONS TO CONCEPT PAPER ON WEIGHTED VOTING RIGHTS (2015).

Figure 16: Number of trades (millions), by region

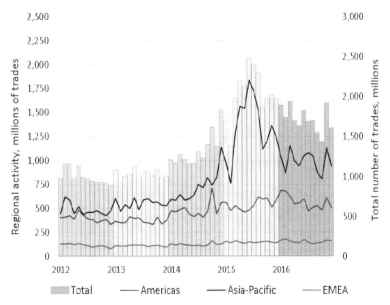

Source: World Federation of Exchanges

Figure 17: Number of new listings, by region

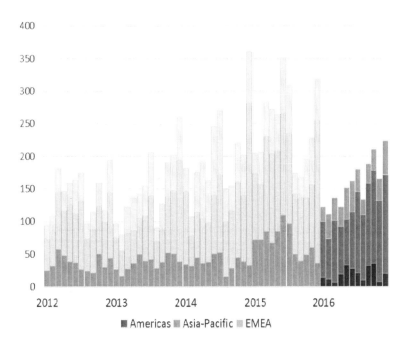

Source: World Federation of Exchanges

Commission did not support the proposal,[1150] and since its approval was required to amend the listing standards of the exchange, the HKEx was forced to abandon the project. As a result of the one-share-one-vote requirement, several significant technology firms, such as Alibaba, Baidu, JD.com and Weibo have instead opted to list in the U.S.

Asian stock markets have been found to be more subject to "idiosyncratic" influences in pricing, and more detached from fundamentals, than other stock markets in the G-7.[1151] IMF researchers have recommended improvements to securities regulation to reduce the observed "noise" in stock pricing.[1152] The Hong Kong market has recently exhibited several unusual events, including inexplicable rallies and crashes.[1153] The Hong Kong market is also idiosyncratic in that much of the equity placed in IPOs in the last year was sold to cornerstone investors who enter into lock-up agreements and do not trade (reducing the free float), and in that the government controls the board of the exchange.

5.5 The Impact of *Morrison*

For a foreign issuer choosing how to enter the U.S. capital markets, the Supreme Court's decision in *Morrison v. NAB* and decisions of lower courts have chiseled out some relatively clear boundaries for when and how § 10(b) liability will apply.

Morrison established a "transactional test" for § 10(b) such that it applies to "transactions in securities listed on domestic exchanges, and domestic transactions in other securities."[1154] The first prong ("domestic exchanges") has been interpreted narrowly to exclude transactions in securities not listed on a

---

[1150] SECURITIES AND FUTURES COMMISSION, SFC STATEMENT ON THE SEHK'S DRAFT PROPOSAL ON WEIGHTED VOTING RIGHTS (2015), https://www.sfc.hk/edistributionWeb/gateway/EN/news-and-announcements/news/doc?refNo=15PR69.

[1151] Fabian Lipinsky & Li Lian Ong, *Asia's Stock Markets: Are There Crouching Tigers and Hidden Dragons?* (working paper, 2014), https://www.imf.org/external/pubs/ft/wp/2014/wp1437.pdf.

[1152] *Id.*

[1153] Jennifer Hughes, *Hong Kong Struggles with Proposed IPO Shake-Up*, FIN. TIMES, Sept. 20, 2016.

[1154] 561 U.S. 247, 267 (2010).

U.S. exchange.¹¹⁵⁵ Further, a cross-listing on a U.S. exchange will not be sufficient to fulfil this test if the plaintiff transacted in such securities on a non-U.S. exchange.¹¹⁵⁶ This has been explicitly confirmed in a case where plaintiffs purchased foreign shares of an issuer with American Depositary Receipts (ADRs) listed on a U.S. exchange.¹¹⁵⁷

Issuer-sponsored ADR programs come in three types. Level III ADRs permit capital raising and are listed on a stock exchange. Level I and Level II ADRs do not permit capital raising; the difference between them is that Level II ADRs are listed on a stock exchange while Level I ADRs may only be quoted OTC.¹¹⁵⁸ Since Level III and Level II ADRs are listed on a U.S. exchange, they would be covered by the first prong of *Morrison* and § 10(b) claims would not suffer automatic preclusion due to extraterritoriality. Level I ADRs, which trade OTC and therefore are not 'listed" as required under the first prong, would instead need to be covered by the second ("domestic transactions") prong. The Second Circuit has elucidated that it will find a "domestic transaction" when "irrevocable liability is incurred or title passes" in the U.S.¹¹⁵⁹ This formulation

---

¹¹⁵⁵ Absolute Activist Value Master Fund Ltd v. Ficeto, 677 F.3d 60, 66 (2d Cir. 2012); United States v. Georgiou, 777 F3d 125, 134 (3d Cir. 2015) (simply noting that the OTC Bullein Board and the Pink Sheets were not among the eighteen national securities exchanges registered with the SEC).

¹¹⁵⁶ City of Pontiac Policemen's & Firemen's Ret Sys v. UBS AG, 752 F.3d 173 (2d Cir. 2014). The court clarified that both prongs of *Morrison* should be read to take aim at domestic transactions, and that the first prong's "domestic listing" phrase should be considered a proxy for a domestic transaction. *Id.* at 180. The court also held that the placing of a buy order in the U.S. for the purchase of a foreign security on a foreign exchange was not sufficient to allege that irrevocable liability was transferred under *Absolute Activist. Id.*

¹¹⁵⁷ *In re* Royal Bank of Scotland Grp PLC Sec Litig, 765 F. Supp. 2d 327, 336 (S.D.N.Y. 2011) ("The idea that a foreign company is subject to U.S. [s]ecurities laws everywhere it conducts foreign transactions merely because it has 'listed' some securities in the United States is simply contrary to the spirit of *Morrison*.")

¹¹⁵⁸ For Level I, only a Form F-6 needs to be filed with the SEC to establish the ADR facility (17 CFR 239.36). This is a short form that is focused only on the ADR arrangements; no information about the company's business is necessary. For Level II, the company must also annually register and file Form 20-F and ongoing disclosures.

¹¹⁵⁹ Absolute Activist Value Master Fund Ltd v. Ficeto, 677 F.3d 60 (2d Cir. 2012). The court noted that, in order to allege that irrevocable liability was incurred or that title was transferred within the U.S., the plaintiff would need to

inevitably leads to deeper inquiries into the specific facts than the transaction test's first prong.

In addition, in *Parkcentral v. Porsche*, the Second Circuit held that "a domestic transaction is necessary but not necessarily sufficient" to bring a § 10(b) claim where the transaction is "predominantly foreign" in character.[1160] In *United States v. Georgiou*, the Third Circuit found that this second prong applied to transactions in the U.S. OTC markets, since the transactions took place through U.S.-based market-makers.[1161] In a recent Californian case relating to Volkswagen's Level I ADRs trading in the OTCQX market, the parties agreed that the first prong was unavailable and the defendants did not dispute that the transaction was domestic under the second prong.[1162] Instead, the defendants argued that the transaction was predominantly foreign under *Parkcentral*, on the basis that Volkswagen's Level I ADR program did not allow it to raise capital in the U.S. and only required compliance with German disclosure laws. The court rejected this argument, concluding that Volkswagen, by sponsoring the ADR program, had taken "affirmative steps" to allow U.S. investors to buy its securities. Unsponsored ADRs, discussed further in Section 7, have been found not to create a domestic transaction under the second prong due to a lack of issuer involvement.[1163]

From the perspective of a foreign issuer considering whether to enter the U.S. capital markets, *Morrison*'s first prong appears settled: listing on a U.S.

---

allege that some of the following took place in the US: the "formation of the contracts, the placement of purchase orders, the passing of title, or the exchange of money." *Id.* at 70. In *United States v. Vilar*, 729 F.3d 62, 77 n. 11 (2d Cir. 2013), the Second Circuit has also held that "territoriality under *Morrison* concerns where, physically, the purchaser or seller committed him or herself, not where, as a matter of law, a contract is said to have been executed."

[1160] Parkcentral Global Hub v. Porsche Auto Holdings, 763 F.3d 198 (2014) (finding that the German company Porsche could not be held liable for securities fraud in the U.S. for statements it had made in relation to its intentions to take over Volkswagen when international hedge funds suffered losses on a securities-based swap agreement entered into in the U.S. which referenced Volkswagen's share price when Porsche was unaware of, and not a party to, such swap agreement).

[1161] United States v. Georgiou, 777 F.3d 125, 134 (3d Cir. 2015).

[1162] Order Re: Motions to Dismiss the Consolidated Securities Class Action Complaint, In re: Volkswagen "Clean Diesel" Marketing, Sales Practices, and Products Liability Litigation, MDL No. 2672 CRB. (C.D. Cal. Jan. 4, 2017).

[1163] Stoyas v. Toshiba Corp., 191 F. Supp. 3d 1080 (C.D. Cal. 2016).

exchange means entering the purview of the private right of action under § 10(b). As regards the second prong, *Volkswagen* is the only case available on Level I ADRs to date, which may mean that the case law is less settled.[1164] To summarize, the post-*Morrison* regulatory environment appears to allow issuers to estimate their U.S. liability exposure with reference to the proportion of their securities that they decide to actually make available in the U.S.

6 Secondary Market Trading

In this Section, we consider global issues in the regulation of trading venues. We first examine the "menu" of trading venues on offer in the U.S. and the EU; next we briefly discuss the new EU rules on dark pools and concentration of trading on multilateral trading venues; finally, we offer a substantive comparison of the regulation of high frequency trading and insider trading and reflect upon the significance, if any, of these differences for the operation of international markets.

6.1 Investor Choice: the U.S. Venue Menu

From a regulatory perspective, there are two main types of U.S. stock markets: national securities exchanges (such as NYSE and Nasdaq)[1165] and Alternative Trading Systems (ATSs), such as Electronic Communication Networks (ECNs) and dark pools. In addition, broker-dealers can quote stocks on non-ATS systems as OTC market-makers or block positioners.[1166] The 21 national securities exchanges are the only venues where equity securities can be

---

[1164] Dudek has recently argued that Level I ADR programs should not, without more, give rise to a § 10(b) claim, since the SEC itself has long considered issuers behind such programs not to actively access the U.S. capital markets. *See* Paul Dudek, *Applying Morrison to American Depositary Receipts*, 31:2 INSIGHTS 9 (Feb. 2017).

[1165] An *exchange* is defined as "any organization . . . which constitutes, maintains or provides a market place or facilities for bringing together purchasers and sellers of securities or for otherwise performing with respect to securities the functions commonly performed by a stock exchange as that term is generally understood." Section 3(a)(1) of the Exchange Act. A *national securities exchange* is an exchange registered with the SEC, Section 6(a) of the Exchange Act.

[1166] For a description of the features of the different types of venues, see SEC, Concept Release on Equity Market Structure; Proposed Rule, 75 Fed. Regulation 3594 (Jan 21, 2010).

listed,[1167] although exchanges' revenue from listing services have generally decreased in importance in recent years.[1168]

ATSs technically fall within the statutory definition of an "exchange," but do not have to register as such if they instead comply with Regulation ATS.[1169] Among the more significant differences between exchanges and ATSs are that exchanges must undertake self-regulatory obligations over their members and that ATSs do not have to publicly disclose details about their services or fees. In addition, ATSs have greater control over which traders to allow access to.[1170]

However, significant amounts of trading occur beyond both exchanges and ATSs; in fact more off-exchange trading of listed stocks occurs off, than on, ATSs.[1171] Such trading includes inter-dealer quotation systems where dealers may post quotes for securities.[1172] One of these over-the-counter markets is the Pink Open Market ("POM"), where the equity of foreign firms not listed on a U.S. exchange is quoted by brokers. OTC Markets Inc., which operates POM and other OTC markets, compares itself to the UK AIM market.[1173] OTC Markets

---

[1167] The SEC provides a list of regulated exchanges at https://www.sec.gov/divisions/marketreg/mrexchanges.shtml.

[1168] OECD, BUSINESS AND FINANCE OUTLOOK 2016 122-23 (comparing the revenue structure of 18 listed stock exchanges in 2004 and 2014 and finding that listing fees on average decreased as a percentage of revenue from 14% in 2004 to 8% in 2014).

[1169] 17 CFR § 242.300-303. Regulation ATS requires ATSs to register as broker-dealers. *See* 17 CFR § 242.301(b)(1).

[1170] In 2015, the SEC proposed to amend Regulation ATS to increase ATS transparency. SEC, Regulation of NMS Stock Alternative Trading Systems; Proposed Rule, 80 Fed. Regulation 80998 (Dec. 28, 2015). If an ATS has more than 5% of the average daily volume of an exchange-listed stock, however, it becomes subject to a rule to not unreasonably limit access. *See* Regulation ATS Rule 17 CFR § 242.301(b)(5). In contrast, exchanges are required to allow any qualified broker-dealer to become a member. Section 6(a)(2) of the Exchange Act.

[1171] LAURA TUTTLE, OTC TRADING: DESCRIPTION OF NON-ATS OTC TRADING IN NATIONAL MARKET SYSTEM STOCKS (2014).

[1172] 17 CFR § 240.15c2-11(e)(2) ("any system of general circulation to brokers or dealers which regularly disseminates quotations of identified brokers or dealers").

[1173] *See supra* Section 5.3; *see also* OTC Markets, Presentation to SEC Advisory Committee on Small and Emerging Companies (presentation by Dan Zinn, General Counsel, arguing that OTC Markets had 60 issuers that "graduated" to a

Inc. has established various market segments and criteria, of which POM is the segment subject to the least requirements.[1174] As of February 2017, POM had 8,245 securities quoted, of which 670 were from the UK. It was recently announced that a leading provider of automated trading systems would incorporate OTC Markets Inc. data into its order book,[1175] a move which could facilitate cross-border arbitrage in foreign securities quoted in POM and listed abroad.[1176] Retail investors are able to buy unlisted equities quoted on the OTC Markets through their regular brokers, and are the predominant owners of such equities.[1177]

6.2 Investor Choice: The EU Venue Menu

Under EU rules, two types of multilateral trading venues are available for equity trading: regulated markets (RMs) and multilateral trading facilities (MTFs). These are neutral venues that may not execute client orders against proprietary capital and must provide traders access on a non-discriminatory basis.[1178] In addition, investment firms that deal on their own account to execute client orders outside an RM or MTF on an "organized, frequent, systematic and substantial" basis are subject to a regulatory framework for "systematic internalizers" (SIs).[1179]

---

national exchange in 2015, compared to just 4 for the AIM Market), https://www.sec.gov/info/smallbus/acsec-071916-otc-zinn-reg-a.pdf.

[1174] The POM in turn has three tiers, where the least onerous tier is called "No Information" and includes firms that do not provide disclosure to investors. *See* https://www.otcmarkets.com/marketplaces/otc-pink.

[1175] Press Release, OTC Markets, OTC Markets Group Data Now Available Via Redline Trading Solutions (Mar. 30, 2016), https://www.redlinetrading.com/s/Redline-OTC-pr-1603.pdf.

[1176] ADRs established on the basis of 12g3-2(b) require a listing in the home country.

[1177] Andrew Ang, Assaf A. Shtauber & Paul C. Tetlock, *Asset Pricing in the Dark: The Cross-Section of OTC Stocks*, 26 REV. FIN. STUD. 2985 (2013).

[1178] MiFID II, Art. 53(1) (RMs), Art. 18(3) (MTFs), Recital (7) (principles). MiFID II, which together with the companion regulation MIFIR will replace what is now known as MiFID I, will come into force on January 1, 2018. We refer to MiFID II and MIFIR in the footnotes. Unless we indicate otherwise, the forthcoming rules described in the text do not innovate on the MiFID I regime.

[1179] MiFID II, Art. 4(1)(20), Art. 14.

The regime in force until the end of 2017 puts a premium on competition among trading venues and other liquidity services providers, by banning any concentration rule across the EU. It does so in the absence of a consolidated tape and with weak enforcement of the best execution rule. Reacting to widespread concerns about the unfairness of this open-architecture framework for retail investors, the forthcoming MiFID II regime makes a U-turn and, with due exceptions, mandates equity trading on organized trading venues with the purpose of reducing market fragmentation and facilitating efficient price discovery. The new regime also promotes the private supply of a consolidated tape of executed trades by channeling post-trade transparency reporting via specified routes which should facilitate private party solutions to data consolidation.[1180] Nevertheless, it is interesting to note that in contrast to the U.S., a consolidated tape of trading quotes—and hence a "European Market System"—is not yet part of the EU equity markets environment and is unlikely to operate before the next decade.[1181]

6.3 Old and New Topics in the Regulation of Cross-Border Trading

In comparing U.S. and EU trading regulation, we have identified four areas of diverging approaches that may affect cross-border coordination or competition or anyhow deserve further reflections and analysis in a New Special Study. We discuss dark pools, the EU's new trading obligation, high-frequency trading (HFT), and insider trading prohibitions.

6.3.1 Dark Pools

With MiFID II, the EU will introduce limits on trading in dark pools, with the goal of protecting price formation on organized trading venues.[1182] All trading venues will generally be required to provide pre-trade transparency on a continuous basis,[1183] but competent authorities will be permitted to waive this requirement for (a) reference price trades (where dark orders are matched at a price set at another venue); (b) negotiated transactions (e.g., where orders are matched within the volume-weighted spread of quotes of market makers of the

---

[1180] MiFIR, Arts. 20-22.

[1181] *See, e.g.,* HOGAN LOVELLS, MIFID II DATA REPORTING SERVICES (2017), http://hoganlovells.com/~/media/hogan-lovells/pdf/mifid/subtopic-pdf/lwdlib01-4925126-v1-mifid_ii_data_publication_v2.pdf.

[1182] MiFIR, Art. 5 gives this rationale.

[1183] MiFIR, Art. 3.

trading venue operating the system); (c) large-scale orders; and (d) orders held in an order management facility (such as "iceberg orders" where only a portion of the full order is initially displayed and gradually revealing new portions as it executes). Waivers under (a) and (b) will be capped at a maximum of 4 per cent of an equity security's total trading volume, and no more than 8 per cent of all trading in any equity security may take place under such waivers.[1184] This is known as the "double volume cap" (DVC). If trading exceeds these limits in a 12-month period, dark trading will be suspended on the venue in question or across the EU, depending on the cap exceeded.

As this type of cap is a new technique to regulate trading in dark liquidity pools, the change of EU regimes may serve as a natural experiment to see whether the new market structure framework results in improved price formation.[1185] The double volume cap also raises the question whether EU trading in dark pools could move to third countries if the EU suspends dark trading in a security. It appears that EU market participants have prepared new order types and functionality to maintain opportunities for dark trading, so this may not be an immediate risk.[1186]

6.3.2 The New Trading Concentration Rule

While the double volume cap rule is aimed at trading venues, MiFIR also introduces a requirement, known as the share trading obligation (STO), that where shares are available for trading on organized EU trading venues, or a third-country venue that has been assessed as equivalent, EU investment firms must actually trade them on such organized venues.[1187]

[1184] MiFIR, Arts 4-5.

[1185] *See also* SEC Commissioner Luis A. Aguilar, Public Statement: Shedding Light on Dark Pools (Nov. 18, 2015) (suggesting that the SEC should monitor the effects of EU initiatives), https://www.sec.gov/news/statement/shedding-light-on-dark-pools.html. For a discussion of how studies of the EU framework could be designed, see Merritt B. Fox, *MiFID II and Equity Trading: A U.S. View, in* REGULATION OF THE EU FINANCIAL MARKETS: MIFID II AND MIFIR 519 (Busch & Ferrarini eds., 2017).

[1186] *See* Peter Gomber & Ilya Gvozdevskiy, *Dark Trading Under MiFID II, in* REGULATION OF THE EU FINANCIAL MARKETS: MIFID II AND MIFIR 386-88 (Busch & Ferrarini eds., 2017).

[1187] Art. 23 provides two limited exceptions to this obligation: (1) non-systematic, ad-hoc, irregular, and infrequent trades, and (2) trades between eligible counterparties that do not contribute to price discovery.

The STO could have significant effects on cross-border trading because of its bias toward EU trading venues. Where U.S. and other "third country" stocks are also traded on EU trading venues, the STO would require EU investment firms to trade them on the EU venues, regardless of how its pricing and market depth compares to non-EU venues (save those designated as "equivalent"). For example, in the last 12 months there has been a relatively small amount of trading of Apple stock on EU venues.[1188] Under the STO, unless and until Nasdaq is assessed as equivalent to a EU trading venue, EU trading would have to be directed to EU venues.

The STO is currently a source of significant uncertainty for EU investment firms, since it is unclear both to what extent there will be equivalence decisions in place when it comes into effect in January 2018 and how it relates to best execution obligations that would designate a non-EU venue. In particular, unless the UK following Brexit is immediately deemed equivalent, EU investment firms would be required to avoid trading on the London Stock Exchange when the relevant equity security is available on alternative EU trading venues.

The EU rule could also impact U.S. equity market structure. If the EU were to take a selective approach and grant equivalence only to certain U.S. exchanges,[1189] trading of U.S. stocks by EU investment firms could only take place on such venues, meaning that EU regulation would drive inbound U.S. liquidity to the venues deemed equivalent.

6.3.3 Algorithmic and High-Frequency Trading

Exchanges and trading venues compete for volume, both intra- and inter-jurisdictionally. Attracting high-frequency traders (HFTs) can add

---

[1188] For example, data from the Fidessa Fragulator indicates that a relatively small portion of the volume in Apple stock (typically less than 0.20%) trades over the Deutsche Börse. *See* http://fragmentation.fidessa.com/fragulator/.

[1189] The equivalence assessment will proceed under Art. 23(1) MiFIR, which directs to Art. 4(1) of the Prospectus Directive 2003/71 via Art. 25(4)(a) MiFID II. The process entails an assessment by the Commission of whether the third country trading venue is equivalent with an EU regulated market (i.e., not an MTF), which suggests that it is more likely that a U.S. exchange will be deemed equivalent than an ATS.

significantly to such volume. In fact, they are estimated to account for between 24 and 43 per cent of the value traded within the EU.[1190]

In the aftermath of the financial crisis, European policymakers addressed the regulatory challenges posed by HFT by applying the "precautionary principle": they viewed HFTs as capable of exacerbating market volatility and malfunctioning, which could create systemic risk.[1191] Hence, they targeted HFTs with *ex ante* regulatory strategies in order to prevent or reduce harm rather than having to respond to issues in real time (which is difficult, given that "real time" for HFTs is milliseconds or less):[1192] more precisely, they deployed, first, *entry regulation*, which includes the requirement to be licensed by the regulator. Second, they resorted to *conduct regulation*, such as restrictions on cancellations of orders or market maker obligations to post quotes. Finally, in a subset of countries, including France and Italy, a structural restriction in the form of a financial transaction tax (FTT) aimed at curbing undesirably excessive activity was introduced.

The first European country to tackle HFTs was Germany, in 2013.[1193] Its legislation served as a model for the subsequent EU-wide regime, which will enter into force in 2018. HFTs on German markets are required to obtain authorization and are supervised by the German regulator, regardless of where they are physically located. In addition, HFTs must flag orders generated by algorithms to allow market surveillance of individual algorithms, while trading venues are required to determine a minimum tick size, establish an order-to-trade ratio for each traded instrument, charge separate fees for excessive usage of their systems, and have circuit breakers in place. The German Act is only applicable to German markets, a fact used in a study of its effects which reported that it had

---

[1190] ESMA, ECONOMIC REPORT 1/2014: HIGH-FREQUENCY TRADING ACTIVITY IN EU EQUITY MARKETS, 4 (the two figures reflect two different approaches to identify HFT activity).

[1191] MiFIR, Recital 32.

[1192] Oliver Linton, Maureen O'Hara & J. P. Zigrand, *The Regulatory Challenge of High-Frequency Markets*, in HIGH-FREQUENCY TRADING: NEW REALITIES FOR TRADERS, MARKETS AND REGULATORS 208-09 (Easley, López de Prado & O'Hara eds., 2013).

[1193] An English translation of the German law is available at the German regulator's website: https://www.bafin.de/SharedDocs/Veroeffentlichungen/EN/Aufsichtsrecht/Gesetz/hft_en.html.

reduced the amount of intraday messages, but had only a small impact on trade execution in the form of a negligible widening of the bid-ask spread.[1194]

Similarly, the new MiFID II regime will introduce specific EU rules for algorithmic trading (AT)[1195] and HFT,[1196] where the latter is a subset of the former. The new regime will harmonize EU rules, bringing to an end a period of varied regulatory approaches to HFT across EU member states, ranging from permissive (UK) to uncertain (France),[1197] to prescriptive (as in Germany).

[1194] Martin Haferkorn & Kai Zimmermann, *The German High-Frequency Trading Act: Implications for Market Quality* (working paper, 2014), https://papers.ssrn.com/sol3/papers.cfm?abstract_id=2514334 (noting that many HFTs in Germany already had prior regulatory authorization in another capacity).

[1195] The EU defines "algorithmic trading" as "trading in financial instruments where a computer algorithm automatically determines individual parameters of orders such as whether to initiate the order, the timing, price or quantity of the order or how to manage the order after its submission, with limited or no human intervention." MiFID II, Art. 4(1)(39).

[1196] The EU defines HFT as "an algorithmic trading technique characterised by: (a) infrastructure intended to minimise network and other types of latencies, including at least one of the following facilities for algorithmic order entry: co-location, proximity hosting or high-speed direct electronic access; (b) system-determination of order initiation, generation, routing or execution without human intervention for individual trades or orders; and (c) high message intraday rates which constitute orders, quotes or cancellations." MiFID II, Art. 4(1)(40). The EU considers high message intraday rates to be two messages per second for any single financial instrument or four messages per second for all financial instruments. Art. 19 of the Commission Delegated Regulation (EU) of 25.4.2016 supplementing Directive 2014/65/EU of the European Parliament and of the Council as regards organisational requirements and operating conditions for investment firms and defined terms for the purposes of that Directive, [C(2016) 2398].

[1197] A December 2015 decision by the French financial regulator has been described as a "*de facto* ban on HFT in France." *See* Pierre-Henri Conac, *Algorithmic Trading and High-Frequency Trading (HFT)*, *in* REGULATION OF THE EU FINANCIAL MARKETS: MIFID II AND MIFIR 519 (Busch & Ferrarini eds., 2017). However, a recent study by the French regulator did not appear to treat HFT as banned, noting that "high-frequency traders . . . are . . . best able to offer effective inventory management in an increasingly fast-moving and fragmented market." *See* AUTORITÉ DES MARCHÉS FINANCIERS, STUDY OF THE BEHAVIOUR OF HIGH-FREQUENCY TRADERS ON EURONEXT PARIS (2017).

The new European rules will treat HFT as a regulated investment activity,[1198] and require HFTs to be authorized as investment firms and comply with rules on minimum initial capital, comprehensive obligations with respect to organizational and risk-management matters, "fit and proper" requirements for management and qualifying shareholders, and numerous reporting and disclosure requirements. Firms engaging in AT will have to notify this to competent authorities both in their home state (which acts as the primary regulator) and in the state of the relevant trading venue. AT firms will be subject to specific requirements on systems and risk controls and are required to test algorithms before deployment. Further, they will be subject to specific reporting requirements allowing authorities to request, regularly or episodically, detailed descriptions of their trading strategies including parameters, limits and risk controls.[1199] HFTs are, in addition, required to keep records of all orders placed and make such records available to authorities on request.[1200] Further, AT firms pursuing market-making strategies[1201] must enter into written agreements with the relevant trading venues, containing express obligations to provide liquidity on a "regular and predictable basis," save under exceptional circumstances.[1202]

In addition to entry rules, again following the German model, MiFID II requires regulated exchanges to have circuit breakers in place,[1203] to have a minimum tick size,[1204] to be able to identify orders generated by algorithmic trading,[1205] and to limit the ratio of unexecuted orders to transactions that may be entered into the system by a member or participant.[1206] MiFID II also explicitly

---

[1198] MiFID II, Recital (18), Art. 2(1)(d).

[1199] MiFID II, Art. 17(1), 17(2).

[1200] MiFID II, Art. 17.

[1201] An investment firm pursues a market-making strategy when "as a member or participant of one or more trading venues, its strategy, when dealing on own account, involves posting firm, simultaneous two-way quotes of comparable size and at competitive prices relating to one or more financial instruments on a single trading venue or across different trading venues, with the result of providing liquidity on a regular and frequent basis to the overall market." MiFID II, Art. 17(4).

[1202] MiFID II, Art. 17(3).

[1203] MiFID II, Art. 48(5).

[1204] MiFID II, Art. 49.

[1205] MiFID II, Art. 48(10). This may be by means of flagging from members or from participants.

[1206] MiFID II, Art. 48(6).

preserves Member States' ability to permit "a regulated market to impose a higher fee for placing an order that is subsequently cancelled than an order which is executed and to impose a higher fee on participants placing a high ratio of cancelled orders to executed orders and on those operating a high-frequency algorithmic trading technique in order to reflect the additional burden on system capacity."[1207] Regulation that raises the cost of running HFT businesses will create barriers to entry, but is neutral to the extent that it merely codifies pre-existing practices (such as requiring the testing of algorithms). While entry barriers can trigger industry consolidation, reduce competition, and increase margins (and market share) for significant players, entry regulation has no impact *per se* on the "disruption" HFTs may bring to securities markets, or any negative impact they may have on other market participants. However, structural barriers that instead curb HFT by reducing the available revenue (such as a FTT), and conduct regulation (such as tick size rules, restrictions on cancellations of orders, or obligations on market makers) will directly affect the size of the HFT market.

After the EU rules enter into force, we may expect less liquidity (and perhaps less volatility in abnormal times) in European markets. This means that the EU may be an interesting source of data when considering alternative models of regulation.[1208] Similarly, while we would not expect any interjurisdictional spill-overs to the U.S. to follow from the EU's forthcoming stringent rules, cross-listed stocks may provide useful data for research.[1209]

6.3.4 Insider Trading Regulation and Enforcement

At the time of the first Special Study, the prohibition of insider trading (or at least its enforcement) was a novel U.S. idiosyncrasy.[1210] Following the SEC's efforts,[1211] it has become global. Perhaps because the SEC was behind

---

[1207] MiFID II, Art. 48(9), third para.

[1208] *See also* Fox, *supra* note 1185, at 523 (noting that it may be instructive to study the market reaction in France to a ruling that HFT order cancellation constituted market abuse).

[1209] For example, it may be interesting to see (as a measurement of market interconnectedness via cross-border arbitrage) whether liquidity decreases in stocks cross-listed on U.S. markets when HFT activity becomes costlier in EU markets.

[1210] The SEC had, in effect, launched the "disclose or abstain" policy two years earlier. *See In re* Cady, Roberts & Co., 40 SEC 907 (1961).

[1211] *See, e.g.*, Luca Enriques, Gerard Hertig, Reinier Kraakman & Edward Rock, *Corporate Law and Securities Markets, in* THE ANATOMY OF CORPORATE LAW: A

global adoption,[1212] however, the philosophy adopted across the rest of the globe is the SEC's "market egalitarianism" model, rather than the Supreme Court's more restrictive theory. The EU has a broad prohibition on trading on inside information, regardless of how the information was acquired. So too do Australia, Brazil, Hong Kong, and Singapore.[1213] The Japanese approach is limited to enumerated categories of insiders and shareholders, but still prohibits tippees from knowingly trading on material information,[1214] which is not always the result under the U.S. framework.[1215]

The global picture is thus one in which the U.S. stands alone in its unique approach to insider trading, whereas many other countries have theoretically simpler and functionally similar frameworks employing the SEC's "disclose or abstain" model (simplifying just to "abstain" for individuals with inside information considering whether to trade in anonymous securities markets). Since most other countries have a ban on insider trading that extends beyond the scope of the U.S. prohibition, the lack of a globally accepted and readily-comprehensible framework for insider trading in today's integrated capital markets is likely only to cause practical problems for Americans.[1216]

COMPARATIVE AND FUNCTIONAL APPROACH 257-58 (Kraakman, Armour, Davies, Enriques, Hansmann, Hertig, Hopt, Kanda, Pargendler, Ringe & Rock eds., 2017) (hereinafter THE ANATOMY OF CORPORATE LAW).

[1212] An investigation of how insider trading law enactment and enforcement spread found that having an MoU with the U.S. SEC made a country four times more likely to adopt insider trading laws, whereas membership of IOSCO significantly increased the likelihood of enforcement. David Bach & Abraham L. Newman, *Transgovernmental Networks and Domestic Policy Convergence: Evidence from Insider Trading Regulation*, 64 INT'L ORG. 505 (2010).

[1213] *See* DOUGLAS ARNER, BERRY HSU, SAY H. GOO, SYREN JOHNSTONE & PAUL LEJOT, FINANCIAL MARKETS IN HONG KONG 538 et seq. (2016) (Hong Kong); Luca Enriques, Gerard Hertig, Hideki Kanda & Mariana Pargendler, *Related-Party Transactions*, *in* THE ANATOMY OF CORPORATE LAW, *supra* note 1211, 159-161 (Brazil); Alexander F. Loke, *From the Fiduciary Theory to Information Abuse: The Changing Fabric of Insider Trading Law in the U.K., Australia and Singapore*, 54 AM. J. COMP. L. 123 (2006) (Australia and Singapore).

[1214] Enriques et al., *supra* note 1213, at 159-61.

[1215] Martin Bengtzen, *Private Investor Meetings in Public Firms: The Case for Increasing Transparency*, 22 FORDHAM J. CORP. & FIN. L. 33 (2017).

[1216] Indeed, it has. *See* Financial Services Authority, In the Matter of David Einhorn (Jan. 12, 2012), where a U.S. hedge fund manager refused to sign a confidentiality agreement with a UK public firm but received inside information

In the EU, rules on insider trading are closely connected with those governing *ad hoc* corporate disclosure. The same materiality threshold simultaneously activates a requirement for a firm to disclose the information and the blanket ban on trading.[1217] In contrast, the U.S. has no general requirement to disclose information as soon as it becomes material.[1218] Of course, certain categories of information must be disclosed on Form 8-K (such as entering into a material agreement), but even here there is a difference, in that U.S. companies have four business days to make such information public.[1219] To see this, imagine that a U.S. and an EU firm enter into a mutually material agreement on a Thursday morning in New York. The EU firm would need to issue a press release immediately, whereas the U.S. firm need only to file its 8-K by the following Wednesday. It is unclear why U.S. firms need so much longer to prepare announcements than do their EU counterparts. This account of the law on the books implies that disclosure dynamics are radically different on the different sides of the Atlantic. It may be fruitful to investigate whether this is the case in practice, and whether there is scope to reduce the lead-times in the U.S. disclosure framework.[1220]

The U.S. is undoubtedly the most zealous of jurisdictions when it comes to insider trading enforcement.[1221] One study has found that, as a functional

---

regardless, traded on it (allegedly in good faith), and was found to have breached UK rules on market abuse.

[1217] Arts. 14 and 17 Market Abuse Regulation 596/2014, 2014 O.J. (L 173) 1.

[1218] While U.S. stock exchanges typically require prompt issuer disclosure of material information as part of their listing rules, they do not appear to enforce these rules. For example, NYSE Rule 202.05 requires "quick" disclosure, but has never been used to sanction an issuer. *See, e.g.,* Gill North, *National Company Disclosure Regulatory Frameworks: Superficially Similar but Substantively Different*, 3 J. MARSHALL GLOBAL MKTS. L.J. 187, 194 (noting that all NYSE disciplinary actions related to the conduct of intermediaries).

[1219] 17 C.F.R. § 249.308.

[1220] Reducing disclosure lead times may also be of interest in light of a recent study that found that U.S. insiders trade profitably in the time period between the occurrence of an event and its subsequent public disclosure. *See* Alma Cohen, Robert J. Jackson, Jr. & Joshua R. Mitts, *The 8-K Trading Gap* (working paper, 2015), https://ssrn.com/abstract_id=2657877. Donald Langevoort's chapter, *supra*, also highlights these issues.

[1221] *See* Enriques et al., *supra* note 1213, at 160; *see also* Lev Bromberg, George Gilligan & Ian Ramsay, *The Extent and Intensity of Insider Trading Enforcement – an International Comparison*, 2016 J. CORP. L. STUD. 1 (2016) (comparing public

matter, enforcement is particularly important, such that firms' cost of capital decreases not with a country's adoption of insider trading laws, but on its first prosecution of violators.[1222] This may raise the question whether the U.S. would find it difficult to designate another country as equivalent for the purposes of mutual recognition.

7 Intermediaries

This section considers global regulatory issues in relation to *intermediaries* and focuses on (i) a comparative overview of U.S. and EU regulation of cross-border broker-dealer services relating to equity markets; (ii) the U.S. regulation of foreign broker-dealers; (iii) an analysis of the implications of Brexit; and (iv) an account of fiduciary duties owed to clients by EU "investment firms" (encompassing broker-dealers, investment advisers and portfolio managers) and banks engaging in investment services.[1223]

7.1 The Regulation of U.S./EU Cross-Border Broker-Dealer Services

A key policy question for regulators is whether, and to what, extent domestic investors need access to international intermediaries, or whether access to domestic intermediaries which can themselves invest internationally will suffice. In this subsection, we review the respective approaches of the U.S. and the EU to regulation of cross-border broker-dealer services in the equity markets. We focus on the U.S. federal securities regulation and the EU MiFID II/MiFIR regime which will come into effect from January 2018.[1224] This new EU regime brings significant changes, among them a new framework pertaining to non-EU investment firms (so-called third country firms) seeking to do business in the EU.

---

enforcement of insider trading in Australia, Canada, Hong Kong, Singapore, the UK and the U.S.; concluding that the U.S. imposes the greatest dollar value, but not always the most severe, sanctions).

[1222] Utpal Bhattacharya & Hazem Daouk, *The World Price of Insider Trading*, 57 J. FIN. 75 (2002).

[1223] "Investment services" include broker-dealer, underwriting and placement of securities, including securities issued by the investment services provider itself, and investment advice and portfolio management services. *See* MiFID II, Annex 1, Section A.

[1224] Directive 2014/65/EU of the European Parliament and of the Council of 15 May 2014 (MiFID II) and the Regulation (EU) No 600/2014 of the European Parliament and of the Council of 15 May 2014 ('MIFIR').

7.1.1 Investment Services Provision by Non-EU Firms Within the EU

Retail clients. MiFID II gives each EU member state the right to regulate third country firms by devolving to them the decision of whether third country firms intending to provide investment services to clients in their territory shall be required to establish a branch.[1225] If a branch is required (and authorization to open it is granted),[1226] then the firm can provide investment services to all types of clients—retail and sophisticated—within that country's territory. If a branch is not established, the third country firm will operate outside of MiFID II and must comply with national rules, which must be no less stringent than MiFID II.

Sophisticated clients. For transactions with sophisticated clients, MiFIR provides for a harmonized third country regime under which an eligible third country investment firm can obtain a passport to operate across the EU.[1227] For a third country firm to be eligible, various conditions must be satisfied in relation both to the firm and as to the country in which its head office is located (its "home country"). First, the Commission must have assessed the firm's home country's regulatory regime and concluded that it is *equivalent* to the EU regime.[1228] Such an equivalence determination itself has three components: (i) *substantive equivalence*: that the home country rules have equivalent effect to the prudential and conduct of business rules of MiFiD II and MiFIR; (ii) *Compliance*: that the legal and supervisory arrangements in the home country ensure that firms authorized there actually comply with these requirements; and (iii) *Reciprocity*: that the third country's legal framework provides for reciprocal recognition of EU firms.[1229] Second, there must be a *cooperation* agreement in place between ESMA and the third country's regulatory authorities encompassing information exchange regarding relevant firms.[1230] Third, the firm must either have registered a branch under MiFID II in an EU Member State, or must register with ESMA.[1231]

[1225] MiFID II, Arts. 39-43.

[1226] Subject to the conditions set out in Article 39(2) MiFID II, which inter alia requires that a cooperation agreement is entered into between the competent authority of the EU state and the one in the third country (Article 39(2)(b)).

[1227] MiFIR, Arts. 46-49 (and transitional rules in Art. 54).

[1228] MiFIR, Art. 46(2)(a).

[1229] *Id.*, Art. 47(1).

[1230] *Id.*, Arts 47(2); MiFID II, Art. 39(2)(b).

[1231] MiFIR, Arts. 46, 47(3).

7.1.2 Broker-Dealers' Cross-Border Direct Access to Stock-Exchanges

We now consider the respective EU and U.S. regulation of a foreign broker-dealer (for the EU, a "third country" investment firm) seeking to become a member of an exchange in the region in order to execute orders electronically there.

Our first scenario is where a U.S. broker-dealer seeks to become a member of an EU exchange in order to execute orders from its U.S. clients. This situation is, as noted above, not regulated by MiFID II but left to each EU member state. In the UK, for example, a U.S. broker-dealer that seeks to execute orders for a U.S. client on the London Stock Exchange does not require any regulatory authorization,[1232] but will (of course) need to fulfil the membership requirements of the exchange. However, the SEC restricts direct cross-border trading from the U.S. on an EU exchange by prohibiting foreign exchanges from placing trading terminals in the U.S. without registering as a U.S. exchange that becomes subject to its regulation and supervision.[1233]

The U.S. regulates the reverse first scenario, where an EU broker seeks to execute EU orders on a U.S. exchange, in a less permissive fashion than the EU. Brokers may not solicit transactions in any security unless they are registered with the SEC.[1234] While Rule 15a-6(a)(1) offers a general exemption for foreign broker-dealers that effect transactions with or for persons they have not solicited, for practical purposes the SEC's broad definition of solicitation restricts that possibility to cases where foreign broker-dealers' quotations are distributed by third parties through systems that do not allow for execution.[1235] In addition, Section 6(c)(1) of the Exchange Act stipulates that an exchange may not grant membership to anyone who is not a registered broker or dealer. The effect of these provisions is that an EU broker cannot access a U.S. exchange without registration as (or cooperation with) a U.S. broker-dealer.

[1232] While buying or selling securities is a regulated activity, there are exemptions for an "Overseas Person" that apply in this case.

[1233] *See* Howell E. Jackson, Andreas M. Fleckner & Mark Gurevich, *Foreign Trading Screens in the United States*, 1 CAPITAL MKTS. L.J. 54 (2006).

[1234] Section 15(a)(1) of the Exchange Act. Section 3(a)(4)(A) of the Exchange Act defines a broker as "any person engaged in the business of effecting transactions in securities for the account of others." Section 3(a)(17) of the Exchange Act defines interstate commerce to include communication between any foreign country and any U.S. state.

[1235] Securities and Exchange Commission, Final Rule: Registration Requirements for Foreign Broker-Dealers, Exchange Act Release No. 34-27017, 54 Fed. Reg. 30013, 30018 (July 18, 1989).

Our second scenario is where a U.S. broker-dealer is approached by EU investors to engage in securities trading on a U.S. stock exchange. In this case, MiFID II stipulates that such *reverse* solicitation (solicitation by EU clients of third country firms) shall not require authorization.[1236] It appears that MiFID II may have arrived at this approach by taking the perspective of the client requesting the service, since that is how Article 42 is drafted, but the outcome is that EU member states are proscribed from regulating foreign firms in this respect. The reverse second scenario is where an EU broker-dealer is approached by U.S. investors to engage in securities trading on an EU stock exchange. As we have seen, EU broker-dealers may execute such trades provided they do not engage in any solicitation in the U.S., as broadly defined by the SEC.[1237]

Our third scenario is where a U.S. broker seeks to approach EU investors to engage in securities trading on a U.S. stock exchange. MiFID II directs the regulation of this issue to each member state.[1238] The UK regime, for example, provides that a U.S. broker may solicit business from sophisticated investors without authorization.[1239] The reverse third scenario is where an EU broker seeks to approach U.S. investors to engage in securities trading on an EU stock exchange. Again, the U.S. SEC's regulation on solicitation prohibits such activity.

7.1.3 Investors' Cross-Border Direct Access to Stock Exchanges

Can investors trade directly on exchanges abroad, without the intermediation of a broker? Neither the EU nor the UK have any regulatory requirements that serve to prevent its investors from trading on exchanges abroad. U.S. exchange membership requires registration as a broker-dealer, however, a requirement which also applies to EU investors.

[1236] MiFID II, Art. 42.

[1237] The SEC views "solicitation" as "any affirmative effort by a broker or dealer intended to induce transactional business for the broker-dealer or its affiliates," including "the dissemination in the United States of a broker-dealer's quotes for a security" 54 Fed. Reg. 30017-18. *But see* text preceding *supra* note 1235.

[1238] MiFID II, Art. 39.

[1239] This is the case as long as the U.S. broker-dealer can establish on reasonable grounds that the recipient is sufficiently knowledgeable to understand the risks of the activity, has informed the investor about the lack of protection under the UK Financial Services and Markets Act, and the investor has agreed to such terms. *See* Art. 33 of the Financial Services and Markets Act 2000 (Financial Promotion) Order 2005.

The U.S. also takes a stricter approach in relation to U.S. investors' ability to access foreign exchanges directly. Foreign exchanges may not provide for the dissemination of quotes in the U.S. without registering with the SEC as an exchange. The practical effect of this is that U.S. investors cannot get direct access to foreign exchanges.

7.1.4 Broker-Dealers' Facilitation of Cross-Border Investment

There are various ways in which a country's domestic broker-dealer may facilitate cross-border trading by its clients. One is by making an OTC market for a foreign security.[1240] The other is to set up an unsponsored American Depositary Receipts (UADR) program. Following amendments to SEC Rule 12g3-2(b) in 2008, foreign private issuers are automatically exempted from registration so long as they have their shares listed on a non-U.S. exchange, publish all their material mandatory disclosures under local law on their website, and are not otherwise required to report under the Exchange Act. This exemption is therefore available to ADRs that are not listed in the U.S., including UADRs. Following the SEC rule change there has indeed been a significant increase in UADR programs, from 169 programs before the change to 1,579 programs as of February, 2015.[1241] UADRs appear to fulfil an important role for smaller U.S. asset managers, allowing them to compete with larger investors who can access foreign equities overseas, and also for other investor types, such as those that are restricted to buying U.S. securities.[1242] Yet, it should be noted that the laws of some countries, notably Brazil, Russia and Malaysia, reportedly prohibit the establishment of UADR programs.[1243]

A study of firms that had their securities become subject to UADR programs following the SEC's rule change found that firms with such "involuntary cross-listing" experienced a decrease in firm value, attributed to increased perceived litigation risk.[1244]

[1240] *See* text associated with *supra* notes 1172-1177.

[1241] DEUTSCHE BANK, UNSPONSORED ADRS, MARKET REVIEW (2015).

[1242] Steve Johnson, *Unprecedented Demand for Unsponsored ADRs*, FIN. TIMES, June 1, 2014.

[1243] *See* UNSPONSORED ADRS, *supra* note 1241 at 4.

[1244] Peter Iliev, Darius P. Miller & Lukas Roth, *Uninvited U.S. Investors? Economic Consequences of Involuntary Cross-Listings*, 52 J. ACC. RES. 473 (2014).

7.2 The U.S. Exemption for Foreign Broker-Dealers

While Section 15 of the Exchange Act requires brokers or dealers providing services to U.S. investors to be registered with the SEC, a general exemption from such registration has been available since 1989 for foreign intermediaries that have only limited interactions with U.S. investors (Rule 15a-6). Interactions that are generally permitted without registration include effecting unsolicited transactions, transacting with registered broker-dealers and certain other persons, and providing research reports.

Foreign broker-dealers may solicit securities transactions from certain U.S. institutional investors provided that they enter into a chaperone agreement with a U.S. broker-dealer.[1245] The chaperone must then effect all transactions with such investors and take on certain responsibilities, including issuing confirmations to the institutional investors and maintaining a consent to service of process from the foreign broker-dealer.[1246] If the foreign broker-dealer would like to visit institutional investors in the U.S., a representative of the chaperoning broker-dealer must be present and take responsibility for its communications. The chaperone must also participate in any phone calls the foreign broker-dealer makes to U.S. institutional investors, unless such investors have more than $100 million of assets under management.[1247] In 2008, against the backdrop of "ever increasing market globalization" and advances in technology, the SEC proposed to expand the 15a-6 exemptions for foreign intermediaries to allow targeting of "qualified investors" with more than $25 million in investments,[1248] reduce the role of chaperones in order to "allow qualified investors the more direct contact they seek with those expert in foreign markets and foreign securities,"[1249] and somewhat soften the SEC's interpretation of what constitutes solicitation so that quotes for securities could be disseminated in systems that did not allow for execution. These proposals were never enacted.

[1245] 17 CFR 240.15a-6(a)(3).

[1246] The chaperoning U.S. broker-dealer may delegate to the foreign broker-dealer the actual execution of the foreign securities trades and processing of records. *See* GREENE ET AL., *supra* note 1101, at 45-46.

[1247] Chaperoning is not required for phone calls that take place outside of U.S. business hours and do not involve transactions in U.S. securities. *See id.* at 14-43.

[1248] *See* Section 3(a)(54) of the Securities Exchange Act for the full definition of "qualified investor." 15 U.S.C. §78c(a)(54).

[1249] SEC Proposed Rule, Exemption of Certain Foreign Brokers or Dealers, Release No 34-58047, 73 Fed. Reg. 39182, 39188 (July 8, 2008).

A separate but fundamental question relating to Rule 15a-6 is how to reconcile its aim to regulate overseas conduct relating to overseas transactions with *Morrison v. NAB*. In *SEC v. Benger*,[1250] the court held that, following *Morrison*'s pronouncements on the scope of the Exchange Act, it could not find any Congressional intent to require registration under the Act of "brokers involved in foreign transactions on foreign exchanges."[1251] The SEC has not commented on the issue, but there is clearly significant uncertainty about the continued applicability of the rule.[1252]

7.3 U.S. Investor Access to Off-Shore Liquidity and Investment Services

In a framework where retail investors have indirect access to capital markets via institutional investors, it is less important to allow retail investors direct access to the services of foreign broker-dealers and/or to foreign trading venues (via domestic or foreign brokers). The relevant question is rather whether the regulatory restrictions for institutional investors (including investment advisers, who are treated like institutional investors under the relevant exemption rules) are justified or whether they impose unduly high costs to protect the business of domestic broker-dealers.

Table 2 summarizes the inbound and outbound interactions between investors, intermediaries and issuers according to rules in force on the two sides of the Atlantic. The SEC does not allow trading screens of foreign exchanges to be placed in the U.S. unless such exchanges choose to opt into its regulations.[1253] Hence, U.S. investors cannot transact on European exchanges via such trading screens, but can execute transactions via other methods. For example, they can engage foreign broker-dealers either from their own overseas offices or through execution-only interactions from their U.S. offices which avoid triggering SEC registration requirements as long as the foreign broker-dealer does not actively

---

[1250] SEC v. Benger, 934 F. Supp. 2d 1008 (N.D. Ill. 2013).

[1251] *Id.* at 1012; *see also id.* at 1013 ("[I]n light of *Morrison*, a broker's failure to register under Section 15(a) of the Act is not actionable in those cases where the ultimate and intended purchase and sale was foreign and thus, itself, outside the scope of the Act.")

[1252] LOUIS LOSS, JOEL SELIGMAN & TROY PAREDES, VI SECURITIES REGULATION 691-94 & n. 297 (5th ed. 2014); *see also* Edward Greene & Arpan Patel, *Consequences of Morrison v. NAB, Securities Litigation and Beyond*, 11 CAP. MKTS. L.J. 145, at 167-68 (2016) (describing difficulties in applying *Morrison*'s transactional approach to intermediary registration provisions).

[1253] *See* Jackson et al., *supra* note 1233.

Table 2. Overview of U.S.-EU Regulation of Cross-Border Investment Activity.

	EU Clients	EU Brokers	EU Exchanges	EU Issuers
U.S. Clients		If exemption applies, or reverse solicitation, and only for foreign securities	Direct access via membership for some institutional investors under EU rules (but U.S. prohibits trading screens)	U.S. Prospectus exemptions (including for qualified buyers)
U.S. Brokers	MiFID rules apply for securities transactions to be carried out on U.S. markets, unless reverse solicitation		Direct access via membership, on behalf of U.S. clients (but U.S. prohibits trading screens)	Yes, after U.S. resale restrictions cease to apply; UADRs can be traded in the U.S. upon U.S. brokers' initiative.
U.S. Exchanges	Not an issue under EU rules; through U.S. brokers under U.S. rules	Not unless authorized as U.S. brokers		No specific EU regulation of issuer that only lists outside EU
U.S. Issuers	Prospectus exemptions (including for qualified buyers)	No resale restrictions under EU rules	SEC registration required unless limited holders of record.	

solicit such business.[1254] This latter method would also apply to individual investors. The SEC's current approach may thus mainly have the effect of making trading of foreign securities costlier, particularly for retail investors.

7.4 Implications of Brexit

Brexit now looks likely to involve the UK leaving the European single market, in which case it will become a third country. This raises the question of the extent to which the new MiFIR third country passport regime for sophisticated client business could be used to provide UK investment firms with continued EU market access.[1255]

The UK government has announced that its likely strategy on exit from the EU will be a wholesale enactment of all previously-binding EU law into domestic UK law. It follows that, at the point of exit, the UK will have in place a body of financial regulation that necessarily will be substantively equivalent to EU law. The UK's FCA and PRA have larger enforcement budgets than many other EU Member States' financial regulators, which should suffice to meet the Commission's enquiries regarding compliance. And it will naturally be in the UK government's interests to agree, where necessary, to reciprocity for EU financial services firms wishing to do business in the UK.

There is a widely held fear that the process of determining equivalence may become politicized in the context of a messy Brexit negotiation. Yet this likely under-appreciates the merits of leaving decisions to technocrats, which is precisely what the democratically-opaque structure of the Commission, and a fortiori, the delegation of the initial assessment to the European Supervisory Authorities, is intended to achieve.[1256] The Commission have already made equivalence decisions in favor of many of the G20 countries and other international financial centers in respect of other provisions of EU financial regulation.[1257]

A more plausible concern is whether the Commission will have completed the necessary equivalence determinations by the time the UK's two-year "exit period" is completed. Neither a third country, nor its firms, have any right to compel the Commission to start the process of making an equivalence determination, even if the third country would manifestly meet the criteria. The

---

[1254] *Id.* at 69-75.

[1255] The following text draws on Armour, *supra* note 996, at S61-S64.

[1256] Niamh Moloney, *Financial Services, the EU, and Brexit: An Uncertain Future for the City?*, 17 GERM. L.J. 75 (2016).

[1257] Armour, *supra* note 996, at S62.

very earliest equivalence decisions under EMIR, for Australia, Hong Kong and Singapore, took two years from when the legislation came into force.

A further concern relates to the future beyond the short term. Equivalence must be reviewed periodically, and an initial decision in favor of the UK may be withdrawn by the Commission at will. While the regimes will be equivalent on exit, they may rapidly diverge. The EU has produced new legislation governing the financial sector at an astonishing rate since the financial crisis, and this shows little sign of abating. On ceasing to be hardwired into the system, the UK will rapidly fall behind unless it adopts a mechanism for automatic implementation of new EU financial regulation initiatives into domestic law, likely along with some kind of enforcement machinery.

This would on the face of it relegate the UK to a "rule-taker." However, outside the single market, the UK would have another option if it was dissatisfied with actual or proposed EU rules in a particular area. It could cease to maintain equivalence with the EU in that particular area, while continuing to do so in other areas. This would harm EU-UK trade, but potentially put the UK in a competitive position vis-à-vis the EU in relation to other third countries. Maintaining the possibility of a la carte non-equivalence of this sort would give the UK a credible "threat" in any informal discussions regarding proposed new EU rules. Some commentators have floated the idea of a "parallel regime" within the UK, one EU-compliant and one not.[1258]

7.5 EU-Style Broker-Dealer Fiduciary Duties

One of the most debated issues in recent years by U.S. securities law scholars and policymakers is whether broker-dealers and others providing similar services to clients should be subject to a fiduciary duty towards their clients. In referring the reader to the relevant chapter of this book for a discussion, we focus here on the European rules that, since the 1990s, have imposed obligations akin to fiduciary duties on European investment firms and banks (here, together, investment firms) engaged in investment services.

More precisely, EU investment firms must "act honestly, fairly and professionally in accordance with the best interests of [their] clients"[1259] (hereinafter: the fiduciary duty). Not only does breach of such duties typically entail private enforcement by investment firms' clients, but it also triggers administrative sanctions.[1260]

[1258] *See* Ferran, *supra* note 996.

[1259] MiFID II, Art. 24(1).

[1260] *See* MiFID II Art. 69(2); MiFID II Art. 70(3)(a)(x).

The fiduciary duty co-exists with more specific duties that apply to investment firms depending on the individual services they provide and which can be held to be a specification thereof: for instance, they are subject to a suitability rule if they provide advisory or portfolio management services,[1261] while for other services, with due exceptions, they must apply an appropriateness test before assisting clients in the purchase of a given financial instrument.[1262] When these or any of the other MiFID II specific conduct of business rules apply, but circumstances are such that compliance with those rules is insufficient to ensure that the investor's interest is duly protected, the client can invoke the fiduciary duty to obtain redress.[1263]

Whenever MiFID II permits waiver of specific obligations, the fiduciary duty may still apply, in whole or in part. For instance, the duty to assess the appropriateness of investment services and financial instruments is waived for the execution of trading orders concerning non-complex financial instruments,[1264] to the extent that such activities are performed at the initiative of the clients.[1265] However, even for such "execution-only" services, MiFID II does not exempt investment firms from the fiduciary duty, which may hence support clients' claims, for instance, in situations where the investment firm somehow promoted the purchase of the financial instrument without providing advice to the client.[1266]

The fiduciary duty applies, with narrowly defined exceptions, whatever the client's characteristics—that is, regardless of whether the client is "professional" or not.[1267] Of the two exemptions from the duty, the more salient

---

[1261] MiFID II, Art. 25(2).

[1262] MiFID II, Art. 25(3).

[1263] *See* Luca Enriques & Matteo Gargantini, *The Overarching Duty to Act in the Best Interest of the Client in MiFID II*, in REGULATION OF EU FINANCIAL MARKETS: MIFID II AND MIFIR 85, at 88 (Busch & Ferrarini eds., 2017).

[1264] As defined by MiFID II Art. 25(4)(a).

[1265] MiFID II, Art. 25(4).

[1266] *See* Enriques & Gargantini, *supra* note 1263, at 95.

[1267] "Professional clients" are defined by MiFID's Annex II to include, in addition to financial institutions, large non-financial firms, governments, and wealthy individuals who are particularly active on securities markets and have requested to be treated as such.

one is partial in both content and scope:[1268] investment firms are exempted from the duty to act in clients' best interests, but not from the duty to act honestly, fairly and professionally, when they engage in execution of orders (whether by matching the client with another trader or entering the contract as dealers) with "eligible counterparties,"—that is, clients that are themselves financial institutions, such as other banks and investment firms, and asset managers and insurance companies.[1269]

While the operation of the fiduciary duty is unproblematic in relation to the provision of investment advice and portfolio management services, reconciling its implications with transactional relationships such as dealing on one's own account and the placement of the investment firms' own securities—which is also qualified as an investment service[1270]—is rather more difficult.

Where firms are operating as counterparties to their clients, the duty to put their clients' "best interests" first can scarcely be reconciled with the duties trading desk employees owe to their principals. So much so that doubts have been raised, including by some national competent authorities under the previous regime, over whether conduct of business rules, including the fiduciary duty, apply at all when investment firms merely act as dealers. Nevertheless, first the Commission and then ESMA have clearly adhered to view that they do.[1271]

The irreconcilable tension between the transactional nature of the service and the content of the fiduciary duty means that the duty sometimes serves as an indirect prohibition on certain activities. Two case studies serve to illustrate these difficulties.

First, ESMA has opined that when an investment firm acts as counterparty to retail clients in contracts for differences (CFD)—where a client's losses are obviously the investment firm's gains—the incentives to profit at investors' expense implies a *per se* breach of the fiduciary duty. ESMA's conclusion is that the offer of CFDs and other speculative products to retail clients should therefore be avoided altogether.[1272]

[1268] A full exemption is only provided for the non-discretionary crossing of buying and selling interests within trading venues. *See* MiFID II, Arts. 19(4) & 53(4).

[1269] MiFID II, Art. 30(2).

[1270] MiFID II, Art. 4(1)(5).

[1271] *See* Enriques & Gargantini, *supra* note 1263, at 112.

[1272] *See* ESMA, QUESTIONS AND ANSWERS RELATING TO THE PROVISION OF CFDS AND OTHER SPECULATIVE PRODUCTS TO RETAIL INVESTORS UNDER MiFID 18, 20 (ESMA/2016/590) (2016).

Second, in combination with rules setting out obligations to consider clients' interests in the process of developing new investment products, the fiduciary duty affects their commercial policies as well: according to ESMA, when it would be impossible not to breach the duty to act in the client's best interest for any possible target clientele of a given new product, a ban on the selling of that product may ensue.[1273]

To conclude, the EU has long since imposed a fiduciary duty on investment firms, and this duty is now an important pillar of broker-dealer client-facing regulations within the EU. We have hinted here at some of the implications of a broad duty of this kind and, specifically, how it can shape the boundaries of permissible services, marketing practices, and financial products. This is an area where comparative research, both legal and empirical, may shed some light on the merits of policy proposals currently debated in the U.S.

8 Supervision and Enforcement in Global Securities Regulation

Our final substantive Section considers issues of enforcement and the implications of the *Morrison* decision. We ask whether the "new structure" we have identified for global securities regulation means that the model of the U.S. as "global enforcer" of securities regulation is now outmoded.

8.1 The U.S.: An Outlier?

The influential role played by the U.S. in global securities regulation is perhaps most keenly felt in enforcement. Foreign issuers' securities law transgressions may often be acted upon sooner, and with more meaningful consequences, by the U.S. SEC than by these firms' domestic regulators.

The literature on comparative financial supervision and enforcement places the U.S. as both a global leader and a global outlier. For example, both the number of enforcement actions by the public regulator and the dollar amount of assessed sanctions has been found to be significantly higher in the U.S. than in the UK and Germany.[1274] For a full picture, private sanctions should also be

---

[1273] *See* ESMA, MiFID PRACTICES FOR FIRMS SELLING COMPLEX PRODUCTS 3 (ESMA/2014/146) (2014).

[1274] Howell E. Jackson, *Variation in the Intensity of Financial Regulation: Preliminary Evidence and Potential Implications*, 24 YALE J. REG. 253, 281-85 (2007) (scaling data by stock market capitalization). Looking specifically at the costs of operating the securities regulator (scaled by the size of the stock market in respective countries), the U.S. does not stand out, however. *See id.* at 269 (estimating the securities budget per $bn of market cap at $98,000 for the U.S., compared to $138,000 in the UK and $280,000 in Australia).

considered, but there is little doubt that the U.S. leads the way also in this respect.[1275] It has been suggested that these disparities in enforcement activity could make it difficult for other countries to be considered equivalent to the U.S. under a substituted compliance approach.[1276]

However, institutional differences between countries may make direct comparisons difficult. The UK system of financial regulation, for example, relies significantly on informal, difficult-to-quantify enforcement mechanisms that may make an apples-to-apples cross-country comparison of enforcement intensity less straightforward than it appears.[1277] Further, as globalization increases, so too does the difficulty of conducting meaningful international comparisons. For example, some national regulators invest more in policy analysis and/or international harmonization efforts, the results of which may be available to others to draw upon at low cost, and increasing amounts of cross-border transactions mean that national regulators cooperate more with their foreign counterparts.[1278] Another confounding factor is that a country whose larger issuers are cross-listed in the U.S. may save on regulatory costs by deferring to the enforcement efforts of the U.S. SEC.[1279] The SEC's enforcement intensity towards foreign firms has increased significantly during the last fifteen years.[1280] Non-targeted foreign firms see their value increase on the announcement of such enforcement actions. In particular, firms with weaker domestic regimes gain relatively more in value. This implies these firms' domestic regulators are effectively delegating enforcement to the SEC.[1281]

In conclusion, if or when the SEC resumes its consideration of substituted compliance as a regulatory strategy, research regarding the details of comparative financial regulation, supervision and enforcement in key

---

[1275] *See, e.g.*, Coffee, *supra* note 1018, at 267.

[1276] *Id.* at 307-08.

[1277] *See, e.g.*, John Armour, *Enforcement Strategies in UK Corporate Governance, in* RATIONALITY IN COMPANY LAW – ESSAYS IN HONOUR OF DD PRENTICE 71 (Armour & Payne eds., 2009) (describing the several institutions that form part of the UK supervision and enforcement framework and detailing how informal enforcement, both by public enforcement agencies and private investors, plays a more important role than formal enforcement).

[1278] Jackson, *supra* note 1118, at 408-09.

[1279] *Id.*

[1280] *See* Silvers, *supra* note 1106.

[1281] *Id.*

jurisdictions would be highly useful, if not necessary, for its assessment of their regulatory quality.[1282]

8.2 The Impact of *Morrison*

The U.S. Supreme Court's 2010 decision in *Morrison v. NAB*[1283] was an earthquake that significantly changed the global securities litigation landscape, and although the tremors may not yet have finished entirely, we will briefly survey the emerging topography.

In the pre-*Morrison* era, behavior that had been conducted,[1284] or had effects,[1285] in the U.S. was accepted as founding jurisdiction for U.S. courts under § 10(b) of the Exchange Act. These "conduct" and "effects" tests were originally developed in the Second Circuit, but were widely embraced. In *Morrison*, the Supreme Court rejected them both in favor of a new "transactional test," under which § 10(b) applies only to purchases and sales of securities taking place in the United States. This, the court explained, covers "transactions in securities listed on domestic exchanges, and domestic transactions in other securities."[1286]

The Dodd-Frank Act required the SEC to study the international scope of the private right of action under § 10(b).[1287] As part of this study, it analyzed the impact of *Morrison* on the share prices of cross-listed firms and found no

---

[1282] *Cf.* Jackson, *Variation*, *supra* note 1274, at 289 (suggesting that the U.S. could benefit from an international comparison of its system for financial regulation and enforcement in order to benchmark its costs and benefits).

[1283] 561 U.S. 247 (2010).

[1284] Leasco Data Processing Equipment v. Maxwell, 468 F.2d 1326 (2d Cir. 1972) (fraudulent representations made in the U.S. by the British media proprietor Robert Maxwell, the relevant securities were foreign and traded only in foreign markets; court found U.S. subject matter jurisdiction).

[1285] Schoenbaum v. Firstbrook, 405 F.2d 215 (2d Cir. 1968) (sufficient domestic "effects" even though the conduct occurred outside the U.S.).

[1286] *Morrison*, 561 U.S. at 267.

[1287] Section 929Y of the Dodd-Frank Act. We note that § 929P(b)(2) of the Dodd-Frank Act (purporting to grant extraterritorial jurisdiction to the SEC and the Department of Justice to U.S. conduct or effects that violate the § 10(b) antifraud provision) has been described as unlikely to offset any impact of *Morrison* since it only confers subject-matter jurisdiction. *See, e.g.*, Richard W. Painter, *The Dodd-Frank Extraterritorial Jurisdiction Provision: Was it Effective, Needed or Sufficient?*, 1 HARV. BUS. L. REV. 195 (2011).

statistically significant costs or benefits to shareholders of foreign companies with listings on both a non-U.S. and a U.S. exchange stemming from the *Morrison* decision. An analysis of whether *Morrison* prompted institutional investors to reallocate their investments in cross-listed firms to U.S.-traded securities in order to preserve their rights to participate in 10b-5 actions did not find any evidence to support that claim.[1288]

Commentators predicted that *Morrison* would result in increasing globalization of securities litigation and that European litigation would increase to make up for the unavailability of U.S. actions,[1289] but it was less obvious that the U.S. plaintiffs' bar would lead the way. However, as recently detailed by Coffee, American law firms have created innovative structures to allow for global securities settlements building on a Dutch statute, announcing a European record $1.3 billion settlement in 2016.[1290]

9 Research Agenda

9.1 Introduction

In this chapter, we have explored the effects of globalization on the operation of securities markets and the challenges this poses for their regulation. We have argued that three macro-level trends—capital market liberalization, institutionalization of investment, and technologization of market activity—have severed the link between listing on a particular exchange and having access to the capital base originating in the country where that exchange is located. They have simultaneously increased the attractiveness of alternative (private) forums for capital-raising. Thanks to the removal of barriers to free movement of capital, the intermediation of professional managers who have the skills and the scale to invest internationally, and the digital interconnection of markets across the globe, investors can reach all markets and issuers, regardless of where the issuers raise

---

[1288] Robert P. Bartlett III, *Do Institutional Investors Value the Rule 10b-5 Private Right of Action? Evidence from Investors' Trading Behavior following Morrison v. National Australia Bank Ltd.*, 44 J. LEGAL STUD. 183 (2015).

[1289] *See, e.g.*, Vincent Smith, *"Bridging the Gap": Contrasting Effects of U.S. Supreme Court Territorial Restraint on European Collective Claims*, in EXTRATERRITORIALITY AND COLLECTIVE REDRESS 389 (Fairgrieve & Lein eds., 2012) (predicting that London, Amsterdam, and Germany would become the main fora for collective actions in Europe).

[1290] John C. Coffee, Jr., *The Globalization of Entrepreneurial Litigation: Law, Culture, and Incentives* (working paper, 2017), http://ssrn.com/abstract=2857258 (describing various steps taken to create a "synthetic" opt-out class action).

capital and have their securities traded, or which securities laws apply on the issuers' side.

Many of the issues we have reviewed in this chapter raise important questions for further research. As the research agenda for the New Special Study of the Securities Markets is drawn up, international aspects are bound to feature in many areas. In the remainder of this concluding Section, we identify, under the same section headings used earlier in this chapter, the questions that we believe are particularly worthy of scholarly attention.

9.2 Macro-Level Issues

The secular trends driving globalization that we identified and discussed in Section 2 raise fundamental questions for further research. First, the trend towards collectivization of investments and the concomitant institutionalization of the stock market mean that retail investors are decreasingly directly active in the trading of individual stocks. This raises two important questions.

> 1   To what extent are current securities regulation provisions dealing with market access based on the view that retail investor protection is needed, and are these measures still appropriate, necessary, and beneficial?[1291]
> 2   As the institutionalization of the securities market means that investment capital is increasingly held through institutions that qualify for participation in exempt securities offerings (which provide more flexibility than the public markets to tailor investor protection to requirements), what role is envisaged for public securities markets in the future?

Increasing institutionalization means that investment intermediaries increasingly become the market entry point for retail investors and are likely to continue to grow in size and influence, which merits an analysis of the suitability of their regulation:

> 3   Following from question 1 above, should the focus of retail investor protection be shifted towards intermediaries? If so, is the current regulation adequate?
> 4   Is the regulation of intermediaries satisfactory for purposes of reducing systemic risk and ensuring financial stability or may, for example, micro-prudential regulation be warranted?[1292]

[1291] Needless to say, this is the kind of question that a New Special Study will have to ask in relation to many areas of securities regulation.

The ongoing technologization of society and markets is another important development where we believe the NSS would benefit from addressing important questions such as the following:

> 5. The regulatory perimeter will come into the spotlight as technological innovations attempt to substitute for various functions currently performed by more established players in the securities markets. How do new FinTech equivalents work, and how do they work in different countries? Do new products warrant a review of the perimeter of securities regulation (such as the definition of a security)?[1293]
> 6. With global capital raising becoming technically possible, does nationally-bounded regulation actually become a major impediment?
> 7. Online offerings are segmented across geographic lines. Can technology (e.g., the algorithms in peer-to-peer lending) substitute for creditor protection rules, making geographic segmentation of these markets obsolete?
> 8. In light of increasing global interconnectedness, is it desirable for the U.S. stock market to become further globalized, both as regards issuers and investors?[1294] What might be the costs and benefits of this for the U.S., and for other nations? With nationalistic positions being adopted in political discourse, this appears a particularly salient normative issue.

[1292] *See* FINANCIAL STABILITY BOARD, POLICY RECOMMENDATIONS TO ADDRESS STRUCTURAL VULNERABILITIES FROM ASSET MANAGEMENT ACTIVITIES (2017), http://www.fsb.org/wp-content/uploads/FSB-Policy-Recommendations-on-Asset-Management-Structural-Vulnerabilities.pdf.

[1293] The issues here are certainly not exclusively international, but there may be benefits in studying the experiences in countries that have been early adopters of promising new technology. As just one example, proxy voting via distributed ledger technology has been successfully trialed in Estonia. *See* Nasdaq MarketInsite, *Is Blockchain the Answer to E-Voting? Nasdaq Believes So*, Jan. 23, 2017, http://business.nasdaq.com/marketinsite/2017/Is-Blockchain-the-Answer-to-E-voting-Nasdaq-Believes-So.html.

[1294] For an interesting recent contribution to this literature, see, e.g., Jan Bena, Miguel A. Ferriera, Pedro Matos & Pedro Pires, *Are Foreign Investors Locusts? The Long-Term Effects of Foreign Institutional Ownership*, 126 J. FIN. ECON. 122 (2017) (finding that greater foreign ownership supports long-term investments).

9.3 Market Access and Extraterritoriality

> 9. What drives cross-border investment structuring for U.S. institutional investors? In which cases and why do U.S. institutional investors choose to operate from foreign countries? When do they invest via ADRs and when do they invest directly in foreign stock? Is regulation driving structuring and, if so, is it desirable?[1295] This is an area where interviews with market participants, including institutional investors and issuers, could provide an up-to-date account of market practices to inform regulation.[1296]
> 10. To what extent should financial stability be a concern for global securities markets and international securities regulation?
> 11. What tools and powers should the SEC have available to deal with cross-border issues (in their prudential implications)? For example, does the transaction-focused approach in *Morrison*, as further developed by the lower courts, provide the SEC with the tools necessary to mitigate systemic risks to the U.S. financial system wherever they arise in the world?

9.4 Regulatory Coordination

> 12. Where does regulation still make a difference to outcomes, given that much of the domestic investor protection edifice is optional in institutional markets? Does it affect innovation?
> 13. Against the backdrop of the various EU initiatives described in Section 6.3, how will regulatory heterogeneity affect outcomes?

9.5 Primary Markets and Cross-Listings

The secular trends discussed in Section 2 have also played a part in the declining amounts of U.S. IPOs and cross-listings. The following research questions are particularly relevant:

[1295] To give an example of the sort of adaption to regulation that we have in mind here, it was suggested during discussions at the New Special Study Initiating Conference that the Reg. S safe harbor for offshore offerings led U.S. investors to set up offices abroad.

[1296] For an earlier and highly successful application of this methodology, see Jackson & Pan, Parts & II, *supra* note 959.

> 14 How do countries' industrial and financial structures relate – to each other and to growth over time? This may be a useful starting point in establishing what may be the theoretically optimal footprint for securities markets (as opposed to other types of capital-raising) and whether the maximization of IPOs (by dollars or volume) is a valuable regulatory goal.
>
> 15 What are the overall welfare implications of reduced cross-listings?[1297] Foreign firms' decisions not to list in the U.S. could be rooted in globalization, in that U.S. institutional investors may now be able to invest more efficiently in foreign issuers through these issuers' home markets (which are often more liquid and therefore preferable), rendering a U.S. listing unnecessary. If that is the case, U.S. trading venues and broker-dealers may see less U.S. business,[1298] but if the investment opportunity is still available to U.S. investors, albeit in a foreign country, there may not be much cause for alarm.[1299]

If more cross-listings are considered desirable (following an inquiry such as that outlined in question 15), further research along the following lines could elucidate how best to design policy.

> 16 What is the main motivation for those foreign firms choosing to conduct IPOs or to cross-list in the U.S. today? Are they choosing a U.S. listing

---

[1297] Another issue that might usefully be explored is the desirable role of the listing function in future equity markets. *See, e.g.,* Onnig H. Dombalagian, *Exchanges, Listless?: The Disintermediation of the Listing Function*, 50 WAKE FOREST L. REV. 579 (2015).

[1298] We say "U.S. business" since U.S. broker-dealers have strong market positions across the world (*see supra* Section 4.4). They may thus be involved in foreign issuers' home country listings, the subsequent trading of their stocks, and provide a variety of investment banking services to them abroad.

[1299] We note that the new Chairman of the SEC (previously a transactional securities lawyer) as part of his Senate confirmation hearing highlighted that U.S. capital markets "faced growing competition from abroad" and that "U.S.-listed IPOs by non-U.S. companies have slowed dramatically"; a situation which had reduced the "investment opportunities [available to] Main Street investors" but provides "meaningful room for improvement." *See* OPENING STATEMENT OF JAY CLAYTON, NOMINEE FOR CHAIRMAN, SECURITIES AND EXCHANGE COMMISSION, SENATE COMMITTEE ON BANKING, HOUSING AND URBAN AFFAIRS (Mar. 23, 2017).

> because of the attractiveness of the U.S. regime or the unattractiveness of the home country regime,[1300] and what does the answer to that question imply for the future of cross-listings as a phenomenon? Is legal bonding or reputational bonding more important for issuers seeking a U.S. listing? Are there regulatory levers available to attract more foreign issuers? Are there significant foreign stock markets that U.S. institutional investors are unable to access? If so, what are the reasons and are they likely to persist in the medium to long term?
>
> 17 Has *Morrison* changed the risk-benefit tradeoff for foreign issuers by providing greater certainty as regards litigation risk? Does it affect U.S. listings at the margin?
>
> 18 Can factors such as the availability of passive investment funds (such as ETFs that invest in certain indices) or the persistence of home bias explain the choice of listing venue?
>
> 19 Increased cross-border investment flows imply that issuers may not need to list abroad to get access to capital. What is the nature of these investment flows? How do they vary by country? How do they relate to domestic corporate finance?

9.6 Secondary Market Trading

Section 6.3 noted various few areas where the new EU approach in MiFID II may provide useful insights regarding market structure.

9.7 Intermediaries

> 20 Consideration could be given to whether foreign models of regulation might offer lessons for the US—in particular, the EU's unified approach to regulating investment firms rather than broker-dealers and investment advisors in separate regimes.

[1300] Although most commentators tend to see the U.S. as a regime that combines strong regulation and enforcement, foreign issuers' domestic regimes could, at least in theory, be stronger or weaker than the U.S. regime, meaning that issuers may choose the U.S. either to avoiding a weak home country regime or to avoid a strong home country regime.

9.8 Supervision and Enforcement

> 21 What types of enforcement actions (*ex ante* or *ex post*; private or public; formal or informal) really make a difference? A comparative inquiry could provide further insights.
>
> 22 Securities law practitioners interviewed two years before *Morrison* were very clear that U.S. class actions acted as a significant deterrent to foreign firms entering the U.S. capital markets.[1301] In light of competition between international listing venues, and considering that the SEC may exempt classes of persons and transactions from the Exchange Act,[1302] it may be informative to conduct new practitioner interviews to see to what extent *Morrison* has alleviated concerns regarding the perimeter of liability.
>
> 23 What are the longer term effects of *Morrison*? Has it led to changes in market practices?
>
> 24 How does international data protection law, such as the EU General Data Protection Regulation,[1303] affect cross-border securities supervision and enforcement?

[1301] Howell E. Jackson, *Summary of Research Findings on Extra-Territorial Application of Federal Securities Law*, in GLOBAL CAPITAL MARKETS & THE U.S. SECURITIES LAWS (2009) (presenting information received from interviews with twenty-two leading practitioners and academics, seventeen of whom were practicing lawyers).

[1302] Section 36 of the Exchange Act. 15 U.S.C. § 78mm.

[1303] Regulation (EU) 2016/679.

Made in United States
North Haven, CT
09 February 2022

15935060R00290